CALIFORNIA

FAMILY CODE

2026 EDITION

I0894885

League Publishing Inc.

ISBN: 979-8-90113-053-7
www.californiafamilycodebook.com

EDITORIAL NOTE

This book compiles the California Family Code as in effect on January 1, 2026. The statutory text is presented in its enacted form and organized for reference. No commentary, analysis, or interpretation is intended.

The California Family Code is a work of the public domain. This publication does not claim authorship of the statutory text. The material has been compiled, organized, and formatted for usability and reference purposes.

This compilation was prepared by Jeremy J. Salvador, who served solely in an editorial and organizational capacity. Responsibility for the content of the law remains with the Legislature of the State of California. Users should consult applicable case law, court rules, and other authorities when applying the Code to specific matters.

The Code is organized in accordance with its official statutory divisions.

OVERVIEW OF CHANGES

(2025 → 2026)

Here are the Legislative Updates and Amendments to the California Family Code (Effective January 1, 2026):

Section	Type of Change	Summary of Change / New Text	Notes on 2025 Applicability
2040	Amended Text	Paragraph (3) adds nonpayment lapses and renewal failures as a restraint in the interest of the child in Version 2 of 2040. Version 1 of 2040 adds subdivision (f), stating the section is only in effect until January 1, 2027. Version 2 of 2040 adds subdivision (f), stating "this section shall become operative on January 1, 2027."	Updates restraints; effective on January 1, 2026
2211	Amended Text	Adds subdivision (g) with paragraphs (1) and (2), to include court permission and modifications. Version 1 of 2211 adds subdivision (h), stating the section is only in effect until January 1, 2027. Version 2 of 2211 adds subdivision (h), stating "this section shall become operative on January 1, 2027."	Updates proceeding reasons for nullity of marriage; effective on Jan 1, 2026
2342.5	Newly Added	(a) Defines the first joint petitioner as the	Entirely new section.

Section	Type of Change	Summary of Change / New Text	Notes on 2025 Applicability
		petitioner and the second as the respondent. Requires a joint summons to include a temporary restraining order. Section 412.20 does not apply. (b) Allows amended petitions or responses before entry of judgment. (i) Effective January 1, 2026.	
2342.51	Newly Added	Requires the Judicial Council to adopt or amend rules or forms necessary to implement §2342.5 on or before January 1, 2026.	Procedural only; supports §2342.5; entirely new section.
3040.5	Newly Added	Grants the court permission to, "consider any relevant, admissible evidence that a parent has caused human trafficking of the child or other parent."	Entirely new section.
3044	Repealed and Amended Text	Version 1 of Section 3044 expired and was repealed as of January 1, 2026, pursuant to its sunset clause. A revised version of Section 3044 in subdivision (G) adds the Code of Civil Procedure and the Penal Code to be valid violations if the perpetrator has a firearm.	The repeal of Version 1 and the operative effect of the amended version both take effect on January 1, 2026.

Section	Type of Change	Summary of Change / New Text	Notes on 2025 Applicability
6307	Amended Text	Adds subdivision (B), stating that there will be no charges for petitions and filings commencing January 1, 2027.	New wording is effective January 1, 2026.
6308	Amended Text	Adds subdivision (b), stating that there not be a fee to appear remotely at a hearing commencing January 1, 2027.	New wording is effective January 1, 2026.
6320	Amended Text	Adds to subdivision (c) definitions of internet-connected devices referred to in Section 22948.30 of the Business and Professions Code.	New wording is effective January 1, 2026.
6380.5	Newly Added	Section 6380.5 is known as Wylands' Law, and allows a department to establish a notification system to provide a petitioner or protected person with access to information about their case.	Entirely new section
6389	Repealed and Amended Text	Version 1 of Section 6389 expired and was repealed as of January 1, 2026, pursuant to its sunset clause. A revised version of Section 6389 replaces the prior text and includes stricter firearm regulations, including updates to subdivision (l).	The repeal of Version 1 and the operative effect of the amended version both take effect on January 1, 2026.

Section	Type of Change	Summary of Change / New Text	Notes on 2025 Applicability
6550	Amended Text	Paragraph (3) now includes specific care methods such as "immunizations, physical examinations, and medical examinations."	New wording is effective January 1, 2026.
6552	Amended Text	#5 of the Caregiver Authorization Affidavit now begins with, "I am a relative of the child." Adds "Warning to Caregiver" and "Warning to Local Educational Agencies and Health Care Providers." Updates wording in multiple subsections, including caregiver definitions, affidavit validity, acceptable identification, school official requirements, and health care provider provisions.	All updated language is effective January 1, 2026.
8626	Newly Added	Addition of a new statement regarding adoption laws beginning with: "Notwithstanding any other law…".	Entirely new section.
8807	Newly Added	Additional subdivision (d) to include "home study reports" in adoption proceedings.	Entirely new provision.
9210	Newly Added & Amended Text	Addition of new paragraph (5) with subparagraphs (A) and (B) regarding adoption	Updated and new language is effective January 1, 2026.

Section	Type of Change	Summary of Change / New Text	Notes on 2025 Applicability
		jurisdiction when a minor is born in the state. Renumbers former paragraph (5) as (6) and updates cross-references. Additional new subdivision (e) clarifying jurisdictional limits.	

CONTENTS

DIVISION 1: PRELIMINARY PROVISIONS AND DEFINITION

ENACTED BY STATS. 1992, CH. 162, SEC. 10
SECTION 1-185

PART 1: PRELIMINARY PROVISIONS

enacted by Stats. 1992, Ch. 162, Sec. 10

1. This code shall be known as the Family Code.[1]

2. A provision of this code, insofar as it is substantially the same as a previously existing provision relating to the same subject matter, shall be considered as a restatement and continuation thereof and not as a new enactment, and a reference in a statute to the provision of this code shall be deemed to include a reference to the previously existing provision unless a contrary intent appears.[5]

3. A provision of this code, insofar as it is the same in substance as a provision of a uniform act, shall be construed to effectuate the general purpose to make uniform the law in those states which enact that provision.[1]

4. (a) As used in this section:
(1) "New law" means either of the following, as the case may be:
(A) The act that enacted this code.
(B) The act that makes a change in this code, whether effectuated by amendment, addition, or repeal of a provision of this code.
(2) "Old law" means the applicable law in effect before the operative date of the new law.
(3) "Operative date" means the operative date of the new law.
(b) This section governs the application of the new law except to the extent otherwise expressly provided in the new law.
(c) Subject to the limitations provided in this section, the new law applies on the operative date to all matters governed by the new law, regardless of whether an event occurred or circumstance existed before, on, or after the operative date, including, but not limited to, commencement of a proceeding, making of an order, or taking of an action.
(d) If a document or paper is filed before the operative date, the contents, execution, and notice thereof are governed by the old law and not by the new law; but subsequent proceedings taken after the operative date concerning the document or paper, including an objection or response, a hearing, an order, or other matter relating thereto is governed by the new law and not by the old law.
(e) If an order is made before the operative date, or an action on an order is taken before the operative date, the validity of the order or action is governed by the old law and not by the new law. Nothing in this subdivision precludes proceedings after the operative date to modify an order made, or alter a course of action commenced, before the operative date to the extent proceedings for modification of an order or alteration of a course of action of that type are otherwise provided in the new law.
(f) No person is liable for an action

taken before the operative date that was proper at the time the action was taken, even though the action would be improper if taken on or after the operative date, and the person has no duty, as a result of the enactment of the new law, to take any step to alter the course of action or its consequences.

(g) If the new law does not apply to a matter that occurred before the operative date, the old law continues to govern the matter notwithstanding its repeal or amendment by the new law.

(h) If a party shows, and the court determines, that application of a particular provision of the new law or of the old law in the manner required by this section or by the new law would substantially interfere with the effective conduct of the proceedings or the rights of the parties or other interested persons in connection with an event that occurred or circumstance that existed before the operative date, the court may, notwithstanding this section or the new law, apply either the new law or the old law to the extent reasonably necessary to mitigate the substantial interference.[1]

5. Division, part, chapter, article, and section headings do not in any manner affect the scope, meaning, or intent of this code.[1]

6. Unless the provision or context otherwise requires, the general provisions and rules of construction in this part govern the construction of this code.[1]

7. Whenever a reference is made to a portion of this code or to another law, the reference applies to all amendments and additions regardless of when made.[1]

8. Unless otherwise expressly stated:

(a) "Division" means a division of this code.

(b) "Part" means a part of the division in which that term occurs.

(c) "Chapter" means a chapter of the division or part, as the case may be, in which that term occurs.

(d) "Article" means an article of the chapter in which that term occurs.

(e) "Section" means a section of this code.

(f) "Subdivision" means a subdivision of the section in which that term occurs.

(g) "Paragraph" means a paragraph of the subdivision in which that term occurs.

(h) "Subparagraph" means a subparagraph of the paragraph in which that term occurs.[1]

9. The present tense includes the past and future tenses, and the future, the present.[1]

10. The singular number includes the plural, and the plural, the singular.[1]

11. A reference to "husband" and "wife," "spouses," or "married persons," or a comparable term, includes persons who are lawfully married to each other and persons who were previously lawfully married to each other, as is appropriate under the circumstances of the particular case.[1]

12. "Shall" is mandatory and "may" is permissive. "Shall not" and "may not" are prohibitory.[1]

13. If a provision or clause of this code or its application to any person or circumstances is held invalid, the invalidity does not affect other provisions or applications of the code which can be given effect without the

invalid provision or application, and to this end the provisions of this code are severable.

PART 2: DEFINITIONS

enacted by Stats. 1992, Ch. 162, Sec. 10

50. Unless the provision or context otherwise requires, the definitions and rules of construction in this part govern the construction of this code.[1]

58. "Child for whom support may be ordered" means a minor child and a child for whom support is authorized under Section 3587, 3901, or 3910.[5]

63. "Community estate" includes both community property and quasi-community property.[6]

65. "Community property" is property that is community property under Part 2 (commencing with Section 760) of Division 4.[1]

67. "County" includes city and county.[1]

70. (a) "Date of separation" means the date that a complete and final break in the marital relationship has occurred, as evidenced by both of the following:
(1) The spouse has expressed to the other spouse the intent to end the marriage.
(2) The conduct of the spouse is consistent with the intent to end the marriage.
(b) In determining the date of separation, the court shall take into consideration all relevant evidence.
(c) It is the intent of the Legislature in enacting this section to abrogate the decisions in *In re Marriage of Davis* (2015) 61 Cal. 4th 846 and *In re Marriage of Norviel* (2002) 102 Cal. App. 4th 1152.[413]

80. "Employee benefit plan" includes public and private retirement, pension, annuity, savings, profit sharing, stock bonus, stock option, thrift, vacation pay, and similar plans of deferred or fringe benefit compensation, whether of the defined contribution or defined benefit type whether or not such plan is qualified under the Employee Retirement Income Security Act of 1974 (P.L. 93-406) (ERISA), as amended. The term also includes "employee benefit plan" as defined in Section 3 of ERISA (29 U.S.C.A. Sec. 1002(3)).[43]

92. "Family support" means an agreement between the parents, or an order or judgment, that combines child support and spousal support without designating the amount to be paid for child support and the amount to be paid for spousal support.[1]

95."Income and expense declaration" means the form for an income and expense declaration in family law matters adopted by the Judicial Council.[1]

100. "Judgment" and "order" include a decree, as appropriate under the circumstances.[1]

105. "Person" includes a natural person, firm, association, organization, partnership, business trust, corporation, limited liability company, or public entity.

110. "Proceeding" includes an action.[7]

113. "Property" includes real and personal property and any interest therein.[78]

115. "Property declaration" means the

form for a property declaration in family law matters adopted by the Judicial Council.[1]

125. "Quasi-community property" means all real or personal property, wherever situated, acquired before or after the operative date of this code in any of the following ways:
(a) By either spouse while domiciled elsewhere which would have been community property if the spouse who acquired the property had been domiciled in this state at the time of its acquisition.
(b) In exchange for real or personal property, wherever situated, which would have been community property if the spouse who acquired the property so exchanged had been domiciled in this state at the time of its acquisition.[1]

126. "Petitioner" includes plaintiff, where appropriate.

127. "Respondent" includes defendant, where appropriate.

130. "Separate property" is property that is separate property under Part 2 (commencing with Section 760) of Division 4.[1]

142. "Spousal support" means support of the spouse of the obligor.[1]

143. "Spouse" includes "registered domestic partner," as required by Section 297.5.[344]

145. "State" means a state of the United States, the District of Columbia, or a commonwealth, territory, or insular possession subject to the jurisdiction of the United States.

150. "Support" refers to a support obligation owing on behalf of a child, spouse, or family, or an amount owing pursuant to Section 17402. It also includes past due support or arrearage when it exists. "Support," when used with reference to a minor child or a child described in Section 3901, includes maintenance and education.

155. "Support order" means a judgment or order of support in favor of an obligee, whether temporary or final, or subject to modification, termination, or remission, regardless of the kind of action or proceeding in which it is entered. For the purposes of Section 685.020 of the Code of Civil Procedure, only the initial support order, whether temporary or final, whether or not the order is contained in a judgment, shall be considered an installment judgment. No support order or other order or notice issued, which sets forth the amount of support owed for prior periods of time or establishes a periodic payment to liquidate the support owed for prior periods, shall be considered a money judgment for purposes of subdivision (b) of Section 685.020 of the Code of Civil Procedure.

PART 3: INDIAN CHILDREN

added by Stats. 2006, Ch. 838, Sec. 1.

170. (a) As used in this code, unless the context otherwise requires, the terms "Indian," "Indian child," "Indian child's tribe," "Indian custodian," "Indian organization," "Indian tribe," "reservation," and "tribal court" shall be defined as provided in Section 1903 of the Indian Child Welfare Act (25 U.S.C. Sec. 1901 et seq.).
(b) When used in connection with an Indian child custody proceeding, the

terms "extended family member" and "parent" shall be defined as provided in Section 1903 of the Indian Child Welfare Act.

(c) "Indian child custody proceeding" means a "child custody proceeding" within the meaning of Section 1903 of the Indian Child Welfare Act, including a voluntary or involuntary proceeding that may result in an Indian child's temporary or long-term foster care or guardianship placement if the parent or Indian custodian cannot have the child returned upon dem and, termination of parental rights, or adoptive placement. An "Indian child custody proceeding" does not include a proceeding under this code commenced by the parent of an Indian child to determine the custodial rights of the child's parents, unless the proceeding involves a petition to declare an Indian child free from the custody or control of a parent or involves a grant of custody to a person or persons other than a parent, over the objection of a parent.

(d) If an Indian child is a member of more than one tribe or is eligible for membership in more than one tribe, the court shall make a determination, in writing together with the reasons for it, as to which tribe is the Indian child's tribe for purposes of the Indian child custody proceeding. The court shall make that determination as follows:

(1) If the Indian child is or becomes a member of only one tribe, that tribe shall be designated as the Indian child's tribe, even though the child is eligible for membership in another tribe.

(2) If an Indian child is or becomes a member of more than one tribe, or is not a member of any tribe but is eligible for membership in more than one tribe, the tribe with which the child has the more significant contacts shall be designated as the Indian child's tribe. In determining which tribe the child has the more significant contacts with, the court shall consider, among other things, the following factors:

(A) The length of residence on or near the reservation of each tribe and frequency of contact with each tribe.

(B) The child's participation in activities of each tribe.

(C) The child's fluency in the language of each tribe.

(D) Whether there has been a previous adjudication with respect to the child by a court of one of the tribes.

(E) Residence on or near one of the tribes' reservations by the child's parents, Indian custodian or extended family members.

(F) Tribal membership of custodial parent or Indian custodian.

(G) Interest asserted by each tribe in response to the notice specified in Section 180.

(H) The child's self-identification.

(3) If an Indian child becomes a member of a tribe other than the one designated by the court as the Indian child's tribe under paragraph (2), actions taken based on the court's determination prior to the child's becoming a tribal member shall continue to be valid.[143]

175. (a) The Legislature finds and declares the following:

(1) There is no resource that is more vital to the continued existence and integrity of recognized Indian tribes than their children, and the State of California has an interest in protecting

Indian children who are members of, or are eligible for membership in, an Indian tribe. The state is committed to protecting the essential tribal relations and best interest of an Indian child by promoting practices, in accordance with the Indian Child Welfare Act (25 U.S.C. Sec. 1901 et seq.) and other applicable law, designed to prevent the child's involuntary out-of-home placement and, whenever the placement is necessary or ordered, by placing the child, whenever possible, in a placement that reflects the unique values of the child's tribal culture and is best able to assist the child in establishing, developing, and maintaining a political, cultural, and social relationship with the child's tribe and tribal community.

(2) It is in the interest of an Indian child that the child's membership in the child's Indian tribe and connection to the tribal community be encouraged and protected, regardless of any of the following:

(A) Whether the child is in the physical custody of an Indian parent or Indian custodian at the commencement of a child custody proceeding.

(B) Whether the parental rights of the child's parents have been terminated.

(C) Where the child has resided or been domiciled.

(b) In all Indian child custody proceedings the court shall consider all of the findings contained in subdivision (a), strive to promote the stability and security of Indian tribes and families, comply with the federal Indian Child Welfare Act, and seek to protect the best interest of the child. Whenever an Indian child is removed from a foster care home or institution, guardianship, or adoptive placement for the purpose of further foster care, guardianship, or adoptive placement, placement of the child shall be in accordance with the Indian Child Welfare Act.

(c) A determination by an Indian tribe that an unmarried person, who is under the age of 18 years, is either (1) a member of an Indian tribe or (2) eligible for membership in an Indian tribe and a biological child of a member of an Indian tribe shall constitute a significant political affiliation with the tribe and shall require the application of the federal Indian Child Welfare Act to the proceedings.

(d) In any case in which this code or other applicable state or federal law provides a higher standard of protection to the rights of the parent or Indian custodian of an Indian child, or the Indian child's tribe, than the rights provided under the Indian Child Welfare Act, the court shall apply the higher standard.

(e) Any Indian child, the Indian child's tribe, or the parent or Indian custodian from whose custody the child has been removed, may petition the court to invalidate an action in an Indian child custody proceeding for foster care, guardianship placement, or termination of parental rights if the action violated Sections 1911, 1912, and 1913 of the Indian Child Welfare Act (25 U.S.C. Sec. 1901 et seq.). Nothing in this section is intended to prohibit, restrict, or otherwise limit any rights under Section 1914 of the Indian Child Welfare Act (25 U.S.C. Sec. 1901 et seq.).[143]

177. (a) In an Indian child custody proceeding, the court shall apply Sections 224.2 to 224.6, inclusive, and Sections 305.5, 361.31, and 361.7 of the Welfare and Institutions Code, and the following rules from the California Rules of Court, as they read on January 1, 2007:

(1) Paragraph (7) of subdivision (b) of Rule 5.530.

(2) Subdivision (i) of Rule 5.534.

(b) In the provisions cited in subdivision (a), references to social workers, probation officers, county welfare department, or probation department shall be construed as meaning the party seeking a foster care placement, guardianship, or adoption under this code.

(c) This section shall only apply to proceedings involving an Indian child.[171]

180. (a) In an Indian child custody proceeding notice shall comply with subdivision (b) of this section.

(b) Any notice sent under this section shall be sent to the minor's parent or legal guardian, Indian custodian, if any, and the Indian child's tribe and shall comply with all of the following requirements:

(1) Notice shall be sent by registered or certified mail with return receipt requested. Additional notice by first-class mail is recommended, but not required.

(2) Notice to the tribe shall be to the tribal chairperson, unless the tribe has designated another agent for service.

(3) Notice shall be sent to all tribes of which the child may be a member or eligible for membership until the court makes a determination as to which tribe is the Indian child's tribe in accordance with subdivision (d) of Section 170, after which notice need only be sent to the tribe determined to be the Indian child's tribe.

(4) Notice, to the extent required by federal law, shall be sent to the Secretary of the Interior's designated agent, the Sacramento Area Director, Bureau of Indian Affairs. If the identity or location of the Indian child's tribe is known, a copy of the notice shall also be sent directly to the Secretary of the Interior unless the Secretary of the Interior has waived that notice in writing and the person responsible for giving notice under this section has filed proof of the waiver with the court.

(5) In addition to the information specified in other sections of this article, notice shall include all of the following information:

(A) The name, birthdate, and birthplace of the Indian child, if known.

(B) The name of any Indian tribe in which the child is a member or may be eligible for membership, if known.

(C) All names known of the Indian child's biological parents, grand-parents, and great-grandparents, or Indian custodians, including maiden, married, and former names or aliases, as well as their current and former addresses, birthdates, places of birth and death, tribal enrollment numbers, and any other identifying information, if known.

(D) A copy of the petition by which the proceeding was initiated.

(E) A copy of the child's birth certificate, if available.

(F) The location, mailing address, and telephone number of the court and all parties notified pursuant to this section.

(G) A statement of the following:

(i) The absolute right of the child's parents, Indian custodians, and tribe to intervene in the proceeding.

(ii) The right of the child's parents, Indian custodians, and tribe to petition the court to transfer the proceeding to the tribal court of the Indian child's tribe, absent objection by either parent and subject to declination by the tribal court.

(iii) The right of the child's parents, Indian custodians, and tribe to, upon request, be granted up to an additional 20 days from the receipt of the notice to prepare for the proceeding.

(iv) The potential legal consequences of the proceedings on the future custodial rights of the child's parents or Indian custodians.

(v) That if the parents or Indian custodians are unable to afford counsel, counsel will be appointed to represent the parents or Indian custodians pursuant to Section 1912 of the Indian Child Welfare Act (25 U.S.C. Sec. 1901 et seq.)

(vi) That the information contained in the notice, petition, pleading, and other court documents is confidential, so any person or entity notified shall maintain the confidentiality of the information contained in the notice concerning the particular proceeding and not reveal it to anyone who does not need the information in order to exercise the tribe's rights under the Indian Child Welfare Act (25 U.S.C. Sec. 1901 et seq.).

(c) Notice shall be sent whenever it is known or there is reason to know that an Indian child is involved, and for every hearing thereafter, including, but not limited to, the hearing at which a final adoption order is to be granted. After a tribe acknowledges that the child is a member or eligible for membership in that tribe, or after the Indian child's tribe intervenes in a proceeding, the information set out in subparagraphs (C), (D), (E), and (G) of paragraph (5) of subdivision (b) need not be included with the notice.

(d) Proof of the notice, including copies of notices sent and all return receipts and responses received, shall be filed with the court in advance of the hearing except as permitted under subdivision (e).

(e) No proceeding shall be held until at least 10 days after receipt of notice by the parent, Indian custodian, the tribe, or the Bureau of Indian Affairs. The parent, Indian custodian, or the tribe shall, upon request, be granted up to 20 additional days to prepare for the proceeding. Nothing herein shall be construed as limiting the rights of the parent, Indian custodian, or tribe to 10 days' notice if a lengthier notice period is required under this code.

(f) With respect to giving notice to Indian tribes, a party shall be subject to court sanctions if that person knowingly and willfully falsifies or conceals a material fact concerning whether the child is an Indian child, or counsels a party to do so.

(g) The inclusion of contact information of any adult or child that would otherwise be required to be included in the notification pursuant to this section, shall not be required if that person is at risk of harm as a result of domestic violence, child abuse, sexual abuse, or stalking.[143]

185. (a) In a custody proceeding

involving a child who would otherwise be an Indian child based on the definition contained in paragraph (4) of Section 1903 of the federal Indian Child Welfare Act (25 U.S.C. Sec. 1901 et seq.), but is not an Indian child based on status of the child's tribe, as defined in paragraph (8) of Section 1903 of the federal Indian Child Welfare Act (25 U.S.C. Sec. 1901 et seq.), the court may permit the tribe from which the child is descended to participate in the proceeding upon request of the tribe.

(b) If the court permits a tribe to participate in a proceeding, the tribe may do all of the following, upon consent of the court:

(1) Be present at the hearing.

(2) Address the court.

(3) Request and receive notice of hearings.

(4) Request to examine court documents relating to the proceeding.

(5) Present information to the court that is relevant to the proceeding.

(6) Submit written reports and recommendations to the court.

(7) Perform other duties and responsibilities as requested or approved by the court.

(c) If more than one tribe requests to participate in a proceeding under subdivision (a), the court may limit participation to the tribe with which the child has the most significant contacts, as determined in accordance with paragraph (2) of subdivision (d) of Section 170.

(d) This section is intended to assist the court in making decisions that are in the best interest of the child by permitting a tribe in the circumstances set out in subdivision (a) to inform the court and parties to the proceeding about placement options for the child within the child's extended family or the tribal community, services and programs available to the child and the child's parents as Indians, and other unique interests the child or the child's parents may have as Indians. This section shall not be construed to make the Indian Child Welfare Act (25 U.S.C. Sec. 1901 et seq.), or any state law implementing the Indian Child Welfare Act, applicable to the proceedings, or to limit the court's discretion to permit other interested persons to participate in these or any other proceedings.

(e) This section shall only apply to proceedings involving an Indian child.[143]

DIVISION 2: GENERAL PROVISIONS

ENACTED BY STATS. 1992, CH. 162, SEC. 10.
SECTION 200-295

PART 1: JURISDICTION

enacted by Stats. 1992, Ch. 162, Sec. 10

200. The superior court has jurisdiction in proceedings under this code.[1]

PART 2: GENERAL PROCEDURAL PROVISIONS

enacted by Stats. 1992, Ch. 162, Sec. 10

210. Except to the extent that any other statute or rules adopted by the Judicial Council provide applicable rules, the rules of practice and procedure applicable to civil actions generally, including the provisions of Title 3a (commencing with Section 391) of Part 2 of the Code of Civil Procedure, apply to, and constitute the rules of practice and procedure in, proceedings under this code.[95]

211. Notwithstanding any other provision of law, the Judicial Council may provide by rule for the practice and procedure in proceedings under this code.[1]

211.5. (a) (1) Commencing January 1, 2024, in proceedings under this code, a court shall provide self-identified veterans with a list of resources for veterans, including information about how to contact the local office of the Department of Veterans Affairs.

(2) The veteran may, at their discretion, provide the information about their veteran status on the Judicial Council military service form, file the form with the court, and serve it on the other parties to the action.

(b) (1) When a person files a form identifying the person as a veteran pursuant to paragraph (2) of subdivision (a), the court shall transmit a copy of the form to the Department of Veterans Affairs.

(2) Upon receipt of a copy of the form, the Department of Veterans Affairs shall, within a reasonable time, contact the person using the information provided on the form.

(c) On or before January 1, 2024, the Judicial Council may amend or develop the rules and forms necessary to implement this section.[515]

212. A petition, response, application, opposition, or other pleading filed with the court under this code shall be verified.[1]

213. (a) In a hearing on an order to show cause, or on a modification thereof, or in a hearing on a motion, other than for contempt, the responding party may seek affirmative relief alternative to that requested by the moving party, on the same issues raised by the moving party, by filing a responsive declaration within the time set by statute or rules of court.

(b) This section applies in any of the following proceedings:

(1) A proceeding for dissolution of marriage, for nullity of marriage, or for legal separation of the parties.

(2) A proceeding relating to a

protective order described in Section 6218.

(3) Any other proceeding in which there is at issue the visitation, custody, or support of a child.

214. Except as otherwise provided in this code or by court rule, the court may, when it considers it necessary in the interests of justice and the persons involved, direct the trial of any issue of fact joined in a proceeding under this code to be private, and may exclude all persons except the officers of the court, the parties, their witnesses, and counsel.[1]

215. (a) Except as provided in subdivision (b) or (c), after entry of a judgment of dissolution of marriage, nullity of marriage, legal separation of the parties, or paternity, or after a permanent order in any other proceeding in which there was at issue the visitation, custody, or support of a child, no modification of the judgment or order, and no subsequent order in the proceedings, is valid unless any prior notice otherwise required to be given to a party to the proceeding is served, in the same manner as the notice is otherwise permitted by law to be served, upon the party. For the purposes of this section, service upon the attorney of record is not sufficient.

(b) A post judgment motion to modify a custody, visitation, or child support order may be served on the other party or parties by first-class mail or airmail, postage prepaid, to the persons to be served. For any party served by mail, the proof of service shall include an address verification.

(c) This section does not apply if the court has ordered an issue or issues bifurcated for separate trial in advance of the disposition of the entire case. In those cases, service of a motion on any outstanding matter shall be served either upon the attorney of record, if the parties are represented, or upon the parties, if unrepresented. However, if there has been no pleading filed in the action for a period of six months after the entry of the bifurcated judgment, service shall be upon both the party, at the party's last known address, and the attorney of record.[345]

216. (a) In the absence of a stipulation by the parties to the contrary, there shall be no ex parte communication between the attorneys for any party to an action and any court-appointed or court-connected evaluator or mediator, or between a court-appointed or court-connected evaluator or mediator and the court, in any proceedings under this code, except with regard to the scheduling of appointments.

(b) There shall be no ex parte communications between counsel appointed by the court pursuant to Section 3150 and a court-appointed or court-connected evaluator or mediator, except when it is expressly authorized by the court or undertaken pursuant to paragraph (5) of subdivision (c) of Section 3151.

(c) Subdivisions (a) and (b) shall not apply in the following situations:

(1) To allow a mediator or evaluator to address a case involving allegations of domestic violence as set forth in Sections 3113, 3181, and 3192.

(2) To allow a mediator or evaluator to address a case involving allegations of domestic violence as set forth in Rule 5.215 of the California Rules of Court.

(3) If the mediator or evaluator determines that ex parte communication is

needed to inform the court of the mediator's or evaluator's belief that a restraining order is necessary to prevent an imminent risk to the physical safety of the child or the party.
(d) This section shall not be construed to limit the responsibilities a mediator or evaluator may have as a mandated reporter pursuant to Section 11165.9 of the Penal Code or the responsibilities a mediator or evaluator have to warn under *Tarasoff v. Regents of the University of California* (1976) 17 Cal. 3d 425, *Hedlund v. Superior Court* (1983) 34 Cal. 3d 695, and Section 43.92 of the Civil Code.
(e) The Judicial Council shall, by July 1, 2006, adopt a rule of court to implement this section.[414]

217. (a) At a hearing on any order to show cause or notice of motion brought pursuant to this code, absent a stipulation of the parties or a finding of good cause pursuant to subdivision (b), the court shall receive any live, competent testimony that is relevant and within the scope of the hearing and the court may ask questions of the parties.
(b) In appropriate cases, a court may make a finding of good cause to refuse to receive live testimony and shall state its reasons for the finding on the record or in writing. The Judicial Council shall, by January 1, 2012, adopt a statewide rule of court regarding the factors a court shall consider in making a finding of good cause.
(c) A party seeking to present live testimony from witnesses other than the parties shall, prior to the hearing, file and serve a witness list with a brief description of the anticipated testimony. If the witness list is not served prior to the hearing, the court may, on request, grant a brief continuance and may make appropriate temporary orders pending the continued hearing.[198]

218. With respect to the ability to conduct formal discovery in family law proceedings, when a request for order or other motion is filed and served after entry of judgment, discovery shall automatically reopen as to the issues raised in the post judgment pleadings currently before the court. The date initially set for trial of the action specified in subdivision (a) of Section 2024.020 of the Code of Civil Procedure shall mean the date the post judgment proceeding is set for hearing on the motion or any continuance thereof, or evidentiary trial, whichever is later.[309]

PART 3: TEMPORARY RESTRAINING ORDER IN SUMMONS

enacted by Stats. 1992, Ch. 162, Sec. 10

231. This part applies to a temporary restraining order in a summons issued under any of the following provisions:
(a) Section 2040 (proceeding for dissolution of marriage, for nullity of marriage, or for legal separation of the parties).
(b) Section 7700 (proceeding under Uniform Parentage Act).

232. The summons shall state on its face that the order is enforceable in any place in this state by any law enforcement agency that has received mailed notice of the order or has otherwise received a copy of the order and any officer who has been shown a copy of the order.[1]

233. (a) Upon filing the petition and issuance of the summons and upon personal service of the petition and summons on the respondent or upon waiver and acceptance of service by the respondent, the temporary restraining order under this part shall be in effect against the parties until the final judgment is entered or the petition is dismissed, or until further order of the court.
(b) The temporary restraining order is enforceable in any place in this state, but is not enforceable by a law enforcement agency of a political subdivision unless that law enforcement agency has received mailed notice of the order or has otherwise received a copy of the order or the officer enforcing the order has been shown a copy of the order.
(c) A willful and knowing violation of the order included in the summons by removing a child from the state without the written consent of the other party or an order of the court is punishable as provided in Section 278.5 of the Penal Code. A willful and knowing violation of any of the other orders included in the summons is punishable as provided in Section 273.6 of the Penal Code.[1]

234. The automatic granting of the ex parte temporary restraining order under this part is not a court determination or competent evidence in any proceeding of any prior history of the conduct so proscribed occurring between the parties.[1]

235. Nothing in this part precludes either party from applying to the court for modification or revocation of the temporary restraining order provided for in this part or for further temporary orders or an expanded temporary ex parte order.[1]

PART 4: EX PARTE TEMPORARY RESTRAINING ORDERS

enacted by Stats. 1993, Ch. 219, Sec. 84.7

240. This part applies where a temporary restraining order, including a protective order as defined in Section 6218, is issued under any of the following provisions:
(a) Article 2 (commencing with Section 2045) of Chapter 4 of Part 1 of Division 6 (dissolution of marriage, nullity of marriage, or legal separation of the parties).
(b) Article 3 (commencing with Section 4620) of Chapter 3 of Part 5 of Division 9 (deposit of assets to secure future child support payments).
(c) Article 1 (commencing with Section 6320) of Chapter 2 of Part 4 of Division 10 (Domestic Violence Prevention Act), other than an order under Section 6322.5.
(d) Article 2 (commencing with Section 7710) of Chapter 6 of Part 3 of Division 12 (Uniform Parentage Act).[69]

241. Except as provided in Section 6300, an order described in Section 240 may not be granted without notice to the respondent unless it appears from facts shown by the declaration in support of the petition for the order, or in the petition for the order, that great or irreparable injury would result to the petitioner before the matter can be heard on notice.[213]

242. (a) Within 21 days, or, if good cause appears to the court, 25 days from the date that a temporary restraining order is granted or denied,

a hearing shall be held on the petition. If no request for a temporary restraining order is made, the hearing shall be held within 21 days, or, if good cause appears to the court, 25 days from the date that the petition is filed.
(b) If a hearing is not held within the time provided in subdivision (a), the court may nonetheless hear the matter, but the temporary restraining order shall no longer be enforceable unless it is extended under Section 245.[334]

243. (a) If a petition under this part has been filed, the respondent shall be personally served with a copy of the petition, the temporary restraining order, if any, and the notice of hearing on the petition. Service shall be made at least five days before the hearing.
(b) On motion of the petitioner or on its own motion, the court may shorten the time for service on the respondent.
(c) If service on the respondent is made, the respondent may file a response that explains or denies the allegations in the petition.[335]

244. (a) On the day of the hearing, the hearing on the petition shall take precedence over all other matters on the calendar that day, except older matters of the same character, and matters to which special precedence may be given by law.
(b) The hearing on the petition shall be set for trial at the earliest possible date and shall take precedence over all other matters, except older matters of the same character, and matters to which special precedence may be given by law.[214]

245. (a) The respondent shall be entitled, as a matter of course, to one continuance for a reasonable period, to respond to the petition.
(b) Either party may request a continuance of the hearing, which the court shall grant on a showing of good cause. The request may be made in writing before or at the hearing or orally at the hearing. The court may also grant a continuance on its own motion.
(c) If the court grants a continuance, any temporary restraining order that has been issued shall remain in effect until the end of the continued hearing, unless otherwise ordered by the court. In granting a continuance, the court may modify or terminate a temporary restraining order.
(d) If the court grants a continuance, the extended temporary restraining order shall state on its face the new date of expiration of the order.
(e) A fee shall not be charged for the extension of the temporary restraining order.[336]

246. A request for a temporary restraining order described in Section 240, issued without notice, shall be granted or denied on the same day that the petition is submitted to the court, unless the petition is filed too late in the day to permit effective review, in which case the order shall be granted or denied on the next day of judicial business in sufficient time for the order to be filed that day with the clerk of the court.[215]

PART 5: ATTORNEY'S FEES AND COSTS

repealed and added by Stats. 1993, Ch. 219, Sec. 8

270. If a court orders a party to pay attorney's fees or costs under this code, the court shall first determine

that the party has or is reasonably likely to have the ability to pay.[8]

271. (a) Notwithstanding any other provision of this code, the court may base an award of attorney's fees and costs on the extent to which any conduct of each party or attorney furthers or frustrates the policy of the law to promote settlement of litigation and, where possible, to reduce the cost of litigation by encouraging cooperation between the parties and attorneys. An award of attorney's fees and costs pursuant to this section is in the nature of a sanction. In making an award pursuant to this section, the court shall take into consideration all evidence concerning the parties' incomes, assets, and liabilities. The court shall not impose a sanction pursuant to this section that imposes an unreasonable financial burden on the party against whom the sanction is imposed. In order to obtain an award under this section, the party requesting an award of attorney's fees and costs is not required to demonstrate any financial need for the award.
(b) An award of attorney's fees and costs as a sanction pursuant to this section shall be imposed only after notice by the requesting party or the court to the party against whom the sanction is proposed and opportunity for that party to be heard is provided by the court.
(c) An award of attorney's fees and costs as a sanction pursuant to this section is payable only from the property or income of the party against whom the sanction is imposed, except that the award may be against the sanctioned party's share of the community property.[541]

272. (a) Where the court orders one of the parties to pay attorney's fees and costs for the benefit of the other party, the fees and costs may, in the discretion of the court, be made payable in whole or in part to the attorney entitled thereto.
(b) Subject to subdivision (c), the order providing for payment of the attorney's fees and costs may be enforced directly by the attorney in the attorney's own name or by the party in whose behalf the order was made.
(c) If the attorney has ceased to be the attorney for the party in whose behalf the order was made, the attorney may enforce the order only if it appears of record that the attorney has given to the former client or successor counsel 10 days' written notice of the application for enforcement of the order. During the 10-day period, the client may file in the proceeding a motion directed to the former attorney for partial or total reallocation of fees and costs to cover the services and cost of successor counsel. On the filing of the motion, the enforcement of the order by the former attorney shall be stayed until the court has resolved the motion.[8]

273. Notwithstanding any other provision of this code, the court shall not award attorney's fees against any governmental agency involved in a family law matter or child support proceeding except when sanctions are appropriate pursuant to Section 128.5 of the Code of Civil Procedure or Section 271 of this code.[44]

274. (a) Notwithstanding any other provision of law, if the injured spouse is entitled to a remedy authorized pursuant to Section 4324, the injured

spouse shall be entitled to an award of reasonable attorney's fees and costs as a sanction pursuant to this section.

(b) An award of attorney's fees and costs as a sanction pursuant to this section shall be imposed only after notice to the party against whom the sanction is proposed to be imposed and opportunity for that party to be heard.

(c) An award of attorney's fees and costs as a sanction pursuant to this section is payable only from the property or income of the party against whom the sanction is imposed, except that the award may be against the sanctioned party's share of the community property. In order to obtain an award under this section, the party requesting an award of attorney's fees and costs is not required to demonstrate any financial need for the award.[137]

PART 6: ENFORCEMENT OF JUDGMENTS AND ORDERS

enacted by Stats. 1992, Ch. 162, Sec. 10.

290. A judgment or order made or entered pursuant to this code may be enforced by the court by execution, the appointment of a receiver, or contempt, or by any other order as the court in its discretion determines from time to time to be necessary.[130]

291. (a) A money judgment or judgment for possession or sale of property that is made or entered under this code, including a judgment for child, family, or spousal support, is enforceable until paid in full or otherwise satisfied.

(b) A judgment described in this section is exempt from any requirement that a judgment be renewed. Failure to renew a judgment described in this section has no effect on the enforceability of the judgment.

(c) A judgment described in this section may be renewed pursuant to Article 2 (commencing with Section 683.110) of Chapter 3 of Division 1 of Title 9 of Part 2 of the Code of Civil Procedure. An application for renewal of a judgment described in this section, whether or not payable in installments, may be filed:

(1) If the judgment has not previously been renewed as to past due amounts, at any time.

(2) If the judgment has previously been renewed, the amount of the judgment as previously renewed and any past due amount that became due and payable after the previous renewal may be renewed at any time after a period of at least five years has elapsed from the time the judgment was previously renewed.

(d) In an action to enforce a judgment for child, family, or spousal support, the defendant may raise, and the court may consider, the defense of laches only with respect to any portion of the judgment that is owed to the state.

(e) Nothing in this section supersedes the law governing enforcement of a judgment after the death of the judgment creditor or judgment debtor.

(f) On or before January 1, 2008, the Judicial Council shall develop self-help materials that include: (1) a description of the remedies available for enforcement of a judgment under this code, and (2) practical advice on how to avoid disputes relating to the enforcement of a support obligation. The self-help materials shall be made available to the public through the

Judicial Council self-help Internet Web site.

(g) As used in this section, "judgment" includes an order.[172]

292. (a) The Judicial Council shall modify the title of its existing form, "Order to Show Cause and Declaration for Contempt (Family Law)," to "Order to Show Cause and Affidavit for Contempt (Family Law)."

(b) The Judicial Council shall prescribe a form entitled "Affidavit of Facts Constituting Contempt" that a party seeking to enforce a judgment or order made or entered pursuant to this code by contempt may use as an attachment to the Judicial Council form entitled "Order to Show Cause and Affidavit for Contempt (Family Law)." The form shall provide in the simplest language possible:

(1) The basic information needed to sustain a cause of action for contempt, including, but not limited to, the elements of a cause of action for contempt.

(2) Instructions on how to prepare and submit the Order to Show Cause and Affidavit for Contempt (Family Law) and the Affidavit of Facts Constituting Contempt.

(3) Lines for the date and a signature made under penalty of perjury.

(c) Section 1211.5 of the Code of Civil Procedure shall apply to the Order to Show Cause and Affidavit for Contempt (Family Law) and the Affidavit of Facts Constituting Contempt.[59]

PART 7: TRIBAL MARRIAGES AND DIVORCES

enacted by Stats. 1992, Ch. 162, Sec. 10.

295. (a) For the purpose of application of the laws of succession set forth in the Probate Code to a decedent, and for the purpose of determining the validity of a marriage under the laws of this state, an alliance entered into before 1958, which, by custom of the Indian tribe, band, or group of which the parties to the alliance, or either of them, are members, is commonly recognized in the tribe, band, or group as marriage, is deemed a valid marriage under the laws of this state.

(b) In the case of these marriages and for the purposes described in subdivision (a), a separation, which, by custom of the Indian tribe, band, or group of which the separating parties, or either of them, are members, is commonly recognized in the tribe, band, or group as a dissolution of marriage, is deemed a valid divorce under the laws of this state.[1]

DIVISION 2.5: DOMESTIC PARTNER REGISTRATION

ADDED BY STATS. 1999, CH. 588, SEC. 2.
SECTION 297-299.6

PART 1: DEFINITIONS

added by Stats. 1999, Ch. 588, Sec. 2.

297. (a) Domestic partners are two adults who have chosen to share one another's lives in an intimate and committed relationship of mutual caring.
(b) A domestic partnership shall be established in California when both persons file a Declaration of Domestic Partnership with the Secretary of State pursuant to this division, and, at the time of filing, all of the following requirements are met:
(1) Neither person is married to someone else or is a member of another domestic partnership with someone else that has not been terminated, dissolved, or adjudged a nullity.
(2) The two persons are not related by blood in a way that would prevent them from being married to each other in this state.
(3) Both persons are at least 18 years of age, except as provided in Section 297.1.
(4) Both persons are capable of consenting to the domestic partnership.[467]

297.1. (a) A person under 18 years of age who, together with the other proposed domestic partner, otherwise meets the requirements for a domestic partnership other than the requirement of being at least 18 years of age, may establish a domestic partnership upon obtaining a court order granting permission to the underage person or persons to establish a domestic partnership.
(b) (1) The court order and written consent of the parents of each person under 18 years of age or of one of the parents or the guardian of each person under 18 years of age, except as provided in paragraph (2), shall be filed with the clerk of the court, and a certified copy of the order shall be filed with the Secretary of State with the Declaration of Domestic Partnership.
(2) If it appears to the satisfaction of the court by application of a person under 18 years of age that the person requires a written consent to establish a domestic partnership and that the minor has no parent or guardian, or has no parent or guardian capable of consenting, the court may make an order consenting to establishing the domestic partnership. The order shall be filed with the clerk of the court and a certified copy of the order shall be filed with the Secretary of State with the Declaration of Domestic Partnership.
(3) Notwithstanding any other law, immediately after the Secretary of State creates or updates the document described in Section 298.8 using the information required for the document and that is contained in a certified copy of a court order filed with the Secretary of State with the Declaration of Domestic Partnership pursuant to this subdivision, the Secretary of State may dispose of the certified copy of the court order.

(c) In determining whether to issue a court order granting permission to establish a domestic partnership, the court shall do all of the following:

(1) Require Family Court Services to separately interview the parties intending to establish a domestic partnership and, if applicable, at least one of the parents or the guardian of each party who is a minor. If more than one parent or guardian is interviewed, the parents or guardians shall be interviewed separately.

(2) Require Family Court Services to prepare and submit to the court a written report, containing any assessment of potential force, threat, persuasion, fraud, coercion, or duress by either of the parties or their family members relating to the intended domestic partnership. The report shall also contain recommendations of Family Court Services for either granting or denying the parties permission to establish a domestic partnership. If Family Court Services knows or reasonably suspects that either party is a victim of child abuse or neglect, Family Court Services shall submit a report of the known or suspected child abuse or neglect to the county child protective services agency.

(3) After receiving the report of the assessments of Family Court Services, as described in paragraph (2), separately interview in camera each of the parties prior to making a final determination regarding the court order.

(4) Consider whether there is evidence of coercion or undue influence on the minor.

(d) If the court issues an order granting the parties permission to establish a domestic partnership, and if one or both of the parties are 17 years of age or younger, the parties shall be eligible to file a Declaration of Domestic Partnership with the Secretary of State no earlier than 30 days from the time the court order was issued.

(e) As part of the court order granting permission to establish a domestic partnership, the court shall, if it considers it necessary, require the parties to the prospective domestic partnership of a minor to participate, before the domestic partnership is established, in counseling concerning social, economic, and personal responsibilities incident to the domestic partnership. The parties shall not be required to confer with counselors provided by religious organizations of any denomination. In determining whether to order the parties to participate in the counseling, the court shall consider, among other factors, the ability of the parties to pay for the counseling. The court may impose a reasonable fee to cover the cost of counseling provided by the county or the court. The fees shall be used exclusively to cover the cost of the counseling services authorized by this section.

(f) (1) Only for purposes of completing the document described in Section 298.8, and not for purposes of making a determination regarding the court order, the gender of each party intending to establish a domestic partnership, if provided, shall be documented on the court order granting permission to establish the domestic partnership.

(2) The date of birth of each party intending to establish a domestic partnership shall also be documented

on the court order granting permission to establish the domestic partnership.

(g) Upon issuance of the order granting permission to establish a domestic partnership, the minor shall be provided with the following information:

(1) The rights and responsibilities of an emancipated minor, including, but not limited to, the effects of emancipation as described in Chapter 2 (commencing with Section 7050) of Part 6 of Division 11.

(2) (A) The circumstances under which a domestic partnership may be determined by a court to be void or voidable and adjudged a nullity and the procedure for obtaining that judicial determination.

(B) The procedures for termination of a domestic partnership.

(3) Telephone numbers for the National Domestic Violence Hotline and the National Sexual Assault Hotline.

(4) The conditions under which an unemancipated minor may leave home and seek to remain in a shelter or otherwise live separately from the minor's parent or guardian, and whether the consent or acquiescence of a parent or guardian is required to remain away from the home of the parent or guardian, the rights of an unemancipated minor to apply for a protective or restraining order to prevent abuse, and the rights of a minor to enter into contracts, including contracts for legal services and mental health counseling.

(h) (1) Subdivisions (c) and (d) do not apply to a minor who is 17 years of age and who has achieved a high school diploma or a high school equivalency certificate.

(2) Subdivision (d) does not apply to a minor who is 16 or 17 years of age and who is pregnant or whose prospective domestic partner is pregnant.[468]

297.5. (a) Registered domestic partners shall have the same rights, protections, and benefits, and shall be subject to the same responsibilities, obligations, and duties under law, whether they derive from statutes, administrative regulations, court rules, government policies, common law, or any other provisions or sources of law, as are granted to and imposed upon spouses.

(b) Former registered domestic partners shall have the same rights, protections, and benefits, and shall be subject to the same responsibilities, obligations, and duties under law, whether they derive from statutes, administrative regulations, court rules, government policies, common law, or any other provisions or sources of law, as are granted to and imposed upon former spouses.

(c) A surviving registered domestic partner, following the death of the other partner, shall have the same rights, protections, and benefits, and shall be subject to the same responsibilities, obligations, and duties under law, whether they derive from statutes, administrative regulations, court rules, government policies, common law, or any other provisions or sources of law, as are granted to and imposed upon a widow or a widower.

(d) The rights and obligations of registered domestic partners with respect to a child of either of them shall be the same as those of spouses. The rights and obligations of former or surviving registered domestic partners with respect to a child of either of them shall be the same as those of former or surviving spouses.

(e) To the extent that provisions of California law adopt, refer to, or rely upon, provisions of federal law in a way that otherwise would cause registered domestic partners to be treated differently than spouses, registered domestic partners shall be treated by California law as if federal law recognized a domestic partnership in the same manner as California law.

(f) Registered domestic partners shall have the same rights regarding nondiscrimination as those provided to spouses.

(g) No public agency in this state may discriminate against any person or couple on the ground that the person is a registered domestic partner rather than a spouse or that the couple are registered domestic partners rather than spouses, except that nothing in this section applies to modify eligibility for long-term care plans pursuant to Chapter 15 (commencing with Section 21660) of Part 3 of Division 5 of Title 2 of the Government Code.

(h) This act does not preclude any state or local agency from exercising its regulatory authority to implement statutes providing rights to, or imposing responsibilities upon, domestic partners.

(i) This section does not amend or modify any provision of the California Constitution or any provision of any statute that was adopted by initiative.

(j) Where necessary to implement the rights of registered domestic partners under this act, gender-specific terms referring to spouses shall be construed to include domestic partners.

(k) (1) For purposes of the statutes, administrative regulations, court rules, government policies, common law, and any other provision or source of law governing the rights, protections, and benefits, and the responsibilities, obligations, and duties of registered domestic partners in this state, as effectuated by this section, with respect to community property, mutual responsibility for debts to third parties, the right in particular circumstances of either partner to seek financial support from the other following the dissolution of the partnership, and other rights and duties as between the partners concerning ownership of property, any reference to the date of a marriage shall be deemed to refer to the date of registration of a domestic partnership with the state.

(2) Notwithstanding paragraph (1), for domestic partnerships registered with the state before January 1, 2005, an agreement between the domestic partners that the partners intend to be governed by the requirements set forth in Sections 1600 to 1620, inclusive, and which complies with those sections, except for the agreement's effective date, shall be enforceable as provided by Sections 1600 to 1620, inclusive, if that agreement was fully executed and in force as of June 30, 2005.[140]

PART 2: REGISTRATION

added by Stats. 1999, Ch. 588, Sec. 2.

298. (a) (1) The Secretary of State shall prepare forms entitled "Declaration of Domestic Partnership" and "Notice of Termination of Domestic Partnership" to meet the requirements of this division. These forms shall

require the signature and seal of an acknowledgment by a notary public to be binding and valid.

(2) The instructions on the "Declaration of Domestic Partnership" form shall include both of the following:

(A) An explanation that registered domestic partners have the same rights, protections, and benefits, and are subject to the same responsibilities, obligations, and duties under law as are granted to and imposed upon spouses.

(B) An explanation of how to terminate a registered domestic partnership.

(3) When funding allows, the Secretary of State shall include on the form notice that a lesbian, gay, bisexual, and transgender specific domestic abuse brochure is available upon request.

(b) (1) These forms shall be available to the public at the office of the Secretary of State or on the Secretary of State's internet website. The Secretary of State's internet website shall include all of the information required in paragraph (2) of subdivision (a).

(2) The Secretary of State shall, by regulation, establish fees for the actual costs of processing each of these forms and shall charge these fees to persons filing the forms.

(3) There is hereby established a fee of twenty-three dollars ($23) to be charged in addition to the existing fees established by regulation to persons filing domestic partner registrations pursuant to Section 297 for development and support of a lesbian, gay, bisexual, and transgender curriculum for training workshops on domestic violence, conducted pursuant to Section 13823.15 of the Penal Code, and for the support of a grant program to promote healthy nonviolent relationships in the lesbian, gay, bisexual, and transgender community. This paragraph does not apply to persons filing a domestic partner registration when one or both of the domestic partners are 62 years of age or older.

(4) The fee established by paragraph (3) shall be deposited in the Equality in Prevention and Services for Domestic Abuse Fund, which is hereby established. The fund shall be administered by the Office of Emergency Services, and expenditures from the fund shall be used to support the purposes of paragraph (3).

(c) The Declaration of Domestic Partnership shall require each person who wants to become a domestic partner to (1) state that the person meets the requirements of Section 297 at the time the form is signed, (2) provide a mailing address, (3) state that the person consents to the jurisdiction of the Superior Courts of California for the purpose of a proceeding to obtain a judgment of dissolution or nullity of the domestic partnership or for legal separation of partners in the domestic partnership, or for any other proceeding related to the partners' rights and obligations, even if one or both partners ceases to be a resident of, or to maintain a domicile in, this state, (4) sign the form with a declaration that representations made therein are true, correct, and contain no material omissions of fact to the best knowledge and belief of the applicant, and (5) have a notary public acknowledge the signature. Both partners' signatures shall be affixed to one Declaration of Domestic Partnership form, which shall then be transmitted to the Secretary of State according to the instructions provided on the form. Filing an intentionally and materially false Declaration of Domestic Partnership shall be punishable as a misdemeanor.

(d) The Declaration of Domestic Partnership form shall contain an optional section for either party or both parties to indicate a change in name pursuant to Section 298.6. The optional section shall require a party indicating a change in name to provide the person's date of birth.[469]

298.5. (a) Two persons desiring to become domestic partners may complete and file a Declaration of Domestic Partnership with the Secretary of State.

(b) The Secretary of State shall register the Declaration of Domestic Partnership in a registry for those partnerships, and shall return a copy of the registered form, a Certificate of Registered Domestic Partnership, and a copy of the brochure that is made available to county clerks and the Secretary of State by the State Department of Public Health pursuant to Section 358 and distributed to individuals receiving a confidential marriage license pursuant to Section 503, to the domestic partners at the mailing address provided by the domestic partners.

(c) A person who has filed a Declaration of Domestic Partnership may not file a new Declaration of Domestic Partnership or enter a civil marriage with someone other than their registered domestic partner unless the most recent domestic partnership has been terminated or a final judgment of dissolution or nullity of the most recent domestic partnership has been entered. This prohibition does not apply if the previous domestic partnership ended because one of the partners died.

(d) When funding allows, the Secretary of State shall print and make available upon request, pursuant to Section 358, a lesbian, gay, bisexual, and transgender specific domestic abuse brochure developed by the State Department of Public Health and made available to the Secretary of State to domestic partners who qualify pursuant to Section 297.

(e) The Certificate of Registered Domestic Partnership shall include the name used by each party before registration of the domestic partnership and the new name, if any, selected by each party upon registration of the domestic partnership.[470]

298.6. (a) Parties to a registered domestic partnership shall not be required to have the same name. Neither party shall be required to change their name. A person's name shall not change upon registration as a domestic partner unless that person elects to change their name pursuant to subdivision (b).

(b) (1) One party or both parties to a registered domestic partnership may elect to change the middle or last names by which that party wishes to be known after registration of the domestic partnership by entering the new name in the space provided on the Declaration of Domestic Partnership form without intent to defraud.

(2) A person may adopt any of the following middle or last names

pursuant to paragraph (1):

(A) The current last name of the other domestic partner.

(B) The last name of either domestic partner given at birth.

(C) A name combining into a single last name all or a segment of the current last name or the last name of either domestic partner given at birth.

(D) A hyphenated combination of last names.

(3) (A) An election by a person to change the person's name pursuant to paragraph (1) shall serve as a record of the name change. A certified copy of the Declaration of Domestic Partnership containing the new name, or retaining the former name, shall constitute proof that the use of the new name or retention of the former name is lawful.

(B) A certified copy of a Declaration of Domestic Partnership shall be accepted as identification establishing a true, full name for purposes of Section 12800.7 of the Vehicle Code.

(C) This section does not prohibit the Department of Motor Vehicles from accepting as identification other documents establishing a true, full name for purposes of Section 12800.7 of the Vehicle Code. Those documents may include, without limitation, a certified copy of a document that is substantially equivalent to a Certificate of Registered Domestic Partnership that records either of the following:

(i) A legal union of two persons that was validly formed in another jurisdiction and is recognized as a valid domestic partnership in this state pursuant to Section 299.2.

(ii) A legal union of domestic partners as defined by a local jurisdiction pursuant to Section 299.6.

(D) This section shall be applied in a manner consistent with the requirements of Sections 1653.5 and 12801 of the Vehicle Code.

(4) The adoption of a new name, or the choice not to adopt a new name, by means of a Declaration of Domestic Partnership pursuant to paragraph (1) shall not abrogate the right of either party to adopt a different name through usage at a future date, or to petition the superior court for a change of name pursuant to Title 8 (commencing with Section 1275) of Part 3 of the Code of Civil Procedure.

(c) This section does not abrogate the common law right of a person to change the person's name, or the right of a person to petition the superior court for a change of name pursuant to Title 8 (commencing with Section 1275) of Part 3 of the Code of Civil Procedure.[471]

298.7. The Secretary of State shall establish a process by which two persons, who have been living together as domestic partners and who meet the requirements of paragraphs (1) to (4), inclusive, of subdivision (b) of Section 297, may enter into a confidential domestic partnership. This process shall do all of the following:

(a) Maintain each confidential Declaration of Domestic Partnership as a permanent record that is not open to public inspection except upon order of the court issued upon a showing of good cause.

(b) Authorize the Secretary of State to charge a reasonable fee to offset costs directly connected with maintaining confidentiality of a Declaration of

Domestic Partnership.[472]

298.8. (a) The Secretary of State shall create a document no later than March 1, 2020, with annual updates no later than March 1 of each year thereafter, disaggregated by county, containing only the following information concerning domestic partnerships that were registered during the preceding calendar year and in which one or both of the parties were minors at the time the domestic partnership was established:

(1) The total number of those registered domestic partnerships.

(2) Itemized for each of those registered domestic partnerships, the age of each party at the time the domestic partnership was established.

(3) Itemized for each of those registered domestic partnerships, the gender of each party as documented on the court order pursuant to Section 297.1, unless the court order does not include the gender.

(b) The document shall not contain the names, addresses, or other personal identifying information of parties to a registered domestic partnership, or any information identifying a registered domestic partnership. The document shall not contain a registered domestic partnership or a copy of the court order described in Section 297.1.

(c) The Secretary of State shall make the document available to the public upon request.[380]

PART 3: TERMINATION

added by Stats. 1999, Ch. 588, Sec. 2.

299. (a) A registered domestic partnership may be terminated without filing a proceeding for dissolution of domestic partnership by the filing of a Notice of Termination of Domestic Partnership with the Secretary of State pursuant to this section, provided that all of the following conditions exist at the time of the filing:

(1) The Notice of Termination of Domestic Partnership is signed by both registered domestic partners.

(2) There are no children of the relationship of the parties born before or after registration of the domestic partnership or adopted by the parties after registration of the domestic partnership, and neither of the registered domestic partners, to their knowledge, is pregnant.

(3) The registered domestic partnership is not more than five years in duration.

(4) Neither party has any interest in real property wherever situated, with the exception of the lease of a residence occupied by either party which satisfies the following requirements:

(A) The lease does not include an option to purchase.

(B) The lease terminates within one year from the date of filing of the Notice of Termination of Domestic Partnership.

(5) There are no unpaid obligations in excess of the amount described in paragraph (6) of subdivision (a) of Section 2400, as adjusted by subdivision (b) of Section 2400, incurred by either or both of the parties after registration of the domestic partnership, excluding the amount of any unpaid obligation with respect to an automobile.

(6) The total fair market value of community property assets, excluding

all encumbrances and automobiles, including any deferred compensation or retirement plan, is less than the amount described in paragraph (7) of subdivision (a) of Section 2400, as adjusted by subdivision (b) of Section 2400, and neither party has separate property assets, excluding all encumbrances and automobiles, in excess of that amount.

(7) The parties have executed an agreement setting forth the division of assets and the assumption of liabilities of the community property, and have executed any documents, title certificates, bills of sale, or other evidence of transfer necessary to effectuate the agreement.

(8) The parties waive any rights to support by the other domestic partner.

(9) The parties have read and understand a brochure prepared by the Secretary of State describing the requirements, nature, and effect of terminating a domestic partnership.

(10) Both parties desire that the domestic partnership be terminated.

(b) The registered domestic partnership shall be terminated effective six months after the date of filing of the Notice of Termination of Domestic Partnership with the Secretary of State pursuant to this section, provided that neither party has, before that date, filed with the Secretary of State a notice of revocation of the termination of domestic partnership, in the form and content as shall be prescribed by the Secretary of State, and sent to the other party a copy of the notice of revocation by first-class mail, postage prepaid, at the other party's last known address. The effect of termination of a domestic partnership pursuant to this section shall be the same as, and shall be treated for all purposes as, the entry of a judgment of dissolution of a domestic partnership.

(c) The termination of a domestic partnership pursuant to subdivision (b) does not prejudice nor bar the rights of either of the parties to institute an action in the superior court to set aside the termination for fraud, duress, mistake, or any other ground recognized at law or in equity. A court may set aside the termination of domestic partnership and declare the termination of the domestic partnership null and void upon proof that the parties did not meet the requirements of subdivision (a) at the time of the filing of the Notice of Termination of Domestic Partnership with the Secretary of State.

(d) The superior courts shall have jurisdiction over all proceedings relating to the dissolution of domestic partnerships, nullity of domestic partnerships, and legal separation of partners in a domestic partnership. The dissolution of a domestic partner-ship, nullity of a domestic partnership, and legal separation of partners in a domestic partnership shall follow the same procedures, and the partners shall possess the same rights, protections, and benefits, and be subject to the same responsibilities, obligations, and duties, as apply to the dissolution of marriage, nullity of marriage, and legal separation of spouses in a marriage, respectively, except as provided in subdivision (a), and except that, in accordance with the consent acknowledged by domestic partners in the Declaration of Domestic Partnership form, proceedings for dissolution, nullity, or legal separation of a domestic partnership registered in this state

may be filed in the superior courts of this state even if neither domestic partner is a resident of, or maintains a domicile in, the state at the time the proceedings are filed.
(e) Parties to a registered domestic partnership who are also married to one another may petition the court to dissolve both their domestic partnership and their marriage in a single proceeding, in a form that shall be prescribed by the Judicial Council.

299.2. A legal union of two persons, other than a marriage, that was validly formed in another jurisdiction, and that is substantially equivalent to a domestic partnership as defined in this part, shall be recognized as a valid domestic partnership in this state regardless of whether it bears the name domestic partnership.[473]

PART 4: LEGAL EFFECT

PART 5: PREEMPTION

added by Stats. 1999, Ch. 588, Sec. 2.

299.6. (a) Any local ordinance or law that provides for the creation of a "domestic partnership" shall be preempted on and after July 1, 2000, except as provided in subdivision (c).
(b) Domestic partnerships created under any local domestic partnership ordinance or law before July 1, 2000, shall remain valid. On and after July 1, 2000, domestic partnerships previously established under a local ordinance or law shall be governed by this division and the rights and duties of the partners shall be those set out in this division, except as provided in subdivision (c), provided a Declaration of Domestic Partnership is filed by the domestic partners under Section 298.5.
(c) Any local jurisdiction may retain or adopt ordinances, policies, or laws that offer rights within that jurisdiction to domestic partners as defined by Section 297 or as more broadly defined by the local jurisdiction's ordinances, policies, or laws, or that impose duties upon third parties regarding domestic partners as defined by Section 297 or as more broadly defined by the local jurisdiction's ordinances, policies, or laws, that are in addition to the rights and duties set out in this division, and the local rights may be conditioned upon the agreement of the domestic partners to assume the additional obligations set forth in this division.

DIVISION 3: MARRIAGE

ENACTED BY STATS. 1992, CH. 162, SEC. 10.
SECTION 300-560

PART 1: VALIDITY OF MARRIAGE

enacted by Stats. 1992, Ch. 162, Sec. 10

300. (a) Marriage is a personal relation arising out of a civil contract between two persons, to which the consent of the parties capable of making that contract is necessary. Consent alone does not constitute marriage. Consent must be followed by the issuance of a license and solemnization as authorized by this division, except as provided by Section 425 and Part 4 (commencing with Section 500).
(b) For purposes of this part, the document issued by the county clerk is a marriage license until it is registered with the county recorder, at which time the license becomes a marriage certificate.[282]

301. Two unmarried persons 18 years of age or older, who are not otherwise disqualified, are capable of consenting to and consummating marriage.[283]

302. (a) An unmarried person under 18 years of age may be issued a marriage license upon obtaining a court order granting permission to the underage person or persons to marry, in accordance with the requirements described in Section 304.
(b) The court order and written consent of at least one of the parents or the guardian of each underage person shall be filed with the clerk of the court, and a certified copy of the order shall be presented to the county clerk at the time the marriage license is issued.[381]

303. If it appears to the satisfaction of the court by application of a minor that the minor requires a written consent to marry and that the minor has no parent or has no parent capable of consenting, the court may make an order consenting to the issuance of a marriage license and granting permission to the minor to marry, in accordance with the requirements described in Section 304. The order shall be filed with the clerk of the court and a certified copy of the order shall be presented to the county clerk at the time the marriage license is issued.[382]

304. (a) In determining whether to issue a court order granting permission to marry pursuant to Section 302 or 303, the court shall do all of the following:
(1) Require Family Court Services to separately interview the parties intending to marry and, if applicable, at least one of the parents or the guardian of each party who is a minor. If more than one parent or guardian is interviewed, the parents or guardians shall be interviewed separately.
(2) Require Family Court Services to prepare and submit to the court a written report, containing any assessment of potential force, threat, persuasion, fraud, coercion, or duress by either of the parties or their family members relating to the intended

marriage. The report shall also contain recommendations of Family Court Services for either granting or denying the parties permission to marry. If Family Court Services knows or reasonably suspects that either party is a victim of child abuse or neglect, Family Court Services shall submit a report of the known or suspected child abuse or neglect to the county child protective services agency.

(3) After receiving the report of the assessments of Family Court Services, as described in paragraph (2), separately interview in camera each of the parties prior to making a final determination regarding the court order.

(4) Consider whether there is evidence of coercion or undue influence on the minor.

(b) If the court issues an order granting the parties permission to marry pursuant to Section 302 or 303, and if one or both of the parties are 17 years of age or younger, the parties shall be eligible to request a marriage license no earlier than 30 days from the time the court order was issued.

(c) As part of the court order granting permission to marry under Section 302 or 303, the court shall, if it considers it necessary, require the parties to the prospective marriage of a minor to participate in premarital counseling concerning social, economic, and personal responsibilities incident to marriage. The parties shall not be required to confer with counselors provided by religious organizations of any denomination. In determining whether to order the parties to participate in the premarital counseling, the court shall consider, among other factors, the ability of the parties to pay for the counseling. The court may impose a reasonable fee to cover the cost of premarital counseling provided by the county or the court. The fees shall be used exclusively to cover the cost of the counseling services authorized by this section.

(d) (1) Only for purposes of completing the document described in Section 102233 of the Health and Safety Code, and not for purposes of making a determination regarding the court order, the gender of each party intending to marry, if provided, shall be documented on the court order granting permission to marry.

(2) The date of birth of each party intending to marry shall also be documented on the court order granting permission to marry.

(3) For purposes of the requirements on the person solemnizing the marriage under subdivision (b) of Section 423, and the requirements on the local registrar under subdivision (a) of Section 102356 of the Health and Safety Code, the court shall provide parties who are granted permission to marry with a copy of the court order granting permission to marry.

(e) Upon issuance of the order granting permission to marry, the minor shall be provided with the following information:

(1) The rights and responsibilities of an emancipated minor, including, but not limited to, the effects of emancipation as described in Chapter 2 (commencing with Section 7050) of Part 6 of Division 11.

(2) (A) The circumstances under which a marriage may be determined by a court to be void or voidable and

adjudged a nullity and the procedure for obtaining that judicial determination.

(B) The procedures for legal separation or dissolution of marriage.

(3) Telephone numbers for the National Domestic Violence Hotline and the National Sexual Assault Hotline.

(4) The conditions under which an unemancipated minor may leave home and seek to remain in a shelter or otherwise live separately from the minor's parent or guardian, and whether the consent or acquiescence of a parent or guardian is required to remain away from the home of the parent or guardian, the rights of an unemancipated minor to apply for a protective or restraining order to prevent abuse, and the rights of a minor to enter into contracts, including contracts for legal services and mental health counseling.

(f) (1) Subdivisions (a) and (b) do not apply to a minor who is 17 years of age and who has achieved a high school diploma or a high school equivalency certificate.

(2) Subdivision (b) does not apply to a minor who is 16 or 17 years of age and who is pregnant or whose prospective spouse is pregnant.[415]

305. Consent to and solemnization of marriage may be proved under the same general rules of evidence as facts are proved in other cases.[1]

306. Except as provided in Section 307, a marriage shall be licensed, solemnized, and authenticated, and the authenticated marriage license shall be returned to the county recorder of the county where the marriage license was issued, as provided in this part. Noncompliance with this part by a nonparty to the marriage does not invalidate the marriage.[149]

306.5. (a) Parties to a marriage shall not be required to have the same name. Neither party shall be required to change their name. A person's name shall not change upon marriage unless that person elects to change their name pursuant to subdivision (b).

(b) (1) One party or both parties to a marriage may elect to change the middle or last names, or both, by which that party wishes to be known after solemnization of the marriage by entering the new name in the spaces provided on the marriage license application without intent to defraud.

(2) A person may adopt any of the following last names pursuant to paragraph (1):

(A) The current last name of the other spouse.

(B) The last name of either spouse given at birth.

(C) A name combining into a single last name all or a segment of the current last name or the last name of either spouse given at birth.

(D) A combination of last names.

(3) A person may adopt any of the following middle names pursuant to paragraph (1):

(A) The current last name of either spouse.

(B) The last name of either spouse given at birth.

(C) A combination of the current middle name and the current last name of the person or spouse.

(D) A combination of the current middle name and the last name given at birth of the person or spouse.

(4) (A) An election by a person to change their name pursuant to

paragraph (1) shall serve as a record of the name change. A certified copy of a marriage certificate containing the new name, or retaining the former name, shall constitute proof that the use of the new name or retention of the former name is lawful.

(B) A certified copy of a marriage certificate shall be accepted as identification establishing a true, full name for purposes of Section 12800.7 of the Vehicle Code.

(C) This section does not prohibit the Department of Motor Vehicles from accepting as identification other documents establishing a true, full name for purposes of Section 12800.7 of the Vehicle Code. Those documents may include, without limitation, a certified copy of a marriage certificate recording a marriage outside of this state.

(D) This section shall be applied in a manner consistent with the requirements of Sections 1653.5 and 12801 of the Vehicle Code.

(5) The adoption of a new name, or the choice not to adopt a new name, by means of a marriage license application pursuant to paragraph (1) shall only be made at the time the marriage license is issued. After a marriage certificate is registered by the local registrar, the certificate shall not be amended to add a new name or change the name adopted pursuant to paragraph (1). An amendment may be issued to correct a clerical error in the new name fields on the marriage license. In this instance, the amendment shall be signed by one of the parties to the marriage and the county clerk or a deputy clerk, and the reason for the amendment shall be stated as correcting a clerical error. A clerical error as used in this part is an error made by the county clerk, a deputy clerk, or a notary authorized to issue confidential marriage licenses, whereby the information shown in the new name field does not match the information shown on the marriage license application. This requirement does not abrogate the right of either party to adopt a different name through usage at a future date, or to petition the superior court for a change of name pursuant to Title 8 (commencing with Section 1275) of Part 3 of the Code of Civil Procedure.

(c) This section does not abrogate the common law right of a person to change their name, or the right of a person to petition the superior court for a change of name pursuant to Title 8 (commencing with Section 1275) of Part 3 of the Code of Civil Procedure.[416]

307. This division, so far as it relates to the solemnizing of marriage, is not applicable to members of a particular religious society or denomination not having clergy for the purpose of solemnizing marriage or entering the marriage relation, if all of the following requirements are met:

(a) The parties to the marriage sign and endorse on the form prescribed by the State Department of Public Health, showing all of the following:

(1) The fact, time, and place of entering into the marriage.

(2) The printed names, signatures, and mailing addresses of two witnesses to the ceremony.

(3) The religious society or denomination of the parties to the marriage, and that the marriage was entered into in accordance with the

rules and customs of that religious society or denomination. The statement of the parties to the marriage that the marriage was entered into in accordance with the rules and customs of the religious society or denomination is conclusively presumed to be true.

(b) The License and Certificate of Non-Clergy Marriage, endorsed pursuant to subdivision (a), is returned to the county recorder of the county in which the license was issued within 10 days after the ceremony.[174]

308. A marriage contracted outside this state that would be valid by laws of the jurisdiction in which the marriage was contracted is valid in California.[352]

309. If either party to a marriage denies the marriage, or refuses to join in a declaration of the marriage, the other party may proceed, by action pursuant to Section 103450 of the Health and Safety Code, to have the validity of the marriage determined and declared.[150]

310. Marriage is dissolved only by one of the following:

(a) The death of one of the parties.

(b) A judgment of dissolution of marriage.

(c) A judgment of nullity of marriage.[1]

PART 2: MARRIAGE LICENSES

amended by Stats. 2006, Ch. 816, Sec. 7.

350. (a) Before entering a marriage, or declaring a marriage pursuant to Section 425, the parties shall first obtain a marriage license from a county clerk.

(b) If a marriage is to be entered into pursuant to subdivision (b) of Section 420, the attorney-in-fact shall appear before the county clerk on behalf of the party who is overseas, as prescribed in subdivision (a).[111]

351. The marriage license shall show all of the following:

(a) The identity of the parties to the marriage.

(b) The parties' full given names at birth or by court order, and mailing addresses.

(c) The parties' dates of birth.[151]

351.5. Notwithstanding subdivision (b) of Section 351 or 359 of this code, or Section 103175 of the Health and Safety Code, if either of the applicants for, or any witness to, a certificate of registry of marriage and a marriage license requests, the certificate of registry and the marriage license shall show the business address or United States Postal Service post office box for that applicant or witness instead of the residential address of that person.[128]

351.6. Notwithstanding Section 307, 351, 351.5, 359, or 422 of this code, or Section 103175 or 103180 of the Health and Safety Code, a mailing address used by an applicant, witness, or person solemnizing or performing the marriage ceremony shall be a residential address, a business address, or a United States Postal Service post office box.[152]

352. No marriage license shall be granted if either of the applicants lacks the capacity to enter into a valid marriage or is, at the time of making the application for the license, under the influence of an intoxicating liquor or narcotic drug.[1]

354.(a) Each applicant for a marriage license shall be required to present

authentic photo identification acceptable to the county clerk as to name and date of birth. A credible witness affidavit or affidavits may be used in lieu of authentic photo identification.
(b) For the purpose of ascertaining the facts mentioned or required in this part, if the clerk deems it necessary, the clerk may examine the applicants for a marriage license on oath at the time of the application. The clerk shall reduce the examination to writing and the applicants shall sign it.
(c) If necessary, the clerk may request additional documentary proof as to the accuracy of the facts stated.
(d) Applicants for a marriage license shall not be required to state, for any purpose, their race or color.
(e) If a marriage is to be entered into pursuant to subdivision (b) of Section 420, the attorney in fact shall comply with the requirements of this section on behalf of the applicant who is overseas, if necessary.[153]

355. (a) The forms for the marriage license shall be prescribed by the State Department of Public Health, and shall be adapted to set forth the facts required in this part.
(b) The marriage license shall include an affidavit, which the applicants shall sign, affirming that they have received the brochure provided for in Section 358. If the marriage is to be entered into pursuant to subdivision (b) of Section 420, the attorney in fact shall sign the affidavit on behalf of the applicant who is overseas.
(c) The forms for the marriage license shall contain spaces for either party or both parties to indicate a change in name pursuant to Section 306.5.[176]

356. A marriage license issued pursuant to this part expires 90 days after its issuance. The calendar date of expiration shall be clearly noted on the face of the license.[1]

357. (a) The county clerk shall number each marriage license issued and shall transmit at periodic intervals to the county recorder a list or copies of the licenses issued.
(b) Not later than 60 days after the date of issuance, the county recorder shall notify license holders whose marriage license has not been returned of that fact and that the marriage license will automatically expire on the date shown on its face.
(c) The county recorder shall notify the license holders of the obligation of the person solemnizing their marriage to return the marriage license to the recorder's office within 10 days after the ceremony.[153]

358. (a) The State Department of Public Health shall prepare and publish a brochure that shall contain the following:
(1) Information concerning the possibilities of genetic defects and diseases and a listing of centers available for the testing and treatment of genetic defects and diseases.
(2) Information concerning acquired immunodeficiency syndrome (AIDS) and the availability of testing for antibodies to the probable causative agent of AIDS.
(3) Information concerning domestic violence, including resources available to victims and a statement that physical, emotional, psychological, and sexual abuse, and assault and battery, are against the law.
(4) Information concerning options for changing a name upon

solemnization of marriage pursuant to Section 306.5, or upon registration of a domestic partnership pursuant to Section 298.6. That information shall include a notice that the recording of a change in name or the absence of a change in name on a marriage license application and certificate pursuant to Section 306.5 may not be amended once the marriage license is issued, but that options to adopt a change in name in the future through usage, common law, or petitioning the superior court are preserved, as set forth in Section 306.5.

(b) The State Department of Public Health shall make the brochures available to county clerks who shall distribute a copy of the brochure to each applicant for a marriage license, including applicants for a confidential marriage license and notaries public receiving a confidential marriage license pursuant to Section 503. The department shall also make the brochure available to the Secretary of State, who shall distribute a copy of the brochure to persons who qualify as domestic partners pursuant to Section 297 and shall make the brochure available electronically on the Internet Web site of the Secretary of State.

(c) The department shall prepare a lesbian, gay, bisexual, and transgender specific domestic abuse brochure and make the brochure available to the Secretary of State who shall print and make available the brochure, as funding allows, pursuant to Section 298.5.

(d) Each notary public issuing a confidential marriage license under Section 503 shall distribute a copy of the brochure to the applicants for a confidential marriage license.

(e) To the extent possible, the State Department of Public Health shall seek to combine in a single brochure all statutorily required information for marriage license applicants.[177]

359. (a) Except as provided in Sections 420 and 426, applicants to be married shall first appear together in person before the county clerk to obtain a marriage license.

(b) The contents of the marriage license are provided in Part 1 (commencing with Section 102100) of Division 102 of the Health and Safety Code.

(c) The issued marriage license shall be presented to the person solemnizing the marriage by the parties to be married.

(d) The person solemnizing the marriage shall complete the solemnization sections on the marriage license, and shall cause to be entered on the marriage license the printed name, signature, and mailing address of at least one, and no more than two, witnesses to the marriage ceremony.

(e) The marriage license shall be returned by the person solemnizing the marriage to the county recorder of the county in which the license was issued within 10 days after the ceremony.

(f) As used in this division, "returned" means presented to the appropriate person in person, or postmarked, before the expiration of the specified time period.

(g) This section shall become operative on January 1, 2024.[539]

360. (a) If a marriage license is lost, damaged, or destroyed after the marriage ceremony, but before it is returned to the county recorder, or

deemed unacceptable for registration by the county recorder, the person solemnizing the marriage, in order to comply with Section 359, shall obtain a duplicate marriage license by filing an affidavit setting forth the facts with the county clerk of the county in which the license was issued.

(b) The duplicate marriage license shall not be issued later than one year after the date of marriage and shall be returned by the person solemnizing the marriage to the county recorder within one year of the date of marriage.

(c) The county clerk may charge a fee to cover the actual costs of issuing a duplicate marriage license.

(d) If a marriage license is lost, damaged, or destroyed before a marriage ceremony takes place, the applicants shall purchase a new marriage license and the old license shall be voided.[353]

PART 3: SOLEMNIZATION OF MARRIAGE

enacted by Stats. 1992, Ch. 162, Sec. 10.

Chapter 1: Persons Authorized to Solemnize Marriage

400. (a) Although marriage is a personal relation arising out of a civil, and not a religious, contract, a marriage may be solemnized by a priest, minister, rabbi, or authorized person of any religious denomination who is 18 years of age or older. A person authorized by this subdivision shall not be required to solemnize a marriage that is contrary to the tenets of the person's faith. Refusal to solemnize a marriage under this subdivision, either by an individual or by a religious denomination, shall not affect the tax-exempt status of any entity.

(b) Consistent with Section 94.5 of the Penal Code and provided that any compensation received is reasonable, including payment of actual expenses, a marriage may also be solemnized by any of the following persons:

(1) A judge or retired judge, commissioner of civil marriages or retired commissioner of civil marriages, commissioner or retired commissioner, or assistant commissioner of a court of record in this state.

(2) A judge or magistrate who has resigned from office.

(3) Any of the following judges or magistrates of the United States:

(A) A justice or retired justice of the United States Supreme Court.

(B) A judge or retired judge of a court of appeals, a district court, or a court created by an act of the United States Congress the judges of which are entitled to hold office during good behavior.

(C) A judge or retired judge of a bankruptcy court or a tax court.

(D) A United States magistrate or retired magistrate.

(c) Except as provided in subdivision (d), a marriage may also be solemnized by any of the following persons who are 18 years of age or older:

(1) A Member of the Legislature or constitutional officer of this state or a Member of Congress of the United States who represents a district within this state, or a former Member of the Legislature or constitutional officer of this state or a former Member of Congress of the United States who represented a district within this state.

(2) A person that holds or formerly

held an elected office of a city, county, or city and county.

(3) A city clerk of a charter city or serving in accordance with subdivision (b) of Section 36501 of the Government Code, while that person holds office.

(d) (1) A person listed in subdivision (c) shall not accept compensation for solemnizing a marriage while holding office.

(2) A person listed in subdivision (c) shall not solemnize a marriage pursuant to this section if they have been removed from office due to committing an offense or have been convicted of an offense that involves moral turpitude, dishonesty, or fraud.[417]

401. (a) For each county, the county clerk is designated as a commissioner of civil marriages.

(b) The commissioner of civil marriages may appoint deputy commissioners of civil marriages who may solemnize marriages under the direction of the commissioner of civil marriages and shall perform other duties directed by the commissioner.[1]

402. In addition to the persons permitted to solemnize marriages under Section 400, a county may license officials of a nonprofit religious institution, whose articles of incorporation are registered with the Secretary of State, to solemnize the marriages of persons who are affiliated with or are members of the religious institution. The licensee shall possess the degree of doctor of philosophy and must perform religious services or rites for the institution on a regular basis. The marriages shall be performed without fee to the parties.[1]

Chapter 2: Solemnization of Marriage

enacted by Stats. 1992, Ch. 162, Sec. 10.

420. (a) No particular form for the ceremony of marriage is required for solemnization of the marriage, but the parties shall declare, in the physical presence of the person solemnizing the marriage and necessary witnesses, that they take each other as spouses.

(b) Notwithstanding subdivision (a), a member of the Armed Forces of the United States who is stationed overseas and serving in a conflict or a war and is unable to appear for the licensure and solemnization of the marriage may enter into that marriage by the appearance of an attorney in fact, commissioned and empowered in writing for that purpose through a power of attorney. The attorney in fact shall personally appear at the county clerk's office with the party who is not stationed overseas and present the original power of attorney duly signed by the party stationed overseas and acknowledged before a notary or witnessed by two officers of the United States Armed Forces. Copies in any form, including by facsimile, are not acceptable. The power of attorney shall state the full given names at birth, or by court order, of the parties to be married, and that the power of attorney is solely for the purpose of authorizing the attorney in fact to obtain a marriage license on the person's behalf and participate in the solemnization of the marriage. The original power of attorney shall be a part of the marriage certificate upon registration. The completion of a power of attorney shall be the sole determinant as to whether the county clerk's office and the State Registrar

will accept the power of attorney.
(c) A contract of marriage, if otherwise duly made, shall not be invalidated for want of conformity to the requirements of any religious sect.[350]

421. Before solemnizing a marriage, the person solemnizing the marriage shall require the presentation of the marriage license. If the person solemnizing the marriage has reason to doubt the correctness of the statement of facts in the marriage license, the person must be satisfied as to the correctness of the statement of facts before solemnizing the marriage. For this purpose, the person may administer oaths and examine the parties and witnesses in the same manner as the county clerk does before issuing the license.

422. The person solemnizing a marriage shall sign and print or type upon the marriage license a statement, in the form prescribed by the State Department of Public Health, showing all of the following:
(a) The fact, date (month, day, year), and place (city and county) of solemnization.
(b) The printed names, signatures, and mailing addresses of at least one, and no more than two, witnesses to the ceremony.
(c) The official position of the person solemnizing the marriage, or of the denomination of which that person is a priest, minister, rabbi, or other authorized person of any religious denomination.
(d) The person solemnizing the marriage shall also type or print their name and mailing address.[418]

423. (a) The person solemnizing the marriage shall return the marriage license, endorsed as required in Section 422, to the county recorder of the county in which the license was issued within 10 days after the ceremony.
(b) For purposes of Section 102356 of the Health and Safety Code, the person solemnizing the marriage shall include with the marriage license described in subdivision (a) a copy of the court order granting permission to marry described in Section 304, if one or both of the parties to the marriage were minors at the time of solemnization of the marriage.[383]

425. If no record of the solemnization of a California marriage previously contracted under this division for that marriage is known to exist, the parties may purchase a License and Certificate of Declaration of Marriage from the county clerk in the parties' county of residence one year or more from the date of the marriage. The license and certificate shall be returned to the county recorder of the county in which the license was issued.[154]

426. If for sufficient reason, as described in subdivision (d), either or both of the parties to be married are physically unable to appear in person before the county clerk, a marriage license may be issued by the county clerk to the person solemnizing the marriage if the following requirements are met:
(a) The person solemnizing the marriage physically presents an affidavit to the county clerk explaining the reason for the inability to appear.
(b) The affidavit is signed under penalty of perjury by the person solemnizing the marriage and by both parties.
(c) The signature of any party to be

married who is unable to appear in person before the county clerk is authenticated by a notary public or a court prior to the county clerk issuing the marriage license.

(d) Sufficient reason includes proof of hospitalization, incarceration, or any other reason proved to the satisfaction of the county clerk.[155]

PART 4: CONFIDENTIAL MARRIAGE

enacted by Stats. 1992, Ch. 162, Sec. 10.

Chapter 1: General Provisions

500. When two unmarried people, not minors, have been living together as spouses, they may be married pursuant to this chapter by a person authorized to solemnize a marriage under Chapter 1 (commencing with Section 400) of Part 3.[354]

500.5. For purposes of this part, the document issued by the county clerk is a marriage license until it is registered with the county clerk, at which time the license becomes a marriage certificate.[156]

501. (a) Except as provided in Section 502, a confidential marriage license shall be issued by the county clerk upon the personal appearance together of the parties to be married and their payment of the fees required by Sections 26840.1 and 26840.8 of the Government Code and any fee imposed pursuant to the authorization of Section 26840.3 of the Government Code.

(b) This section shall become operative on January 1, 2024.[540]

502. If for sufficient reason, as described in subdivision (d), either or both of the parties to be married are physically unable to appear in person before the county clerk, a confidential marriage license may be issued by the county clerk to the person solemnizing the marriage if the following requirements are met:

(a) The person solemnizing the marriage physically presents an affidavit to the county clerk explaining the reason for the inability to appear.

(b) The affidavit is signed under penalty of perjury by the person solemnizing the marriage and by both parties.

(c) The signature of any party to be married who is unable to appear in person before the county clerk is authenticated by a notary public or a court prior to the county clerk issuing the confidential marriage license.

(d) Sufficient reason includes proof of hospitalization, incarceration, or any other reason proved to the satisfaction of the county clerk.[157]

503. The county clerk shall issue a confidential marriage license upon the request of a notary public approved by the county clerk to issue confidential marriage licenses pursuant to Chapter 2 (commencing with Section 530) and upon payment by the notary public of the fees specified in Sections 26840.1 and 26840.8 of the Government Code. The parties shall reimburse a notary public who issues a confidential marriage license for the amount of the fees.[158]

504. A confidential marriage license is valid only for a period of 90 days after its issuance by the county clerk.[325]

505. (a) The form of the confidential marriage license shall be prescribed by the State Registrar of Vital Statistics.

(b) The form shall be designed to

require that the parties to be married declare or affirm that they meet all of the requirements of this chapter.
(c) The form shall include an affidavit, which the bride and groom shall sign, affirming that they have received the brochure provided for in Section 358.[159]

506. (a) The confidential marriage license shall be presented to the person solemnizing the marriage.
(b) Upon performance of the ceremony, the solemnization section on the confidential marriage license shall be completed by the person solemnizing the marriage.
(c) The confidential marriage license shall be returned by the person solemnizing the marriage to the office of the county clerk in the county in which the license was issued within 10 days after the ceremony.[160]

508. Upon issuance of a confidential marriage license, parties shall be provided with an application to obtain a certified copy of the confidential marriage certificate from the county clerk.[161]

509. (a) A party to a confidential marriage may obtain a certified copy of the confidential marriage certificate from the county clerk of the county in which the certificate is filed by submitting an application that satisfies the requirements of Chapter 14 (commencing with Section 103525) of Part 1 of Division 102 of the Health and Safety Code.
(b) Copies of a confidential marriage certificate may be issued to the parties to the marriage upon payment of the fee equivalent to that charged for copies of a marriage certificate.[191]

510. (a) If a confidential marriage license is lost, damaged, or destroyed after the performance of the marriage, but before it is returned to the county clerk, or deemed unacceptable for registration by the county clerk, the person solemnizing the marriage, in order to comply with Section 506, shall obtain a duplicate marriage license by filing an affidavit setting forth the facts with the county clerk of the county in which the license was issued.
(b) The duplicate license may not be issued later than one year after the date of the marriage and shall be returned by the person solemnizing the marriage to the county clerk within one year of the date of the marriage.
(c) The county clerk may charge a fee to cover the actual costs of issuing a duplicate marriage license.
(d) If a marriage license is lost, damaged, or destroyed before a marriage ceremony takes place, the applicants shall purchase a new marriage license and the old license shall be voided.[478]

511. (a) Except as provided in subdivision (b), the county clerk shall maintain confidential marriage certificates filed pursuant to Section 506 as permanent records which shall not be open to public inspection except upon order of the court issued upon a showing of good cause. The confidential marriage license is a confidential record and not open to public inspection without an order from the court.
(b) The county clerk shall keep all original certificates of confidential marriages for one year from the date of filing. After one year, the clerk may reproduce the certificates pursuant to Section 26205 of the Government

Code, and dispose of the original certificates. The county clerk shall promptly seal and store at least one original negative of each microphotographic film made in a manner and place as reasonable to ensure its preservation indefinitely against loss, theft, defacement, or destruction. The microphotograph shall be made in a manner that complies with the minimum standards or guidelines, or both, recommended by the American National Standards Institute or the Association for Information and Image Management. Every reproduction shall be deemed and considered an original. A certified copy of any repro-duction shall be deemed and considered a certified copy of the original.

(c) The county clerk may conduct a search for a confidential marriage certificate for the purpose of confirming the existence of a marriage, but the date of the marriage and any other information contained in the certificate shall not be disclosed except upon order of the court.

(d) The county clerk shall, not less than quarterly, transmit copies of all original confidential marriage certificates retained, or originals of reproduced confidential marriage certificates filed after January 1, 1982, to the State Registrar of Vital Statistics. The registrar may destroy the copies so transmitted after they have been indexed. The registrar may respond to an inquiry as to the existence of a marriage performed pursuant to this chapter, but shall not disclose the date of the marriage.[162]

Chapter 2: Approval of Notaries to Authorize Confidential Marriages

530. (a) No notary public shall issue a confidential marriage license pursuant to this part unless the notary public is approved by the county clerk to issue confidential marriage licenses pursuant to this chapter.

(b) A violation of subdivision (a) is a misdemeanor punishable by a fine not to exceed one thousand dollars ($1,000) or six months in jail.[163]

531.(a) An application for approval to authorize confidential marriages pursuant to this part shall be submitted to the county clerk in the county in which the notary public who is applying for the approval resides. The county clerk shall exercise reasonable discretion as to whether to approve applications.

(b) The application shall include all of the following:

(1) The full name of the applicant.

(2) The date of birth of the applicant.

(3) The applicant's current residential address and telephone number.

(4) The address and telephone number of the place where the applicant will issue confidential marriage licenses.

(5) The full name of the applicant's employer if the applicant is employed by another person.

(6) Whether or not the applicant has engaged in any of the acts specified in Section 8214.1 of the Government Code.

(c) The application shall be accompanied by the fee provided for in Section 536.[164]

532. No approval, or renewal of the approval, shall be granted pursuant to this chapter unless the notary public

shows evidence of successful completion of a course of instruction concerning the issuance of confidential marriage licenses that was conducted by the county clerk in the county of registration. The course of instruction shall not exceed six hours in duration.[165]

533. An approval to issue confidential marriage licenses pursuant to this chapter is valid for one year. The approval may be renewed for additional one-year periods provided the following conditions are met:
(a) The applicant has not violated any of the provisions provided for in Section 531.
(b) The applicant has successfully completed the course prescribed in Section 532.
(c) The applicant has paid the renewal fee provided for in Section 536.[166]

534. (a) The county clerk shall maintain a list of the notaries public who are approved to issue confidential marriage licenses. The list shall be available for inspection by the public.
(b) It is the responsibility of a notary public approved to issue confidential marriage licenses pursuant to this chapter to keep current the information required in paragraphs (1), (3), (4), and (5) of subdivision (b) of Section 531. This information shall be used by the county clerk to update the list required to be maintained by this section.[167]

535. (a) If, after an approval to issue confidential marriage licenses is granted pursuant to this chapter, it is discovered that the notary public has engaged in any of the actions specified in Section 8214.1 of the Government Code, the approval shall be revoked, and the county clerk shall notify the Secretary of State for whatever action the Secretary of State deems appropriate. Any fees paid by the notary public shall be retained by the county clerk.
(b) If a notary public who is approved to authorize confidential marriages pursuant to this chapter is alleged to have violated a provision of this division, the county clerk shall conduct a hearing to determine if the approval of the notary public should be suspended or revoked. The notary public may present any evidence as is necessary in the notary public's defense. If the county clerk determines that the notary public has violated a provision of this division, the county clerk may place the notary public on probation or suspend or revoke the notary public's registration, and any fees paid by the notary public shall be retained by the county clerk. The county clerk shall report the findings of the hearing to the Secretary of State for whatever action the Secretary of State deems appropriate.[168]

536. (a) The fee for an application for approval to authorize confidential marriages pursuant to this chapter is three hundred dollars ($300).
(b) The fee for renewal of an approval is three hundred dollars ($300).
(c) Fees received pursuant to this chapter shall be deposited in a trust fund established by the county clerk. The money in the trust fund shall be used exclusively for the administration of the programs described in this chapter.[169]

PART 5: REMOTE MARRIAGE LICENSE ISSUANCE AND SOLEMNIZATION

added by Stats. 2021, Ch. 620, Sec. 5.

550. Notwithstanding any other law, including, but not limited to, Section 420, a county clerk may issue a marriage license, including a confidential marriage license, or solemnize or witness a marriage ceremony under state law using remote technology pursuant to this part, except for a marriage of a minor, as set forth in Sections 302 to 304, inclusive, or any successor provisions.[485]

552. A couple seeking a marriage license or solemnization pursuant to this part shall present, in the manner requested by the county clerk, a copy of a valid government-issued photo identification to verify their identity and any additional documentary proof requested by the county clerk.[485]

554. (a) Each member of the couple shall be physically located in the State of California while using remote technology to obtain a marriage license pursuant to this part.
(b) (1) Each member of the couple shall be in the same physical location in the State of California while using remote technology to solemnize their marriage pursuant to this part.
(2) The person solemnizing the marriage, any necessary witnesses, and the county clerk shall all be physically located in the State of California, but may be at separate physical locations from each other and the couple solemnizing their marriage.
(c) The county clerk may require a couple to complete an affidavit, in a form provided by the county clerk, affirming that they and each individual participating in a marriage solemnization using remote technology are physically present within the State of California in compliance with this part.[485]

556. (a) At the discretion of the county clerk, a couple applying for a marriage license using remote technology may sign their marriage license electronically or by original wet signature. The couple shall transmit a signed, legible copy of their marriage license by United States mail, fax, or electronic means directly to the county clerk, in the manner required by the county clerk.
(b) At the discretion of the county clerk, a marriage license issued using the procedure described in this part may be transmitted to the applicants by United States mail, fax, or electronic means.
(c) Before the solemnization of a marriage pursuant to this part, one or both of the parties to be married shall transmit the marriage license by United States mail, fax, or electronic means to the person solemnizing the marriage and any necessary witnesses, in the manner required by the county clerk.
(d) At the discretion of the county clerk, the person solemnizing the marriage or any necessary witnesses may sign the marriage license electronically or by original wet signature and transmit the signed marriage license by United States mail, fax, or electronic means, in the manner required by the county clerk.
(e) A county clerk who witnesses a marriage solemnized by someone other than the county clerk using remote technology may apply an

electronic signature to the marriage license as a witness, and transmit the signed license to the person solemnizing the marriage by United States mail, fax, or electronic means.[485]

558. A county clerk may provide guidance relating to marriage license applications, marriage license issuance, and the witnessing or solemnizing of the marriage ceremony when the guidance relates to the use of their remote technology pursuant to this part.[485]

560. For purposes of this part, "remote technology" means audio video technology that is provided by a county clerk and allows the couple, or the couple and others participating in a marriage solemnization, as applicable, to appear together from the same physical location and directly interact with each other and the county clerk.[485]

DIVISION 4:
RIGHTS AND OBLIGATION DURING MARRIAGE

ENACTED BY STATS. 1992, CH. 162, SEC. 10
SECTION 700-1620

PART 1:
GENERAL PROVISIONS

enacted by Stats. 1992, Ch. 162, Sec. 10.

Chapter 1: Definitions

700. For the purposes of this division, a leasehold interest in real property is real property, not personal property.[1]

Chapter 2: Relation of Spouses

720. Spouses contract toward each other obligations of mutual respect, fidelity, and support.[284]

721. (a) Subject to subdivision (b), either spouse may enter into any transaction with the other, or with any other person, respecting property, which either might if unmarried.
(b) Except as provided in Sections 143, 144, 146, 16040, 16047, and 21385 of the Probate Code, in transactions between themselves, spouses are subject to the general rules governing fiduciary relationships that control the actions of persons occupying confidential relations with each other. This confidential relationship imposes a duty of the highest good faith and fair dealing on each spouse, and neither shall take any unfair advantage of the other. This confidential relationship is a fiduciary relationship subject to the same rights and duties of nonmarital business partners, as provided in Sections 16403, 16404, and 16503 of the Corporations Code, including, but not limited to, the following:
(1) Providing each spouse access at all times to any books kept regarding a transaction for the purposes of inspection and copying.
(2) Rendering upon request, true and full information of all things affecting any transaction that concerns the community property. Nothing in this section is intended to impose a duty for either spouse to keep detailed books and records of community property transactions.
(3) Accounting to the spouse, and holding as a trustee, any benefit or profit derived from any transaction by one spouse without the consent of the other spouse that concerns the community property.[412]

Chapter 3: Property Rights during Marriage

750. Spouses may hold property as joint tenants or tenants in common, or as community property, or as community property with a right of survivorship.[285]

751. The respective interests of each spouse in community property during continuance of the marriage relation are present, existing, and equal interests.[286]

752. Except as otherwise provided by statute, neither spouse has any interest in the separate property of the other.[287]

753. Notwithstanding Section 752 and

except as provided in Article 2 (commencing with Section 2045), Article 3 (commencing with Section 2047), or Article 4 (commencing with Section 2049) of Chapter 4 of Part 1 of Division 6, neither spouse may be excluded from the other's dwelling.[9]

754. If notice of the pendency of a proceeding for dissolution of the marriage, for nullity of the marriage, or for legal separation of the parties is recorded in any county in which either spouse resides on real property that is the separate property of the other, the real property shall not for a period of three months thereafter be transferred, encumbered, or otherwise disposed of voluntarily or involuntarily without the joinder of both spouses, unless the court otherwise orders.[288]

755. (a) The terms "participant," "beneficiary," "employer," "employee organization," "named fiduciary," "fiduciary," and "administrator," as used in subdivision (b), have the same meaning as provided in Section 3 of the Employee Retirement Income Security Act of 1974 (P.L. 93-406) (ERISA), as amended (29 U.S.C.A. Sec. 1002). The term "employee benefit plan" has the same meaning as provided in Section 80 of this code. The term "trustee" shall include a "named fiduciary" as that term is employed in ERISA. The term "plan sponsor" shall include an "employer" or "employee organization," as those terms are used in ERISA (29 U.S.C.A. Sec. 1002).
(b) Notwithstanding Sections 751 and 1100, if payment or refund is made to a participant or the participant's, employee's, or former employee's beneficiary or estate pursuant to an employee benefit plan including a plan governed by the Employee Retirement Income Security Act of 1974 (P.L. 93-406), as amended, the payment or refund fully discharges the plan sponsor and the administrator, trustee, or insurance company making the payment or refund from all adverse claims thereto unless, before the payment or refund is made, the plan sponsor or the administrator of the plan has received written notice by or on behalf of some other person that the other person claims to be entitled to the payment or refund or some part thereof. Nothing in this section affects or releases the participant from claims which may exist against 'the participant by a person other than the plan sponsor, trustee, administrator, or other person making the benefit payment.[45]

PART 2: CHARACTERIZATION OF MARITAL PROPERTY

enacted by Stats. 1992, Ch. 162, Sec. 10.

Chapter 1: Community Property

760. Except as otherwise provided by statute, all property, real or personal, wherever situated, acquired by a married person during the marriage while domiciled in this state is community property.[1]

761. (a) Unless the trust instrument or the instrument of transfer expressly provides otherwise, community property that is transferred in trust remains community property during the marriage, regardless of the identity of the trustee, if the trust, originally or as amended before or after the transfer, provides that the trust is revocable as to that property during

the marriage and the power, if any, to modify the trust as to the rights and interests in that property during the marriage may be exercised only with the joinder or consent of both spouses.
(b) Unless the trust instrument expressly provides otherwise, a power to revoke as to community property may be exercised by either spouse acting alone. Community property, including any income or appreciation, that is distributed or withdrawn from a trust by revocation, power of withdrawal, or otherwise, remains community property unless there is a valid transmutation of the property at the time of distribution or withdrawal.
(c) The trustee may convey and otherwise manage and control the trust property in accordance with the provisions of the trust without the joinder or consent of either spouse unless the trust expressly requires the joinder or consent of one or both spouses.
(d) This section applies to a transfer made before, on, or after July 1, 1987.
(e) Nothing in this section affects the community character of property that is transferred before, on, or after July 1, 1987, in any manner or to a trust other than described in this section.[289]

Chapter 2: Separate Property

770. (a) Separate property of a married person includes all of the following:
(1) All property owned by the person before marriage.
(2) All property acquired by the person after marriage by gift, bequest, devise, or descent.
(3) The rents, issues, and profits of the property described in this section.
(b) A married person may, without the consent of the person's spouse, convey the person's separate property.[1]

771. (a) The earnings and accumulations of a spouse and the minor children living with, or in the custody of, the spouse, after the date of separation of the spouses, are the separate property of the spouse.
(b) Notwithstanding subdivision (a), the earnings and accumulations of an unemancipated minor child related to a contract of a type described in Section 6750 shall remain the sole legal property of the minor child.[346]

772. After entry of a judgment of legal separation of the parties, the earnings or accumulations of each party are the separate property of the party acquiring the earnings or accumulations.[1]

Chapter 3: Damages for Injuries to Married Person

780. Except as provided in Section 781 and subject to the rules of allocation set forth in Section 2603, money and other property received or to be received by a married person in satisfaction of a judgment for damages for personal injuries, or pursuant to an agreement for the settlement or compromise of a claim for such damages, is community property if the cause of action for the damages arose during the marriage.[1]

781. (a) Money or other property received or to be received by a married person in satisfaction of a judgment for damages for personal injuries, or pursuant to an agreement for the settlement or compromise of a claim for those damages, is the separate property of the injured person if the cause of action for the damages arose

as follows:

(1) After the entry of a judgment of dissolution of a marriage or legal separation of the parties.

(2) While the injured spouse is living separate from the other spouse.

(b) Notwithstanding subdivision (a), if the spouse of the injured person has paid expenses by reason of the personal injuries from separate property or from the community property, the spouse is entitled to reimbursement of the separate property or the community property for those expenses from the separate property received by the injured person under subdivision (a).

(c) Notwithstanding subdivision (a), if one spouse has a cause of action against the other spouse that arose during the marriage of the parties, money or property paid or to be paid by or on behalf of a party to the party's spouse of that marriage in satisfaction of a judgment for damages for personal injuries to that spouse, or pursuant to an agreement for the settlement or compromise of a claim for the damages, is the separate property of the injured spouse.[419]

782. (a) Where an injury to a married person is caused in whole or in part by the negligent or wrongful act or omission of the person's spouse, the community property may not be used to discharge the liability of the tortfeasor spouse to the injured spouse or the liability to make contribution to a joint tortfeasor until the separate property of the tortfeasor spouse, not exempt from enforcement of a money judgment, is exhausted.

(b) This section does not prevent the use of community property to discharge a liability referred to in subdivision (a) if the injured spouse gives written consent thereto after the occurrence of the injury.

(c) This section does not affect the right to indemnity provided by an insurance or other contract to discharge the tortfeasor spouse's liability, whether or not the consideration given for the contract consisted of community property.[1]

782.5. In addition to any other remedy authorized by law, when a spouse is convicted of attempting to murder the other spouse, as punishable pursuant to subdivision (a) of Section 664 of the Penal Code, or of soliciting the murder of the other spouse, as punishable pursuant to subdivision (b) of Section 653f of the Penal Code, the injured spouse shall be entitled to an award to the injured spouse of 100 percent of the community property interest in the retirement and pension benefits of the injured spouse.

As used in this section, "injured spouse" has the same meaning as defined in Section 4324.[195]

783. If a married person is injured by the negligent or wrongful act or omission of a person other than the married person's spouse, the fact that the negligent or wrongful act or omission of the spouse of the injured person was a concurring cause of the injury is not a defense in an action brought by the injured person to recover damages for the injury except in cases where the concurring negligent or wrongful act or omission would be a defense if the marriage did not exist.[1]

Chapter 4: Presumptions Concerning Nature of Property

802. The presumption that property acquired during marriage is community property does not apply to any property to which legal or equitable title is held by a person at the time of the person's death if the marriage during which the property was acquired was terminated by dissolution of marriage more than four years before the death.[1]

803. Notwithstanding any other provision of this part, whenever any real or personal property, or any interest therein or encumbrance thereon, was acquired before January 1, 1975, by a married woman by an instrument in writing, the following presumptions apply, and are conclusive in favor of any person dealing in good faith and for a valuable consideration with the married woman or her legal representatives or successors in interest, regardless of any change in her marital status after acquisition of the property:
(a) If acquired by the married woman, the presumption is that the property is the married woman's separate property.
(b) If acquired by the married woman and any other person, the presumption is that the married woman takes the part acquired by her as tenant in common, unless a different intention is expressed in the instrument.
(c) If acquired by husband and wife by an instrument in which they are described as husband and wife, the presumption is that the property is the community property of the husband and wife, unless a different intention is expressed in the instrument.[1]

Chapter 5: Transmutation of Property

850. Subject to Sections 851 to 853, inclusive, married persons may by agreement or transfer, with or without consideration, do any of the following:
(a) Transmute community property to separate property of either spouse.
(b) Transmute separate property of either spouse to community property.
(c) Transmute separate property of one spouse to separate property of the other spouse.[1]

851. A transmutation is subject to the laws governing fraudulent transfers. [1]

852. (a) A transmutation of real or personal property is not valid unless made in writing by an express declaration that is made, joined in, consented to, or accepted by the spouse whose interest in the property is adversely affected.
(b) A transmutation of real property is not effective as to third parties without notice thereof unless recorded.
(c) This section does not apply to a gift between the spouses of clothing, wearing apparel, jewelry, or other tangible articles of a personal nature that is used solely or principally by the spouse to whom the gift is made and that is not substantial in value taking into account the circumstances of the marriage.
(d) Nothing in this section affects the law governing characterization of property in which separate property and community property are commingled or otherwise combined.
(e) This section does not apply to or affect a transmutation of property made before January 1, 1985, and the law that would otherwise be applicable to that transmutation shall continue to

apply.[1]

853. (a) A statement in a will of the character of property is not admissible as evidence of a transmutation of the property in a proceeding commenced before the death of the person who made the will.
(b) A waiver of a right to a joint and survivor annuity or survivor's benefits under the federal Retirement Equity Act of 1984 (Public Law 98-397) is not a transmutation of the community property rights of the person executing the waiver.
(c) A written joinder or written consent to a nonprobate transfer of community property on death that satisfies Section 852 is a transmutation and is governed by the law applicable to transmutations and not by Chapter 2 (commencing with Section 5010) of Part 1 of Division 5 of the Probate Code.

PART 3: LIABILITY OF MARITAL PROPERTY

enacted by Stats. 1992, Ch. 162, Sec. 10.

Chapter 1: Definitions

900. Unless the provision or context otherwise requires, the definitions in this chapter govern the construction of this part.[1]

902 "Debt" means an obligation incurred by a married person before or during marriage, whether based on contract, tort, or otherwise.[1]

903. A debt is "incurred" at the following time:
(a) In the case of a contract, at the time the contract is made.
(b) In the case of a tort, at the time the tort occurs.
(c) In other cases, at the time the obligation arises.[1]

Chapter 2: General Rules of Liability

910. (a) Except as otherwise expressly provided by statute, the community estate is liable for a debt incurred by either spouse before or during marriage, regardless of which spouse has the management and control of the property and regardless of whether one or both spouses are parties to the debt or to a judgment for the debt.
(b) "During marriage" for purposes of this section does not include the period after the date of separation, as defined in Section 70, and before a judgment of dissolution of marriage or legal separation of the parties.[347]

911. (a) The earnings of a married person during marriage are not liable for a debt incurred by the person's spouse before marriage. After the earnings of the married person are paid, they remain not liable so long as they are held in a deposit account in which the person's spouse has no right of withdrawal and are uncommingled with other property in the community estate, except property insignificant in amount.
(b) As used in this section:
(1) "Deposit account" has the meaning prescribed in paragraph (29) of subdivision (a) of Section 9102 of the Commercial Code.
(2) "Earnings" means compensation for personal services performed, whether as an employee or otherwise.

912. For the purposes of this part, quasi-community property is liable to the same extent, and shall be treated the same in all other respects, as

community property.[1]

913. (a) The separate property of a married person is liable for a debt incurred by the person before or during marriage.
(b) Except as otherwise provided by statute:
(1) The separate property of a married person is not liable for a debt incurred by the person's spouse before or during marriage.
(2) The joinder or consent of a married person to an encumbrance of community estate property to secure payment of a debt incurred by the person's spouse does not subject the person's separate property to liability for the debt unless the person also incurred the debt.[1]

914. (a) Notwithstanding Section 913, a married person is personally liable for the following debts incurred by the person's spouse during marriage:
(1) A debt incurred for necessaries of life of the person's spouse before the date of separation of the spouses.
(2) Except as provided in Section 4302, a debt incurred for common necessaries of life of the person's spouse after the date of separation of the spouses.
(b) The separate property of a married person may be applied to the satisfaction of a debt for which the person is personally liable pursuant to this section. If separate property is so applied at a time when nonexempt property in the community estate or separate property of the person's spouse is available but is not applied to the satisfaction of the debt, the married person is entitled to reimbursement to the extent such property was available.
(c) (1) Except as provided in paragraph (2), the statute of limitations set forth in Section 366.2 of the Code of Civil Procedure shall apply if the spouse for whom the married person is personally liable dies.
(2) If the surviving spouse had actual knowledge of the debt prior to expiration of the period set forth in Section 366.2 of the Code of Civil Procedure and the personal representative of the deceased spouse's estate failed to provide the creditor asserting the claim under this section with a timely written notice of the probate administration of the estate in the manner provided for pursuant to Section 9050 of the Probate Code, the statute of limitations set forth in Section 337 or 339 of the Code of Civil Procedure, as applicable, shall apply.
(d) For purposes of this section, "date of separation" has the same meaning as set forth in Section 70.[348]

915. (a) For the purpose of this part, a child or spousal support obligation of a married person that does not arise out of the marriage shall be treated as a debt incurred before marriage, regardless of whether a court order for support is made or modified before or during marriage and regardless of whether any installment payment on the obligation accrues before or during marriage.
(b) If property in the community estate is applied to the satisfaction of a child or spousal support obligation of a married person that does not arise out of the marriage, at a time when nonexempt separate income of the person is available but is not applied to the satisfaction of the obligation, the community estate is entitled to

reimbursement from the person in the amount of the separate income, not exceeding the property in the community estate so applied.

(c) Nothing in this section limits the matters a court may take into consideration in determining or modifying the amount of a support order, including, but not limited to, the earnings of the spouses of the parties.

916. (a) Notwithstanding any other provision of this chapter, after division of community and quasi-community property pursuant to Division 7 (commencing with Section 2500):

(1) The separate property owned by a married person at the time of the division and the property received by the person in the division is liable for a debt incurred by the person before or during marriage and the person is personally liable for the debt, whether or not the debt was assigned for payment by the person's spouse in the division.

(2) The separate property owned by a married person at the time of the division and the property received by the person in the division is not liable for a debt incurred by the person's spouse before or during marriage, and the person is not personally liable for the debt, unless the debt was assigned for payment by the person in the division of the property. Nothing in this paragraph affects the liability of property for the satisfaction of a lien on the property.

(3) The separate property owned by a married person at the time of the division and the property received by the person in the division is liable for a debt incurred by the person's spouse before or during marriage, and the person is personally liable for the debt, if the debt was assigned for payment by the person in the division of the property. If a money judgment for the debt is entered after the division, the property is not subject to enforcement of the judgment and the judgment may not be enforced against the married person, unless the person is made a party to the judgment for the purpose of this paragraph.

(b) If property of a married person is applied to the satisfaction of a money judgment pursuant to subdivision (a) for a debt incurred by the person that is assigned for payment by the person's spouse, the person has a right of reimbursement from the person's spouse to the extent of the property applied, with interest at the legal rate, and may recover reasonable attorney's fees incurred in enforcing the right of reimbursement.[1]

Chapter 3: Reimbursement

920. A right of reimbursement provided by this part is subject to the following provisions:

(a) The right arises regardless of which spouse applies the property to the satisfaction of the debt, regardless of whether the property is applied to the satisfaction of the debt voluntarily or involuntarily, and regardless of whether the debt to which the property is applied is satisfied in whole or in part. The right is subject to an express written waiver of the right by the spouse in whose favor the right arises.

(b) The measure of reimbursement is the value of the property or interest in property at the time the right arises.

(c) The right shall be exercised not later than the earlier of the following times:

(1) Within three years after the spouse in whose favor the right arises has actual knowledge of the application of the property to the satisfaction of the debt.
(2) In proceedings for division of community and quasi-community property pursuant to Division 7 (commencing with Section 2500) or in proceedings upon the death of a spouse.[1]

Chapter 4: Transitional Provisions

930. Except as otherwise provided by statute, this part governs the liability of separate property and property in the community estate and the personal liability of a married person for a debt enforced on or after January 1, 1985, regardless of whether the debt was incurred before, on, or after that date.

931. The provisions of this part that govern reimbursement apply to all debts, regardless of whether satisfied before, on, or after January 1, 1985.[1]

Chapter 5: Liability for Death or Injury

1000. (a) A married person is not liable for any injury or damage caused by the other spouse except in cases where the married person would be liable therefor if the marriage did not exist.
(b) The liability of a married person for death or injury to person or property shall be satisfied as follows:
(1) If the liability of the married person is based upon an act or omission which occurred while the married person was performing an activity for the benefit of the community, the liability shall first be satisfied from the community estate and second from the separate property of the married person.
(2) If the liability of the married person is not based upon an act or omission which occurred while the married person was performing an activity for the benefit of the community, the liability shall first be satisfied from the separate property of the married person and second from the community estate.
(c) This section does not apply to the extent the liability is satisfied out of proceeds of insurance for the liability, whether the proceeds are from property in the community estate or from separate property. Notwithstanding Section 920, no right of reimbursement under this section shall be exercised more than seven years after the spouse in whose favor the right arises has actual knowledge of the application of the property to the satisfaction of the debt.

PART 4: MANAGEMENT AND CONTROL OF MARITAL PROPERTY

enacted by Stats. 1992, Ch. 162, Sec. 10.

1100. (a) Except as provided in subdivisions (b), (c), and (d) and Sections 761 and 1103, either spouse has the management and control of the community personal property, whether acquired prior to or on or after January 1, 1975, with like absolute power of disposition, other than testamentary, as the spouse has of the separate estate of the spouse.
(b) A spouse may not make a gift of community personal property, or dispose of community personal property for less than fair and reasonable value, without the written consent of the other spouse. This

subdivision does not apply to gifts mutually given by both spouses to third parties and to gifts given by one spouse to the other spouse.

(c) A spouse may not sell, convey, or encumber community personal property used as the family dwelling, or the furniture, furnishings, or fittings of the home, or the clothing or wearing apparel of the other spouse or minor children which is community personal property, without the written consent of the other spouse.

(d) Except as provided in subdivisions (b) and (c), and in Section 1102, a spouse who is operating or managing a business or an interest in a business that is all or substantially all community personal property has the primary management and control of the business or interest. Primary management and control means that the managing spouse may act alone in all transactions but shall give prior written notice to the other spouse of any sale, lease, exchange, encumberance, or other disposition of all or substantially all of the personal property used in the operation of the business (including personal property used for agricultural purposes), whether or not title to that property is held in the name of only one spouse. Written notice is not, however, required when prohibited by the law otherwise applicable to the transaction.

Remedies for the failure by a managing spouse to give prior written notice as required by this subdivision are only as specified in Section 1101. A failure to give prior written notice shall not adversely affect the validity of a transaction nor of any interest transferred.

(e) Each spouse shall act with respect to the other spouse in the management and control of the community assets and liabilities in accordance with the general rules governing fiduciary relationships which control the actions of persons having relationships of personal confidence as specified in Section 721, until such time as the assets and liabilities have been divided by the parties or by a court. This duty includes the obligation to make full disclosure to the other spouse of all material facts and information regarding the existence, characterization, and valuation of all assets in which the community has or may have an interest and debts for which the community is or may be liable, and to provide equal access to all information, records, and books that pertain to the value and character of those assets and debts, upon request.

1101. (a) A spouse has a claim against the other spouse for any breach of the fiduciary duty that results in impairment to the claimant spouse's present undivided one-half interest in the community estate, including, but not limited to, a single transaction or a pattern or series of transactions, which transaction or transactions have caused or will cause a detrimental impact to the claimant spouse's undivided one-half interest in the community estate.

(b) A court may order an accounting of the property and obligations of the parties to a marriage and may determine the rights of ownership in, the beneficial enjoyment of, or access to, community property, and the classification of all property of the parties to a marriage.

(c) A court may order that the name of

a spouse shall be added to community property held in the name of the other spouse alone or that the title of community property held in some other title form shall be reformed to reflect its community character, except with respect to any of the following:

(1) A partnership interest held by the other spouse as a general partner.

(2) An interest in a professional corporation or professional association.

(3) An asset of an unincorporated business if the other spouse is the only spouse involved in operating and managing the business.

(4) Any other property, if the revision would adversely affect the rights of a third person.

(d) (1) Except as provided in paragraph (2), any action under subdivision (a) shall be commenced within three years of the date a petitioning spouse had actual knowledge that the transaction or event for which the remedy is being sought occurred.

(2) An action may be commenced under this section upon the death of a spouse or in conjunction with an action for legal separation, dissolution of marriage, or nullity without regard to the time limitations set forth in paragraph (1).

(3) The defense of laches may be raised in any action brought under this section.

(4) Except as to actions authorized by paragraph (2), remedies under subdivision (a) apply only to transactions or events occurring on or after July 1, 1987.

(e) In any transaction affecting community property in which the consent of both spouses is required, the court may, upon the motion of a spouse, dispense with the requirement of the other spouse's consent if both of the following requirements are met:

(1) The proposed transaction is in the best interest of the community.

(2) Consent has been arbitrarily refused or cannot be obtained due to the physical incapacity, mental incapacity, or prolonged absence of the nonconsenting spouse.

(f) Any action may be brought under this section without filing an action for dissolution of marriage, legal separation, or nullity, or may be brought in conjunction with the action or upon the death of a spouse.

(g) Remedies for breach of the fiduciary duty by one spouse, including those set out in Sections 721 and 1100, shall include, but not be limited to, an award to the other spouse of 50 percent, or an amount equal to 50 percent, of any asset undisclosed or transferred in breach of the fiduciary duty plus attorney's fees and court costs. The value of the asset shall be determined to be its highest value at the date of the breach of the fiduciary duty, the date of the sale or disposition of the asset, or the date of the award by the court.

(h) Remedies for the breach of the fiduciary duty by one spouse, as set forth in Sections 721 and 1100, when the breach falls within the ambit of Section 3294 of the Civil Code shall include, but not be limited to, an award to the other spouse of 100 percent, or an amount equal to 100 percent, of any asset undisclosed or transferred in breach of the fiduciary duty.

1102. (a) Except as provided in Sections 761 and 1103, either spouse has the management and control of the community real property, whether acquired prior to, or on or after

January 1, 1975, but both spouses, either personally or by a duly authorized agent, are required to join in executing an instrument by which that community real property or an interest therein is leased for a longer period than one year, or is sold, conveyed, or encumbered.

(b) This section does not apply to a lease, mortgage, conveyance, or transfer of real property, or of an interest in real property, between spouses.

(c) Notwithstanding subdivision (b), both of the following shall apply:

(1) The sole lease, contract, mortgage, or deed of the husband, holding the record title to community real property, to a lessee, purchaser, or encumbrancer, in good faith without knowledge of the marriage relation, shall be presumed to be valid if executed prior to January 1, 1975.

(2) The sole lease, contract, mortgage, or deed of either spouse, holding the record title to community real property to a lessee, purchaser, or encumbrancer, in good faith without knowledge of the marriage relation, shall be presumed to be valid if executed on or after January 1, 1975.

(d) An action to avoid an instrument mentioned in this section, affecting any property standing of record in the name of either spouse alone, executed by the spouse alone, shall not be commenced after the expiration of one year from the filing for record of that instrument in the recorder's office in the county in which the land is situated.

(e) This section does not preclude either spouse from encumbering that spouse's interest in community real property, as provided in Section 2033, to pay reasonable attorney's fees in order to retain or maintain legal counsel in a proceeding for dissolution of marriage, for nullity of marriage, or for legal separation of the parties.[420]

1103. (a) Where one or both of the spouses either has a conservator of the estate or lacks legal capacity to manage and control community property, the procedure for management and control (which includes disposition) of the community property is that prescribed in Part 6 (commencing with Section 3000) of Division 4 of the Probate Code.

(b) Where one or both spouses either has a conservator of the estate or lacks legal capacity to give consent to a gift of community personal property or a disposition of community personal property without a valuable consideration as required by Section 1100 or to a sale, conveyance, or encumbrance of community personal property for which a consent is required by Section 1100, the procedure for that gift, disposition, sale, conveyance, or encumbrance is that prescribed in Part 6 (commencing with Section 3000) of Division 4 of the Probate Code.

(c) Where one or both spouses either has a conservator of the estate or lacks legal capacity to join in executing a lease, sale, conveyance, or encumberance of community real property or any interest therein as required by Section 1102, the procedure for that lease, sale, conveyance, or encumberance is that prescribed in Part 6 (commencing with Section 3000) of Division 4 of the Probate Code.[1]

PART 5: MARITAL AGREEMENTS

enacted by Stats. 1992, Ch. 162, Sec. 10.

Chapter 1: General Provisions

1500. The property rights of spouses prescribed by statute may be altered by a premarital agreement or other marital property agreement.[290]

1501. A minor may make a valid premarital agreement or other marital property agreement if the minor is emancipated, is otherwise capable of contracting marriage pursuant to Section 302 or 303, or has entered or is entering a marriage that is valid in the jurisdiction where the marriage is solemnized.[384]

1502. (a) A premarital agreement or other marital property agreement that is executed and acknowledged or proved in the manner that a grant of real property is required to be executed and acknowledged or proved may be recorded in the office of the recorder of each county in which real property affected by the agreement is situated.
(b) Recording or nonrecording of a premarital agreement or other marital property agreement has the same effect as recording or nonrecording of a grant of real property.[1]

1503. Nothing in this chapter affects the validity or effect of premarital agreements made before January 1, 1986, and the validity and effect of those agreements shall continue to be determined by the law applicable to the agreements before January 1, 1986.[1]

Chapter 2: Uniform Premarital Agreement Act

Article 1: Preliminary Provisions

1600. This chapter may be cited as the Uniform Premarital Agreement Act.[1]

1601. This chapter is effective on and after January 1, 1986, and applies to any premarital agreement executed on or after that date.[1]

Article 2: Premarital Agreements

1610. As used in this chapter:
(a) "Premarital agreement" means an agreement between prospective spouses made in contemplation of marriage and to be effective upon marriage.
(b) "Property" means an interest, present or future, legal or equitable, vested or contingent, in real or personal property, including income and earnings.[1]

1611. A premarital agreement shall be in writing and signed by both parties. It is enforceable without consideration.[1]

1612. (a) Parties to a premarital agreement may contract with respect to all of the following:
(1) The rights and obligations of each of the parties in any of the property of either or both of them whenever and wherever acquired or located.
(2) The right to buy, sell, use, transfer, exchange, abandon, lease, consume, expend, assign, create a security interest in, mortgage, encumber, dispose of, or otherwise manage and control property.
(3) The disposition of property upon separation, marital dissolution, death, or the occurrence or nonoccurrence

of any other event.

(4) The making of a will, trust, or other arrangement to carry out the provisions of the agreement.

(5) The ownership rights in and disposition of the death benefit from a life insurance policy.

(6) The choice of law governing the construction of the agreement.

(7) Any other matter, including their personal rights and obligations, not in violation of public policy or a statute imposing a criminal penalty.

(b) The right of a child to support may not be adversely affected by a premarital agreement.

(c) Any provision in a premarital agreement regarding spousal support, including, but not limited to, a waiver of it, is not enforceable if the party against whom enforcement of the spousal support provision is sought was not represented by independent counsel at the time the agreement containing the provision was signed, or if the provision regarding spousal support is unconscionable at the time of enforcement. An otherwise unenforceable provision in a premarital agreement regarding spousal support may not become enforceable solely because the party against whom enforcement is sought was represented by independent counsel.

1613. A premarital agreement becomes effective upon marriage.[1]

1614. After marriage, a premarital agreement may be amended or revoked only by a written agreement signed by the parties. The amended agreement or the revocation is enforceable without consideration.[1]

1615. (a) A premarital agreement is not enforceable if the party against whom enforcement is sought proves either of the following:

(1) That party did not execute the agreement voluntarily.

(2) The agreement was unconscionable when it was executed and, before execution of the agreement, all of the following applied to that party:

(A) That party was not provided a fair, reasonable, and full disclosure of the property or financial obligations of the other party.

(B) That party did not voluntarily and expressly waive, in writing, any right to disclosure of the property or financial obligations of the other party beyond the disclosure provided.

(C) That party did not have, or reasonably could not have had, an adequate knowledge of the property or financial obligations of the other party.

(b) An issue of unconscionability of a premarital agreement shall be decided by the court as a matter of law.

(c) For the purposes of subdivision (a), it shall be deemed that a premarital agreement was not executed voluntarily unless the court finds in writing or on the record all of the following:

(1) The party against whom enforcement is sought was represented by independent legal counsel at the time of signing the agreement or, after being advised to seek independent legal counsel, expressly waived, in a separate writing, representation by independent legal counsel. The advisement to seek independent legal counsel shall be made at least seven calendar days before the final

agreement is signed.

(2) One of the following:

(A) For an agreement executed between January 1, 2002, and January 1, 2020, the party against whom enforcement is sought had not less than seven calendar days between the time that party was first presented with the final agreement and advised to seek independent legal counsel and the time the agreement was signed. This requirement does not apply to nonsubstantive amendments that do not change the terms of the agreement.

(B) For an agreement executed on or after January 1, 2020, the party against whom enforcement is sought had not less than seven calendar days between the time that party was first presented with the final agreement and the time the agreement was signed, regardless of whether the party is represented by legal counsel. This requirement does not apply to nonsubstantive amendments that do not change the terms of the agreement.

(3) The party against whom enforcement is sought, if unrepresented by legal counsel, was fully informed of the terms and basic effect of the agreement as well as the rights and obligations the party was giving up by signing the agreement, and was proficient in the language in which the explanation of the party's rights was conducted and in which the agreement was written. The explanation of the rights and obligations relinquished shall be memorialized in writing and delivered to the party prior to signing the agreement. The unrepresented party shall, on or before the signing of the premarital agreement, execute a document declaring that the party received the information required by this paragraph and indicating who provided that information.

(4) The agreement and the writings executed pursuant to paragraphs (1) and (3) were not executed under duress, fraud, or undue influence, and the parties did not lack capacity to enter into the agreement.

(5) Any other factors the court deems relevant.[474]

1616. If a marriage is determined to be void, an agreement that would otherwise have been a premarital agreement is enforceable only to the extent necessary to avoid an inequitable result.[1]

1617. Any statute of limitations applicable to an action asserting a claim for relief under a premarital agreement is tolled during the marriage of the parties to the agreement. However, equitable defenses limiting the time for enforcement, including laches and estoppel, are available to either party.[1]

Chapter 3: Agreements between Spouses

1620. Except as otherwise provided by law, spouses cannot, by a contract with each other, alter their legal relations, except as to property.[291]

DIVISION 5: CONCILIATION PROCEEDINGS

ENACTED BY STATS. 1992, CH. 162, SEC. 10.
SECTION 1800-1852

PART 1: FAMILY CONCILIATION COURT LAW

enacted by Stats. 1992, Ch. 162, Sec. 10.

Chapter 1: General Provisions

1800. This part may be cited as the Family Conciliation Court Law.[1]

1801. The purposes of this part are to protect the rights of children and to promote the public welfare by preserving, promoting, and protecting family life and the institution of matrimony, and to provide means for the reconciliation of spouses and the amicable settlement of domestic and family controversies.[1]

1802. (a) This part applies only in counties in which the superior court determines that the social conditions in the county and the number of domestic relations cases in the courts render the procedures provided in this part necessary to the full and proper consideration of those cases and the effectuation of the purposes of this part.
(b) The determination under subdivision (a) shall be made annually in the month of January by:
(1) The judge of the superior court in counties having only one superior court judge.
(2) A majority of the judges of the superior court in counties having more than one superior court judge.[1]

Chapter 2: Family Conciliation Courts

1810. Each superior court shall exercise the jurisdiction conferred by this part. While sitting in the exercise of this jurisdiction, the court shall be known and referred to as the "family conciliation court."[1]

1811. The presiding judge of the superior court shall annually, in the month of January, designate at least one judge to hear all cases under this part.

1812. (a) The judge of the family conciliation court may transfer any case before the family conciliation court pursuant to this part to the department of the presiding judge of the superior court for assignment for trial or other proceedings by another judge of the court, whenever in the opinion of the judge of the family conciliation court the transfer is necessary to expedite the business of the family conciliation court or to ensure the prompt consideration of the case.
(b) When a case is transferred pursuant to subdivision (a), the judge to whom it is transferred shall act as the judge of the family conciliation court in the matter.[1]

1813. (a) The presiding judge of the superior court may appoint a judge of the superior court other than the judge of the family conciliation court to act as judge of the family conciliation court during any period when the judge of the family conciliation court is on vacation, absent, or for any reason unable to perform the duties as judge of the family conciliation court.

(b) The judge appointed under subdivision (a) has all of the powers and authority of a judge of the family conciliation court in cases under this part.[1]

1814. (a) In each county in which a family conciliation court is established, the superior court may appoint one supervising counselor of conciliation and one secretary to assist the family conciliation court in disposing of its business and carrying out its functions. When superior courts by contract have established joint family conciliation court services, the contracting courts jointly may make the appointments under this subdivision.

(b) The supervising counselor of conciliation has the power to do all of the following:

(1) Hold conciliation conferences with parties to, and hearings in, proceedings under this part, and make recommendations concerning the proceedings to the judge of the family conciliation court.

(2) Provide supervision in connection with the exercise of the counselor's jurisdiction as the judge of the family conciliation court may direct.

(3) Cause reports to be made, statistics to be compiled, and records to be kept as the judge of the family conciliation court may direct.

(4) Hold hearings in all family conciliation court cases as may be required by the judge of the family conciliation court, and make investigations as may be required by the court to carry out the intent of this part.

(5) Make recommendations relating to marriages where one or both parties are underage.

(6) Make investigations, reports, and recommendations as provided in Section 281 of the Welfare and Institutions Code under the authority provided the probation officer in that code.

(7) Act as domestic relations cases investigator.

(8) Conduct mediation of child custody and visitation disputes.

(c) The superior court, or contracting superior courts, may also appoint associate counselors of conciliation and other office assistants as may be necessary to assist the family conciliation court in disposing of its business. The associate counselors shall carry out their duties under the supervision of the supervising counselor of con-ciliation and have the powers of the supervising counselor of conciliation. Office assistants shall work under the supervision and direction of the supervising counselor of conciliation.

(d) The classification and salaries of persons appointed under this section shall be determined by:

(1) The superior court of the county in which a noncontracting family conciliation court operates.

(2) The superior court of the county which by contract has the responsibility to administer funds of the joint family conciliation court service.[256]

1815. (a) A person employed as a supervising counselor of conciliation or as an associate counselor of conciliation shall have all of the following minimum qualifications:

(1) A master's degree in psychology,

social work, marriage, family and child counseling, or other behavioral science substantially related to marriage and family interpersonal relationships.

(2) At least two years of experience in counseling or psychotherapy, or both, preferably in a setting related to the areas of responsibility of the family conciliation court and with the ethnic population to be served.

(3) Knowledge of the court system of California and the procedures used in family law cases.

(4) Knowledge of other resources in the community that clients can be referred to for assistance.

(5) Knowledge of adult psychopathology and the psychology of families.

(6) Knowledge of child development, child abuse, clinical issues relating to children, the effects of divorce on children, the effects of domestic violence on children, and child custody research sufficient to enable a counselor to assess the mental health needs of children.

(7) Training in domestic violence issues as described in Section 1816.

(b) The family conciliation court may substitute additional experience for a portion of the education, or additional education for a portion of the experience, required under subdivision (a).

(c) This section does not apply to any supervising counselor of conciliation who was in office on March 27, 1980.[132]

1816. (a) For purposes of this section, the following definitions apply:

(1) "Eligible provider" means the Administrative Office of the Courts or an educational institution, professional association, professional continuing education group, a group connected to the courts, or a public or private group that has been authorized by the Administrative Office of the Courts to provide domestic violence training.

(2) "Evaluator" means a supervising or associate counselor described in Section 1815, a mediator described in Section 3164, a court-connected or private child custody evaluator described in Section 3110.5, or a court-appointed investigator or evaluator as described in Section 3110 or Section 730 of the Evidence Code.

(b) An evaluator shall participate in a program of continuing instruction in domestic violence, including child abuse, as may be arranged and provided to that evaluator. This training may utilize domestic violence training programs conducted by nonprofit community organizations with an expertise in domestic violence issues.

(c) Areas of basic instruction shall include, but are not limited to, the following:

(1) The effects of domestic violence on children.

(2) The nature and extent of domestic violence.

(3) The social and family dynamics of domestic violence.

(4) Techniques for identifying and assisting families affected by domestic violence.

(5) Interviewing, documentation of, and appropriate recommendations for, families affected by domestic violence.

(6) The legal rights of, and remedies available to, victims.

(7) Availability of community and legal domestic violence resources.

(d) An evaluator shall also complete 16

hours of advanced training within a 12-month period. Four hours of that advanced training shall include community resource networking intended to acquaint the evaluator with domestic violence resources in the geographical communities where the family being evaluated may reside. Twelve hours of instruction, as approved by the Administrative Office of the Courts, shall include all of the following:

(1) The appropriate structuring of the child custody evaluation process, including, but not limited to, all of the following:

(A) Maximizing safety for clients, evaluators, and court personnel.

(B) Maintaining objectivity.

(C) Providing and gathering balanced information from the parties and controlling for bias.

(D) Providing separate sessions at separate times as described in Section 3113.

(E) Considering the impact of the evaluation report and recommendations with particular attention to the dynamics of domestic violence.

(2) The relevant sections of local, state, and federal laws, rules, or regulations.

(3) The range, availability, and applicability of domestic violence resources available to victims, including, but not limited to, all of the following:

(A) Domestic violence shelter-based programs.

(B) Counseling, including drug and alcohol counseling.

(C) Legal assistance.

(D) Job training.

(E) Parenting classes.

(F) Resources for a victim who is an immigrant.

(4) The range, availability, and applicability of domestic violence intervention available to perpetrators, including, but not limited to, all of the following:

(A) Certified treatment programs described in subdivision (c) of Section 1203.097 of the Penal Code.

(B) Drug and alcohol counseling.

(C) Legal assistance.

(D) Job training.

(E) Parenting classes.

(5) The unique issues in a family and psychological assessment in a domestic violence case, including all of the following:

(A) The effects of exposure to domestic violence and psychological trauma on children, the relationship between child physical abuse, child sexual abuse, and domestic violence, the differential family dynamics related to parent-child attachments in families with domestic violence, intergenerational transmission of familial violence, and manifestations of post-traumatic stress disorders in children.

(B) The nature and extent of domestic violence, and the relationship of gender, class, race, culture, and sexual orientation to domestic violence.

(C) Current legal, psychosocial, public policy, and mental health research related to the dynamics of family violence, the impact of victimization, the psychology of perpetration, and the dynamics of power and control in battering relationships.

(D) The assessment of family history based on the type, severity, and frequency of violence.

(E) The impact on parenting abilities of being a victim or perpetrator of domestic violence.

(F) The uses and limitations of psychological testing and psychiatric diagnosis in assessing parenting abilities in domestic violence cases.

(G) The influence of alcohol and drug use and abuse on the incidence of domestic violence.

(H) Understanding the dynamics of high conflict relationships and relationships between an abuser and victim.

(I) The importance of, and procedures for, obtaining collateral information from a probation department, children's protective services, police incident report, a pleading regarding a restraining order, medical records, a school, and other relevant sources.

(J) Accepted methods for structuring safe and enforceable child custody and parenting plans that ensure the health, safety, welfare, and best interest of the child, and safeguards for the parties.

(K) The importance of discouraging participants in child custody matters from blaming victims of domestic violence for the violence and from minimizing allegations of domestic violence, child abuse, or abuse against a family member.

(L) The risks associated with access to firearms and ways to reduce those risks.

(e) After an evaluator has completed the advanced training described in subdivision (d), that evaluator shall complete four hours of updated training annually that shall include, but is not limited to, all of the following:

(1) Changes in local court practices, case law, and state and federal legislation related to domestic violence.

(2) An update of current social science research and theory, including the impact of exposure to domestic violence on children.

(f) Training described in this section shall be acquired from an eligible provider and that eligible provider shall comply with all of the following:

(1) Ensure that a training instructor or consultant delivering the education and training programs either meets the training requirements of this section or is an expert in the subject matter.

(2) Monitor and evaluate the quality of courses, curricula, training, instructors, and consultants.

(3) Emphasize the importance of focusing child custody evaluations on the health, safety, welfare, and best interest of the child.

(4) Develop a procedure to verify that an evaluator completes the education and training program.

(5) Distribute a certificate of completion to each evaluator who has completed the training. That certificate shall document the number of hours of training offered, the number of hours the evaluator completed, the dates of the training, and the name of the training provider.

(g) (1) If there is a local court rule regarding the procedure to notify the court that an evaluator has completed training as described in this section, the evaluator shall comply with that local court rule.

(2) Except as provided in paragraph (1), an evaluator shall attach copies of the certificates of completion of the

training described in subdivision (d) and the most recent updated training described in subdivision (e).

(h) An evaluator may satisfy the requirement for 12 hours of instructtion described in subdivision (d) by training from an eligible provider that was obtained on or after January 1, 1996. The advanced training of that evaluator shall not be complete until that evaluator completes the four hours of community resource net-working described in subdivision (d).

(i) The Judicial Council shall develop standards for the training programs. The Judicial Council shall solicit the assistance of community organizations concerned with domestic violence and child abuse and shall seek to develop training programs that will maximize coordination between conciliation courts and local agencies concerned with domestic violence.[585]

1817. The probation officer in every county shall do all of the following:

(a) Give assistance to the family conciliation court that the court may request to carry out the purposes of this part, and to that end shall, upon request, make investigations and reports as requested.

(b) In cases pursuant to this part, exercise all the powers and perform all the duties granted or imposed by the laws of this state relating to probation or to probation officers.[1]

1818. (a) All superior court hearings or conferences in proceedings under this part shall be held in private and the court shall exclude all persons except the officers of the court, the parties, their counsel, and witnesses. The court shall not allow ex parte communications, except as authorized by Section 216. All communications, verbal or written, from parties to the judge, commissioner, or counselor in a proceeding under this part shall be deemed to be official information within the meaning of Section 1040 of the Evidence Code.

(b) The files of the family conciliation court shall be closed. The petition, supporting affidavit, conciliation agreement, and any court order made in the matter may be opened to inspection by a party or the party's counsel upon the written authority of the judge of the family conciliation court.[125]

1819. (a) Except as provided in subdivision (b), upon order of the judge of the family conciliation court, the supervising counselor of conciliation may destroy any record, paper, or document filed or kept in the office of the supervising counselor of conciliation which is more than two years old.

(b) Records described in subdivision (a) of child custody or visitation mediation may be destroyed when the minor or minors involved are 18 years of age.

(c) In the judge's discretion, the judge of the family conciliation court may order the microfilming of any record, paper, or document described in subdivision (a) or (b).[1]

1820. (a) A court may contract with any other court or courts to provide joint family conciliation court services.

(b) An agreement between two or more courts for the operation of a joint family conciliation court service may provide that one participating court shall be the custodian of moneys made available for the purposes of the joint services, and that the custodian court may make payments from the moneys upon audit of the appropriate auditing officer or body of the court.

(c) An agreement between two or more courts for the operation of a joint family conciliation court service may also provide:

(1) For the joint provision or operation of services and facilities or for the provision or operation of services and facilities by one participating court under contract for the other participating courts.

(2) For appointments of members of the staff of the family conciliation court including the supervising counselor.

(3) That, for specified purposes, the members of the staff of the family conciliation court including the supervising counselor, but excluding the judges of the family conciliation court, shall be considered to be employees of one participating court.

(4) For other matters that are necessary or proper to effectuate the purposes of the Family Conciliation Court Law.

(d) The provisions of this part relating to family conciliation court services provided by a single court shall be equally applicable to courts which contract, pursuant to this section, to provide joint family conciliation court services.[257]

Chapter 3: Proceedings for Conciliation

1830. (a) When a controversy exists between spouses, or when a controversy relating to child custody or visitation exists between parents regardless of their marital status, and the controversy may, unless a reconciliation is achieved, result in dissolution of the marriage, nullity of the marriage, or legal separation of the parties, or in the disruption of the household, and there is a minor child of the spouses or parents or of either of them whose welfare might be affected thereby, the family conciliation court has jurisdiction as provided in this part over the controversy and over the parties to the controversy and over all persons having any relation to the controversy.

(b) The family conciliation court also has jurisdiction over the controversy, whether or not there is a minor child of the parties or either of them, where the controversy involves domestic violence.[1]

1831. Before the filing of a proceeding for determination of custody or visitation rights, for dissolution of marriage, for nullity of a voidable marriage, or for legal separation of the parties, either spouse or parent, or both, may file in the family conciliation court a petition invoking the jurisdiction of the court for the purpose of preserving the marriage by effecting a reconciliation between the parties, or for amicable settlement of the controversy between the spouses or parents, so as to avoid further litigation over the issue involved.[1]

1832. The petition shall be captioned substantially as follows:

In the Superior Court of the State of California

in and for the County of ________

Upon the petition of)	
________________________________)	Petition for
(Petitioner))	Conciliation
And concerning)	(Under the Family
_____________________________ and)	Conciliation
________________________________)	Court Law)
____________________, Respondents)	

To the Family Conciliation Court:

(Enacted by Stats. 1992, Ch. 162, Sec. 10. Operative January 1, 1994.)

1833. The petition shall:
(a) Allege that a controversy exists between the spouses or parents and request the aid of the court to effect a reconciliation or an amicable settlement of the controversy.
(b) State the name and age of each minor child whose welfare may be affected by the controversy.
(c) State the name and address of the petitioner or the names and addresses of the petitioners.
(d) If the petition is presented by one spouse or parent only, the name of the other spouse or parent as a respondent, and state the address of that spouse or parent.
(e) Name as a respondent any other person who has any relation to the controversy, and state the address of the person if known to the petitioner.
(f) If the petition arises out of an instance of domestic violence, so state generally and without specific allegations as to the incident.
(g) State any other information the court by rule requires.[1]

1834. (a) The clerk of the court shall provide, at the expense of the court, blank forms for petitions for filing pursuant to this part.
(b) The probation officers of the county and the attachés and employees of the family conciliation court shall assist a person in the preparation and presentation of a petition under this part if the person requests assistance.
(c) All public officers in each county shall refer to the family conciliation court all petitions and complaints made to them in respect to controversies within the jurisdiction of the family conciliation court.
(d) The jurisdiction of the family conciliation court in respect to controversies arising out of an instance of domestic violence is not exclusive but is coextensive with any other remedies either civil or criminal in nature that may be available.[258]

1835. No fee shall be charged by any officer for filing the petition.[1]

1836. (a) The court shall fix a reasonable time and place for hearing on the petition. The court shall cause notice to be given to the respondents of the filing of the petition and of the time and place of the hearing that the court deems necessary.
(b) The court may, when it deems it necessary, issue a citation to a respondent requiring the respondent to appear at the time and place stated in the citation. The court may require the attendance of witnesses as in other civil cases.[1]

1837. (a) Except as provided in subdivision (b), for the purpose of conducting hearings pursuant to this part, the family conciliation court may be convened at any time and place within the county, and the hearing may be had in chambers or otherwise.
(b) The time and place for hearing shall not be different from the time and place provided by law for the trial of civil actions if any party, before the hearing, objects to any different time or place.[1]

1838. (a) The hearing shall be conducted informally as a conference or a series of conferences to effect a reconciliation of the spouses or an amicable adjustment or settlement of the issues in controversy.
(b) To facilitate and promote the purposes of this part, the court may,

with the consent of both parties to the proceeding, recommend or invoke the aid of medical or other specialists or scientific experts, or of the pastor or director of any religious denomination to which the parties may belong. Aid under this subdivision shall not be at the expense of the court unless the presiding judge specifically authorizes the aid, nor at the expense of the county unless the board of supervisors of the county specifically provides and authorizes the aid.[259]

1839. (a) At or after the hearing, the court may make orders in respect to the conduct of the spouses or parents and the subject matter of the controversy that the court deems necessary to preserve the marriage or to implement the reconciliation of the spouses. No such order shall be effective for more than 30 days from the hearing of the petition unless the parties mutually consent to a continuation of the time the order remains effective.
(b) A reconciliation agreement between the parties may be reduced to writing and, with the consent of the parties, a court order may be made requiring the parties to comply fully with the agreement.
(c) During the pendency of a proceeding under this part, the superior court may order a spouse or parent, as the case may be, to pay an amount necessary for the support and maintenance of the other spouse and for the support, maintenance, and education of the minor children, as the case may be. In determining the amount, the superior court may take into consideration the recommendations of a financial referee if one is available to the court. An order made pursuant to this subdivision shall not prejudice the rights of the parties or children with respect to any subsequent order that may be made. An order made pursuant to this subdivision may be modified or terminated at any time except as to an amount that accrued before the date of filing of the notice of motion or order to show cause to modify or terminate.[292]

1840. (a) During a period beginning upon the filing of the petition for conciliation and continuing until 30 days after the hearing of the petition for conciliation, neither spouse shall file a petition for dissolution of marriage, for nullity of a voidable marriage, or for legal separation of the parties.
(b) After the expiration of the period under subdivision (a), if the controversy between the spouses, or the parents, has not been terminated, either spouse may institute a proceeding for dissolution of marriage, for nullity of a void-able marriage, or for legal separation of the parties, or a proceeding to determine custody or visitation of the minor child or children.
(c) The pendency of a proceeding for dissolution of marriage, for nullity of marriage, or for legal separation of the parties, or a proceeding to determine custody or visitation of the minor child or children, does not operate as a bar to the instituting of proceedings for conciliation under this part.[1]

1841. If a petition for dissolution of marriage, for nullity of marriage, or for legal separation of the parties is filed, the case may be transferred at any time during the pendency of the proceeding to the family conciliation court for

proceedings for reconciliation of the spouses or amicable settlement of issues in controversy in accordance with this part if both of the following appear to the court:
(a) There is a minor child of the spouses, or of either of them, whose welfare may be adversely affected by the dissolution of the marriage or the disruption of the household or a controversy involving child custody.
(b) There is some reasonable possibility of a reconciliation being effected.[1]

1842. (a) If an application is made to the family conciliation court for conciliation proceedings in respect to a controversy between spouses, or a contested proceeding for dissolution of marriage, for nullity of a voidable marriage, or for legal separation of the parties, but there is no minor child whose welfare may be affected by the results of the controversy, and it appears to the court that reconciliation of the spouses or amicable adjustment of the controversy can probably be achieved, and that the work of the court in cases involving children will not be seriously impeded by acceptance of the case, the court may accept and dispose of the case in the same manner as similar cases involving the welfare of children are disposed of.
(b) If the court accepts the case under subdivision (a), the court has the same jurisdiction over the controversy and the parties to the controversy and those having a relation to the controversy that it has under this part in similar cases involving the welfare of children.[1]

PART 2: STATEWIDE COORDINATION OF FAMILY MEDIATION AND CONCILIATION SERVICES

enacted by Stats. 1992, Ch. 162, Sec. 10.

1850. The Judicial Council shall do all of the following:
(a) Assist courts in implementing mediation and conciliation proceedings under this code.
(b) Establish and implement a uniform statistical reporting system relating to proceedings brought for dissolution of marriage, for nullity of marriage, or for legal separation of the parties, including, but not limited to, a custody disposition survey.
(c) Administer a program of grants to public and private agencies submitting proposals for research, study, and demonstration projects in the area of family law, including, but not limited to, all of the following:
(1) The development of conciliation and mediation and other newer dispute resolution techniques, particularly as they relate to child custody and to avoidance of litigation.
(2) The establishment of criteria to ensure that a child support order is adequate.
(3) The development of methods to ensure that a child support order is paid.
(4) The study of the feasibility and desirability of guidelines to assist judges in making custody decisions.
(d) Administer a program for the training of court personnel involved in family law proceedings, which shall be available to the court personnel and which shall be totally funded from funds specified in Section 1852. The training shall include, but not be limited to, the order of preference for

custody of minor children and the meaning of the custody arrangements under Part 2 (commencing with Section 3020) of Division 8.
(e) Conduct research on the effectiveness of current family law for the purpose of shaping future public policy.[260]

1851. The Judicial Council shall establish an advisory committee of persons representing a broad spectrum of interest in and knowledge about family law. The committee shall recommend criteria for determining grant recipients pursuant to subdivision (c) of Section 1850, which shall include proposal evaluation guidelines and procedures for submission of the results to the Legislature, the Governor, and family law courts. In accordance with established criteria, the committee shall receive grant proposals and shall recommend the priority of submitted proposals.[1]

1852. (a) There is in the State Treasury the Family Law Trust Fund.
(b) Moneys collected by the state pursuant to subdivision (c) of Section 103625 of the Health and Safety Code, Section 70674 of the Government Code, and grants, gifts, or devises made to the state from private sources to be used for the purposes of this part shall be deposited into the Family Law Trust Fund.
(c) Moneys deposited in the Family Law Trust Fund shall be placed in an interest-bearing account. Any interest earned shall accrue to the fund and shall be disbursed pursuant to subdivision (d).
(d) Money deposited in the Family Law Trust Fund shall be disbursed for purposes specified in this part and for other family law related activities.
(e) Moneys deposited in the Family Law Trust Fund shall be administered by the Judicial Council. The Judicial Council may, with appropriate guidelines, delegate the administration of the fund to the Administrative Office of the Courts.
(f) Any moneys in the Family Law Trust Fund that are unencumbered at the end of the fiscal year are automatically appropriated to the Family Law Trust Fund of the following year.
(g) In order to defray the costs of collection of these funds, pursuant to this section, the local registrar, county clerk, or county recorder may retain a percentage of the funds collected, not to exceed 10 percent of the fee payable to the state pursuant to subdivision (c) of Section 103625 of the Health and Safety Code.[121]

DIVISION 6: NULLITY, DISSOLUTION, AND LEGAL SEPARATION

ENACTED BY STATS. 1992, CH. 162, SEC. 10.
SECTION 2000-2452

PART 1: GENERAL PROVISIONS

enacted by Stats. 1992, Ch. 162, Sec. 10.

Chapter 1: Application of Part

2000. This part applies to a proceeding for dissolution of marriage, for nullity of marriage, or for legal separation of the parties.[1]

Chapter 2: Jurisdiction

2010. In a proceeding for dissolution of marriage, for nullity of marriage, or for legal separation of the parties, the court has jurisdiction to inquire into and render any judgment and make orders that are appropriate concerning the following:
(a) The status of the marriage, including any marriage under subdivision (c) of Section 308.
(b) The custody of minor children of the marriage.
(c) The support of children for whom support may be ordered, including children born after the filing of the initial petition or the final decree of dissolution.
(d) The support of either party.
(e) The settlement of the property rights of the parties.
(f) The award of attorney's fees and costs.[210]

2011. When service of summons on a spouse is made pursuant to Section 415.50 of the Code of Civil Procedure, the court, without the aid of attachment or the appointment of a receiver, shall have and may exercise the same jurisdiction over:
(a) The community real property of the spouse so served situated in this state as it has or may exercise over the community real property of a spouse who is personally served with process within this state.
(b) The quasi-community real property of the spouse so served situated in this state as it has or may exercise over the quasi-community real property of a spouse who is personally served with process within this state.[1]

2012. (a) During the time a motion pursuant to Section 418.10 of the Code of Civil Procedure is pending, the respondent may appear in opposition to an order made during the pendency of the proceeding and the appearance shall not be deemed a general appearance by the respondent.
(b) As used in this section, a motion pursuant to Section 418.10 of the Code of Civil Procedure is pending from the time notice of motion is served and filed until the time within which to petition for a writ of mandate has expired or, if a petition is made, until the time final judgment in the mandate proceeding is entered.[1]

2013. (a) If a written agreement is entered into by the parties, the parties may utilize a collaborative law process to resolve any matter governed by this code over which the court is granted

jurisdiction pursuant to Section 2000.
(b) "Collaborative law process" means the process in which the parties and any professionals engaged by the parties to assist them agree in writing to use their best efforts and to make a good faith attempt to resolve disputes related to the family law matters as referenced in subdivision (a) on an agreed basis without resorting to adversary judicial intervention.[135]

Chapter 3: Procedural Provisions

2020. A responsive pleading, if any, shall be filed and a copy served on the petitioner within 30 days of the date of the service on the respondent of a copy of the petition and summons.[70]

2021. (a) Subject to subdivision (b), the court may order that a person who claims an interest in the proceeding be joined as a party to the proceeding in accordance with rules adopted by the Judicial Council pursuant to Section 211.
(b) An employee benefit plan may be joined as a party only in accordance with Chapter 6 (commencing with Section 2060).

2022. (a) Evidence collected by eavesdropping in violation of Chapter 1.5 (commencing with Section 630) of Title 15 of Part 1 of the Penal Code is inadmissible.
(b) If it appears that a violation described in subdivision (a) exists, the court may refer the matter to the proper authority for investigation and prosecution.[1]

2023. (a) On a determination that payment of an obligation of a party would benefit either party or a child for whom support may be ordered, the court may order one of the parties to pay the obligation, or a portion thereof, directly to the creditor.
(b) The creditor has no right to enforce the order made under this section, nor are the creditor's rights affected by the determination made under this section.

2024. (a) A petition for dissolution of marriage, nullity of marriage, or legal separation of the parties, or a joint petition for summary dissolution of marriage, shall contain the following notice:
"Dissolution or annulment of your marriage may automatically cancel your spouse's rights under your will, trust, retirement benefit plan, power of attorney, pay on death bank account, transfer on death vehicle registration, survivorship rights to any property owned in joint tenancy, and any other similar thing. It does not automatically cancel your spouse's rights as beneficiary of your life insurance policy. If these are not the results that you want, you must change your will, trust, account agreement, or other similar document to reflect your actual wishes.
Dissolution or annulment of your marriage may also automatically cancel your rights under your spouse's will, trust, retirement benefit plan, power of attorney, pay on death bank account, transfer on death vehicle registration, and survivorship rights to any property owned in joint tenancy, and any other similar thing. It does not automatically cancel your rights as beneficiary of your spouse's life insurance policy.
You should review these matters, as well as any credit cards, other credit accounts, insurance policies, retirement benefit plans, and credit

reports to determine whether they should be changed or whether you should take any other actions in view of the dissolution or annulment of your marriage, or your legal separation. However, some changes may require the agreement of your spouse or a court order (see Part 3 (commencing with Section 231) of Division 2 of the Family Code)."

(b) A judgment for dissolution of marriage, for nullity of marriage, or for legal separation of the parties shall contain the following notice:

"Dissolution or annulment of your marriage may automatically cancel your spouse's rights under your will, trust, retirement benefit plan, power of attorney, pay on death bank account, transfer on death vehicle registration, survivorship rights to any property owned in joint tenancy, and any other similar thing. It does not automatically cancel your spouse's rights as beneficiary of your life insurance policy. If these are not the results that you want, you must change your will, trust, account agreement, or other similar document to reflect your actual wishes.

Dissolution or annulment of your marriage may also automatically cancel your rights under your spouse's will, trust, retirement benefit plan, power of attorney, pay on death bank account, transfer on death vehicle registration, survivorship rights to any property owned in joint tenancy, and any other similar thing. It does not automatically cancel your rights as beneficiary of your spouse's life insurance policy.

You should review these matters, as well as any credit cards, other credit accounts, insurance policies, retirement benefit plans, and credit reports to determine whether they should be changed or whether you should take any other actions in view of the dissolution or annulment of your marriage, or your legal separation."

2024.5. (a) Except as provided in subdivision (b), the petitioner or respondent may redact any social security number from any pleading, attachment, document, or other written material filed with the court pursuant to a petition for dissolution of marriage, nullity of marriage, or legal separation. The Judicial Council form used to file such a petition, or a response to such a petition, shall contain a notice that the parties may redact any social security numbers from those pleadings, attachments, documents, or other material filed with the court.

(b) An abstract of support judgment, the form required pursuant to subdivision (b) of Section 4014, or any similar form created for the purpose of collecting child or spousal support payments may not be redacted pursuant to subdivision (a).[110]

2024.6. (a) Upon request by a party to a petition for dissolution of marriage, nullity of marriage, or legal separation, the court shall order a pleading that lists the parties' financial assets and liabilities and provides the location or identifying information about those assets and liabilities sealed. The request may be made by ex parte application. Nothing sealed pursuant to this section may be unsealed except upon petition to the court and good cause shown.

(b) Commencing not later than July 1, 2005, the Judicial Council form used to

declare assets and liabilities of the parties in a proceeding for dissolution of marriage, nullity of marriage, or legal separation of the parties shall require the party filing the form to state whether the declaration contains identifying information on the assets and liabilities listed therein. If the party making the request uses a pleading other than the Judicial Council form, the pleading shall exhibit a notice on the front page, in bold capital letters, that the pleading lists and identifies financial information and is therefore subject to this section.
(c) For purposes of this section, "pleading" means a document that sets forth or declares the parties' assets and liabilities, income and expenses, a marital settlement agreement that lists and identifies the parties' assets and liabilities, or any document filed with the court incidental to the declaration or agreement that lists and identifies financial information.
(d) The party making the request to seal a pleading pursuant to subdivision (a) shall serve a copy of the pleading on the other party to the proceeding and file a proof of service with the request to seal the pleading.
(e) Nothing in this section precludes a party to a proceeding described in this section from using any document or information contained in a sealed pleading in any manner that is not otherwise prohibited by law.[119]

2024.7. On and after January 1, 2014, upon the filing of a petition for dissolution of marriage, nullity of marriage, or legal separation, the court shall provide to the petitioner and the respondent a notice informing them that they may be eligible for reduced-cost coverage through the California Health Benefit Exchange established under Title 22 (commencing with Section 100500) of the Government Code or no-cost coverage through Medi-Cal. The notice shall include information on obtaining coverage pursuant to those programs, and shall be developed by the California Health Benefit Exchange.[421]

2025. Notwithstanding any other provision of law, if the court has ordered an issue or issues bifurcated for separate trial or hearing in advance of the disposition of the entire case, a court of appeal may order an issue or issues transferred to it for hearing and decision when the court that heard the issue or issues certifies that the appeal is appropriate. Certification by the court shall be in accordance with rules promulgated by the Judicial Council.[1]

2026. The reconciliation of the parties, whether conditional or unconditional, is an ameliorating factor to be considered by the court in considering a contempt of an existing court order.[1]

Chapter 3.5: Attorney's Fees and Cost

2030. (a) (1) In a proceeding for dissolution of marriage, nullity of marriage, or legal separation of the parties, and in any proceeding subsequent to entry of a related judgment, the court shall ensure that each party has access to legal representation, including access early in the proceedings, to preserve each party's rights by ordering, if necessary based on the income and needs assessments, one party, except a governmental entity, to pay to the other party, or to the other party's attorney, whatever amount is reasonably necessary for attorney's fees and for the cost of maintaining or defending the proceeding during the pendency of the proceeding.

(2) When a request for attorney's fees and costs is made, the court shall make findings on whether an award of attorney's fees and costs under this section is appropriate, whether there is a disparity in access to funds to retain counsel, and whether one party is able to pay for legal representation of both parties. If the findings demonstrate disparity in access and ability to pay, the court shall make an order awarding attorney's fees and costs. A party who lacks the financial ability to hire an attorney may request, as an in pro per litigant, that the court order the other party, if that other party has the financial ability, to pay a reasonable amount to allow the unrepresented party to retain an attorney in a timely manner before proceedings in the matter go forward.

(b) Attorney's fees and costs within this section may be awarded for legal services rendered or costs incurred before or after the commencement of the proceeding.

(c) The court shall augment or modify the original award for attorney's fees and costs as may be reasonably necessary for the prosecution or defense of the proceeding, or any proceeding related thereto, including after any appeal has been concluded.

(d) Any order requiring a party who is not the spouse of another party to the proceeding to pay attorney's fees or costs shall be limited to an amount reasonably necessary to maintain or defend the action on the issues relating to that party.

(e) The Judicial Council shall, by January 1, 2012, adopt a statewide rule of court to implement this section and develop a form for the information that shall be submitted to the court to obtain an award of attorney's fees under this section.[199]

2031. (a) (1) Except as provided in subdivision (b), during the pendency of a proceeding for dissolution of marriage, for nullity of marriage, for legal separation of the parties, or any proceeding subsequent to entry of a related judgment, an application for a temporary order making, augmenting, or modifying an award of attorney's fees, including a reasonable retainer to hire an attorney, or costs or both shall be made by motion on notice or by an order to show cause.

(2) The court shall rule on an application within 15 days of the hearing on the motion or order to show cause.

(b) An order described in subdivision (a) may be made without notice by an oral motion in open court at either of the following times:

(1) At the time of the hearing of the cause on the merits.

(2) At any time before entry of judgment against a party whose default has been entered pursuant to Section 585 or 586 of the Code of Civil Procedure. The court shall rule on any motion made pursuant to this subdivision within 15 days and prior to the entry of any judgment.[116]

2032. (a) The court may make an award of attorney's fees and costs under Section 2030 or 2031 where the making of the award, and the amount of the award, are just and reasonable under the relative circumstances of the respective parties.

(b) In determining what is just and reasonable under the relative circumstances, the court shall take into consideration the need for the award to enable each party, to the extent practical, to have sufficient financial resources to present the party's case adequately, taking into consideration, to the extent relevant, the circumstances of the respective parties described in Section 4320. The fact that the party requesting an award of attorney's fees and costs has resources from which the party could pay the party's own attorney's fees and costs is not itself a bar to an order that the other party pay part or all of the fees and costs requested. Financial resources are only one factor for the court to consider in determining how to apportion the overall cost of the litigation equitably between the parties under their relative circumstances.

(c) The court may order payment of an award of attorney's fees and costs from any type of property, whether community or separate, principal or income.

(d) Either party may, at any time before the hearing of the cause on the merits, on noticed motion, request the court to make a finding that the case involves complex or substantial issues of fact or law related to property rights, visitation, custody, or support. Upon that finding, the court may in its discretion determine the appropriate, equitable allocation of attorney's fees, court costs, expert fees, and consultant fees between the parties. The court order may provide for the allocation of separate or community assets, security against these assets, and for payments from income or anticipated income of either party for the purpose described in this subdivision and for the benefit of one or both parties. Payments shall be authorized only on agreement of the parties or, in the absence thereof, by court order. The court may order that a referee be appointed pursuant to Section 639 of the Code of Civil Procedure to oversee the allocation of fees and costs.

2033. (a) Either party may encumber the party's interest in community real property to pay reasonable attorney's fees in order to retain or maintain legal counsel in a proceeding for dissolution of marriage, for nullity of marriage, or for legal separation of the parties. This encumbrance shall be known as a "family law attorney's real property lien" and attaches only to the encumbering party's interest in the community real property.

(b) Notice of a family law attorney's real property lien shall be served either personally or on the other party's attorney of record at least 15 days before the encumbrance is recorded. This notice shall contain a declaration signed under penalty of perjury containing all of the following:

(1) A full description of the real property.

(2) The party's belief as to the fair market value of the property and documentation supporting that belief.

(3) Encumbrances on the property as of the date of the declaration.

(4) A list of community assets and liabilities and their estimated values as of the date of the declaration.

(5) The amount of the family law attorney's real property lien.

(c) The nonencumbering party may file an ex parte objection to the family law attorney's real property lien. The objection shall include a request to stay the recordation until further notice of the court and shall contain a copy of the notice received. The objection shall also include a declaration signed under penalty of perjury as to all of the following:

(1) Specific objections to the family law attorney's real property lien and to the specific items in the notice.

(2) The objector's belief as to the appropriate items or value and documentation supporting that belief.

(3) A declaration specifically stating why recordation of the encumbrance at this time would likely result in an unequal division of property or would otherwise be unjust under the circumstances of the case.

(d) Except as otherwise provided by this section, general procedural rules regarding ex parte motions apply.

(e) An attorney for whom a family law attorney's real property lien is obtained shall comply with Rule 3-300 of the Rules of Professional Conduct of the State Bar of California.[422]

2034. (a) On application of either party, the court may deny the family law attorney's real property lien described in Section 2033 based on a finding that the encumbrance would likely result in an unequal division of property because it would impair the encumbering party's ability to meet the party's fair share of the community obligations or would otherwise be unjust under the circumstances of the case. The court may also, for good cause, limit the amount of the family law attorney's real property lien. A limitation by the court is not to be construed as a determination of reasonable attorney's fees.

(b) On receiving an objection to the establishment of a family law attorney's real property lien, the court may, on its own motion, determine whether the case involves complex or substantial issues of fact or law related to property rights, visitation, custody, or support. If the court finds that the case involves one or more of these complex or substantial issues, the court may determine the appropriate, equitable allocation of fees and costs as provided in subdivision (d) of Section 2032.

(c) The court has jurisdiction to resolve any dispute arising from the existence of a family law attorney's real property lien.[423]

Chapter 4: Protective and Restraining Orders

Article 1: Orders in Summons

2040. (a) In addition to the contents required by Section 412.20 of the Code of Civil Procedure, the summons shall contain a temporary restraining order:

(1) Restraining both parties from removing the minor child or children of the parties, if any, from the state, or from applying for a new or replacement passport for the minor child or children, without the prior written consent of the other party or an order of the court.

(2) (A) Restraining both parties from transferring, encumbering, hypothecating, concealing, or in any way disposing of, any property, real or personal, whether community, quasi-community, or separate, without the written consent of the other party or an order of the court, except in the usual course of business or for the necessities of life, and requiring each party to notify the other party of proposed extraordinary expenditures at

least five business days before incurring those expenditures and to account to the court for all extraordinary expenditures made after service of the summons on that party.

(B) Notwithstanding subparagraph (A), the restraining order shall not preclude a party from using community property, quasi-community property, or the party's own separate property to pay reasonable attorney's fees and costs in order to retain legal counsel in the proceeding. A party who uses community property or quasi-community property to pay the party's attorney's retainer for fees and costs under this provision shall account to the community for the use of the property. A party who uses other property that is subsequently determined to be the separate property of the other party to pay the party's attorney's retainer for fees and costs under this provision shall account to the other party for the use of the property.

(3) Restraining both parties from cashing, borrowing against, canceling, transferring, disposing of, or changing the beneficiaries of insurance or other coverage, including life, health, automobile, and disability, held for the benefit of the parties and their child or children for whom support may be ordered.

(4) Restraining both parties from creating a nonprobate transfer or modifying a nonprobate transfer in a manner that affects the disposition of property subject to the transfer, without the written consent of the other party or an order of the court.

(b) This section does not restrain any of the following:

(1) Creation, modification, or revocation of a will.

(2) Revocation of a nonprobate transfer, including a revocable trust, pursuant to the instrument, provided that notice of the change is filed and served on the other party before the change takes effect.

(3) Elimination of a right of survivorship to property, provided that notice of the change is filed and served on the other party before the change takes effect.

(4) Creation of an unfunded revocable or irrevocable trust.

(5) Execution and filing of a disclaimer pursuant to Part 8 (commencing with Section 260) of Division 2 of the Probate Code.

(c) In all actions filed on and after January 1, 1995, the summons shall contain the following notice:

"WARNING: California law provides that, for purposes of division of property upon dissolution of marriage or legal separation, property acquired by the parties during marriage in joint form is presumed to be community property. If either party to this action should die before the jointly held community property is divided, the language of how title is held in the deed (i.e., joint tenancy, tenants in common, or community property) will be controlling and not the community property presumption. You should consult your attorney if you want the community property presumption to be written into the recorded title to the property."

(d) For the purposes of this section:

(1) "Nonprobate transfer" means an instrument, other than a will, that makes a transfer of property on death, including a revocable trust, pay on

death account in a financial institution, Totten trust, transfer on death registration of personal property, revocable transfer on death deed, or other instrument of a type described in Section 5000 of the Probate Code.

(2) "Nonprobate transfer" does not include a provision for the transfer of property on death in an insurance policy or other coverage held for the benefit of the parties and their child or children for whom support may be ordered, to the extent that the provision is subject to paragraph (3) of subdivision (a).

(e) The restraining order included in the summons shall include descriptions of the notices required by paragraphs (2) and (3) of subdivision (b).

(f) This section shall remain in effect only until January 1, 2027, and as of that date is repealed.[424]

2040. (a) In addition to the contents required by Section 412.20 of the Code of Civil Procedure, the summons shall contain a temporary restraining order:

(1) Restraining both parties from removing the minor child or children of the parties, if any, from the state, or from applying for a new or replacement passport for the minor child or children, without the prior written consent of the other party or an order of the court.

(2) (A) Restraining both parties from transferring, encumbering, hypothecating, concealing, or in any way disposing of, any property, real or personal, whether community, quasi-community, or separate, without the written consent of the other party or an order of the court, except in the usual course of business or for the necessities of life, and requiring each party to notify the other party of proposed extraordinary expenditures at least five business days before incurring those expenditures and to account to the court for all extraordinary expenditures made after service of the summons on that party.

(B) Notwithstanding subparagraph (A), the restraining order shall not preclude a party from using community property, quasi-community property, or the party's own separate property to pay reasonable attorney's fees and costs in order to retain legal counsel in the proceeding. A party who uses community property or quasi-community property to pay the party's attorney's retainer for fees and costs under this provision shall account to the community for the use of the property. A party who uses other property that is subsequently determined to be the separate property of the other party to pay the party's attorney's retainer for fees and costs under this provision shall account to the other party for the use of the property.

(3) Restraining both parties from cashing, borrowing against, canceling, allowing to lapse for nonpayment of premiums, failing to renew, transferring, disposing of, or changing the beneficiaries of insurance or other coverage, including life, health, automobile, and disability, held for the benefit of the parties and their child or children for whom support may be ordered.

(4) Restraining both parties from creating a nonprobate transfer or modifying a nonprobate transfer in a

manner that affects the disposition of property subject to the transfer, without the written consent of the other party or an order of the court.

(b) This section does not restrain any of the following:

(1) Creation, modification, or revocation of a will.

(2) Revocation of a nonprobate transfer, including a revocable trust, pursuant to the instrument, provided that notice of the change is filed and served on the other party before the change takes effect.

(3) Elimination of a right of survivorship to property, provided that notice of the change is filed and served on the other party before the change takes effect.

(4) Creation of an unfunded revocable or irrevocable trust.

(5) Execution and filing of a disclaimer pursuant to Part 8 (commencing with Section 260) of Division 2 of the Probate Code.

(c) In all actions filed on and after January 1, 1995, the summons shall contain the following notice:

"WARNING: California law provides that, for purposes of division of property upon dissolution of marriage or legal separation, property acquired by the parties during marriage in joint form is presumed to be community property. If either party to this action should die before the jointly held community property is divided, the language of how title is held in the deed (i.e., joint tenancy, tenants in common, or community property) will be controlling and not the community property presumption. You should consult your attorney if you want the community property presumption to be written into the recorded title to the property."

(d) For the purposes of this section:

(1) "Nonprobate transfer" means an instrument, other than a will, that makes a transfer of property on death, including a revocable trust, pay on death account in a financial institution, Totten trust, transfer on death registration of personal property, revocable transfer on death deed, or other instrument of a type described in Section 5000 of the Probate Code.

(2) "Nonprobate transfer" does not include a provision for the transfer of property on death in an insurance policy or other coverage held for the benefit of the parties and their child or children for whom support may be ordered, to the extent that the provision is subject to paragraph (3) of subdivision (a).

(e) The restraining order included in the summons shall include descriptions of the notices required by paragraphs (2) and (3) of subdivision (b).

(f) This section shall become operative on January 1, 2027.

2041. Nothing in Section 2040 adversely affects the rights, title, and interest of a purchaser for value, encumbrancer for value, or lessee for value who is without actual knowledge of the restraining order.[10]

Article 2: Ex Parte Orders

2045. During the pendency of the proceeding, on application of a party in the manner provided by Part 4 (commencing with Section 240) of Division 2, the court may issue ex parte any of the following orders:

(a) An order restraining any person

from transferring, encumbering, hypothecating, concealing, or in any way disposing of any property, real or personal, whether community, quasi-community, or separate, except in the usual course of business or for the necessities of life, and if the order is directed against a party, requiring that party to notify the other party of any proposed extraordinary expenditures and to account to the court for all extraordinary expenditures.

(b) A protective order, as defined in Section 6218, and any other order as provided in Article 1 (commencing with Section 6320) of Chapter 2 of Part 4 of Division 10.[10]

Article 3: Orders After Notice and Hearing

2047. (a) After notice and a hearing, the court may issue a protective order, as defined in Section 6218, and any other restraining order as provided in Article 2 (commencing with Section 6340) of Chapter 2 of Part 4 of Division 10.

(b) The court may not issue a mutual protective order pursuant to subdivision (a) unless it meets the requirements of Section 6305.[56]

Article 4: Orders Included in Judgment

2049. A judgment may include a protective order, as defined in Section 6218, and any other restraining order as provided in Article 3 (commencing with Section 6360) of Chapter 2 of Part 4 of Division 10.[10]

Chapter 5: Notice to Insurance Carriers

2050. Upon filing of the petition, or at any time during the proceeding, a party may transmit to, or the court may order transmittal to, a health, life, or disability insurance carrier or plan the following notice in substantially the following form:

"YOU ARE HEREBY NOTIFIED, PURSUANT TO A PENDING PROCEEDING, IN RE MARRIAGE OF ____, CASE NUMBER ____, FILED IN THE SUPERIOR COURT OF THE STATE OF CALIFORNIA, COUNTY OF ____, THAT OWNERSHIP OF, OR BENEFITS PAYABLE UNDER, A POLICY OF HEALTH, LIFE, OR DISABILITY INSURANCE WHICH YOU HAVE ISSUED TO ONE OF THE PARTIES TO THIS PROCEEDING, POLICY NO. ____, IS AT ISSUE OR MAY BE AT ISSUE IN THE PROCEEDING.

YOU ARE HEREBY INSTRUCTED TO MAINTAIN THE NAMED BENEFICIARIES OR COVERED DEPENDENTS UNDER THE POLICY, UNLESS THE TERMS OF THE POLICY OR OTHER PROVISIONS OF LAW REQUIRE OTHERWISE, OR UNTIL RECEIPT OF A COURT ORDER, JUDGMENT, OR STIPULATION BETWEEN THE PARTIES PROVIDING OTHER INSTRUCTIONS.

YOU ARE FURTHER INSTRUCTED TO SEND NOTICE TO THE NAMED BENEFICIARIES, COVERED DEPENDENTS, OR OTHER SPECIFIED PERSONS UPON CANCELLATION, LAPSE, OR CHANGE OF THE COVERAGE, OR CHANGE OF DESIGNATED BENEFICIARIES UNDER THE

POLICY."[1]

2051. Upon the entry of an order or judgment in the proceeding requiring a party to maintain existing health, life, or disability insurance coverage for a spouse or children or after an order or judgment in the proceeding requiring a party to purchase life or disability insurance and name the spouse or children as beneficiaries and upon receipt of the name, title, and address of the insurer, or the name of the plan's trustee, administrator, or agent for service of process, a party may transmit to, or the court may order transmittal to, the insurer or plan a copy of the order or judgment endorsed by the court, together with the following notice in substantially the following form:

"PURSUANT TO A PROCEEDING, IN RE MARRIAGE OF ____, CASE NUMBER ____, IN THE SUPERIOR COURT OF THE STATE OF CALIFORNIA, COUNTY OF ____, YOUR INSURED, ____, HAS BEEN ORDERED TO MAINTAIN THE EXISTING (HEALTH) (LIFE) (DISABILITY) INSURANCE COVERAGE, POLICY NO. ____, IN FORCE FOR THE NAMED BENEFICIARIES OR COVERED DEPENDENTS AS SPECIFIED IN THE ATTACHED ORDER OR JUDGMENT.

THE ATTACHED ORDER OR JUDGMENT REQUIRES YOU TO MAINTAIN THE NAMED BENEFICIARIES UNDER THE POLICY AS IRREVOCABLE BENEFICIARIES OR COVERED DEPENDENTS OF THE POLICY AND YOU MUST ADMINISTER THE COVERAGE ACCORDINGLY, UNTIL THE DATE SPECIFIED, IF ANY, IN THE ORDER OR JUDGMENT, OR UNTIL THE RECEIPT OF A COURT ORDER, JUDGMENT, OR STIPULATION PROVIDING OTHER INSTRUCTIONS.

YOU ARE FURTHER INSTRUCTED TO SEND NOTICE TO THE NAMED BENEFICIARIES, COVERED DEPENDENTS, OR OTHER SPECIFIED PERSONS UPON ANY CANCELLATION, LAPSE, OR CHANGE OF COVERAGE, OR CHANGE OF DESIGNATED BENEFICIARIES UNDER THIS POLICY."[1]

2052. Notice pursuant to this chapter may be sent by first-class mail, postage prepaid, to the last known address of the covered dependents, named beneficiaries, or other specified persons who have requested receipt of notification.[1]

2053. The insured or policyholder who is a party to the proceeding shall furnish to the other party the name, title, and address of the insurer or the insurer's agent for service of process.[1]

Chapter 6: Employee Pension Benefit Plan as Party

Article 1: Joinder of Plan

2060. (a) Upon written application by a party, the clerk shall enter an order joining as a party to the proceeding any employee benefit plan in which either party to the proceeding claims an interest that is or may be subject to disposition by the court.

(b) An order or judgment in the proceeding is not enforceable against an employee benefit plan unless the plan has been joined as a party to the proceeding.

2061. Upon entry of the order under Section 2060, the party requesting joinder shall file an appropriate pleading setting forth the party's claim against the plan and the nature of the relief sought.[1]

2062. (a) The party requesting joinder shall serve all of the following upon the employee benefit plan:
(1) A copy of the pleading on joinder.
(2) A copy of the request for joinder and order of joinder.
(3) A copy of the summons (joinder).
(4)A blank copy of a notice of appearance in form and content approved by the Judicial Council.
(b) Service shall be made in the same manner as service of papers generally. Service of the summons upon a trustee or administrator of the plan in its capacity as trustee or administrator, or upon an agent designated by the plan for service of process in its capacity as agent, constitutes service upon the plan.
(c) To facilitate identification and service, the employee spouse shall furnish to the nonemployee spouse within 30 days after written request, as to each employee benefit plan covering the employee, the name of the plan, the name, title, address, and telephone number of the plan's trustee, administrator, or agent for service of process. If necessary, the employee shall obtain the information from the plan or plan sponsor.[46]

2063. (a) The employee benefit plan shall file and serve a copy of a notice of appearance upon the party requesting joinder within 30 days of the date of the service upon the plan of a copy of the joinder request and summons.
(b) The employee benefit plan may, but need not, file an appropriate responsive pleading with its notice of appearance. If the plan does not file a responsive pleading, all statements of fact and requests for relief contained in any pleading served on the plan are deemed to be controverted by the plan's notice of appearance.[47]

2064. Notwithstanding any contrary provision of law, the employee benefit plan is not required to pay any fee to the clerk of the court as a condition to filing the notice of appearance or any subsequent paper in the proceeding.[48]

2065. If the employee benefit plan has been served and no notice of appearance, notice of motion to quash service of summons pursuant to Section 418.10 of the Code of Civil Procedure, or notice of the filing of a petition for writ of mandate as provided in that section, has been filed with the clerk of the court within the time specified in the summons or such further time as may be allowed, the clerk, upon written application of the party requesting joinder, shall enter the default of the employee benefit plan in accordance with Chapter 2 (commencing with Section 585) of Title 8 of Part 2 of the Code of Civil Procedure.[49]

Article 2: Proceedings After Joinder

2070. (a) This article governs a proceeding in which an employee benefit plan has been joined as a party.
(b) To the extent not in conflict with this article and except as otherwise provided by rules adopted by the

Judicial Council pursuant to Section 211, all provisions of law applicable to civil actions generally apply, regardless of nomenclature, to the portion of the proceeding as to which an employee benefit plan has been joined as a party if those provisions would otherwise apply to the proceeding without reference to this article.[50]

2071. Either party or their representatives may notify the employee benefit plan of any proposed property settlement as it concerns the plan before any hearing at which the proposed property settlement will be a matter before the court. If so notified, the plan may stipulate to the proposed settlement or advise the representative that it will contest the proposed settlement.[51]

2072. The employee benefit plan is not required to, but may, appear at any hearing in the proceeding. For purposes of the Code of Civil Procedure, the plan shall be considered a party appearing at the trial with respect to any hearing at which the interest of the parties in the plan is an issue before the court.[52]

2073. (a) Subject to subdivisions (b) and (c), the provisions of an order entered by stipulation of the parties or entered at or as a result of a hearing not attended by the employee benefit plan (whether or not the plan received notice of the hearing) which affect the plan or which affect any interest either the petitioner or respondent may have or claim under the plan, shall be stayed until 30 days after the order has been served upon the plan.

(b) The plan may waive all or any portion of the 30-day period under subdivision (a).

(c) If within the 30-day period, the plan files in the proceeding a motion to set aside or modify those provisions of the order affecting it, those provisions shall be stayed until the court has resolved the motion.

(d) The duration of the stay described in subdivision (a), and the time period for filing the motion to set aside or modify provisions of the order, shall be extended to 60 days if the plan files with the court and serves on all affected parties a request for extension within the 30-day period.

(e) Either spousal party may seek an order staying any other provisions of the order and associated orders or judgments related to or affected by the provisions to which the plan has objected, until the court has resolved the motion, in order to protect the right of the party to seek relief under subdivision (c) of Section 2074.[53]

2074. (a) At any hearing on a motion to set aside or modify an order pursuant to Section 2073, any party may present further evidence on any issue relating to the rights of the parties under the employee benefit plan or the extent of the parties' community or quasi-community property interest in the plan, except where the parties have agreed in writing to the contrary.

(b) Any statement of decision issued by the court with respect to the order which is the subject of the motion shall take account of the evidence referred to in subdivision (a).

(c) If the provisions of the order affecting the employee benefit plan are modified or set aside, the court, on motion by either party, may set aside or modify other provisions of the order and associated orders or judgments related to or affected by the provisions affecting the plan.[54]

Chapter 7: Restoration of Spouse's Former Name

2080. In a proceeding for dissolution of marriage or for nullity of marriage, but not in a proceeding for legal separation of the parties, the court, upon the request of a party, shall restore the birth name or former name of that party, regardless of whether a request for restoration of the name was included in the petition.[597]

2081. The restoration of a former name or birth name requested under Section 2080 shall not be denied on the basis that the party has custody of a minor child who bears a different name, or for any other reason except fraud.[598]

2082. This code does not abrogate the common law right of any person to change one's name.[599]

Chapter 8: Uniform Divorce Recognition Act

2090. This chapter may be cited as the Uniform Divorce Recognition Act.[1]

2091. A divorce obtained in another jurisdiction shall be of no force or effect in this state if both parties to the marriage were domiciled in this state at the time the proceeding for the divorce was commenced.[1]

2092. Proof that a person hereafter obtaining a divorce from the bonds of matrimony in another jurisdiction was (a) domiciled in this state within 12 months before the commencement of the proceeding therefor, and resumed residence in this state within 18 months after the date of the person's departure therefrom, or (b) at all times after the person's departure from this state and until the person's return maintained a place of residence within this state, shall be prima facie evidence that the person was domiciled in this state when the divorce proceeding was commenced.[1]

2093. The application of this chapter is limited by the requirement of the Constitution of the United States that full faith and credit shall be given in each state to the public acts, records, and judicial proceedings of every other state.[1]

Chapter 9: Disclosure of Assets and Liabilities

2100. The Legislature finds and declares the following:
(a) It is the policy of the State of California (1) to marshal, preserve, and protect community and quasi-community assets and liabilities that exist at the date of separation so as to avoid dissipation of the community estate before distribution, (2) to ensure fair and sufficient child and spousal support awards, and (3) to achieve a division of community and quasi-community assets and liabilities on the dissolution or nullity of marriage or legal separation of the parties as provided under California law.
(b) Sound public policy further favors the reduction of the adversarial nature of marital dissolution and the attendant costs by fostering full disclosure and cooperative discovery.
(c) In order to promote this public policy, a full and accurate disclosure of all assets and liabilities in which one or both parties have or may have an interest must be made in the early

stages of a proceeding for dissolution of marriage or legal separation of the parties, regardless of the characterization as community or separate, together with a disclosure of all income and expenses of the parties. Moreover, each party has a continuing duty to immediately, fully, and accurately update and augment that disclosure to the extent there have been any material changes so that at the time the parties enter into an agreement for the resolution of any of these issues, or at the time of trial on these issues, each party will have a full and complete knowledge of the relevant underlying facts.[79]

2101. Unless the provision or context otherwise requires, the following definitions apply to this chapter:
(a) "Asset" includes, but is not limited to, any real or personal property of any nature, whether tangible or intangible, and whether currently existing or contingent.
(b) "Default judgment" does not include a stipulated judgment or any judgment pursuant to a marital settlement agreement.
(c) "Earnings and accumulations" includes income from whatever source derived, as provided in Section 4058.
(d) "Expenses" includes, but is not limited to, all personal living expenses, but does not include business related expenses.
(e) "Income and expense declaration" includes the Income and Expense Declaration forms approved for use by the Judicial Council, and any other financial statement that is approved for use by the Judicial Council in lieu of the Income and Expense Declaration, if the financial statement form satisfies all other applicable criteria.
(f) "Liability" includes, but is not limited to, any debt or obligation, whether currently existing or contingent.[71]

2102. (a) From the date of separation to the date of the distribution of the community or quasi-community asset or liability in question, each party is subject to the standards provided in Section 721, as to all activities that affect the assets and liabilities of the other party, including, but not limited to, the following activities:
(1) The accurate and complete disclosure of all assets and liabilities in which the party has or may have an interest or obligation and all current earnings, accumulations, and expenses, including an immediate, full, and accurate update or augmentation to the extent there have been material changes.
(2) The accurate and complete written disclosure of any investment opportunity, business opportunity, or other income-producing opportunity that presents itself after the date of separation, but that results from any investment, significant business activity outside the ordinary course of business, or other income-producing opportunity of either spouse from the date of marriage to the date of separation, inclusive. The written disclosure shall be made in sufficient time for the other spouse to make an informed decision as to whether the spouse desires to participate in the investment opportunity, business, or other potential income-producing opportunity, and for the court to resolve any dispute regarding the right of the other spouse to participate in the opportunity. In the event of

nondisclosure of an investment opportunity, the division of any gain resulting from that opportunity is governed by the standard provided in Section 2556.

(3) The operation or management of a business or an interest in a business in which the community may have an interest.

(b) From the date that a valid, enforceable, and binding resolution of the disposition of the asset or liability in question is reached, until the asset or liability has actually been distributed, each party is subject to the standards provided in Section 721 as to all activities that affect the assets or liabilities of the other party. Once a particular asset or liability has been distributed, the duties and standards set forth in Section 721 shall end as to that asset or liability.

(c) From the date of separation to the date of a valid, enforceable, and binding resolution of all issues relating to child or spousal support and professional fees, each party is subject to the standards provided in Section 721 as to all issues relating to the support and fees, including immediate, full, and accurate disclosure of all material facts and information regarding the income or expenses of the party.[425]

2103. In order to provide full and accurate disclosure of all assets and liabilities in which one or both parties may have an interest, each party to a proceeding for dissolution of the marriage or legal separation of the parties shall serve on the other party a preliminary declaration of disclosure under Section 2104, unless service of the preliminary declaration of disclosure is waived as provided in Section 2107 or is not required pursuant to Section 2110, and a final declaration of disclosure under Section 2105, unless service of the final declaration of disclosure is waived pursuant to Section 2105, 2107, or 2110, and shall file proof of service of each with the court.[355]

2104. (a) Except by court order for good cause, as provided in Section 2107, or when service of the preliminary declaration of disclosure is not required pursuant to Section 2110, in the time period set forth in subdivision (f), each party shall serve on the other party a preliminary declaration of disclosure, executed under penalty of perjury on a form prescribed by the Judicial Council. The commission of perjury on the preliminary declaration of disclosure may be grounds for setting aside the judgment, or any part or parts thereof, pursuant to Chapter 10 (commencing with Section 2120), in addition to any and all other remedies, civil or criminal, that otherwise are available under law for the commission of perjury. The preliminary declaration of disclosure shall include all tax returns filed by the declarant within the two years prior to the date that the party served the declaration.

(b) The preliminary declaration of disclosure shall not be filed with the court, except on court order. However, the parties shall file proof of service of the preliminary declaration of disclosure with the court.

(c) The preliminary declaration of disclosure shall set forth with sufficient particularity, that a person of reasonable and ordinary intelligence can ascertain, all of the following:

(1) The identity of all assets in which

the declarant has or may have an interest and all liabilities for which the declarant is or may be liable, regardless of the characterization of the asset or liability as community, quasi-community, or separate.

(2) The declarant's percentage of ownership in each asset and percentage of obligation for each liability when property is not solely owned by one or both of the parties. The preliminary declaration may also set forth the declarant's characterization of each asset or liability.

(d) A declarant may amend the preliminary declaration of disclosure without leave of the court. Proof of service of an amendment shall be filed with the court.

(e) Along with the preliminary declaration of disclosure, each party shall provide the other party with a completed income and expense declaration unless an income and expense declaration has already been provided and is current and valid.

(f) The petitioner shall serve the other party with the preliminary declaration of disclosure either concurrently with the petition for dissolution or legal separation, or within 60 days of filing the petition. When a petitioner serves the summons and petition by publication or posting pursuant to court order and the respondent files a response prior to a default judgment being entered, the petitioner shall serve the other party with the preliminary declaration of disclosure within 30 days of the response being filed. The respondent shall serve the other party with the preliminary declaration of disclosure either concurrently with the response to the petition, or within 60 days of filing the response. The time periods specified in this subdivision may be extended by written agreement of the parties or by court order.[426]

2105. (a) Except by court order for good cause, before or at the time the parties enter into an agreement for the resolution of property or support issues other than pendente lite support, or, if the case goes to trial, no later than 45 days before the first assigned trial date, each party, or the attorney for the party in this matter, shall serve on the other party a final declaration of disclosure and a current income and expense declaration, executed under penalty of perjury on a form prescribed by the Judicial Council, unless the parties mutually waive the final declaration of disclosure. The commission of perjury on the final declaration of disclosure by a party may be grounds for setting aside the judgment, or any part or parts thereof, pursuant to Chapter 10 (commencing with Section 2120), in addition to any and all other remedies, civil or criminal, that otherwise are available under law for the commission of perjury.

(b) The final declaration of disclosure shall include all of the following information:

(1) All material facts and information regarding the characterization of all assets and liabilities.

(2) All material facts and information regarding the valuation of all assets that are contended to be community property or in which it is contended the community has an interest.

(3) All material facts and information regarding the amounts of all obligations that are contended to be community obligations or for which it

is contended the community has liability.

(4) All material facts and information regarding the earnings, accumulate-ions, and expenses of each party that have been set forth in the income and expense declaration.

(c) In making an order setting aside a judgment for failure to comply with this section, the court may limit the set aside to those portions of the judgment materially affected by the nondisclosure.

(d) The parties may stipulate to a mutual waiver of the requirements of subdivision (a) concerning the final declaration of disclosure, by execution of a waiver under penalty of perjury entered into in open court or by separate stipulation. The waiver shall include all of the following representations:

(1) Both parties have complied with Section 2104 and the preliminary declarations of disclosure have been completed and exchanged.

(2) Both parties have completed and exchanged a current income and expense declaration, that includes all material facts and information regarding that party's earnings, accumulations, and expenses.

(3) Both parties have fully complied with Section 2102 and have fully augmented the preliminary declarant-ions of disclosure, including disclosure of all material facts and information regarding the characterization of all assets and liabilities, the valuation of all assets that are contended to be community property or in which it is contended the community has an interest, and the amounts of all obligations that are contended to be community obligations or for which it is contended the community has liability.

(4) The waiver is knowingly, intelligently, and voluntarily entered into by each of the parties.

(5) Each party understands that this waiver does not limit the legal disclosure obligations of the parties, but rather is a statement under penalty of perjury that those obligations have been fulfilled. Each party further understands that noncompliance with those obligations will result in the court setting aside the judgment.[80]

2106. Except as provided in subdivision (d) of Section 2105, Section 2110, or absent good cause as provided in Section 2107, judgment shall not be entered with respect to the parties' property rights without each party, or the attorney for that party in this matter, having executed and served a copy of the final declaration of disclosure and current income and expense declaration. Each party, or the party's attorney, shall execute and file with the court a declaration signed under penalty of perjury stating that service of the final declaration of disclosure and current income and expense declaration was made on the other party or that service of the final declaration of disclosure has been waived pursuant to subdivision (d) of Section 2105 or in Section 2110.[427]

2107. (a) If one party fails to serve on the other party a preliminary declarant-ion of disclosure under Section 2104, unless that party is not required to serve a preliminary declaration of disclosure pursuant to Section 2110, or a final declaration of disclosure under Section 2105, or fails to provide the information required in the respective declarations with sufficient particularity, and if the other party has served the respective declaration of disclosure on the noncomplying party, the complying party may, within a reasonable time, request preparation of the appropriate declaration of disclosure or further particularity.

(b) If the noncomplying party fails to comply with a request under subdivision (a), the complying party may do one or more of the following:

(1) File a motion to compel a further response.

(2) File a motion for an order preventing the noncomplying party from presenting evidence on issues that should have been covered in the declaration of disclosure.

(3) File a motion showing good cause for the court to grant the complying party's voluntary waiver of receipt of the noncomplying party's preliminary declaration of disclosure pursuant to Section 2104 or final declaration of disclosure pursuant to Section 2105. The voluntary waiver does not affect the rights enumerated in subdivision (d).

(c) If a party fails to comply with any provision of this chapter, the court shall, in addition to any other remedy provided by law, impose money sanctions against the noncomplying party. Sanctions shall be in an amount sufficient to deter repetition of the conduct or comparable conduct, and shall include reasonable attorney's fees, costs incurred, or both, unless the court finds that the noncomplying party acted with substantial justification or that other circumstances make the imposition of the sanction unjust.

(d) Except as otherwise provided in this subdivision, if a court enters a judgment when the parties have failed to comply with all disclosure requirements of this chapter, the court shall set aside the judgment. The failure to comply with the disclosure requirements does not constitute harmless error. If the court granted the complying party's voluntary waiver of receipt of the noncomplying party's preliminary declaration of disclosure pursuant to paragraph (3) of subdivision (b), the court shall set aside the judgment only at the request of the complying party, unless the motion to set aside the judgment is based on one of the following:

(1) Actual fraud if the defrauded party was kept in ignorance or in some other manner was fraudulently prevented from fully participating in the proceeding.

(2) Perjury, as defined in Section 118 of the Penal Code, in the preliminary or final declaration of disclosure, in the waiver of the final declaration of disclosure, or in the current income and expense statement.

(e) Upon the motion to set aside judgment, the court may order the parties to provide the preliminary and final declarations of disclosure that were exchanged between them. Absent a court order to the contrary, the disclosure declarations shall not be filed with the court and shall be returned to the parties.[326]

2108. At any time during the proceeding, the court has the authority, on application of a party and for good cause, to order the liquidation of community or quasi-community assets so as to avoid unreasonable market or investment risks, given the relative nature, scope, and extent of the community estate. However, in no event shall the court grant the application unless, as provided in this chapter, the appropriate declaration of disclosure has been served by the moving party.[11]

2109. The provisions of this chapter requiring a final declaration of disclosure do not apply to a summary dissolution of marriage, but a preliminary declaration of disclosure is required.[2]

2110. In the case of a default judgment, the petitioner may waive the final declaration of disclosure requirements provided in this chapter, and shall not be required to serve a final declaration of disclosure on the respondent nor receive a final declaration of disclosure from the respondent. However, a preliminary declaration of disclosure by the petitioner is required unless the petitioner served the summons and petition by publication or posting pursuant to court order and the respondent has defaulted.[327]

2111. A disclosure required by this chapter does not abrogate the attorney work product privilege or impede the power of the court to issue protective orders.[3]

2112. The Judicial Council shall adopt appropriate forms and modify existing forms to effectuate the purposes of this chapter.[4]

2113. This chapter applies to any proceeding commenced on or after January 1, 1993.

Chapter 10: Relief From Judgment

2120. The Legislature finds and declares the following:
(a) The State of California has a strong policy of ensuring the division of community and quasi-community property in the dissolution of a marriage as set forth in Division 7 (commencing with Section 2500), and of providing for fair and sufficient child and spousal support awards. These policy goals can only be implemented with full disclosure of community, quasi-community, and separate assets, liabilities, income, and expenses, as provided in Chapter 9 (commencing with Section 2100), and decisions freely and knowingly made.
(b) It occasionally happens that the division of property or the award of support, whether made as a result of agreement or trial, is inequitable when made due to the nondisclosure or other misconduct of one of the parties.
(c) The public policy of assuring finality of judgments must be balanced against the public interest in ensuring proper division of marital property, in ensuring sufficient support awards, and in deterring misconduct.
(d) The law governing the circumstances under which a judgment can be set aside, after the time for relief under Section 473 of the Code of Civil Procedure has passed, has been the subject of considerable confusion which has led to increased litigation and unpredictable and inconsistent decisions at the trial and appellate levels.

2121. (a) In proceedings for dissolution of marriage, for nullity of marriage, or for legal separation of the parties, the court may, on any terms

that may be just, relieve a spouse from a judgment, or any part or parts thereof, adjudicating support or division of property, after the six-month time limit of Section 473 of the Code of Civil Procedure has run, based on the grounds, and within the time limits, provided in this chapter.
(b) In all proceedings under this chapter, before granting relief, the court shall find that the facts alleged as the grounds for relief materially affected the original outcome and that the moving party would materially benefit from the granting of the relief.

2122. The grounds and time limits for a motion to set aside a judgment, or any part or parts thereof, are governed by this section and shall be one of the following:
(a) Actual fraud where the defrauded party was kept in ignorance or in some other manner was fraudulently prevented from fully participating in the proceeding. An action or motion based on fraud shall be brought within one year after the date on which the complaining party either did discover, or should have discovered, the fraud.
(b) Perjury. An action or motion based on perjury in the preliminary or final declaration of disclosure, the waiver of the final declaration of disclosure, or in the current income and expense statement shall be brought within one year after the date on which the complaining party either did discover, or should have discovered, the perjury.
(c) Duress. An action or motion based upon duress shall be brought within two years after the date of entry of judgment.
(d) Mental incapacity. An action or motion based on mental incapacity shall be brought within two years after the date of entry of judgment.
(e) As to stipulated or uncontested judgments or that part of a judgment stipulated to by the parties, mistake, either mutual or unilateral, whether mistake of law or mistake of fact. An action or motion based on mistake shall be brought within one year after the date of entry of judgment.
(f) Failure to comply with the disclosure requirements of Chapter 9 (commencing with Section 2100). An action or motion based on failure to comply with the disclosure requirements shall be brought within one year after the date on which the complaining party either discovered, or should have discovered, the failure to comply.[81]

2123. Notwithstanding any other provision of this chapter, or any other law, a judgment may not be set aside simply because the court finds that it was inequitable when made, nor simply because subsequent circumstances caused the division of assets or liabilities to become inequitable, or the support to become inadequate.

2124. The negligence of an attorney shall not be imputed to a client to bar an order setting aside a judgment, unless the court finds that the client knew, or should have known, of the attorney's negligence and unreasonably failed to self-protect.[428]

2125. When ruling on an action or motion to set aside a judgment, the court shall set aside only those provisions materially affected by the circumstances leading to the court's decision to grant relief. However, the court has discretion to set aside the entire judgment, if necessary, for equitable considerations.

2126. As to assets or liabilities for which a judgment or part of a judgment is set aside, the date of valuation shall be subject to equitable considerations. The court shall equally divide the asset or liability, unless the court finds upon good cause shown that the interests of justice require an unequal division.

2127. As to actions or motions filed under this chapter, if a timely request is made, the court shall render a statement of decision where the court has resolved controverted factual evidence.

2128. (a) Nothing in this chapter prohibits a party from seeking relief under Section 2556.
(b) Nothing in this chapter changes existing law with respect to contract remedies where the contract has not been merged or incorporated
into a judgment.
(c) Nothing in this chapter is intended to restrict a family law court from acting as a court of equity.
(d) Nothing in this chapter is intended to limit existing law with respect to the modification or enforcement of support orders.
(e) Nothing in this chapter affects the rights of a bona fide lessee, purchaser, or encumbrancer for value of real property.[12]

2129. This chapter applies to judgments entered on or after January 1, 1993.[12]

PART 2: JUDICIAL DETERMINATION OF VOID OR VOIDABLE MARRIAGE

enacted by Stats. 1992, Ch. 162, Sec. 10.

Chapter 1: Void Marriage

2200. Marriages between parents and children, ancestors and descendants of every degree, and between siblings of the half as well as the whole blood, and between uncles or aunts and nieces or nephews, are incestuous, and void from the beginning, whether the relationship is legitimate or illegitimate.[293]

2201. (a) A subsequent marriage contracted by a person during the life of his or her former spouse, with a person other than the former spouse, is illegal and void, unless:
(1) The former marriage has been dissolved or adjudged a nullity before the date of the subsequent marriage.
(2) The former spouse (A) is absent, and not known to the person to be living for the period of five successive years immediately preceding the subsequent marriage, or (B) is generally reputed or believed by the person to be dead at the time the subsequent marriage was contracted.
(b) In either of the cases described in paragraph (2) of subdivision (a), the subsequent marriage is valid until its nullity is adjudged pursuant to subdivision (b) of Section 2210.[294]

Chapter 2: Voidable Marriage

2210. A marriage is voidable and may be adjudged a nullity if any of the following conditions existed at the time of the marriage:
(a) The party who commences the

proceeding or on whose behalf the proceeding is commenced was under 18 years of age, unless the party entered into the marriage pursuant to Section 302 or 303.

(b) The spouse of either party was living and the marriage with that spouse was then in force and that spouse (1) was absent and not known to the party commencing the proceeding to be living for a period of five successive years immediately preceding the subsequent marriage for which the judgment of nullity is sought or (2) was generally reputed or believed by the party commencing the proceeding to be dead at the time the subsequent marriage was contracted.

(c) Either party was of unsound mind, unless the party of unsound mind, after coming to reason, freely cohabited with the other as his or her spouse.

(d) The consent of either party was obtained by fraud, unless the party whose consent was obtained by fraud afterwards, with full knowledge of the facts constituting the fraud, freely cohabited with the other as his or her spouse.

(e) The consent of either party was obtained by force, unless the party whose consent was obtained by force afterwards freely cohabited with the other as his or her spouse.

(f) Either party was, at the time of marriage, physically incapable of entering into the marriage state, and that incapacity continues, and appears to be incurable.

2211. A proceeding to obtain a judgment of nullity of marriage, for causes set forth in Section 2210, must be commenced within the periods and by the parties, as follows:

(a) For causes mentioned in subdivision (a) of Section 2210, by any of the following:

(1) The party to the marriage who was married under the age of legal consent, within four years after arriving at the age of consent.

(2) A parent, guardian, conservator, or other person having charge of the minor, at any time before the married minor has arrived at the age of legal consent.

(b) For causes mentioned in subdivision (b) of Section 2210, by either of the following:

(1) Either party during the life of the other.

(2) The former spouse.

(c) For causes mentioned in subdivision (c) of Section 2210, by the party injured, or by a relative or conservator of the party of unsound mind, at any time before the death of either party.

(d) For causes mentioned in subdivision (d) of Section 2210, by the party whose consent was obtained by fraud, within four years after the discovery of the facts constituting the fraud.

(e) For causes mentioned in subdivision (e) of Section 2210, by the party whose consent was obtained by force, within four years after the marriage.

(f) For causes mentioned in subdivision (f) of Section 2210, by the injured party, within four years after the marriage.

(g) This section shall remain in effect only until January 1, 2027, and as of that date is repealed.[295]

2211. A proceeding to obtain a judgment of nullity of marriage, for causes set forth in Section 2210, shall be commenced within the periods and by the parties, as follows:

(a) For causes mentioned in subdivision (a) of Section 2210, by any of the following:

(1) The party to the marriage who was married under the age of legal consent, within four years after arriving at the age of consent.

(2) A parent, guardian, conservator, or other person having charge of the minor, at any time before the married minor has arrived at the age of legal consent.

(b) For causes mentioned in subdivision (b) of Section 2210, by either of the following:

(1) Either party during the life of the other.

(2) The former spouse.

(c) For causes mentioned in subdivision (c) of Section 2210, by the party injured, or by a relative or conservator of the party of unsound mind, at any time before the death of either party.

(d) For causes mentioned in subdivision (d) of Section 2210, by the party whose consent was obtained by fraud, within four years after the discovery of the facts constituting the fraud.

(e) For causes mentioned in subdivision (e) of Section 2210, by the party whose consent was obtained by force, within four years after the marriage.

(f) For causes mentioned in subdivision (f) of Section 2210, by the injured party, within four years after the marriage.

(g) (1) If the petition for nullity of marriage on the grounds identified in subdivision (e) is filed beyond the relevant period provided, a court may grant permission for a party to proceed with the petition upon a showing of good cause.

(2) The Judicial Council shall modify or develop the forms necessary to implement this subdivision.

(h) This section shall become operative on January 1, 2027.[610]

2212. (a) The effect of a judgment of nullity of marriage is to restore the parties to the status of unmarried persons.

(b) A judgment of nullity of marriage is conclusive only as to the parties to the proceeding and those claiming under them.[1]

Chapter 3: Procedural Provisions

2250. (a) A proceeding based on void or voidable marriage is commenced by filing a petition entitled "In re the marriage of ____ and ____" which shall state that it is a petition for a judgment of nullity of the marriage.

(b) A copy of the petition together with a copy of a summons in form and content approved by the Judicial Council shall be served upon the other party to the marriage in the same manner as service of papers in civil actions generally.[1]

2251. (a) If a determination is made that a marriage is void or voidable and the court finds that either party or both parties believed in good faith that the marriage was valid, the court shall:

(1) Declare the party or parties, who believed in good faith that the marriage was valid, to have the status of a putative spouse.

(2) If the division of property is in issue, divide, in accordance with Division 7 (commencing with Section 2500), that property acquired during the union that would have been community property or quasi-

community property if the union had not been void or voidable, only upon request of a party who is declared a putative spouse under paragraph (1). This property is known as "quasi-marital property."

(b) If the court expressly reserves jurisdiction, it may make the property division at a time after the judgment.[330]

2252. The property divided pursuant to Section 2251 is liable for debts of the parties to the same extent as if the property had been community property or quasi-community property.[1]

2253. In a proceeding under this part, custody of the children shall be determined according to Division 8 (commencing with Section 3000).[1]

2254. The court may, during the pendency of a proceeding for nullity of marriage or upon judgment of nullity of marriage, order a party to pay for the support of the other party in the same manner as if the marriage had not been void or voidable if the party for whose benefit the order is made is found to be a putative spouse.[1]

2255. The court may grant attorney's fees and costs in accordance with Chapter 3.5 (commencing with Section 2030) of Part 1 in proceedings to have the marriage adjudged void and in those proceedings based upon voidable marriage in which the party applying for attorney's fees and costs is found to be innocent of fraud or wrongdoing in inducing or entering into the marriage, and free from knowledge of the then existence of any prior marriage or other impediment to the contracting of the marriage for which a judgment of nullity is sought.[13]

PART 3: DISSOLUTION OF MARRIAGE AND LEGAL SEPARATION

enacted by Stats. 1992, Ch. 162, Sec. 10.

Chapter 1: Effect of Dissolution

2300. The effect of a judgment of dissolution of marriage when it becomes final is to restore the parties to the state of unmarried persons.[1]

Chapter 2: Grounds for Dissolution or Legal Separation

2310. Dissolution of the marriage or legal separation of the parties may be based on either of the following grounds, which shall be pleaded generally:

(a) Irreconcilable differences, which have caused the irremediable breakdown of the marriage.

(b) Permanent legal incapacity to make decisions.[305]

2311. Irreconcilable differences are those grounds which are determined by the court to be substantial reasons for not continuing the marriage and which make it appear that the marriage should be dissolved.[1]

2312. A marriage may be dissolved on the grounds of permanent legal incapacity to make decisions only upon proof, including competent medical or psychiatric testimony, that the spouse was at the time the petition was filed, and remains, permanently lacking the legal capacity to make decisions.[306]

2313. No dissolution of marriage granted on the ground of permanent legal incapacity to make decisions relieves a spouse from any obligation imposed by law as a result of the marriage for the support of the spouse who lacks legal capacity to make decisions, and the court may make an order for support, or require a bond therefor, as the circumstances require.[307]

Chapter 3: Residence Requirements

2320. (a) Except as provided in subdivision (b), a judgment of dissolution of marriage may not be entered unless one of the parties to the marriage has been a resident of this state for six months and of the county in which the proceeding is filed for three months next preceding the filing of the petition.
(b) (1) A judgment for dissolution, nullity, or legal separation of a marriage between persons of the same sex may be entered, even if neither spouse is a resident of, or maintains a domicile in, this state at the time the proceedings are filed, if the following apply:
(A) The marriage was entered in California.
(B) Neither party to the marriage resides in a jurisdiction that will dissolve the marriage. If the jurisdiction does not recognize the marriage, there shall be a rebuttable presumption that the jurisdiction will not dissolve the marriage.
(2) For the purposes of this subdivision, the superior court in the county where the marriage was entered shall be the proper court for the proceeding. The dissolution, nullity, or legal separation shall be adjudicated in accordance with California law.[225]

2321. (a) In a proceeding for legal separation of the parties in which neither party, at the time the proceeding was commenced, has complied with the residence requirements of Section 2320, either party may, upon complying with the residence requirements, amend the party's petition or responsive pleading in the proceeding to request that a judgment of dissolution of the marriage be entered. The date of the filing of the amended petition or pleading shall be deemed to be the date of commencement of the proceeding for the dissolution of the marriage for the purposes only of the residence requirements of Section 2320.
(b) If the other party has appeared in the proceeding, notice of the amendment shall be given to the other party in the manner provided by rules adopted by the Judicial Council. If no appearance has been made by the other party in the proceeding, notice of the amendment may be given to the other party by mail to the last known address of the other party, or by personal service, if the intent of the party to so amend upon satisfaction of the residence requirements of Section 2320 is set forth in the initial petition or pleading in the manner provided by rules adopted by the Judicial Council.[1]

2322. For the purpose of a proceeding for dissolution of marriage, each spouse may have a separate domicile or residence depending upon proof of the fact and not upon legal presumptions.[296]

Chapter 4: General Procedural Provisions

2330. (a) A proceeding for dissolution of marriage or for legal separation of the parties is commenced by filing a petition or joint petition entitled "In re the marriage of ____ and ____," which shall state whether it is a petition for dissolution of the marriage or for legal separation of the parties.

(b) In a proceeding for dissolution of marriage or for legal separation of the parties, the petition shall set forth, among other matters, as nearly as can be ascertained, the following facts:

(1) The date of marriage.

(2) The date of separation.

(3) The number of years from marriage to separation.

(4) The number of children of the marriage, if any, and if none a statement of that fact.

(5) The age and birth date of each minor child of the marriage.

(c) In a joint petition proceeding for dissolution of marriage or for legal separation of the parties, the joint petition shall set forth, among other matters, as nearly as can be ascertained, the following facts:

(1) The date of the marriage.

(2) (A) If there are children of the marriage, all of the following information:

(i) The number of children.

(ii) The age of each child.

(iii) The date of birth of each child.

(B) If there are no children of the marriage, a statement of that fact.

(3) (A) A list of issues upon which the parties intend to resolve by agreement, which may include, but is not limited to, the following:

(i) The legal grounds for dissolution or legal separation.

(ii) The date of separation.

(iii) Child custody.

(iv) Child support.

(v) Spousal support or domestic partner support.

(vi) Separate property.

(vii) Community and quasi-community property.

(viii) Restoration of former name.

(ix) Attorney's fees and costs.

(B) The list of issues required by subparagraph (A) shall represent all of the matters at issue in the dissolution. If the parties have an issue that they do not intend to resolve by agreement, they shall file a petition pursuant to subdivision (b).[578]

2330.1. In any proceeding for dissolution of marriage, for legal separation of the parties, or for the support of children, the petition or complaint may list children born before the marriage to the same parties and, pursuant to the terms of the Uniform Parentage Act, a determination of paternity may be made in the action. In addition, a supplemental complaint may be filed, in any of those proceedings, pursuant to Section 464 of the Code of Civil Procedure, seeking a judgment or order of paternity or support for a child of the mother and father of the child whose paternity and support are already in issue before the court. A supplemental complaint for paternity or support of children may be filed without leave of court either before or after final judgment in the underlying action. Service of the supplemental summons and complaint shall be made in the manner provided for the initial service of a summons by this code.[72]

2330.3. (a) All dissolution actions, to the greatest extent possible, shall be assigned to the same superior court department for all purposes, in order

that all decisions in a case through final judgment shall be made by the same judicial officer. However, if the assignment will result in a significant delay of any family law matter, the dissolution action need not be assigned to the same superior court department for all purposes, unless the parties stipulate otherwise.
(b) The Judicial Council shall adopt a standard of judicial administration prescribing a minimum length of assignment of a judicial officer to a family law assignment.
(c) This section shall be operative on July 1, 1997.[200]

2330.5. Notwithstanding any other provision of law, if no demand for money, property, costs, or attorney's fees is contained in the petition and the judgment of dissolution of marriage is entered by default, the filing of income and expense declarations and property declarations in connection therewith shall not be required.[1]

2331. (a) A copy of the petition, together with a copy of a summons, in a form and content approved by the Judicial Council, shall be served upon the other party to the marriage in the same manner as service of papers in civil actions generally.
(b) If the parties file a joint petition and joint summons, in a form and content approved by the Judicial Council, the joint petition shall be deemed to be served on both parties upon the filing of the joint petition with the court and both parties shall be determined to have appeared in the matter.[579]

2332. (a) If the petition for dissolution of the marriage is based on the ground of permanent legal incapacity to make decisions and the spouse who lacks legal capacity to make decisions has a guardian or conservator, other than the spouse filing the petition, the petition and summons shall be served upon the spouse and the guardian or conservator. The guardian or conservator shall defend and protect the interests of the spouse who lacks legal capacity to make decisions.
(b) If the spouse who lacks legal capacity to make decisions has no guardian or conservator, or if the spouse filing the petition is the guardian or conservator, the court shall appoint a guardian ad litem, who may be the district attorney or the county counsel, if any, to defend and protect the interests of the spouse who lacks legal capacity to make decisions. If a district attorney or county counsel is appointed guardian ad litem pursuant to this subdivision, the successor in the office of district attorney or county counsel, as the case may be, succeeds as guardian ad litem, without further action by the court or parties.
(c) "Guardian or conservator" as used in this section means:
(1) With respect to the issue of the dissolution of the marriage relationship, the guardian or conservator of the person.
(2) With respect to support and property division issues, the guardian or conservator of the estate.[308]

2333. Subject to Section 2334, if from the evidence at the hearing the court finds that there are irreconcilable differences which have caused the irremediable breakdown of the marriage, the court shall order the dissolution of the marriage or a legal separation of the parties.

2334. (a) If it appears that there is a reasonable possibility of reconciliation, the court shall continue the proceeding for the dissolution of the marriage or for a legal separation of the parties for a period not to exceed 30 days.

(b) During the period of the continuance, the court may make orders for the support and maintenance of the parties, the custody of the minor child-ren of the marriage, the support of children for whom support may be ordered, attorney's fees, and for the preservation of the property of the parties.

(c) At any time after the termination of the period of the continuance, either party may move for the dissolution of the marriage or a legal separation of the parties, and the court may enter a judgment of dissolution of the marri-age or legal separation of the parties.

2335. Except as otherwise provided by statute, in a pleading or proceeding for dissolution of marriage or legal separation of the parties, including deposit-ions and discovery proceedings, evidence of specific acts of misconduct is improper and inadmissible.[14]

2335.5. In a proceeding for dissolution of marriage or legal separation of the parties, where the judgment is to be entered by default, the petitioner shall provide the court clerk with a stamped envelope bearing sufficient postage addressed to the spouse who has defaulted, with the address of the court clerk as the return address, and the court clerk shall mail a copy of the request to enter default to that spouse in the envelope provided. A judgment of dissolution or legal separation, including relief requested in the petition, shall not be denied solely on the basis that the request to enter default was returned unopened to the court. The court clerk shall maintain any such document returned by the post office as part of the court file in the case.

2336. (a) No judgment of dissolution or of legal separation of the parties may be granted upon the default of one of the parties or upon a statement or finding of fact made by a referee; but the court shall, in addition to the statement or finding of the referee, require proof of the grounds alleged, and the proof, if not taken before the court, shall be by affidavit. In all cases where there are minor children of the parties, each affidavit or offer of proof shall include an estimate by the declarant or affiant of the monthly gross income of each party. If the declarant or affiant has no knowledge of the estimated monthly income of a party, the declarant or affiant shall state why he or she has no knowledge. In all cases where there is a community estate, each affidavit or offer of proof shall include an estimate of the value of the assets and the debts the declarant or affiant proposes to be distributed to each party, unless the declarant or affiant has filed, or con-currently files, a complete and accurate property declaration with the court.

(b) If the proof is by affidavit, the personal appearance of the affiant is required only when it appears to the court that any of the following circumstances exist:

(1) Reconciliation of the parties is reasonably possible.

(2) A proposed child custody order is not in the best interest of the child.

(3) A proposed child support order is less than a noncustodial parent is capable of paying.

(4) A personal appearance of a party or interested person would be in the best interests of justice.

(c) An affidavit submitted pursuant to this section shall contain a stipulation by the affiant that the affiant understands that proof will be by affidavit and that the affiant will not appear before the court unless so ordered by the court.[73]

2337. (a) In a proceeding for dissolution of marriage, the court, upon noticed motion, may sever and grant an early and separate trial on the issue of the dissolution of the status of the marriage apart from other issues.

(b) A preliminary declaration of disclosure with a completed schedule of assets and debts shall be served on the nonmoving party with the noticed motion unless it has been served previously, or unless the parties stipulate in writing to defer service of the preliminary declaration of disclosure until a later time.

(c) The court may impose upon a party any of the following conditions on granting a severance of the issue of the dissolution of the status of the marriage, and in case of that party's death, an order of any of the following conditions continues to be binding upon that party's estate:

(1) The party shall indemnify and hold the other party harmless from any taxes, reassessments, interest, and penalties payable by the other party in connection with the division of the community estate that would not have been payable if the parties were still married at the time the division was made.

(2) Until judgment has been entered on all remaining issues and has become final, the party shall maintain all existing health and medical insurance coverage for the other party and any minor children as named dependents, so long as the party is eligible to do so. If at any time during this period the party is not eligible to maintain that coverage, the party shall, at the party's sole expense, provide and maintain health and medical insurance coverage that is comparable to the existing health and medical insurance coverage to the extent it is available. To the extent that coverage is not available, the party shall be responsible to pay, and shall demonstrate to the court's satisfaction the ability to pay, for the health and medical care for the other party and the minor children, to the extent that care would have been covered by the existing insurance coverage but for the dissolution of marital status, and shall otherwise indemnify and hold the other party harmless from any adverse consequences resulting from the loss or reduction of the existing coverage. For purposes of this subdivision, "health and medical insurance coverage" includes any coverage for which the parties are eligible under any group or individual health or other medical plan, fund, policy, or program.

(3) Until judgment has been entered on all remaining issues and has become final, the party shall indemnify and hold the other party harmless from any adverse consequences to the other party if the bifurcation results in a termination of the other party's right to a probate

homestead in the residence in which the other party resides at the time the severance is granted.

(4) Until judgment has been entered on all remaining issues and has become final, the party shall indemnify and hold the other party harmless from any adverse consequences to the other party if the bifurcation results in the loss of the rights of the other party to a probate family allowance as the surviving spouse of the party.

(5) Until judgment has been entered on all remaining issues and has become final, the party shall indemnify and hold the other party harmless from any adverse consequences to the other party if the bifurcation results in the loss of the other party's rights with respect to any retirement, survivor, or deferred compensation benefits under any plan, fund, or arrangement, or to any elections or options associated therewith, to the extent that the other party would have been entitled to those benefits or elections as the spouse or surviving spouse of the party.

(6) The party shall indemnify and hold the other party harmless from any adverse consequences if the bifurcation results in the loss of rights to social security benefits or elections to the extent the other party would have been entitled to those benefits or elections as the surviving spouse of the party.

(7) (A) The court may make an order pursuant to paragraph (3) of subdivision (b) of Section 5040 of the Probate Code, if appropriate, that a party maintain a beneficiary designation for a nonprobate transfer, as described in Section 5000 of the Probate Code, for a spouse or domestic partner for up to one-half of or, upon a showing of good cause, for all of a nonprobate transfer asset until judgment has been entered with respect to the community ownership of that asset, and until the other party's interest therein has been distributed to him or her.

(B) Except upon a showing of good cause, this paragraph does not apply to any of the following:

(i) A nonprobate transfer described in Section 5000 of the Probate Code that was not created by either party or that was acquired by either party by gift, descent, or devise.

(ii) An irrevocable trust.

(iii) A trust of which neither party is the grantor.

(iv) Powers of appointment under a trust instrument that was not created by either party or of which neither party is a grantor.

(v) The execution and filing of a disclaimer pursuant to Part 8 (commencing with Section 260) of Division 2 of the Probate Code.

(vi) The appointment of a party as a trustee.

(8) In order to preserve the ability of the party to defer the distribution of the Individual Retirement Account or annuity (IRA) established under Section 408 or 408A of the Internal Revenue Code of 1986, as amended, (IRC) upon the death of the other party, the court may require that one-half, or all upon a showing of good cause, of the community interest in any IRA, by or for the benefit of the party, be assigned and transferred to the other party pursuant to Section 408(d)(6) of the Internal Revenue Code. This paragraph does not limit the power granted pursuant to

subdivision (g).

(9) Upon a showing that circumstances exist that would place a substantial burden of enforcement upon either party's community property rights or would eliminate the ability of the surviving party to enforce his or her community property rights if the other party died before the division and distribution or compliance with any court-ordered payment of any community property interest therein, including, but not limited to, a situation in which preemption under federal law applies to an asset of a party, or purchase by a bona fide purchaser has occurred, the court may order a specific security interest designed to reduce or eliminate the likelihood that a postmortem enforcement proceeding would be ineffective or unduly burdensome to the surviving party. For this purpose, those orders may include, but are not limited to, any of the following:

(A) An order that the party provide an undertaking.

(B) An order to provide a security interest by Qualified Domestic Relations Order from that party's share of a retirement plan or plans.

(C) An order for the creation of a trust as defined in paragraph (2) of subdivision (a) of Section 82 of the Probate Code.

(D) An order for other arrangements as may be reasonably necessary and feasible to provide appropriate security in the event of the party's death before judgment has been entered with respect to the community ownership of that asset, and until the other party's interest therein has been distributed to him or her.

(E) If a retirement plan is not subject to an enforceable court order for the payment of spousal survivor benefits to the other party, an interim order requiring the party to pay or cause to be paid, and to post adequate security for the payment of, any survivor benefit that would have been payable to the other party on the death of the party but for the judgment granting a dissolution of the status of the marriage, pending entry of judgment on all remaining issues.

(10) Any other condition the court determines is just and equitable.

(d) Prior to, or simultaneously with, entry of judgment granting dissolution of the status of the marriage, all of the following shall occur:

(1) The party's retirement or pension plan shall be joined as a party to the proceeding for dissolution, unless joinder is precluded or made unnecessary by Title 1 of the federal Employee Retirement Income Security Act of 1974 (29 U.S.C. Sec. 1001 et seq.), as amended (ERISA), or any other applicable law.

(2) To preserve the claims of each spouse in all retirement plan benefits upon entry of judgment granting a dissolution of the status of the marriage, the court shall enter one of the following in connection with the judgment for each retirement plan in which either party is a participant:

(A) An order pursuant to Section 2610 disposing of each party's interest in retirement plan benefits, including survivor and death benefits.

(B) An interim order preserving the nonemployee party's right to retirement plan benefits, including survivor and death benefits, pending entry of judgment on all remaining issues.

(C) An attachment to the judgment granting a dissolution of the status of the marriage, as follows:

EACH PARTY (insert names and addresses) IS PROVISIONALLY AWARDED WITHOUT PREJUDICE AND SUBJECT TO ADJUSTMENT BY A SUBSEQUENT DOMESTIC RELATIONS ORDER, A SEPARATE INTEREST EQUAL TO ONE-HALF OF ALL BENEFITS ACCRUED OR TO BE ACCRUED UNDER THE PLAN (name each plan individually) AS A RESULT OF EMPLOYMENT OF THE OTHER PARTY DURING THE MARRIAGE OR DOMESTIC PARTNERSHIP AND PRIOR TO THE DATE OF SEPARATION. IN ADDITION, PENDING FURTHER NOTICE, THE PLAN SHALL, AS ALLOWED BY LAW, OR IN THE CASE OF A GOVERNMENTAL PLAN, AS ALLOWED BY THE TERMS OF THE PLAN, CONTINUE TO TREAT THE PARTIES AS MARRIED OR DOMESTIC PARTNERS FOR PURPOSES OF ANY SURVIVOR RIGHTS OR BENEFITS AVAILABLE UNDER THE PLAN TO THE EXTENT NECESSARY TO PROVIDE FOR PAYMENT OF AN AMOUNT EQUAL TO THAT SEPARATE INTEREST OR FOR ALL OF THE SURVIVOR BENEFIT IF AT THE TIME OF THE DEATH OF THE PARTICIPANT, THERE IS NO OTHER ELIGIBLE RECIPIENT OF THE SURVIVOR BENEFIT.

(e) The moving party shall promptly serve a copy of any order, interim order, or attachment entered pursuant to paragraph (2) of subdivision (d), and a copy of the judgment granting a dissolution of the status of the marriage, on the retirement or pension plan administrator.

(f) A judgment granting a dissolution of the status of the marriage shall expressly reserve jurisdiction for later determination of all other pending issues.

(g) If the party dies after the entry of judgment granting a dissolution of marriage, any obligation imposed by this section shall be enforceable against any asset, including the proceeds thereof, against which these obligations would have been enforceable prior to the person's death.[331]

2338. (a) In a proceeding for dissolution of the marriage or legal separation of the parties, the court shall file its decision and any statement of decision as in other cases.

(b) If the court determines that no dissolution should be granted, a judgment to that effect only shall be entered.

(c) If the court determines that a dissolution should be granted, a judgment of dissolution of marriage shall be entered. After the entry of the judgment and before it becomes final, neither party has the right to dismiss the proceeding without the consent of the other.[1]

2338.5. Where a judgment of dissolution or nullity of marriage or legal separation of the parties is to be granted upon the default of one of the parties:

(a) The signature of the spouse who

has defaulted on any marital settlement agreement or on any stipulated judgment shall be notarized.

(b) The court clerk shall give notice of entry of judgment of dissolution of marriage, nullity of marriage, or legal separation to the attorney for each party or to the party, if unrepresented.

(c) For the purpose of mailing the notice of entry of judgment, the party submitting the judgment shall provide the court clerk with a stamped envelope bearing sufficient postage addressed to the attorney for the other party or to the party, if unrepresented, with the address of the court clerk as the return address. The court clerk shall maintain any such document returned by the post office as part of the court file in the case.

2339. (a) Subject to subdivision (b) and to Sections 2340 to 2344, inclusive, no judgment of dissolution is final for the purpose of terminating the marriage relationship of the parties until six months have expired from the date of service of a copy of summons and petition or the date of appearance of the respondent, whichever occurs first.

(b) The court may extend the six-month period described in subdivision (a) for good cause shown.[1]

2340. A judgment of dissolution of marriage shall specify the date on which the judgment becomes finally effective for the purpose of terminating the marriage relationship of the parties.[1]

2341. (a) Notwithstanding Section 2340, if an appeal is taken from the judgment or a motion for a new trial is made, the dissolution of marriage does not become final until the motion or appeal has been finally disposed of, nor then, if the motion has been granted or judgment reversed.

(b) Notwithstanding any other provision of law, the filing of an appeal or of a motion for a new trial does not stay the effect of a judgment insofar as it relates to the dissolution of the marriage status and restoring the parties to the status of unmarried persons, unless the appealing or moving party specifies in the notice of appeal or motion for new trial an objection to the termination of the marriage status. No party may make such an objection to the termination of the marriage status unless such an objection was also made at the time of trial.[1]

2342. Where a joint petition for summary dissolution under Chapter 5 (commencing with Section 2400) is thereafter revoked and either party commences a proceeding pursuant to Section 2330 within 90 days from the date of the filing of the revocation, the date the judgment becomes a final judgment under Section 2339 shall be calculated by deducting the period of time that has elapsed from the date of filing the joint petition to the date of filing the revocation.[580]

2342.5. (a) (1) If the parties file a joint petition for dissolution of marriage or for legal separation of the parties and joint summons in accordance with Sections 2330 and 2331, for identification purposes, including, but not limited to, identification on a Judicial Council form, the first joint petitioner shall be deemed petitioner and the other joint petitioner shall be deemed respondent.

(2) A joint summons shall include the temporary restraining order required

by Section 2040.

(3) Section 412.20 of the Code of Civil Procedure does not apply to a joint summons.

(b) (1) At any time before the entry of judgment on the joint petition, without leave of court, in a form and content approved by the Judicial Council, a petitioner may file an amended petition or the respondent may file an amended response.

(2) (A) If either party is served with an amended petition or amended response, the party served shall file and serve an amended petition or amended response, as applicable, within 30 days, in accordance with Section 2020, in a form and content approved by the Judicial Council.

(B) Subject to the court's discretion to regulate the order of proof, pursuant to Section 320 of the Evidence Code, the order of proof shall be determined by the order of service of the amended pleadings.

(3) If an amended petition or amended response is filed pursuant to paragraph (1), the joint petition for dissolution or for legal separation of the parties is deemed revoked and the proceeding shall proceed as a petition for dissolution or for legal separation of the parties under Section 2330. The filing date of the joint petition shall be considered the filing date for the action and all relevant deadlines, including, but not limited to, the deadlines set forth in Section 2339.

(4) A temporary restraining order included in the summons shall remain in effect if a party files an amended petition or amended response.

(c) The parties may file an amended joint petition. The filing of an amended joint petition does not affect the parties' ability to proceed pursuant to a joint petition.

(d) Either party may seek discovery, as set forth in the Code of Civil Procedure, under the joint petition process.

(e) If either party files a request for order, including, but not limited to, a request for a motion to compel or other discovery motion, or request for trial setting with the court, that party shall file an amended petition or amended response, pursuant to subdivision (b), before making, or simultaneously with, the request.

(f) A judgment based on the agreement of the parties shall be in the same form as if one party had filed a petition for dissolution of marriage or legal separation and the other party had filed a response to the petition for dissolution of marriage or legal separation or otherwise appeared prior to entry of judgment because both joint petitioners will have appeared in the matter pursuant to subdivision (b) of Section 2331 due to the filing of a joint petition.

(g) The provisions of Division 6 (commencing with Section 2000) of this code that apply to a petition for dissolution of marriage or for the legal separation of the parties also apply to a joint petition for dissolution of marriage or for legal separation of the parties unless otherwise provided for by this section, in which case the provisions of this section shall supersede.

(h) The filing of a joint petition shall be accompanied by the fees provided in subdivisions (b) and (d) of Section 70670 of the Government Code and the supplemental fees provided in Sections 70602.5 and 70602.6 of the

Government Code unless both parties have been granted a fee waiver pursuant to Section 68632 of the Government Code.
(i) This section shall become operative on January 1, 2026.[581]

2342.51. The Judicial Council shall adopt or amend any rules or forms necessary to implement Section 2342.5 on or before January 1, 2026.[582]

2343. The court may, upon notice and for good cause shown, or on stipulation of the parties, retain jurisdiction over the date of termination of the marital status, or may order that the marital status be terminated at a future specified date. On the date of termination of the marital status, the parties are restored to the status of unmarried persons.[1]

2344. (a) The death of either party after entry of the judgment does not prevent the judgment from becoming a final judgment under Sections 2339 to 2343, inclusive.
(b) Subdivision (a) does not validate a marriage by either party before the judgment becomes final, nor does it constitute a defense in a criminal prosecution against either party.[1]

2345. The court may not render a judgment of the legal separation of the parties without the consent of both parties unless one party has not made a general appearance and the petition is one for legal separation.[1]

2346. (a) If the court determines that a judgment of dissolution of the marriage should be granted, but by mistake, negligence, or inadvertence, the judgment has not been signed, filed, and entered, the court may cause the judgment to be signed, dated, filed, and entered in the proceeding as of the date when the judgment could have been signed, dated, filed, and entered originally, if it appears to the satisfaction of the court that no appeal is to be taken in the proceeding or motion made for a new trial, to annul or set aside the judgment, or for relief under Chapter 8 (commencing with Section 469) of Title 6 of Part 2 of the Code of Civil Procedure.
(b) The court may act under subdivision (a) on its own motion or upon the motion of either party to the proceeding. In contested cases, the motion of a party shall be with notice to the other party.
(c) The court may cause the judgment to be entered nunc pro tunc as provided in this section, even though the judgment may have been previously entered, where through mistake, negligence, or inadvertence the judgment was not entered as soon as it could have been entered under the law if applied for.
(d) The court shall not cause a judgment to be entered nunc pro tunc as provided in this section as of a date before trial in the matter, before the date of an uncontested judgment hearing in the matter, or before the date of submission to the court of an application for judgment on affidavit pursuant to Section 2336. Upon the entry of the judgment, the parties have the same rights with regard to the dissolution of marriage becoming final on the date that it would have become final had the judgment been entered upon the date when it could have been originally entered.[1]

2347. A judgment of legal separation of the parties does not bar a subsequent judgment of dissolution of the marriage granted pursuant to a petition for dissolution filed by either party.[1]

2348. (a) In addition to the requirements of Section 103200 of the Health and Safety Code, the clerk of the superior court of each county shall report annually to the Judicial Council the number of judgments entered in the county during the preceding calendar year or other 12-month period as required by the Judicial Council for each of the following:
(1) Dissolution of marriage.
(2) Legal separation of the parties.
(3) Nullity of marriage.
(b) After the Judicial Branch Statistical Information System (JBSIS) is operational statewide, the clerk of the superior court of each county shall also report annually to the Judicial Council the number of each of those judgments specified in paragraphs (1), (2), and (3) of subdivision (a), entered in the county during the preceding calendar year or other 12-month period as required by the Judicial Council, that include orders relating to child custody, visitation, or support.
(c) The Judicial Council shall include in its annual report to the Legislature on court statistics the number of each of the types of judgments entered in the state reported pursuant to subdivisions (a) and (b).
(d) The Judicial Council shall establish the applicable 12-month reporting period, the due date, and forms to be used, for submission of data pursuant to subdivisions (a) and (b). Until the Judicial Branch Statistical Information System (JBSIS) is operational statewide, the clerk of the superior court may report the data described in subdivision (a) using existing data collection systems, according to current Judicial Council statistical reporting regulations.[67]

Chapter 5: Summary Dissolution

2400. (a) A marriage may be dissolved by the summary dissolution procedure provided in this chapter if all of the following conditions exist at the time the proceeding is commenced:
(1) Either party has met the jurisdictional requirements of Chapter 3 (commencing with Section 2320) with regard to dissolution of marriage.
(2) Irreconcilable differences have caused the irremediable breakdown of the marriage and the marriage should be dissolved.
(3) There are no children of the relationship of the parties born before or during the marriage or adopted by the parties during the marriage, and neither party, to that party's knowledge, is pregnant.
(4) The marriage is not more than five years in duration as of the date of separation of the parties.
(5) Neither party has any interest in real property wherever situated, with the exception of the lease of a residence occupied by either party which satisfies the following requirements:
(A) The lease does not include an option to purchase.
(B) The lease terminates within one year from the date of the filing of the petition.
(6) There are no unpaid obligations in excess of four thousand dollars ($4,000) incurred by either or both of the parties after the date of their marriage, excluding the amount of any unpaid obligation with respect to an automobile.

(7) The total fair market value of community property assets, excluding all encumbrances and automobiles, including any deferred compensation or retirement plan, is less than twenty-five thousand dollars ($25,000), and neither party has separate property assets, excluding all encumbrances and automobiles, in excess of twenty-five thousand dollars ($25,000).
(8) The parties have executed an agreement setting forth the division of assets and the assumption of liabilities of the community, and have executed any documents, title certificates, bills of sale, or other evidence of transfer necessary to effectuate the agreement.
(9) The parties waive any rights to spousal support.
(10) The parties, upon entry of the judgment of dissolution of marriage pursuant to Section 2403, irrevocably waive their respective rights to appeal and their rights to move for a new trial.
(11) The parties have read and understand the summary dissolution brochure provided for in Section 2406.
(12) The parties desire that the court dissolve the marriage.
(b) On January 1, 1985, and on January 1 of each odd-numbered year thereafter, the amounts in paragraph (6) of subdivision (a) shall be adjusted to reflect any change in the value of the dollar. On January 1, 1993, and on January 1 of each odd-numbered year thereafter, the amounts in paragraph (7) of subdivision (a) shall be adjusted to reflect any change in the value of the dollar. The adjustments shall be made by multiplying the base amounts by the percentage change in the California Consumer Price Index as compiled by the Department of Industrial Relations, with the result rounded to the nearest thousand dollars. The Judicial Council shall compute and publish the amounts.[297]

2401. (a) A proceeding for summary dissolution of the marriage shall be commenced by filing a joint petition for summary dissolution in the form prescribed by the Judicial Council.
(b) The petition shall be signed under oath by both spouses and shall include all of the following:
(1) A statement that as of the date of the filing of the joint petition all of the conditions set forth in Section 2400 have been met.
(2) The mailing address of each spouse.
(3) A statement whether a spouse elects to have their former name restored and, if so, the name to be restored.[583]

2402. (a) At any time before the filing of application for judgment pursuant to Section 2403, either party to the marriage may revoke the joint petition for summary dissolution and thereby terminate the summary dissolution proceeding filed pursuant to this chapter.
(b) The revocation shall be effected by filing with the clerk of the court where the proceeding was commenced a notice of revocation in a form and content as shall be prescribed by the Judicial Council.
(c) The revoking party shall send a copy of the notice of revocation to the other party by first-class mail, postage prepaid, at the other party's last known address.[584]

2403. When six months have expired

from the date of the filing of the joint petition for summary dissolution, the court shall, unless a revocation has been filed pursuant to Section 2402, enter the judgment dissolving the marriage. The judgment restores to the parties the status of single persons, and either party may marry after the entry of the judgment. The clerk shall send a notice of entry of judgment to each of the parties at the party's last known address.[201]

2404. Entry of the judgment pursuant to Section 2403 constitutes:
(a) A final adjudication of the rights and obligations of the parties with respect to the status of the marriage and property rights.
(b) A waiver of their respective rights to spousal support, rights to appeal, and rights to move for a new trial.[1]

2405. (a) Entry of the judgment pursuant to Section 2403 does not prejudice nor bar the rights of either of the parties to institute an action to set aside the judgment for fraud, duress, accident, mistake, or other grounds recognized at law or in equity or to make a motion pursuant to Section 473 of the Code of Civil Procedure.
(b) The court shall set aside a judgment entered pursuant to Section 2403 regarding all matters except the status of the marriage, upon proof that the parties did not meet the requirements of Section 2400 at the time the petition was filed.[1]

2406. (a) Each superior court shall make available a brochure, the contents and form of which shall be prescribed by the Judicial Council, describing the requirements, nature, and effect of proceedings under this chapter. The brochure shall be printed and distributed by the Judicial Council in both English and Spanish.
(b) The brochure shall state, in nontechnical language, all the following:
(1) It is in the best interests of the parties to consult an attorney regarding the dissolution of their marriage. The services of an attorney may be obtained through lawyer referral services, group or prepaid legal services, or legal aid organizations.
(2) The parties should not rely exclusively on this brochure which is not intended as a guide for self-representation in proceedings under this chapter.
(3) A concise summary of the provisions and procedures of this chapter and Sections 2320 and 2322 and Sections 2339 to 2344, inclusive.
(4) The nature of services of the conciliation court, where available.
(5) Neither party to the marriage can in the future obtain spousal support from the other.
(6) A statement in boldface type to the effect that upon entry of the judgment, the rights and obligations of the parties to the marriage with respect to the marriage, including property and spousal support rights, will be permanently adjudicated without right of appeal, except that neither party will be barred from instituting an action to set aside the judgment for fraud, duress, accident, mistake, or other grounds at law or in equity, or to make a motion pursuant to Section 473 of the Code of Civil Procedure.
(7) The parties to the marriage retain the status of married persons and cannot remarry until the judgment

dissolving the marriage is entered.
(8) Other matters as the Judicial Council considers appropriate.[1]

Chapter 6: Case Management

2450. (a) The purpose of family centered case resolution is to benefit the parties by providing judicial assistance and management to the parties in actions for dissolution of marriage for the purpose of expediting the processing of the case, reducing the expense of litigation, and focusing on early resolution by settlement. Family centered case resolution is a tool to allow the courts to better assist families. It does not increase the authority of the court to appoint any third parties to the case.
(b) The court may order a family centered case resolution plan as provided in Section 2451. If the court orders family centered case resolution, it shall state the family centered case resolution plan in writing or on the record.[202]

2451. (a) A court-ordered family centered case resolution plan must be in conformance with due process requirements and may include, but is not limited to, all of the following:
(1) Early neutral case evaluation.
(2) Alternative dispute resolution consistent with the requirements of subdivision (a) of Section 3181.
(3) Limitations on discovery, including temporary suspension pending exploration of settlement. There is a rebuttable presumption that an attorney who carries out discovery as provided in a family centered case resolution plan has fulfilled his or her duty of care to the client as to the existence of community property.
(4) Use of telephone conference calls to ascertain the status of the case, encourage cooperation, and assist counsel in reaching agreement. However, if the court is required to issue an order other than by stipulation, a hearing shall be held.
(5) If stipulated by the parties, modification or waiver of the requirements of procedural statutes.
(6) A requirement that any expert witness be selected by the parties jointly or be appointed by the court. However, if at any time the court determines that the issues for which experts are required cannot be settled under these conditions, the court shall permit each party to employ his or her own expert.
(7) Bifurcation of issues for trial.
(b) This section does not provide any additional authority to the court to appoint experts beyond that permitted under other provisions of law.
(c) The Judicial Council shall, by January 1, 2012, adopt a statewide rule of court to implement this section.
(d) The changes made to this section by the act adding this subdivision shall become operative on January 1, 2012.[212]

2452. The Judicial Council may, by rule, increase the procedures set forth in this chapter.[310]

DIVISION 7: DIVISION OF PROPERTY

ENACTED BY STATS. 1992, CH. 162, SEC. 10.
SECTION 2500-2660

PART 1: DEFINITIONS

enacted by Stats. 1992, Ch. 162, Sec. 10.

2500. Unless the provision or context otherwise requires, the definitions in this part govern the construction of this division.[1]

2502. "Separate property" does not include quasi-community property.[1]

PART 2: GENERAL PROVISIONS

enacted by Stats. 1992, Ch. 162, Sec. 10.

2550. Except upon the written agreement of the parties, or on oral stipulation of the parties in open court, or as otherwise provided in this division, in a proceeding for dissolution of marriage or for legal separation of the parties, the court shall, either in its judgment of dissolution of the marriage, in its judgment of legal separation of the parties, or at a later time if it expressly reserves jurisdiction to make such a property division, divide the community estate of the parties equally.[1]

2551. For the purposes of division and in confirming or assigning the liabilities of the parties for which the community estate is liable, the court shall characterize liabilities as separate or community and confirm or assign them to the parties in accordance with Part 6 (commencing with Section 2620).[1]

2552. (a) For the purpose of division of the community estate upon dissolution of marriage or legal separation of the parties, except as provided in subdivision (b), the court shall value the assets and liabilities as near as practicable to the time of trial.
(b) Upon 30 days' notice by the moving party to the other party, the court for good cause shown may value all or any portion of the assets and liabilities at a date after separation and before trial to accomplish an equal division of the community estate of the parties in an equitable manner.[1]

2553. The court may make any orders the court considers necessary to carry out the purposes of this division.[1]

2554. (a) Notwithstanding any other provision of this division, in any case in which the parties do not agree in writing to a voluntary division of the community estate of the parties, the issue of the character, the value, and the division of the community estate may be submitted by the court to arbitration for resolution pursuant to Chapter 2.5 (commencing with Section 1141.10) of Title 3 of Part 3 of the Code of Civil Procedure, if the total value of the community and quasi-community property in controversy in the opinion of the court does not exceed fifty thousand dollars ($50,000). The decision of the court regarding the value of the community and quasi-community property for purposes of this section is not

appealable.
(b) The court may submit the matter to arbitration at any time it believes the parties are unable to agree upon a division of the property.[1]

2555. The disposition of the community estate, as provided in this division, is subject to revision on appeal in all particulars, including those which are stated to be in the discretion of the court.[1]

2556. In a proceeding for dissolution of marriage, for nullity of marriage, or for legal separation of the parties, the court has continuing jurisdiction to award community estate assets or community estate liabilities to the parties that have not been previously adjudicated by a judgment in the proceeding. A party may file a postjudgment motion or order to show cause in the proceeding in order to obtain adjudication of any community estate asset or liability omitted or not adjudicated by the judgment. In these cases, the court shall equally divide the omitted or unadjudicated community estate asset or liability, unless the court finds upon good cause shown that the interests of justice require an unequal division of the asset or liability.[15]

PART 3: PRESUMPTION CONCERNING PROPERTY HELD IN JOINT FORM

enacted by Stats. 1992, Ch. 162, Sec. 10.

2580. The Legislature hereby finds and declares as follows:
(a) It is the public policy of this state to provide uniformly and consistently for the standard of proof in establishing the character of property acquired by spouses during marriage in joint title form, and for the allocation of community and separate interests in that property between the spouses.
(b) The methods provided by case and statutory law have not resulted in consistency in the treatment of spouses' interests in property they hold in joint title, but rather, have created confusion as to which law applies to property at a particular point in time, depending on the form of title, and, as a result, spouses cannot have reliable expectations as to the characterization of their property and the allocation of the interests therein, and attorneys cannot reliably advise their clients regarding applicable law.
(c) Therefore, a compelling state interest exists to provide for uniform treatment of property. Thus, former Sections 4800.1 and 4800.2 of the Civil Code, as operative on January 1, 1987, and as continued in Sections 2581 and 2640 of this code, apply to all property held in joint title regardless of the date of acquisition of the property or the date of any agreement affecting the character of the property, and those sections apply in all proceedings commenced on or after January 1, 1984. However, those sections do not apply to property settlement agreements executed before January 1, 1987, or proceedings in which judgments were rendered before January 1, 1987, regardless of whether those judgments have become final.

2581. For the purpose of division of property on dissolution of marriage or legal separation of the parties, property acquired by the parties during marriage in joint form, including property held in tenancy in common, joint tenancy, or tenancy by the entirety, or as

community property, is presumed to be community property. This presumption is a presumption affecting the burden of proof and may be rebutted by either of the following:
(a) A clear statement in the deed or other documentary evidence of title by which the property is acquired that the property is separate property and not community property.
(b) Proof that the parties have made a written agreement that the property is separate property.

PART 4: SPECIAL RULES FOR DIVISION OF COMMUNITY ESTATE

enacted by Stats. 1992, Ch. 162, Sec. 10.

2600. Notwithstanding Sections 2550 to 2552, inclusive, the court may divide the community estate as provided in this part.[1]

2601. Where economic circumstances warrant, the court may award an asset of the community estate to one party on such conditions as the court deems proper to effect a substantially equal division of the community estate.[1]

2602. As an additional award or offset against existing property, the court may award, from a party's share, the amount the court determines to have been deliberately misappropriated by the party to the exclusion of the interest of the other party in the community estate.[1]

2603. (a) "Community estate personal injury damages" as used in this section means all money or other property received or to be received by a person in satisfaction of a judgment for damages for the person's personal injuries or pursuant to an agreement for the settlement or compromise of a claim for the damages, if the cause of action for the damages arose during the marriage but is not separate property as described in Section 781, unless the money or other property has been commingled with other assets of the community estate.
(b) Community estate personal injury damages shall be assigned to the party who suffered the injuries unless the court, after taking into account the economic condition and needs of each party, the time that has elapsed since the recovery of the damages or the accrual of the cause of action, and all other facts of the case, determines that the interests of justice require another disposition. In such a case, the community estate personal injury damages shall be assigned to the respective parties in such proportions as the court determines to be just, except that at least one-half of the damages shall be assigned to the party who suffered the injuries.[1]

2603.5. The court may, if there is a judgment for civil damages for an act of domestic violence perpetrated by one spouse against the other spouse, enforce that judgment against the abusive spouse's share of community property, if a proceeding for dissolution of marriage or legal separation of the parties is pending prior to the entry of final judgment.[112]

2604. If the net value of the community estate is less than five thousand dollars ($5,000) and one party cannot be located through the exercise of reasonable diligence, the court may award all the community estate to the other party on conditions the court deems proper in its judgment of dissolution of marriage or legal separation of the parties.[1]

2605. (a) The court, at the request of a party to proceedings for dissolution of marriage or for legal separation of the parties, may enter an order, prior to the final determination of ownership of a pet animal, to require a party to care for the pet animal. The existence of an order providing for the care of a pet animal during the course of proceedings for dissolution of marriage or for legal separation of the parties shall not have any impact on the court's final determination of ownership of the pet animal.
(b) Notwithstanding any other law, including, but not limited to, Section 2550, the court, at the request of a party to proceedings for dissolution of marriage or for legal separation of the parties, may assign sole or joint ownership of a pet animal taking into consideration the care of the pet animal.
(c) For purposes of this section, the following definitions shall apply:
(1) "Care" includes, but is not limited to, the prevention of acts of harm or cruelty, as described in Section 597 of the Penal Code, and the provision of food, water, veterinary care, and safe and protected shelter.
(2) "Pet animal" means any animal that is community property and kept as a household pet.[386]

PART 5: RETIREMENT PLAN BENEFITS

enacted by Stats. 1992, Ch. 162, Sec. 10.

2610. (a) Except as provided in subdivision (b), the court shall make whatever orders are necessary or appropriate to ensure that each party receives the party's full community property share in any retirement plan, whether public or private, including all survivor and death benefits, including, but not limited to, any of the following:
(1) Order the disposition of retirement benefits payable upon or after the death of either party in a manner consistent with Section 2550.
(2) Order a party to elect a survivor benefit annuity or other similar election for the benefit of the other party, as specified by the court, when a retirement plan provides for that election, provided that no court shall order a retirement plan to provide increased benefits determined on the basis of actuarial value.
(3) Upon the agreement of the nonemployee spouse, order the division of accumulated community property contributions and service credit as provided in the following or similar enactments:
(A) Article 2 (commencing with Section 21290) of Chapter 9 of Part 3 of Division 5 of Title 2 of the Government Code.
(B) Chapter 12 (commencing with Section 22650) of Part 13 of Division 1 of Title 1 of the Education Code.
(C) Article 8.4 (commencing with Section 31685) of Chapter 3 of Part 3 of Division 4 of Title 3 of the Government Code.
(D) Article 2.5 (commencing with Section 75050) of Chapter 11 of Title 8 of the Government Code.
(E) Chapter 15 (commencing with Section 27400) of Part 14 of Division 1 of Title 1 of the Education Code.
(4) Order a retirement plan to make

payments directly to a nonmember party of the nonmember party's community property interest in retirement benefits.

(b) A court shall not make an order that requires a retirement plan to do either of the following:

(1) Make payments in a manner that will result in an increase in the amount of benefits provided by the plan.

(2) Make the payment of benefits to a party at any time before the member retires, except as provided in paragraph (3) of subdivision (a), unless the plan so provides.

(c) This section shall not be applied retroactively to payments made by a retirement plan to a person who retired or died prior to January 1, 1987, or to payments made to a person who retired or died prior to June 1, 1988, for plans subject to paragraph (3) of subdivision (a).[429]

2611. (a) A final order of a tribal court that creates or recognizes the existence of the right of a spouse, former spouse, child, or other dependent of a participant in a retirement plan or other plan of deferred compensation to receive all or a portion of the benefits payable with respect to such plan participant, and that relates to the provision of child support, spousal support payments, or marital property rights to such spouse, former spouse, child, or other dependent, that is filed in accordance with Section 1733.1 of the Code of Civil Procedure shall be recognized as an order made pursuant to the domestic relations laws of this state.

(b) The filing of the tribal court order does not confer any jurisdiction on a court of this state to modify or enforce the tribal court order.[488]

PART 6: DEBTS AND LIABILITIES

enacted by Stats. 1992, Ch. 162, Sec. 10.

2620. The debts for which the community estate is liable which are unpaid at the time of trial, or for which the community estate becomes liable after trial, shall be confirmed or divided as provided in this part.[1]

2621. Debts incurred by either spouse before the date of marriage shall be confirmed without offset to the spouse who incurred the debt.[1]

2622. (a) Except as provided in subdivision (b), debts incurred by either spouse after the date of marriage but before the date of separation shall be divided as set forth in Sections 2550 to 2552, inclusive, and Sections 2601 to 2604, inclusive.

(b) To the extent that community debts exceed total community and quasi-community assets, the excess of debt shall be assigned as the court deems just and equitable, taking into account factors such as the parties' relative ability to pay.[1]

2623. Debts incurred by either spouse after the date of separation but before entry of a judgment of dissolution of marriage or legal separation of the parties shall be confirmed as follows:

(a) Debts incurred by either spouse for the common necessaries of life of either spouse or the necessaries of life of the children of the marriage for whom support may be ordered, in the absence of a court order or written agreement for support or for the payment of these debts, shall be confirmed to either spouse according to the parties' respective needs and abilities to pay at the time the debt was incurred.

(b) Debts incurred by either spouse for nonnecessaries of that spouse or children of the marriage for whom support may be ordered shall be confirmed without offset to the spouse who incurred the debt.

2624. Debts incurred by either spouse after entry of a judgment of dissolution of marriage but before termination of the parties' marital status or after entry of a judgment of legal separation of the parties shall be confirmed without offset to the spouse who incurred the debt.[1]

2625. Notwithstanding Sections 2620 to 2624, inclusive, all separate debts, including those debts incurred by a spouse during marriage and before the date of separation that were not incurred for the benefit of the community, shall be confirmed without offset to the spouse who incurred the debt. [1]

2626. The court has jurisdiction to order reimbursement in cases it deems appropriate for debts paid after separation but before trial.[1]

2627. Notwithstanding Sections 2550 to 2552, inclusive, and Sections 2620 to 2624, inclusive, educational loans shall be assigned pursuant to Section 2641 and liabilities subject to paragraph (2) of subdivision (b) of Section 1000 shall be assigned to the spouse whose act or omission provided the basis for the liability, without offset.[1]

2628. Notwithstanding Sections 2550 to 2552, inclusive, and Sections 2620 to 2624, inclusive, joint California income tax liabilities may be revised by a court in a proceeding for dissolution of marriage, provided the requirements of Section 19006 of the Revenue and Taxation Code are satisfied.[84]

PART 7: REIMBURSEMENTS

enacted by Stats. 1992, Ch. 162, Sec. 10.

2640. (a) "Contributions to the acquisition of property," as used in this section, include downpayments, payments for improvements, and payments that reduce the principal of a loan used to finance the purchase or improvement of the property but do not include payments of interest on the loan or payments made for maintenance, insurance, or taxation of the property.

(b) In the division of the community estate under this division, unless a party has made a written waiver of the right to reimbursement or has signed a writing that has the effect of a waiver, the party shall be reimbursed for the party's contributions to the acquisition of property of the community property estate to the extent the party traces the contributions to a separate property source. The amount reimbursed shall be without interest or adjustment for change in monetary values and may not exceed the net value of the property at the time of the division.

(c) A party shall be reimbursed for the party's separate property contributions to the acquisition of property of the other spouse's separate property estate during the marriage, unless there has been a transmutation in writing pursuant to Chapter 5 (commencing with Section 850) of Part 2 of Division 4, or a written waiver of the right to reimbursement. The amount reimbursed shall be without interest or adjustment for change in monetary values and may not exceed the net value of the property at the time of the division.[113]

2641. (a) "Community contributions to education or training" as used in this section means payments made with community or quasi-community property for education or training or for the repayment of a loan incurred for education or training, whether the payments were made while the parties were resident in this state or resident outside this state.

(b) Subject to the limitations provided in this section, upon dissolution of marriage or legal separation of the parties:

(1) The community shall be reimbursed for community contributions to education or training of a party that substantially enhances the earning capacity of the party. The amount reimbursed shall be with interest at the legal rate, accruing from the end of the calendar year in which the contributions were made.

(2) A loan incurred during marriage for the education or training of a party shall not be included among the liabilities of the community for the purpose of division pursuant to this division but shall be assigned for payment by the party.

(c) The reimbursement and assignment required by this section shall be reduced or modified to the extent circumstances render such a disposition unjust, including, but not limited to, any of the following:

(1) The community has substantially benefited from the education, training, or loan incurred for the education or training of the party. There is a rebuttable presumption, affecting the burden of proof, that the community has not substantially benefited from community contributions to the education or training made less than 10 years before the commencement of the proceeding, and that the community has substantially benefit-ed from community contributions to the education or training made more than 10 years before the commencement of the proceeding.

(2) The education or training received by the party is offset by the education or training received by the other party for which community contributions have been made.

(3) The education or training enables the party receiving the education or training to engage in gainful employment that substantially reduces the need of the party for support that would otherwise be required.

(d) Reimbursement for community contributions and assignment of loans pursuant to this section is the exclusive remedy of the community or a party for the education or training and any resulting enhancement of the earning capacity of a party. However, nothing in this subdivision limits consideration of the effect of the education, training, or enhancement, or the amount reimbursed pursuant to this section, on the circumstances of the parties for the purpose of an order for support pursuant to Section 4320.

(e) This section is subject to an express written agreement of the parties to the contrary.[1]

PART 8: JOINTLY HELD SEPARATE PROPERTY

enacted by Stats. 1992, Ch. 162, Sec. 10.

2650. In a proceeding for division of the community estate, the court has jurisdiction, at the request of either party, to divide the separate property interests of the parties in real and personal property, wherever situated and whenever acquired, held by the parties as joint tenants or tenants in common. The property shall be divided together with, and in accordance with the same procedure for and limitations on, division of community estate.[1]

PART 9: REAL PROPERTY LOCATED IN ANOTHER STATE

enacted by Stats. 1992, Ch. 162, Sec. 10.

2660. (a) Except as provided in subdivision (b), if the property subject to division includes real property situated in another state, the court shall, if possible, divide the community property and quasi-community property as provided for in this division in such a manner that it is not necessary to change the nature of the interests held in the real property situated in the other state.

(b) If it is not possible to divide the property in the manner provided for in subdivision (a), the court may do any of the following in order to effect a division of the property as provided for in this division:

(1) Require the parties to execute conveyances or take other actions with respect to the real property situated in the other state as are necessary.

(2) Award to the party who would have been benefited by the conveyances or other actions the money value of the interest in the property that the party would have received if the conveyances had been executed or other actions taken.[1]

DIVISION 8: CUSTODY OF CHILDREN

ENACTED BY STATS. 1992, CH. 162, SEC. 10.
SECTION 3000-3465

PART 1: DEFINITIONS AND GENERAL PROVISIONS

enacted by Stats. 1992, Ch. 162, Sec. 10.

Chapter 1: Definitions

3000. Unless the provision or context otherwise requires, the definitions in this chapter govern the construction of this division.[1]

3002. "Joint custody" means joint physical custody and joint legal custody.[1]

3003. "Joint legal custody" means that both parents shall share the right and the responsibility to make the decisions relating to the health, education, and welfare of a child.[1]

3004. "Joint physical custody" means that each of the parents shall have significant periods of physical custody. Joint physical custody shall be shared by the parents in such a way so as to assure a child of frequent and continuing contact with both parents, subject to Sections 3011 and 3020.

3006. "Sole legal custody" means that one parent shall have the right and the responsibility to make the decisions relating to the health, education, and welfare of a child.[1]

3007. "Sole physical custody" means that a child shall reside with and be under the supervision of one parent, subject to the power of the court to order visitation.[1]

Chapter 2: General Provisions

3010. (a) The mother of an unemancipated minor child and the father, if presumed to be the father under Section 7611, are equally entitled to the custody of the child.
(b) If one parent is dead, is unable or refuses to take custody, or has abandoned the child, the other parent is entitled to custody of the child.[16]

3011. (a) In making a determination of the best interests of the child in a proceeding described in Section 3021, the court shall, among any other factors it finds relevant and consistent with Section 3020, consider all of the following:
(1) The health, safety, and welfare of the child.
(2) (A) A history of abuse by one parent or any other person seeking custody against any of the following:
(i) A child to whom the parent or person seeking custody is related by blood or affinity or with whom the parent or person seeking custody has had a caretaking relationship, no matter how temporary.
(ii) The other parent.
(iii) A parent, current spouse, or cohabitant, of the parent or person seeking custody, or a person with whom the parent or person seeking custody has a dating or engagement relationship.
(B) As a prerequisite to considering allegations of abuse, the court may require independent corroboration, including, but not limited to, written

reports by law enforcement agencies, child protective services or other social welfare agencies, courts, medical facilities, or other public agencies or private nonprofit organizations providing services to victims of sexual assault or domestic violence. As used in this paragraph, "abuse against a child" means "child abuse and neglect" as defined in Section 11165.6 of the Penal Code and abuse against any other person described in clause (ii) or (iii) of subparagraph (A) means "abuse" as defined in Section 6203.

(3) The nature and amount of contact with both parents, including as provided in Sections 3046 and 3100.

(4) The habitual or continual illegal use of controlled substances, the habitual or continual abuse of alcohol, or the habitual or continual abuse of prescribed controlled substances by either parent. Before considering these allegations, the court may first require independent corroboration, including, but not limited to, written reports from law enforcement agencies, courts, probation departments, social welfare agencies, medical facilities, rehabilitation facilities, or other public agencies or nonprofit organizations providing drug and alcohol abuse services. As used in this paragraph, "controlled substances" has the same meaning as defined in the California Uniform Controlled Substances Act (Division 10 (commencing with Section 11000) of the Health and Safety Code).

(5) (A) When allegations about a parent pursuant to paragraph (2) or (4) have been brought to the attention of the court in the current proceeding, and the court makes an order for sole or joint custody or unsupervised visitation to that parent, the court shall state its reasons in writing or on the record that the order is in the best interest of the child and protects the safety of the parties and the child. In these circumstances, the court shall ensure that any order regarding custody or visitation is specific as to time, day, place, and manner of transfer of the child as set forth in subdivision (c) of Section 6323.

(B) Nothing in this paragraph eliminates the requirement that the contents of the stipulation be in the best interest of the child and be specific as to time, day, place, and manner of transfer of the child if the parties do stipulate in writing or on the record regarding custody or visitation.

(b) Notwithstanding subdivision (a), the court shall not consider the sex, gender identity, gender expression, or sexual orientation of a parent, legal guardian, or relative in determining the best interests of the child.[571]

3012. (a) If a party's deportation or detention by the United States Immigration and Customs Enforcement of the Department of Homeland Security will have a material effect on the person's ability, or anticipated ability, to appear in person at a child custody proceeding, the court shall, upon motion of the party, allow the party to present testimony and evidence and participate in mandatory child custody mediation by electronic means, including, but not limited to, telephone, video teleconferencing, or other electronic means that provide remote access to the hearing, to the extent that this technology is reasonably available to the court and protects the due process rights of all parties.

(b) This section does not authorize the use of electronic recording for the purpose of taking the official record of these proceedings.[430]

PART 2: RIGHT TO CUSTODY OF MINOR CHILD

enacted by Stats. 1992, Ch. 162, Sec. 10.

Chapter 1: General Provisions

3020. (a) The Legislature finds and declares that it is the public policy of this state to ensure that the health, safety, and welfare of children shall be the court's primary concern in determining the best interests of children when making any orders regarding the physical or legal custody or visitation of children. The Legislature further finds and declares that children have the right to be safe and free from abuse, and that the perpetration of child abuse or domestic violence in a household where a child resides is detrimental to the health, safety, and welfare of the child.

(b) The Legislature finds and declares that it is the public policy of this state to ensure that children have frequent and continuing contact with both parents after the parents have separated or dissolved their marriage, or ended their relationship, and to encourage parents to share the rights and responsibilities of child rearing in order to effect this policy, except when the contact would not be in the best interests of the child, as provided in subdivisions (a) and (c) of this section and Section 3011.

(c) When the policies set forth in subdivisions (a) and (b) of this section are in conflict, a court's order regarding physical or legal custody or visitation shall be made in a manner that ensures the health, safety, and welfare of the child and the safety of all family members.

(d) The Legislature finds and declares that it is the public policy of this state to ensure that the sex, gender identity, gender expression, or sexual orientation of a parent, legal guardian, or relative is not considered in determining the best interests of the child.[476]

3021. This part applies in any of the following:

(a) A proceeding for dissolution of marriage.

(b) A proceeding for nullity of marriage.

(c) A proceeding for legal separation of the parties.

(d) An action for exclusive custody pursuant to Section 3120.

(e) A proceeding to determine physical or legal custody or for visitation in a proceeding pursuant to the Domestic Violence Prevention Act (Division 10 (commencing with Section 6200)).

In an action under Section 6323, nothing in this subdivision shall be construed to authorize physical or legal custody, or visitation rights, to be granted to any party to a Domestic Violence Prevention Act proceeding who has not established a parent and child relationship pursuant to paragraph (2) of subdivision (a) of Section 6323.

(f) A proceeding to determine physical or legal custody or visitation in an action pursuant to the Uniform Parentage Act (Part 3 (commencing with Section 7600) of Division 12).

(g) A proceeding to determine physical

or legal custody or visitation in an action brought by the district attorney pursuant to Section 17404.

3022. The court may, during the pendency of a proceeding or at any time thereafter, make an order for the custody of a child during minority that seems necessary or proper.[17]

3022.3. Upon the trial of a question of fact in a proceeding to determine the custody of a minor child, the court shall, upon the request of either party, issue a statement of the decision explaining the factual and legal basis for its decision pursuant to Section 632 of the Code of Civil Procedure.[136]

3022.5. A motion by a parent for reconsideration of an existing child custody order shall be granted if the motion is based on the fact that the other parent was convicted of a crime in connection with falsely accusing the moving parent of child abuse.

3023. (a) If custody of a minor child is the sole contested issue, the case shall be given preference over other civil cases, except matters to which special precedence may be given by law, for assigning a trial date and shall be given an early hearing.
(b) If there is more than one contested issue and one of the issues is the custody of a minor child, the court, as to the issue of custody, shall order a separate trial. The separate trial shall be given preference over other civil cases, except matters to which special precedence may be given by law, for assigning a trial date.[18]

3024. In making an order for custody, if the court does not consider it inappropriate, the court may specify that a parent shall notify the other parent if the parent plans to change the residence of the child for more than 30 days, unless there is prior written agreement to the removal. The notice shall be given before the contemplated move, by mail, return receipt requested, postage prepaid, to the last known address of the parent to be notified. A copy of the notice shall also be sent to that parent's counsel of record. To the extent feasible, the notice shall be provided within a minimum of 45 days before the proposed change of residence so as to allow time for mediation of a new agreement concerning custody. This section does not affect orders made before January 1, 1989.[1]

3025. Notwithstanding any other provision of law, access to records and information pertaining to a minor child, including, but not limited to, medical, dental, and school records, shall not be denied to a parent because that parent is not the child's custodial parent.[1]

3025.5. (a) In a proceeding involving child custody or visitation rights, if a report containing psychological evaluations of a child or recommendations regarding custody of, or visitation with, a child is submitted to the court, including, but not limited to, a report created pursuant to Chapter 6 (commencing with Section 3110) of this part and a recommendation made to the court pursuant to Section 3183, that information shall be contained in a document that shall be placed in the confidential portion of the court file of the proceeding, and may not be disclosed, except to the following persons:
(1) A party to the proceeding and the

party's attorney.

(2) A federal or state law enforcement officer, the licensing entity of a child custody evaluator, a judicial officer, court employee, or family court facilitator of the superior court of the county in which the action was filed, or an employee or agent of that facilitator, acting within the scope of the facilitator's duties.

(3) Counsel appointed for the child pursuant to Section 3150.

(4) Any other person upon order of the court for good cause.

(b) Confidential information contained in a report prepared pursuant to Section 3111 that is disclosed to the licensing entity of a child custody evaluator pursuant to subdivision (a) shall remain confidential and shall only be used for purposes of investigating allegations of unprofessional conduct by the child custody evaluator, or in a criminal, civil, or administrative proceeding involving the child custody evaluator. All confidential information, including, but not limited to, the identity of any minors, shall retain their confidential nature in a criminal, civil, or administrative proceeding resulting from the investigation of unprofessional conduct and shall be sealed at the conclusion of the proceeding and shall not subsequently be released. Names that are confidential shall be listed in attachments separate from the general pleadings. If the confidential information does not result in a criminal, civil, or administrative proceeding, it shall be sealed after the licensing entity decides that no further action will be taken in the matter of suspected licensing violations.[431]

3026. Family reunification services shall not be ordered as a part of a child custody or visitation rights proceeding. Nothing in this section affects the applicability of Section 16507 of the Welfare and Institutions Code.[19]

3027. (a) If allegations of child abuse, including child sexual abuse, are made during a child custody proceeding and the court has concerns regarding the child's safety, the court may take any reasonable, temporary steps as the court, in its discretion, deems appropriate under the circumstances to protect the child's safety until an investigation can be completed. Nothing in this section shall affect the applicability of Section 16504 or 16506 of the Welfare and Institutions Code.

(b) If allegations of child abuse, including child sexual abuse, are made during a child custody proceeding, the court may request that the local child welfare services agency conduct an investigation of the allegations pursuant to Section 328 of the Welfare and Institutions Code. Upon completion of the investigation, the agency shall report its findings to the court.[203]

3027.1. (a) If a court determines, based on the investigation described in Section 3027 or other evidence presented to it, that an accusation of child abuse or neglect made during a child custody proceeding is false and the person making the accusation knew it to be false at the time the accusation was made, the court may impose reasonable money sanctions, not to exceed all costs incurred by the party accused as a direct result of defending the accusation, and reasonable attorney's fees incurred in recovering the sanctions, against the person making the accusation. For the purposes of this section, "person" includes a witness, a party, or a party's attorney.

(b) On motion by any person requesting sanctions under this section, the court shall issue its order to show cause why the requested sanctions should not be imposed. The order to show cause shall be served on the person against whom the sanctions are sought and a hearing thereon shall be scheduled by the court to be conducted at least 15 days after the order is served.

(c) The remedy provided by this section is in addition to any other remedy provided by law.

3027.5. (a) A parent shall not be placed on supervised visitation, or be denied custody of or visitation with the parent's child, and custody or visitation rights shall not be limited, solely because the parent did any of the following:

(1) Lawfully reported suspected sexual abuse of the child.

(2) Otherwise acted lawfully, based on a reasonable belief, to determine if the child was the victim of sexual abuse.

(3) Sought treatment for the child from a licensed mental health professional for suspected sexual abuse.

(b) The court may order supervised visitation or limit a parent's custody or visitation if the court finds substantial evidence that the parent, with the intent to interfere with the other parent's lawful contact with the child, made a report of child sexual abuse, during a child custody proceeding or at any other time, that the reporting parent knew was false at the time it was made. A limitation of custody or visitation, including an order for supervised visitation, pursuant to this subdivision, or a statute regarding the making of a false child abuse report, shall be imposed only after the court has determined that the limitation is necessary to protect the health, safety, and welfare of the child, and the court has considered the state's policy of ensuring that children have frequent and continuing contact with both parents as declared in subdivision (b) of Section 3020.[432]

3028. (a) The court may order financial compensation for periods when a parent fails to assume the caretaker responsibility or when a parent has been thwarted by the other parent when attempting to exercise custody or visitation rights contemplated by a custody or visitation order, including, but not limited to, an order for joint physical custody, or by a written or oral agreement between the parents.

(b) The compensation shall be limited to (1) the reasonable expenses incurred for or on behalf of a child, resulting from the other parent's failure to assume caretaker responsibility or (2) the reasonable expenses incurred by a parent for or on behalf of a child, resulting from the other parent's thwarting of the parent's efforts to exercise custody or visitation rights. The expenses may include the value of caretaker services but are not limited to the cost of services provided by a third party during the relevant period.

(c) The compensation may be requested by noticed motion or an order to show cause, which shall allege, under penalty of perjury, (1) a minimum of one hundred dollars ($100) of expenses incurred or (2) at least three occurrences of failure to exercise custody or visitation rights or (3) at least three occurrences of the thwarting of efforts to exercise custody or visitation rights within the six months before filing of the motion or order.

(d) Attorney's fees shall be awarded to the prevailing party upon a showing of the nonprevailing party's ability to pay as required by Section 270.

3029. An order granting custody to a parent who is receiving, or in the opinion of the court is likely to receive, assistance pursuant to the Family Economic Security Act of 1982 (Chapter 2 (commencing with Section 11200) of Part 3 of Division 9 of the Welfare and Institutions Code) for the maintenance of the child shall include an order pursuant to Chapter 2 (commencing with Section 4000) of Part 2 of Division 9 of this code, directing the noncustodial parent to pay any amount necessary for the support of the child, to the extent of the noncustodial parent's ability to pay.[21]

3030. (a) (1) No person shall be granted physical or legal custody of, or unsupervised visitation with, a child if the person is required to be registered as a sex offender under Section 290 of the Penal Code where the victim was a minor, or if the person has been convicted under Section 273a, 273d, or 647.6 of the Penal Code, unless the court finds that there is no significant risk to the child and states its reasons in writing or on the record. The child may not be placed in a home in which that person resides, nor permitted to have unsupervised visitation with that person, unless the court states the reasons for its findings in writing or on the record.

(2) No person shall be granted physical or legal custody of, or unsupervised visitation with, a child if anyone residing in the person's household is required, as a result of a felony conviction in which the victim was a minor, to register as a sex offender under Section 290 of the Penal Code, unless the court finds there is no significant risk to the child and states its reasons in writing or on the record. The child may not be placed in a home in which that person resides, nor permitted to have unsupervised visitation with that person, unless the court states the reasons for its findings in writing or on the record.

(3) The fact that a child is permitted unsupervised contact with a person who is required, as a result of a felony conviction in which the victim was a minor, to be registered as a sex offender under Section 290 of the Penal Code, shall be prima facie evidence that the child is at significant risk. When making a determination regarding significant risk to the child, the prima facie evidence shall constitute a presumption affecting the burden of producing evidence. However, this presumption shall not apply if there are factors mitigating against its application, including whether the party seeking custody or visitation is also required, as the result of a felony conviction in which the victim was a minor, to register as a sex offender under Section 290 of the Penal Code.

(b) No person shall be granted custody of, or visitation with, a child if the person has been convicted under Section 261 of the Penal Code and the child was conceived as a result of that violation.

(c) No person shall be granted custody of, or unsupervised visitation with, a child if the person has been convicted of murder in the first degree, as defined in Section 189 of the Penal Code, and the victim of the murder was the other parent of the child who is the subject of the order, unless the court finds that there is no risk to the child's health, safety, and welfare, and states the reasons for its finding in writing or on the record. In making its finding, the court may consider, among other things, the following:

(1) The wishes of the child, if the child is of sufficient age and capacity to reason so as to form an intelligent preference.

(2) Credible evidence that the convicted parent was a victim of abuse, as defined in Section 6203, committed by the deceased parent. That evidence may include, but is not limited to, written reports by law enforcement agencies, child protective services or other social welfare agencies, courts, medical facilities, or other public agencies or private nonprofit organizations providing services to victims of domestic abuse.

(3) Testimony of an expert witness, qualified under Section 1107 of the Evidence Code, that the convicted parent experiences intimate partner battering.

Unless and until a custody or visitation order is issued pursuant to this subdivision, no person shall permit or cause the child to visit or remain in the custody of the convicted parent without the consent of the child's custodian or legal guardian.

(d) The court may order child support that is to be paid by a person subject to subdivision (a), (b), or (c) to be paid through the local child support agency, as authorized by Section 4573 of the Family Code and Division 17 (commencing with Section 17000) of this code.

(e) The court shall not disclose, or cause to be disclosed, the custodial parent's place of residence, place of employment, or the child's school, unless the court finds that the disclosure would be in the best interest of the child.[134]

3030.5. (a) Upon the motion of one or both parents, or the legal guardian or custodian, or upon the court's own motion, an order granting physical or legal custody of, or unsupervised visitation with, a child may be modified or terminated if either of the following circumstances has occurred since the order was entered, unless the court finds that there is no significant risk to the child and states its reasons in writing or on the record:

(1) The person who has been granted physical or legal custody of, or unsupervised visitation with the child is required, as a result of a felony conviction in which the victim was a minor, to be registered as a sex offender under Section 290 of the Penal Code.

(2) The person who has been granted physical or legal custody of, or unsupervised visitation with, the child resides with another person who is required, as a result of a felony conviction in which the victim was a minor, to be registered as a sex offender under Section 290 of the Penal Code.

(b) The fact that a child is permitted unsupervised contact with a person who is required, as a result of a felony conviction in which the victim was a minor, to be registered as a sex offender under Section 290 of the Penal Code, shall be prima facie evidence that the child is at significant risk. When making a determination regarding significant risk to the child, the prima facie evidence shall constitute a presumption affecting the burden of producing evidence. However, this presumption shall not apply if there are factors mitigating against its application, including whether the party seeking custody or visitation is also required, as the result of a felony conviction in which the victim was a minor, to register as a sex offender under Section 290 of the Penal Code.

(c) The court shall not modify an existing custody or visitation order upon the ex parte petition of one party pursuant to this section without providing notice to the other party and an opportunity to be heard. This notice provision applies only when the mot-ion for custody or visitation change is based solely on the fact that the child is allowed unsupervised contact with a person required, as a result of a felony conviction in which the victim was a minor, to register as a sex offender under Section 290 of the Penal Code and does not affect the court's ability to remove a child upon an ex parte motion when there is a showing of immediate harm to the child.[123]

3031. (a) Where the court considers the issue of custody or visitation the court is encouraged to make a reasonable effort to ascertain whether or not any emergency protective order, protective order, or other restraining order is in effect that concerns the parties or the minor. The court is encouraged not to make a custody or visitation order that is inconsistent with the emergency protective order, protective order, or other restraining order, unless the court makes both of the following findings:

(1) The custody or visitation order cannot be made consistent with the emergency protective order, protective order, or other restraining order.

(2) The custody or visitation order is in the best interest of the minor.

(b) Whenever custody or visitation is granted to a parent in a case in which domestic violence is alleged and an emergency protective order, protective order, or other restraining order has been issued, the custody or visitation order shall specify the time, day, place, and manner of transfer of the child for custody or visitation to limit the child's exposure to potential domestic conflict or violence and to ensure the safety of all family members. Where the court finds a party is staying in a place designated as a shelter for victims of domestic violence or other confidential location, the court's order for time, day, place, and manner of transfer of the child for custody or visitation shall be designed to prevent disclosure of the location of the shelter or other confidential location.

(c) When making an order for custody or visitation in a case in which domestic violence is alleged and an emergency protective order, protective order, or other restraining order has been issued, the court shall consider whether the best interest of the child, based upon the circumstances of the case, requires that any custody or visitation arrangement shall be limited to situations in which a third person, specified by the court, is present, or whether custody or visitation shall be suspended or denied.

3032. (a) The Judicial Council shall establish a state-funded one-year pilot project beginning July 1, 1999, in at least two counties, including Los Angeles County, pursuant to which, in any child custody proceeding, including mediation proceedings pursuant to Section 3170, any action or proceeding under Division 10 (commencing with Section 6200), any action or proceeding under the Uniform Parentage Act (Part 3 (commencing with Section 7600) of Division 12), and any proceeding for dissolution or nullity of marriage or legal separation of the parties in which a protective order as been granted or is being sought pursuant to Section 6221, the court shall, notwithstanding Section 68092 of the Government Code, appoint an interpreter to interpret the proceedings at court expense, if both of the following conditions are met:

(1) One or both of the parties is unable to participate fully in the proceeding due to a lack of proficiency in the English language.

(2) The party who needs an interpreter appears in forma pauperis, pursuant to Section 68511.3 of the Government Code, or the court otherwise determines that the parties are financially unable to pay the cost of an interpreter. In all other cases where an interpreter is required pursuant to this section, interpreter fees shall be paid as provided in Section 68092 of the Government Code.

(3) This section shall not prohibit the court doing any of the following when an interpreter is not present:

(A) Issuing an order when the necessity for the order outweighs the necessity for an interpreter.

(B) Extending the duration of a previously issued temporary order if an interpreter is not readily available.

(C) Issuing a permanent order where a party who requires an interpreter fails to make appropriate arrangements for an interpreter after receiving proper notice of the hearing, including notice of the requirement to have an interpreter present, along with information about obtaining an interpreter.

(b) The Judicial Council shall submit its findings and recommendations with respect to the pilot project to the Legislature by January 31, 2001. Measurable objectives of the program may include increased utilization of the court by parties not fluent in English, increased efficiency in proceedings, increased compliance with orders, enhanced coordination between courts and culturally relevant services in the community, increased client satisfaction, and increased public satisfaction.[74]

Chapter 2: Matters To Be Considered in Granting Custody

3040. (a) Custody should be granted in the following order of preference according to the best interest of the child as provided in Sections 3011 and 3020:

(1) To both parents jointly pursuant to Chapter 4 (commencing with Section 3080) or to either parent. In making an order granting custody to either parent, the court shall consider, among other factors, which parent is more likely to allow the child frequent

and continuing contact with the noncustodial parent, consistent with Sections 3011 and 3020. The court, in its discretion, may require the parents to submit to the court a plan for the implementation of the custody order.

(2) If to neither parent, to the person or persons in whose home the child has been living in a wholesome and stable environment.

(3) To any other person or persons deemed by the court to be suitable and able to provide adequate and proper care and guidance for the child.

(b) The immigration status of a parent, legal guardian, or relative shall not disqualify the parent, legal guardian, or relative from receiving custody under subdivision (a).

(c) The court shall not consider the sex, gender identity, gender expression, or sexual orientation of a parent, legal guardian, or relative in determining the best interest of the child under subdivision (a).

(d) (1) Commencing January 1, 2024, if a court finds that the effects of a parent's, legal guardian's, or relative's history of or current mental illness are a factor in determining the best interest of the child under subdivision (a), the court shall do both of the following:

(A) Provide the parent, legal guardian, or relative with a list of local resources for mental health treatment.

(B) State its reasons for the finding in writing or on the record.

(2) This subdivision does not relieve a court from ensuring that the health, safety, and welfare of the child is the court's primary concern in determining the best interests of children when making any order regarding the physical or legal custody, or visitation, of the child.

(e) This section establishes neither a preference nor a presumption for or against joint legal custody, joint physical custody, or sole custody, but allows the court and the family the widest discretion to choose a parenting plan that is in the best interest of the child, consistent with this section.

(f) In cases where a child has more than two parents, the court shall allocate custody and visitation among the parents based on the best interest of the child, including, but not limited to, addressing the child's need for continuity and stability by preserving established patterns of care and emotional bonds. The court may order that not all parents share legal or physical custody of the child if the court finds that it would not be in the best interest of the child as provided in Sections 3011 and 3020.[516]

3040.5. When making a determination of the best interests of a child pursuant to Section 3011, the court shall consider any relevant, admissible evidence that a parent has caused human trafficking of the child or other parent.[611]

3041. (a) Before making an order granting custody to a person other than a parent, over the objection of a parent, the court shall make a finding that granting custody to a parent would be detrimental to the child and that granting custody to the nonparent is required to serve the best interest of the child. Allegations that parental custody would be detrimental to the child, other than a statement of that ultimate fact, shall not appear in the pleadings. The court may, in its discretion, exclude the public from the hearing on this issue.

(b) Subject to subdivision (d), a finding that parental custody would be detrimental to the child shall be supported by clear and convincing evidence.

(c) As used in this section, "detriment to the child" includes the harm of removal from a stable placement of a child with a person who has assumed, on a day-to-day basis, the role of the child's parent, fulfilling both the child's physical needs and the child's psychological needs for care and affection, and who has assumed that role for a substantial period of time. A finding of detriment does not require a finding of unfitness of the parents.

(d) Notwithstanding subdivision (b), if the court finds by a preponderance of the evidence that the person to whom custody may be given is a person described in subdivision (c), this finding shall constitute a finding that the custody is in the best interest of the child and that parental custody would be detrimental to the child absent a showing by a preponderance of the evidence to the contrary.

(e) Notwithstanding subdivisions (a) to (d), inclusive, if the child is an Indian child, when an allegation is made that parental custody would be detrimental to the child, before making an order granting custody to a person other than a parent, over the objection of a parent, the court shall apply the evidentiary standards described in subdivisions (d), (e), and (f) of Section 1912 of the Indian Child Welfare Act (25 U.S.C. Sec. 1901 et seq.) and Sections 224.6 and 361.7 of the Welfare and Institutions Code and the placement preferences and standards set out in Section 361.31 of the Welfare and Institutions Code and Section 1922 of the Indian Child Welfare Act (25 U.S.C. Sec. 1901 et seq.).[433]

3041.5. In any custody or visitation proceeding brought under this part, as described in Section 3021, or any guardianship proceeding brought under the Probate Code, the court may order any person who is seeking custody of, or visitation with, a child who is the subject of the proceeding to undergo testing for the illegal use of controlled substances and the use of alcohol if there is a judicial determination based upon a preponderance of evidence that there is the habitual, frequent, or continual illegal use of controlled substances or the habitual or continual abuse of alcohol by the parent, legal custodian, person seeking guardianship, or person seeking visitation in a guardianship. This evidence may include, but may not be limited to, a conviction within the last five years for the illegal use or possession of a controlled substance. The court shall order the least intrusive method of testing for the illegal use of controlled substances or the habitual or continual abuse of alcohol by either or both parents, the legal custodian, person seeking guardianship, or person seeking visitation in a guardianship. If substance abuse testing is ordered by the court, the testing shall be performed in conformance with procedures and standards established by the United States Department of Health and Human Services for drug testing of federal employees. The parent, legal custodian, person seeking guardianship, or person seeking visitation in a guardianship who has undergone drug testing shall have the right to a hearing, if requested, to challenge a positive test result. A positive test result, even if challenged and upheld, shall not, by itself, constitute grounds for an adverse custody or guardianship decision. Determining the best interests of the child requires weighing all relevant factors. The court shall also consider any reports provided to the court pursuant to the Probate Code. The results of this testing shall be confidential, shall be maintained as a sealed record in the court file, and may not be released to any person except the court, the parties, their attorneys, the Judicial Council, until completion of its authorized study of the testing process, and any person to whom the court expressly grants access by written order made with prior notice to all parties. Any person who has access to the test results may not disseminate copies or disclose information about the test results to any person other than a person who is authorized to receive the test results pursuant to this section. Any breach of the confidentiality of the test results shall be punishable by civil sanctions not to exceed two thousand five hundred dollars ($2,500). The results of the testing may not be used for any purpose, including any criminal, civil, or administrative proceeding, except to assist the court in determining, for purposes of the proceeding, the best interest of the child pursuant to Section 3011 and the content of the order or judgment determining custody or visitation. The court may order either party, or both parties, to pay the costs of the drug or alcohol testing ordered pursuant to this section. As used in this section, "controlled substances" has the same meaning as defined in the California Uniform Controlled Substances Act (Division 10 (commencing with Section 11000) of the Health and Safety Code).[254]

3042. (a) If a child is of sufficient age and capacity to reason so as to form an intelligent preference as to custody or visitation, the court shall consider, and give due weight to, the wishes of the child in making an order granting or modifying custody or visitation.
(b) In addition to the requirements of subdivision (b) of Section 765 of the Evidence Code, the court shall control the examination of a child witness so as to protect the best interest of the child.
(c) If the child is 14 years of age or older and wishes to address the court regarding custody or visitation, the child shall be permitted to do so, unless the court determines that doing so is not in the child's best interest, in which case, the court shall state its reasons for that finding on the record.
(d) This section does not prevent a child who is less than 14 years of age from addressing the court regarding custody or visitation, if the court determines that is appropriate pursuant to the child's best interest.
(e) If the court precludes the calling of a child as a witness, the court shall provide alternative means of obtaining input from the child and other information regarding the child's preferences.
(f) (1) Except as provided in paragraph (2), the court shall not permit a child addressing the court regarding custody or visitation to do so in the presence

of the parties. The court shall provide an alternative to having the child address the court in the presence of the parties in order to obtain input directly from the child.

(2) Notwithstanding paragraph (1), the court may permit the child addressing the court regarding custody or visitation to do so in the presence of the parties if the court determines that doing so is in the child's best interest and states its reasons for that finding on the record. In determining the child's best interest under this paragraph, the court shall consider whether addressing the court regarding custody or visitation in the presence of the parties is likely to be detrimental to the child.

(g) To assist the court in determining whether the child wishes to express a preference or to provide other input regarding custody or visitation to the court, a minor's counsel, an evaluator, an investigator, or a child custody recommending counselor shall indicate to the judge that the child wishes to address the court, or the judge may make that inquiry in the absence of that request. A party or a party's attorney may also indicate to the judge that the child wishes to address the court or judge.

(h) If a child informs the minor's counsel, an evaluator, an investigator, or a child custody recommending counselor at any point that the child has changed their choice with respect to addressing the court, the minor's counsel, evaluator, investigator, or child custody recommending counselor shall, as soon as feasible, indicate to the judge, the parties or their attorneys, and other professionals serving on the case that the child has changed their preference.

(i) This section does not require the child to express to the court a preference or to provide other input regarding custody or visitation.

(j) The Judicial Council shall, no later than January 1, 2023, develop or amend rules as necessary to implement this section.[504]

3043. In determining the person or persons to whom custody should be granted under paragraph (2) or (3) of subdivision (a) of Section 3040, the court shall consider and give due weight to the nomination of a guardian of the person of the child by a parent under Article 1 (commencing with Section 1500) of Chapter 1 of Part 2 of Division 4 of the Probate Code.[22]

3044. (a) Upon a finding by the court that a party seeking custody of a child has perpetrated domestic violence within the previous five years against the other party seeking custody of the child, or against the child or the child's siblings, or against a person in subparagraph (A) of paragraph (2) of subdivision (a) of Section 3011 with whom the party has a relationship, there is a rebuttable presumption that an award of sole or joint physical or legal custody of a child to a person who has perpetrated domestic violence is detrimental to the best interest of the child, pursuant to Sections 3011 and 3020. This presumption may only be rebutted by a preponderance of the evidence.

(b) To overcome the presumption set forth in subdivision (a), the court shall find that paragraph (1) is satisfied and shall find that the factors in paragraph (2), on balance, support the legislative findings in Section 3020.

(1) The perpetrator of domestic violence has demonstrated that giving sole or joint physical or legal custody of a child to the perpetrator is in the best interest of the child pursuant to Sections 3011 and 3020. In determining the best interest of the child, the preference for frequent and continuing contact with both parents, as set forth in subdivision (b) of Section 3020, or with the noncustodial parent, as set forth in paragraph (1) of subdivision (a) of Section 3040, may not be used to rebut the presumption, in whole or in part.

(2) Additional factors:

(A) The perpetrator has successfully completed a batterer's treatment program that meets the criteria outlined in subdivision (c) of Section 1203.097 of the Penal Code.

(B) The perpetrator has successfully completed a program of alcohol or drug abuse counseling, if the court determines that counseling is appropriate.

(C) The perpetrator has successfully completed a parenting class, if the court determines the class to be appropriate.

(D) The perpetrator is on probation or parole, and has or has not complied with the terms and conditions of probation or parole.

(E) The perpetrator is restrained by a protective order or restraining order, and has or has not complied with its terms and conditions.

(F) The perpetrator of domestic violence has committed further acts of domestic violence.

(G) The court has determined, pursuant to Section 6322.5, that the perpetrator is a restrained person in possession or control of a firearm or ammunition in violation of Section 6389, Section 527.9 of the Code of Civil Procedure, or Section 18120 of the Penal Code.

(c) For purposes of this section, a person has "perpetrated domestic violence" when the person is found by the court to have intentionally or recklessly caused or attempted to cause bodily injury, or sexual assault, or to have placed a person in reasonable apprehension of imminent serious bodily injury to that person or to another, or to have engaged in behavior involving, but not limited to, threatening, striking, harassing, destroying personal property, or disturbing the peace of another, for which a court may issue an ex parte order pursuant to Section 6320 to protect the other party seeking custody of the child or to protect the child and the child's siblings.

(d) (1) For purposes of this section, the requirement of a finding by the court shall be satisfied by, among other things, and not limited to, evidence that a party seeking custody has been convicted within the previous five years, after a trial or a plea of guilty or no contest, of a crime against the other party that comes within the definition of domestic violence contained in Section 6211 and of abuse contained in Section 6203, including, but not limited to, a crime described in subdivision (e) of Section 243 of, or Section 261, 273.5, 422, or 646.9 of, or former Section 262 of, the Penal Code.

(2) The requirement of a finding by the court shall also be satisfied if a court, whether that court hears or has heard the child custody proceedings or

not, has made a finding pursuant to subdivision (a) based on conduct occurring within the previous five years.

(e) When a court makes a finding that a party has perpetrated domestic violence, the court may not base its findings solely on conclusions reached by a child custody evaluator or on the recommendation of the Family Court Services staff, but shall consider any relevant, admissible evidence submitted by the parties.

(f) (1) It is the intent of the Legislature that this subdivision be interpreted consistently with the decision in Jaime G. v. H.L. (2018) 25 Cal.App.5th 794, which requires that the court, in determining that the presumption in subdivision (a) has been overcome, make specific findings on each of the factors in subdivision (b).

(2) If the court determines that the presumption in subdivision (a) has been overcome, the court shall state its reasons in writing or on the record as to why paragraph (1) of subdivision (b) is satisfied and why the factors in paragraph (2) of subdivision (b), on balance, support the legislative findings in Section 3020.

(g) In an evidentiary hearing or trial in which custody orders are sought and where there has been an allegation of domestic violence, the court shall make a determination as to whether this section applies prior to issuing a custody order, unless the court finds that a continuance is necessary to determine whether this section applies, in which case the court may issue a temporary custody order for a reasonable period of time, provided the order complies with Sections 3011 and 3020.

(h) In a custody or restraining order proceeding in which a party has alleged that the other party has perpetrated domestic violence in accordance with the terms of this section, the court shall inform the parties of the existence of this section and shall give them a copy of this section prior to custody mediation in the case.

(i) This section shall become effective on January 1, 2026.[591]

3046. (a) If a party is absent or relocates from the family residence, the court shall not consider the absence or relocation as a factor in determining custody or visitation in either of the following circumstances:

(1) The absence or relocation is of short duration and the court finds that, during the period of absence or relocation, the party has demonstrated an interest in maintaining custody or visitation, the party maintains, or makes reasonable efforts to maintain, regular contact with the child, and the party's behavior demonstrates no intent to abandon the child.

(2) The party is absent or relocates because of an act or acts of actual or threatened domestic or family violence by the other party.

(b) The court may consider attempts by one party to interfere with the other party's regular contact with the child in determining if the party has satisfied the requirements of subdivision (a).

(c)This section does not apply to either of the following:

(1) A party against whom a protective or restraining order has been issued excluding the party from the dwelling of the other party or the child, or otherwise enjoining the party from assault or harassment against the other party or the child, including, but

not limited to, orders issued under Part 4 (commencing with Section 6300) of Division 10, orders preventing civil harassment or workplace violence issued pursuant to Section 527.6 or 527.8 of the Code of Civil Procedure, and criminal protective orders issued pursuant to Section 136.2 of the Penal Code.
(2) A party who abandons a child as provided in Section 7822.[138]

3047. (a) A party's absence, relocation, or failure to comply with custody and visitation orders shall not, by itself, be sufficient to justify a modification of a custody or visitation order if the reason for the absence, relocation, or failure to comply is the party's activation to military duty or temporary duty, mobilization in support of combat or other military operation, or military deployment out of state.
(b) (1) If a party with sole or joint physical custody or visitation receives temporary duty, deployment, or mobilization orders from the military that require the party to move a substantial distance from the party's residence or otherwise has a material effect on the ability of the party to exercise custody or visitation rights, any necessary modification of the existing custody order shall be deemed a temporary custody order made without prejudice, which shall be subject to review and reconsideration upon the return of the party from military deployment, mobilization, or temporary duty.
(2) If the temporary order is reviewed upon return of the party from military deployment, mobilization, or temporary duty, there shall be a presumption that the custody order shall revert to the order that was in place before the modification, unless the court determines that it is not in the best interest of the child. The court shall not, as part of its review of the temporary order upon the return of the deploying party, order a child custody evaluation under Section 3111 of this code or Section 730 of the Evidence Code, unless the party opposing reversion of the order makes a prima facie showing that reversion is not in the best interest of the child.
(3) (A) If the court makes a temporary custody order, it shall consider any appropriate orders to ensure that the relocating party can maintain frequent and continuing contact with the child by means that are reasonably available.
(B) Upon a motion by the relocating party, the court may grant reasonable visitation rights to a stepparent, grandparent, or other family member if the court does all of the following:
(i) Finds that there is a preexisting relationship between the family member and the child that has engendered a bond such that visitation is in the best interest of the child.
(ii) Finds that the visitation will facilitate the child's contact with the relocating party.
(iii) Balances the interest of the child in having visitation with the family member against the right of the parents to exercise parental authority.
(C) This paragraph does not increase the authority of the persons described in subparagraph (B) to seek visitation orders independently.
(D) The granting of visitation rights

to a nonparent pursuant to subparagraph (B) shall not impact the calculation of child support.

(c) If a party's deployment, mobilization, or temporary duty will have a material effect on the party's ability, or anticipated ability, to appear in person at a regularly scheduled hearing, the court shall do either of the following:

(1) Upon motion of the party, hold an expedited hearing to determine custody and visitation issues prior to the departure of the party.

(2) Upon motion of the party, allow the party to present testimony and evidence and participate in court-ordered child custody mediation by electronic means, including, but not limited to, telephone, video teleconferencing, or the internet, to the extent that this technology is reasonably available to the court and protects the due process rights of all parties.

(d) A relocation by a nondeploying parent during a period of a deployed parent's absence while a temporary modification order for a parenting plan is in effect shall not, by itself, terminate the exclusive and continuing jurisdiction of the court for purposes of later determining custody or parenting time under this chapter.

(e) When a court of this state has issued a custody or visitation order, the absence of a child from this state during the deployment of a parent shall be considered a "temporary absence" for purposes of the Uniform Child Custody Jurisdiction and Enforcement Act (Part 3 (commencing with Section 3400)), and the court shall retain exclusive continuing jurisdiction under Section 3422.

(f) The deployment of a parent shall not be used as a basis to assert inconvenience of the forum under Section 3427.

(g) For purposes of this section, the following terms have the following meanings:

(1) "Deployment" means the temporary transfer of a member of the Armed Forces in active-duty status in support of combat or some other military operation.

(2) "Mobilization" means the transfer of a member of the National Guard or Military Reserve to extended active-duty status, but does not include National Guard or Military Reserve annual training.

(3) "Temporary duty" means the transfer of a servicemember from one military base to a different location, usually another base, for a limited period of time to accomplish training or to assist in the performance of a noncombat mission.

(h) It is the intent of the Legislature that this section provide a fair, efficient, and expeditious process to resolve child custody and visitation issues when a party receives temporary duty, deployment, or mobilization orders from the military, as well as at the time that the party returns from service and files a motion to revert back to the custody order in place before the deployment. The Legislature intends that family courts shall, to the extent feasible within existing resources and court practices, prioritize the calendaring of these cases, avoid unnecessary delay or continuances, and ensure that parties who serve in the military are not penalized for their service by a delay in appropriate access to their children.[434]

3048. (a) Notwithstanding any other law, in a proceeding to determine child custody or visitation with a child, every custody or visitation order shall contain all of the following:

(1) The basis for the court's exercise of jurisdiction.

(2) The manner in which notice and opportunity to be heard were given.

(3) A clear description of the custody and visitation rights of each party.

(4) A provision stating that a violation of the order may subject the party in violation to civil or criminal penalties, or both.

(5) Identification of the country of habitual residence of the child or children.

(b) (1) In cases in which the court becomes aware of facts that may indicate that there is a risk of abduction of a child, the court shall, either on its own motion or at the request of a party, determine whether measures are needed to prevent the abduction of the child by one parent. To make that determination, the court shall consider the risk of abduction of the child, obstacles to location, recovery, and return if the child is abducted, and potential harm to the child if the child is abducted. To determine whether there is a risk of abduction, the court shall consider the following factors:

(A) Whether a party has previously taken, enticed away, kept, withheld, or concealed a child in violation of the right of custody or of visitation of a person.

(B) Whether a party has previously threatened to take, entice away, keep, withhold, or conceal a child in violation of the right of custody or of visitation of a person.

(C) Whether a party lacks strong ties to this state.

(D) Whether a party has strong familial, emotional, or cultural ties to another state or country, including foreign citizenship. This factor shall be considered only if evidence exists in support of another factor specified in this section.

(E) Whether a party has no financial reason to stay in this state, including whether the party is unemployed, is able to work anywhere, or is financially independent.

(F) Whether a party has engaged in planning activities that would facilitate the removal of a child from the state, including quitting a job, selling the primary residence, terminating a lease, closing a bank account, liquidating other assets, hiding or destroying documents, applying for a passport, applying to obtain a birth certificate or school or medical records, or purchasing airplane or other travel tickets, with consideration given to whether a party is carrying out a safety plan to flee from domestic violence.

(G) Whether a party has a history of a lack of parental cooperation or child abuse, or there is substantiated evidence that a party has perpetrated domestic violence.

(H) Whether a party has a criminal record.

(2) If the court makes a finding that there is a need for preventative measures after considering the factors listed in paragraph (1), the court shall consider taking one or more of the following measures to prevent the abduction of the child:

(A) Ordering supervised visitation.

(B) Requiring a parent to post a bond

in an amount sufficient to serve as a financial deterrent to abduction, the proceeds of which may be used to offset the cost of recovery of the child in the event there is an abduction.

(C) Restricting the right of the custodial or noncustodial parent to remove the child from the county, the state, or the country.

(D) Restricting the right of the custodial parent to relocate with the child, unless the custodial parent provides advance notice to, and obtains the written agreement of, the noncustodial parent, or obtains the approval of the court, before relocating with the child.

(E) Requiring the surrender of passports and other travel documents.

(F) Prohibiting a parent from applying for a new or replacement passport for the child.

(G) Requiring a parent to notify a relevant foreign consulate or embassy of passport restrictions and to provide the court with proof of that notification.

(H) Requiring a party to register a California order in another state as a prerequisite to allowing a child to travel to that state for visits, or to obtain an order from another country containing terms identical to the custody and visitation order issued in the United States (recognizing that these orders may be modified or enforced pursuant to the laws of the other country), as a prerequisite to allowing a child to travel to that country for visits.

(I) Obtaining assurances that a party will return from foreign visits by requiring the traveling parent to provide the court or the other parent or guardian with any of the following:

(i) The travel itinerary of the child.

(ii) Copies of round trip airline tickets.

(iii) A list of addresses and telephone numbers where the child can be reached at all times.

(iv) An open airline ticket for the left-behind parent in case the child is not returned.

(J) Including provisions in the custody order to facilitate use of the Uniform Child Custody Jurisdiction and Enforcement Act (Part 3 (commencing with Section 3400)) and the Hague Convention on the Civil Aspects of International Child Abduction (implemented pursuant to 42 U.S.C. Sec. 11601 et seq.), such as identifying California as the home state of the child or otherwise defining the basis for the California court's exercise of jurisdiction under Part 3 (commencing with Section 3400), identifying the United States as the country of habitual residence of the child pursuant to the Hague Convention, defining custody rights pursuant to the Hague Convention, obtaining the express agreement of the parents that the United States is the country of habitual residence of the child, or that California or the United States is the most appropriate forum for addressing custody and visitation orders.

(K) Authorizing the assistance of law enforcement.

(3) If the court imposes any or all of the conditions listed in paragraph (2), those conditions shall be specifically noted on the minute order of the court proceedings.

(4) If the court determines there is a risk of abduction that is sufficient to warrant the application of one or more of the prevention measures authorized by this section, the court shall inform the parties of the telephone number and address of the Child Abduction Unit in the office of the district attorney in the county where the custody or visitation order is being entered.

(c) The Judicial Council shall make the changes to its child custody order forms that are necessary for the implementation of subdivision (b).

(d) This section does not affect the applicability of Section 278.7 of the Penal Code.[435]

3049. It is the intent of the Legislature in enacting this section to codify the decision of the California Supreme Court in *In re Marriage of Carney* (1979) 24 Cal.3d 725, with respect to custody and visitation determinations by the court involving a disabled parent.[197]

Chapter 3: Temporary Custody Order during Pendency of Proceeding

3060. A petition for a temporary custody order, containing the statement required by Section 3429, may be included with the initial filing of the petition or action or may be filed at any time after the initial filing.[475]

3061. If the parties have agreed to or reached an understanding on the custody or temporary custody of their children, a copy of the agreement or an affidavit as to their understanding shall be attached to the petition or action. As promptly as possible after this filing, the court shall, except in exceptional circumstances, enter an order granting temporary custody in accordance with the agreement or understanding or in accordance with any stipulation of the parties.[23]

3062. (a) In the absence of an agreement, understanding, or stipulation, the court may, if jurisdiction is appropriate, enter an ex parte temporary custody order, set a hearing date within 20 days, and issue an order to show cause on the responding party. If the responding party does not appear or respond within the time set, the temporary custody order may be extended as necessary, pending the termination of the proceedings.

(b) If, despite good faith efforts, service of the ex parte order and order to show cause has not been effected in a timely fashion and there is reason to believe, based on an affidavit, or other manner of proof made under penalty of perjury, by the petitioner, that the responding party has possession of the minor child and seeks to avoid the jurisdiction of the court or is concealing the whereabouts of the child, then the hearing date may be reset and the ex parte order extended up to an additional 90 days. After service has been effected, either party may request ex parte that the hearing date be advanced or the ex parte order be dissolved or modified.[1]

3063. In conjunction with any ex parte order seeking or modifying an order of custody, the court shall enter an order restraining the person receiving custody from removing the child from the state pending notice and a hearing on the order seeking or modifying custody.[1]

3064. (a) The court shall refrain from making an order granting or modifying a custody order on an ex parte basis unless there has been a showing of immediate harm to the child or immediate risk that the child will be removed from the State of California.

(b) (1) "Immediate harm to the child" includes, but is not limited to, either of the following:

(A) Having a parent who has committed acts of domestic violence, if the court determines that the acts of domestic violence are of recent origin or are part of a demonstrated and continuing pattern of acts of domestic violence.(B) Sexual abuse of the child, if the court determines that the acts of sexual abuse are of recent origin or are part of a demonstrated and continuing pattern of acts of sexual abuse.

(2) (A) In determining whether there is a showing of immediate harm to the child, the court shall consider a parent's illegal access to firearms and ammunition, including, but not limited to, whether a parent is prohibited from having firearms and ammunition.

(B) "Illegal access to firearms and ammunition" includes the possession, purchase, or receipt of a firearm or ammunition in violation of state or federal law, a restraining order, a protective order, or an injunction, or a condition of probation or parole.[586]

Chapter 4: Joint Custody

3080. There is a presumption, affecting the burden of proof, that joint custody is in the best interest of a minor child, subject to Section 3011, where the parents have agreed to joint custody or so agree in open court at a hearing for the purpose of determining the custody of the minor child.[24]

3081. On application of either parent, joint custody may be ordered in the discretion of the court in cases other than those described in Section 3080, subject to Section 3011. For the purpose of assisting the court in making a determination whether joint custody is appropriate under this section, the court may direct that an investigation be conducted pursuant to Chapter 6 (commencing with Section 3110).[25]

3082. When a request for joint custody is granted or denied, the court, upon the request of any party, shall state in its decision the reasons for granting or denying the request. A statement that joint physical custody is, or is not, in the best interest of the child is not sufficient to satisfy the requirements of this section.[1]

3083. In making an order of joint legal custody, the court shall specify the circumstances under which the consent of both parents is required to be obtained in order to exercise legal control of the child and the consequences of the failure to obtain mutual consent. In all other circumstances, either parent acting alone may exercise legal control of the child. An order of joint legal custody shall not be construed to permit an action that is inconsistent with the physical custody order unless the action is expressly authorized by the court.[1]

3084. In making an order of joint physical custody, the court shall specify the rights of each parent to physical control of the child in sufficient detail to enable a parent deprived of that control to implement laws for relief of child snatching and kidnapping.[1]

3085. In making an order for custody with respect to both parents, the court may grant joint legal custody without granting joint physical custody.[26]

3086. In making an order of joint physical custody or joint legal custody, the court may specify one parent as the primary caretaker of the child and one home as the primary home of the child, for the purposes of determining eligibility for public assistance.[1]

3087. An order for joint custody may be modified or terminated upon the petition of one or both parents or on the court's own motion if it is shown that the best interest of the child requires modification or termination of the order. If either parent opposes the modification or termination order, the court shall state in its decision the reasons for modification or termination of the joint custody order.[1]

3088. An order for the custody of a minor child entered by a court in this state or any other state may, subject to the jurisdictional requirements in Sections 3403 and 3414, be modified at any time to an order for joint custody in accordance with this chapter.[27]

3089. In counties having a conciliation court, the court or the parties may, at any time, pursuant to local rules of court, consult with the conciliation court for the purpose of assisting the parties to formulate a plan for implementation of the custody order or to resolve a controversy which has arisen in the implementation of a plan for custody.[1]

Chapter 5: Visitation Rights

3100. (a) In making an order pursuant to Chapter 4 (commencing with Section 3080), the court shall grant reasonable visitation rights to a parent when it is shown that the visitation would be in the best interest of the child, as defined in Section 3011, and consistent with Section 3020. In the discretion of the court, reasonable visitation rights may be granted to any other person having an interest in the welfare of the child.

(b) (1) (A) If a protective order, as defined in Section 6218 of this code or Section 136.2 of the Penal Code, has been issued restraining a parent, the court shall consider whether the best interest of the child requires that visitation by that parent be suspended, denied, or limited to situations in which a third person, specified by the court, is present, including virtual visitation.

(B) A parent may submit to the court the name of a person who the parent deems suitable to be present during visitation.

(C) The court may order supervised visitation with the person whose name was submitted, but the submission of a name does not require the court to order supervised visitation if it is not in the best interest of the child, nor does a parent's submission of a name constitute agreement or stipulation to supervised visitation.

(2) In determining the type of visitation with the restrained party, if any, is in the best interest of the child pursuant to paragraph (1), the court shall consider the nature of the acts that led to the protective order, the period of time that has elapsed since

that order, and whether the restrained party has committed further acts of abuse.

(c) (1) (A) If the court has found that circumstances warrant making an order granting or modifying a custody order on an ex parte basis under Section 3064, the court shall consider whether the best interest of the child requires that visitation by the party whose conduct presents a risk of immediate harm to the child or immediate risk that the child will be removed from the State of California should be suspended, denied, or limited to situations in which a third person, specified by the court, is present, including virtual visitation.

(B) A parent may submit to the court the name of a person who the parent deems suitable to be present during visitation, which may be accepted or rejected by the court as set forth in subparagraph (C) of paragraph (1) of subdivision (b).

(2) In determining the type of visitation with the party whose conduct presents a risk of immediate harm to the child or immediate risk that the child will be removed from the State of California, if any, is in the best interest of the child pursuant to paragraph (1), the court shall consider the nature of the acts that led to the finding of the risk of immediate harm or immediate risk of removal.

(d) If visitation is ordered in a case in which domestic violence is alleged and an emergency protective order, protective order, or other restraining order has been issued, the visitation order shall specify the time, day, place, and manner of the visitation, including virtual visitation, or any transfer of the child, so as to limit the child's exposure to potential domestic conflict or abuse, to ensure the safety of all family members, and to minimize any opportunity for the use of abuse, including coercive control. If a criminal protective order has been issued pursuant to Section 136.2 of the Penal Code, the visitation order shall make reference to, and, unless there is an emergency protective order that has precedence in enforcement pursuant to paragraph (1) of subdivision (c) of Section 136.2 of the Penal Code or a no-contact order, as described in Section 6320, acknowledge the precedence of enforcement of, an appropriate criminal protective order.

(e) (1) If the court finds a party is staying in a place designated as a shelter for victims of domestic violence or other confidential location, the court's order shall be designed to prevent disclosure of the location of the shelter or other confidential location and to protect all adults and children living in that location.

(2) If a court finds that a parent is residing in a confidential shelter due to domestic violence or fear of domestic violence from the other parent, the court shall order in-person visitation with the other parent only if the court finds that in-person visitation is in the best interest of the child, taking into account all of the following:

(A) The other parent's access to firearms and ammunition, including, but not limited to, whether the other parent is prohibited from having firearms and ammunition.

(B) If a parent is the subject of an emergency protective order, protective order, or other restraining order, whether that parent has violated that order, and the nature of any violation.

(C) Information obtained pursuant to Section 6306, the requirements of this section, and the information obtained pursuant to Section 3011.

(D) The potential for disclosure of the confidential location.

(3) A court shall make its findings pursuant to paragraphs (1) and (2) in writing or on the record.

(f) For purposes of this section, "virtual visitation" means use of audiovisual electronic communication tools to provide contact between a parent and their children as part of a parenting plan or custody order. Virtual visitation may be supervised or unsupervised, based on the court's determination of what is in the best interest of the child.[587]

3101. (a) Notwithstanding any other provision of law, the court may grant reasonable visitation to a stepparent, if visitation by the stepparent is determined to be in the best interest of the minor child.

(b) If a protective order, as defined in Section 6218, has been directed to a stepparent to whom visitation may be granted pursuant to this section, the court shall consider whether the best interest of the child requires that any visitation by the stepparent be denied.

(c) Visitation rights may not be ordered under this section that would conflict with a right of custody or visitation of a birth parent who is not a party to the proceeding.

(d) As used in this section:

(1) "Birth parent" means "birth parent" as defined in Section 8512.

(2) "Stepparent" means a person who is a party to the marriage that is the subject of the proceeding, with respect to a minor child of the other party to the marriage.[28]

3102. (a) If either parent of an unemancipated minor child is deceased, the children, siblings, parents, and grandparents of the deceased parent may be granted reasonable visitation with the child during the child's minority upon a finding that the visitation would be in the best interest of the minor child.

(b) In granting visitation pursuant to this section to a person other than a grandparent of the child, the court shall consider the amount of personal contact between the person and the child before the application for the visitation order.

(c) This section does not apply if the child has been adopted by a person other than a stepparent or grandparent of the child. Any visitation rights granted pursuant to this section before the adoption of the child automatically terminate if the child is adopted by a person other than a stepparent or grandparent of the child.

3103. (a) Notwithstanding any other provision of law, in a proceeding described in Section 3021, the court may grant reasonable visitation to a grandparent of a minor child of a party to the proceeding if the court determines that visitation by the grandparent is in the best interest of the child.

(b) If a protective order as defined in Section 6218 has been directed to the grandparent during the pendency of the proceeding, the court shall consider whether the best interest of the child requires that visitation by the grandparent be denied.

(c) The petitioner shall give notice of the petition to each of the parents of the child, any stepparent, and any person who has physical custody of the child, by certified mail, return receipt requested, postage prepaid, to the person's last known address, or to the attorneys of record of the parties to the proceeding.

(d) There is a rebuttable presumption affecting the burden of proof that the visitation of a grandparent is not in the best interest of a minor child if the child's parents agree that the grandparent should not be granted visitation rights.

(e) Visitation rights may not be ordered under this section if that would conflict with a right of custody or visitation of a birth parent who is not a party to the proceeding.

(f) Visitation ordered pursuant to this section shall not create a basis for or against a change of residence of the child, but shall be one of the factors for the court to consider in ordering a change of residence.

(g) When a court orders grandparental visitation pursuant to this section, the court in its discretion may, based upon the relevant circumstances of the case:

(1) Allocate the percentage of grandparental visitation between the parents for purposes of the calculation of child support pursuant to the statewide uniform guideline (Article 2 (commencing with Section 4050) of Chapter 2 of Part 2 of Division 9).

(2) Notwithstanding Sections 3930 and 3951, order a parent or grandparent to pay to the other, an amount for the support of the child or grandchild. For purposes of this paragraph, "support" means costs related to visitation such as any of the following:

(A) Transportation.

(B) Provision of basic expenses for the child or grandchild, such as medical expenses, day care costs, and other necessities.

(h) As used in this section, "birth parent" means "birth parent" as defined in Section 8512.

3104. (a) On petition to the court by a grandparent of a minor child, the court may grant reasonable visitation rights to the grandparent if the court does both of the following:

(1) Finds that there is a preexisting relationship between the grandparent and the grandchild that has engendered a bond such that visitation is in the best interest of the child.

(2) Balances the interest of the child in having visitation with the grandparent against the right of the parents to exercise their parental authority.

(b) A petition for visitation under this section shall not be filed while the natural or adoptive parents are married, unless one or more of the following circumstances exist:

(1) The parents are currently living separately and apart on a permanent or indefinite basis.

(2) One of the parents has been absent for more than one month without the other spouse knowing the whereabouts of the absent spouse.

(3) One of the parents joins in the petition with the grandparents.

(4) The child is not residing with either parent.

(5) The child has been adopted by a stepparent.

(6) One of the parents is incarcerated or involuntarily institutionalized.

At any time that a change of circumstances occurs such that none of these circumstances exist, the parent or parents may move the court to terminate grandparental visitation and the court shall grant the termination.

(c) The petitioner shall give notice of the petition to each of the parents of the child, any stepparent, and any person who has physical custody of the child, by personal service pursuant to Section 415.10 of the Code of Civil Procedure.

(d) If a protective order as defined in Section 6218 has been directed to the grandparent during the pendency of the proceeding, the court shall consider whether the best interest of the child requires that any visitation by that grandparent should be denied.

(e) There is a rebuttable presumption that the visitation of a grandparent is not in the best interest of a minor child if the natural or adoptive parents agree that the grandparent should not be granted visitation rights.

(f) There is a rebuttable presumption affecting the burden of proof that the visitation of a grandparent is not in the best interest of a minor child if the parent who has been awarded sole legal and physical custody of the child in another proceeding, or the parent with whom the child resides if there is currently no operative custody order objects to visitation by the grandparent.

(g) Visitation rights may not be ordered under this section if that would conflict with a right of custody or visitation of a birth parent who is not a party to the proceeding.

(h) Visitation ordered pursuant to this section shall not create a basis for or against a change of residence of the child, but shall be one of the factors for the court to consider in ordering a change of residence.

(i) When a court orders grandparental visitation pursuant to this section, the court in its discretion may, based upon the relevant circumstances of the case:

(1) Allocate the percentage of grandparental visitation between the parents for purposes of the calculation of child support pursuant to the statewide uniform guideline (Article 2 (commencing with Section 4050) of Chapter 2 of Part 2 of Division 9).

(2) Notwithstanding Sections 3930 and 3951, order a parent or grandparent to pay to the other, an amount for the support of the child or grandchild. For purposes of this paragraph, "support" means costs related to visitation such as any of the following:

(A) Transportation.

(B) Provision of basic expenses for the child or grandchild, such as medical expenses, day care costs, and other necessities.

(j) As used in this section, "birth parent" means "birth parent" as defined in Section 8512.[311]

3105. (a) The Legislature finds and declares that a parent's fundamental right to provide for the care, custody, companionship, and management of the parent's children, while compelling, is not absolute. Children have a fundamental right to maintain healthy, stable relationships with a person who has served in a significant, judicially approved parental role.

(b) The court may grant reasonable visitation rights to a person who previously served as the legal guardian of a child, if visitation is determined to be in the best interest of the minor child.

(c) In the absence of a court order granting or denying visitation between a former legal guardian and a former minor ward, and if a dependency proceeding is not pending, a former legal guardian may maintain an independent action for visitation with the former minor ward. If the child does not have at least one living parent, visitation shall not be determined in a proceeding under the Family Code, but shall instead be determined in a guardianship proceeding that may be initiated for that purpose.[436]

Chapter 6: Custody Investigation and Report

3110. As used in this chapter, "court-appointed investigator" means a probation officer, domestic relations investigator, or court-appointed evaluator directed by the court to conduct an investigation pursuant to this chapter.[29]

3110.5. (a) A person may be a court-connected or private child custody evaluator under this chapter only if the person has completed the domestic violence and child abuse training program described in Section 1816 and has complied with Rules 5.220 and 5.230 of the California Rules of Court.
(b) (1) On or before January 1, 2002, the Judicial Council shall formulate a statewide rule of court that establishes education, experience, and training requirements for all child custody evaluators appointed pursuant to this chapter, Section 730 of the Evidence Code, or Chapter 15 (commencing with Section 2032.010) of Title 4 of Part 4 of the Code of Civil Procedure.
(A) The rule shall require a child custody evaluator to declare under penalty of perjury that the evaluator meets all of the education, experience, and training requirements specified in the rule and, if applicable, possesses a license in good standing. The Judicial Council shall establish forms to implement this section. The rule shall permit court-connected evaluators to conduct evaluations if they meet all of the qualifications established by the Judicial Council. The education, experience, and training requirements to be specified for court-connected evaluators shall include, but not be limited to, knowledge of the psychological and developmental needs of children and parent and child relationships.
(B) The rule shall require all evaluators to utilize comparable interview, assessment, and testing procedures for all parties that are consistent with generally accepted clinical, forensic, scientific, diagnostic, or medical standards. The rule shall also require evaluators to inform each adult party of the purpose, nature, and method of the evaluation.
(C) The rule may allow courts to permit the parties to stipulate to an evaluator of their choosing with the approval of the court under the circumstances set forth in subdivision (d). The rule may require courts to provide general information about how parties can contact qualified child custody evaluators in their county.
(2) On or before January 1, 2004, the Judicial Council shall include in the statewide rule of court created pursuant to this section a requirement that all court-connected and private

child custody evaluators receive training in the nature of child sexual abuse. The Judicial Council shall develop standards for this training that shall include, but not be limited to, the following:

(A) Children's patterns of hiding and disclosing sexual abuse occurring in a family setting.

(B) The effects of sexual abuse on children.

(C) The nature and extent of child sexual abuse.

(D) The social and family dynamics of child sexual abuse.

(E) Techniques for identifying and assisting families affected by child sexual abuse.

(F) Legal rights, protections, and remedies available to victims of child sexual abuse.

(c) In addition to the education, experience, and training requirements established by the Judicial Council pursuant to subdivision (b), on or after January 1, 2005, a person may be a child custody evaluator under this chapter, Section 730 of the Evidence Code, or Chapter 15 (commencing with Section 2032.010) of Title 4 of Part 4 of the Code of Civil Procedure only if the person meets one of the following criteria:

(1) The person is licensed as a physician under Chapter 5 (commencing with Section 2000) of Division 2 of the Business and Professions Code and either is a board-certified psychiatrist or has completed a residency in psychiatry.

(2) The person is licensed as a psychologist under Chapter 6.6 (commencing with Section 2900) of Division 2 of the Business and Professions Code.

(3) The person is licensed as a marriage and family therapist under Chapter 13 (commencing with Section 4980) of Division 2 of the Business and Professions Code.

(4) The person is licensed as a clinical social worker under Article 4 (commencing with Section 4996) of Chapter 14 of Division 2 of the Business and Professions Code.

(5) The person is licensed as a professional clinical counselor under Chapter 16 (commencing with Section 4999.10) of Division 2 of the Business and Professions Code.

(6) The person is a court-connected evaluator who has been certified by the court as meeting all of the qualifications for court-connected evaluators as specified by the Judicial Council pursuant to subdivision (b).

(d) Subdivision (c) does not apply in a case in which the court determines that there are no evaluators who meet the criteria of subdivision (c) who are willing and available, within a reasonable period of time, to perform child custody evaluations. In those cases, the parties may stipulate to an individual who does not meet the criteria of subdivision (c), subject to approval by the court.

(e) A child custody evaluator who is licensed by the Medical Board of California, the Board of Psychology, or the Board of Behavioral Sciences shall be subject to disciplinary action by that board for unprofessional conduct, as defined in the licensing law applicable to that licensee.

(f) On or after January 1, 2005, a court-connected or private child custody evaluator may not evaluate, investigate, or mediate an issue of child custody in a proceeding pursuant to this division unless that person has completed child sexual abuse training as required by this section.[494]

3111. (a) In a contested proceeding involving child custody or visitation rights, the court may appoint a child custody evaluator to conduct a child custody evaluation in cases where the court determines it is in the best interest of the child. The child custody evaluation shall be conducted in accordance with the standards adopted by the Judicial Council pursuant to Section 3117, and all other standards adopted by the Judicial Council regarding child custody evaluations. If directed by the court, the court-appointed child custody evaluator shall file a written confidential report on the evaluation. At least 10 days before a hearing regarding custody of the child, the report shall be filed with the clerk of the court in which the custody hearing will be conducted and served on the parties or their attorneys, and any other counsel appointed for the child pursuant to Section 3150. A child custody evaluation, investigation, or assessment, and a resulting report, may be considered by the court only if it is conducted in accordance with the requirements set forth in the standards adopted by the Judicial Council pursuant to Section 3117; however, this does not preclude the consideration of a child custody evaluation report that contains nonsubstantive or inconsequential errors or both.

(b) The report shall not be made available other than as provided in subdivision (a) or Section 3025.5, or as described in Section 204 of the Welfare and Institutions Code or Section 1514.5 of the Probate Code. Any information obtained from access to a juvenile court case file, as defined in subdivision (e) of Section 827 of the Welfare and Institutions Code, is confidential and shall only be disseminated as provided by paragraph (4) of subdivision (a) of Section 827 of the Welfare and Institutions Code.

(c) The report may be received in evidence on stipulation of all interested parties and is competent evidence as to all matters contained in the report.

(d) If the court determines that an unwarranted disclosure of a written confidential report has been made, the court may impose a monetary sanction against the disclosing party. The sanction shall be in an amount sufficient to deter repetition of the conduct, and may include reasonable attorney's fees, costs incurred, or both, unless the court finds that the disclosing party acted with substantial justification or that other circumstances make the imposition of the sanction unjust. The court shall not impose a sanction pursuant to this subdivision that imposes an unreasonable financial burden on the party against whom the sanction is imposed.

(e) The Judicial Council shall, by January 1, 2010, do the following:

(1) Adopt a form to be served with every child custody evaluation report that informs the report recipient of the confidentiality of the report and the potential consequences for the unwarranted disclosure of the report.

(2) Adopt a rule of court to require that, when a court-ordered child custody evaluation report is served on the parties, the form specified in paragraph (1) shall be included with

the report.

(f) For purposes of this section, a disclosure is unwarranted if it is done either recklessly or maliciously, and is not in the best interest of the child. [437]

3112. (a) Where a court-appointed investigator is directed by the court to conduct a custody investigation or evaluation pursuant to this chapter or to undertake visitation work, including necessary evaluation, supervision, and reporting, the court shall inquire into the financial condition of the parent, guardian, or other person charged with the support of the minor. If the court finds the parent, guardian, or other person able to pay all or part of the expense of the investigation, report, and recommendation, the court may make an order requiring the parent, guardian, or other person to repay the court the amount the court determines proper.

(b) The repayment shall be made to the court. The court shall keep suitable accounts of the expenses and repayments and shall deposit the collections as directed by the Judicial Council.

3113. Where there has been a history of domestic violence between the parties, or where a protective order as defined in Section 6218 is in effect, at the request of the party alleging domestic violence in a written declaration under penalty of perjury or at the request of a party who is protected by the order, the parties shall meet with the court-appointed investigator separately and at separate times. [29]

3114. Nothing in this chapter prohibits a court-appointed investigator from recommending to the court that counsel be appointed pursuant to Chapter 10 (commencing with Section 3150) to represent the minor child. In making that recommendation, the court-appointed investigator shall inform the court of the reasons why it would be in the best interest of the child to have counsel appointed.[29]

3115. A statement, whether written or oral, or conduct shall not be held to constitute a waiver by a party of the right to cross-examine the court-appointed investigator, unless the statement is made, or the conduct occurs, after the report has been received by a party or the party's attorney.[438]

3116. Nothing in this chapter limits the duty of a court-appointed investigator to assist the appointing court in the transaction of the business of the court.[29]

3117. The Judicial Council shall, by January 1, 1999, do both of the following:

(a) Adopt standards for full and partial court-connected evaluations, investigations, and assessments related to child custody.

(b) Adopt procedural guidelines for the expeditious and cost-effective cross-examination of court-appointed investigators, including, but not limited to, the use of electronic technology whereby the court-appointed investigator may not need to be present in the courtroom. These guidelines shall in no way limit the requirement that the court-appointed investigator be available for the purposes of cross-examination. These guidelines shall also provide for written notification to the parties of the right to cross-examine these investigators after the parties have had a reasonable time to review the investigator's report.[61]

3118. (a) In any contested proceeding involving child custody or visitation rights, where the court has appointed a child custody evaluator or has referred a case for a full or partial court-connected evaluation, investigation, or assessment, and the court determines that there is a serious allegation of child sexual abuse, the court shall require an evaluation, investigation, or assessment pursuant to this section. When the court has determined that there is a serious allegation of child sexual abuse, any child custody evaluation, investigation, or assessment conducted subsequent to that determination shall be considered by the court only if the evaluation, investigation, or assessment is conducted in accordance with the minimum requirements set forth in this section in determining custody or visitation rights, except as specified in paragraph (1). For purposes of this section, a serious allegation of child sexual abuse means an allegation of child sexual abuse, as defined in Section 11165.1 of the Penal Code, that is based in whole or in part on statements made by the child to law enforcement, a child welfare services agency investigator, any person required by statute to report suspected child abuse, or any other court-appointed personnel, or that is supported by substantial independent corroboration as provided for in subparagraph (B) of paragraph (2) of subdivision (a) of Section 3011. When an allegation of child abuse arises in any other circumstances in any proceeding involving child custody or visitation rights, the court may require an evaluator or investigator to conduct an evaluation, investigation, or assessment pursuant to this section. The order appointing a child custody evaluator or investigator pursuant to this section shall provide that the evaluator or investigator have access to all juvenile court records pertaining to the child who is the subject of the evaluation, investigation, or assessment. The order shall also provide that any juvenile court records or information gained from those records remain confidential and shall only be released as specified in Section 3111.

(1) This section does not apply to any emergency court-ordered partial investigation that is conducted for the purpose of assisting the court in determining what immediate temporary orders may be necessary to protect and meet the immediate needs of a child. This section does apply when the emergency is resolved and the court is considering permanent child custody or visitation orders.

(2) This section does not prohibit a court from considering evidence relevant to determining the safety and protection needs of the child.

(3) Any evaluation, investigation, or assessment conducted pursuant to this section shall be conducted by an evaluator or investigator who meets the qualifications set forth in Section 3110.5.

(b) The evaluator or investigator shall, at a minimum, do all of the following:

(1) Consult with the agency providing child welfare services and law enforcement regarding the allegations of child sexual abuse, and obtain recommendations from these professionals regarding the child's safety and the child's need for

protection.

(2) Review and summarize the child welfare services agency file. No document contained in the child welfare services agency file may be photocopied, but a summary of the information in the file, including statements made by the children and the parents, and the recommendations made or anticipated to be made by the child welfare services agency to the juvenile court, may be recorded by the evaluator or investigator, except for the identity of the reporting party. The evaluator's or investigator's notes summarizing the child welfare services agency information shall be stored in a file separate from the evaluator's or investigator's file and may only be released to either party under order of the court.

(3) Obtain from a law enforcement investigator all available information obtained from criminal background checks of the parents and any suspected perpetrator that is not a parent, including information regarding child abuse, domestic violence, or substance abuse.

(4) Review the results of a multidisciplinary child interview team (hereafter MDIT) interview if available, or if not, or if the evaluator or investigator believes the MDIT interview is inadequate for purposes of the evaluation, investigation, or assessment, interview the child or request an MDIT interview, and shall wherever possible avoid repeated interviews of the child.

(5) Request a forensic medical examination of the child from the appropriate agency, or include in the report required by paragraph (6) a written statement explaining why the examination is not needed.

(6) File a confidential written report with the clerk of the court in which the custody hearing will be conducted and which shall be served on the parties or their attorneys at least 10 days prior to the hearing. On and after January 1, 2021, this report shall be made on the form adopted pursuant to subdivision (i). This report may not be made available other than as provided in this subdivision. This report shall address the safety of the child and shall include, but not be limited to, the following:

(A) Documentation of material interviews, including any MDIT interview of the child or the evaluator or investigator, written documentation of interviews with both parents by the evaluator or investigator, and interviews with other witnesses who provided relevant information.

(B) A summary of any law enforcement investigator's investigation, including information obtained from the criminal background check of the pa-rents and any suspected perpetrator that is not a parent, including in-formation regarding child abuse, domestic violence, or substance abuse.

(C) Relevant background material, including, but not limited to, a summary of a written report from any therapist treating the child for suspected child sexual abuse, excluding any communication subject to Section 1014 of the Evidence Code, reports from other professionals, and the results of any forensic medical examination and any other medical examination or treatment that could help establish or disprove whether the child has been the victim of sexual abuse.

(D) The written recommendations of the evaluator or investigator regarding the therapeutic needs of the child and how to ensure the safety of the child.

(E) A summary of the following information: whether the child and the child's parents are or have been the subject of a child abuse investigation and the disposition of that investigation; the name, location, and telephone number of the children's services worker; the status of the investigation and the recommendations made or anticipated to be made regarding the child's safety; and any dependency court orders or findings that might have a bearing on the custody dispute.

(F) Any information regarding the presence of domestic violence or substance abuse in the family that has been obtained from a child protective agency in accordance with paragraphs (1) and (2), a law enforcement agency, medical personnel or records, prior or currently treating therapists, excluding any communication subject to Section 1014 of the Evidence Code, or from interviews conducted or reviewed for this evaluation, investigation, or assessment.

(G) Which, if any, family members are known to have been deemed eligible for assistance from the Victims of Crime Program due to child abuse or domestic violence.

(H) Any other information the evaluator or investigator believes would be helpful to the court in determining what is in the best interests of the child.

(c) If the evaluator or investigator obtains information as part of a family court mediation, that information shall be maintained in the family court file, which is not subject to subpoena by either party. If, however, the members of the family are the subject of an ongoing child welfare services investigation, or the evaluator or investigator has made a child welfare services referral, the evaluator or investigator shall so inform the family law judicial officer in writing and this information shall become part of the family law file. This subdivision may not be construed to authorize or require a mediator to disclose any information not otherwise authorized or required by law to be disclosed.

(d) In accordance with subdivision (d) of Section 11167 of the Penal Code, the evaluator or investigator may not disclose any information regarding the identity of any person making a report of suspected child abuse. This section is not intended to limit any disclosure of information by any agency that is otherwise required by law or court order.

(e) The evaluation, investigation, or assessment standards set forth in this section represent minimum requirements of evaluation and the court shall order further evaluation beyond these minimum requirements when necessary to determine the safety needs of the child.

(f) If the court orders an evaluation, investigation, or assessment pursuant to this section, the court shall consider whether the best interests of the child require that a temporary order be issued that limits visitation with the parent against whom the allegations have been made to situations in which a third person specified by the court is present or whether visitation will be suspended or denied in accordance with Section 3011.

(g) An evaluation, investigation, or assessment pursuant to this section shall be suspended if a petition is filed to declare the child a dependent child of the juvenile court pursuant to Section 300 of the Welfare and Institutions Code, and all information gathered by the evaluator or investigator shall be made available to the juvenile court.

(h) This section shall not be construed to authorize a court to issue any orders in a proceeding pursuant to this division regarding custody or visitation with respect to a minor child who is the subject of a dependency hearing in juvenile court or to otherwise supersede Section 302 of the Welfare and Institutions Code.

(i) On or before January 1, 2021, the Judicial Council shall adopt a mandatory form that shall be used for all evaluations, investigations, or assessments conducted pursuant to this section. The form shall provide a standardized template for all information necessary to provide a full and complete analysis of the allegations raised in the proceeding.[489]

Chapter 7: Action for Exclusive Custody

3120. Without filing a petition for dissolution of marriage or legal separation of the parties, a spouse may bring an action for the exclusive custody of the children of the marriage. The court may, during the pendency of the action, or at the final hearing thereof, or afterwards, make such order regarding the support, care, custody, education, and control of the children of the marriage as may be just and in accordance with the natural rights of the parents and the best interest of the children. The order may be modified or terminated at any time thereafter as the natural rights of the parties and the best interest of the children may require.[298]

3121. (a) In any proceeding pursuant to Section 3120, and in any proceeding subsequent to entry of a related judgment, the court shall ensure that each party has access to legal representation, including access early in the proceedings, to preserve each party's rights by ordering, if necessary based on the income and needs assessments, one party, except a government entity, to pay to the other party, or to the other party's attorney, whatever amount is reasonably necessary for attorney's fees and for the cost of maintaining or defending the proceeding during the pendency of the proceeding.

(b) When a request for attorney's fees and costs is made, the court shall make findings on whether an award of attorney's fees and costs under this section is appropriate, whether there is a disparity in access to funds to retain counsel, and whether one party is able to pay for legal representation of both parties. If the findings demonstrate disparity in access and ability to pay, the court shall make an order awarding attorney's fees and costs. A party who lacks the financial ability to hire an attorney may request, as an in pro per litigant, that the court order the other party, if that other party has the financial ability, to pay a reasonable amount to allow the unrepresented party to retain an attorney in a timely manner before proceedings in the matter go forward.

(c) Attorney's fees and costs within this section may be awarded for legal services rendered or costs incurred before or after the commencement of the proceeding.

(d) The court shall augment or modify the original award for attorney's fees and costs as may be reasonably necessary for the prosecution or defense of a proceeding described in Section 3120, or any proceeding related thereto, including after any appeal has been concluded.

(e) Except as provided in subdivision (f), an application for a temporary order making, augmenting, or modifying an award of attorney's fees, including a reasonable retainer to hire an attorney, or costs, or both, shall be made by motion on notice or by an order to show cause during the pendency of any proceeding described in Section 3120.

(f) The court shall rule on an application for fees under this section within 15 days of the hearing on the motion or order to show cause. An order described in subdivision (a) may be made without notice by an oral motion in open court at either of the following times:

(1) At the time of the hearing of the cause on the merits.

(2) At any time before entry of judgment against a party whose default has been entered pursuant to Section 585 or 586 of the Code of Civil Procedure. The court shall rule on any motion made pursuant to this subdivision within 15 days and prior to the entry of any judgment.

(g) The Judicial Council shall, by January 1, 2012, adopt a statewide rule of court to implement this section and develop a form for the information that shall be submitted to the court to obtain an award of attorney's fees under this section.[204]

Chapter 8: Location of Missing Party or Child

3130. If a petition to determine custody of a child has been filed in a court of competent jurisdiction, or if a temporary order pending determination of custody has been entered in accordance with Chapter 3 (commencing with Section 3060), and the whereabouts of a party in possession of the child are not known, or there is reason to believe that the party may not appear in the proceedings although ordered to appear personally with the child pursuant to Section 3430, the district attorney shall take all actions necessary to locate the party and the child and to procure compliance with the order to appear with the child for purposes of adjudication of custody. The petition to determine custody may be filed by the district attorney.[188]

3131. If a custody or visitation order has been entered by a court of competent jurisdiction and the child is taken or detained by another person in violation of the order, the district attorney shall take all actions necessary to locate and return the child and the person who violated the order and to assist in the enforcement of the custody or visitation order or other order of the court by use of an appropriate civil or criminal proceeding.[1]

3132. In performing the functions described in Sections 3130 and 3131, the district attorney shall act on behalf of the court and shall not represent any party to the custody proceedings.[1]

3133. If the district attorney represents to the court, by a written declaration under penalty of perjury, that a temporary custody order is needed to recover a child who is being detained or concealed in violation of a court order or a parent's right to custody, the court may issue an order, placing temporary sole physical custody in the parent or person recommended by the district attorney to facilitate the return of the child to the jurisdiction of the court, pending further hearings. If the court determines that it is not in the best interest of the child to place temporary sole physical custody in the parent or person recommended by the district attorney, the court shall appoint a person to take charge of the child and return the child to the jurisdiction of the court.[1]

3134. (a) When the district attorney incurs expenses pursuant to this chapter, including expenses incurred in a sister state, payment of the expenses may be advanced by the county subject to reimbursement by the state, and shall be audited by the Controller and paid by the State Treasury according to law.
(b) The court in which the custody proceeding is pending or which has continuing jurisdiction shall, if appropriate, allocate liability for the reimbursement of actual expenses incurred by the district attorney to either or both parties to the proceedings, and that allocation shall constitute a judgment for the state for the funds advanced pursuant to this section. The county shall take reasonable action to enforce that liability and shall transmit all recovered funds to the state.[1]

3134.5. (a) Upon request of the district attorney, the court may issue a protective custody warrant to secure the recovery of an unlawfully detained or concealed child. The request by the district attorney shall include a written declaration under penalty of perjury that a warrant for the child is necessary in order for the district attorney to perform the duties described in Sections 3130 and 3131. The protective custody warrant for the child shall contain an order that the arresting agency shall place the child in protective custody, or return the child as directed by the court. The protective custody warrant for the child may also contain an order to freeze the California assets of the party alleged to be in possession of the child. The protective custody warrant may be served in any county in the same manner as a warrant of arrest and may be served at any time of the day or night. For purposes of this subdivision, "assets" means funds held in a depository institution, as defined in subdivision (a) of Section 1420 of the Financial Code, in California.
(b) Upon a declaration of the district attorney that the child has been recovered or that the warrant is otherwise no longer required, the court may dismiss the warrant without further court proceedings.
(c) Upon noticed motion, any order to freeze assets pursuant to subdivision (a) may be terminated, modified, or vacated by the court upon a finding that the release of the assets will not jeopardize the safety or best interest of the child.
(d) If an asset freeze order is entered

pursuant to subdivision (a), and the court subsequently dismisses the warrant pursuant to subdivision (b), notice of the dismissal shall be immediately served on the depository institutions holding any assets pursuant to the freeze order.[255]

3135. Part 3 (commencing with Section 3400) does not limit the authority of a district attorney or arresting agency to act pursuant to this chapter, Section 279.6 of the Penal Code, or any other applicable law.

Chapter 9: Check to Determine Whether Child is Missing Person

3140. (a) Subject to subdivisions (b) and (c), before granting or modifying a custody order in a case in which one or both parents of the child have not appeared either personally or by counsel, the court shall require the parent, petitioner, or other party appearing in the case to submit a certified copy of the child's birth certificate to the court. The court or its designee shall forward the certified copy of the birth certificate to the local police or sheriff's department which shall check with the National Crime Information Center Missing Person System to ascertain whether the child has been reported missing or is the victim of an abduction and shall report the results of the check to the court.
(b) If the custody matter before the court also involves a petition for the dissolution of marriage or the adjudication of paternity rights or duties, this section applies only to a case in which there is no proof of personal service of the petition on the absent parent.
(c) For good cause shown, the court may waive the requirements of this section.[1]

Chapter 10: Appointment of Counsel to Represent Child

3150. (a) If the court determines that it would be in the best interest of the minor child, the court may appoint private counsel to represent the interests of the child in a custody or visitation proceeding, provided that the court and counsel comply with the requirements set forth in Rules 5.240, 5.241, and 5.242 of the California Rules of Court.
(b) Upon entering an appearance on behalf of a child pursuant to this chapter, counsel shall continue to represent that child unless relieved by the court upon the substitution of other counsel by the court or for cause.[205]

3151. (a) The child's counsel appointed under this chapter is charged with the representation of the child's best interests. The role of the child's counsel is to gather evidence that bears on the best interests of the child, and present that admissible evidence to the court in any manner appropriate for the counsel of a party. If the child so desires, the child's counsel shall present the child's wishes to the court. The counsel's duties, unless under the circumstances it is inappropriate to exercise the duty, include interviewing the child, reviewing the court files and all accessible relevant records available to both parties, and making any further investigations as the counsel considers necessary to ascertain evidence relevant to the custody or visitation hearings.
(b) Counsel shall serve notices and

pleadings on all parties, consistent with requirements for parties. Counsel shall not be called as a witness in the proceeding. Counsel may introduce and examine counsel's own witnesses, present arguments to the court concerning the child's welfare, and participate further in the proceeding to the degree necessary to represent the child adequately.

(c) The child's counsel shall have the following rights:

(1) Reasonable access to the child.

(2) Standing to seek affirmative relief on behalf of the child.

(3) Notice of any proceeding, and all phases of that proceeding, including a request for examination affecting the child.

(4) The right to take any action that is available to a party to the proceeding, including, but not limited to, the following: filing pleadings, making evidentiary objections, and presenting evidence and being heard in the proceeding, which may include, but shall not be limited to, presenting motions and orders to show cause, and participating in settlement conferences, trials, seeking writs, appeals, and arbitrations.

(5) Access to the child's medical, dental, mental health, and other health care records, school and educational records, and the right to interview school personnel, caretakers, health care providers, mental health professionals, and others who have assessed the child or provided care to the child. The release of this information to counsel shall not constitute a waiver of the confidentiality of the reports, files, and any disclosed communications. Counsel may interview mediators; however, the provisions of Sections 3177 and 3182 shall apply.

(6) The right to reasonable advance notice of and the right to refuse any physical or psychological examination or evaluation, for purposes of the proceeding, which has not been ordered by the court.

(7) The right to assert or waive any privilege on behalf of the child.

(8) The right to seek independent psychological or physical examination or evaluation of the child for purposes of the pending proceeding, upon approval by the court.[206]

3152. (a) The child's counsel may, upon noticed motion to all parties and the local child protective services agency, request the court to authorize release of relevant reports or files, concerning the child represented by the counsel, of the relevant local child protective services agency.

(b) The court shall review the reports or files in camera in order to determine whether they are relevant to the pending action and whether and to what extent they should be released to the child's counsel.

(c) Neither the review by the court nor the release to counsel shall constitute a waiver of the confidentiality of the reports and files. Counsel shall not disclose the contents or existence of the reports or files to anyone unless otherwise permitted by law.[1]

3153. (a) If the court appoints counsel under this chapter to represent the child, counsel shall receive a reasonable sum for compensation and expenses, the amount of which shall be determined by the court. Except as provided in subdivision (b), this amount shall be paid by the parties in

the proportions the court deems just.
(b) Upon its own motion or that of a party, the court shall determine whether both parties together are financially unable to pay all or a portion of the cost of counsel appointed pursuant to this chapter, and the portion of the cost of that counsel which the court finds the parties are unable to pay shall be paid by the county. The Judicial Council shall adopt guidelines to assist in determining financial eligibility for county payment of counsel appointed by the court pursuant to this chapter.[1]

Chapter 11: Mediation of Custody and Visitation Issues

Article 1: General Provisions

3160. Each superior court shall make a mediator available. The court is not required to institute a family conciliation court in order to provide mediation services.[30]

3161. The purposes of a mediation proceeding are as follows:
(a) To reduce acrimony that may exist between the parties.
(b) To develop an agreement assuring the child close and continuing contact with both parents that is in the best interest of the child, consistent with Sections 3011 and 3020.
(c) To effect a settlement of the issue of visitation rights of all parties that is in the best interest of the child.[65]

3162. (a) Mediation of cases involving custody and visitation concerning children shall be governed by uniform standards of practice adopted by the Judicial Council.
(b) The standards of practice shall include, but not be limited to, all of the following:
(1) Provision for the best interest of the child and the safeguarding of the rights of the child to frequent and continuing contact with both parents, consistent with Sections 3011 and 3020.
(2) Facilitation of the transition of the family by detailing factors to be considered in decisions concerning the child's future.
(3) The conducting of negotiations in such a way as to equalize power relationships between the parties.
(c) In adopting the standards of practice, the Judicial Council shall consider standards developed by recognized associations of mediators and attorneys and other relevant standards governing mediation of proceedings for the dissolution of marriage.
(d) The Judicial Council shall offer training with respect to the standards to mediators.[66]

3163. Courts shall develop local rules to respond to requests for a change of mediators or to general problems relating to mediation. [30]

3164. (a) The mediator may be a member of the professional staff of a family conciliation court, probation department, or mental health services agency, or may be any other person or agency designated by the court.
(b) The mediator shall meet the minimum qualifications required of a counselor of conciliation as provided in Section 1815.[30]

3165. Any person, regardless of administrative title, hired on or after January 1, 1998, who is responsible for clinical supervision of evaluators, investigators, or mediators or who directly supervises or administers the

Family Court Services evaluation or mediation programs shall meet the same continuing education requirements specified in Section 1816 for supervising and associate counselors of conciliation.[62]

Article 2: Availability of Mediation

3170. (a) If it appears on the face of a petition, application, or other pleading to obtain or modify a temporary or permanent custody or visitation order that custody, visitation, or both are contested, the court shall set the contested issues for mediation.
(b) Domestic violence cases shall be handled by Family Court Services in accordance with a separate written protocol approved by the Judicial Council. The Judicial Council shall adopt guidelines for services, other than services provided under this chapter, that courts or counties may offer to parents who have been unable to resolve their disputes. These services may include, but are not limited to, parent education programs, booklets, video recordings, or referrals to additional community resources.
(c) This section shall become operative on January 1, 2020.[411]

3171. (a) If a stepparent or grandparent has petitioned, or otherwise applied, for a visitation order pursuant to Chapter 5 (commencing with Section 3100), the court shall set the matter for mediation.
(b) A natural or adoptive parent who is not a party to the proceeding is not required to participate in the mediation proceeding, but failure to participate is a waiver of that parent's right to object to a settlement reached by the other parties during mediation or to require a hearing on the matter.[30]

3172. Mediation shall not be denied to the parties on the basis that paternity is at issue in a proceeding before the court.[30]

3173. (a) Upon an order of the presiding judge of a superior court authorizing the procedure in that court, a petition may be filed pursuant to this chapter for mediation of a dispute relating to an existing order for custody, visitation, or both.
(b) The mediation of a dispute concerning an existing order shall be set not later than 60 days after the filing of the petition.[30]

Article 3: Mediation Proceedings

3175. If a matter is set for mediation pursuant to this chapter, the mediation shall be set before or concurrent with the setting of the matter for hearing.[30]

3176. (a) Notice of mediation and of any hearing to be held pursuant to this chapter shall be given to the following persons:
(1) Where mediation is required to settle a contested issue of custody or visitation, to each party and to each party's counsel of record.
(2) Where a stepparent or grandparent seeks visitation rights, to the stepparent or grandparent seeking visitation rights, to each parent of the child, and to each parent's counsel of record.
(b) Notice shall be given by certified mail, return receipt requested, postage prepaid, to the last known address.
(c) Notice of mediation pursuant to Section 3188 shall state that all communications involving the mediator shall be kept confidential between

the mediator and the disputing parties.

3177. Mediation proceedings pursuant to this chapter shall be held in private and shall be confidential. All communications, verbal or written, from the parties to the mediator made in the proceeding are official information within the meaning of Section 1040 of the Evidence Code.[30]

3178. An agreement reached by the parties as a result of mediation shall be limited as follows:
(a) Where mediation is required to settle a contested issue of custody or visitation, the agreement shall be limited to the resolution of issues relating to parenting plans, custody, visitation, or a combination of these issues.
(b) Where a stepparent or grandparent seeks visitation rights, the agreement shall be limited to the resolution of issues relating to visitation.[30]

3179. A custody or visitation agreement reached as a result of mediation may be modified at any time at the discretion of the court, subject to Chapter 1 (commencing with Section 3020), Chapter 2 (commencing with Section 3040), Chapter 4 (commencing with Section 3080), and Chapter 5 (commencing with Section 3100).[30]

3180. (a) In mediation proceedings pursuant to this chapter, the mediator has the duty to assess the needs and interests of the child involved in the controversy, and is entitled to interview the child when the mediator considers the interview appropriate or necessary.
(b) The mediator shall use their best efforts to effect a settlement of the custody or visitation dispute that is in the best interest of the child, as provided in Section 3011.[439]

3181. (a) In a proceeding in which mediation is required pursuant to this chapter, where there has been a history of domestic violence between the parties or where a protective order as defined in Section 6218 is in effect, at the request of the party alleging domestic violence in a written declaration under penalty of perjury or protected by the order, the mediator appointed pursuant to this chapter shall meet with the parties separately and at separate times.
(b) Any intake form that an agency charged with providing family court services requires the parties to complete before the commencement of mediation shall state that, if a party alleging domestic violence in a written declaration under penalty of perjury or a party protected by a protective order so requests, the mediator will meet with the parties separately and at separate times.[30]

3182. (a) The mediator has authority to exclude counsel from participation in the mediation proceedings pursuant to this chapter if, in the mediator's discretion, exclusion of counsel is appropriate or necessary.
(b) The mediator has authority to exclude a domestic violence support person from a mediation proceeding as provided in Section 6303.[30]

3183. (a) Except as provided in Section 3188, the mediator may, consistent with local court rules, submit a recommendation to the court as to the custody of or visitation with the child, if the mediator has first provided the parties and their attorneys, including counsel for any minor children, with

the recommendations in writing in advance of the hearing. The court shall make an inquiry at the hearing as to whether the parties and their attorneys have received the recommendations in writing. If the mediator is authorized to submit a recommendation to the court pursuant to this subdivision, the mediation and recommendation process shall be referred to as "child custody recommending counseling" and the mediator shall be referred to as a "child custody recommending counselor." Mediators who make those recommendations are considered mediators for purposes of Chapter 11 (commencing with Section 3160), and shall be subject to all requirements for mediators for all purposes under this code and the California Rules of Court. On and after January 1, 2012, all court communications and information regarding the child custody recommending counseling process shall reflect the change in the name of the process and the name of the providers.
(b) If the parties have not reached agreement as a result of the mediation proceedings, the mediator may recommend to the court that an investigation be conducted pursuant to Chapter 6 (commencing with Section 3110) or that other services be offered to assist the parties to effect a resolution of the controversy before a hearing on the issues.
(c) In appropriate cases, the mediator may recommend that restraining orders be issued, pending determination of the controversy, to protect the well-being of the child involved in the controversy.[207]

3184. Except as provided in Section 3188, nothing in this chapter prohibits the mediator from recommending to the court that counsel be appointed, pursuant to Chapter 10 (commencing with Section 3150), to represent the minor child. In making this recommendation, the mediator shall inform the court of the reasons why it would be in the best interest of the minor child to have counsel appointed.[94]

3185. (a) If issues that may be resolved by agreement pursuant to Section 3178 are not resolved by an agreement of all the parties who participate in mediation, the mediator shall inform the court in writing and the court shall set the matter for hearing on the unresolved issues.
(b) Where a stepparent or grandparent requests visitation, each natural or adoptive parent and the stepparent or grandparent shall be given an opportunity to appear and be heard on the issue of visitation.[30]

3186. (a) An agreement reached by the parties as a result of mediation shall be reported to counsel for the parties by the mediator on the day set for mediation or as soon thereafter as practical, but before the agreement is reported to the court.
(b) An agreement may not be confirmed or otherwise incorporated in an order unless each party, in person or by counsel of record, has affirmed and assented to the agreement in open court or by written stipulation.
(c) An agreement may be confirmed or otherwise incorporated in an order if a party fails to appear at a noticed hearing on the issue involved in the agreement.[30]

3188. (a)Any court selected by the

Judicial Council under subdivision (c) may voluntarily adopt a confidential mediation program that provides for all of the following:

(1) The mediator may not make a recommendation as to custody or visitation to anyone other than the disputing parties, except as otherwise provided in this section.

(2) If total or partial agreement is reached in mediation, the mediator may report this fact to the court. If both parties consent in writing, where there is a partial agreement, the mediator may report to the court a description of the issues still in dispute, without specific reference to either party.

(3) In making the recommendation described in Section 3184, the mediator may not inform the court of the reasons why it would be in the best interest of the minor child to have counsel appointed.

(4) If the parties have not reached agreement as a result of the initial mediation, this section does not prohibit the court from requiring subsequent mediation that may result in a recommendation as to custody or visitation with the child if the subsequent mediation is conducted by a different mediator with no prior involvement with the case or knowledge of any communications, as defined in Section 1040 of the Evidence Code, with respect to the initial mediation. The court, however, shall inform the parties that the mediator will make a recommendation to the court regarding custody or visitation in the event that the parties cannot reach agreement on these issues.

(5) If an initial screening or intake process indicates that the case involves serious safety risks to the child, such as domestic violence, sexual abuse, or serious substance abuse, the mediator may provide an initial emergency assessment service that includes a recommendation to the court concerning temporary custody or visitation orders in order to expeditiously address those safety issues.

(b) This section shall become operative upon the appropriation of funds in the annual Budget Act sufficient to implement this section.

(c) This section shall apply only in four or more superior courts selected by the Judicial Council that currently allow a mediator to make custody recommendations to the court and have more than 1,000 family law case filings per year. The Judicial Council may also make this section applicable to additional superior courts that have fewer than 1,000 family law case filings per year.[261]

Chapter 12: Counseling of Parents and Child

3190. (a) The court may require parents or any other party involved in a custody or visitation dispute, and the minor child, to participate in outpatient counseling with a licensed mental health professional, or through other community programs and services that provide appropriate counseling, including, but not limited to, mental health or substance abuse services, for not more than one year, provided that the program selected has counseling available for the designated period of time, if the court finds both of the following:

(1) The dispute between the parents,

between the parent or parents and the child, between the parent or parents and another party seeking custody or visitation rights with the child, or between a party seeking custody or visitation rights and the child, poses a substantial danger to the best interest of the child.

(2) The counseling is in the best interest of the child.

(b) In determining whether a dispute, as described in paragraph (1) of subdivision (a), poses a substantial danger to the best interest of the child, the court shall consider, in addition to any other factors the court determines relevant, any history of domestic violence, as defined in Section 6211, within the past five years between the parents, between the parent or parents and the child, between the parent or parents and another party seeking custody or visitation rights with the child, or between a party seeking custody or visitation rights and the child.

(c) Subject to Section 3192, if the court finds that the financial burden created by the order for counseling does not otherwise jeopardize a party's other financial obligations, the court shall fix the cost and shall order the entire cost of the services to be borne by the parties in the proportions the court deems reasonable.

(d) The court, in its finding, shall set forth reasons why it has found both of the following:

(1) The dispute poses a substantial danger to the best interest of the child and the counseling is in the best interest of the child.

(2) The financial burden created by the court order for counseling does not otherwise jeopardize a party's other financial obligations.

(e) The court shall not order the parties to return to court upon the completion of counseling. Any party may file a new order to show cause or motion after counseling has been completed, and the court may again order counseling consistent with this chapter.[68]

3191. The counseling pursuant to this chapter shall be specifically designed to facilitate communication between the parties regarding their minor child's best interest, to reduce conflict regarding custody or visitation, and to improve the quality of parenting skills of each parent.

3192. In a proceeding in which counseling is ordered pursuant to this chapter, where there has been a history of abuse by either parent against the child or by one parent against the other parent and a protective order, as defined in Section 6218, is in effect, the court may order the parties to participate in counseling separately and at separate times. Each party shall bear the cost of the party's own counseling separately, unless good cause is shown for a different apportionment. The costs associated with a minor child participating in counseling shall be apportioned in accordance with Section 4062.[440]

3193. (a) Notwithstanding any other law, a court shall not order family reunification treatments, programs, or services, including, but not limited to, camps, workshops, therapeutic vacations, or educational programs that, as a condition of enrollment or participation, require or result in any of the following:

(1) A no-contact order.

(2) An overnight, out-of-state, or

multiday stay.

(3) A transfer of physical or legal custody of the child.

(4) The use of private youth transporters or private transportation agents engaged in the use of force, threat of force, physical obstruction, acutely distressing circumstances, or circumstances that place the safety of the child at risk.

(5) The use of threats of physical force, undue coercion, verbal abuse, isolation from the child's family, community, or other sources of support, or other acutely distressing circumstances.

(b) This section does not affect the applicability of Section 16507 of the Welfare and Institutions Code.

Chapter 13: Supervised Visitation and Exchange Services, Education, and Counseling

3200. The Judicial Council shall develop standards for supervised visitation providers in accordance with the guidelines set forth in this section. For the purposes of the development of these standards, the term "provider" shall include any individual who functions as a visitation monitor, as well as supervised visitation centers, including those housed in superior court locations. Provisions shall be made within the standards to allow for the diversity of supervised visitation providers.

(a) When developing standards, the Judicial Council shall consider all of the following issues:

(1) The provider's qualifications, experience, and education.

(2) Safety and security procedures, including ratios of children per supervisor.

(3) Any conflict of interest.

(4) Maintenance and disclosure of records, including confidentiality policies.

(5) Procedures for screening, delineation of terms and conditions, and termination of supervised visitation services.

(6) Procedures for emergency or extenuating situations.

(7) Orientation to and guidelines for cases in which there are allegations of domestic violence, child abuse, substance abuse, or special circumstances.

(8) The legal obligations and responsibilities of supervisors.

(b) The Judicial Council shall consult with visitation centers, mothers' groups, fathers' groups, judges, the State Bar of California, children's advocacy groups, domestic violence prevention groups, Family Court Services, and other groups it regards as necessary in connection with these standards.

(c) It is the intent of the Legislature that the safety of children, adults, and visitation supervisors be a precondition to providing visitation services. Once safety is assured, the best interest of the child is the paramount consideration at all stages and particularly in deciding the manner in which supervision is provided.

(d) Superior court locations may serve as supervised visitation and exchange locations. Superior courts may designate employees and contractors to provide supervised visitation and exchange services or assistance with those services.[572]

3200.5. (a) Any standards for supervised visitation providers adopted by the Judicial Council pursuant to Section 3200 shall conform to this section. A provider, as described in Section 3200, shall be a professional provider or nonprofessional provider.

(b) In any case in which the court has determined that there is domestic violence or child abuse or neglect, as defined in Section 11165.6 of the Penal Code, and the court determines supervision is necessary, the court shall consider whether to use a professional or nonprofessional provider based upon the child's best interest.

(c) For the purposes of this section, the following definitions apply:

(1) "Nonprofessional provider" means any person who is not paid for providing supervised visitation services.

(2) "Professional provider" means any person paid for providing supervised visitation services, or an independent contractor, employee, intern, or volunteer operating independently or through a supervised visitation center or agency.

(d) Unless otherwise ordered by the court or stipulated by the parties, a nonprofessional provider shall:

(1) Have no record of a conviction for child molestation, child abuse, or other crimes against a person.

(2) Have proof of automobile insurance if transporting the child.

(3) Have no current or past court order in which the provider is the person being supervised.

(4) Agree to adhere to and enforce the court order regarding supervised visitation.

(e) A professional provider shall:

(1) Be at least 21 years of age.

(2) Have no record of a conviction for driving under the influence (DUI) within the last five years.

(3) Not have been on probation or parole for the last 10 years.

(4) Have no record of a conviction for child molestation, child abuse, or other crimes against a person.

(5) Have proof of automobile insurance if transporting the child.

(6) Have no civil, criminal, or juvenile restraining orders within the last 10 years.

(7) Have no current or past court order in which the provider is the person being supervised.

(8) Be able to speak the language of the party being supervised and of the child, or the provider must provide a neutral interpreter over 18 years of age who is able to do so.

(9) Agree to adhere to and enforce the court order regarding supervised visitation.

(10) (A) Complete 24 hours of training prior to providing visitation services, including at least 12 hours of classroom instruction in the following subjects:

(i) The role of a professional provider.

(ii) Child abuse reporting laws.

(iii) Recordkeeping procedures.

(iv) Screening, monitoring, and termination of visitation.

(v) Developmental needs of children.

(vi) Legal responsibilities and obligations of a provider.

(vii) Cultural sensitivity.

(viii) Conflicts of interest, including the acceptance of gifts.

(ix) Confidentiality.

(x) Issues relating to substance abuse, child abuse, sexual abuse, and domestic violence.

(xi) Basic knowledge of family and

juvenile law.

(B) Of the 24 hours of training required pursuant to subparagraph (A), at a minimum, three hours shall be on the screening, monitoring, and termination of visitation, three hours shall be on the developmental needs of children, three hours shall be on issues relating to substance abuse, child abuse, sexual abuse, and domestic violence, and one hour shall be on basic knowledge of family law.

(C) Notwithstanding the requirement for classroom instruction in subparagraph (A), on and after January 1, 2021, a professional provider shall complete the training required pursuant to clause (ii) of subparagraph (A), relating to child abuse reporting laws, by completing an online training course required for mandated reporters that is provided by the State Department of Social Services. This online training requirement is not intended to increase the total number of training hours required by this paragraph.

(11) Complete a Live Scan criminal background check, at the expense of the provider or the supervised visitation center or agency, prior to providing visitation services.

(12) Sign the Judicial Council Declaration of Supervised Visitation Provider form that the person meets the training and qualifications of a provider. A professional provider shall sign a separate, updated form each time the professional provider submits a report to the court.

(13) (A) Beginning January 1, 2021, be registered as a trustline provider pursuant to Chapter 3.35 (commencing with Section 1596.60) of Divis-ion 2 of the Health and Safety Code.

(B) Notwithstanding any other law, if a person is denied trustline registration by the State Department of Social Services pursuant to Section 1596.605 or 1596.607 of the Health and Safety Code, or if the State Department of Social Services revokes a person's trustline registration pursuant to Section 1596.608 of the Health and Safety Code, that person shall be ineligible to be a professional provider.

(f) The ratio of children to a professional provider shall be contingent on:

(1) The degree of risk factors present in each case.

(2) The nature of supervision required in each case.

(3) The number and ages of the children to be supervised during a visit.

(4) The number of people visiting the child during the visit.

(5) The duration and location of the visit.

(6) The experience of the provider.

(g) Professional providers of supervised visitation shall:

(1) Advise the parties before commencement of supervised visitation that no confidential privilege exists.

(2) Report suspected child abuse to the appropriate agency, as provided by law, and inform the parties of the provider's obligation to make those reports.

(3) Suspend or terminate visitation under subdivision (h).

(h) Professional providers shall:

(1) Prepare a written contract to be signed by the parties before

commencement of the supervised visitation. The contract should inform each party of the terms and conditions of supervised visitation.

(2) Review custody and visitation orders relevant to the supervised visitation.

(3) Keep a record for each case, including, at least, all of the following:

(A) A written record of each contact and visit.

(B) Who attended the visit.

(C) Any failure to comply with the terms and conditions of the visitation.

(D) Any incidence of abuse, as required by law.

(i) (1) Each provider shall make every reasonable effort to provide a safe visit for the child and the noncustodial party.

(2) If a provider determines that the rules of the visit have been violated, the child has become acutely distressed, or the safety of the child or the provider is at risk, the visit may be temporarily interrupted, rescheduled at a later date, or terminated.

(3) All interruptions or terminations of visits shall be recorded in the case file.

(4) All providers shall advise both parties of the reasons for the interruption or termination of a visit.

(j) A professional provider shall state the reasons for temporary suspension or termination of supervised visitation in writing and shall provide the written statement to both parties, their attorneys, the attorney for the child, and the court.[477]

3201. Any supervised visitation maintained or imposed by the court shall be administered in accordance with Standard 5.20 of the California Standards of Judicial Administration recommended by the Judicial Council.[493]

3201.5. (a) The programs described in this chapter shall be administered by the family law division of the superior court in the county.

(b) For purposes of this chapter, "education about protecting children during family disruption" includes education on parenting skills and the impact of parental conflict on children, how to put a parenting agreement into effect, and the responsibility of both parents to comply with custody and visitation orders.[332]

3202. (a) All supervised visitation and exchange programs funded pursuant to this chapter shall comply with all requirements of the Uniform Standards of Practice for Providers of Supervised Visitation set forth in Standard 5.20 of the Standards of Judicial Administration as amended. The family law division of the superior court may contract with eligible providers of supervised visitation and exchange services, education, and group counseling to provide services under this chapter.

(b) As used in this section, "eligible provider" means:

(1) For providers of supervised visitation and exchange services, a local public agency or nonprofit entity that satisfies the Uniform Standards of Practice for Providers of Supervised Visitation.

(2) For providers of group counseling, a professional licensed to practice psychotherapy in this state, including, but not limited to, a licensed psychiatrist, licensed psychologist, licensed clinical social

worker, licensed marriage and family therapist, or licensed professional clinical counselor; or a mental health intern working under the direct supervision of a professional licensed to practice psychotherapy.

(3) For providers of education, a professional with a bachelor's or master's degree in human behavior, child development, psychology, counseling, family-life education, or a related field, having specific training in issues relating to child and family development, substance abuse, child abuse, domestic violence, effective parenting, and the impact of divorce and interparental conflict on children; or an intern working under the supervision of that professional.[266]

3203. Subject to the availability of federal funding for the purposes of this chapter, the family law division of the superior court in each county may establish and administer a supervised visitation and exchange program, programs for education about protecting children during family disruption, and group counseling programs for parents and children under this chapter. The programs shall allow parties and children to participate in supervised visitation between a custodial party and a noncustodial party or joint custodians, and to participate in the education and group counseling programs, irrespective of whether the parties are or are not married to each other or are currently living separately and apart on a permanent or temporary basis.[77]

3204. (a) The Judicial Council shall annually submit an application to the federal Administration for Children and Families, pursuant to Section 669B of the "1996 Federal Personal Responsibility and Work Opportunity Recovery Act" (PRWORA), for a grant to fund child custody and visitation programs pursuant to this chapter.

The Judicial Council shall be charged with the administration of the grant funds.

(b) (1) It is the intention of the Legislature that, effective October 1, 2000, the grant funds described in subdivision (a) shall be used to fund the following three types of programs: supervised visitation and exchange services, education about protecting children during family disruption, and group counseling for parents and children, as set forth in this chapter. Contracts shall follow a standard request for proposal procedure, that may include multiple year funding. Requests for proposals shall meet all state and federal requirements for receiving access and visitation grant funds.

(2) The grant funds shall be awarded with the intent of approving as many requests for proposals as possible while assuring that each approved proposal would provide beneficial services and satisfy the overall goals of the program under this chapter. The Judicial Council shall determine the final number and amount of grants. Requests for proposals shall be evaluated based on the following criteria:

(A) Availability of services to a broad population of parties.

(B) The ability to expand existing services.

(C) Coordination with other community services.

(D) The hours of service delivery.

(E) The number of counties or regions participating.

(F) Overall cost-effectiveness.

(G) The purpose of the program to promote and encourage healthy parent and child relationships between noncustodial parents and their children, while ensuring the health, safety, and welfare of the children.

(3) Special consideration for grant funds shall be given to proposals that coordinate supervised visitation and exchange services, education, and group counseling with existing court-based programs and services.

(c) The family law division of the superior court in each county shall approve sliding scale fees that are based on the ability to pay for all parties, including low-income families, participating in a supervised visitation and exchange, education, and group counseling programs under this chapter.

(d) The Judicial Council shall, on March 1, 2002, and on the first day of March of each subsequent even-numbered year, report to the Legislature on the programs funded pursuant to this chapter and whether and to what extent those programs are achieving the goal of promoting and encouraging healthy parent and child relationships between noncustodial or joint custodial parents and their children while ensuring the health, safety, and welfare of children, and the other goals described in this chapter.[184]

PART 3: UNIFORM CHILD CUSTODY JURISDICTION AND ENFORCEMET ACT

repealed and added by Stats. 1999, Ch. 867, Sec. 3

Chapter 1: General Provisions

3400. This part may be cited as the Uniform Child Custody Jurisdiction and Enforcement Act.[76]

3402. As used in this part:

(a) "Abandoned" means left without provision for reasonable and necessary care or supervision.

(b) "Child" means an individual who has not attained 18 years of age.

(c) "Child custody determination" means a judgment, decree, or other order of a court providing for the legal custody, physical custody, or visitation with respect to a child. The term includes a permanent, temporary, initial, and modification order. The term does not include an order relating to child support or other monetary obligation of an individual.

(d) "Child custody proceeding" means a proceeding in which legal custody, physical custody, or visitation with respect to a child is an issue. The term includes a proceeding for dissolution of marriage, legal separation of the parties, neglect, abuse, dependency, guardianship, paternity, termination of parental rights, and protection from domestic violence, in which the issue may appear. The term does not include a proceeding involving juvenile delinquency, contractual emancipation, or enforcement under Chapter 3 (commencing with Section 3441).

(e) "Commencement" means the filing of the first pleading in a proceeding.

(f) "Court" means an entity authorized under the law of a state to establish, enforce, or modify a child custody determination.
(g) "Home state" means the state in which a child lived with a parent or a person acting as a parent for at least six consecutive months immediately before the commencement of a child custody proceeding. In the case of a child less than six months of age, the term means the state in which the child lived from birth with any of the persons mentioned. A period of temporary absence of any of the mentioned persons is part of the period.
(h) "Initial determination" means the first child custody determination concerning a particular child.
(i) "Issuing court" means the court that makes a child custody determination for which enforcement is sought under this part.
(j) "Issuing state" means the state in which a child custody determination is made.
(k) "Modification" means a child custody determination that changes, replaces, supersedes, or is otherwise made after a previous determination concerning the same child, whether or not it is made by the court that made the previous determination.
(l) "Person" means an individual, corporation, business trust, estate, trust, partnership, limited liability company, association, joint venture, or government; governmental subdivision, agency, or instrumentality; public corporation; or any other legal or commercial entity.
(m) "Person acting as a parent" means a person, other than a parent, who: (1) has physical custody of the child or has had physical custody for a period of six consecutive months, including any temporary absence, within one year immediately before the commencement of a child custody proceeding; and (2) has been awarded legal custody by a court or claims a right to legal custody under the law of this state.
(n) "Physical custody" means the physical care and supervision of a child.
(o) "State" means a state of the United States, the District of Columbia, Puerto Rico, the United States Virgin Islands, or any territory or insular possession subject to the jurisdiction of the United States.
(p) "Tribe" means an Indian tribe or band, or Alaskan Native village, that is recognized by federal law or formally acknowledged by a state.
(q) "Warrant" means an order issued by a court authorizing law enforcement officers to take physical custody of a child.[76]

3403. This part does not govern an adoption proceeding or a proceeding pertaining to the authorization of emergency medical care for a child. [76]

3404. (a) A child custody proceeding that pertains to an Indian child as defined in the Indian Child Welfare Act (25 U.S.C. Sec. 1901 et seq.) is not subject to this part to the extent that it is governed by the Indian Child Welfare Act.
(b) A court of this state shall treat a tribe as if it were a state of the United States for the purpose of applying this chapter and Chapter 2 (commencing with Section 3421).
(c) A child custody determination made by a tribe under factual circumstances in substantial

conformity with the jurisdictional standards of this part must be recognized and enforced under Chapter 3 (commencing with Section 3441).[76]

3405. (a) A court of this state shall treat a foreign country as if it were a state of the United States for the purpose of applying this chapter and Chapter 2 (commencing with Section 3421).
(b) Except as otherwise provided in subdivision (c), a child custody determination made in a foreign country under factual circumstances in substantial conformity with the jurisdictional standards of this part must be recognized and enforced under Chapter 3 (commencing with Section 3441).
(c) A court of this state need not apply this part if the child custody law of a foreign country violates fundamental principles of human rights.[76]

3406. A child custody determination made by a court of this state that had jurisdiction under this part binds all persons who have been served in accordance with the laws of this state or notified in accordance with Section 3408 or who have submitted to the jurisdiction of the court, and who have been given an opportunity to be heard. As to those persons, the determination is conclusive as to all decided issues of law and fact except to the extent the determination is modified.[76]

3407. If a question of existence or exercise of jurisdiction under this part is raised in a child custody proceeding, the question, upon request of a party, must be given priority on the calendar and handled expeditiously.[76]

3408. (a) Notice required for the exercise of jurisdiction when a person is outside this state may be given in a manner prescribed by the law of this state for service of process or by the law of the state in which the service is made. Notice must be given in a manner reasonably calculated to give actual notice but may be by publication if other means are not effective.
(b) Proof of service may be made in the manner prescribed by the law of this state or by the law of the state in which the service is made.
(c) Notice is not required for the exercise of jurisdiction with respect to a person who submits to the jurisdiction of the court.[76]

3409. (a) A party to a child custody proceeding, including a modification proceeding, or a petitioner or respondent in a proceeding to enforce or register a child custody determination, is not subject to personal jurisdiction in this state for another proceeding or purpose solely by reason of having participated, or of having been physically present for the purpose of participating, in the proceeding.
(b) A person who is subject to personal jurisdiction in this state on a basis other than physical presence is not immune from service of process in this state. A party present in this state who is subject to the jurisdiction of another state is not immune from service of process allowable under the laws of that state.
(c) The immunity granted by subdivision (a) does not extend to civil litigation based on acts unrelated to the participation in a proceeding under this part committed by an individual while present in this state.[76]

3410. (a) A court of this state may communicate with a court in another state concerning a proceeding arising under this part.

(b) The court may allow the parties to participate in the communication. If the parties are not able to participate in the communication, they must be given the opportunity to present facts and legal arguments before a decision on jurisdiction is made.

(c) Communication between courts on schedules, calendars, court records, and similar matters may occur without informing the parties. A record need not be made of the communication.

(d) Except as otherwise provided in subdivision (c), a record must be made of a communication under this section. The parties must be informed promptly of the communication and granted access to the record.

(e) For the purposes of this section, "record" means information that is inscribed on a tangible medium or that is stored in an electronic or other medium and is retrievable in perceivable form.[76]

3411. (a) In addition to other procedures available to a party, a party to a child custody proceeding may offer testimony of witnesses who are located in another state, including testimony of the parties and the child, by deposition or other means allowable in this state for testimony taken in another state. The court, on its own motion, may order that the testimony of a person be taken in another state and may prescribe the manner in which and the terms upon which the testimony is taken.

(b) A court of this state may permit an individual residing in another state to be deposed or to testify by telephone, audiovisual means, or other electronic means before a designated court or at another location in that state. A court of this state shall cooperate with courts of other states in designating an appropriate location for the deposition or testimony.

(c) Documentary evidence transmitted from another state to a court of this state by technological means that do not produce an original writing may not be excluded from evidence on an objection based on the means of transmission.[76]

3412. (a) A court of this state may request the appropriate court of another state to do all of the following:

(1) Hold an evidentiary hearing.

(2) Order a person to produce or give evidence pursuant to procedures of that state.

(3) Order that an evaluation be made with respect to the custody of a child involved in a pending proceeding.

(4) Forward to the court of this state a certified copy of the transcript of the record of the hearing, the evidence otherwise presented, and any evaluation prepared in compliance with the request.

(5) Order a party to a child custody proceeding or any person having physical custody of the child to appear in the proceeding with or without the child.

(b) Upon request of a court of another state, a court of this state may hold a hearing or enter an order described in subdivision (a).

(c) Travel and other necessary and reasonable expenses incurred under subdivisions (a) and (b) may be assessed against the parties according to the law of this state.

(d) A court of this state shall preserve

the pleadings, orders, decrees, records of hearings, evaluations, and other pertinent records with respect to a child custody proceeding until the child attains 18 years of age. Upon appropriate request by a court or law enforcement official of another state, the court shall forward a certified copy of those records.[76]

Chapter 2: Jurisdiction

3421. (a) Except as otherwise provided in Section 3424, a court of this state has jurisdiction to make an initial child custody determination only if any of the following are true:

(1) This state is the home state of the child on the date of the commencement of the proceeding, or was the home state of the child within six months before the commencement of the proceeding and the child is absent from this state but a parent or person acting as a parent continues to live in this state.

(2) A court of another state does not have jurisdiction under paragraph (1), or a court of the home state of the child has declined to exercise jurisdiction on the grounds that this state is the more appropriate forum under Section 3427 or 3428, and both of the following are true:

(A) The child and the child's parents, or the child and at least one parent or a person acting as a parent, have a significant connection with this state other than mere physical presence.

(B) Substantial evidence is available in this state concerning the child's care, protection, training, and personal relationships.

(3) All courts having jurisdiction under paragraph (1) or (2) have declined to exercise jurisdiction on the ground that a court of this state is the more appropriate forum to determine the custody of the child under Section 3427 or 3428.

(4) No court of any other state would have jurisdiction under the criteria specified in paragraph (1), (2), or (3).

(b) Subdivision (a) is the exclusive jurisdictional basis for making a child custody determination by a court of this state.

(c) Physical presence of, or personal jurisdiction over, a party or a child is not necessary or sufficient to make a child custody determination.

(d) The presence of a child in this state for the purpose of obtaining gender-affirming health care or gender-affirming mental health care, as defined by Section 16010.2 of the Welfare and Institutions Code, is sufficient to meet the requirements of paragraph (2) of subdivision (a).[524]

3422. (a) Except as otherwise provided in Section 3424, a court of this state that has made a child custody determination consistent with Section 3421 or 3423 has exclusive, continuing jurisdiction over the determination until either of the following occurs:

(1) A court of this state determines that neither the child, nor the child and one parent, nor the child and a person acting as a parent have a significant connection with this state and that substantial evidence is no longer available in this state concerning the child's care, protection, training, and personal relationships.

(2) A court of this state or a court of another state determines that the child, the child's parents, and any person acting as a parent do not presently reside in this state.

(b) A court of this state that has made a child custody determination and does not have exclusive, continuing jurisdiction under this section may modify that determination only if it has jurisdiction to make an initial determination under Section 3421.[76]

3423. Except as otherwise provided in Section 3424, a court of this state may not modify a child custody determination made by a court of another state unless a court of this state has jurisdiction to make an initial determination under paragraph (1) or (2) of subdivision (a) of Section 3421 and either of the following determinations is made:

(a) The court of the other state determines it no longer has exclusive, continuing jurisdiction under Section 3422 or that a court of this state would be a more convenient forum under Section 3427.

(b) A court of this state or a court of the other state determines that the child, the child's parents, and any person acting as a parent do not presently reside in the other state.[76]

3424. (a) A court of this state has temporary emergency jurisdiction if the child is present in this state and the child has been abandoned or it is necessary in an emergency to protect the child because the child, or a sibling or parent of the child, is subjected to, or threatened with, mistreatment or abuse, or because the child has been unable to obtain gender-affirming health care or gender-affirming mental health care, as defined by Section 16010.2 of the Welfare and Institutions Code.

(b) If there is no previous child custody determination that is entitled to be enforced under this part and a child custody proceeding has not been commenced in a court of a state having jurisdiction under Sections 3421 to 3423, inclusive, a child custody determination made under this section remains in effect until an order is obtained from a court of a state having jurisdiction under Sections 3421 to 3423, inclusive. If a child custody proceeding has not been or is not commenced in a court of a state having jurisdiction under Sections 3421 to 3423, inclusive, a child custody determination made under this section becomes a final determination, if it so provides and this state becomes the home state of the child.

(c) If there is a previous child custody determination that is entitled to be enforced under this part, or a child custody proceeding has been commenced in a court of a state having jurisdiction under Sections 3421 to 3423, inclusive, any order issued by a court of this state under this section must specify in the order a period that the court considers adequate to allow the person seeking an order to obtain an order from the state having jurisdiction under Sections 3421 to 3423, inclusive. The order issued in this state remains in effect until an order is obtained from the other state within the period specified or the period expires.

(d) A court of this state that has been asked to make a child custody determination under this section, upon being informed that a child custody proceeding has been commenced in, or a child custody determination has been made by, a court of a state having jurisdiction under Sections 3421 to 3423, inclusive, shall immediately

communicate with the other court. A court of this state which is exercising jurisdiction pursuant to Sections 3421 to 3423, inclusive, upon being informed that a child custody proceeding has been commenced in, or a child custody determination has been made by, a court of another state under a statute similar to this section shall immediately communicate with the court of that state to resolve the emergency, protect the safety of the parties and the child, and determine a period for the duration of the temporary order.
(e) It is the intent of the Legislature in enacting subdivision (a) that the grounds on which a court may exercise temporary emergency jurisdiction be expanded. It is further the intent of the Legislature that these grounds include those that existed under Section 3403 of the Family Code as that section read on December 31, 1999, particularly including cases involving domestic violence.[525]

3425. (a) Before a child custody determination is made under this part, notice and an opportunity to be heard in accordance with the standards of Section 3408 must be given to all persons entitled to notice under the law of this state as in child custody proceedings between residents of this state, any parent whose parental rights have not been previously terminated, and any person having physical custody of the child.
(b) This part does not govern the enforceability of a child custody determination made without notice or an opportunity to be heard.
(c) The obligation to join a party and the right to intervene as a party in a child custody proceeding under this part are governed by the law of this state as in child custody proceedings between residents of this state.[189]

3426. (a) Except as otherwise provided in Section 3424, a court of this state may not exercise its jurisdiction under this chapter if, at the time of the commencement of the proceeding, a proceeding concerning the custody of the child has been commenced in a court of another state having jurisdiction substantially in conformity with this part, unless the proceeding has been terminated or is stayed by the court of the other state because a court of this state is a more convenient forum under Section 3427.
(b) Except as otherwise provided in Section 3424, a court of this state, before hearing a child custody proceeding, shall examine the court documents and other information supplied by the parties pursuant to Section 3429. If the court determines that a child custody proceeding has been commenced in a court in another state having jurisdiction substantially in accordance with this part, the court of this state shall stay its proceeding and communicate with the court of the other state. If the court of the state having jurisdiction substantially in accordance with this part does not determine that the court of this state is a more appropriate forum, the court of this state shall dismiss the proceeding.
(c) In a proceeding to modify a child custody determination, a court of this state shall determine whether a proceeding to enforce the determination has been commenced in another state. If a proceeding to enforce a child custody determination has been commenced in another state, the court may do any of the following:

(1) Stay the proceeding for modification pending the entry of an order of a court of the other state enforcing, staying, denying, or dismissing the proceeding for enforcement.

(2) Enjoin the parties from continuing with the proceeding for enforcement.

(3) Proceed with the modification under conditions it considers appropriate.[76]

3427. (a) A court of this state that has jurisdiction under this part to make a child custody determination may decline to exercise its jurisdiction at any time if it determines that it is an inconvenient forum under the circumstances and that a court of another state is a more appropriate forum. The issue of inconvenient forum may be raised upon motion of a party, the court's own motion, or request of another court.

(b) Before determining whether it is an inconvenient forum, a court of this state shall consider whether it is appropriate for a court of another state to exercise jurisdiction. For this purpose, the court shall allow the parties to submit information and shall consider all relevant factors, including:

(1) Whether domestic violence has occurred and is likely to continue in the future and which state could best protect the parties and the child.

(2) The length of time the child has resided outside this state.

(3) The distance between the court in this state and the court in the state that would assume jurisdiction.

(4) The degree of financial hardship to the parties in litigating in one forum over the other.

(5) Any agreement of the parties as to which state should assume jurisdiction.

(6) The nature and location of the evidence required to resolve the pending litigation, including testimony of the child.

(7) The ability of the court of each state to decide the issue expeditiously and the procedures necessary to present the evidence.

(8) The familiarity of the court of each state with the facts and issues in the pending litigation.

(c) If a court of this state determines that it is an inconvenient forum and that a court of another state is a more appropriate forum, it shall stay the proceedings upon condition that a child custody proceeding be promptly commenced in another designated state and may impose any other condition the court considers just and proper.

(d) A court of this state may decline to exercise its jurisdiction under this part if a child custody determination is incidental to an action for dissolution of marriage or another proceeding while still retaining jurisdiction over the dissolution of marriage or other proceeding.

(e) If it appears to the court that it is clearly an inappropriate forum, the court may require the party who commenced the proceeding to pay, in addition to the costs of the proceeding in this state, necessary travel and other expenses, including attorney's fees, incurred by the other parties or their witnesses. Payment is to be made to the clerk of the court for remittance to the proper party.

(f) (1) In a case where the provision of gender-affirming health care or gender-affirming mental health care to the child is at issue, a court of this state shall not determine that it is an inconvenient forum where the law or policy of the other state that may take jurisdiction limits the ability of a parent to obtain gender-affirming health care or gender-affirming mental health care for their child.

(2) For the purposes of this section, "gender-affirming health care" and "gender-affirming mental health care" have the same meaning as defined by Section 16010.2 of the Welfare and Institutions Code.[526]

3428. (a) Except as otherwise provided in Section 3424 or by any other law of this state, if a court of this state has jurisdiction under this part because a person seeking to invoke its jurisdiction has engaged in unjustifiable conduct, the court shall decline to exercise its jurisdiction unless one of the following are true:

(1) The parents and all persons acting as parents have acquiesced in the exercise of jurisdiction.

(2) A court of the state otherwise having jurisdiction under Sections 3421 to 3423, inclusive, determines that this state is a more appropriate forum under Section 3427.

(3) No court of any other state would have jurisdiction under the criteria specified in Sections 3421 to 3423, inclusive.

(b) If a court of this state declines to exercise its jurisdiction pursuant to subdivision (a), it may fashion an appropriate remedy to ensure the safety of the child and prevent a repetition of the unjustifiable conduct, including staying the proceeding until a child custody proceeding is commenced in a court having jurisdiction under Sections 3421 to 3423, inclusive.

(c) If a court dismisses a petition or stays a proceeding because it declines to exercise its jurisdiction pursuant to subdivision (a), it shall assess against the party seeking to invoke its jurisdiction necessary and reasonable expenses including costs, communication expenses, attorney's fees, investigative fees, expenses for witnesses, travel expenses, and child care during the course of the proceedings, unless the party from whom fees are sought establishes that the assessment would be clearly inappropriate. The court may not assess fees, costs, or expenses against this state unless authorized by law other than this part.

(d) In making a determination under this section, a court shall not consider as a factor weighing against the petitioner any taking of the child, or retention of the child after a visit or other temporary relinquishment of physical custody, from the person who has legal custody, if there is evidence that the taking or retention of the child was a result of domestic violence against the petitioner, as defined in Section 6211, or for the purposes of obtaining gender-affirming health care or gender-affirming mental health care, as defined by Section 16010.2 of the Welfare and Institutions Code, for the child and the law or policy of the other state limits the ability of a parent to obtain gender-affirming health care or gender-affirming mental health care for their child.[527]

3429. (a) In a child custody proceeding, each party, in its first pleading or in an attached affidavit, shall give information, if reasonably ascertainable, under oath as to the child's present address or whereabouts, the places where the child has lived during the last five years, and the names and present addresses of the persons with whom the child has lived during that period. However, where there are allegations of domestic violence or child abuse, any addresses of the party alleging violence or abuse and of the child which are unknown to the other party are confidential and may not be disclosed in the pleading or affidavit. The pleading or affidavit must state whether the party:

(1) Has participated, as a party or witness or in any other capacity, in any other proceeding concerning the custody of, or visitation with, the child and, if so, identify the court, the case number, and the date of the child custody determination, if any.

(2) Knows of any proceeding that could affect the current proceeding, including proceedings for enforcement and proceedings relating to domestic violence, protective orders, termination of parental rights, and adoptions and, if so, identify the court, the case number, and the nature of the proceeding.

(3) Knows the names and addresses of any person not a party to the proceeding who has physical custody of the child or claims rights of legal custody or physical custody of, or visitation with, the child and, if so, the names and addresses of those persons.

(b) If the information required by subdivision (a) is not furnished, the court, upon motion of a party or its own motion, may stay the proceeding until the information is furnished.

(c) If the declaration as to any of the items described in paragraphs (1) to (3), inclusive, of subdivision (a) is in the affirmative, the declarant shall give additional information under oath as required by the court. The court may examine the parties under oath as to details of the information furnished and other matters pertinent to the court's jurisdiction and the disposition of the case.

(d) Each party has a continuing duty to inform the court of any proceeding in this or any other state that could affect the current proceeding.

3430. (a) In a child custody proceeding in this state, the court may order a party to the proceeding who is in this state to appear before the court in person with or without the child. The court may order any person who is in this state and who has physical custody or control of the child to appear in person with the child.

(b) If a party to a child custody proceeding whose presence is desired by the court is outside this state, the court may order that a notice given pursuant to Section 3408 include a statement directing the party to appear in person with or without the child and informing the party that failure to appear may result in a decision adverse to the party.

(c) The court may enter any orders necessary to ensure the safety of the child and of any person ordered to appear under this section.

(d) If a party to a child custody proceeding who is outside this state is directed to appear under subdivision (b) or desires to appear personally before the court with or without the child, the court may require another party to pay reasonable and necessary travel and other expenses of the party so appearing and of the child.[76]

Chapter 3: Enforcement

3441. In this chapter:
(a) "Petitioner" means a person who seeks enforcement of an order for return of a child under the Hague Convention on the Civil Aspects of International Child Abduction or enforcement of a child custody determination.
(b) "Respondent" means a person against whom a proceeding has been commenced for enforcement of an order for return of a child under the Hague Convention on the Civil Aspects of International Child Abduction or enforcement of a child custody determination.[76]

3442. Under this chapter, a court of this state may enforce an order for the return of a child made under the Hague Convention on the Civil Aspects of International Child Abduction as if it were a child custody determination.[76]

3443. (a) A court of this state shall recognize and enforce a child custody determination of a court of another state if the latter court exercised jurisdiction in substantial conformity with this part or the determination was made under factual circumstances meeting the jurisdictional standards of this part and the determination has not been modified in accordance with this part.
(b) A court of this state may utilize any remedy available under other laws of this state to enforce a child custody determination made by a court of another state. The remedies provided in this chapter are cumulative and do not affect the availability of other remedies to enforce a child custody determination.[76]

3444. (a) A court of this state which does not have jurisdiction to modify a child custody determination may issue a temporary order enforcing either:
(1) A visitation schedule made by a court of another state.
(2) The visitation provisions of a child custody determination of another state that does not provide for a specific visitation schedule.
(b) If a court of this state makes an order under paragraph (2) of subdivision (a), it shall specify in the order a period that it considers adequate to allow the petitioner to obtain an order from a court having jurisdiction under the criteria specified in Chapter 2 (commencing with Section 3421). The order remains in effect until an order is obtained from the other court or the period expires.[76]

3445. (a) A child custody determination issued by a court of another state may be registered in this state, with or without a simultaneous request for enforcement, by sending all of the following to the appropriate court in this state:
(1) A letter or other document requesting registration.
(2) Two copies, including one certified copy, of the determination sought to be registered, and a statement under penalty of perjury that to the best of the knowledge and belief of the person seeking registration the order has not been modified.
(3) Except as otherwise provided in Section 3429, the name and address of the person seeking registration and any parent or person acting as a parent who has been awarded custody or visitation in the child custody determination sought to be registered.

(b) On receipt of the documents required by subdivision (a), the registering court shall do both of the following:

(1) Cause the determination to be filed as a foreign judgment, together with one copy of any accompanying documents and information, regardless of their form.

(2) Serve notice upon the persons named pursuant to paragraph (3) of subdivision (a) and provide them with an opportunity to contest the registration in accordance with this section.

(c) The notice required by paragraph (2) of subdivision (b) shall state all of the following:

(1) That a registered determination is enforceable as of the date of the registration in the same manner as a determination issued by a court of this state.

(2) That a hearing to contest the validity of the registered determination must be requested within 20 days after service of the notice.

(3) That failure to contest the registration will result in confirmation of the child custody determination and preclude further contest of that determination with respect to any matter that could have been asserted.

(d) A person seeking to contest the validity of a registered order must request a hearing within 20 days after service of the notice. At that hearing, the court shall confirm the registered order unless the person contesting registration establishes any of the following:

(1) That the issuing court did not have jurisdiction under Chapter 2 (commencing with Section 3421).

(2) That the child custody determination sought to be registered has been vacated, stayed, or modified by a court having jurisdiction to do so under Chapter 2 (commencing with Section 3421).

(3) That the person contesting registration was entitled to notice, but notice was not given in accordance with the standards of Section 3408, in the proceedings before the court that issued the order for which registration is sought.

(e) If a timely request for a hearing to contest the validity of the registration is not made, the registration is confirmed as a matter of law and the person requesting registration and all persons served shall be notified of the confirmation.

(f) Confirmation of a registered order, whether by operation of law or after notice and hearing, precludes further contest of the order with respect to any matter that could have been asserted at the time of registration.[76]

3446. (a) A court of this state may grant any relief normally available under the law of this state to enforce a registered child custody determination made by a court of another state.

(b) A court of this state shall recognize and enforce, but may not modify, except in accordance with Chapter 2 (commencing with Section 3421), a registered child custody determination of a court of another state.[76]

3447. If a proceeding for enforcement under this chapter is commenced in a court of this state and the court determines that a proceeding to modify the determination is pending in a court of another state having jurisdiction to modify the determination under Chapter 2 (commencing with Section 3421), the enforcing court shall immediately communicate with the modifying court. The proceeding for enforcement continues unless the enforcing court, after consultation with the modifying court, stays or dismisses the proceeding.[76]

3448. (a) A petition under this chapter must be verified. Certified copies of all orders sought to be enforced and of any order confirming registration must be attached to the petition. A copy of a certified copy of an order may be attached instead of the original.

(b) A petition for enforcement of a child custody determination must state all of the following:

(1) Whether the court that issued the determination identified the jurisdictional basis it relied upon in exercising jurisdiction and, if so, what the basis was.

(2) Whether the determination for which enforcement is sought has been vacated, stayed, or modified by a court whose decision must be enforced under this part and, if so, identify the court, the case number, and the nature of the proceeding.

(3) Whether any proceeding has been commenced that could affect the current proceeding, including proceedings relating to domestic violence, protective orders, termination of parental rights, and adoptions and, if so, identify the court, the case number, and the nature of the proceeding.

(4) The present physical address of the child and the respondent, if known.

(5) Whether relief in addition to the immediate physical custody of the child and attorney's fees is sought, including a request for assistance from law enforcement officials and, if so, the relief sought.

(6) If the child custody determination has been registered and confirmed under Section 3445, the date and place of registration.

(c) Upon the filing of a petition, the court shall issue an order directing the respondent to appear in person with or without the child at a hearing and may enter any order necessary to ensure the safety of the parties and the child. The hearing must be held on the next judicial day after service of the order unless that date is impossible. In that event, the court shall hold the hearing on the first judicial day possible. The court may extend the date of hearing at the request of the petitioner.

(d) An order issued under subdivision (c) must state the time and place of the hearing and advise the respondent that, at the hearing, the court will order that the petitioner may take immediate physical custody of the child and the payment of fees, costs, and expenses under Section 3452, and may schedule a hearing to determine whether further relief is appropriate, unless the respondent appears and establishes either of the following:

(1) That the child custody determination has not been registered and confirmed under Section 3445 and all of the following are true:

(A) The issuing court did not have jurisdiction under Chapter 2 (commencing with Section 3421).

(B) The child custody determination for which enforcement is sought has been vacated, stayed, or modified by a court having jurisdiction to do so under Chapter 2 (commencing with

Section 3421).

(C) The respondent was entitled to notice, but notice was not given in accordance with the standards of Section 3408, in the proceedings before the court that issued the order for which enforcement is sought.

(2) That the child custody determination for which enforcement is sought was registered and confirmed under Section 3445, but has been vacated, stayed, or modified by a court of a state having jurisdiction to do so under Chapter 2 (commencing with Section 3421).

3449. Except as otherwise provided in Section 3451, the petition and order shall be served, by any method authorized by the law of this state, upon the respondent and any person who has physical custody of the child.[76]

3450. (a) Unless the court issues a temporary emergency order pursuant to Section 3424, upon a finding that a petitioner is entitled to immediate physical custody of the child, the court shall order that the petitioner may take immediate physical custody of the child unless the respondent establishes either of the following:

(1) That the child custody determination has not been registered and confirmed under Section 3445 and one of the following is true:

(A) The issuing court did not have jurisdiction under Chapter 2 (commencing with Section 3421).

(B) The child custody determination for which enforcement is sought has been vacated, stayed, or modified by a court of a state having jurisdiction to do so under Chapter 2 (commencing with Section 3421).

(C) The respondent was entitled to notice, but notice was not given in accordance with the standards of Section 3408, in the proceedings before the court that issued the order for which enforcement is sought.

(2) That the child custody determination for which enforcement is sought was registered and confirmed under Section 3445 but has been vacated, stayed, or modified by a court of a state having jurisdiction to do so under Chapter 2 (commencing with Section 3421).

(b) The court shall award the fees, costs, and expenses authorized under Section 3452 and may grant additional relief, including a request for the assistance of law enforcement officials, and set a further hearing to determine whether additional relief is appropriate.

(c) If a party called to testify refuses to answer on the ground that the testimony may be self-incriminating, the court may draw an adverse inference from the refusal.

(d) A privilege against disclosure of communications between spouses and a defense of immunity based on the relationship of spouses or parent and child may not be invoked in a proceeding under this chapter.[299]

3451. (a) Upon the filing of a petition seeking enforcement of a child custody determination, the petitioner may file a verified application for the issuance of a warrant to take physical custody of the child if the child is imminently likely to suffer serious physical harm or be removed from this state.

(b) If the court, upon the testimony of the petitioner or other witness, finds that the child is imminently likely to suffer serious physical harm or be removed from this state, it may issue a warrant to take physical custody of the child. The petition must be heard on the next judicial day after the warrant is executed unless that date is impossible. In that event, the court shall hold the hearing on the first judicial day possible. The application for the warrant must include the statements required by subdivision (b) of Section 3448.

(c) A warrant to take physical custody of a child must do all of the following:

(1) Recite the facts upon which a conclusion of imminent serious physical harm or removal from the jurisdiction is based.

(2) Direct law enforcement officers to take physical custody of the child immediately.

(3) Provide for the placement of the child pending final relief.

(d) The respondent must be served with the petition, warrant, and order immediately after the child is taken into physical custody.

(e) A warrant to take physical custody of a child is enforceable throughout this state. If the court finds on the basis of the testimony of the petitioner or other witness that a less intrusive remedy is not effective, it may authorize law enforcement officers to enter private property to take physical custody of the child. If required by exigent circumstances of the case, the court may authorize law enforcement officers to make a forcible entry at any hour.

(f) The court may impose conditions upon placement of a child to ensure the appearance of the child and the child's custodian.[76]

3452. (a) The court shall award the prevailing party, including a state, necessary and reasonable expenses incurred by or on behalf of the party, including costs, communication expenses, attorney's fees, investigative fees, expenses for witnesses, travel expenses, and child care during the course of the proceedings, unless the party from whom fees or expenses are sought establishes that the award would be clearly inappropriate.

(b) The court may not assess fees, costs, or expenses against a state unless authorized by law other than this part.[76]

3453. A court of this state shall accord full faith and credit to an order issued by another state, and consistent with this part, enforce a child custody determination by a court of another state unless the order has been vacated, stayed, or modified by a court having jurisdiction to do so under Chapter 2 (commencing with Section 3421).[76]

3453.5. (a) A law of another state that authorizes a state agency to remove a child from their parent or guardian based on the parent or guardian allowing their child to receive gender-affirming health care or gender-affirming mental health care is against the public policy of this state and shall not be enforced or applied in a case pending in a court in this state.

(b) For the purpose of this subdivision, "gender-affirming health care" and "gender-affirming mental health care" shall have the same meaning as provided in Section 16010.2 of the Welfare and Institutions Code.[528]

3454. An appeal may be taken from a final order in a proceeding under this chapter in accordance with expedited appellate procedures in other civil cases. Unless the court enters a temporary emergency order under Section 3424, the enforcing court may not stay an order enforcing a child custody determination pending appeal.[76]

3455. (a) In a case arising under this part or involving the Hague Convention on the Civil Aspects of International Child Abduction, a district attorney is authorized to proceed pursuant to Chapter 8 (commencing with Section 3130) of Part 2.
(b) A district attorney acting under this section acts on behalf of the court and may not represent any party.[76]

3456. At the request of a district attorney acting under Section 3455, a law enforcement officer may take any lawful action reasonably necessary to locate a child or a party and assist the district attorney with responsibilities under Section 3455.[76]

3457. The court may assess all direct expenses and costs incurred by a district attorney under Section 3455 or 3456 pursuant to the provisions of Section 3134.[76]

Chapter 4: Miscellaneous Provisions

3461. In applying and construing this Uniform Child Custody Jurisdiction and Enforcement Act, consideration shall be given to the need to promote uniformity of the law with respect to its subject matter among states that enact it.[76]

3462. If any provision of this part or its application to any person or circumstance is held invalid, the invalidity does not affect other provisions or applications of this part that can be given effect without the invalid provision or application, and to this end the provisions of this part are severable.[76]

3465. A motion or other request for relief made in a child custody proceeding or to enforce a child custody determination that was commenced before the effective date of this part is governed by the law in effect at the time the motion or other request was made.[76]

DIVISION 9: SUPPORT

ENACTED BY STATS. 1992, CH. 162, SEC. 10.
SECTION 3500 - 5700.905

PART 1: DEFINITIONS AND GENERAL PROVISIONS

enacted by Stats. 1992, Ch. 162, Sec. 10.

Chapter 1: Definitions

3500. Unless the provision or context otherwise requires, the definitions in this chapter govern the construction of this division.[1]

3515. "Separate property" does not include quasi-community property.[1]

Chapter 2: General Provisions

3550. (a) As used in this section:
(1) "Obligee" means a person to whom a duty of support is owed.
(2) "Obligor" means a person who owes a duty of support.
(b) An obligor present or resident in this state has the duty of support as defined in Sections 3900, 3901, 3910, 4300, and 4400, regardless of the presence or residence of the obligee.[1]

3551. Laws attaching a privilege against the disclosure of communications between spouses are inapplicable under this division. Spouses are competent witnesses to testify to any relevant matter, including marriage and parentage.[300]

3552. (a) In a proceeding involving child, family, or spousal support, no party to the proceeding may refuse to submit copies of the party's state and federal income tax returns to the court, whether individual or joint.
(b) The tax returns may be examined by the other party and are discoverable by the other party. A party also may be examined by the other party as to the contents of a tax return submitted pursuant to this section.
(c) If the court finds that it is relevant to the case to retain the tax return, the tax return shall be sealed and maintained as a confidential record of the court. If the court finds that the tax return is not relevant to disposition of the case, all copies of the tax return shall be returned to the party who submitted it.[1]

3554. An appeal may be taken from an order or judgment under this division as in other civil actions.[1]

3555. Where support is ordered to be paid through the county officer designated by the court on behalf of a child or other party not receiving public assistance pursuant to the Family Economic Security Act of 1982 (Chapter 2 (commencing with Section 11200) of Part 3 of Division 9 of the Welfare and Institutions Code), the designated county officer shall forward the support received to the designated payee within the time standards prescribed by federal law and the Department of Child Support Services.

3556. The existence or enforcement of a duty of support owed by a noncustodial parent for the support of a minor child is not affected by a failure or refusal by the custodial parent to implement any rights as to custody or visitation granted by a court to the noncustodial parent.[1]

3557. (a) Notwithstanding any other provision of law, absent good cause to the contrary, the court, in order to ensure that each party has access to legal representation to preserve each party's rights, upon determining (1) an award of attorney's fees and cost under this section is appropriate, (2) there is a disparity in access to funds to retain counsel, and (3) one party is able to pay for legal representation for both parties, shall award reasonable attorney's fees to any of the following persons:

(1) A custodial parent or other person to whom payments should be made in any action to enforce any of the following:

(A) An existing order for child support.

(B) A penalty incurred pursuant to Chapter 5 (commencing with Section 4720) of Part 5 of Division 9.

(2) A supported spouse in an action to enforce an existing order for spousal support.

(b) This section shall not be construed to allow an award of attorney's fees to or against a governmental entity.[208]

3558. In a proceeding involving child or family support, a court may require either parent to attend job training, job placement and vocational rehabilitation, and work programs, as designated by the court, at regular intervals and times and for durations specified by the court, and provide documentation of participation in the programs, in a format that is acceptable to the court, in order to enable the court to make a finding that good faith attempts at job training and placement have been undertaken by the parent.[60]

Chapter 3: Support Agreements

Article 1: General Provisions

3580. Subject to this chapter and to Section 3651, spouses may agree, in writing, to an immediate separation, and may provide in the agreement for the support of either of them and of their children during the separation or upon the dissolution of their marriage. The mutual consent of the parties is sufficient consideration for the agreement.[301]

Article 2: Child Support

3585. The provisions of an agreement between the parents for child support shall be deemed to be separate and severable from all other provisions of the agreement relating to property and support of either spouse. An order for child support based on the agreement shall be imposed by law and shall be made under the power of the court to order child support.[302]

3586. If an agreement between the parents combines child support and spousal support without designating the amount to be paid for child support and the amount to be paid for spousal support, the court is not required to make a separate order for child support.[1]

3587. Notwithstanding any other provision of law, the court has the authority to approve a stipulated agreement by the parents to pay for the support of an adult child or for the continuation of child support after a child attains the age of 18 years and to make a support order to effectuate the agreement.[1]

Article 3: Spousal Support

3590. The provisions of an agreement for support of either party shall be deemed to be separate and severable from the provisions of the agreement relating to property. An order for support of either party based on the agreement shall be law-imposed and shall be made under the power of the court to order spousal support.[1]

3591. (a) Except as provided in subdivisions (b) and (c), the provisions of an agreement for the support of either party are subject to subsequent modification or termination by court order.
(b) An agreement may not be modified or terminated as to an amount that accrued before the date of the filing of the notice of motion or order to show cause to modify or terminate.
(c) An agreement for spousal support may not be modified or revoked to the extent that a written agreement, or, if there is no written agreement, an oral agreement entered into in open court between the parties, specifically provides that the spousal support is not subject to modification or termination.[1]

3592. If an obligation under an agreement for settlement of property to a spouse or for support of a spouse is discharged in bankruptcy, the court may make all proper orders for the support of the spouse, as the court determines are just, having regard for the circumstances of the parties and the amount of the obligations under the agreement that are discharged.[1]

3593. Sections 3590 and 3591 are effective only with respect to a property settlement agreement entered into on or after January 1, 1970, and do not affect an agreement entered into before January 1, 1970, as to which Chapter 1308 of the Statutes of 1967 shall apply.[1]

Chapter 4: Spousal and Child Support During Pendency of Proceeding

3600. During the pendency of any proceeding for dissolution of marriage or for legal separation of the parties or under Division 8 (commencing with Section 3000) (custody of children) or in any proceeding where there is at issue the support of a minor child or a child for whom support is authorized under Section 3901 or 3910, the court may order (a) either spouse to pay any amount that is necessary for the support of the other spouse, consistent with the requirements of subdivisions (i) and (m) of Section 4320 and Section 4325, or (b) either or both parents to pay any amount necessary for the support of the child, as the case may be.[303]

3601. (a) An order for child support entered pursuant to this chapter continues in effect until the order (1) is terminated by the court or (2) terminates by operation of law pursuant to Sections 3900, 3901, 4007, and 4013.
(b) Subject to Section 3602, subdivision (a) applies notwithstanding any other provision of law and notwithstanding that the proceeding has not been brought to trial within the time limits specified in Chapter 1.5 (commencing with Section 583.110) of Title 8 of Part 2 of the Code of Civil Procedure.[31]

3602. Unless the order specifies

otherwise, an order made pursuant to this chapter is not enforceable during any period in which the parties have reconciled and are living together.[1]

3603. An order made pursuant to this chapter may be modified or terminated at any time except as to an amount that accrued before the date of the filing of the notice of motion or order to show cause to modify or terminate.[1]

3604. An order made pursuant to this chapter does not prejudice the rights of the parties or the child with respect to any subsequent order which may be made.[1]

Chapter 6: Modification, Termination, or Set Aside of Support Orders

Article 1: General Provisions

3650. Unless the provision or context otherwise requires, as used in this chapter, "support order" means a child, family, or spousal support order.

3651. (a) Except as provided in subdivisions (c) and (d) and subject to Article 3 (commencing with Section 3680) and Sections 3552, 3587, and 4004, a support order may be modified or terminated at any time as the court determines to be necessary.
(b) Upon the filing of a supplemental complaint pursuant to Section 2330.1, a child support order in the original proceeding may be modified in conformity with the statewide uniform guideline for child support to provide for the support of all of the children of the same parents who were named in the initial and supplemental pleadings, to consolidate arrearages and wage assignments for children of the parties, and to consolidate orders for support.
(c) (1) Except as provided in paragraph (2) and subdivision (b), a support order may not be modified or terminated as to an amount that accrued before the date of the filing of the notice of motion or order to show cause to modify or terminate.
(2) If a party to a support order is activated to United States military duty or National Guard service and deployed out of state, the servicemember may file and serve a notice of activation of military service and request to modify a support order, in lieu of a notice of motion or order to show cause, by informing the court and the other party of the request to modify the support order based on the change in circumstance. The servicemember shall indicate the date of deployment and, if possible, the court shall schedule the hearing prior to that date. If the court cannot hear the matter prior to the date of deployment out of state, and the servicemember complies with the conditions set forth in the Servicemembers Civil Relief Act, Section 522 of the Appendix of Title 50 of the United States Code, the court shall grant a stay of proceedings consistent with the timelines for stays set forth in that section. If, after granting the mandatory stay required by Section 522 of the Appendix of Title 50 of the United States Code, the court fails to grant the discretionary stay described under the law, it shall comply with the federal mandate to appoint counsel to represent the interests of the deployed servicemember. The court may not proceed with the matter if it does not appoint counsel, unless the servicemember is represented by

other counsel. If the court stays the proceeding until after the return of the service member, the servicemember shall request the court to set the matter for hearing within 90 days of return from deployment or the matter shall be taken off calendar and the existing order may not be made retroactive pursuant to subdivision (c) of Section 3653.

(3) A servicemember who does not file a notice of activation of military service and request to modify a support order or order to show cause or notice of motion prior to deployment out of state nonetheless shall not be subject to penalties otherwise authorized by Chapter 5 (commencing with Section 4720) of Part 5 on the amount of child support that would not have accrued if the order had been modified pursuant to paragraph (2), absent a finding by the court of good cause. Any such finding shall be stated on the record.

(4) Notwithstanding any other law, interest shall not accrue on that amount of a child support obligation that would not have become due and owing if the activated servicemember modified the support order upon activation to reflect the change in income due to the activation. Upon a finding by the court that good cause did not exist for the servicemember's failure to seek, or delay in seeking, the modification, interest shall accrue as otherwise allowed by law.

(d) An order for spousal support may not be modified or terminated to the extent that a written agreement or, if there is no written agreement, an oral agreement entered into in open court between the parties, specifically provides that the spousal support is not subject to modification or termination.

(e) This section applies whether or not the support order is based upon an agreement between the parties.

(f) This section is effective only with respect to a property settlement agreement entered into on or after January 1, 1970, and does not affect an agreement entered into before January 1, 1970, as to which Chapter 1308 of the Statutes of 1967 shall apply.

(g) (1) The Judicial Council, no later than 90 days after the effective date of the act adding this section, shall develop forms and procedures necessary to implement paragraph (2) of subdivision (c). The Judicial Council shall ensure that all forms adopted pursuant to this section are in plain language.

(2) The form developed by the Judicial Council, in addition to other items the Judicial Council determines to be necessary or appropriate, shall include the following:

(A) The date of deployment and all information relevant to the determination of the amount of child support, including whether the servicemember's employer will supplement the servicemember's income during the deployment.

(B) A notice informing the opposing party that, absent a finding of good cause, the order will be made retroactive to the date of service of the form or the date of deployment, whichever is later.

(C) Notice that the requesting party must notify the court and the other party upon return from military duty and seek to bring any unresolved request for modification to hearing within 90 days of return, or else lose the right to modify the order pursuant to this section. [441]

3652. Except as against a governmental agency, an order modifying, terminating, or setting aside a support order may include an award of attorney's fees and court costs to the prevailing party.

3653. (a) An order modifying or terminating a support order may be made retroactive to the date of the filing of the notice of motion or order to show cause to modify or terminate, or to any subsequent date, except as provided in subdivision (b) or by federal law (42 U.S.C. Sec. 666(a)(9)).
(b) If an order modifying or terminating a support order is entered due to the unemployment of either the support obligor or the support obligee, the order shall be made retroactive to the later of the date of the service on the opposing party of the notice of motion or order to show cause to modify or terminate or the date of unemployment, subject to the notice requirements of federal law (42 U.S.C. Sec. 666(a)(9)), unless the court finds good cause not to make the order retroactive and states its reasons on the record.
(c) If an order modifying or terminating a support order is entered due to a change in income resulting from the activation to United States military service or National Guard duty and deployment out of state for either the support obligor or the support obligee, the order shall be made retroactive to the later of the date of the service on the opposing party of the notice of activation, notice of motion, order to show cause to modify or terminate, or the date of activation, subject to the notice requirements of federal law (42 U.S.C. Sec. 666(a)(9)), unless the court finds good cause not to make the order retroactive and states its reasons on the record. Good cause shall include, but not be limited to, a finding by the court that the delay in seeking the modification was not reasonable under the circumstances faced by the service member.
(d) If an order decreasing or terminating a support order is entered retroactively pursuant to this section, the support obligor may be entitled to, and the support obligee may be ordered to repay, according to the terms specified in the order, any amounts previously paid by the support obligor pursuant to the prior order that are in excess of the amounts due pursuant to the retroactive order. The court may order that the repayment by the support obligee shall be made over any period of time and in any manner, including, but not limited to, by an offset against future support payments or wage assignment, as the court deems just and reasonable. In determining whether to order a repayment, and in establishing the terms of repayment, the court shall consider all of the following factors:
(1) The amount to be repaid.
(2) The duration of the support order prior to modification or termination.
(3) The financial impact on the support obligee of any particular method of repayment such as an offset against future support payments or wage assignment.
(4) Any other facts or circumstances that the court deems relevant. [118]

3654. At the request of either party, an order modifying, terminating, or setting aside a support order shall include a statement of decision.

Article 2: Discovery Before Commencing Modification or Termination Proceeding

3660. The purpose of this article is to permit inexpensive discovery of facts before the commencement of a proceeding for modification or termination of an order for child, family, or spousal support.[1]

3662. Methods of discovery other than that described in this article may only be used if a motion for modification or termination of the support order is pending.[1]

3663. In the absence of a pending motion for modification or termination of a support order, a request for discovery pursuant to this article may be undertaken not more frequently than once every 12 months.

3664. (a) At any time following a judgment of dissolution of marriage or legal separation of the parties, or a determination of parentage, that provides for payment of support, either the party ordered to pay support or the party to whom support was ordered to be paid or that party's assignee, without leave of court, may serve a request on the other party for the production of a completed current income and expense declaration in the form adopted by the Judicial Council.
(b) If there is no response within 35 days of service of the request or if the responsive income and expense declaration is incomplete as to any wage information, including the attachment of pay stubs and income tax returns, the requesting party may serve a request on the employer of the other party for information limited to the income and benefits provided to the party in the form adopted by the Judicial Council. The employer may require the requesting party to pay the reasonable costs of copying this information for the requesting party. The date specified in the request served on the employer for the production of income and benefit information shall not be less than 15 days from the date this request is issued.
(c) The requesting party shall serve or cause to be served on the employee described in this section, or on the employee's attorney, a copy of the request served on the employer prior to the date specified in the request served on the employer for the production of income and benefit information. This copy shall be accompanied by a notice, in a typeface that is intended to call attention to its terms, that indicates all of the following:
(1) That information limited to the income and benefits provided to the employee by the employer is being sought from the employer named in the request for production.
(2) That the information may be protected by right of privacy.
(3) That, if the employee objects to the production of this information by the employer to the requesting party, the employee shall notify the court, in writing, of this objection prior to the date specified in the request served on the employer for the production of income and benefit information.
(4) That, if the requesting party does not agree, in writing, to cancel or narrow the scope of the request for the production of this information by the employer, the employee should

consult an attorney regarding the employee's right to privacy and how to protect this right.

(d) The employee described in this section may, prior to the date specified in the request served on the employer for the production of income and benefit information, bring a motion pursuant to Section 1987.1 of the Code of Civil Procedure to quash or modify this request in the same manner as a subpoena duces tecum. Notice of this motion shall be given to the employer prior to the date specified in the request served on the employer for the production of income and benefit information. An employer is not required to produce information limited to the income and benefits of the employee, except upon order of the court or upon agreement of the parties, employers, and employee affected.

(e) Service of a request for production of an income and expense declaration or for income and benefit information pursuant to this section or a copy thereof shall be by certified mail, postage prepaid, return receipt requested, to the last known address of the party to be served, or by personal service.

(f) The form adopted by the Judicial Council for purposes of the request on an employer described in subdivision (b) shall state that compliance with the request is voluntary, except upon order of the court or upon agreement of the parties, employers, and employee affected.[442]

3665. (a) A copy of the prior year's federal and state personal income tax returns shall be attached to the income and expense declaration of each party.

(b) A party shall not disclose the contents or provide copies of the other party's tax returns to anyone except the court, the party's attorney, the party's accountant, or other financial consultant assisting with matters relating to the proceeding, or any other person permitted by the court.

(c) The tax returns shall be controlled by the court as provided in Section 3552.[1]

3666. This article may be enforced in the manner specified in Sections 1991, 1991.1, 1991.2, 1992, and 1993 of the Code of Civil Procedure and in the Civil Discovery Act (Title 4 (commencing with Section 2016.010) of Part 4 of the Code of Civil Procedure), and any other statutes applicable to the enforcement of procedures for discovery.[117]

3667. Upon the subsequent filing of a motion for modification or termination of the support order by the requesting party, if the court finds that the income and expense declaration submitted by the responding party pursuant to this article was incomplete, inaccurate, or missing the prior year's federal and state personal income tax returns, or that the declaration was not submitted in good faith, the court may order sanctions against the responding party in the form of payment of all costs of the motion, including the filing fee and the costs of the depositions and subpoenas necessary to be utilized in order to obtain complete and accurate information. This section is applicable regardless of whether a party has utilized subdivision (b) of Section 3664.[57]

3668. The Judicial Council shall adopt forms which shall be used in the procedure provided by this article.[1]

Article 3: Simplified Procedure for Modification of Support Order

3680. (a) The Legislature finds and declares the following:

(1) There is currently no simple method available to parents to quickly modify their support orders when circumstances warrant a change in the amount of support.

(2) The lack of a simple method for parents to use to modify support orders has led to orders in which the amount of support ordered is inappropriate based on the parents' financial circumstances.

(3) Parents should not have to incur significant costs or experience significant delays in obtaining an appropriate support order.

(b) Therefore, it is the intent of the Legislature that the Judicial Council adopt rules of court and forms for a simplified method to modify support orders. This simplified method should be designed to be used by parents who are not represented by counsel.[63]

3680.5. (a) The local child support agency shall monitor child support cases and seek modifications, when needed.

(b) At least once every three years, the local child support agency shall review, and, if appropriate, seek modification of, each child support case for which assistance is being provided under the CalWORKs program, pursuant to Chapter 2 (commencing with Section 11200) of Part 3 of Division 9 of the Welfare and Institutions Code.[175]

Article 4: Relief From Orders

3690. (a) The court may, on any terms that may be just, relieve a party from a support order, or any part or parts thereof, after the six-month time limit of Section 473 of the Code of Civil Procedure has run, based on the grounds, and within the time limits, provided in this article.

(b) In all proceedings under this division, before granting relief, the court shall find that the facts alleged as the grounds for relief materially affected the original order and that the moving party would materially benefit from the granting of the relief.

(c) Nothing in this article shall limit or modify the provisions of Section 17432 or 17433.

(d) This section shall only be operative if Assembly Bill 196, of the 1999–2000 Regular Session, is enacted and becomes operative.

3691. The grounds and time limits for an action or motion to set aside a support order, or part thereof, are governed by this section and shall be one of the following:

(a) Actual fraud. Where the defrauded party was kept in ignorance or in some other manner, other than through the party's own lack of care or attention, was fraudulently prevented from fully participating in the proceeding. An action or motion based on fraud shall be brought within six months after the date on which the complaining party discovered or reasonably should have discovered the fraud.

(b) Perjury. An action or motion based on perjury shall be brought within six months after the date on which the complaining party discovered or reasonably should have discovered the perjury.

(c) Lack of Notice.

(1) When service of a summons has not resulted in notice to a party in time to defend the action for support and a default or default judgment has been entered against the party in the action, the party may serve and file a notice of motion to set aside the default and for leave to defend the action. The notice of motion shall be served and filed within a reasonable time, but in no event later than six months after the party obtains or reasonably should have obtained notice (A) of the support order, or (B) that the party's income and assets are subject to attachment pursuant to the order.

(2) A notice of motion to set aside a support order pursuant to this subdivision shall be accompanied by an affidavit showing, under oath, that the party's lack of notice in time to defend the action was not caused by avoidance of service or inexcusable neglect. The party shall serve and file with the notice a copy of the answer, motion, or other pleading proposed to be filed in the action.

(3) The court may not set aside or otherwise relieve a party from a support order pursuant to this subdivision if service of the summons was accomplished in accordance with existing requirements of law regarding service of process. [443]

3692. Notwithstanding any other provision of this article, or any other law, a support order may not be set aside simply because the court finds that it was inequitable when made, nor simply because subsequent circumstances caused the support ordered to become excessive or inadequate.

3693. When ruling on an action or motion to set aside a support order, the court shall set aside only those provisions materially affected by the circumstances leading to the court's decision to grant relief. However, the court has discretion to set aside the entire order, if necessary, for equitable considerations.

Chapter 7: Health Insurance

Article 1: Health Insurance Coverage for Supported Child

3750. "Health insurance coverage" as used in this article includes all of the following:

(a) Vision care and dental care coverage whether the vision care or dental care coverage is part of existing health insurance coverage or is issued as a separate policy or plan.

(b) Provision for the delivery of health care services by a fee for service, health maintenance organization, preferred provider organization, or any other type of health care delivery system under which medical services could be provided to a dependent child of an absent parent.

3751. (a) (1) Support orders issued or modified pursuant to this chapter shall include a provision requiring the child support obligor to keep the agency designated under Title IV-D of the Social Security Act (42 U.S.C. Sec. 651 et seq.) informed of whether the obligor has health insurance coverage at a reasonable cost and, if so, the health insurance policy information.

(2) When an amount is set for current support, the court shall require that health insurance coverage for a supported child shall be maintained

by either or both parents if that insurance is available at no cost or at a reasonable cost to the parent. Health insurance coverage shall be rebuttably presumed to be reasonable in cost if the cost to the responsible parent providing medical support does not exceed 5 percent of the parent's gross income. In applying the 5 percent for the cost of health insurance, the cost is the difference between self-only and family coverage. If the obligor is entitled to a low-income adjustment as provided in paragraph (7) of subdivision (b) of Section 4055, medical support shall be deemed not reasonable, unless the court determines that not requiring medical support would be unjust and inappropriate in the particular case. If the court determines that the cost of health insurance coverage is not reasonable, the court shall state its reasons on the record. If the court determines that, although the obligor is entitled to a low-income adjustment, not requiring medical support would be unjust and inappropriate, the court shall state its reasons on the record.

(b) If the court determines that health insurance coverage is not available at no cost or at a reasonable cost, the court's order for support shall contain a provision that specifies that health insurance coverage shall be obtained if it becomes available at no cost or at a reasonable cost. Upon health insurance coverage at no cost or at a reasonable cost becoming available to a parent, the parent shall apply for that coverage.

(c) The court's order for support shall require the parent who, at the time of the order or subsequently, provides health insurance coverage for a supported child to seek continuation of coverage for the child upon attainment of the limiting age for a dependent child under the health insurance coverage if the child meets the criteria specified under Section 1373 of the Health and Safety Code or Section 10277 or 10278 of the Insurance Code and that health insurance coverage is available at no cost or at a reasonable cost to the parent or parents, as applicable.[444]

3751.5. (a) Notwithstanding any other provision of law, an employer or insurer shall not deny enrollment of a child under the health insurance coverage of a child's parent on any of the following grounds:

(1) The child was born out of wedlock.

(2) The child is not claimed as a dependent on the parent's federal income tax return.

(3) The child does not reside with the parent or within the insurer's service area.

(b) Notwithstanding any other provision of law, in any case in which a parent is required by a court or administrative order to provide health insurance coverage for a child and the parent is eligible for family health coverage through an employer or an insurer, the employer or insurer shall do all of the following, as applicable:

(1) Permit the parent to enroll under health insurance coverage any child who is otherwise eligible to enroll for that coverage, without regard to any enrollment period restrictions.

(2) If the parent is enrolled in health insurance coverage but fails to apply to obtain coverage of the child, enroll that child under the health coverage upon presentation of the court order

or request by the local child support agency, the other parent or person having custody of the child, or the Medi-Cal program.

(3) The employer or insurer shall not disenroll or eliminate coverage of a child unless either of the following applies:

(A) The employer has eliminated family health insurance coverage for all of the employer's employees.

(B) The employer or insurer is provided with satisfactory written evidence that either of the following apply:

(i) The court order or administrative order is no longer in effect or is terminated pursuant to Section 3770.

(ii) The child is or will be enrolled in comparable health insurance coverage through another insurer that will take effect not later than the effective date of the child's disenrollment.

(c) In any case in which health insurance coverage is provided for a child pursuant to a court or administrative order, the insurer shall do all of the following:

(1) Provide any information, including, but not limited to, the health insurance membership or identification card regarding the child, the evidence of coverage and disclosure form, and any other information provided to the covered parent about the child's health care coverage to the noncovered parent having custody of the child or any other person having custody of the child and to the local child support agency when requested by the local child support agency.

(2) Permit the noncovered parent or person having custody of the child, or a provider with the approval of the noncovered parent or person having custody, to submit claims for covered services without the approval of the covered parent.

(3) Make payment on claims sub-mitted in accordance with subparagraph (2) directly to the noncovered parent or person having custody, the provider, or to the Medi-Cal program. Payment on claims for services provided to the child shall be made to the covered parent for claims sub-mitted or paid by the covered parent.

(d) For purposes of this section, "insurer" includes every health care service plan, self-insured welfare benefit plan, including those regulated pursuant to the Employee Retirement Income Security Act of 1974 (29 U.S.C. Sec. 1001, et seq.), self-funded employer plan, disability insurer, nonprofit hospital service plan, labor union trust fund, employer, and any other similar plan, insurer, or entity offering a health coverage plan.

(e) For purposes of this section, "person having custody of the child" is defined as a legal guardian, a caregiver who is authorized to enroll the child in school or to authorize medical care for the child pursuant to Section 6550, or a person with whom the child resides.

(f) For purposes of this section, "employer" has the meaning provided in Section 5210.

(g) For purposes of this section, the insurer shall notify the covered parent and noncovered parent having custody of the child or any other person having custody of the child in writing at any time that health insurance for the child is terminated.

(h) The requirements of subdivision (g) shall not apply unless the court, employer, or person having custody of the child provides the insurer with one of the following:

(1) A qualified medical child support order that meets the requirements of subdivision (a) of Section 1169 of Title 29 of the United States Code.

(2) A health insurance coverage assignment or assignment order made pursuant to Section 3761.

(3) A national medical support notice made pursuant to Section 3773.

(i) The noncovered parent or person having custody of the child may contact the insurer, by telephone or in writing, and request information about the health insurance coverage for the child. Upon request of the noncovered parent or person having custody of the child, the insurer shall provide the requested information that is specific to the health insurance coverage for the child.

3752. (a) If the local child support agency has been designated as the assigned payee for child support, the court shall order the parent to notify the local child support agency upon applying for and obtaining health insurance coverage for the child within a reasonable period of time.

(b) The local child support agency shall obtain a completed medical form from the parent in accordance with Section 17422 and shall forward the completed form to the State Department of Health Services.

(c) In those cases where the local child support agency is providing medical support enforcement services, the local child support agency shall provide the parent or person having custody of the child with information pertaining to the health insurance policy that has been secured for the child.

3752.5. (a) A child support order issued or modified pursuant to this division shall include a provision requiring the child support obligor to keep the obligee informed of whether the obligor has health insurance made available through the obligor's employer or has other group health insurance and, if so, the health insurance policy information. The support obligee under a child support order shall inform the support obligor of whether the obligee has health insurance made available through the employer or other group health insurance and, if so, the health insurance policy information.

(b) A child support order issued or modified pursuant to this division shall include a provision requiring the child support obligor and obligee to provide the information described in subdivision (a) for a child or an adult who meets the criteria for continuation of health insurance coverage upon attaining the limiting age pursuant to Section 1373 of the Health and Safety Code or Section 10277 or 10278 of the Insurance Code.

(c) The Judicial Council shall modify the form of the order for health insurance coverage (family law) to notify child support obligors of the requirements of this section and of Section 3752. Notwithstanding any other provision of law, the Judicial Council shall not be required to modify the form of the order for health insurance coverage (family law) to include the provisions described in subdivision (b) until January 1, 2010.[183]

3753. The cost of the health insurance shall be in addition to the child support amount ordered under Article 2 (commencing with Section 4050), with allowance for the costs of health insurance actually obtained given due consideration under subdivision (d) of Section 4059.

Article 2: Health Insurance Coverage Assignment

3760. As used in this article, unless the provision or context otherwise requires:
(a) "Employer" includes the United States government and any public entity as defined in Section 811.2 of the Government Code.
(b) "Health insurance," "health insurance plan," "health insurance coverage," "health care services," or "health insurance coverage assignment" includes vision care and dental care coverage whether the vision care or dental care coverage is part of existing health insurance coverage or is issued as a separate policy or plan.
(c) "Health insurance coverage assignment" or "assignment order" means an order made under Section 3761.
(d) "National medical support notice" means the notice required by Section 666(a)(19) of Title 42 of the United States Code with respect to an order made pursuant to Section 3773.

3761. (a) Upon application by a party or local child support agency in any proceeding where the court has ordered either or both parents to maintain health insurance coverage under Article 1 (commencing with Section 3750), the court shall order the employer of the obligor parent or other person providing health insurance to the obligor to enroll the supported child in the health insurance plan available to the obligor through the employer or other person and to deduct the appropriate premium or costs, if any, from the earnings of the obligor unless the court makes a finding of good cause for not making the order.
(b) (1) The application shall state that the party or local child support agency seeking the assignment order has given the obligor a written notice of the intent to seek a health insurance coverage assignment order in the event of a default in instituting coverage required by court order on behalf of the parties' child and that the notice was transmitted by first-class mail, postage prepaid, or personally served at least 15 days before the date of the filing of the application for the order. The written notice of the intent to seek an assignment order required by this subdivision may be given at the time of filing a petition or complaint for support or at any later time, but shall be given at least 15 days before the date of filing the application under this section. The obligor may at any time waive the written notice required by this subdivision.
(2) The party or local child support agency seeking the assignment order shall file a certificate of service showing the method and date of service of the order and the statements required under Section 3772 upon the employer or provider of health insurance.
(c) The total amount that may be withheld from earnings for all obligations, including health insurance

assignments, is limited by subdivision (a) of Section 706.052 of the Code of Civil Procedure or Section 1673 of Title 15 of the United States Code, whichever is less.

3762. Good cause for not making a health insurance coverage assignment order shall be limited to either of the following:
(a) The court finds that one of the conditions listed in subdivision (a) of Section 3765 or in Section 3770 exists.
(b) The court finds that the health insurance coverage assignment order would cause extraordinary hardship to the obligor. The court shall specify the nature of the extraordinary hardship and, whenever possible, a date by which the obligor shall obtain health insurance coverage or be subject to a health insurance coverage assignment.

3763. (a) The health insurance coverage assignment order may be ordered at the time of trial or entry of a judgment ordering health insurance coverage. The order operates as an assignment and is binding on any existing or future employer of the obligor parent, or other person providing health insurance to the obligor, upon whom a copy of the order has been served.
(b) The order of assignment may be modified at any time by the court.

3764. (a) A health insurance coverage assignment order does not become effective until 20 days after service by the applicant of the assignment order on the employer.
(b) Within 10 days after service of the order, the employer or other person providing health insurance to the obligor shall deliver a copy of the order to the obligor, together with a written statement of the obligor's rights and the relevant procedures under the law to move to quash the order.
(c) Service of a health insurance coverage assignment order on any employer or other person providing health insurance may be made by first class mail in the manner prescribed in Section 1013 of the Code of Civil Procedure.

3765. (a) The obligor may move to quash a health insurance coverage assignment order as provided in this section if the obligor declares under penalty of perjury that there is error on any of the following grounds:
(1) No order to maintain health insurance has been issued under Article 1 (commencing with Section 3750).
(2) The amount to be withheld for premiums is greater than that permissible under Article 1 (commencing with Section 3750) or greater than the amount otherwise ordered by the court.
(3) The amount of the increased premium is unreasonable.
(4) The alleged obligor is not the obligor from whom health insurance coverage is due.
(5) The child is or will be otherwise provided health care coverage.
(6) The employer's choice of coverage is inappropriate.
(b) The motion and notice of motion to quash the assignment order, including the declaration required by subdivision (a), shall be filed with the court issuing the assignment order within 15 days after delivery of a copy of the order to the obligor pursuant to subdivision (b) of Section 3764. The court clerk shall set the motion for hearing not less than 15 days, nor more

than 30 days, after receipt of the notice of motion. The clerk shall, within five days after receipt of the notice of motion, deliver a copy of the notice of motion to (1) the district attorney personally or by first-class mail, and (2) the applicant and the employer or other person providing health insurance, at the appropriate addresses contained in the application, by first-class mail.

(c) Upon a finding of error described in subdivision (a), the court shall quash the assignment.

3766. (a) The employer, or other person providing health insurance, shall take steps to commence coverage, consistent with the order for the health insurance coverage assignment, within 30 days after service of the assignment order upon the obligor under Section 3764 unless the employer or other person providing health insurance coverage receives an order issued pursuant to Section 3765 to quash the health insurance coverage assignment. The employer, or the person providing health insurance, shall commence coverage at the earliest possible time and, if applicable, consistent with the group plan enrollment rules.

(b) If the obligor has made a selection of health coverage prior to the issuance of the court order, the selection shall not be superseded unless the child to be enrolled in the plan will not be provided benefits or coverage where the child resides or the court order specifically directs other health coverage.

(c) If the obligor has not enrolled in an available health plan, there is a choice of coverage, and the court has not ordered coverage by a specific plan, the employer or other person providing health insurance shall enroll the child in the plan that will provide reasonable benefits or coverage where the child resides. If that coverage is not available, the employer or other person providing health insurance shall, within 20 days, return the assignment order to the attorney or person initiating the assignment.

(d) If an assignment order is served on an employer or other person providing health insurance and no coverage is available for the supported child, the employer or other person shall, within 20 days, return the assignment to the attorney or person initiating the assignment.[92]

3767. The employer or other person providing health insurance shall do all of the following:

(a) Notify the applicant for the assignment order or notice of assignment of the commencement date of the coverage of the child.

(b) Provide evidence of coverage and any information necessary for the child to obtain benefits through the coverage to both parents or the person having custody of the child and to the local child support agency when requested by the local child support agency.

(c) Upon request by the parents or person having custody of the child, provide all forms and other documentation necessary for the purpose of submitting claims to the insurance carrier which the employer or other person providing health insurance usually provides to insureds.

3768. (a) An employer or other person providing health insurance who willfully fails to comply with a valid

health insurance coverage assignment order entered and served on the employer or other person pursuant to this article is liable to the applicant for the amount incurred in health care services that would otherwise have been covered under the insurance policy but for the conduct of the employer or other person that was contrary to the assignment order.
(b) Willful failure of an employer or other person providing health insurance to comply with a health insurance coverage assignment order is punishable as contempt of court under Section 1218 of the Code of Civil Procedure.

3769. No employer shall use a health insurance coverage assignment order as grounds for refusing to hire a person or for discharging or taking disciplinary action against an employee. An employer who violates this section may be assessed a civil penalty of a maximum of five hundred dollars ($500).

3770. Upon notice of motion by the obligor, the court shall terminate a health insurance coverage assignment order if any of the following conditions exist:
(a) A new order has been issued under Article 1 (commencing with Section 3750) that is inconsistent with the existing assignment.
(b) The employer or other person providing health insurance has discontinued that coverage to the obligor.
(c) The court determines that there is good cause, consistent with Section 3762, to terminate the assignment.
(d) The death or emancipation of the child for whom the health insurance has been obtained.

3771. Upon request of the local child support agency the employer shall provide the following information to the local child support agency within 30 days:
(a) The social security number of the absent parent.
(b) The home address of the absent parent.
(c) Whether the absent parent has a health insurance policy and, if so, the policy names and numbers, and the names of the persons covered.
(d) Whether the health insurance policy provides coverage for dependent children of the absent parent who do not reside in the absent parent's home.
(e) If there is a subsequent lapse in health insurance coverage, the employer shall notify the local child support agency, giving the date the coverage ended, the reason for the lapse in coverage and, if the lapse is temporary, the date upon which coverage is expected to resume.

3772. The Judicial Council shall adopt forms for the health insurance coverage assignment required or authorized by this article, including, but not limited to, the application, the order, the statement of the obligor's rights, and an employer's return form which shall include information on the limitations on the total amount that may be withheld from earnings for obligations, including health insurance assignments, under subdivision (a) of Section 706.052 of the Code of Civil Procedure and Section 1673 of Title 15 of the United States Code, and the information required by Section 3771. The parties and child shall be sufficiently identified on the forms by the inclusion of birth dates, social security numbers, and any other information the Judicial Council determines is necessary.

3773. (a) This section applies only to Title IV-D cases where support enforcement services are being provided by the local child support agency pursuant to Section 17400.
(b) After the court has ordered that a parent provide health insurance coverage, the local child support agency shall serve on the employer a national medical support notice in lieu of the health insurance coverage assignment order. The national medical support notice may be combined with the order/notice to withhold income for child support that is authorized by Section 5246.
(c) A national medical support notice shall have the same force and effect as a health insurance coverage assignment order.
(d) The obligor shall have the same right to move to quash or terminate a national medical support notice as provided in this article for a health insurance coverage assignment order.

Chapter 8: Deferred Sale of Home Order

3800. As used in this chapter:
(a) "Custodial parent" means a party awarded physical custody of a child.
(b) "Deferred sale of home order" means an order that temporarily delays the sale and awards the temporary exclusive use and possession of the family home to a custodial parent of a minor child or child for whom support is authorized under Sections 3900 and 3901 or under Section 3910, whether or not the custodial parent has sole or joint custody, in order to minimize the adverse impact of dissolution of marriage or legal separation of the parties on the welfare of the child.
(c) "Resident parent" means a party who has requested or who has already been awarded a deferred sale of home order.[1]

3801. (a) If one of the parties has requested a deferred sale of home order pursuant to this chapter, the court shall first determine whether it is economically feasible to maintain the payments of any note secured by a deed of trust, property taxes, insurance for the home during the period the sale of the home is deferred, and the condition of the home comparable to that at the time of trial.
(b) In making this determination, the court shall consider all of the following:
(1) The resident parent's income.
(2) The availability of spousal support, child support, or both spousal and child support.
(3) Any other sources of funds available to make those payments.
(c) It is the intent of the Legislature, by requiring the determination under this section, to do all of the following:
(1) Avoid the likelihood of possible defaults on the payments of notes and resulting foreclosures.
(2) Avoid inadequate insurance coverage.
(3) Prevent deterioration of the condition of the family home.
(4) Prevent any other circumstance which would jeopardize both parents' equity in the home.[1]

3802. (a) If the court determines pursuant to Section 3801 that it is economically feasible to consider ordering a deferred sale of the family home, the court may grant a deferred sale of home order to a custodial parent if the court determines that the order is necessary in order to minimize the adverse impact of dissolution of marriage or legal separation of the parties on the child.

(b) In exercising its discretion to grant or deny a deferred sale of home order, the court shall consider all of the following:

(1) The length of time the child has resided in the home.

(2) The child's placement or grade in school.

(3) The accessibility and convenience of the home to the child's school and other services or facilities used by and available to the child, including child care.

(4) Whether the home has been adapted or modified to accommodate any physical disabilities of a child or a resident parent in a manner that a change in residence may adversely affect the ability of the resident parent to meet the needs of the child.

(5) The emotional detriment to the child associated with a change in residence.

(6) The extent to which the location of the home permits the resident parent to continue employment.

(7) The financial ability of each parent to obtain suitable housing.

(8) The tax consequences to the parents.

(9) The economic detriment to the nonresident parent in the event of a deferred sale of home order.

(10) Any other factors the court deems just and equitable.[1]

3803. A deferred sale of home order shall state the duration of the order and may include the legal description and assessor's parcel number of the real property which is subject to the order.[1]

3804. A deferred sale of home order may be recorded in the office of the county recorder of the county in which the real property is located.[1]

3806. The court may make an order specifying the parties' respective responsibilities for the payment of the costs of routine maintenance and capital improvements.[1]

3807. Except as otherwise agreed to by the parties in writing, a deferred sale of home order may be modified or terminated at any time at the discretion of the court.[1]

3808. Except as otherwise agreed to by the parties in writing, if the party awarded the deferred sale of home order remarries, or if there is otherwise a change in circumstances affecting the determinations made pursuant to Section 3801 or 3802 or affecting the economic status of the parties or the children on which the award is based, a rebuttable presumption, affecting the burden of proof, is created that further deferral of the sale is no longer an equitable method of minimizing the adverse impact of the dissolution of marriage or legal separation of the parties on the children.[1]

3809. In making an order pursuant to this chapter, the court shall reserve jurisdiction to determine any issues that arise with respect to the deferred sale of home order including, but not limited to, the maintenance of the home and the tax consequences to each party.[1]

3810. This chapter is applicable

regardless of whether the deferred sale of home order is made before or after January 1, 1989.[1]

Chapter 9: Software Used to Determine Support

3830. (a) On and after January 1, 1994, no court shall use any computer software to assist in determining the appropriate amount of child support or spousal support obligations, unless the software conforms to rules of court adopted by the Judicial Council prescribing standards for the software, which shall ensure that it performs in a manner consistent with the applicable statutes and rules of court for determination of child support or spousal support.
(b) The Judicial Council may contract with an outside agency or organization to analyze software to ensure that it conforms to the standards established by the Judicial Council. The cost of this analysis shall be paid by the applicant software producers and fees therefor shall be established by the Judicial Council in an amount that in the aggregate will defray its costs of administering this section.

PART 2: CHILD SUPPORT

enacted by Stats. 1992, Ch. 162, Sec. 10.

Chapter 1: Duty of parent to Support Child

Article 1: Support Minor Child

3900. Subject to this division, the father and mother of a minor child have an equal responsibility to support their child in the manner suitable to the child's circumstances.[1]

3901. (a) (1) The duty of support imposed by Section 3900 continues as to an unmarried child who has attained 18 years of age, is a full-time high school student, unless excused pursuant to paragraph (2), and who is not self-supporting, until the time the child completes the 12th grade or attains 19 years of age, whichever occurs first.
(2) A child is excused from the requirement to be a full-time high school student for purposes of paragraph (1) if the child has a medical condition documented by a physician that prevents full-time school attendance.
(b) This section does not limit a parent's ability to agree to provide additional support or the court's power to inquire whether an agreement to provide additional support has been made.[377]

3902. The court may direct that an allowance be made to the parent of a child for whom support may be ordered out of the child's property for the child's past or future support, on conditions that are proper, if the direction is for the child's benefit.

Article 2: Support of Adult Child

3910. (a) Each parent of a child has an equal responsibility to maintain, to the extent of their ability, their child of whatever age who is incapacitated from earning a living and without sufficient means.
(b) The court may order that a support payment be paid to a special needs trust. For purposes of this section, "special needs trust" means a trust that meets the requirements described in subparagraph (A) or (C) of paragraph (4) of subsection (d) of Section 1396p

of Title 42 of the United States Code and paragraph (3) or (4) of subdivision (a) of Section 50489.9 of Title 22 of the California Code of Regulations.
(c) This section does not limit the duty of support under Sections 3900 and 3901.[607]

Article 3: Support of Grandchildren

3930. A parent does not have the duty to support a child of the parent's child.

Article 4: Liability to Others Who Provide Support for Child

3950. If a parent neglects to provide articles necessary for the parent's child who is under the charge of the parent, according to the circumstances of the parent, a third person may in good faith supply the necessaries and recover their reasonable value from the parent.[1]

3951. (a) A parent is not bound to compensate the other parent, or a relative, for the voluntary support of the parent's child, without an agreement for compensation.
(b) A parent is not bound to compensate a stranger for the support of a child who has abandoned the parent without just cause.
(c) Nothing in this section relieves a parent of the obligation to support a child during any period in which the state, county, or other governmental entity provides support for the child.[1]

3952. If a parent chargeable with the support of a child dies leaving the child chargeable to the county or leaving the child confined in a state institution to be cared for in whole or in part at the expense of the state, and the parent leaves an estate sufficient for the child's support, the supervisors of the county or the director of the state department having jurisdiction over the institution may claim provision for the child's support from the parent's estate, and for this purpose has the same remedies as a creditor against the estate of the parent and may obtain reimbursement from the successor of the deceased parent to the extent provided in Division 8 (commencing with Section 13000) of the Probate Code.[1]

Chapter 2: Court-Ordered Child Support

Article 1: General provisions

4000. If a parent has the duty to provide for the support of the parent's child and willfully fails to so provide, the other parent, or the child by a guardian ad litem, may bring an action against the parent to enforce the duty.[1]

4001. In any proceeding where there is at issue the support of a minor child or a child for whom support is authorized under Section 3901 or 3910, the court may order either or both parents to pay an amount necessary for the support of the child.[1]

4002. (a) The county may proceed on behalf of a child to enforce the child's right of support against a parent.
(b) If the county furnishes support to a child, the county has the same right as the child to secure reimbursement and obtain continuing support. The right of the county to reimbursement is subject to any limitation otherwise imposed by the law of this state.
(c) The court may order the parent to pay the county reasonable attorney's fees and court costs in a proceeding brought by the county pursuant to this

section.[1]

4003. In any case in which the support of a child is at issue, the court may, upon a showing of good cause, order a separate trial on that issue. The separate trial shall be given preference over other civil cases, except matters to which special precedence may be given by law, for assigning a trial date. If the court has also ordered a separate trial on the issue of custody pursuant to Section 3023, the two issues shall be tried together.

4004. In a proceeding where there is at issue the support of a child, the court shall require the parties to reveal whether a party is currently receiving, or intends to apply for, public assistance under the Family Economic Security Act of 1982 (Chapter 2 (commencing with Section 11200) of Part 3 of Division 9 of the Welfare and Institutions Code) for the maintenance of the child.

4005. At the request of either party, the court shall make appropriate findings with respect to the circumstances on which the order for support of a child is based.

4006. In a proceeding for child support under this code, including, but not limited to, Division 17 (commencing with Section 17000), the court shall consider the health insurance coverage, if any, of the parties to the proceeding.

4007. (a) If a court orders a person to make specified payments for support of a child during the child's minority, or until the child is married or otherwise emancipated, or until the death of, or the occurrence of a specified event as to, a child for whom support is authorized under Section 3901 or 3910, the obligation of the person ordered to pay support terminates on the happening of the contingency. The court may, in the original order for support, order the custodial parent or other person to whom payments are to be made to notify the person ordered to make the payments, or the person's attorney of record, of the happening of the contingency.

(b) If the custodial parent or other person having physical custody of the child, to whom payments are to be made, fails to notify the person ordered to make the payments, or the attorney of record of the person ordered to make the payments, of the happening of the contingency and continues to accept support payments, the person shall refund all moneys received that accrued after the happening of the contingency, except that the overpayments shall first be applied to any support payments that are then in default.[1]

4007.5. (a) Every money judgment or order for support of a child shall be suspended, by operation of law, for any period exceeding 90 consecutive days in which the person ordered to pay support is incarcerated or involuntarily institutionalized, unless the person owing support has the means to pay support while incarcerated or involuntarily institutionalized.

(b) (1) The child support obligation shall be suspended effective on the first day of the first full month of incarceration or involuntary institutionalization.

(2) For persons owing support who are released from incarceration or

involuntary institutionalization on or after January 1, 2024, the child support obligation shall resume on the first day of the 10th month after release from incarceration or involuntary institutionalization of the person owing support.

(3) If the person owing support obtains employment prior to the date set for reinstatement, the person to whom the support is owed or the local child support agency may seek a court order reinstating child support obligations at the amount determined by the court pursuant to Article 2 (commencing with Section 4050).

(4) This section does not preclude a person owing support or the local child support agency from seeking a modification of the child support order pursuant to Section 3651, based on a change in circumstances or any other appropriate reason.

(c) (1) A local child support agency enforcing a child support order under Title IV-D of the Social Security Act (42 U.S.C. Sec. 651 et seq.) may, upon written notice of the proposed adjustment to the support obligor and obligee along with a blank form provided for the support obligor or obligee to object to the administrative adjustment to the local child support agency, administratively adjust account balances for a money judgment or order for support of a child suspended pursuant to subdivision (a) if all of the following occurs:

(A) The agency verifies that arrears and interest were accrued in violation of this section.

(B) The agency verifies that, to the extent known to the agency, the person owing support does not have the means to pay support while incarcerated or involuntarily institutionalized.

(C) Neither the support obligor nor obligee objects, within 30 days of receipt of the notice of proposed adjustment, whether in writing or by telephone, to the administrative adjustment by the local child support agency.

(2) If either the support obligor or obligee objects to the administrative adjustment set forth in this subdivision, the agency shall not adjust the order, but shall file a motion with the court to seek to adjust the arrears and shall serve copies of the motion on the parties, who may file an objection to the agency's motion with the court. The obligor's arrears shall not be adjusted unless the court approves the adjustment.

(3) The agency may perform this adjustment without regard to whether it was enforcing the child support order at the time the parent owing support qualified for relief under this section.

(d) This section does not prohibit the local child support agency or a party from petitioning a court for a determination of child support or arrears amounts.

(e) For purposes of this section, the following definitions shall apply:

(1) "Incarcerated or involuntarily institutionalized" includes, but is not limited to, involuntary confinement to a federal or state prison, a county jail, a juvenile facility operated by the Division of Juvenile Facilities in the Department of Corrections and Rehabilitation, or a mental health facility.

(2) "Suspend" means that the

payment due on the current child support order, an arrears payment on a preexisting arrears balance, or interest on arrears created during a qualifying period of incarceration pursuant to this section is, by operation of law, set to zero dollars ($0) for the period in which the person owing support is incarcerated or involuntarily institutionalized.

(f) This section applies to any child support obligation that accrues on or after the enactment of this section regardless of when the child support order was established.

(g) The Department of Child Support Services shall, by July 1, 2023, and in consultation with the Judicial Council, develop forms to implement this section.

(h) On or before January 1, 2026, the Department of Child Support Services, in consultation with the Judicial Council, shall conduct an evaluation of the effectiveness of the administrative adjustment process authorized by this section and shall report the results of the review, as well as any recommended changes, to the Assembly Judiciary Committee and the Senate Judiciary Committee. The evaluation shall include a review of the ease of the process to both the obligor and obligee, as well as an analysis of the number of cases administratively adjusted, the number of cases adjusted in court, and the number of cases not adjusted.

(i) It is the intent of the Legislature to ensure qualified persons are provided the support suspension by operation of law for qualified periods of incarceration or involuntary institutionalization that existed during the operative terms of the earlier versions of this statute regardless of whether the judicial or administrative determination of arrears is made before or after the repeal of the statute, if the earlier version of the statute provided for the money judgment or order for support to be suspended by operation of law. This subdivision is declarative of existing law.[574]

4008. The community property, the quasi-community property, and the separate property may be subjected to the support of the children in the proportions the court determines are just.[1]

4009. An original order for child support may be made retroactive to the date of filing the petition, complaint, or other initial pleading. If the parent ordered to pay support was not served with the petition, complaint, or other initial pleading within 90 days after filing and the court finds that the parent was not intentionally evading service, the child support order shall be effective no earlier than the date of service.[113]

4010. In a proceeding in which the court orders a payment for the support of a child, the court shall, at the time of providing written notice of the order, provide the parties with a document describing the procedures by which the order may be modified.

4011. Payment of child support ordered by the court shall be made by the person owing the support payment before payment of any debts owed to creditors.[1]

4012. Upon a showing of good cause, the court may order a parent required to make a payment of child support to give reasonable security for the payment.[1]

4013. If obligations for support of a child are discharged in bankruptcy, the court may make all proper orders for the support of the child that the court determines are just.[1]

4014. (a) An order for child support issued or modified pursuant to this chapter shall include a provision requiring the obligor and child support obligee to notify the other parent or, if the order requires payment through an agency designated under Title IV-D of the Social Security Act (42 U.S.C. Sec. 651 et seq.), the agency named in the order, of the name and address of the person's current employer.
(b) The requirements set forth in this subdivision apply only in cases when the local child support agency is not providing child support services pursuant to Section 17400. To the extent required by federal law, and subject to applicable confidentiality provisions of state or federal law, a judgment for paternity and an order for child support entered or modified pursuant to any law shall include a provision requiring the child support obligor and obligee to file with the court all of the following information:
(1) Residential and mailing address.
(2) Social security number, individual taxpayer identification number, or other uniform identification number.
(3) Telephone number.
(4) Driver's license number or identification card number issued by the Department of Motor Vehicles.
(5) Name, address, and telephone number of the employer.
(6) Any other information prescribed by the Judicial Council.
The judgment or order shall specify that each parent is responsible for providing the parent's own information, that the information must be filed with the court within 10 days of the court order, and that new or different information must be filed with the court within 10 days after any event causing a change in the previously provided information.
(c) The requirements set forth in this subdivision shall only apply in cases in which the local child support agency is not providing child support services pursuant to Section 17400. Once the child support registry, as described in Section 17391 is operational, a judgment for parentage and an order for child support entered or modified pursuant to any law shall include a provision requiring the child support obligor and obligee to file and keep updated the information specified in subdivision (b) with the child support registry.
(d) The Judicial Council shall develop forms to implement this section. The forms shall be developed so as not to delay the implementation of the Statewide Child Support Registry described in Section 17391 and shall be available no later than 30 days prior to the implementation of the Statewide Child Support Registry.[445]

Article 2: Statewide Uniform Guideline

4050. In adopting the statewide uniform guideline provided in this article, it is the intention of the Legislature to ensure that this state remains in compliance with federal regulations for child support guidelines.

4052. The court shall adhere to the statewide uniform guideline and may depart from the guideline only in the special circumstances set forth in this article.

4052.5. (a) The statewide uniform guideline, as required by federal regulations, shall apply in any case in which a child has more than two parents. The court shall apply the guideline by dividing child support obligations among the parents based on income and amount of time spent with the child by each parent, pursuant to Section 4053.
(b) Consistent with federal regulations, after calculating the amount of support owed by each parent under the guideline, the presumption that the guideline amount of support is correct may be rebutted if the court finds that the application of the guideline in that case would be unjust or inappropriate due to special circumstances, pursuant to Section 4057. If the court makes that finding, the court shall divide child support obligations among the parents in a manner that is just and appropriate based on income and amount of time spent with the child by each parent, applying the principles set forth in Section 4053 and this article.
(c) Nothing in this section shall be construed to require reprogramming of the California Child Support Enforcement System, a change to the statewide uniform guideline for determining child support set forth in Section 4055, or a revision by the Department of Child Support Services of its regulations, policies, procedures, forms, or training materials.[356]

4053. In implementing the statewide uniform guideline, the courts shall adhere to the following principles:
(a) A parent's first and principal obligation is to support the parent's minor children according to the parent's circumstances and station in life.
(b) Both parents are mutually responsible for the support of their children.
(c) The guideline takes into account each parent's actual income and level of responsibility for the children.
(d) Each parent should pay for the support of the children according to the parent's ability.
(e) The guideline seeks to place the interests of children as the state's top priority.
(f) Children should share in the standard of living of both parents. Child support may therefore appropriately improve the standard of living of the custodial household to improve the lives of the children.
(g) Child support orders in cases in which both parents have high levels of responsibility for the children should reflect the increased costs of raising the children in two homes and should minimize significant disparities in the children's living standards in the two homes.
(h) The financial needs of the children should be met through private financial resources as much as possible.
(i) It is presumed that a parent having primary physical responsibility for the children contributes a significant portion of available resources for the support of the children.
(j) The guideline seeks to encourage fair and efficient settlements of conflicts between parents and seeks to minimize the need for litigation.
(k) The guideline is intended to be presumptively correct in all cases, and

only under special circumstances should child support orders fall below the child support mandated by the guideline formula.

(l) Child support orders shall ensure that children actually receive fair, timely, and sufficient support reflecting the state's high standard of living and high costs of raising children compared to other states.[446]

4054. (a) The Judicial Council shall periodically review the statewide uniform guideline to recommend to the Legislature appropriate revisions.

(b) The review shall include all of the following:

(1) Economic data on the cost of raising children.

(2) Labor market data, such as unemployment rates, employment rates, hours worked, and earnings, by occupation and skill level for the state and local job markets.

(3) The impact of guideline policies and amounts on custodial and noncustodial parents who have family incomes below 200 percent of the federal poverty level.

(4) Factors that influence employment rates among custodial and noncustodial parents and compliance with child support orders.

(5) An analysis of case data, gathered through sampling or other methods, on the actual application of, and deviations from, the guideline after the guideline's operative date, as well as the rates of orders entered by default, orders entered based on presumed income and earning capacity, and orders determined using the low-income adjustment.

(6) An analysis of guidelines and studies from other states, and other research and studies available to or undertaken by the Judicial Council.

(7) A comparison of payments on child support orders by case characteristics, including whether the order was entered by default, based on earning capacity or presumed income, or determined using the low-income adjustment.

(8) Any additional factors required by federal regulations.

(c) Any recommendations for revisions to the guideline shall be made to ensure that the guideline results in appropriate child support orders, to limit deviations from the guideline, or otherwise to help ensure that the guideline is in compliance with federal law.

(d) The Judicial Council may also review and report on other matters, including, but not limited to, the following:

(1) The treatment of the income of a subsequent spouse or nonmarital partner.

(2) The treatment of children from prior or subsequent relationships.

(3) The application of the guideline in a case where a payer parent has extraordinarily low or extraordinarily high income, or where each parent has primary physical custody of one or more of the children of the marriage.

(4) The benefits and limitations of a uniform statewide spousal support guideline and the interrelationship of that guideline with the state child support guideline.

(5) Whether the use of gross or net income in the guideline is preferable.

(6) Whether the guideline affects child custody litigation or the efficiency of the judicial process.

(7) Whether the various assumptions

used in computer software used by some courts to calculate child support comport with state law and should be made available to parties and counsel.

(e) The initial review by the Judicial Council shall be submitted to the Legislature and to the Department of Child Support Services on or before December 31, 1993, and subsequent reviews shall occur at least every four years thereafter unless federal law requires a different interval.

(f) In developing its recommendations, the Judicial Council shall consult with a broad cross-section of groups involved in child support issues, including, but not limited to, the following:

(1) Custodial and noncustodial parents.

(2) Representatives of established women's rights and fathers' rights groups.

(3) Representatives of established organizations that advocate for the economic well-being of children.

(4) Members of the judiciary, district attorney's offices, the Attorney General's office, and the Department of Child Support Services.

(5) Certified family law specialists.

(6) Academicians specializing in family law.

(7) Persons representing low-income parents.

(8) Persons representing recipients of assistance under the CalWORKs program seeking child support services.

(9) Persons representing currently or formerly incarcerated parents.

(g) In developing its recommendations, the Judicial Council shall seek public comment and shall be guided by the legislative intent that children share in the standard of living of both of their parents.[506]

4055. (a) The statewide uniform guideline for determining child support orders is as follows:

CS = K[HN - (H%)(TN)].

(b) (1) The components of the formula are as follows:

(A) CS = child support amount.

(B) K = amount of both parents' income to be allocated for child support as set forth in paragraph (3).

(C) HN = high earner's net monthly disposable income.

(D) H% = approximate percentage of time that the high earner has or will have primary physical responsibility for the children compared to the other parent. In cases in which parents have different time-sharing arrangements for different children, H% equals the average of the approximate percentages of time the high earner parent spends with each child.

(E) TN = total net monthly disposable income of both parties.

(2) To compute net disposable income, see Section 4059.

(3) K (amount of both parents' income allocated for child support) equals one plus H% (if H% is less than or equal to 50 percent) or two minus H% (if H% is greater than 50 percent) times the following fraction:

Total Net Disposable Income Per Month	K
$0–2,900	0.165 + TN/82,857
$2,901–5,000	0.131 + TN/42,149
$5,001–10,000	0.250
$10,001–15,000	0.10 + 1,499/TN
Over $15,000	0.12 + 1,200/TN

For example, if H% equals 20 percent

and the total monthly net disposable income of the parents is $1,000, K = (1 + 0.20) × (0.165 + 1,000/82,857), or 0.21. If H% equals 80 percent and the total monthly net disposable income of the parents is $1,000, K = (2 - 0.80) × (0.165 + 1,000/82,857), or 0.21.

(4) For more than one child, multiply CS by:

2 children	1.6
3 children	2
4 children	2.3
5 children	2.5
6 children	2.625
7 children	2.75
8 children	2.813
9 children	2.844
10 children	2.86

(5) If the amount calculated under the formula results in a positive number, the higher earner shall pay that amount to the lower earner. If the amount calculated under the formula results in a negative number, the lower earner shall pay the absolute value of that amount to the higher earner.

(6) In any default proceeding where proof is by affidavit pursuant to Section 2336, or in any proceeding for child support in which a party fails to appear after being duly noticed, H% shall be set at zero in the formula if the noncustodial parent is the higher earner or at 100 if the custodial parent is the higher earner, where there is no evidence presented demonstrating the percentage of time that the noncustodial parent has primary physical responsibility for the children. H% shall not be set as described in paragraph (3) if the moving party in a default proceeding is the noncustodial parent or if the party who fails to appear after being duly noticed is the custodial parent. A statement by the party who is not in default as to the percentage of time that the noncustodial parent has primary physical responsibility for the children shall be deemed sufficient evidence.

(7) In all cases in which the net disposable income per month of the obligor is less than the amount of monthly gross income earned from full-time minimum wage, established by Section 1182.12 of the Labor Code, at 40 hours per week, 52 weeks per year, there is a rebuttable presumption that the obligor is entitled to a low-income adjustment. The presumption may be rebutted by evidence showing that the application of the lowest amount of child support permitted pursuant to this paragraph would be unjust and inappropriate in the particular case. In determining whether the presumption is rebutted, the court shall consider the principles provided in Section 4053, and the impact of the contemplated adjustment on the respective net incomes of the obligor and the obligee. The low-income adjustment shall reduce the child support amount otherwise determined under this section by an amount that is no greater than the amount calculated by multiplying the child support amount otherwise determined under this section by a fraction, the numerator of which is the amount of monthly gross income earned from full-time minimum wage, established by Section 1182.12 of the Labor Code, at 40 hours per week, 52 weeks per year, minus the obligor's net disposable

income per month, and the denominator of which is the amount of monthly gross income earned from full-time minimum wage, established by Section 1182.12 of the Labor Code, at 40 hours per week, 52 weeks per year.

(8) Unless the court orders otherwise, the order for child support shall allocate the support amount so that the amount of support for the youngest child is the amount of support for one child, and the amount for the next youngest child is the difference between that amount and the amount for two children, with similar allocations for additional children. However, this paragraph does not apply to cases in which there are different time-sharing arrangements for different children or where the court determines that the allocation would be inappropriate in the particular case.

(c) If a court uses a computer to calculate the child support order and the obligor's income qualifies for a low-income adjustment, the computer program shall provide the range of the adjustment permitted by paragraph (7) of subdivision (b).

(d) This section shall be operative September 1, 2024.[547]

4056. (a) To comply with federal law, the court shall state, in writing or on the record, the following information whenever the court is ordering an amount for support that differs from the statewide uniform guideline formula amount under this article:

(1) The amount of support that would have been ordered under the guideline formula.

(2) The reasons the amount of support ordered differs from the guideline formula amount.

(3) The reasons the amount of support ordered is consistent with the best interests of the children.

(b) At the request of any party, the court shall state in writing or on the record the following information used in determining the guideline amount under this article:

(1) The net monthly disposable income of each parent.

(2) The actual federal income tax filing status of each parent (for example, single, married, married filing separately, or head of household and number of exemptions).

(3) Deductions from gross income for each parent.

(4) The approximate percentage of time pursuant to paragraph (1) of subdivision (b) of Section 4055 that each parent has primary physical responsibility for the children compared to the other parent.

4057. (a) The amount of child support established by the formula provided in subdivision (a) of Section 4055 is presumed to be the correct amount of child support to be ordered.

(b) The presumption of subdivision (a) is a rebuttable presumption affecting the burden of proof and may be rebutted by admissible evidence showing that application of the formula would be unjust or inappropriate in the particular case, consistent with the principles set forth in Section 4053, because one or more of the following factors is found to be applicable by a preponderance of the evidence, and the court states in writing or on the record the information required in subdivision (a) of Section 4056:

(1) The parties have stipulated to a

different amount of child support under subdivision (a) of Section 4065.

(2) The sale of the family residence is deferred pursuant to Chapter 8 (commencing with Section 3800) of Part 1 and the rental value of the family residence where the children reside exceeds the mortgage payments, homeowner's insurance, and property taxes. The amount of any adjustment pursuant to this paragraph shall not be greater than the excess amount.

(3) The parent being ordered to pay child support has an extraordinarily high income and the amount determined under the formula would exceed the needs of the children.

(4) A party is not contributing to the needs of the children at a level commensurate with that party's custodial time.

(5) A support obligor qualifies for the low-income adjustment pursuant to paragraph (7) of subdivision (b) of Section 4055 and the amount of child support established by the formula exceeds 50 percent of the support obligor's net disposable income as defined in Section 4059 after application of the low-income adjustment. The amount of any adjustment pursuant to this paragraph shall not be greater than the amount exceeding 50 percent of the support obligor's net disposable income.

(6) Application of the formula would be unjust or inappropriate due to special circumstances in the particular case. These special circumstances include, but are not limited to, the following:

(A) Cases in which the parents have different time-sharing arrangements for different children.

(B) Cases in which both parents have substantially equal time-sharing of the children and one parent has a much lower or higher percentage of income used for housing than the other parent.

(C) Cases in which the children have special medical or other needs that could require child support that would be greater than the formula amount.

(D) Cases in which a child is found to have more than two parents.

(c) If the court is made aware that a parent is subject to multiple court orders to pay child support arising from a different case or cases, the court may take steps to determine how to allocate the parent's income and support obligation appropriately across the cases. A court that continues a hearing based on a party's representation that it will file an appropriate request to modify support in a related case may issue a temporary support order.

(d) This section shall be operative September 1, 2024.[548]

4057.5. (a) (1) The income of the obligor parent's subsequent spouse or nonmarital partner shall not be considered when determining or modifying child support, except in an extraordinary case where excluding that income would lead to extreme and severe hardship to any child subject to the child support award, in which case the court shall also consider whether including that income would lead to extreme and severe hardship to any child supported by the obligor or by the obligor's subsequent spouse or nonmarital partner.

(2) The income of the obligee parent's subsequent spouse or nonmarital

partner shall not be considered when determining or modifying child support, except in an extraordinary case where excluding that income would lead to extreme and severe hardship to any child subject to the child support award, in which case the court shall also consider whether including that income would lead to extreme and severe hardship to any child supported by the obligee or by the obligee's subsequent spouse or nonmarital partner.

(b) For purposes of this section, an extraordinary case may include a parent who voluntarily or intentionally quits work or reduces income, or who intentionally remains unemployed or underemployed and relies on a subsequent spouse's income.

(c) If any portion of the income of either parent's subsequent spouse or nonmarital partner is allowed to be considered pursuant to this section, discovery for the purposes of determining income shall be based on W2 and 1099 income tax forms, except where the court determines that application would be unjust or inappropriate.

(d) If any portion of the income of either parent's subsequent spouse or nonmarital partner is allowed to be considered pursuant to this section, the court shall allow a hardship deduction based on the minimum living expenses for one or more stepchildren of the party subject to the order.

(e) The enactment of this section constitutes cause to bring an action for modification of a child support order entered prior to the operative date of this section.

4058. (a) The annual gross income of each parent means income from whatever source derived, except as specified in subdivision (c) and includes, but is not limited to, the following:

(1) Income such as commissions, salaries, royalties, wages, bonuses, rents, dividends, pensions, interest, trust income, annuities, workers' compensation benefits, unemployment insurance benefits, disability insurance benefits, social security benefits, severance pay, veterans benefits that are not based on need, military allowances for housing and food, and spousal support actually received from a person not a party to the proceeding to establish a child support order pursuant to this article.

(2) Income from the proprietorship of a business, such as gross receipts from the business reduced by expenditures required for the operation of the business.

(3) In the discretion of the court, employee benefits or self-employment benefits, taking into consideration the benefit to the employee, any corresponding reduction in living expenses, and other relevant facts.

(b) (1) (A) In a case when a parent's annual gross income is unknown, the court shall consider the earning capacity of the parent.

(B) In a case when a parent's annual gross income is known, the court may, in its discretion, consider the earning capacity of a parent in lieu of the parent's income, consistent with the best interests of the children, taking into consideration the overall welfare and developmental needs of the children, and the time that parent spends with the children.

(2) When determining the earning capacity of the parent pursuant to this subdivision, the court shall consider the specific circumstances of the parent, to the extent known. Those circumstances include, but are not limited to, evidence of the parent's assets, residence, employment and earnings history, job skills, educational attainment, literacy, age, health, criminal record and other employment barriers, and record of seeking work, as well as the local job market, the availability of employers willing to hire the parent, prevailing earnings levels in the local community, and other relevant background factors affecting the parent's ability to earn.

(3) Notwithstanding any other law, the incarceration or involuntary institutionalization of a parent shall not be treated as voluntary unemployment in establishing or modifying support orders regardless of the nature of the offense. "Incarcerated or involuntarily institutionalized" has the same meaning as subdivision (e) of Section 4007.5.

(c) Annual gross income does not include any income derived from child support payments actually received, and income derived from any public assistance program, eligibility for which is based on a determination of need. Child support received by a party for children from another relationship shall not be included as part of that party's gross or net income.

(d) This section shall be operative September 1, 2024.[549]

4059. The annual net disposable income of each parent shall be computed by deducting from the parent's annual gross income the actual amounts attributable to the following items or other items permitted under this article:

(a) The state and federal income tax liability resulting from the parties' taxable income. Federal and state income tax deductions shall bear an accurate relationship to the tax status of the parties (that is, single, married, married filing separately, or head of household) and number of dependents. State and federal income taxes shall be those actually payable (not necessarily current withholding) after considering appropriate filing status, all available exclusions, deductions, and credits. Unless the parties stipulate otherwise, the tax effects of spousal support shall not be considered in determining the net disposable income of the parties for determining child support, but shall be considered in determining spousal support consistent with Chapter 3 (commencing with Section 4330) of Part 3.

(b) Deductions attributed to the employee's contribution or the self-employed worker's contribution pursuant to the Federal Insurance Contributions Act (FICA), or an amount not to exceed that allowed under FICA for persons not subject to FICA, provided that the deducted amount is used to secure retirement or disability benefits for the parent.

(c) Deductions for mandatory union dues and retirement benefits, provided that they are required as a condition of employment.

(d) Deductions for health insurance or health plan premiums for the parent and for any children the parent has an obligation to support and deductions for state disability insurance premiums.

(e) Any child or spousal support actually being paid by the parent pursuant to a court order, to or for the benefit of a person who is not a subject of the order to be established by the court. In the absence of a court order, child support actually being paid, not to exceed the amount established by the guideline, for natural or adopted children of the parent not residing in that parent's home, who are not the subject of the order to be established by the court, and of whom the parent has a duty of support. Unless the parent proves payment of the support, a deduction shall not be allowed under this subdivision.

(f) Job-related expenses, if allowed by the court after consideration of whether the expenses are necessary, the benefit to the employee, and any other relevant facts.

(g) A deduction for hardship, as defined by Sections 4070 to 4073, inclusive, and applicable published appellate court decisions. The amount of the hardship shall not be deducted from the amount of child support, but shall be deducted from the income of the party to whom it applies. In applying any hardship under paragraph (2) of subdivision (a) of Section 4071, the court shall seek to provide equity between competing child support orders. The Judicial Council shall develop a formula for calculating the maximum hardship deduction and shall submit it to the Legislature for its consideration on or before July 1, 1995.[447]

4060. The monthly net disposable income shall be computed by dividing the annual net disposable income by 12. If the monthly net disposable income figure does not accurately reflect the actual or prospective earnings of the parties at the time the determination of support is made, the court may adjust the amount appropriately.

4061. The amounts in Section 4062 shall be considered additional support for the children and shall be computed in accordance with the following:

(a) If there needs to be an apportionment of expenses pursuant to Section 4062, the expenses shall be divided in proportion to the parents' net incomes as adjusted pursuant to subdivisions (c) and (d), unless a party requests or the court finds on its own motion that expenses should be divided in a different manner.

(b) (1) The basic child support obligation shall first be computed using the formula set forth in subdivision (a) of Section 4055, as adjusted for any appropriate rebuttal factors in subdivision (b) of Section 4057.

(2) Any additional child support required for expenses pursuant to Section 4062 shall thereafter be ordered to be paid by the parents in proportion to their net disposable incomes as adjusted pursuant to subdivisions (c) and (d).

(c) In cases when spousal support is or has been ordered to be paid by one parent to the other, for purposes of allocating additional expenses pursuant to Section 4062, the gross income of the parent paying spousal support shall be decreased by the amount of the spousal support paid and the gross income of the parent receiving the spousal support shall be increased by the amount of the spousal support received for as long as the spousal support order is in effect and is paid.

(d) For purposes of computing the adjusted net disposable income of the parent paying child support for allocating any additional expenses pursuant to Section 4062, the net disposable income of the parent paying child support shall be reduced by the amount of any basic child support ordered to be paid under subdivision (a) of Section 4055. However, the net disposable income of the parent receiving child support shall not be increased by any amount of child support received.

(e) This section shall be operative September 1, 2024.[550]

4062. (a) The court shall order the following as additional child support:

(1) Childcare costs, if those expenses are actually incurred, related to employment or to reasonably necessary education or training for employment skills, as described in Section 4063, unless those costs are specifically included in the guideline calculation itself.

(2) The reasonable uninsured health care costs for the children as provided in Section 4063.

(b) The court may order the following as additional child support:

(1) Costs related to the educational or other special needs of the children.

(2) Travel expenses for visitation.

(c) This section shall be operative September 1, 2024.[551]

4063. (a) When making an order pursuant to subdivision (a) of Section 4062, the court shall:

(1) Advise each parent, in writing or on the record, of the parent's rights and liabilities, including financial responsibilities.

(2) Include in its order the time period for a parent to reimburse the other parent for the reimbursing parent's share of the reasonable additional child support costs subject to the requirements of this section.

(b) Unless there has been an assignment of rights pursuant to Section 11477 of the Welfare and Institutions Code, when either parent accrues or pays costs pursuant to an order under this section, that parent shall provide the other parent with an itemized statement of the costs within a reasonable time, but not more than 90 days after accruing the costs. These costs shall then be paid as follows:

(1) If a parent has already paid all of these costs, that parent shall provide proof of payment and a request for reimbursement of that parent's court-ordered share to the other parent.

(2) If a parent has paid the parent's court-ordered share of the costs only, that parent shall provide proof of payment to the other parent, request the other parent to pay the remainder of the costs directly to the provider, and provide the reimbursing parent with any necessary information about how to make the payment to the provider.

(3) The other parent shall make the reimbursement or pay the remaining costs within the time period specified by the court, or, if no period is specified, within a reasonable time not to exceed 30 days from notification of the amount due, or according to any payment schedule set by the health care provider for either parent unless the parties agree in writing to another payment

schedule or the court finds good cause for setting another payment schedule.

(4) If the reimbursing parent disputes a request for payment, that parent shall pay the requested amount and thereafter may seek judicial relief under this section and Section 290. If the reimbursing parent fails to pay the other parent as required by this subdivision, the other parent may seek judicial relief under this section and Section 290.

(c) Either parent may file a noticed motion to enforce an order issued pursuant to this section. In addition to the court's powers under Section 290, the court may award filing costs and reasonable attorney's fees if it finds that either party acted without reasonable cause regarding the party's obligations pursuant to this section.

(d) There is a rebuttable presumption that the costs actually paid for the uninsured health care needs of the children and for childcare that is for employment or reasonably necessary for education or training for employment skills are reasonable, except as provided in subdivision (e).

(e) Except as provided in subdivision (g):

(1) The health care insurance coverage, including, but not limited to, coverage for emergency treatment, provided by a parent pursuant to a court order, shall be the coverage to be utilized at all times, consistent with the requirements of that coverage, unless the other parent can show that the health care insurance coverage is inadequate to meet the child's needs.

(2) If either parent obtains health care insurance coverage in addition to that provided pursuant to the court order, that parent shall bear sole financial responsibility for the costs of that additional coverage and the costs of any care or treatment obtained pursuant thereto in excess of the costs that would have been incurred under the health care insurance coverage provided for in the court order.

(f) Except as provided in subdivision (g):

(1) If the health care insurance coverage provided by a parent pursuant to a court order designates a preferred health care provider, that preferred provider shall be used at all times, consistent with the terms and requirements of that coverage.

(2) If either parent uses a health care provider other than the preferred provider inconsistent with the terms and requirements of the court-ordered health care insurance coverage, the parent obtaining that care shall bear the sole responsibility for any nonreimbursable health care costs in excess of the costs that would have been incurred under the court-ordered health care insurance coverage had the preferred provider been used.

(g) When ruling on a motion made pursuant to this section, in order to ensure that the health care needs of the child and the need for childcare for employment or reasonably necessary for education or training for employment skills pursuant to this section are met, the court shall consider all relevant facts, on both of the following categories:

(1) With regard to health care, the court shall consider all relevant facts, including, but not limited to, the following:

(A) The geographic access and

reasonable availability of necessary health care for the child that complies with the terms of the health care insurance coverage paid for by either parent pursuant to a court order. Health insurance shall be rebuttably presumed to be accessible if services to be provided are within 50 miles of the residence of the child subject to the support order. If the court determines that health insurance is not accessible, the court shall state the reason on the record.

(B) The necessity of emergency medical treatment that may have precluded the use of the health care insurance, or the preferred health care provider required under the insurance, provided by either parent pursuant to a court order.

(C) The special medical needs of the child.

(D) The reasonable inability of a parent to pay the full amount of reimbursement within a 30-day period and the resulting necessity for a court-ordered payment schedule.

(2) With regard to childcare costs for employment or that are reasonably necessary for education or training for employment skills, the court shall consider all relevant facts, including, but not limited to, the following:

(A) The nature and extent of job-related childcare needs, including, but not limited to, work schedule needs and the duration of education or training for employment skills.

(B) The necessity and reasonableness of the cost under the circumstances of the case.

(C) The special needs of the child.

(D) The reasonable inability of a parent to pay the full amount of reimbursement within a 30-day period and the resulting necessity for a court-ordered payment schedule.

(h) This section shall become operative September 1, 2024.[552]

4064. The court may adjust the child support order as appropriate to accommodate seasonal or fluctuating income of either parent.

4065. (a) Unless prohibited by applicable federal law, the parties may stipulate to a child support amount subject to approval of the court. However, the court shall not approve a stipulated agreement for child support below the guideline formula amount unless the parties declare all of the following:

(1) They are fully informed of their rights concerning child support.

(2) The order is being agreed to without coercion or duress.

(3) The agreement is in the best interests of the children involved.

(4) The needs of the children will be adequately met by the stipulated amount.

(5) The right to support has not been assigned to the county pursuant to Section 11477 of the Welfare and Institutions Code and no public assistance application is pending.

(b) The parties may, by stipulation, require the child support obligor to designate an account for the purpose of paying the child support obligation by electronic funds transfer pursuant to Section 4508.

(c) A stipulated agreement of child support is not valid unless the local child support agency has joined in the stipulation by signing it in any case in which the local child support agency is providing services pursuant to Section 17400. The local child support agency shall not stipulate to a child support order below the guideline amount if the children are receiving assistance under the CalWORKs program, if an application for public assistance is pending, or if the parent receiving support has not consented to the order.

(d) If the parties to a stipulated agreement stipulate to a child support order below the amount established by the statewide uniform guideline, no change of circumstances need be demonstrated to obtain a modification of the child support order to the applicable guideline level or above.

4066. Orders and stipulations otherwise in compliance with the statewide uniform guideline may designate as "family support" an unallocated total sum for support of the spouse and any children without specifically labeling all or any portion as "child support" as long as the amount is adjusted to reflect the effect of additional deductibility. The amount of the order shall be adjusted to maximize the tax benefits for both parents.

4067. It is the intent of the Legislature that the statewide uniform guideline shall be reviewed by the Legislature at least every four years and shall be revised by the Legislature as appropriate to ensure that its application results in the determination of appropriate child support amounts. The review shall include consideration of changes required by applicable federal laws and regulations or recommended from time to time by the Judicial Council pursuant to Section 4054.

4068. (a) The Judicial Council may develop the following:

(1) Model worksheets to assist parties in determining the approximate amount of child support due under the formula provided in subdivision (a) of Section 4055 and the approximate percentage of time each parent has primary physical responsibility for the children.

(2) A form to assist the courts in making the findings and orders required by this article.

(b) The Judicial Council, in consultation with representatives of the State Department of Social Services, the California Family Support Council, the Senate Judiciary Committee, the Assembly Judiciary Committee, the Family Law Section of the State Bar of California, a legal services organization providing representation on child support matters, a custodial parent group, and a noncustodial parent group, shall develop a simplified income and expense form for determining child support under the formula provided in subdivision (a) of Section 4055, by June 1, 1995. The Judicial Council, also in consultation with these groups, shall develop factors to use to determine when the simplified income and expense form may be used and when the standard income and expense form must be used.

4069. The establishment of the statewide uniform guideline constitutes a change of circumstances.

4070. If a parent is experiencing extreme financial hardship due to justifiable expenses resulting from the circumstances enumerated in Section 4071, on the request of a party, the court may allow the income deductions under Section 4059 that may be necessary to accommodate those circumstances.

4071. (a) Circumstances evidencing hardship include the following:

(1) Extraordinary health expenses for which the parent is financially responsible, and uninsured catastrophic losses.

(2) The minimum basic living expenses of either parent's natural or adopted children for whom the parent has the obligation to support from other marriages or relationships who reside with the parent. The court, on its own motion or on the request of a party, may allow these income deductions as necessary to accommodate these expenses after making the deductions allowable under paragraph (1).

(b) The maximum hardship deduction under paragraph (2) of subdivision (a) for each child who resides with the parent may be equal to, but shall not exceed, the support allocated each child subject to the order. For purposes of calculating this deduction, the amount of support per child established by the statewide uniform guideline shall be the total amount ordered divided by the number of children and not the amount established under paragraph (8) of subdivision (b) of Section 4055.

(c) The Judicial Council may develop tables in accordance with this section to reflect the maximum hardship deduction, taking into consideration the parent's net disposable income before the hardship deduction, the number of children for whom the deduction is being given, and the number of children for whom the support award is being made.

4072.(a) If a deduction for hardship expenses is allowed, the court shall do both of the following:

(1) State the reasons supporting the deduction in writing or on the record.

(2) Document the amount of the deduction and the underlying facts and circumstances.

(b) Whenever possible, the court shall specify the duration of the deduction.

4073. The court shall be guided by the goals set forth in this article when considering whether or not to allow a financial hardship deduction, and, if allowed, when determining the amount of the deduction.

4074. This article applies to an award for the support of children, including those awards designated as "family support," that contain provisions for the support of children as well as for the support of the spouse.

4075. This article shall not be construed to affect the treatment of spousal support and separate maintenance payments pursuant to Section 71 of the Internal Revenue Code of 1954 (26 U.S.C. Sec. 71).

4076. (a) When the court is requested to modify a child support order issued prior to July 1, 1992, for the purpose of conforming to the statewide child support guideline, and it is not using its discretionary authority to depart from the guideline pursuant to paragraph (3), (4), or (5) of subdivision (b) of Section 4057, and the amount of child support to be ordered is the amount provided under the guideline formula in subdivision (a) of Section 4055, the court may, in its discretion, order a two-step phase-in of the formula amount of support to provide the obligor with time for transition to the full formula amount if all of the following are true:

(1) The period of the phase-in is carefully limited to the time necessary for the obligor to rearrange the obligor's financial obligations in order to meet the full formula amount of support.

(2) The obligor is immediately being ordered to pay not less than 30 percent of the amount of the child support increase, in addition to the amount of child support required under the prior order.

(3) The obligor has not unreasonably increased their financial obligations following notice of the motion for modification of support, has no arrearages owing, and has a history of good faith compliance with prior support orders.

(b) When the court grants a request for a phase-in pursuant to this section, the court shall state the following in writing:

(1) The specific reasons why (A) the immediate imposition of the full formula amount of support would place an extraordinary hardship on the obligor, and (B) this extraordinary hardship on the obligor would outweigh the hardship caused the supported children by the temporary phase-in of the full formula amount of support.

(2) The full guideline amount of support, the date and amount of each phase-in, and the date that the obligor must commence paying the full formula amount of support, which shall not be later than one year after the filing of the motion for modification of support.

(c) When the court orders a phase-in pursuant to this section, and the court thereafter determines that the obligor has violated the phase-in schedule or has intentionally lowered the income available for the payment of child support during the phase-in period, the court may order the immediate payment of the full formula amount of child support and the difference in the amount of support that would have been due without the phase-in and the amount of support due with the phase-in, in addition to any other penalties provided for by law.[448]

4077. The Department of Child Support Services and the Judicial Council shall meet and confer, no later than November 21, 2022, and each entity shall submit its own report to the Assembly Committee on Budget and the Senate Committee on Budget and Fiscal Review and the Assembly and Senate Committees on Judiciary on what additional legislative changes are required to comply with the federal child support regulations revised in 81 Federal Register 93492 (Dec. 20, 2016), if any, which shall consider the most recent review of the statewide child support guideline completed pursuant to Section 4054, and identify any points of agreement and any difference of interpretation, perspective, or opinion between the entities regarding the legislative changes required.[507]

Article 3: Payment to Court Designated County Officer; Enforcement by District Attorney

4200. In any proceeding where a court makes or has made an order requiring the payment of child support to a parent receiving welfare moneys for the maintenance of children for whom

support may be ordered, the court shall do both of the following:
(a) Direct that the payments of support shall be made to the county officer designated by the court for that purpose. Once the State Disbursement Unit is implemented pursuant to Section 17309, all payments shall be directed to the State Disbursement Unit instead of the county officer designated by the court.
(b) Direct the local child support agency to appear on behalf of the welfare recipient in any proceeding to enforce the order.[103]

4201. In any proceeding where a court makes or has made an order requiring the payment of child support to the person having custody of a child for whom support may be ordered, the court may do either or both of the following:
(a) Direct that the payments shall be made to the county officer designated by the court for that purpose. Once the State Disbursement Unit is implemented pursuant to Section 17309, all payments shall be directed to the State Disbursement Unit instead of the county officer designated by the court.
(b) Direct the local child support agency to appear on behalf of the minor children in any proceeding to enforce the order.[103]

4202. (a) Notwithstanding any other provision of law, in a proceeding where the custodial parent resides in one county and the parent ordered to pay support resides in another county, the court may direct payment to be made to the county officer designated by the court for those purposes in the county of residence of the custodial parent, and may direct the local child support agency of either county to enforce the order.
(b) If the court directs the local child support agency of the county of residence of the noncustodial parent to enforce the order, the expenses of the local child support agency with respect to the enforcement is a charge upon the county of residence of the noncustodial parent.[115]

4203. (a) Except as provided in Section 4202, expenses of the county officer designated by the court, and expenses of the local child support agency incurred in the enforcement of an order of the type described in Section 4200 or 4201, are a charge upon the county where the proceedings are pending.
(b) Fees for service of process in the enforcement of an order of the type described in Section 4200 or 4201 are a charge upon the county where the process is served.

4204. Notwithstanding any other law, in any proceeding where the court has made an order requiring the payment of child support and the child support is subsequently assigned to the county pursuant to Section 11477 of the Welfare and Institutions Code or the support obligor or obligee has requested a local child support agency to provide child support enforcement services pursuant to Section 17400, the local child support agency shall issue a notice directing that the payments shall be made to the local child support agency, another county office, or the State Disbursement Unit pursuant to Section 17309. Additionally, the local child support agency shall provide notice when it is no longer providing services under Part D of Title IV of the federal Social Security Act (42 U.S.C. Sec. 651 et seq.). The local child support agency shall serve the notice on both the support obligor and obligee in compliance with Section 1013 of the Code of Civil Procedure and file the notice with the court.[517]

4205. Any notice from the local child support agency requesting a meeting with the support obligor for any purpose authorized under this part shall contain a statement advising the support obligor of the obligor's right to have an attorney present at the meeting.[449]

Article 4: Child Support Commissioners

4250. (a) The Legislature finds and declares the following:

(1) Child and spousal support are serious legal obligations.

(2) The current system for obtaining, modifying, and enforcing child and spousal support orders is inadequate to meet the future needs of California's children due to burgeoning caseloads within local child supp-ort agencies and the growing number of parents who are representing themselves in family law actions.

(3) The success of California's child support enforcement program depends upon its ability to establish and enforce child support orders quickly and efficiently.

(4) There is a compelling state interest in creating an expedited process in the courts that is cost-effective and accessible to families, for establishing and enforcing child support orders in cases being enforced by the local child support agency.

(5) There is a compelling state interest in having a simple, speedy, conflict-reducing system, that is both cost-effective and accessible to families, for resolving all issues concerning children, including support, health insurance, custody, and visitation in family law cases that do not involve enforcement by the local child support agency.

(b) Therefore, it is the intent of the Legislature to: (1) provide for commissioners to hear child support cases being enforced by the local child support agency; (2) adopt uniform and simplified procedures for all child support cases; and (3) create an Office of the Family Law Facilitator in the courts to provide education, information, and assistance to parents with child support issues.

4251. (a) Commencing July 1, 1997, each superior court shall provide sufficient commissioners to hear Title IV-D child support cases filed by the local child support agency. The number of child support commissioners required in each county shall be determined by the Judicial Council as prescribed by paragraph (3) of subdivision (b) of Section 4252. All actions or proceedings filed by the local child support agency in a support action or proceeding in which enforcement services are being provided pursuant to Section 17400, for an order to establish, modify, or enforce child or spousal support, including actions to establish parentage, shall be referred for hearing to a child support commissioner unless a child support commissioner is not available due to exceptional circumstances, as prescribed by the Judicial Council pursuant to paragraph (7) of subdivision (b) of Section 4252. All actions or proceedings filed by a party other than the local child support agency to modify or enforce a support order established by the local child support agency or for which enforcement services are being provided pursuant to Section 17400 shall be referred for hearing to a child support commissioner unless a child support commissioner is not available due to exceptional circumstances, as pre-scribed by the Judicial Council pursuant to paragraph (7) of subdivision (b) of Section 4252.

(b) The commissioner shall act as a temporary judge unless an objection is made by the local child support agency or any other party. The Judicial Council shall develop a notice that shall be included on all forms and pleadings used to initiate a child support action or proceeding that advises the parties of their right to review by a superior court judge and how to exercise that right. The parties shall also be advised by the court prior to the commencement of the hearing that the matter is being heard by a commissioner who shall act as a temporary judge unless any party objects to the commissioner acting as a temporary judge. While acting as a temporary judge, the commissioner shall receive no compensation other than compensation as a commissioner.

(c) If a party objects to the commissioner acting as a temporary judge, the commissioner may hear the matter and make findings of fact and a recommended order. Within 10 court days, a judge shall ratify the recommended order unless either party objects to the recommended order, or where a recommended order is in error. In both cases, the judge shall issue a temporary order and schedule a hearing de novo within 10 court days. A party may waive the right to the review hearing at any time.

(d) The commissioner, where appropriate, shall do any of the following:

(1) Review and determine ex parte applications for orders and writs.

(2) Take testimony.

(3) Establish a record, evaluate evidence, and make recommendations or decisions.

(4) Enter judgments or orders based upon voluntary acknowledgments of support liability and parentage and stipulated agreements respecting the amount of child support to be paid.

(5) Enter default orders and judgments pursuant to Section 4253.

(6) In actions in which parentage is at issue, order the mother, child, and alleged father to submit to genetic tests.

(e) The commissioner shall, upon application of a party, join issues concerning custody, visitation, and protective orders in the action filed by the local child support agency, subject to Section 17404. After joinder, the commissioner shall:

(1) Refer the parents for mediation of disputed custody or visitation issues pursuant to Section 3170.

(2) Accept stipulated agreements concerning custody, visitation, and protective orders and enter orders pursuant to the agreements.

(3) Refer contested issues of custody, visitation, and protective orders to a judge or to another commissioner for hearing. A child support commissioner may hear contested

custody, visitation, and restraining order issues only if the court has adopted procedures to segregate the costs of hearing Title IV-D child support issues from the costs of hearing other issues pursuant to applicable federal requirements.

(f) The local child support agency shall be served notice by the moving party of any proceeding under this section in which support is at issue. An order for support that is entered without the local child support agency having received proper notice shall be voidable upon the motion of the local child support agency.[450]

4252. (a) The superior court shall appoint one or more subordinate judicial officers as child support commissioners to perform the duties specified in Section 4251. The child support commissioners' first priority always shall be to hear Title IV-D child support cases. The child support commissioners shall specialize in hearing child support cases, and their primary responsibility shall be to hear Title IV-D child support cases. Notwithstanding Section 71622 of the Government Code, the number of child support commissioner positions allotted to each court shall be determined by the Judicial Council in accordance with caseload standards developed pursuant to paragraph (3) of subdivision (b), subject to appropriations in the annual Budget Act.

(b) The Judicial Council shall do all of the following:

(1) Establish minimum qualifications for child support commissioners.

(2) Establish minimum educational and training requirements for child support commissioners and other court personnel that are assigned to Title IV-D child support cases. Training programs shall include both federal and state laws concerning child support and related issues.

(3) Establish caseload, case processing, and staffing standards for child support commissioners on or before April 1, 1997, which shall set forth the maximum number of cases that each child support commissioner can process. These standards shall be reviewed and, if appropriate, revised by the Judicial Council every two years.

(4) Adopt uniform rules of court and forms for use in Title IV-D child support cases.

(5) Offer technical assistance to courts regarding issues relating to implementation and operation of the child support commissioner system, including assistance related to funding, staffing, and the sharing of resources between courts.

(6) Establish procedures for the distribution of funding to the courts for child support commissioners, family law facilitators pursuant to Division 14 (commencing with Section 10000), and related allowable costs.

(7) Adopt rules that define the exceptional circumstances in which judges may hear Title IV-D child support matters as provided in subdivision (a) of Section 4251.

(8) Undertake other actions as appropriate to ensure the successful implementation and operation of child support commissioners in the counties.

(c) As used in this article, "Title IV-D" means Title IV-D of the federal Social Security Act (42 U.S.C. Sec. 651 et seq.).[85]

4253. Notwithstanding any other provision of law, when hearing child support matters, a commissioner or referee may enter default orders if the defendant does not respond to notice or other process within the time prescribed to respond to that notice.

PART 3: SPOUSAL SUPPORT

enacted by Stats. 1992, Ch. 162, Sec. 10.

Chapter 1: Duty to Support Spouse

4300. Subject to this division, a person shall support the person's spouse.[1]
4301. Subject to Section 914, a person shall support the person's spouse while they are living together out of the separate property of the person when there is no community property or quasi-community property.[1]

4302. A person is not liable for support of the person's spouse when the person is living separate from the spouse by agreement unless support is stipulated in the agreement.[1]

4303. (a) The obligee spouse, or the county on behalf of the obligee spouse, may bring an action against the obligor spouse to enforce the duty of support.
(b) If the county furnishes support to a spouse, the county has the same right as the spouse to whom the support was furnished to secure reimbursement and obtain continuing support. The right of the county to reimbursement is subject to any limitation other-wise imposed by the law of this state.
(c) The court may order the obligor to pay the county reasonable attorney's fees and court costs in a proceeding brought by the county under this section.[1]

Chapter 2: Factors to be Considered in Ordering Support

4320. In ordering spousal support under this part, the court shall consider all of the following circumstances:
(a) The extent to which the earning capacity of each party is sufficient to maintain the standard of living established during the marriage, taking into account all of the following:
(1) The marketable skills of the supported party; the job market for those skills; the time and expenses required for the supported party to acquire the appropriate education or training to develop those skills; and the possible need for retraining or education to acquire other, more marketable skills or employment.
(2) The extent to which the supported party's present or future earning capacity is impaired by periods of unemployment that were incurred during the marriage to permit the supported party to devote time to domestic duties.
(b) The extent to which the supported party contributed to the attainment of an education, training, a career position, or a license by the supporting party.
(c) The ability of the supporting party to pay spousal support, taking into account the supporting party's earning capacity, earned and unearned income, assets, and standard of living.
(d) The needs of each party based on the standard of living established during the marriage.
(e) The obligations and assets, including the separate property, of

each party.

(f) The duration of the marriage.

(g) The ability of the supported party to engage in gainful employment without unduly interfering with the interests of dependent children in the custody of the party.

(h) The age and health of the parties.

(i) All documented evidence of any history of domestic violence, as defined in Section 6211, between the parties or perpetrated by either party against either party's child, including, but not limited to, consideration of:

(1) A plea of nolo contendere.

(2) Emotional distress resulting from domestic violence perpetrated against the supported party by the supporting party.

(3) Any history of violence against the supporting party by the supported party.

(4) Issuance of a protective order after a hearing pursuant to Section 6340.

(5) A finding by a court during the pendency of a divorce, separation, or child custody proceeding, or other proceeding under Division 10 (commencing with Section 6200), that the spouse has committed domestic violence.

(j) The immediate and specific tax consequences to each party.

(k) The balance of the hardships to each party.

(l) The goal that the supported party shall be self-supporting within a reasonable period of time. Except in the case of a marriage of long duration as described in Section 4336, a "reasonable period of time" for purposes of this section generally shall be one-half the length of the marriage. However, nothing in this section is intended to limit the court's discretion to order support for a greater or lesser length of time, based on any of the other factors listed in this section, Section 4336, and the circumstances of the parties.

(m) The criminal conviction of an abusive spouse shall be considered in making a reduction or elimination of a spousal support award in accordance with Section 4324.5 or 4325.

(n) Any other factors the court determines are just and equitable.[408]

4321. In a judgment of dissolution of marriage or legal separation of the parties, the court may deny support to a party out of the separate property of the other party in any of the following circumstances:

(a) The party has separate property, or is earning the party's own livelihood, or there is community property or quasi-community property sufficient to give the party proper support.

(b) The custody of the children has been awarded to the other party, who is supporting them.

4322. In an original or modification proceeding, where there are no children, and a party has or acquires a separate estate, including income from employment, sufficient for the party's proper support, no support shall be ordered or continued against the other party.[1]

4323. (a) (1) Except as otherwise agreed to by the parties in writing, there is a rebuttable presumption, affecting the burden of proof, of decreased need for spousal support if the supported party is cohabiting with a nonmarital partner. Upon a determination that circumstances have changed, the court may modify or terminate the spousal support as provided for in Chapter 6 (commencing with Section 3650) of Part 1.

(2) Holding oneself out to be the spouse of the person with whom one is cohabiting is not necessary to constitute cohabitation as the term is used in this subdivision.

(b) The income of a supporting spouse's subsequent spouse or nonmarital partner shall not be considered when determining or modifying spousal support.

(c) Nothing in this section precludes later modification or termination of spousal support on proof of change of circumstances.[304]

4324. In addition to any other remedy authorized by law, when a spouse is convicted of attempting to murder the other spouse, as punishable pursuant to subdivision (a) of Section 664 of the Penal Code, or of soliciting the murder of the other spouse, as punishable pursuant to subdivision (b) of Section 653f of the Penal Code, the injured spouse shall be entitled to a prohibition of any temporary or permanent award for spousal support or medical, life, or other insurance benefits or payments from the injured spouse to the other spouse.

As used in this section, "injured spouse" means the spouse who has been the subject of the attempted murder or the solicitation of murder for which the other spouse was convicted, whether or not actual physical injury occurred.[196]

4324.5. (a) In any proceeding for dissolution of marriage where there is a criminal conviction for a violent sexual felony or a domestic violence felony perpetrated by one spouse against the other spouse and the petition for dissolution is filed before five years following the conviction and any time served in custody, on probation, or on parole, the following shall apply:

(1) An award of spousal support to the convicted spouse from the injured spouse is prohibited.

(2) If economic circumstances warrant, the court shall order the attorney's fees and costs incurred by the parties to be paid from the community assets. The injured spouse shall not be required to pay any attorney's fees of the convicted spouse out of the injured spouse's separate property.

(3) At the request of the injured spouse, the date of separation, as defined in Section 70, shall be the date of the incident giving rise to the conviction, or earlier, if the court finds circumstances that justify an earlier date.

(4) The injured spouse shall be entitled to 100 percent of the community property interest in the retirement and pension benefits of the injured spouse.

(b) As used in this section, the following definitions apply:

(1) "Domestic violence felony" means a felony offense for an act of abuse, as described in Section 6203, perpetrated by one spouse against the other spouse.

(2) Injured spouse" means the spouse who has been the subject of the violent sexual felony or domestic violence felony for which the other spouse was convicted.

(3) "Violent sexual felony" means those offenses described in paragraphs (3), (4), (5), (11), and (18)

of subdivision (c) of Section 667.5 of the Penal Code.

(c) If a convicted spouse presents documented evidence of the convicted spouse's history as a victim of a violent sexual offense, as described in paragraphs (3), (4), (5), (11), and (18) of subdivision (c) of Section 667.5 of the Penal Code, or domestic violence, as defined in Section 6211, perpetrated by the other spouse, the court may determine, based on the facts of the particular case, that one or more of paragraphs (1) to (4), inclusive, of subdivision (a) do not apply.

(d) The changes made to this section by the bill that added this subdivision shall only apply to convictions that occur on or after January 1, 2019.[388]

4325. (a) In a proceeding for dissolution of marriage where there is a criminal conviction for a domestic violence misdemeanor or a criminal conviction for a misdemeanor that results in a term of probation pursuant to Section 1203.097 of the Penal Code perpetrated by one spouse against the other spouse entered by the court within five years prior to the filing of the dissolution proceeding or during the course of the dissolution proceeding, there shall be a rebuttable presumption that the following shall apply:

(1) An award of spousal support to the convicted spouse from the injured spouse is prohibited.

(2) If economic circumstances warrant, the court shall order the attorney's fees and costs incurred by the parties to be paid from the community assets. The injured spouse shall not be required to pay any attorney's fees of the convicted spouse out of the injured spouse's separate property.

(3) At the request of the injured spouse, the date of separation, as defined in Section 70, shall be the date of the incident giving rise to the conviction, or earlier, if the court finds circumstances that justify an earlier date.

(b) The court may consider documented evidence of a convicted spouse's history as a victim of domestic violence, as defined in Section 6211, perpetrated by the other spouse, or any other factors the court deems just and equitable, as conditions for rebutting this presumption.

(c) The rebuttable presumption created in this section may be rebutted by a preponderance of the evidence.

(d) The court may determine, based on the facts of a particular case, that the injured spouse is entitled to up to 100 percent of the community property interest in the injured spouse's retirement and pension benefits. In determining whether and how to apportion the community property interest in the retirement and pension benefits of the injured spouse, the court shall consider all of the following factors:

(1) The misdemeanor domestic violence conviction, as well as documented evidence of other instances of domestic violence, as defined in Section 6211, between the parties or perpetrated by either party against either party's child, including, but not limited to, consideration of emotional distress resulting from domestic violence. The court shall also consider documented evidence of a convicted spouse's history as a victim of domestic violence, as defined in Section 6211, perpetrated

by the other spouse.

(2) The duration of the marriage and when, based on documented evidence, incidents of domestic violence, as defined in Section 6211, occurred.

(3) The extent to which the convicted spouse's present or future earning capacity is impaired by periods of unemployment that were incurred during the marriage to permit the convicted spouse to devote time to domestic duties.

(4) The extent to which the convicted spouse contributed to the attainment of an education, training, a career position, or a license by the injured spouse.

(5) The balance of the hardships to each party.

(6) Any other factors the court determines are just and equitable.

(e) As used in this section, the following definitions apply:

(1) "Domestic violence misdemeanor" means a misdemeanor offense for an act of abuse, as described in paragraphs (1) to (3), inclusive, of subdivision (a) of Section 6203, perpetrated by one spouse against the other spouse.

(2) "Injured spouse" means the spouse who has been the subject of the domestic violence misdemeanor for which the other spouse was convicted.

(f) The changes made to this section by the bill that added this subdivision shall only apply to convictions that occur on or after January 1, 2019.[451]

4326. (a) Except as provided in subdivision (d), in a proceeding in which a spousal support order exists or in which the court has retained jurisdiction over a spousal support order, if a companion child support order is in effect, the termination of child support pursuant to subdivision (a) of Section 3901 constitutes a change of circumstances that may be the basis for a request by either party for modification of spousal support.

(b) A motion to modify spousal support based on the change of circumstances described in subdivision (a) shall be filed by either party no later than six months from the date the child support order terminates.

(c) If a motion to modify a spousal support order pursuant to subdivision (a) is filed, either party may request the appointment of a vocational training counselor pursuant to Section 4331.

(d) Notwithstanding subdivision (a), termination of the child support order does not constitute a change of circumstances under subdivision (a) in any of the following circumstances:

(1) The child and spousal support orders are the result of a marital settlement agreement or judgment and the marital settlement agreement or judgment contains a provision regarding what is to occur when the child support order terminates.

(2) The child and spousal support orders are the result of a marital settlement agreement or judgment, which provides that the spousal support order is nonmodifiable or that spousal support is waived and the court's jurisdiction over spousal support has been terminated.

(3) The court's jurisdiction over spousal support was previously terminated.

(e) Notwithstanding subdivision (b), a party whose six-month deadline to file expired between January 1, 2014, and September 30, 2014, may file a motion pursuant to this section until December 31, 2014.[281]

Chapter 3: Spousal Support Upon Dissolution or Legal Separation

4330. (a) In a judgment of dissolution of marriage or legal separation of the parties, the court may order a party to pay for the support of the other party an amount, for a period of time, that the court determines is just and reasonable, based on the standard of living established during the marriage, taking into consideration the circumstances as provided in Chapter 2 (commencing with Section 4320).
(b) When making an order for spousal support, the court may advise the recipient of support that the recipient should make reasonable efforts to assist in providing for their support needs, taking into account the particular circumstances considered by the court pursuant to Section 4320, unless, in the case of a marriage of long duration as provided for in Section 4336, the court decides this warning is inadvisable.[452]

4331. (a) In a proceeding for dissolution of marriage or for legal separation of the parties, the court may order a party to submit to an examination by a vocational training counselor. The examination shall include an assessment of the party's ability to obtain employment based upon the party's age, health, education, marketable skills, employment history, and the current availability of employment opportunities. The focus of the examination shall be on an assessment of the party's ability to obtain employment that would allow the party to maintain their marital standard of living.
(b) The order may be made only on motion, for good cause, and on notice to the party to be examined and to all parties. The order shall specify the time, place, manner, conditions, scope of the examination, and the person or persons by whom it is to be made.
(c) A party who does not comply with an order under this section is subject to the same consequences provided for failure to comply with an examination ordered pursuant to Chapter 15 (commencing with Section 2032.010) of Title 4 of Part 4 of the Code of Civil Procedure.
(d) "Vocational training counselor" for the purpose of this section means an individual with sufficient knowledge, skill, experience, training, or education in interviewing, administering, and interpreting tests for analysis of marketable skills, formulating career goals, planning courses of training and study, and assessing the job market, to qualify as an expert in vocational training under Section 720 of the Evidence Code.
(e) A vocational training counselor shall have at least the following qualifications:
(1) A master's degree in the behavioral sciences, or other postgraduate degree that the court finds provides sufficient training to perform a vocational evaluation.
(2) Qualification to administer and interpret inventories for assessing career potential.
(3) Demonstrated ability in interviewing clients and assessing marketable skills with an understanding of age constraints, physical and mental health, previous education and experience, and time

and geographic mobility constraints.

(4) Knowledge of current employment conditions, job market, and wages in the indicated geographic area.

(5) Knowledge of education and training programs in the area with costs and time plans for these programs.

(f) The court may order the supporting spouse to pay, in addition to spousal support, the necessary expenses and costs of the counseling, retraining, or education.[453]

4332. In a proceeding for dissolution of marriage or for legal separation of the parties, the court shall make specific factual findings with respect to the standard of living during the marriage, and, at the request of either party, the court shall make appropriate factual determinations with respect to other circumstances.[1]

4333. An order for spousal support in a proceeding for dissolution of marriage or for legal separation of the parties may be made retroactive to the date of filing the notice of motion or order to show cause, or to any subsequent date.[1]

4334. (a) If a court orders spousal support for a contingent period of time, the obligation of the supporting party terminates on the happening of the contingency. The court may, in the order, order the supported party to notify the supporting party, or the supporting party's attorney of record, of the happening of the contingency.

(b) If the supported party fails to notify the supporting party, or the attorney of record of the supporting party, of the happening of the contingency and continues to accept spousal support payments, the supported party shall refund payments received that accrued after the happening of the contingency, except that the overpayments shall first be applied to spousal support payments that are then in default.[1]

4335. An order for spousal support terminates at the end of the period provided in the order and shall not be extended unless the court retains jurisdiction in the order or under Section 4336.[1]

4336. (a) Except on written agreement of the parties to the contrary or a court order terminating spousal support, the court retains jurisdiction indefinitely in a proceeding for dissolution of marriage or for legal separation of the parties where the marriage is of long duration.

(b) For the purpose of retaining jurisdiction, there is a presumption affecting the burden of producing evidence that a marriage of 10 years or more, from the date of marriage to the date of separation, is a marriage of long duration. However, the court may consider periods of separation during the marriage in determining whether the marriage is in fact of long duration. Nothing in this subdivision precludes a court from determining that a marriage of less than 10 years is a marriage of long duration.

(c) Nothing in this section limits the court's discretion to terminate spousal support in later proceedings on a showing of changed circumstances.

(d) This section applies to the following:

(1) A proceeding filed on or after January 1, 1988.

(2) A proceeding pending on January

1, 1988, in which the court has not entered a permanent spousal support order or in which the court order is subject to modification.[1]

4337. Except as otherwise agreed by the parties in writing, the obligation of a party under an order for the support of the other party terminates upon the death of either party or the remarriage of the other party.[1]

4338. In the enforcement of an order for spousal support, the court shall resort to the property described below in the order indicated:
(a) The earnings, income, or accumulations of either spouse after the date of separation, as defined in Section 70, which would have been community property if the spouse had not been separated from the other spouse.
(b) The community property.
(c) The quasi-community property.
(d) The other separate property of the party required to make the support payments.[349]

4339. The court may order the supporting party to give reasonable security for payment of spousal support.[1]

Chapter 4: Payment to Court-Designated Officer; Enforcement by District Attorney

4350. In any proceeding where a court makes or has made an order requiring the payment of spousal support, the court may direct that payment shall be made to the county officer designated by the court for that purpose. The court may include in its order made pursuant to this section any service charge imposed under the authority of Section 279 of the Welfare and Institutions Code.[1]

4351. (a) In a proceeding where the court has entered an order pursuant to Section 4350, the court may also refer the matter of enforcement of the spousal support order to the local child support agency. The local child support agency may bring those enforcement proceedings it determines to be appropriate.
(b) Notwithstanding subdivision (a), when the local child support agency is required to appear on behalf of a welfare recipient in a proceeding to enforce an order requiring payment of child support, the local child support agency shall also enforce any order requiring payment to the welfare recipient of spousal support that is in arrears.
(c) This section does not prohibit the district attorney or the local child support agency from bringing an action or initiating process to enforce or punish the failure to obey an order for spousal support under any law that empowers the district attorney or the local child support agency to bring an action or initiate a process, whether or not there has been a referral by the court pursuant to this chapter.
(d) Any notice from the district attorney or the local child support agency requesting a meeting with the support obligor for any purpose authorized under this part shall contain a statement advising the support obligor of the obligor's right to have an attorney present at the meeting.[454]

4352. (a) Insofar as expenses of the county officer designated by the court and expenses of the local child support

agency incurred in the enforcement of an order referred by the court under this chapter exceed any service charge imposed under Section 279 of the Welfare and Institutions Code, the expenses are a charge upon the county where the proceedings are pending.
(b) Fees for service of process in the enforcement of an order referred by the court under this chapter are a charge upon the county where the process is served.

Chapter 5: Provision for Support After Death of Supporting Party

4360. (a) For the purpose of Section 4320, where it is just and reasonable in view of the circumstances of the parties, the court, in determining the needs of a supported spouse, may include an amount sufficient to purchase an annuity for the supported spouse or to maintain insurance for the benefit of the supported spouse on the life of the spouse required to make the payment of support, or may require the spouse required to make the payment of support to establish a trust to provide for the support of the supported spouse, so that the supported spouse will not be left without means of support in the event that the spousal support is terminated by the death of the party required to make the payment of support.
(b) Except as otherwise agreed to by the parties in writing, an order made under this section may be modified or terminated at the discretion of the court at any time before the death of the party required to make the payment of support.[1]

PART 4: SUPPORT PARENTS

enacted by Stats. 1992, Ch. 162, Sec. 10.

Chapter 1: General Provisions

4400. Except as otherwise provided by law, an adult child shall, to the extent of the adult child's ability, support a parent who is in need and unable to self-maintain by work.[455]

4401. The promise of an adult child to pay for necessaries previously furnished to a parent described in Section 4400 is binding.[1]

4402. The duty of support under this part is cumulative and not in substitution for any other duty.[1]

4403. (a) Subject to subdivision (b):
(1) A parent, or the county on behalf of the parent, may bring an action against the child to enforce the duty of support under this part.
(2) If the county furnishes support to a parent, the county has the same right as the parent to whom the support was furnished to secure reimbursement and obtain continuing support.
(b) The right of the county to proceed on behalf of the parent or to obtain reimbursement is subject to any limitation otherwise imposed by the law of this state.
(c) The court may order the child to pay the county reasonable attorney's fees and court costs in a proceeding by the county under this section.[1]

4404. In determining the amount to be ordered for support, the court shall consider the following circumstances of each party:
(a) Earning capacity and needs.
(b) Obligations and assets.

(c) Age and health.
(d) Standard of living.
(e) Other factors the court deems just and equitable.[1]

4405. The court retains jurisdiction to modify or terminate an order for support where justice requires.[1]

Chapter 2: Relief from Duty to Support Parent Who Abandoned Child

4410. An adult child may file a petition in the county where a parent of the child resides requesting that the court make an order freeing the petitioner from the obligation otherwise imposed by law to support the parent. If the parent does not reside in this state, the petition shall be filed in the county where the adult child resides.[1]

4411. The court shall make the order requested pursuant to Section 4410 only if the petition alleges and the court finds all of the following:
(a) The child was abandoned by the parent when the child was a minor.
(b) The abandonment continued for a period of two or more years before the time the child attained the age of 18 years.
(c) During the period of abandonment, the parent was physically and mentally able to provide support for the child.[1]

4412. On the filing of a petition under this chapter, the clerk shall set the matter for hearing by the court and shall issue a citation, stating the time and place of the hearing, directed to the parent and to the parent's conservator, if any, or, if the parent is deceased, the personal representative of the parent's estate. At least five days before the date of the hearing, the citation and a copy of the petition shall be personally served on each person to whom it is directed, in the same manner as provided by law for the service of summons.[1]

4413. If the parent is a resident of this state, the court does not have jurisdiction to make an order under this chapter until 30 days after the county counsel, or the district attorney in a county not having a county counsel, of the county in which the parent resides has been served with notice of the pendency of the proceeding.[1]

4414. (a) If, upon hearing, the court determines that the requirements of Section 4411 are satisfied, the court shall make an order that the petitioner is relieved from the obligation otherwise imposed by law to support the parent.
(b) An order under this section also releases the petitioner with respect to any state law under which a child is required to do any of the following:
(1) Pay for the support, care, maintenance, and the like of a parent.
(2) Reimburse the state or a local public agency for furnishing the support, care, maintenance, or the like of a parent.[1]

PART 5: ENFORCEMENT OF SUPPORT OTHERS

enacted by Stats. 1992, Ch. 162, Sec. 10.

Chapter 1: General Provisions

4500. An order for child, family, or spousal support that is made, entered, or enforceable in this state is enforceable under this code, whether or not the order was made or entered pursuant to this code.[1]

4501. A family support order is enforceable in the same manner and to the same extent as a child support order.[1]

4502. The period for enforcement and procedure for renewal of a judgment or order for child, family, or spousal support is governed by Section 291.[131]

4503. If a parent has been ordered to make payments for the support of a minor child, an action to recover an arrearage in those payments may be maintained at any time within the period otherwise specified for the enforcement of such a judgment, notwithstanding the fact that the child has attained the age of 18 years.[1]

4504. (a) If the noncustodial parent is receiving payments from the federal government pursuant to the Social Security Act or Railroad Retirement Act, or from the Department of Veterans Affairs because of the retirement or disability of the noncustodial parent and the noncustodial parent notifies the custodial person, or notifies the local child support agency in a case being enforced by the local child support agency pursuant to Title IV-D of the Social Security Act, then the custodial parent or other child support obligee shall contact the appropriate federal agency within 30 days of receiving notification that the noncustodial parent is receiving those payments to verify eligibility for each child to receive payments from the federal government because of the disability of the noncustodial parent. If the child is potentially eligible for those payments, the custodial parent or other child support obligee shall apply for and cooperate with the appropriate federal agency for the receipt of those benefits on behalf of each child. The noncustodial parent shall cooperate with the custodial parent or other child support obligee in making that application and shall provide any information necessary to complete the application.

(b) If the court has ordered a noncustodial parent to pay for the support of a child, payments for the support of the child made by the federal government pursuant to the Social Security Act or Railroad Retirement Act, or by the Department of Veterans Affairs because of the retirement or disability of the noncustodial parent and received by the custodial parent or other child support obligee shall be credited toward the amount ordered by the court to be paid by the noncustodial parent for support of the child unless the payments made by the federal government were taken into consideration by the court in determining the amount of support to be paid. Any payments shall be credited in the order set forth in Section 695.221 of the Code of Civil Procedure.

(c) If the custodial parent or other child support obligee refuses to apply for those benefits or fails to cooperate with the appropriate federal agency in completing the application but the child or children otherwise are eligible to receive those benefits, the noncustodial parent shall be credited toward the amount ordered by the court to be paid for that month by the noncustodial parent for support of the child or children in the amount of payment that the child or children would have received that month had the custodial parent or other child support obligee completed an application for the benefits if the noncustodial parent provides evidence to the local child support agency indicating the amount the child or children would have received. The credit for those payments shall continue until the child or children would no longer be eligible for those benefits or the order for child support for the child or children is no longer in effect, whichever occurs first.[114]

4505. (a) A court may require a parent who alleges that the parent's default in a child or family support order is due to the parent's unemployment to submit to the appropriate child support enforcement agency or any other entity designated by the court, including, but not limited to, the court itself, each two weeks, or at a frequency deemed appropriate by the court, a list of at least five different places the parent has applied for employment.
(b) This section shall become operative on January 1, 2011.[194]

4506. (a) An abstract of a judgment ordering a party to pay spousal, child, or family support to the other party shall be certified by the clerk of the court where the judgment was entered and shall contain all of the following:
(1) The title of the court where the judgment is entered and the cause and number of the proceeding.
(2) The date of entry of the judgment and of any renewal of the judgment.
(3) Where the judgment and any renewals are entered in the records of the court.
(4) The name and last known address of the party ordered to pay support.
(5) The name and address of the party to whom support payments are ordered to be paid.
(6) Only the last four digits of the social security number, birth date, and driver's license number of the party who is ordered to pay support. If any of those numbers are not known to the party to whom support payments are to be paid, that fact shall be indicated on the abstract of the court judgment. This paragraph shall not apply to documents created prior to January 1, 2010.
(7) Whether a stay of enforcement has been ordered by the court and, if so, the date the stay ends.
(8) The date of issuance of the abstract.
(9) Any other information deemed reasonable and appropriate by the Judicial Council.
(b) The Judicial Council may develop a form for an abstract of a judgment ordering a party to pay child, family, or spousal support to another party which contains the information required by subdivision (a).
(c) Notwithstanding any other provision of law, when a support obligation is being enforced pursuant to Title IV-D of the Social Security Act, the agency enforcing the obligation may record a notice of support judgment. The notice of support judgment shall contain the same information as the form adopted by the Judicial Council pursuant to subdivision (b) and Section 4506.1. The notice of support judgment shall have the same force and effect as an abstract of judgment certified by the clerk of the court where the judgment

was entered. The local child support agency or other Title IV-D agency shall not be subject to any civil liability as a consequence of causing a notice of support judgment to be recorded.

(d) As used in this section, "judgment" includes an order for child, family, or spousal support.[193]

4506.1. Notwithstanding any other provision of law, when a support obligation is being enforced pursuant to Title IV-D of the Social Security Act, the agency enforcing the obligation may file and record an abstract of support judgment as authorized by Section 4506 and substitute the office address of the agency designated to receive support payments for the address of the party to whom support was ordered to be paid.

4506.2. (a) Notwithstanding any other provision of law, when a support obligation is being enforced pursuant to Title IV-D of the Social Security Act, the agency enforcing the obligation may file and record a substitution of payee, if a judgment or abstract of judgment has previously been recorded pursuant to Section 697.320 of the Code of Civil Procedure by the support obligee or by a different governmental agency.

(b) Notwithstanding any other provision of law, when the Title IV-D agency ceases enforcement of a support obligation at the request of the support obligee, the agency may file and record a substitution of payee, if a judgment or abstract of judgment has been previously recorded pursuant to Section 697.320 of the Code of Civil Procedure.

(c) The substitution of payee shall contain all of the following:

(1) The name and address of the governmental agency or substituted payee filing the substitution and a notice that the substituted payee is to be contacted when notice to a lienholder may or must be given.

(2) The title of the court, the cause, and number of the proceeding where the substituted payee has registered the judgment.

(3) The name and last known address of the party ordered to pay support.

(4) The recorder identification number or book and page of the recorded document to which the substitution of payee applies.

(5) Any other information deemed reasonable and appropriate by the Judicial Council.

(d) The recorded substitution of payee shall not affect the priorities created by earlier recordations of support judgments or abstracts of support judgments.

(e) An agency enforcing the support obligation pursuant to Title IV-D of the Social Security Act is not required to obtain prior court approval or a clerk's certification when filing and recording a substitution of payee under this section.

4506.3. The Judicial Council, in consultation with the California Family Support Council, the Department of Child Support Services, and title insurance industry representatives, shall develop a single form, which conforms with the requirements of Section 27361.6 of the Government Code, for the substitution of payee, for notice directing payment of support to the local child support agency pursuant to Section 4204, and for notice that support has been assigned pursuant to Section 11477 of the Welfare and Institutions Code. The form shall be available no later than July 1, 1998.

4507. When a court orders a person to make payment for child support or family support, the court may order that individual to make that payment as provided in Section 1151.5 of the Government Code.

4508. (a) This section does not apply to any child support obligor who is subject to an earnings assignment order pursuant to Chapter 8 (commencing with Section 5200).
(b) Except as provided in subdivision (a), every order or judgment to pay child support may require a child support obligor to designate an account for the purpose of paying the child support obligation by electronic funds transfer, as defined in subdivision (a) of Section 6479.5 of the Revenue and Taxation Code. The order or judgment may require the obligor to deposit funds in an interest-bearing account with a state or federally chartered commercial bank, a savings and loan association, or in shares of a federally insured credit union doing business in this state, and shall require the obligor to maintain funds in the account sufficient to pay the monthly child support obligation. The court may order that each payment be electronically transferred to either the obligee's account or the local child support agency account. The obligor shall be required to notify the obligee if the depository institution or the account number is changed. No interest shall accrue on any amount subject to electronic funds transfer as long as funds are maintained in the account that are sufficient to pay the monthly child support obligation.

Chapter 2: Deposit of money to Secure Future Child Support Payments

Article 1: General Provisions

4550. "Child support obligee" as used in this chapter means either the parent, guardian, or other person to whom child support has been ordered to be paid or the local child support agency designated by the court to receive the payment. The local child support agency is the "child support obligee" for the purposes of this chapter for all cases in which an application for services has been filed under Part D of Title IV of the Social Security Act (42 U.S.C. Sec. 651 et seq.).

4551. Except as provided in this section, this chapter:
(a) Does not apply to a temporary child support order.
(b) Applies to an application for modification of child support filed on or after January 1, 1992, but this chapter does not constitute the basis for the modification.
(c) Applies to an application for modification of child support in a case where the child support obligee has previously waived the establishment of a child support trust account pursuant to subdivision (b) of Section 4560 and now seeks the establishment of the child support trust account.
(d) Applies to an order or judgment entered by the court on or after January 1, 1993, ordering a child support obligor to pay a then existing child support arrearage that the child support obligor has unlawfully failed to pay as of the date of that order or

judgment, including the arrearages which were incurred before January 1, 1992.[1]

4552. The Judicial Council shall promulgate such rules of court and publish such related judicial forms as the Judicial Council determines are necessary and appropriate to implement this chapter. In taking these steps, the Judicial Council shall ensure the uniform statewide application of this chapter and compliance with Part D of Title IV of the Social Security Act (42 U.S.C. Sec. 651 et seq.) and any regulations promulgated thereunder.[1]

4553. Nothing in this chapter shall be construed to permit any action or omission by the state or any of its political subdivisions that would place the state in noncompliance with any requirement of federal law, including, but not limited to, the state reimbursement requirements of Part D of Title IV of the Social Security Act (42 U.S.C. Sec. 651 et seq.) and any regulations promulgated thereunder.[1]

4554. This chapter applies notwithstanding any other law.[1]

Article 2: Order for Deposit of Money

4560. (a) Except as provided in subdivision (b) or in Article 3 (commencing with Section 4565), every order or judgment to pay child support may also require the payment by the child support obligor of up to one year's child support or such lesser amount as is equal to the child support amount due to be paid by the child support obligor between the time of the date of the order and the date when the support obligation will be terminated by operation of law. This amount shall be known as the "child support security deposit."

(b) Unless expressly waived by the child support obligee, the court may order the establishment of a child support trust account pursuant to this chapter in every proceeding in which a child support obligation is imposed by order of the court. Among other reasons, the court may decline to establish a child support trust account upon its finding that an adequately funded child support trust account already exists pursuant to this chapter for the benefit of the child or children involved in the proceeding or that the child support obligor has provided adequate alternative security which is equivalent to the child support security deposit otherwise required by this chapter.[1]

4561. If a child support security deposit is ordered, the court shall order that the moneys be deposited by the child support obligor in an interest-bearing account with a state or federally chartered commercial bank, a trust company authorized to transact trust business in this state, or a savings and loan association, or in shares of a federally insured credit union doing business in this state and having a trust department, subject to withdrawal only upon authorization of the court. The moneys so deposited shall be used exclusively to guarantee the monthly payment of child support.[1]

4562. The court shall also order that evidence of the deposit shall be provided by the child support obligor in the form specified by the court, which shall be served upon the child support obligee and filed with the court within a reasonable time specified by the court, not to exceed 30 days.[1]

4563. An account established pursuant to this chapter shall be dissolved and any remaining funds in the account shall be returned to the support obligor, with any interest earned thereon, upon the full payment and cessation of the child support obligation as provided by court order or operation of law.[1]

Article 3: Application to Reduce or Eliminate Deposit

4565. (a) Before entry of a child support order pursuant to Section 4560, the court shall give the child support obligor reasonable notice and opportunity to file an application to reduce or eliminate the child support security deposit on either of the following grounds:

(1) The obligor has provided adequate alternative equivalent security to assure timely payment of the amount required by Section 4560.

(2) The obligor is unable, without undue financial hardship, to pay the support deposit required by Section 4560.

(b) The application shall be supported by all reasonable and necessary financial and other information required by the court to establish the existence of either ground for relief.

(c) After the filing of an application, the child support obligor shall also serve the application and supporting financial and other information submitted pursuant to subdivision (b) upon the child support obligee and any other party to the proceeding.[173]

4566. Upon the filing of an application under Section 4565 with the court and the service of the application upon the child support obligee and any other party to the proceedings, the court shall provide notice and opportunity for any party opposing the application to file responsive financial and other information setting forth the factual and legal bases for the party's opposition.[1]

4567. The court shall then provide an opportunity for hearing, and shall thereafter enter its order exercising its discretion under all the facts and circumstances as disclosed in the admissible evidence before it so as to maximize the payment and deposit of the amount required by Section 4560, or an equivalent adequate security for the payment thereof, without imposition of undue financial hardship on the support obligor. If the court finds that the deposit of the amount required by Section 4560 would impose an undue financial hardship upon the child support obligor, the court shall reduce this amount to an amount that the child support obligor can pay as the child support security deposit without undue financial hardship.[1]

Article 4: Use of Deposit to Make Delinquent Support Payment

4570. (a) Upon the application of the child support obligee stating that the support payment is 10 or more days late, the court shall immediately order disbursement of funds from the account established pursuant to this chapter solely for the purpose of providing the amount of child support then in arrears.

(b) Funds so disbursed shall be used exclusively for the support, maintenance, and education of the child or children subject to the child support order.

(c) The court shall also order the account to be replenished by the child support obligor in the same amounts as are expended from the account to pay the amount of child support which the child support obligor has failed to pay the child support obligee in a timely manner.[1]

4571. The court shall cause a copy of the application, as well as its order to disburse and replenish funds, to be served upon the child support obligor, who shall be subject to contempt of court for failure to comply with the order.[1]

4572. The court shall cause a copy of its order to disburse and replenish funds to be served upon the depository institution where the child support security deposit is maintained, and upon the child support agency with jurisdiction over the case.

4573. If support is ordered to be paid through the local child support agency on behalf of a child not receiving public assistance pursuant to the Family Economic Security Act of 1982 (Chapter 2 (commencing with Section 11200) of Part 3 of Division 9 of the Welfare and Institutions Code), the local child support agency shall forward the support received pursuant to this chapter to the custodial parent or other person having care or control of the child or children involved.

Chapter 3: Deposit of Assets to Secure Future Child Support Payments

Article 1: General Provisions

4600. The purpose of this chapter is to provide an extraordinary remedy for cases of bad faith failure to pay child support obligations.[1]

4601. "Deposit holder" as used in this chapter means the district attorney, county officer, or trustee designated by the court to receive assets deposited pursuant to this chapter to secure future support payments.[1]

4602. If requested by an obligor-parent, the deposit holder shall prepare a statement setting forth disbursements and receipts made under this chapter.[1]

4603. The deposit holder who is responsible for any money or property and for any disbursements under this chapter is not liable for any action undertaken in good faith and in conformance with this chapter.[1]

4604. (a) If the deposit holder incurs fees or costs under this chapter which are not compensated by the deduction under subdivision (c) of Section 4630 (including, but not limited to, fees or costs incurred in a sale of assets pursuant to this chapter and in the preparation of a statement pursuant to Section 4602), the court shall, after a hearing, order the obligor-parent to pay the reasonable fees and costs incurred by the deposit holder. The hearing shall be held not less than 20 days after the deposit holder serves notice of motion or order to show cause upon the obligor-parent.

(b) Fees and costs ordered to be paid under this section shall be in addition to any deposit made under this chapter but shall not exceed whichever of the following is less:

(1) Five percent of one year's child support obligation.

(2) The total amount ordered deposited under Section 4614.[1]

Article 2: Order for Deposit of Assets

4610. (a) Subject to Sections 4613, 4614, and 4615, in any proceeding where the court has ordered either or both parents to pay any amount for the support of a child for whom support may be ordered, upon an order to show cause or notice of motion, application, and declaration signed under penalty of perjury by the person or county officer to whom support has been ordered to have been paid stating that the parent or parents so ordered is in arrears in payment in a sum equal to the amount of 60 days of payments, the court shall issue to the parent or parents ordered to pay support, following notice and opportunity for a hearing, an order requiring that the parent or parents deposit assets to secure future support payments with the deposit holder designated by the court.
(b) In a proceeding under this article, upon request of any party, the court may also issue an ex parte restraining order as specified in Section 4620.

4611. In a proceeding under this chapter, an obligor-parent shall rebut both of the following presumptions:
(a) The nonpayment of child support was willful, without good faith.
(b) The obligor had the ability to pay the support.[1]

4612. An obligor-parent alleged to be in arrears may use any of the following grounds as a defense to the motion filed pursuant to this article or as a basis for filing a motion to stop a sale or use of assets under Section 4631:
(a) Child support payments are not in arrears.
(b) Laches.
(c) There has been a change in the custody of the children.
(d) There is a pending motion for reduction in support due to a reduction in income.
(e) Illness or disability.
(f) Unemployment.
(g) Serious adverse impact on the immediate family of the obligor-parent residing with the obligor-parent that outweighs the impact of denial of the motion or stopping the sale on obligee.
(h) Serious impairment of the ability of the obligor-parent to generate income.
(i) Other emergency conditions.[1]

4613. The court shall not issue an order pursuant to this article unless the court determines that one or more of the following conditions exist:
(a) The obligor-parent is not receiving salary or wages subject to an assignment pursuant to Chapter 8 (commencing with Section 5200) and there is reason to believe that the obligor-parent has earned income from some source of employment.
(b) An assignment of a portion of salary or wages pursuant to Chapter 8 (commencing with Section 5200) would not be sufficient to meet the amount of the support obligation, for reasons other than a change of circumstances which would qualify for a reduction in the amount of child support ordered.
(c) The job history of the obligor-parent shows that an assignment of a portion of salary or wages pursuant to Chapter 8 (commencing with Section 5200), would be difficult to enforce or would not be a practical means for securing the payment of the support obligation, due to circumstances including, but not limited to, multiple

concurrent or consecutive employers.[1]

4614. The designation of assets subject to an order pursuant to this article shall be based upon concern for maximizing the liquidity and ready convers-ion into cash of the deposited asset. In all instances, the assets shall include a sum of money up to or equal in value to one year of support payments or six thousand dollars ($6,000) whichever is less, or any other assets, personal or real, designated by the court which equal in value up to one year of payments for support of the child, or six thousand dollars ($6,000), which-ever is less, subject to Section 703.070 of the Code of Civil Procedure.

4615. In lieu of depositing cash or other assets as provided in Section 4614, the obligor-parent may, if approved by the court, provide a performance bond secured by real property or other assets of the obligor-parent and equal in value to one year of payments.[1]

4616. Upon deposit of an asset which is not readily convertible into money, the court may, after a hearing, order the sale of that asset and the deposit of the proceeds with the deposit holder. Not less than 20 days written notice of the hearing shall be served on the obligor-parent.[1]

4617. (a) If the asset ordered to be deposited is real property, the order shall be certified as an abstract of judgment in accordance with Section 674 of the Code of Civil Procedure.
(b) A deposit of real property is made effective by recordation of the certified abstract with the county recorder.
(c) The deposited real property and the rights, benefits, and liabilities attached to that property shall continue in the possession of the legal owner.
(d) For purposes of Section 701.545 of the Code of Civil Procedure, the date of the issuance of the order to deposit assets shall be construed as the date notice of levy on an interest in real property was served on the judgment debtor.[1]

Article 3: Ex Parte Restraining Orders

4620. (a) During the pendency of a proceeding under this chapter, upon the application of either party in the manner provided by Part 4 (commencing with Section 240) of Division 2, the court may, without a hearing, issue ex parte orders restraining any person from transferring, encumbering, hypothecating, concealing, or in any way disposing of any property, real or personal, whether community, quasi-community, or separate, except in the usual course of business or for the necessities of life, and if the order is directed against a party, requiring the party to notify the other party of any proposed extraordinary expenditures and to account to the court for all such extraordinary expenditures.
(b) The matter shall be made returnable not later than 20 days, or if good cause appears to the court, 25 days from the date of the order at which time the ex parte order shall expire.
(c) The court, at the hearing, shall determine for which property the obligor-parent shall be required to report extraordinary expenditures and shall specify what is deemed an extraordinary expenditure for purposes of this subdivision.
(d) An order issued pursuant to this

section after the hearing shall state on its face the date of expiration of the order, which shall expire in one year or upon deposit of assets or money pursuant to Article 2 (commencing with Section 4610), whichever first occurs.[1]

Article 4: Use or Sale of Assets to Make Support Payments

4630. (a) Upon an obligor-parent's failure, within the time specified by the court, to make reasonable efforts to cure the default in child support payments or to comply with a court-approved payment plan, if payments continue in arrears, the deposit holder shall, not less than 25 days after providing the obligor-parent or parents with a written notice served personally or with return receipt requested, unless a motion or order to show cause has been filed to stop the use or sale, use the money or sell or otherwise process the deposited assets for an amount sufficient to pay the arrearage and the amount ordered by the court for the support currently due for the child for whom support may be ordered.
(b) Assets deposited pursuant to an order issued under Article 2 (commencing with Section 4610) shall be construed as being assets subject to levy pursuant to Article 6 (commencing with Section 701.510) of Chapter 3 of Division 2 of Title 9 of Part 2 of the Code of Civil Procedure. The sale of assets shall be conducted in accordance with Article 6 (commencing with Section 701.510) and Article 7 (commencing with Section 701.810) of Chapter 3 of Division 2 of Title 9 of Part 2 of the Code of Civil Procedure.
(c) The deposit holder may deduct from the deposited money the sum of one dollar ($1) for each payment made pursuant to this section.

4631. (a) An obligor-parent may file a motion to stop the use of the money or the sale of the asset under this article within 15 days after service of notice on the obligor-parent pursuant to Section 4630.
(b) The clerk of the court shall set the motion for hearing not less than 20 days after service of the notice of motion and the motion on the person or county officer to whom support has been ordered to have been paid.[1]

4632. An obligor-parent alleged to be in arrears under this article may use any ground set forth in Section 4612 as a basis for filing a motion under Section 4631 to stop a sale or use of assets under this article.[1]

Article 5: Return of Assets of Obligor

4640. The deposit holder shall return all assets subject to court order under Article 2 (commencing with Section 4610) to the obligor-parent when both of the following occur:
(a) One year has elapsed since the court issued the order described under Article 2 (commencing with Section 4610).
(b) The obligor-parent has made all support payments on time during that one-year period.[1]

4641. If the deposited asset is real property and the requirements of Section 4640 have been satisfied, the deposit holder shall do all of the following:
(a) Prepare a release in accordance with Section 697.370 of the Code of

Civil Procedure.
(b) Request the clerk of the court where the order to deposit assets was made to certify the release.
(c) Record the certified release in the office of the county recorder where the certified abstract was recorded under Section 4617.[1]

Chapter 4: Child Support Delinquency Reporting

4700. This chapter may be cited as the Child Support Delinquency Reporting Law.[1]

4701. (a) The Department of Child Support Services shall administer a statewide automated system for the reporting of court-ordered child support obligations to credit reporting agencies.
(b) The department shall design and develop standards for the system in conjunction with representatives of the California Family Support Council and the credit reporting industry.
(c) The standards for the system shall be consistent with credit reporting industry standards and reporting format and with the department's statewide central automated system for support enforcement.
(d) The standards shall include, but not be limited to, all of the following:
(1) Court-ordered child support obligations and delinquent payments, including amounts owed and by whom. The California local child support agencies, on a monthly basis, shall update this information, and then submit it to the department which, in turn, shall consolidate and transmit it to the credit reporting agencies.
(2) Before the initial reporting of a court-ordered child support obligation or a delinquent payment, the local child support agency shall attempt to notify the obligor parent of the proposed action and give 30 days to contest in writing the accuracy of the information, or to pay the arrearage, if any, in compliance with the due process requirements of the laws of this state.
(e) The department and the local child support agencies are responsible for the accuracy of information provided pursuant to this section, and the information shall be based upon the data available at the time the information is provided. Each of these organizations and the credit reporting agencies shall follow reasonable procedures to ensure maximum possible accuracy of the information provided. Neither the department, nor the local child support agencies are liable for any consequences of the failure of a parent to contest the accuracy of the information within the time allowed under paragraph (2) of subdivision (d).

Chapter 5: Civil Penalty for

4720. "Support" for the purposes of this chapter means support as defined in Section 150.[1]

4721. (a) This chapter applies only to installments of child support that are due on or after January 1, 1992.
(b) It is the intent of the Legislature that the penalties provided under this chapter shall be applied in egregious instances of noncompliance with child support orders.
(c) It is the intent of the Legislature that for the purposes of this chapter, payments made through wage

assignments are considered timely regardless of the date of receipt by the local child support agency or obligee.

4722. (a) Any person with a court order for child support, the payments on which are more than 30 days in arrears, may file and then serve a notice of delinquency, as described in this chapter.
(b) Except as provided in Section 4726, and subject to Section 4727, any amount of child support specified in a notice of delinquency that remains unpaid for more than 30 days after the notice of delinquency has been filed and served shall incur a penalty of 6 percent of the delinquent payment for each month that it remains unpaid, up to a maximum of 72 percent of the unpaid balance due.[1]

4723. (a) The notice of delinquency shall be signed under penalty of perjury by the support obligee.
(b) The notice of delinquency shall state all of the following:
(1) The amount that the child support obligor is in arrears.
(2) The installments of support due, the amounts, if any, that have been paid, and the balance due.
(3) That any unpaid installment of child support will incur a penalty of 6 percent of the unpaid support per month until paid, to a maximum of 72 percent of the original amount of the unpaid support, unless the support arrearage is paid within 30 days of the date of service of the notice of delinquency.
(c) In the absence of a protective order prohibiting the support obligor from knowing the whereabouts of the child or children for whom support is payable, or otherwise excusing the requirements of this subdivision, the notice of delinquency shall also include a current address and telephone number of all of the children for whom support is due and, if different from that of the support obligee, the address at which court papers may be served upon the support obligee.[1]

4724. The notice of delinquency may be served personally or by certified mail or in any manner provided for service of summons.[1]

4725. If the child support owed, or any arrearages, interest, or penalty, remains unpaid more than 30 days after serving the notice of delinquency, the support obligee may file a motion to obtain a judgment for the amount owed, which shall be enforceable in any manner provided by law for the enforcement of judgments.[1]

4726. No penalties may be imposed pursuant to this chapter if, in the discretion of the court, all of the following conditions are met:
(a) Within a timely fashion after service of the notice of delinquency, the support obligor files and serves a motion to determine arrearages and to show cause why the penalties provided in this chapter should not be imposed.
(b) At the hearing on the motion filed by the support obligor, the court finds that the support obligor has proved any of the following:
(1) The child support payments were not 30 days in arrears as of the date of service of the notice of delinquency and are not in arrears as of the date of the hearing.
(2) The support obligor suffered serious illness, disability, or unemployment which substantially impaired the ability of the support

obligor to comply fully with the support order and the support obligor has made every possible effort to comply with the support order.
(3) The support obligor is a public employee and for reasons relating to fiscal difficulties of the employing entity the obligor has not received a paycheck for 30 or more days.
(4) It would not be in the interests of justice to impose a penalty.[1]

4727. Any penalty due under this chapter shall not be greater than 6 percent per month of the original amount of support arrearages or support installment, nor may the penalties on any arrearage amount or support installment exceed 72 percent of the original amount due, regardless of whether or not the installments have been listed on more than one notice of delinquency.[1]

4728. Penalties due pursuant to this chapter may be enforced by the issuance of a writ of execution in the same manner as a writ of execution may be issued for unpaid installments of child support, as described in Chapter 7 (commencing with Section 5100), except that payment of penalties under this chapter may not take priority over payment of arrearages or current support.

4729. The local child support agency or any other agency providing support enforcement services pursuant to Title IV-D of the federal Social Security Act may not enforce child support obligations utilizing the penalties provided for by this chapter.

4730. At any hearing to set or modify the amount payable for the support of a child, the court shall not consider any penalties imposed under this chapter in determining the amount of current support to be paid.

4731. A subsequent notice of delinquency may be served and filed at any time. The subsequent notice shall indicate those child support arrearages and ongoing installments that have been listed on a previous notice.[1]

4732. The Judicial Council shall adopt forms or notices for the use of the procedures provided by this chapter.[1]

4733. Penalties collected pursuant to this chapter shall be paid to the custodian of the child who is the subject of the child support judgment or order, whether or not the child is a recipient of public assistance.

Chapter 7: Enforcement by Writ of Execution

5100. Notwithstanding Section 290, a child, family, or spousal support order may be enforced by a writ of execution or a notice of levy pursuant to Section 706.030 of the Code of Civil Procedure or Section 17522 of this code without prior court approval.

5103. (a) Notwithstanding Section 2060, an order for the payment of child, family, or spousal support may be enforced against an employee benefit plan regardless of whether the plan has been joined as a party to the proceeding in which the support order was obtained.
(b) Notwithstanding Section 697.710 of the Code of Civil Procedure, an execution lien created by a levy on the judgment debtor's right to payment of benefits from an employee benefit plan to enforce an order for the payment of child, family, or spousal

support continues until the date the plan has withheld and paid over to the levying officer, as provided in Section 701.010 of the Code of Civil Procedure, the full amount specified in the notice of levy, unless the plan is directed to stop withholding and paying over before that time by court order or by the levying officer.
(c) A writ of execution pursuant to which a levy is made on the judgment debtor's right to payment of benefits from an employee benefit plan under an order for the payment of child, family, or spousal support shall be returned not later than one year after the date the execution lien expires under subdivision (b).

5104. (a) The application for a writ of execution shall be accompanied by an affidavit stating the total amount due and unpaid that is authorized to be enforced pursuant to Sections 5100 to 5103, inclusive, on the date of the application.
(b) If interest on the overdue installments is sought, the affidavit shall state the total amount of the interest and the amount of each due and unpaid installment and the date it became due.
(c) The affidavit shall be filed in the action and a copy shall be attached to the writ of execution delivered to the levying officer. The levying officer shall serve the copy of the affidavit on the judgment debtor when the writ of execution is first served on the judgment debtor pursuant to a levy under the writ.[1]

Chapter 8: Earnings Assignment Order

Article 1: Definitions

5200. Unless the provision or context otherwise requires, the definitions in this article govern the construction of this chapter.[1]

5201. "Arrearage" or "arrearages" is the amount necessary to satisfy a support judgment or order pursuant to Section 695.210 of the Code of Civil Procedure.

5202. "Assignment order" has the same meaning as "earnings assignment order for support."[1]

5204. "Due date of support payments" is the date specifically stated in the order of support or, if no date is stated in the support order, the last day of the month in which the support payment is to be paid.[1]

5206. "Earnings," to the extent that they are subject to an earnings assignment order for support under Chapter 4 (commencing with Section 703.010) of Division 2 of Title 9 of Part 2 of the Code of Civil Procedure, include:
(a) Wages, salary, bonus, money, and benefits described in Sections 704.110, 704.113, and 704.115 of the Code of Civil Procedure.
(b) Payments due for services of independent contractors, interest, dividends, rents, royalties, residuals, patent rights, or mineral or other natural resource rights.
(c) Payments or credits due or becoming due as a result of written or oral contracts for services or sales whether denominated as wages, salary, commission, bonus, or otherwise.
(d) Payments due for workers'

compensation temporary disability benefits.
(e) Payments due as a result of disability from benefits described in Section 704.130 of the Code of Civil Procedure.
(f) Any other payments or credits due or becoming due, regardless of source.

5208. (a) "Earnings assignment order for support" means an order that assigns to an obligee a portion of the earnings of a support obligor due or to become due in the future.
(b) Commencing January 1, 2000, all earnings assignment orders for support in any action in which child support or family support is ordered shall be issued on an "order/notice to withhold income for child support" mandated by Section 666 of Title 42 of the United States Code.

5210. "Employer" includes all of the following:
(a) A person for whom an individual performs services as an employee, as defined in Section 706.011 of the Code of Civil Procedure.
(b) The United States government and any public entity as defined in Section 811.2 of the Government Code.
(c) Any person or entity paying earnings as defined under Section 5206.[1]

5212. "IV-D Case" means any case being established, modified, or enforced by the local child support agency pursuant to Section 654 of Title 42 of the United States Code (Section 454 of the Social Security Act).

5214. "Obligee" or "assigned obligee" means either the person to whom support has been ordered to be paid, the local child support agency, or other person designated by the court to receive the payment. The local child support agency is the obligee for all Title IV-D cases as defined under Section 5212 or in which an application for services has been filed under Part D (commencing with Section 651) and Part E (commencing with Section 670) of Subchapter IV of Chapter 7 of Title 42 of the United States Code (Title IV-D or IV-E of the Social Security Act).

5216. "Obligor" means a person owing a duty of support.[1]

5220. "Timely payment" means receipt of support payments by the obligee or assigned obligee within five days of the due date.[1]

Article 2: General Provisions

5230. (a) When the court orders a party to pay an amount for support or orders a modification of the amount of support to be paid, the court shall include in its order an earnings assignment order for support that orders the employer of the obligor to pay to the obligee that portion of the obligor's earnings due or to become due in the future as will be sufficient to pay an amount to cover both of the following:
(1) The amount ordered by the court for support.
(2) An amount which shall be ordered by the court to be paid toward the liquidation of any arrearage.
(b) An earnings assignment order for support shall be issued, and shall be effective and enforceable pursuant to Section 5231, notwithstanding the absence of the name, address, or other identifying information regarding the obligor's employer.

5230.1. (a) An earnings assignment or income withholding order for support issued by a court or administrative agency of another state is binding upon an employer of the obligor to the same extent as an earnings assignment order made by a court of this state.
(b) When an employer receives an earnings assignment order or an income withholding order for support from a court or administrative agency in another state, all of the provisions of this chapter shall apply.

5230.5. Any obligee alleging arrearages in child support shall specify the amount thereof under penalty of perjury.

5231. Unless stayed pursuant to Article 4 (commencing with Section 5260), an assignment order is effective and binding upon any existing or future employer of the obligor upon whom a copy of the order is served in compliance with Sections 5232 and 5233, notwithstanding the absence of the name, address, or other identifying information regarding the obligor's employer, or the inclusion of incorrect information regarding the support obligor's employer.

5232. Service on an employer of an assignment order may be made by first-class mail in the manner prescribed in Section 1013 of the Code of Civil Procedure. The obligee shall serve the documents specified in Section 5234.

5233. Unless the order states a later date, beginning as soon as possible after service of the order on the employer but not later than 10 days after service of the order on the employer, the employer shall commence withholding pursuant to the assignment order from all earnings payable to the employee.[1]

5234. Within 10 days of service of an assignment order or an order/notice to withhold income for child support on an employer, the employer shall deliver both of the following to the obligor:
(a) A copy of the assignment order or the order/notice to withhold income for child support.
(b) A written statement of the obligor's rights under the law to seek to quash, modify, or stay service of the earnings assignment order, together with a blank form that the obligor can file with the court to request a hearing to quash, modify, or stay service of the earnings assignment order with instructions on how to file the form and obtain a hearing date.

5235. (a) The employer shall continue to withhold and forward support as required by the assignment order until served with notice terminating the assignment order. If an employer withholds support as required by the assignment order, the obligor shall not be held in contempt or subject to criminal prosecution for nonpayment of the support that was withheld by the employer but not received by the obligee. If the employer withheld the support but failed to forward the payments to the obligee, the employer shall be liable for the payments, including interest, as provided in Section 5241.
(b) Within 10 days of service of a substitution of payee on the employer, the employer shall forward all subsequent support to the governmental entity or other payee

that sent the substitution.

(c) The employer shall send the amounts withheld to the obligee within the timeframe specified in federal law and shall report to the obligee the date on which the amount was withheld from the obligor's wages.

(d) The employer may deduct from the earnings of the employee the sum of one dollar and fifty cents ($1.50) for each payment made pursuant to the order.

(e) Once the State Disbursement Unit as required by Section 17309 is operational, the employer shall send all earnings withheld pursuant to this chapter to the State Disbursement Unit instead of the obligee.

5236. The state agency or the local agency, designated to enforce support obligations as required by federal law, shall allow employers to simplify the process of assignment order withholding by forwarding, as ordered by the court, the amounts of support withheld under more than one order in a consolidated check, accompanied by an itemized accounting providing names, social security number or other identifying number, and the amount attributable to each obligor.[1]

5237. (a) Except as provided in subdivisions (b) and (c), the obligee shall notify the employer of the obligor, by first-class mail, postage prepaid, of any change of address within a reasonable period of time after the change.

(b) Where payments have been ordered to be made to a county officer designated by the court, the obligee who is the parent, guardian, or other person entitled to receive payment through the designated county officer shall notify the designated county officer by first-class mail, postage prepaid, of any address change within a reasonable period of time after the change.

(c) If the obligee is receiving support payments from the State Disbursement Unit as required by Section 17309, the obligee shall notify the State Disbursement Unit instead of the employer of the obligor as provided in subdivision (a).

(d) (1) Except as set forth in paragraph (2), if the employer, designated county officer, or the State Disbursement Unit is unable to deliver payments under the assignment order for a period of six months due to the failure of the obligee to notify the employer, designated county officer, or State Disbursement Unit, of a change of address, the employer, designated county officer, or State Disbursement Unit shall not make any further payments under the assignment order and shall return all undeliverable payments to the obligor.

(2) If payments are being directed to the State Disbursement Unit pursuant to subdivision (e) of Section 5235, but the case is not otherwise receiving services from the Title IV-D agency, and the State Disbursement Unit is unable to deliver payments under the assignment order for a period of 45 days due to the failure of the obligee to notify the employer, designated county officer, or State Disbursement Unit of a change of address, the Title IV-D agency shall take the following actions:

(A) Immediately return the undeliverable payments to the obligor if the obligee cannot be located.

(B) Notify the employer to suspend withholding pursuant to the wage assignment until the employer or Title IV-D agency is notified of the obligee's whereabouts.

5238. (a) Where an assignment order or assignment orders include both current support and payments towards the liquidation of arrearages, priority shall be given first to the current child support obligation, then the current spousal support obligation, and thereafter to the liquidation of child and then spousal support arrearages.
(b) Where there are multiple assignment orders for the same employee, the employer shall prorate the withheld payments as follows:
(1) If the obligor has more than one assignment for support, the employer shall add together the amount of support due for each assignment.
(2) If 50 percent of the obligor's net disposable earnings will not pay in full all of the assignments for support, the employer shall prorate it first among all of the current support assignments in the same proportion that each assignment bears to the total current support owed.
(3) The employer shall apply any remainder to the assignments for arrearage support in the same proportion that each assignment bears to the total arrearage owed.

5239. Arrearages of support payments shall be computed on the basis of the payments owed and unpaid on the date that the obligor has been given notice of the assignment order as required by Section 5234.[1]

5240. (a) Upon the filing and service of a motion and a notice of motion by the obligor, the court shall terminate the service of an assignment order if past due support has been paid in full, including any interest due, and if any of the following conditions exist:
(1) With regard to orders for spousal support, the death or remarriage of the spouse to whom support is owed.
(2) With regard to orders for child support, the death or emancipation of the child for whom support is owed.
(3) The court determines that there is good cause, as defined in Section 5260, to terminate the assignment order. This subdivision does not apply if there has been more than one application for an assignment order.
(4) The obligor meets the conditions of an alternative arrangement specified in paragraph (2) of subdivision (b) of Section 5260, and a wage assignment has not been previously terminated and subsequently initiated.
(5) There is no longer a current order for support.
(6) The termination of the stay of an assignment order under Section 5261 was improper, but only if that termination was based upon the obligor's failure to make timely support payments as described in subdivision (b) of Section 5261.
(7) The employer or agency designated to provide services under Title IV-D of the Social Security Act or the State Disbursement Unit is unable to deliver payment for a period of six months due to the failure of the obligee to notify that employer or agency or the State Disbursement Unit of a change in the obligee's address.
(b) In lieu of filing and serving a motion and a notice of motion pursuant to subdivision (a), an obligor

may request ex parte relief, except ex parte relief shall not be available in the circumstances described in paragraphs (3) and (4) of subdivision (a).[251]

5241. (a) An employer who willfully fails to withhold and forward support pursuant to a currently valid assignment order entered and served upon the employer pursuant to this chapter is liable to the obligee for the amount of support not withheld, forwarded, or otherwise paid to the obligee, including any interest thereon.
(b) If an employer withholds support as required by the assignment order, the obligor shall not be held in contempt or subject to criminal prosecution for nonpayment of the support that was withheld by the employer but not received by the obligee. In addition, the employer is liable to the obligee for any interest incurred as a result of the employer's failure to timely forward the withheld support pursuant to an assignment earnings order.
(c) In addition to any other penalty or liability provided by law, willful failure by an employer to comply with an assignment order is punishable as a contempt pursuant to Section 1218 of the Code of Civil Procedure.
(d) If an employer withholds support, as required by the assignment order, but fails to forward the support to the obligee, the local child support agency shall take appropriate action to collect the withheld sums from the employer. The child support obligee or the local child support agency upon application may obtain an order requiring payment of support by electronic transfer from the employer's bank account if the employer has willfully failed to comply with the assignment order or if the employer has failed to comply with the assignment order on three separate occasions within a 12-month period. Where a court finds that an employer has willfully failed to comply with the assignment order or has otherwise failed to comply with the assignment order on three separate occasions within a 12-month period, the court may impose a civil penalty, in addition to any other penalty required by law, of up to 50 percent of the support amount that has not been received by the obligee.
(e) To facilitate employer awareness, the local child support agency shall make reasonable efforts to notify any employer subject to an assignment order pursuant to this chapter of the electronic fund transfer provision and enhanced penalties provided by this act.
(f) Notwithstanding any other provision of law, any penalty payable pursuant to this subdivision shall be payable directly to the obligee. The local child support agency shall not be required to establish or collect this penalty on behalf of the obligee. The penalty shall not be included when determining the income of the obligee for the purpose of determining the eligibility of the obligee for benefits payable pursuant to state supplemental income programs. A court may issue the order requiring payment of support by electronic transfer from the employer's bank account and impose the penalty described in this subdivision, after notice and hearing. This provision shall not be construed to expand or limit the duties and obligations of the Labor Commissioner, as set forth in Section 200 and following of the Labor Code.

5242. Service of the assignment order creates a lien on the earnings of the employee and the property of the employer to the same extent as the service of an earnings withholding order as provided in Section 706.029 of the Code of Civil Procedure.[1]

5243. An assignment order for support has priority as against any attachment, execution, or other assignment as specified in Section 706.031 of the Code of Civil Procedure.

5244. A reference to the local child support agency in this chapter applies only when the local child support agency is otherwise ordered or required to act pursuant to law. Nothing in this chapter shall be deemed to mandate additional enforcement or collection duties upon the local child support agency beyond those otherwise imposed by law.

5245. Nothing in this chapter limits the authority of the local child support agency to use any other civil and criminal remedies to enforce support obligations, regardless of whether or not the child or the obligee who is the parent, guardian, or other person entitled to receive payment is the recipient of welfare moneys.

5246. (a) This section applies only to Title IV-D cases where support enforcement services are being provided by the local child support agency pursuant to Section 17400.

(b) In lieu of an earnings assignment order signed by a judicial officer, the local child support agency may serve on the employer a notice of assignment in the manner specified in Section 5232. An order/notice to withhold income for child support shall have the same force and effect as an earnings assignment order signed by a judicial officer. An order/notice to withhold income for child support, when used under this section, shall be considered a notice and shall not require the signature of a judicial officer.

(c) Pursuant to Section 666 of Title 42 of the United States Code, the federally mandated order/notice to withhold income for child support shall be used for the purposes described in this section.

(d) (1) An order/notice to withhold income may not reduce the current amount withheld for court-ordered child support.

(2) If the underlying court order for support does not provide for an arrearage payment, or if an additional arrearage accrues after the date of the court order for support, the local child support agency may send an order/notice to withhold income for child support that shall be used for the purposes described in this section directly to the employer that specifies the updated arrearage amount and directs the employer to withhold an additional amount to be applied towards liquidation of the arrearages not to exceed the maximum amount permitted by Section 1673(b) of Title 15 of the United States Code.

(3) Notwithstanding paragraph (2), if an obligor is disabled, meets the SSI resource test, and is receiving Supplemental Security Income/State Supplementary Payments (SSI/SSP) or, but for excess income as described in Section 416.1100 et seq. of Part 416 of Title 20 of the Code of Federal Regulations, would be eligible to receive SSI/SSP, pursuant to Section

12200 of the Welfare and Institutions Code, and the obligor has supplied the local child support agency with proof of eligibility for and, if applicable, receipt of, SSI/SSP or Social Security Disability Insurance benefits, then the order/notice to withhold income issued by the local child support agency for the liquidation of the arrearage shall not exceed 5 percent of the obligor's total monthly Social Security Disability payments under Title II of the Social Security Act.

(e) If the obligor requests a hearing, a hearing date shall be scheduled within 20 days of the filing of the request with the court. The clerk of the court shall provide notice of the hearing to the local child support agency and the obligor no later than 10 days prior to the hearing.

(1) If, at the hearing, the obligor establishes that they are not the obligor or good cause or an alternative arrangement as provided in Section 5260, the court may order that service of the order/notice to withhold income for child support be quashed. If the court quashes service of the order/notice to withhold income for child support, the local child support agency shall notify the employer within 10 days.

(2) If the obligor contends at the hearing that the payment of arrearages at the rate specified in the order/notice to withhold income for child support is excessive or that the total arrearages owing is incorrect, and if it is determined that payment of the arrearages at the rate specified in this section creates an undue hardship upon the obligor or that the withholding would exceed the maximum amount permitted by Section 1673(b) of Title 15 of the United States Code Annotated, the rate at which the arrearages must be paid shall be reduced to a rate that is fair and reasonable considering the circumstances of the parties and the best interest of the child. If it is determined at a hearing that the total amount of arrearages calculated is erroneous, the court shall modify the amount calculated to the correct amount. If the court modifies the total amount of arrearages owed or reduces the monthly payment due on the arrearages, the local child support agency shall serve the employer with an amended order/notice to withhold income for child support within 10 days.

(f) If an obligor's current support obligation has terminated by operation of law, the local child support agency may serve an order/notice to withhold income for child support on the employer that directs the employer to continue withholding from the obligor's earnings an amount to be applied towards liquidation of the arrearages, not to exceed the maximum amount permitted by Section 1673(b) of Title 15 of the United States Code, until the employer is notified by the local child support agency that the arrearages have been paid in full. The employer shall provide the obligor with a copy of the order/notice to withhold income for child support and a blank form that the obligor may file with the court to request a hearing to modify or quash the assignment with instructions on how to file the form and obtain a hearing date. The obligor shall be entitled to the same rights to a hearing as specified in subdivision (e).

(g) The local child support agency shall retain a copy of the order/notice to withhold income for child support and shall file a copy with the court whenever a hearing concerning the order/notice to withhold income for child support is requested.
(h) The local child support agency may transmit an order/notice to withhold income for child support and other forms required by this section to the employer through electronic means.[456]

5247. Neither the local child support agency nor an employer shall be subject to any civil liability for any amount withheld and paid to the obligee, the local child support agency, or the State Disbursement Unit pursuant to an earnings assignment order or notice of assignment.

Article 3: Support Orders Issued or Modified Before July 1, 1990

5250. For a support order first issued or modified before July 1, 1990, this article provides a procedure for obtaining an earnings assignment order for support when the court in ordering support or modification of support did not issue an assignment order.[1]

5251. The obligee seeking issuance of an assignment order to enforce a supp-ort order described in Section 5250 may use the procedure set forth in this article by filing an application under Section 5252, or by notice of motion or order to show cause, or pursuant to subdivision (b) of Section 5230.[1]

5252. (a) An assignment order under this article may be issued only upon an application signed under penalty of perjury by the obligee that the obligor is in default in support payments in a sum equal to the amount of support payable for one month, for any other occurrence specified by the court in the support order, or earlier by court order if requested by the local child support agency or the obligor.
(b) If the order for support does not contain a provision for an earnings assignment order for support, the application shall state that the obligee has given the obligor a written notice of the obligee's intent to seek an assignment order if there is a default in support payments and that the notice was transmitted by first-class mail, postage prepaid, or personally served at least 15 days before the date of the filing of the application. The written notice of the intent to seek an assignment order may be given at any time, including at the time of filing a petition or complaint in which support is requested or at any time subsequent thereto. The obligor may at any time waive the written notice required by this subdivision.
(c) In addition to any other penalty provided by law, the filing of the application with knowledge of the falsity of the declaration or notice is punishable as a contempt pursuant to Section 1209 of the Code of Civil Procedure.

5253. Upon receipt of the application, the court shall issue, without notice to the obligor, an assignment order requiring the employer of the obligor to pay to the obligee or the State Disbursement Unit that portion of the earnings of the obligor due or to become due in the future as will be sufficient to pay an amount to cover both of the following:
(a) The amount ordered by the court

for support.

(b) An amount which shall be ordered by the court to be paid toward the liquidation of any arrearage or past due support amount.[105]

Article 4: Stay of Service of Assignment Order

5260. (a) The court may order that service of the assignment order be stayed only if the court makes a finding of good cause or if an alternative arrangement exists for payment in accordance with paragraph (2) of subdivision (b). Notwithstanding any other provision of law, service of wage assignments issued for foreign orders for support, and service of foreign orders for the assignment of wages registered pursuant to Chapter 6 (commencing with Section 5700.601) of Part 6 shall not be stayed pursuant to this subdivision.

(b) For purposes of this section, good cause or an alternative arrangement for staying an assignment order is as follows:

(1) Good cause for staying a wage assignment exists only when all of the following conditions exist:

(A) The court provides a written explanation of why the stay of the wage assignment would be in the best interests of the child.

(B) The obligor has a history of uninterrupted, full, and timely payment, other than through a wage assignment or other mandatory process of previously ordered support, during the previous 12 months.

(C) The obligor does not owe an arrearage for prior support.

(D) The obligor proves, and the court finds, by clear and convincing evidence that service of the wage assignment would cause extraordinary hardship upon the obligor. Whenever possible, the court shall specify a date that any stay ordered under this section will automatically terminate.

(2) An alternative arrangement for staying a wage assignment order shall require a written agreement between the parties that provides for payment of the support obligation as ordered other than through the immediate service of a wage assignment. Any agreement between the parties which includes the staying of a service of a wage assignment shall include the concurrence of the local child support agency in any case in which support is ordered to be paid through a county officer designated for that purpose. The execution of an agreement pursuant to this paragraph shall not preclude a party from thereafter seeking a wage assignment in accordance with the procedures specified in Section 5261 upon violation of the agreement.[338]

5261. (a) If service of the assignment order has been ordered stayed, the stay shall terminate pursuant to subdivision (b) upon the obligor's failure to make timely support payments or earlier by court order if requested by the local child support agency or by the obligor. The stay shall terminate earlier by court order if requested by any other obligee who can establish that good cause, as defined in Section 5260, no longer exists.

(b) To terminate a stay of the service of the assignment order, the obligee shall file a declaration signed under penalty of perjury by the obligee that the obligor is in arrears in payment of any portion of the support. At the time of filing the declaration, the stay shall terminate by operation of law without notice to the obligor.

(c) In addition to any other penalty provided by law, the filing of a declaration under subdivision (b) with knowledge of the falsity of its contents is punishable as a contempt pursuant to Section 1209 of the Code of Civil Procedure.

Article 5: Motion to Quash Assignment Order

5270. (a) An obligor may move to quash an assignment order on any of the following grounds:

(1) The assignment order does not correctly state the amount of current or overdue support ordered by the courts.

(2) The alleged obligor is not the obligor from whom support is due.

(3) The amount to be withheld exceeds that allowable under federal law in subsection (b) of Section 1673 of Title 15 of the United States Code.

(b) If an assignment order is sought under Article 3 (commencing with Section 5250), the party ordered to pay support may also move to quash the service of the order based upon Section 5260.

(c) The obligor shall state under oath the ground on which the motion to quash is made.

(d) If an assignment order which has been issued and served on a prior employer is served on the obligor's new employer, the obligor does not have the right to move to quash the assignment order on any grounds which the obligor previously raised when the assignment order was served on the prior employer or on any grounds which the obligor could have raised when the assignment order was served on the prior employer but failed to raise.[1]

5271. (a) The motion and notice of motion to quash the assignment order shall be filed with the court issuing the order within 10 days after delivery of the copy of the assignment order to the obligor by the employer.

(b) The clerk of the court shall set the motion to quash for hearing within not less than 15 days, nor more than 20 days, after receipt of the notice of motion.

(c) The obligor shall serve personally or by first-class mail, postage prepaid, a copy of the motion and notice of motion on the obligee named in the assignment order no less than 10 days before the date of the hearing.[1]

5272. A finding of error in the amount of the current support or arrearage or that the amount exceeds federal or state limits is not grounds to vacate the assignment order. The court shall modify the order to reflect the correct or allowable amount of support or arrearages. The fact that the obligor may have subsequently paid the arrearages does not relieve the court of its duty to enter the assignment order.[1]

Article 6: Information Concerning Address and Employment of Obligor

5280. If the obligee making the application under this chapter also states that the whereabouts of the obligor or the identity of the obligor's employer is unknown to the party to whom support has been ordered to be paid, the local child support agency shall do both of the following:

(a) Contact the California parent locator service maintained by the

Department of Justice in the manner prescribed in Section 17506.
(b) Upon receiving the requested information, notify the court of the last known address of the obligor and the name and address of the obligor's last known employer.

5281. An assignment order required or authorized by this chapter shall include a requirement that the obligor notify the obligee of any change of employment and of the name and address of the obligor's new employer within 10 days of obtaining new employment.[1]

5282. After the obligor has left employment with the employer, the employer, at the time the next payment is due on the assignment order, shall notify the obligee designated in the assignment order by first-class mail, postage prepaid, to the last known address of the obligee that the obligor has left employment.[1]

Article 7: Prohibited Practices

5290. No employer shall use an assignment order authorized by this chapter as grounds for refusing to hire a person, or for discharging, taking disciplinary action against, denying a promotion to, or for taking any other action adversely affecting the terms and conditions of employment of, an employee. An employer who engages in the conduct prohibited by this section may be assessed a civil penalty of a maximum of five hundred dollars ($500).

Article 8: Judicial Council Forms

5295. The Judicial Council shall prescribe forms necessary to carry out the requirements of this chapter, including the following:
(a) The written statement of the obligor's rights.
(b) The earnings assignment order for support.
(c) The instruction guide for obligees and obligors.
(d) The application forms required under Sections 5230, 5252, and 5261.
(e) The notice form required under Section 5252.
(f) Revised judgment and assignment order forms as necessary.[1]

Article 9: Intercounty Support Obligations

5600. (a) A local child support agency or obligee may register an order for support or earnings withholding, or both, obtained in another county of the state.
(b) An obligee may register a support order in the court of another county of this state in the manner, with the effect, and for the purposes provided in this part. The orders may be registered in any county in which the obligor, the obligee, or the child who is the subject of the order resides, or in any county in which the obligor has income, assets, or any other property.

5601. (a) When the local child support agency is responsible for the enforcement of a support order pursuant to Section 17400, the local child support agency may register a support order made in another county by utilizing the procedures set forth in Section 5602 or by filing all of the following in the superior court of the agency's county:
(1) An endorsed file copy of the most recent support order or a copy thereof.

(2) A statement of arrearages, including an accounting of amounts ordered and paid each month, together with any added costs, fees, and interest.

(3) A statement prepared by the local child support agency showing the post office address of the local child support agency, the last known place of residence or post office address of the obligor; the most recent address of the obligor set forth in the licensing records of the Department of Motor Vehicles, if known; and a list of other states and counties in California that are known to the local child support agency in which the original order of support and any modifications are registered.

(b) The filing of the documents described in subdivision (a) constitutes registration under this chapter.

(c) Promptly upon registration, the local child support agency, in compliance with the requirements of Section 1013 of the Code of Civil Procedure, or in any other manner as provided by law, shall serve the obligor with copies of the documents described in subdivision (a).

(d) If a motion to vacate registration is filed under Section 5603, a party may introduce into evidence copies of pleadings, documents, or orders that have been filed in the original court or other courts where the support order has been registered or modified. Certified copies of the documents shall not be required unless a party objects to the authenticity or accuracy of the document, in which case it shall be the responsibility of the party who is asserting the authenticity of the document to obtain a certified copy of the questioned document.

(e) Upon registration, the clerk of the court shall forward a notice of registration to the courts in other counties and states in which the original order for support and any modifications were issued or registered. Further proceedings regarding the obligor's support obligations shall not be filed in other counties.

(f) The procedure prescribed by this section may also be used to register support or wage and earnings assignment orders of other California jurisdictions that previously have been registered for purposes of enforcement only pursuant to the Uniform Interstate Family Support Act (Part 6 (commencing with Section 5700.101)) in another California county. The local child support agency may register such an order by filing an endorsed file copy of the registered California order plus any subsequent orders, including procedural amendments.

(g) The Judicial Council shall develop the forms necessary to effectuate this section. These forms shall be available no later than July 1, 1998.[457]

5602. (a) An obligee other than the local child support agency may register an order issued in this state using the same procedures specified in subdivision (a) of Section 5601, except that the obligee shall prepare and file the statement of registration. The statement shall be verified and signed by the obligee showing the mailing address of the obligee, the last known place of residence or mailing address of the obligor, and a list of other states and counties in California in which, to the obligee's knowledge, the original order of support and any modifications are registered.

(b) Upon receipt of the documents described in subdivision (a) of Section 5601, the clerk of the court shall file them without payment of a filing fee or other cost to the obligee. The filing constitutes registration under this chapter.

(c) Promptly upon registration, the clerk of the court shall send, by any form of mail requiring a return receipt from the addressee only, to the obligor at the address given a notice of the registration with a copy of the registered support order and the post office address of the obligee. Proof shall be made to the satisfaction of the court that the obligor personally received the notice of registration by mail or other method of service. A return receipt signed by the obligor shall be satisfactory evidence of personal receipt.

5603. (a) An obligor shall have 20 days after the service of notice of the registration of a California order of support in which to file a noticed motion requesting the court to vacate the registration or for other relief. In an action under this section, there shall be no joinder of actions, coordination of actions, or cross-complaints, and the claims or defenses shall be limited strictly to the identity of the obligor, the validity of the underlying California support order, or the accuracy of the obligee's statement of the amount of support remaining unpaid unless the amount has been previously established by a judgment or order. The obligor shall serve a copy of the motion, personally or by first-class mail, on the local child support agency, private attorney representing the obligee, or obligee who is self-representing who filed the request for registration of the order, not less than 15 days prior to the date on which the motion is to be heard. If service is by mail, Section 1013 of the Code of Civil Procedure applies. If the obligor does not file the motion within 20 days, the registered California support order and all other documents filed pursuant to subdivision (a) of Section 5601 or Section 5602 are confirmed.

(b) At the hearing on the motion to vacate the registration of the order, the obligor may present only matters that would be available to the obligor as defenses in an action to enforce a support judgment. If the obligor shows, and the court finds, that an appeal from the order is pending or that a stay of execution has been granted, the court shall stay enforcement of the order until the appeal is concluded, the time for appeal has expired, or the order is vacated, upon satisfactory proof that the obligor has furnished security for payment of the support ordered. If the obligor shows, and the court finds, any ground upon which enforcement of a California support order may be stayed, the court shall stay enforcement of the order for an appropriate period if the obligor furnishes security for payment of support.[458]

5604. A previous determination of paternity made by another state, whether established through voluntary acknowledgment procedures in effect in that state or through an administrative or judicial process shall be given full faith and credit by the courts in this state, and shall have the same effect as a paternity determination made in this state and may be enforced and satisfied in a like manner.

Chapter 9: Private Child Support Collectors

5610. For the purposes of this chapter, "private child support collector" means any individual, corporation, attorney, nonprofit organization, or other nongovernmental entity who is engaged by an obligee to collect child support ordered by a court or other tribunal for a fee or other consideration. The term does not include any attorney who addresses issues of ongoing child support or child support arrearages in the course of an action to establish parentage or a child support obligation, a proceeding under Division 10 (commencing with Section 6200), a proceeding for dissolution of marriage, legal separation, or nullity of marriage, or in postjudgment or modification proceedings related to any of those actions. A "private child support collector" includes any private, nongovernmental attorney whose business is substantially comprised of the collection or enforcement of child support. As used in this section, substantially means that at least 50 percent of the attorney's business, either in terms of remuneration or time spent, is comprised of the activity of seeking to collect or enforce child support obligations for other individuals.[139]

5611. (a) A contract for the collection of child support between a private child support collector and an obligee shall be in writing and written in simple language, in at least 10-point type, signed by the private child support collector and the obligee. The contract shall be delivered to the obligee in a paper form that the obligee may retain for their records. The contract shall include all of the following:

(1) An explanation of the fees imposed by contract and otherwise permitted by law and an example of how they are calculated and deducted.

(2) A statement that the amount of fees to be charged is set by the agency and is not set by state law.

(3) A statement that the private child support collector cannot charge fees on current support if the obligee received any current child support during the 6 months preceding execution of the contract with the private collector.

(4) An explanation of the nature of the services to be provided.

(5) The expected duration of the contract, stated as a length of time or as an amount to be collected by the collection agency.

(6) An explanation of the opportunities available to the obligee or private child support collector to cancel the contract or other conditions under which the contract terminates.

(7) The mailing address, street address, telephone numbers, facsimile numbers, and internet address or location of the private child support collector.

(8) A statement that the private child support collector is not a governmental entity and that governmental entities in California provide child support collection and enforcement services free of charge.

(9) A statement that the private child support collector collects only money owed to the obligee and not support

assigned to the state or county due to the receipt of CalWORKs or Temporary Assistance to Needy Families.

(10) A statement that the private child support collector will not retain fees from collections that are primarily attributable to the actions of a governmental entity or any other person or entity and is required by law to refund any fees improperly retained.

(11) A statement that the obligee may continue to receive, or may pursue, services through a governmental entity to collect support, and the private child support collection agency will not require or request that the obligee cease or refrain from engaging those services.

(12) A notice that the private child support collector is required to keep and maintain case records for a period of four years and four months, after the expiration of the contract and may thereafter destroy or otherwise dispose of the records. The obligee may, prior to destruction or disposal, retrieve those portions of the records that are not confidential.

(13) A "Notice of Cancellation," which shall be included with the contract and which shall contain, in the same size font as the contract, the following statement, written in the same language as the contract:

"Notice of Cancellation

You may cancel this contract, without any penalty or obligation, within 15 business days from the date the contract is signed or you receive this notice, whichever is later, or at any time if the private child support collector commits a material breach of any provision of the contract or a material violation of any provision of this chapter with respect to the obligee or the obligor, or ____________________ (all other reasons for cancellation permitted).

To cancel this contract, mail or deliver a signed copy of this cancellation notice or any other written notice to ____________________________ (name of private child support collector) at ____________________________ (address for mail or delivery)

no later than midnight on ______________________ (date).

I am canceling this contract.
______________________ (date)

___________________(signature)"

(14) The following statement by the obligee on the first page of the contract:

"I understand that this contract calls for (name of private child support collector) to collect money owed to me, and not money owed to the state or county. If child support is owed to the state or county because I am receiving or have received program benefits from CalWORKs or Temporary Assistance to Needy Families, then (name of private child support collector) cannot collect that money for me. If I start to receive program benefits from CalWORKs or Temporary Assistance to Needy Families during this contract, I must notify (name of private child support collector) in writing."

"I declare by my signature below that the child support to be collected for me pursuant to this contract is not assigned to the state or county as of the time I sign this contract. I agree that I will give written notice to the private child support collector if I apply for program benefits under CalWORKs or Temporary Assistance to Needy Families during the term of this contract."

(15) (A) The following statement by the obligee immediately above the signature line of the contract:

"I understand that (name of private child support collector) will charge a fee for all the current child support and arrears it collects for me until the entire contract amount is collected or the contract terminates for another reason. I also understand that depending on the frequency and size of payments, it could take years for the amount specified in my contract to be collected. This means that if (name of private child support collector) is collecting my current support by wage withholding or other means, I will not receive the full amount of my periodic court-ordered current support until the contract terminates since (name of private child support collector) will be deducting its fee from the periodic court-ordered current support it collects for me."

(B) The statement required by subparagraph (A) shall:

(i) Be in a type size that is at least equal to one-quarter of the largest type size used in the contract. In no event shall the disclosure be printed in less than 8-point type.

(ii) Be in a contrasting style, and contrasting color or bold type, that is equally or more visible than the type used in the contract.(b) The disclosures required by paragraph (1) of subdivision (a) of Section 5612 shall be printed in the contract, as follows:

(1) In a type size that is at least equal to one-quarter of the largest type size used in the contract. In no event shall the disclosure be printed in less than 8-point type.

(2) In a contrasting style, and contrasting color or bold type that is equally or more visible than the type used in the contract.

(3) Immediately above, below, or beside the stated fee without any intervening words, pictures, marks, or symbols.

(4) In the same language as the contract.[459]

5612. (a) Each private child support collector:

(1) That charges any initial fee, processing fee, application fee, filing

fee, or other fee or assessment that must be paid by an obligee regardless of whether any child support collection is made on behalf of the obligee shall make the following disclosure in every radio, television, or print advertisement intended for a target audience consisting primarily of California residents:

"(Name of private child support collector) is not a governmental entity and charges an upfront fee for its services even if it does not collect anything."

(2) That does not charge any fee or assessment specified in paragraph (1) shall make the following disclosure in every radio, television, or print advertisement aired for a target audience consisting primarily of California residents:

"(Name of private child support collector) is not a governmental entity and charges a fee for its services."

(b) The disclosures required in subdivision (a) shall also be stated during the first 30 seconds of any initial telephone conversation with an obligee and in the private child support collector's contract. [139]

5613. (a) An obligee shall have the right to cancel a contract with a private support collector under either of the following circumstances:

(1) Within 15 business days of the later of signing the contract, or receiving a blank notice of cancellation form, or at any time if the private child support collector commits a material breach of any provision of the contract or a material violation of any provision of this chapter with respect to the obligee or the obligor.

(2) At the end of any 12-month period in which the total amount collected by the private child support collector is less than 50 percent of the amount scheduled to be paid under a payment plan.

(b) A contract shall automatically terminate when the contract term has expired or the contract amount has been collected, whichever occurs first.[139]

5614. (a) A private child support collector shall do all of the following:

(1) (A) Provide to an obligee all of the following information:

(i) The name of, and any other identifying information relating to, an obligor who made child support payments collected by the private child support collector.

(ii) The amount of support collected by the private child support collector.

(iii) The date on which each amount was received by the private child support collector.

(iv) The date on which each amount received by the private child support collector was sent to the obligee.

(v) The amount of the payment sent to the obligee.

(vi) The source of payment of support collected and the actions affirmatively taken by the private child support collector that resulted in the payment.

(vii) The amount and percentage of each payment kept by the private child support collector as its fee.

(B) The information required by subparagraph (A) shall be made available, at the option of the obligee, by mail, telephone, or via secure Internet access. If provided by mail, the notice shall be sent at least quarterly and, if provided by any other method, the information shall be updated and made available at least monthly. Information accessed by telephone and the Internet shall be up to date.

(2) Maintain records of all child support collections made on behalf of a client who is an obligee. The records required under this section shall be maintained by the private child support collector for the duration of the contract plus a period of four years and four months from the date of the last child support payment collected by the private child support collector on behalf of an obligee. In addition to information required by paragraph (1), the private child support collector shall maintain the following:

(A) A copy of the order establishing the child support obligation under which a collection was made by the private child support collector.

(B) Records of all correspondence between the private child support collector and the obligee or obligor in a case.

(C) Any other pertinent information relating to the child support obligation, including any case, cause, or docket number of the court having jurisdiction over the matter and official government payment records obtained by the private child support collector on behalf of, and at the request of, the obligee.

(3) Safeguard case records in a manner reasonably expected to prevent intentional or accidental disclosure of confidential information pertaining to the obligee or obligor, including providing necessary protections for records maintained in an automated system.

(4) Ensure that every person who contracts with a private child support collector has the right to review all files and documents, both paper and electronic, in the possession of the private child support collector for the information specified in this paragraph regarding that obligee's case that are not required by law to be kept confidential. The obligee, during regular business hours, shall be provided reasonable access to and copies of the files and records of the private child support collector regarding all moneys received, collection attempts made, fees retained or paid to the private child support collector, and moneys disbursed to the obligee. The private child support collector may not charge a fee for access to the files and records, but may require the obligee to pay up to three cents ($0.03) per page for the copies prior to their release.

(5) Provide, prior to commencing collection activities, written notice of a contract with an obligee to the local child support agency that is enforcing the obligee's support order, if known, or the local child support agency for the county in which the obligee resides as of the time the contract is signed by the obligee. The notice shall identify the obligee, the obligor, and the amount of the arrearage claimed by the obligee.

(b) A private child support collector shall not do any of the following:

(1) Charge fees on current support if the obligee received any current child support during the six months preceding execution of the contract with the private child support collector. A private child support

collector shall inquire of the obligee and record the month and year of the last current support payment and may rely on information provided by the obligee in determining whether a fee may be charged on current support.

(2) Improperly retain fees from collections that are primarily attributable to the actions of a governmental entity. The private child support collector shall refund all of those fees to the obligee immediately upon discovery or notice of the improper retention of fees.

(3) Collect or attempt to collect child support by means of conduct that is prohibited of a debt collector collecting a consumer debt under Sections 1788.10 to 1788.16, inclusive, of the Civil Code. This chapter does not modify, alter, or amend the definition of a debt or a debt collector under the Rosenthal Fair Debt Collection Practices Act (Title 1.6C (commencing with Section 1788) of Part 4 of Division 3 of the Civil Code).

(4) Misstate the amount of the fee that may be lawfully paid to the private child support collector for the performance of the contract or the identity of the person who is obligated to pay that fee.

(5) Make a false representation of the amount of child support to be collected. A private child support collector is not in violation of this paragraph if it reasonably relied on sufficient documentation provided by the government entity collecting child support, a court with jurisdiction over the support obligation, or from the obligee, or upon sufficient documentation provided by the obligor.

(6) Ask a party other than the obligor to pay the child support obligation, unless that party is legally responsible for the obligation or is the legal representative of the obligor.

(7) On or after January 1, 2007, require, as a condition of providing services to the obligee, that the obligee waive any right or procedure provided for in state law regarding the right to file and pursue a civil action, or that the obligee agree to resolve disputes in a jurisdiction outside of California or to the application of laws other than those of California, as provided by law. Any waiver by the obligee of the right to file and pursue a civil action, the right to file and pursue a civil action in California, or the right to rely upon California law as provided by law must be knowing, voluntary, and not made a condition of doing business with the private child support collector. Any waiver, including, but not limited to, an agreement to arbitrate or regarding choice of forum or choice of law, that is required as a condition of doing business with the private child support collector, shall be presumed involuntary, unconscionable, against public policy, and unenforceable. The private child support collector has the burden of proving that any waiver of rights, including an agreement to arbitrate a claim or regarding choice of forum or choice of law, was knowing, voluntary, and not made a condition of the contract with the obligee.[378]

5615. (a) (1) A person may bring an action for actual damages incurred as a result of a violation of this chapter.

(2) In addition to actual damages, a private child support collector who

willfully and knowingly violates the provisions of this chapter shall be liable for a civil penalty in an amount determined by the court, which may not be less than one hundred dollars ($100) nor more than one thousand dollars ($1,000).

(3) (A) The prevailing party in any action pursuant to this chapter shall be entitled to recover the costs of the action. Reasonable attorney's fees, which shall be based on the time necessarily expended to enforce the liability, shall be awarded to a prevailing party, other than the private child support collector, asserting rights under this chapter. Reasonable attorney's fees may be awarded to a prevailing private child support collector if the court finds that the party bringing the action did not prosecute the action in good faith.

(B) In an action by an obligor under this chapter, the private child support collector shall have no civil liability under this chapter to the obligor under any circumstance in which a debt collector would not have civil liability under Section 1788.30 of the Civil Code.

(4) A private child support collector is not in violation of this chapter if the private child support collector shows, by a preponderance of the evidence, that the action complained of was not intentional and resulted from a bona fide error that occurred notwithstanding the use of reasonable procedures to avoid the error.

(5) The remedies provided in this section are cumulative and are in addition to any other procedures, rights, or remedies available under any other law.

(b) Any waiver of the rights, requirements, and remedies provided by this chapter violates public policy and is void.

(c) Notwithstanding any other provision of this chapter, including provisions establishing a right of cancellation and requiring notice thereof, any contract for the collection of child support between an attorney who is a "private child support collector" pursuant to Section 5610 shall conform to the statutes, rules, and case law governing attorney conduct, including the provisions of law providing that a contract with an attorney is cancelable by the attorney's client at any time. Upon cancellation of that contract, the attorney may seek compensation as provided by law, including, if applicable, a claim for the reasonable value of any services rendered to the attorney's client pursuant to the doctrine of quantum meruit, provided those services lead to the collection of support and the compensation is limited to what would have been collected had the contract been in effect. To the extent that the provisions of this chapter are in conflict with the provisions of state law governing the conduct of attorneys, this chapter shall control. If there is no conflict, an attorney who is a "private child support collector" pursuant to Section 5610 shall conform to the provisions of this chapter.[139]

5616. (a) Every court order for child support issued on or after January 1, 2010, and every child support agreement providing for the payment of child support approved by a court on or after January 1, 2010, shall include a separate money judgment owed by the child support obligor to pay a fee not to exceed 33 and 1/3 percent of the total amount in arrears, and not to exceed 50 percent of the fee as charged by a private child support collector pursuant to a contract complying with this chapter and any other child support collections costs expressly permitted by the child support order for the collection efforts undertaken by the private child support collector. The money judgment shall be in favor of the private child support collector and the child support obligee, jointly, but shall not constitute a private child support collector lien on real property unless an abstract of judgment is recorded pursuant to subdivision (d). Except as provided in subdivision (c), the money judgment may be enforced by the private child support collector by any means available to the obligee for the enforcement of the child support order without any additional action or order by the court. Nothing in this chapter shall be construed to grant the private child support collector any enforcement remedies beyond those authorized by federal or state law. Any fee collected from the obligor pursuant to a contract complying with this chapter, shall not constitute child support.

(b) If the child support order makes the obligor responsible for payment of collection fees and costs, fees that are deducted by a private child support collector may not be credited against child support arrearages or interest owing on arrearages or any other money owed by the obligor to the obligee.

(c) If the order for child support requires payment of collection fees and costs by the obligor, then not later than five days after the date that the private child support collector makes its first collection, written notice shall be provided to the obligor of (1) the amount of arrearages subject to collection, (2) the amount of the collection that shall be applied to the arrearage, and (3) the amount of the collection that shall be applied to the fees and costs of collection. The notice shall provide that, in addition to any other procedures available, the obligor has 30 days to file a motion to contest the amount of collection fees and costs assessed against the obligor.

(d) Any fees or monetary obligations resulting from the contract between an obligee parent and a private child support collector, or moneys owed to a private child support collector by the obligor parent or obligee parent as a result of the private child support collector's efforts, does not create a lien on real property, unless an abstract of judgment is obtained from the court and recorded by the private child support collector against the real property in the county in which it is located, nor shall that amount be added to any existing lien created by a recorded abstract of support or be added to an obligation on any abstract of judgment. A private child support collector lien shall have the force, effect, and priority of a judgment lien.

(e) An assignment to a private child support collector is a voluntary assignment for the purpose of collecting the domestic support obligation as defined in Section 101 of Title 11 of the United States Bankruptcy Code (11 U.S.C. Sec. 101 (14 A)).[220]

PART 6: UNIFORM INTERSTATE FAMILY SUPPORT ACT

added by Stats. 2015, Ch. 493, Sec. 5.

Chapter 1: General Provisions

5700.101. (a) This part may be cited as the Uniform Interstate Family Support Act.
(b) There is a federal mandate set forth in Section 666(f) of Title 42 of the United States Code requiring California to adopt and have in effect the Uni-form Interstate Family Support Act, including any amendments officially adopted by the National Council of Commissioners on Uniform State Laws as of September 30, 2008.[339]

5700.102. In this part:
(1) "Child" means an individual, whether over or under the age of majority, who is or is alleged to be owed a duty of support by the individual's parent or who is or is alleged to be the beneficiary of a support order directed to the parent.
(2) "Child-support order" means a support order for a child, including a child who has attained the age of majority under the law of the issuing state or foreign country.
(3) "Convention" means the Convention on the International Recovery of Child Support and Other Forms of Family Maintenance, concluded at The Hague on November 23, 2007.
(4) "Duty of support" means an obligation imposed or imposable by law to provide support for a child, spouse, or former spouse, including an unsatisfied obligation to provide support.
(5) "Foreign country" means a country, including a political subdivision thereof, other than the United States, that authorizes the issuance of support orders and
(A) Which has been declared under the law of the United States to be a foreign reciprocating country;
(B) Which has established a reciprocal arrangement for child support with this state as provided in Section 5700.308;
(C) Which has enacted a law or established procedures for the issuance and enforcement of support orders which are substantially similar to the procedures under this part; or
(D) In which the Convention is in force with respect to the United States.
(6) "Foreign support order" means a support order of a foreign tribunal.
(7) "Foreign tribunal" means a court, administrative agency, or quasi-judicial entity of a foreign country which is authorized to establish, enforce, or modify support orders or to determine parentage of a child. The term includes a competent authority under the Convention.
(8) "Home state" means the state or foreign country in which a child lived with a parent or a person acting as parent for at least six consecutive months immediately preceding the time of filing of a petition or comparable pleading for support and, if a child is less than six months old, the state or foreign country in which the child lived from birth with any of them. A period of temporary absence of any of them is counted as part of the six-month or other period.
(9) "Income" includes earnings or other periodic entitlements to money

from any source and any other property subject to withholding for support under the law of this state.

(10) "Income-withholding order" means an order or other legal process directed to an obligor's employer, or other debtor, as defined by Section 5208, to withhold support from the income of the obligor.

(11) "Initiating tribunal" means the tribunal of a state or foreign country from which a petition or comparable pleading is forwarded or in which a petition or comparable pleading is filed for forwarding to another state or foreign country.

(12) "Issuing foreign country" means the foreign country in which a tribunal issues a support order or a judgment determining parentage of a child.

(13) "Issuing state" means the state in which a tribunal issues a support order or a judgment determining parentage of a child.

(14) "Issuing tribunal" means the tribunal of a state or foreign country that issues a support order or a judgment determining parentage of a child.

(15) "Law" includes decisional and statutory law and rules and regulations having the force of law.

(16) "Obligee" means:

(A) an individual to whom a duty of support is or is alleged to be owed or in whose favor a support order or a judgment determining parentage of a child has been issued;

(B) a foreign country, state, or political subdivision of a state to which the rights under a duty of support or support order have been assigned or which has independent claims based on financial assistance provided to an individual obligee in place of child support;

(C) an individual seeking a judgment determining parentage of the individual's child; or

(D) a person that is a creditor in a proceeding under Chapter 7.

(17) "Obligor" means an individual, or the estate of a decedent that:

(A) owes or is alleged to owe a duty of support;

(B) is alleged but has not been adjudicated to be a parent of a child;

(C) is liable under a support order; or

(D) is a debtor in a proceeding under Chapter 7.

(18) "Outside this state" means a location in another state or a country other than the United States, whether or not the country is a foreign country.

(19) "Person" means an individual, corporation, business trust, estate, trust, partnership, limited liability company, association, joint venture, public corporation, government or governmental subdivision, agency, or instrumentality, or any other legal or commercial entity.

(20) "Record" means information that is inscribed on a tangible medium or that is stored in an electronic or other medium and is retrievable in perceivable form.

(21) "Register" means to file in a tribunal of this state a support order or judgment determining parentage of a child issued in another state or a foreign country.

(22) "Registering tribunal" means a tribunal in which a support order or judgment determining parentage of a child is registered.

(23) "Responding state" means a state in which a petition or comparable

pleading for support or to determine parentage of a child is filed or to which a petition or comparable pleading is forwarded for filing from another state or a foreign country.

(24) "Responding tribunal" means the authorized tribunal in a responding state or foreign country.

(25) "Spousal-support order" means a support order for a spouse or former spouse of the obligor.

(26) "State" means a state of the United States, the District of Columbia, Puerto Rico, the United States Virgin Islands, or any territory or insular possession under the jurisdiction of the United States. The term includes an Indian nation or tribe.

(27) "Support enforcement agency" means a public official, governmental entity, or private agency authorized to:

(A) seek enforcement of support orders or laws relating to the duty of support;

(B) seek establishment or modification of child support;

(C) request determination of parentage of a child;

(D) attempt to locate obligors or their assets; or

(E) request determination of the controlling child-support order.

(28) "Support order" means a judgment, decree, order, decision, or directive, whether temporary, final, or subject to modification, issued in a state or foreign country for the benefit of a child, a spouse, or a former spouse, which provides for monetary support, health care, arrearages, retroactive support, or reimbursement for financial assistance provided to an individual obligee in place of child support. The term may include related costs and fees, interest, income withholding, automatic adjustment, reasonable attorney's fees, and other relief.

(29) "Tribunal" means a court, administrative agency, or quasi-judicial entity authorized to establish, enforce, or modify support orders or to determine parentage of a child.[339]

5700.103. (a) The superior court is the tribunal of this state.

(b) The Department of Child Support Services is the support enforcement agency of this state.[339]

5700.104. (a) Remedies provided by this part are cumulative and do not affect the availability of remedies under other law or the recognition of a foreign support order on the basis of comity.

(b) This part does not:

(1) provide the exclusive method of establishing or enforcing a support order under the law of this state; or

(2) grant a tribunal of this state jurisdiction to render judgment or issue an order relating to child custody or visitation in a proceeding under this part.[339]

5700.105. (a) A tribunal of this state shall apply Chapters 1 through 6 and, as applicable, Chapter 7, to a support proceeding involving:

(1) a foreign support order;

(2) a foreign tribunal; or

(3) an obligee, obligor, or child residing in a foreign country.

(b) A tribunal of this state that is requested to recognize and enforce a support order on the basis of comity may apply the procedural and substantive provisions of Chapters 1 through 6.

(c) Chapter 7 applies only to a support proceeding under the Convention. In such a proceeding, if a provision of Chapter 7 is inconsistent with Chapters 1 through 6, Chapter 7 controls.[339]

Chapter 2: Jurisdiction

5700.201. (a) In a proceeding to establish or enforce a support order or to determine parentage of a child, a tribunal of this state may exercise personal jurisdiction over a nonresident individual or the individual's guardian or conservator if:

(1) the individual is personally served with notice within this state;

(2) the individual submits to the jurisdiction of this state by consent in a record, by entering a general appearance, or by filing a responsive document having the effect of waiving any contest to personal jurisdiction;

(3) the individual resided with the child in this state;

(4) the individual resided in this state and provided prenatal expenses or support for the child;

(5) the child resides in this state as a result of the acts or directives of the individual;

(6) the individual engaged in sexual intercourse in this state and the child may have been conceived by that act of intercourse;

(7) the individual has filed a declaration of paternity pursuant to Chapter 3 (commencing with Section 7570) of Part 2 of Division 12, maintained in this state by the Department of Child Support Services; or

(8) there is any other basis consistent with the constitutions of this state and the United States for the exercise of personal jurisdiction.

(b) The bases of personal jurisdiction set forth in subsection (a) or in any other law of this state may not be used to acquire personal jurisdiction for a tribunal of this state to modify a child-support order of another state unless the requirements of Section 5700.611 are met, or, in the case of a foreign support order, unless the requirements of Section 5700.615 are met.[339]

5700.202. Personal jurisdiction acquired by a tribunal of this state in a proceeding under this part or other law of this state relating to a support order continues as long as a tribunal of this state has continuing, exclusive jurisdiction to modify its order or continuing jurisdiction to enforce its order as provided by Sections 5700.205, 5700.206, and 5700.211.[339]

5700.203. Under this part, a tribunal of this state may serve as an initiating tribunal to forward proceedings to a tribunal of another state, and as a responding tribunal for proceedings initiated in another state or a foreign country.[339]

5700.204. (a) A tribunal of this state may exercise jurisdiction to establish a support order if the petition or comparable pleading is filed after a pleading is filed in another state or a foreign country only if:

(1) the petition or comparable pleading in this state is filed before the expiration of the time allowed in the other state or the foreign country for filing a responsive pleading challenging the exercise of jurisdiction by the other state or the foreign country;

(2) the contesting party timely challenges the exercise of jurisdiction

in the other state or the foreign country; and

(3) if relevant, this state is the home state of the child.

(b) A tribunal of this state may not exercise jurisdiction to establish a support order if the petition or comparable pleading is filed before a petition or comparable pleading is filed in another state or a foreign country if:

(1) the petition or comparable pleading in the other state or foreign country is filed before the expiration of the time allowed in this state for filing a responsive pleading challenging the exercise of jurisdiction by this state;

(2) the contesting party timely challenges the exercise of jurisdiction in this state; and

(3) if relevant, the other state or foreign country is the home state of the child.[339]

5700.205. (a) A tribunal of this state that has issued a child-support order consistent with the law of this state has and shall exercise continuing, exclusive jurisdiction to modify its child-support order if the order is the controlling order and:

(1) at the time of the filing of a request for modification this state is the residence of the obligor, the individual obligee, or the child for whose benefit the support order is issued; or

(2) even if this state is not the residence of the obligor, the individual obligee, or the child for whose benefit the support order is issued, the parties consent in a record or in open court that the tribunal of this state may continue to exercise jurisdiction to modify its order.

(b) A tribunal of this state that has issued a child-support order consistent with the law of this state may not exercise continuing, exclusive jurisdiction to modify the order if:

(1) all of the parties who are individuals file consent in a record with the tribunal of this state that a tribunal of another state that has jurisdiction over at least one of the parties who is an individual or that is located in the state of residence of the child may modify the order and assume continuing, exclusive jurisdiction; or

(2) its order is not the controlling order.

(c) If a tribunal of another state has issued a child-support order pursuant to the Uniform Interstate Family Support Act or a law substantially similar to that Act which modifies a child-support order of a tribunal of this state, tribunals of this state shall recognize the continuing, exclusive jurisdiction of the tribunal of the other state.

(d) A tribunal of this state that lacks continuing, exclusive jurisdiction to modify a child-support order may serve as an initiating tribunal to request a tribunal of another state to modify a support order issued in that state.

(e) A temporary support order issued ex parte or pending resolution of a jurisdictional conflict does not create continuing, exclusive jurisdiction in the issuing tribunal.[339]

5700.206. (a) A tribunal of this state that has issued a child-support order consistent with the law of this state may serve as an initiating tribunal to request a tribunal of another state to enforce:

(1) the order if the order is the controlling order and has not been modified by a tribunal of another

state that assumed jurisdiction pursuant to the Uniform Interstate Family Support Act; or

(2) a money judgment for arrears of support and interest on the order accrued before a determination that an order of a tribunal of another state is the controlling order.

(b) A tribunal of this state having continuing jurisdiction over a support order may act as a responding tribunal to enforce the order.[339]

5700.207. (a) If a proceeding is brought under this part and only one tribunal has issued a child-support order, the order of that tribunal controls and must be recognized.

(b) If a proceeding is brought under this part, and two or more child-support orders have been issued by tribunals of this state, another state, or a foreign country with regard to the same obligor and same child, a tribunal of this state having personal jurisdiction over both the obligor and individual obligee shall apply the following rules and by order shall determine which order controls and must be recognized:

(1) If only one of the tribunals would have continuing, exclusive jurisdiction under this part, the order of that tribunal controls.

(2) If more than one of the tribunals would have continuing, exclusive jurisdiction under this part:

(A) an order issued by a tribunal in the current home state of the child controls; or

(B) if an order has not been issued in the current home state of the child, the order most recently issued controls.

(3) If none of the tribunals would have continuing, exclusive jurisdiction under this part, the tribunal of this state shall issue a child-support order, which controls.

(c) If two or more child-support orders have been issued for the same obligor and same child, upon request of a party who is an individual or that is a support enforcement agency, a tribunal of this state having personal jurisdiction over both the obligor and the obligee who is an individual shall determine which order controls under subsection (b). The request may be filed with a registration for enforcement or registration for modification pursuant to Chapter 6, or may be filed as a separate proceeding.

(d) A request to determine which is the controlling order must be accompanied by a copy of every child-support order in effect and the applicable record of payments. The requesting party shall give notice of the request to each party whose rights may be affected by the determination.

(e) The tribunal that issued the controlling order under subsection (a), (b), or (c) has continuing jurisdiction to the extent provided in Section 5700.205 or 5700.206.

(f) A tribunal of this state that determines by order which is the controlling order under subsection (b)(1) or (2) or (c), or that issues a new controlling order under subsection(b)(3), shall state in that order:

(1) the basis upon which the tribunal made its determination;

(2) the amount of prospective support, if any; and

(3) the total amount of consolidated arrears and accrued interest, if any, under all of the orders after all payments made are credited as

provided by Section 5700.209.

(g) Within 30 days after issuance of an order determining which is the controlling order, the party obtaining the order shall file a certified copy of it in each tribunal that issued or registered an earlier order of child support. A party or support enforcement agency obtaining the order that fails to file a certified copy is subject to appropriate sanctions by a tribunal in which the issue of failure to file arises. The failure to file does not affect the validity or enforceability of the controlling order.

(h) An order that has been determined to be the controlling order, or a judgment for consolidated arrears of support and interest, if any, made pursuant to this section must be recognized in proceedings under this part.[339]

5700.208. In responding to registrations or petitions for enforcement of two or more child-support orders in effect at the same time with regard to the same obligor and different individual obligees, at least one of which was issued by a tribunal of another state or a foreign country, a tribunal of this state shall enforce those orders in the same manner as if the orders had been issued by a tribunal of this state.[339]

5700.209. A tribunal of this state shall credit amounts collected for a particular period pursuant to any child-support order against the amounts owed for the same period under any other child-support order for support of the same child issued by a tribunal of this state, another state, or a foreign country.[339]

5700.210. A tribunal of this state exercising personal jurisdiction over a nonresident in a proceeding under this part, under other law of this state relating to a support order, or recognizing a foreign support order may receive evidence from outside this state pursuant to Section 5700.316, communicate with a tribunal outside this state pursuant to Section 5700.317, and obtain discovery through a tribunal outside this state pursuant to Section 5700.318. In all other respects, Chapters 3 through 6 do not apply, and the tribunal shall apply the procedural and substantive law of this state.[339]

5700.211. (a) A tribunal of this state issuing a spousal-support order consistent with the law of this state has continuing, exclusive jurisdiction to modify the spousal-support order throughout the existence of the support obligation.

(b) A tribunal of this state may not modify a spousal-support order issued by a tribunal of another state or a foreign country having continuing, exclusive jurisdiction over that order under the law of that state or foreign country.

(c) A tribunal of this state that has continuing, exclusive jurisdiction over a spousal-support order may serve as:

(1) an initiating tribunal to request a tribunal of another state to enforce the spousal-support order issued in this state; or

(2) a responding tribunal to enforce or modify its own spousal-support order.[339]

Chapter 3: Civil Provisions of General Application

5700.301. (a) Except as otherwise provided in this part, this chapter applies to all proceedings under this part.

(b) An individual petitioner or a support enforcement agency may initiate a proceeding authorized under this part by filing a petition in an initiating tribunal for forwarding to a responding tribunal or by filing a petition or a comparable pleading directly in a tribunal of another state or a foreign country which has or can obtain personal jurisdiction over the respondent.[339]

5700.302. A minor parent, or a guardian or other legal representative of a minor parent, may maintain a proceeding on behalf of or for the benefit of the minor's child.[339]

5700.303. Except as otherwise provided in this part, a responding tribunal of this state shall:

(1) apply the procedural and substantive law generally applicable to similar proceedings originating in this state and may exercise all powers and provide all remedies available in those proceedings; and

(2) determine the duty of support and the amount payable in accordance with the law and support guidelines of this state.[339]

5700.304. (a) Upon the filing of a petition authorized by this part, an initiating tribunal of this state shall forward the petition and its accompanying documents:

(1) to the responding tribunal or appropriate support enforcement agency in the responding state; or

(2) if the identity of the responding tribunal is unknown, to the state information agency of the responding state with a request that they be forwarded to the appropriate tribunal and that receipt be acknowledged.

(b) If requested by the responding tribunal, a tribunal of this state shall issue a certificate or other document and make findings required by the law of the responding state. If the responding tribunal is in a foreign country, upon request the tribunal of this state shall specify the amount of support sought, convert that amount into the equivalent amount in the foreign currency under applicable official or market exchange rate as publicly reported, and provide any other documents necessary to satisfy the requirements of the responding foreign tribunal.[339]

5700.305. (a) When a responding tribunal of this state receives a petition or comparable pleading from an initiating tribunal or directly pursuant to Section 5700.301(b), it shall cause the petition or pleading to be filed and notify the petitioner where and when it was filed.

(b) A responding tribunal of this state, to the extent not prohibited by other law, may do one or more of the following:

(1) establish or enforce a support order, modify a child-support order, determine the controlling child-support order, or determine parentage of a child;

(2) order an obligor to comply with a support order, specifying the amount and the manner of compliance;

(3) order income withholding;

(4) determine the amount of any arrearages, and specify a method of payment;

(5) enforce orders by civil or criminal contempt, or both;

(6) set aside property for satisfaction of the support order;

(7) place liens and order execution on the obligor's property;
(8) order an obligor to keep the tribunal informed of the obligor's current residential address, electronic-mail address, telephone number, employer, address of employment, and telephone number at the place of employment;
(9) issue a bench warrant for an obligor who has failed after proper notice to appear at a hearing ordered by the tribunal and enter the bench warrant in any local and state computer systems for criminal warrants;
(10) order the obligor to seek appropriate employment by specified methods;
(11) award reasonable attorney's fees and other fees and costs; and
(12) grant any other available remedy
(c) A responding tribunal of this state shall include in a support order issued under this part, or in the documents accompanying the order, the calculations on which the support order is based.
(d) A responding tribunal of this state may not condition the payment of a support order issued under this part upon compliance by a party with provisions for visitation.
(e) If a responding tribunal of this state issues an order under this part, the tribunal shall send a copy of the order to the petitioner and the respondent and to the initiating tribunal, if any.
(f) If requested to enforce a support order, arrears, or judgment or modify a support order stated in a foreign currency, a responding tribunal of this state shall convert the amount stated in the foreign currency to the equivalent amount in dollars under the applicable official or market exchange rate as publicly reported.[339]

5700.306. If a petition or comparable pleading is received by an inappropriate tribunal of this state, the tribunal shall forward the pleading and accompanying documents to an appropriate tribunal of this state or another state and notify the petitioner where and when the pleading was sent.[339]

5700.307. (a) A support enforcement agency of this state, upon request, shall provide services to a petitioner in a proceeding under this part.
(b) A support enforcement agency of this state that is providing services to the petitioner shall:
(1) take all steps necessary to enable an appropriate tribunal of this state, another state, or a foreign country to obtain jurisdiction over the respondent;
(2) request an appropriate tribunal to set a date, time, and place for a hearing;
(3) make a reasonable effort to obtain all relevant information, including information as to income and property of the parties;
(4) within 14 days, exclusive of Saturdays, Sundays, and legal holidays, after receipt of notice in a record from an initiating, responding, or registering tribunal, send a copy of the notice to the petitioner;
(5) within 14 days, exclusive of Saturdays, Sundays, and legal holidays, after receipt of communication in a record from the respondent or the respondent's attorney, send a copy of the communication to the petitioner; and
(6) notify the petitioner if jurisdiction

over the respondent cannot be obtained.

(c) A support enforcement agency of this state that requests registration of a child-support order in this state for enforcement or for modification shall make reasonable efforts:

(1) to ensure that the order to be registered is the controlling order; or

(2) if two or more child-support orders exist and the identity of the controlling order has not been determined, to ensure that a request for such a determination is made in a tribunal having jurisdiction to do so.

(d) A support enforcement agency of this state that requests registration and enforcement of a support order, arrears, or judgment stated in a foreign currency shall convert the amounts stated in the foreign currency into the equivalent amounts in dollars under the applicable official or market exchange rate as publicly reported.

(e) A support enforcement agency of this state shall issue or request a tribunal of this state to issue a child-support order and an income-withholding order that redirect payment of current support, arrears, and interest if requested to do so by a support enforcement agency of another state pursuant to Section 5700.319.

(f) This part does not create or negate a relationship of attorney and client or other fiduciary relationship between a support enforcement agency or the attorney for the agency and the individual being assisted by the agency.[339]

5700.308. (a) If the Attorney General or the Department of Child Support Services determines that the support enforcement agency is neglecting or refusing to provide services to an individual, the Attorney General or the department may order the agency to perform its duties under this part or may provide those services directly to the individual.

(b) The Department of Child Support Services, in consultation with the Attorney General, may determine that a foreign country has established a reciprocal arrangement for child support with this state and take appropriate action for notification of the determination.[339]

5700.309. An individual may employ private counsel to represent the individual in proceedings authorized by this part.[339]

5700.310. (a) The Department of Child Support Services is the state information agency under this part.

(b) The state information agency shall:

(1) compile and maintain a current list, including addresses, of the tribunals in this state which have jurisdiction under this part and any support enforcement agencies in this state and transmit a copy to the state information agency of every other state;

(2) maintain a register of names and addresses of tribunals and support enforcement agencies received from other states;

(3) forward to the appropriate tribunal in the county in this state in which the obligee who is an individual or the obligor resides, or in which the obligor's property is believed to be located, all documents concerning a proceeding under this part received from another state or a foreign country; and

(4) obtain information concerning the location of the obligor and the

obligor's property within this state not exempt from execution, by such means as postal verification and federal or state locator services, examination of telephone directories, requests for the obligor's address from employers, and examination of governmental records, including, to the extent not prohibited by other law, those relating to real property, vital statistics, law enforcement, taxation, motor vehicles, driver's licenses, and social security.[339]

5700.311. (a) In a proceeding under this part, a petitioner seeking to establish a support order, to determine parentage of a child, or to register and modify a support order of a tribunal of another state or a foreign country must file a petition. Unless otherwise ordered under Section 5700.312, the petition or accompanying documents must provide, so far as known, the name, residential address, and social security numbers of the obligor and the obligee or the parent and alleged parent, and the name, sex, residential address, social security number, and date of birth of each child for whose benefit support is sought or whose parentage is to be determined. Unless filed at the time of registration, the petition must be accompanied by a copy of any support order known to have been issued by another tribunal. The petition may include any other information that may assist in locating or identifying the respondent.
(b) The petition must specify the relief sought. The petition and accompanying documents must conform substantially with the requirements imposed by the forms mandated by federal law for use in cases filed by a support enforcement agency.[339]

5700.312. If a party alleges in an affidavit or a pleading under oath that the health, safety, or liberty of a party or child would be jeopardized by disclosure of specific identifying information, that information must be sealed and may not be disclosed to the other party or the public. After a hearing in which a tribunal takes into consideration the health, safety, or liberty of the party or child, the tribunal may order disclosure of information that the tribunal determines to be in the interest of justice.[339]

5700.313. (a) The petitioner may not be required to pay a filing fee or other costs.
(b) If an obligee prevails, a responding tribunal of this state may assess against an obligor filing fees, reasonable attorney's fees, other costs, and necessary travel and other reasonable expenses incurred by the obligee and the obligee's witnesses. The tribunal may not assess fees, costs, or expenses against the obligee or the support enforcement agency of either the initiating or responding state or foreign country, except as provided by other law. Attorney's fees may be taxed as costs, and may be ordered paid directly to the attorney, who may enforce the order in the attorney's own name. Payment of support owed to the obligee has priority over fees, costs, and expenses.
(c) The tribunal shall order the payment of costs and reasonable attorney's fees if it determines that a hearing was requested primarily for delay. In a proceeding under Chapter 6, a hearing is presumed to have been

requested primarily for delay if a registered support order is confirmed or enforced without change.[339]

5700.314. (a) Participation by a petitioner in a proceeding under this part before a responding tribunal, whether in person, by private attorney, or through services provided by the support enforcement agency, does not confer personal jurisdiction over the petitioner in another proceeding.
(b) A petitioner is not amenable to service of civil process while physically present in this state to participate in a proceeding under this part.
(c) The immunity granted by this section does not extend to civil litigation based on acts unrelated to a proceeding under this part committed by a party while physically present in this state to participate in the proceeding.[339]

5700.315. A party whose parentage of a child has been previously determined by or pursuant to law may not plead nonparentage as a defense to a proceeding under this part.[339]

5700.316. (a) The physical presence of a nonresident party who is an individual in a tribunal of this state is not required for the establishment, enforcement, or modification of a support order or the rendition of a judgment determining parentage of a child.
(b) An affidavit, a document substantially complying with federally mandated forms, or a document incorp-orated by reference in any of them, which would not be excluded under the hearsay rule if given in person, is admissible in evidence if given under penalty of perjury by a party or witness residing outside this state.
(c) A copy of the record of child-support payments certified as a true copy of the original by the custodian of the record may be forwarded to a responding tribunal. The copy is evidence of facts asserted in it, and is admissible to show whether payments were made.
(d) Copies of bills for testing for parentage of a child, and for prenatal and postnatal health care of the mother and child, furnished to the adverse party at least 10 days before trial, are admissible in evidence to prove the amount of the charges billed and that the charges were reasonable, necessary, and customary.
(e) Documentary evidence transmitted from outside this state to a tribunal of this state by telephone, telecopier, or other electronic means that do not provide an original record may not be excluded from evidence on an objection based on the means of transmission.
(f) In a proceeding under this part, a tribunal of this state shall permit a party or witness residing outside this state to be deposed or to testify under penalty of perjury by telephone, audiovisual means, or other electronic means at a designated tribunal or other location. A tribunal of this state shall cooperate with other tribunals in designating an appropriate location for the deposition or testimony.
(g) If a party called to testify at a civil hearing refuses to answer on the ground that the testimony may be self-incriminating, the trier of fact may draw an adverse inference from the refusal.
(h) A privilege against disclosure of communications between spouses

does not apply in a proceeding under this part.
(i) The defense of immunity based on the relationship of husband and wife or parent and child does not apply in a proceeding under this part.
(j) A voluntary acknowledgment of paternity, certified as a true copy, is admissible to establish parentage of the child.[339]

5700.317. A tribunal of this state may communicate with a tribunal outside this state in a record or by telephone, electronic mail, or other means, to obtain information concerning the laws, the legal effect of a judgment, decree, or order of that tribunal, and the status of a proceeding. A tribunal of this state may furnish similar information by similar means to a tribunal outside this state.[339]

5700.318. A tribunal of this state may:
(1) request a tribunal outside this state to assist in obtaining discovery; and
(2) upon request, compel a person over which it has jurisdiction to respond to a discovery order issued by a tribunal outside this state.[339]

5700.319. (a) A support enforcement agency or tribunal of this state shall disburse promptly any amounts received pursuant to a support order, as directed by the order. The agency or tribunal shall furnish to a requesting party or tribunal of another state or a foreign country a certified statement by the custodian of the record of the amounts and dates of all payments received.
(b) If neither the obligor, nor the obligee who is an individual, nor the child resides in this state, upon request from the support enforcement agency of this state or another state, the Department of Child Support Services or a tribunal of this state shall:
(1) direct that the support payment be made to the support enforcement agency in the state in which the obligee is receiving services; and
(2) issue and send to the obligor's employer a conforming income-withholding order or an administrative notice of change of payee, reflecting the redirected payments.
(c) The support enforcement agency of this state receiving redirected payments from another state pursuant to a law similar to subsection (b) shall furnish to a requesting party or tribunal of the other state a certified statement by the custodian of the record of the amount and dates of all payments received.[339]

Chapter 4: Establishment of Support Order or Determination of Parentage

5700.401. (a) If a support order entitled to recognition under this part has not been issued, a responding tribunal of this state with personal jurisdiction over the parties may issue a support order if:
(1) the individual seeking the order resides outside this state; or
(2) the support enforcement agency seeking the order is located outside this state.
(b) The tribunal may issue a temporary child-support order if the tribunal determines that such an order is appropriate and the individual ordered to pay is:
(1) a presumed father of the child;
(2) petitioning to have his paternity adjudicated;
(3) identified as the father of the child

through genetic testing;
(4) an alleged father who has declined to submit to genetic testing;
(5) shown by clear and convincing evidence to be the father of the child;
(6) an acknowledged father as provided by applicable state law;
(7) the mother of the child; or
(8) an individual who has been ordered to pay child support in a previous proceeding and the order has not been reversed or vacated.

(c) Upon finding, after notice and opportunity to be heard, that an obligor owes a duty of support, the tribunal shall issue a support order directed to the obligor and may issue other orders pursuant to Section 5700.305.[339]

5700.402. A tribunal of this state authorized to determine parentage of a child may serve as a responding tribunal in a proceeding to determine parentage of a child brought under this part or a law or procedure substantially similar to this part.[339]

Chapter 5: Enforcement of Support Order Without Registration

5700.501. An income-withholding order issued in another state may be sent by or on behalf of the obligee, or by the support enforcement agency, to the person defined as the obligor's employer under Section 5210 without first filing a petition or comparable pleading or registering the order with a tribunal of this state.[339]

5700.502. (a) Upon receipt of an income-withholding order, the obligor's employer shall immediately provide a copy of the order to the obligor.

(b) The employer shall treat an income-withholding order issued in another state which appears regular on its face as if it had been issued by a tribunal of this state.

(c) Except as otherwise provided in subsection (d) and Section 5700.503, the employer shall withhold and distribute the funds as directed in the withholding order by complying with terms of the order which specify:
(1) the duration and amount of periodic payments of current child support, stated as a sum certain;
(2) the person designated to receive payments and the address to which the payments are to be forwarded;
(3) medical support, whether in the form of periodic cash payment, stated as a sum certain, or ordering the obligor to provide health insurance coverage for the child under a policy available through the obligor's employment;
(4) the amount of periodic payments of fees and costs for a support enforcement agency, the issuing tribunal, and the obligee's attorney, stated as sums certain; and
(5) the amount of periodic payments of arrearages and interest on arrearages, stated as sums certain.

(d) An employer shall comply with the law of the state of the obligor's principal place of employment for with-holding from income with respect to:
(1) the employer's fee for processing an income-withholding order;
(2) the maximum amount permitted to be withheld from the obligor's income; and
(3) the times within which the employer must implement the withholding order and forward the child-support payment.[339]

5700.503. If an obligor's employer receives two or more income-withholding orders with respect to the earnings of the same obligor, the employer satisfies the terms of the orders if the employer complies with the law of the state of the obligor's principal place of employment to establish the priorities for withholding and allocating income withheld for two or more child-support obligees.[339]

5700.504. An employer that complies with an income-withholding order issued in another state in accordance with this chapter is not subject to civil liability to an individual or agency with regard to the employer's withholding of child support from the obligor's income.[339]

5700.505. An employer that willfully fails to comply with an income-withholding order issued in another state and received for enforcement is subject to the same penalties that may be imposed for noncompliance with an order issued by a tribunal of this state.[339]

5700.506. (a) An obligor may contest the validity or enforcement of an income-withholding order issued in another state and received directly by an employer in this state by registering the order in a tribunal of this state and filing a contest to that order as provided in Chapter 6, or otherwise contesting the order in the same manner as if the order had been issued by a tribunal of this state.

(b) The obligor shall give notice of the contest to:

(1) a support enforcement agency providing services to the obligee;

(2) each employer that has directly received an income-withholding order relating to the obligor; and

(3) the person designated to receive payments in the income-withholding order or, if no person is designated, to the obligee.[339]

5700.507. (a) A party or support enforcement agency seeking to enforce a support order or an income-withholding order, or both, issued in another state or a foreign support order may send the documents required for registering the order to a support enforcement agency of this state.

(b) Upon receipt of the documents, the support enforcement agency, without initially seeking to register the order, shall consider and, if appropriate, use any administrative procedure authorized by the law of this state to enforce a support order or an income-withholding order, or both. If the obligor does not contest administrative enforcement, the order need not be registered. If the obligor contests the validity or administrative enforcement of the order, the support enforcement agency shall register the order pursuant to this part.[339]

Chapter 6: Registration, Enforcement, and modification of Support Order

Article 1: Registration for Enforcement of Support Order

5700.601. A support order or income-withholding order issued in another state or a foreign support order may be registered in this state for enforcement.[339]

5700.602. (a) Except as otherwise provided in Section 5700.706, a support order or income-withholding order of another state or a foreign support order may be registered in this state by sending the following records to the appropriate tribunal in this state:

(1) a letter of transmittal to the tribunal requesting registration and enforcement;

(2) two copies, including one certified copy, of the order to be registered, including any modification of the order;

(3) a sworn statement by the person requesting registration or a certified statement by the custodian of the records showing the amount of any arrearage;

(4) the name of the obligor and, if known:

(A) the obligor's address and social security number;

(B) the name and address of the obligor's employer and any other source of income of the obligor; and

(C) a description and the location of property of the obligor in this state not exempt from execution; and

(5) except as otherwise provided in Section 5700.312, the name and address of the obligee and, if applicable, the person to whom support payments are to be remitted.

(b) On receipt of a request for registration, the registering tribunal shall cause the order to be filed as an order of a tribunal of another state or a foreign support order, together with one copy of the documents and information, regardless of their form.

(c) A petition or comparable pleading seeking a remedy that must be affirmatively sought under other law of this state may be filed at the same time as the request for registration or later. The pleading must specify the grounds for the remedy sought.

(d) If two or more orders are in effect, the person requesting registration shall:

(1) furnish to the tribunal a copy of every support order asserted to be in effect in addition to the documents specified in this section;

(2) specify the order alleged to be the controlling order, if any; and

(3) specify the amount of consolidated arrears, if any.

(e) A request for a determination of which is the controlling order may be filed separately or with a request for registration and enforcement or for registration and modification. The person requesting registration shall give notice of the request to each party whose rights may be affected by the determination.[339]

5700.603. (a) A support order or income-withholding order issued in another state or a foreign support order is registered when the order is filed in the registering tribunal of this state.

(b) A registered support order issued in another state or a foreign country is enforceable in the same manner and is subject to the same procedures as an order issued by a tribunal of this state.

(c) Except as otherwise provided in this part, a tribunal of this state shall recognize and enforce, but may not modify, a registered support order if the issuing tribunal had jurisdiction.[339]

5700.604. (a) Except as otherwise provided in subsection (d), the law of the issuing state or foreign country governs:

(1) the nature, extent, amount, and duration of current payments under a registered support order;

(2) the computation and payment of arrearages and accrual of interest on the arrearages under the support

order; and

(3) the existence and satisfaction of other obligations under the support order.

(b) In a proceeding for arrears under a registered support order, the statute of limitation of this state, or of the issuing state or foreign country, whichever is longer, applies.

(c) A responding tribunal of this state shall apply the procedures and remedies of this state to enforce current support and collect arrears and interest due on a support order of another state or a foreign country registered in this state.

(d) After a tribunal of this state or another state determines which is the controlling order and issues an order consolidating arrears, if any, a tribunal of this state shall prospectively apply the law of the state or foreign country issuing the controlling order, including its law on interest on arrears, on current and future support, and on consolidated arrears.[339]

Article 2: Contest of Validity or Enforcement

5700.605. (a) When a support order or income-withholding order issued in another state or a foreign support order is registered, the registering tribunal of this state shall notify the nonregistering party. The notice must be accompanied by a copy of the registered order and the documents and relevant information accompanying the order.

(b) A notice must inform the nonregistering party:

(1) that a registered support order is enforceable as of the date of registration in the same manner as an order issued by a tribunal of this state;

(2) that a hearing to contest the validity or enforcement of the registered order must be requested within 20 days after notice unless the registered order is under Section 5700.707;

(3) that failure to contest the validity or enforcement of the registered order in a timely manner will result in confirmation of the order and enforcement of the order and the alleged arrearages; and

(4) of the amount of any alleged arrearages.

(c) If the registering party asserts that two or more orders are in effect, a notice must also:

(1) identify the two or more orders and the order alleged by the registering party to be the controlling order and the consolidated arrears, if any;

(2) notify the nonregistering party of the right to a determination of which is the controlling order;

(3) state that the procedures provided in subsection (b) apply to the determination of which is the controlling order; and

(4) state that failure to contest the validity or enforcement of the order alleged to be the controlling order in a timely manner may result in confirmation that the order is the controlling order.

(d) Upon registration of an income-withholding order for enforcement, the support enforcement agency or the registering tribunal shall notify the obligor's employer pursuant to Chapter 8 (commencing with Section 5200) of Part 5.[339]

5700.606. (a) A nonregistering party seeking to contest the validity or enforcement of a registered support order in this state shall request a hearing within the time required by Section 5700.605. The nonregistering party may seek to vacate the registration, to assert any defense to an allegation of noncompliance with the registered order, or to contest the remedies being sought or the amount of any alleged arrearages pursuant to Section 5700.607.

(b) If the nonregistering party fails to contest the validity or enforcement of the registered support order in a timely manner, the order is confirmed by operation of law.

(c) If a nonregistering party requests a hearing to contest the validity or enforcement of the registered support order, the registering tribunal shall schedule the matter for hearing and give notice to the parties of the date, time, and place of the hearing.[339]

5700.607. (a) A party contesting the validity or enforcement of a registered support order or seeking to vacate the registration has the burden of proving one or more of the following defenses:

(1) the issuing tribunal lacked personal jurisdiction over the contesting party;

(2) the order was obtained by fraud;

(3) the order has been vacated, suspended, or modified by a later order;

(4) the issuing tribunal has stayed the order pending appeal;

(5) there is a defense under the law of this state to the remedy sought;

(6) full or partial payment has been made;

(7) the statute of limitation under Section 5700.604 precludes enforcement of some or all of the alleged arrearages; or

(8) the alleged controlling order is not the controlling order.

(b) If a party presents evidence establishing a full or partial defense under subsection (a), a tribunal may stay enforcement of a registered support order, continue the proceeding to permit production of additional relevant evidence, and issue other appropriate orders. An uncontested portion of the registered support order may be enforced by all remedies available under the law of this state.

(c) If the contesting party does not establish a defense under subsection (a) to the validity or enforcement of a registered support order, the registering tribunal shall issue an order confirming the order.[339]

5700.608. Confirmation of a registered support order, whether by operation of law or after notice and hearing, precludes further contest of the order with respect to any matter that could have been asserted at the time of registration.[339]

Article 3: Registration and Modification of Child-Support Order of Another State

5700.609. A party or support enforcement agency seeking to modify, or to modify and enforce, a child-support order issued in another state shall register that order in this state in the same manner provided in Sections 5700.601 through 5700.608 if the order has not been registered. A petition for modification may be filed at the same time as a request for registration, or later. The pleading must specify the grounds for modification.[339]

5700.610. A tribunal of this state may enforce a child-support order of another state registered for purposes of modification, in the same manner as if the order had been issued by a tribunal of this state, but the registered support order may be modified only if the requirements of Section 5700.611 or 5700.613 have been met.[339]

5700.611. (a) If Section 5700.613 does not apply, upon petition a tribunal of this state may modify a child-support order issued in another state which is registered in this state if, after notice and hearing, the tribunal finds that:

(1) the following requirements are met:

(A) neither the child, nor the obligee who is an individual, nor the obligor resides in the issuing state;

(B) a petitioner who is a nonresident of this state seeks modification; and

(C) the respondent is subject to the personal jurisdiction of the tribunal of this state; or

(2) this state is the residence of the child, or a party who is an individual is subject to the personal jurisdiction of the tribunal of this state, and all of the parties who are individuals have filed consents in a record in the issuing tribunal for a tribunal of this state to modify the support order and assume continuing, exclusive jurisdiction.

(b) Modification of a registered child-support order is subject to the same requirements, procedures, and defenses that apply to the modification of an order issued by a tribunal of this state and the order may be enforced and satisfied in the same manner.

(c) A tribunal of this state may not modify any aspect of a child-support order that may not be modified under the law of the issuing state, including the duration of the obligation of support. If two or more tribunals have issued child-support orders for the same obligor and same child, the order that controls and must be so recognized under Section 5700.207 establishes the aspects of the support order which are nonmodifiable.

(d) In a proceeding to modify a child-support order, the law of the state that is determined to have issued the initial controlling order governs the duration of the obligation of support. The obligor's fulfillment of the duty of support established by that order precludes imposition of a further obligation of support by a tribunal of this state.

(e) On the issuance of an order by a tribunal of this state modifying a child-support order issued in another state, the tribunal of this state becomes the tribunal having continuing, exclusive jurisdiction.

(f) Notwithstanding subsections (a) through (e) and Section 5700.201(b), a tribunal of this state retains jurisdiction to modify an order issued by a tribunal of this state if:

(1) one party resides in another state; and

(2) the other party resides outside the United States.[339]

5700.612. If a child-support order issued by a tribunal of this state is modified by a tribunal of another state which assumed jurisdiction pursuant to the Uniform Interstate Family Support Act, a tribunal of this state:

(1) may enforce its order that was modified only as to arrears and interest accruing before the modification;

(2) may provide appropriate relief for violations of its order which occurred before the effective date of the modification; and

(3) shall recognize the modifying

order of the other state, upon registration, for the purpose of enforcement.[339]

5700.613. (a) If all of the parties who are individuals reside in this state and the child does not reside in the issuing state, a tribunal of this state has jurisdiction to enforce and to modify the issuing state's child-support order in a proceeding to register that order.
(b) A tribunal of this state exercising jurisdiction under this section shall apply the provisions of Chapters 1 and 2, and this chapter, and the procedural and substantive law of this state to the proceeding for enforcement or modification. Chapters 3, 4, 5, 7, and 8 do not apply.[339]

5700.614. Within 30 days after issuance of a modified child-support order, the party obtaining the modification shall file a certified copy of the order with the issuing tribunal that had continuing, exclusive jurisdiction over the earlier order, and in each tribunal in which the party knows the earlier order has been registered. A party who obtains the order and fails to file a certified copy is subject to appropriate sanctions by a tribunal in which the issue of failure to file arises. The failure to file does not affect the validity or enforceability of the modified order of the new tribunal having continuing, exclusive jurisdiction.[339]

Article 4: Registration and Modification of Foreign Child-Support Order

5700.615. (a) Except as otherwise provided in Section 5700.711, if a foreign country lacks or refuses to exercise jurisdiction to modify its child-support order pursuant to its laws, a tribunal of this state may assume jurisdiction to modify the child-support order and bind all individuals subject to the personal jurisdiction of the tribunal whether the consent to modification of a child-support order otherwise required of the individual pursuant to Section 5700.611 has been given or whether the individual seeking modification is a resident of this state or of the foreign country.
(b) An order issued by a tribunal of this state modifying a foreign child-support order pursuant to this section is the controlling order.[339]

5700.616. A party or support enforcement agency seeking to modify, or to modify and enforce, a foreign child-support order not under the Convent-ion may register that order in this state under Sections 5700.601 through 5700.608 if the order has not been registered. A petition for modification may be filed at the same time as a request for registration, or at another time. The petition must specify the grounds for modification.[339]

Chapter 7: Support Proceeding Under Convention

5700.701. In this chapter:
(1) "Application" means a request under the Convention by an obligee or obligor, or on behalf of a child, made through a central authority for assistance from another central authority.
(2) "Central authority" means the entity designated by the United States or a foreign country described in Section 5700.102(5)(D) to perform the functions specified in the

Convention.

(3) "Convention support order" means a support order of a tribunal of a foreign country described in Section 5700.102(5)(D).

(4) "Direct request" means a petition filed by an individual in a tribunal of this state in a proceeding involving an obligee, obligor, or child residing outside the United States.

(5) "Foreign central authority" means the entity designated by a foreign country described in Section 5700.102(5)(D) to perform the functions specified in the Convention.

(6) "Foreign support agreement":

(A) means an agreement for support in a record that:

(i) is enforceable as a support order in the country of origin;

(ii) has been:

(I) formally drawn up or registered as an authentic instrument by a foreign tribunal; or

(II) authenticated by, or concluded, registered, or filed with a foreign tribunal; and

(iii) may be reviewed and modified by a foreign tribunal; and

(B) includes a maintenance arrangement or authentic instrument under the Convention.

(7) "United States central authority" means the Secretary of the United States Department of Health and Human Services.[339]

5700.702. This chapter applies only to a support proceeding under the Convention. In such a proceeding, if a provision of this chapter is inconsistent with Chapters 1 through 6, this chapter controls.[339]

5700.703. The Department of Child Support Services is recognized as the agency designated by the United States central authority to perform specific functions under the Convention.[339]

5700.704. (a) In a support proceeding under this chapter, the Department of Child Support Services shall:

(1) transmit and receive applications; and

(2) initiate or facilitate the institution of a proceeding regarding an application in a tribunal of this state.

(b) The following support proceedings are available to an obligee under the Convention:

(1) recognition or recognition and enforcement of a foreign support order;

(2) enforcement of a support order issued or recognized in this state;

(3) establishment of a support order if there is no existing order, including, if necessary, determination of parentage of a child;

(4) establishment of a support order if recognition of a foreign support order is refused under Section 5700.708(b)(2), (4), or (9);

(5) modification of a support order of a tribunal of this state; and

(6) modification of a support order of a tribunal of another state or a foreign country.

(c) The following support proceedings are available under the Convention to an obligor against which there is an existing support order:

(1) recognition of an order suspending or limiting enforcement of an existing support order of a tribunal of this state;

(2) modification of a support order of a tribunal of this state; and

(3) modification of a support order of a tribunal of another state or a foreign

country.

(d) A tribunal of this state may not require security, bond, or deposit, however described, to guarantee the payment of costs and expenses in proceedings under the Convention.[339]

5700.705. (a) A petitioner may file a direct request seeking establishment or modification of a support order or determination of parentage of a child. In the proceeding, the law of this state applies.

(b) A petitioner may file a direct request seeking recognition and enforcement of a support order or support agreement. In the proceeding, Sections 5700.706 through 5700.713 apply.

(c) In a direct request for recognition and enforcement of a Convention support order or foreign support agreement:

(1) a security, bond, or deposit is not required to guarantee the payment of costs and expenses; and

(2) an obligee or obligor that in the issuing country has benefited from free legal assistance is entitled to benefit, at least to the same extent, from any free legal assistance provided for by the law of this state under the same circumstances.

(d) A petitioner filing a direct request is not entitled to assistance from the Department of Child Support Services.

(e) This chapter does not prevent the application of laws of this state that provide simplified, more expeditious rules regarding a direct request for recognition and enforcement of a foreign support order or foreign support agreement.[339]

5700.706. (a) Except as otherwise provided in this chapter, a party who is an individual or a support enforcement agency seeking recognition of a Convention support order shall register the order in this state as provided in Chapter 6.

(b) Notwithstanding Sections 5700.311 and 5700.602(a), a request for registration of a Convention support order must be accompanied by:

(1) a complete text of the support order or an abstract or extract of the support order drawn up by the issuing foreign tribunal, which may be in the form recommended by the Hague Conference on Private International Law;

(2) a record stating that the support order is enforceable in the issuing country;

(3) if the respondent did not appear and was not represented in the proceedings in the issuing country, a record attesting, as appropriate, either that the respondent had proper notice of the proceedings and an opportune-ity to be heard or that the respondent had proper notice of the support order and an opportunity to be heard in a challenge or appeal on fact or law before a tribunal;

(4) a record showing the amount of arrears, if any, and the date the amount was calculated;

(5) a record showing a requirement for automatic adjustment of the amount of support, if any, and the information necessary to make the appropriate calculations; and

(6) if necessary, a record showing the extent to which the applicant received free legal assistance in the issuing country.

(c) A request for registration of a

Convention support order may seek recognition and partial enforcement of the order.

(d) A tribunal of this state may vacate the registration of a Convention support order without the filing of a contest under Section 5700.707 only if, acting on its own motion, the tribunal finds that recognition and enforcement of the order would be manifestly incompatible with public policy.

(e) The tribunal shall promptly notify the parties of the registration or the order vacating the registration of a Convention support order.[339]

5700.707. (a) Except as otherwise provided in this chapter, Sections 5700.605 through 5700.608 apply to a contest of a registered Convention support order.

(b) A party contesting a registered Convention support order shall file a contest not later than 30 days after notice of the registration, but if the contesting party does not reside in the United States, the contest must be filed not later than 60 days after notice of the registration.

(c) If the nonregistering party fails to contest the registered Convention support order by the time specified in subsection (b), the order is enforceable.

(d) A contest of a registered Convention support order may be based only on grounds set forth in Section 5700.708. The contesting party bears the burden of proof.

(e) In a contest of a registered Convention support order, a tribunal of this state:

(1) is bound by the findings of fact on which the foreign tribunal based its jurisdiction; and

(2) may not review the merits of the order.

(f) A tribunal of this state deciding a contest of a registered Convention support order shall promptly notify the parties of its decision.

(g) A challenge or appeal, if any, does not stay the enforcement of a Convention support order unless there are exceptional circumstances.[339]

5700.708. (a) Except as otherwise provided in subsection (b), a tribunal of this state shall recognize and enforce a registered Convention support order.

(b) The following grounds are the only grounds on which a tribunal of this state may refuse recognition and enforcement of a registered Convention support order:

(1) recognition and enforcement of the order is manifestly incompatible with public policy, including the failure of the issuing tribunal to observe minimum standards of due process, which include notice and an opportunity to be heard;

(2) the issuing tribunal lacked personal jurisdiction consistent with Section 5700.201;

(3) the order is not enforceable in the issuing country;

(4) the order was obtained by fraud in connection with a matter of procedure;

(5) a record transmitted in accordance with Section 5700.706 lacks authenticity or integrity;

(6) a proceeding between the same parties and having the same purpose is pending before a tribunal of this state and that proceeding was the first to be filed;

(7) the order is incompatible with a more recent support order involving

the same parties and having the same purpose if the more recent support order is entitled to recognition and enforcement under this part in this state;

(8) payment, to the extent alleged arrears have been paid in whole or in part;

(9) in a case in which the respondent neither appeared nor was represented in the proceeding in the issuing foreign country:

(A) if the law of that country provides for prior notice of proceedings, the respondent did not have proper notice of the proceedings and an opportunity to be heard; or

(B) if the law of that country does not provide for prior notice of the proceedings, the respondent did not have proper notice of the order and an opportunity to be heard in a challenge or appeal on fact or law before a tribunal; or

(10) the order was made in violation of Section 5700.711.

(c) If a tribunal of this state does not recognize a Convention support order under subsection (b)(2), (4), or (9):

(1) the tribunal may not dismiss the proceeding without allowing a reasonable time for a party to request the establishment of a new Convention support order; and

(2) the Department of Child Support Services shall take all appropriate measures to request a child-support order for the obligee if the application for recognition and enforcement was received under Section 5700.704.[339]

5700.709. If a tribunal of this state does not recognize and enforce a Convention support order in its entirety, it shall enforce any severable part of the order. An application or direct request may seek recognition and partial enforcement of a Convention support order.[339]

5700.710. (a) Except as otherwise provided in subsections (c) and (d), a tribunal of this state shall recognize and enforce a foreign support agreement registered in this state.

(b) An application or direct request for recognition and enforcement of a foreign support agreement must be accompanied by:

(1) a complete text of the foreign support agreement; and

(2) a record stating that the foreign support agreement is enforceable as an order of support in the issuing country.

(c) A tribunal of this state may vacate the registration of a foreign support agreement only if, acting on its own motion, the tribunal finds that recognition and enforcement would be manifestly incompatible with public policy.

(d) In a contest of a foreign support agreement, a tribunal of this state may refuse recognition and enforcement of the agreement if it finds:

(1) recognition and enforcement of the agreement is manifestly incompatible with public policy;

(2) the agreement was obtained by fraud or falsification;

(3) the agreement is incompatible with a support order involving the same parties and having the same purpose in this state, another state, or a foreign country if the support order is entitled to recognition and enforcement under this act in this state; or

(4) the record submitted under subsection (b) lacks authenticity or integrity.

(e) A proceeding for recognition and enforcement of a foreign support agreement must be suspended during the pendency of a challenge to or appeal of the agreement before a tribunal of another state or a foreign country.[339]

5700.711. (a) A tribunal of this state may not modify a Convention child-support order if the obligee remains a resident of the foreign country where the support order was issued unless:

(1) the obligee submits to the jurisdiction of a tribunal of this state, either expressly or by defending on the merits of the case without objecting to the jurisdiction at the first available opportunity; or

(2) the foreign tribunal lacks or refuses to exercise jurisdiction to modify its support order or issue a new support order.

(b) If a tribunal of this state does not modify a Convention child-support order because the order is not recognized in this state, Section 5700.708(c) applies.[339]

5700.712. Personal information gathered or transmitted under this chapter may be used only for the purposes for which it was gathered or transmitted.[339]

5700.713. A record filed with a tribunal of this state under this chapter must be in the original language and, if not in English, must be accompanied by an English translation.[339]

Chapter 8: Interstate Rendition

5700.801. (a) For purposes of this chapter, "governor" includes an individual performing the functions of governor or the executive authority of a state covered by this part.

(b) The Governor may:

(1) demand that the governor of another state surrender an individual found in the other state who is charged criminally in this state with having failed to provide for the support of an obligee; or

(2) on the demand of the governor of another state, surrender an individual found in this state who is charged criminally in the other state with having failed to provide for the support of an obligee.

(c) A provision for extradition of individuals not inconsistent with this act applies to the demand even if the individual whose surrender is demanded was not in the demanding state when the crime was allegedly committed and has not fled therefrom.[339]

5700.802. (a) Before making a demand that the governor of another state surrender an individual charged criminally in this state with having failed to provide for the support of an obligee, the Governor may require a prosecutor of this state to demonstrate that at least 60 days previously the obligee had initiated proceedings for support pursuant to this act or that the proceeding would be of no avail.

(b) If, under this act or a law substantially similar to this act, the Governor of another state makes a demand that the Governor of this state surrender an individual charged criminally in that state with having failed to provide for the support of a child or other individual to whom a duty of support is owed, the Governor may require a prosecutor to investigate the demand and report whether a proceeding for support has been initiated or would be effective. If it appears that a proceeding would be effective but has not been initiated, the Governor may delay honoring the demand for a reasonable time to permit the initiation of a proceeding.

(c) If a proceeding for support has been initiated and the individual whose rendition is demanded prevails, the Governor may decline to honor the demand. If the petitioner prevails and the individual whose rendition is demanded is subject to a support order, the Governor may decline to honor the demand if the individual is complying with the support order.[339]

Chapter 9: Miscellaneous Provisions

5700.901. In applying and construing this uniform act, consideration must be given to the need to promote uniformity of the law with respect to its subject matter among states that enact it.[339]

5700.902. This part applies to proceedings begun on or after January 1, 2016, to establish a support order or determine parentage of a child or to register, recognize, enforce, or modify a prior support order, determination, or agreement, whenever issued or entered.[339]

5700.903. If any provision of this part or its application to any person or circumstance is held invalid, the invalidity does not affect other provisions or applications of this part which can be given effect without the invalid provision or application, and to this end the provisions of this part are severable.[339]

5700.905. The Department of Child Support Services may adopt emergency regulations as appropriate to implement this part.

DIVISION 10: PREVENTION OF DOMESTIC VIOLENCE

REPEALED AND ADDED BY STATS. 1993, CH. 219 SEC. 154.
SECTION 6200 - 6460

PART 1: SHORT TITLE AND DEFINITIONS

added by Stats. 1993, Ch. 219, Sec. 154

6200. This division may be cited as the Domestic Violence Prevention Act.

6201. Unless the provision or context otherwise requires, the definitions in this part govern the construction of this code.

6203. (a) For purposes of this act, "abuse" means any of the following:
(1) To intentionally or recklessly cause or attempt to cause bodily injury.
(2) Sexual assault.
(3) To place a person in reasonable apprehension of imminent serious bodily injury to that person or to another.
(4) To engage in any behavior that has been or could be enjoined pursuant to Section 6320.
(b) Abuse is not limited to the actual infliction of physical injury or assault.[333]

6205. "Affinity," when applied to the marriage relation, signifies the connection existing in consequence of marriage between each of the married persons and the blood relatives of the other.

6209. "Cohabitant" means a person who regularly resides in the household. "Former cohabitant" means a person who formerly regularly resided in the household.

6210. "Dating relationship" means frequent, intimate associations primarily characterized by the expectation of affection or sexual involvement independent of financial considerations.

6211. "Domestic violence" is abuse perpetrated against any of the following persons:
(a) A spouse or former spouse.
(b) A cohabitant or former cohabitant, as defined in Section 6209.
(c) A person with whom the respondent is having or has had a dating or engagement relationship.
(d) A person with whom the respondent has had a child, where the presumption applies that the male parent is the father of the child of the female parent under the Uniform Parentage Act (Part 3 (commencing with Section 7600) of Division 12).
(e) A child of a party or a child who is the subject of an action under the Uniform Parentage Act, where the presumption applies that the male parent is the father of the child to be protected.
(f) Any other person related by consanguinity or affinity within the second degree.

6215. "Emergency protective order" means an order issued under Part 3 (commencing with Section 6240).

6216. For the purposes of this division, "firearm" includes the frame or receiver of the weapon, including a completed frame or receiver or a firearm precursor part. "Firearm precursor part" has the same meaning as in subdivision (a) of Section 16531 of the Penal Code.[505]

6218. "Protective order" means an order that includes any of the following restraining orders, whether issued ex parte, after notice and hearing, or in a judgment:
(a) An order described in Section 6320 enjoining specific acts of abuse.
(b) An order described in Section 6321 excluding a person from a dwelling.
(c) An order described in Section 6322 enjoining other specified behavior.

6219. Subject to adequate, discretionary funding from a city or a county, the superior courts in San Diego County and in Santa Clara County may develop a demonstration project to identify the best practices in civil, juvenile, and criminal court cases involving domestic violence. The superior courts in any other county that is able and willing may also participate in the demonstration project. The superior courts participating in this demonstration project shall report their findings and recommendations to the Judicial Council and the Legislature on or before May 1, 2004. The Judicial Council may make those recommendations available to any court or county.[82]

PART 2: GENERAL PROVISIONS

added by Stats. 1993, Ch. 219, Sec. 154X

6220. The purpose of this division is to prevent acts of domestic violence, abuse, and sexual abuse and to provide for a separation of the persons involved in the domestic violence for a period sufficient to enable these persons to seek a resolution of the causes of the violence.[312]

6221. (a) Unless the provision or context otherwise requires, this division applies to any order described in this division, whether the order is issued in a proceeding brought pursuant to this division, in an action brought pursuant to the Uniform Parentage Act (Part 3 (commencing with Section 7600) of Division 12), or in a proceeding for dissolution of marriage, for nullity of marriage, or for legal separation of the parties.
(b) Nothing in this division affects the jurisdiction of the juvenile court.
(c) Any order issued by a court to which this division applies shall be issued on forms adopted by the Judicial Council of California and that have been approved by the Department of Justice pursuant to subdivision (i) of Section 6380. However, the fact that an order issued by a court pursuant to this section was not issued on forms adopted by the Judicial Council and approved by the Department of Justice shall not, in and of itself, make the order unenforceable.

6222. There is no filing fee for an application, a responsive pleading, or an order to show cause that seeks to obtain, modify, or enforce a protective order or other order authorized by this division when the request for the other order is necessary to obtain or give effect to a protective order. There is no fee for a subpoena filed in connection with that application, responsive pleading, or order to show cause. There is no fee for any filings related to a petition filed pursuant to Part 4 (commencing with 6300) of this division.[503]

6223. A custody or visitation order issued in a proceeding brought pursuant to this division is subject to Part 2 (commencing with Section 3020) of Division 8 (custody of children).

6224. An order described in this division shall state on its face the date of expiration of the order and the following statements in substantially the following form:
"This order is effective when made. The law enforcement agency shall enforce it immediately on receipt. It is enforceable anywhere in California by any law enforcement agency that has received the order or is shown a copy of the order. If proof of service on the restrained person has not been received, the law enforcement agency shall advise the restrained person of the terms of the order and then shall enforce it."

6225. A petition for an order described in this division is valid and the order is enforceable without explicitly stating the address of the petitioner or the petitioner's place of residence, school, employment, the place where the petitioner's child is provided child care services, or the child's school.

6226. The Judicial Council shall prescribe the form of the orders and any other documents required by this division and shall promulgate forms and instructions for applying for orders described in this division.

6226.5. (a) On or before January 1, 2023, the Judicial Council shall amend the Judicial Council form entitled "Can a Domestic Violence Restraining Order Help Me?" to include a brief description of the address confidentiality program established under Chapter 3.1 (commencing with Section 6205) of Division 7 of Title 1 of the Government Code, the benefits of enrollment in the program for victims of domestic violence, and the internet address for the Secretary of State's internet web page that contains more detailed information about the program.
(b) On or before January 1, 2023, the Judicial Council shall make the Judicial Council form available in English and in at least the other languages describeed in Section 1632 of the Civil Code. The Judicial Council may make the form available in additional languages.[495]

6227. The remedies provided in this division are in addition to any other civil or criminal remedies that may be available to the petitioner.

6228. (a) State and local law enforcement agencies shall provide, upon request and without charging a fee, one copy of all incident report face sheets, one copy of all incident reports, a copy of any accompanying or related photographs of a victim's injuries, property damage, or any other photo-graphs that are noted in the incident report, and a copy of 911 recordings, if any, to a victim, or the victim's representative as defined in subdivision (g), of a crime that constitutes an act of any of the following:
(1) Domestic violence, as defined in Section 6211.
(2) Sexual assault, as defined in Sections 261, 261.5, 265, 266, 266a, 266b, 266c, 266g, 266j, 267, 269, 273.4, 285, 286, 287, 288, 288.5, 289, or 311.4 of, or former Section 262 or 288a of, the Penal Code.
(3) Stalking, as defined in Section 1708.7 of the Civil Code or Section

646.9 of the Penal Code.

(4) Human trafficking, as defined in Section 236.1 of the Penal Code.

(5) Abuse of an elder or a dependent adult, as defined in Section 15610.07 of the Welfare and Institutions Code.

(b) (1) A copy of an incident report face sheet shall be made available during regular business hours to a victim or the victim's representative no later than 48 hours after being requested, unless the state or local law enforcement agency informs the victim or the victim's representative of the reasons why, for good cause, the incident report face sheet is not available, in which case the incident report face sheet shall be made available no later than five working days after the request is made.

(2) A copy of the incident report, any accompanying or related photographs of a victim's injuries, property damage, or any other photographs that are noted in the incident report, and a copy of 911 recordings, if any, shall be made available during regular business hours to a victim or the victim's representative no later than five working days after being requested, unless the state or local law enforcement agency informs the victim or the victim's representative of the reasons why, for good cause, the items are not available, in which case the items shall be made available no later than 10 working days after the request is made.

(c) A person requesting copies under this section shall present state or local law enforcement with the person's identification, including a current, valid driver's license, a state-issued identification card, or a passport. If the person is a representative of the victim and the victim is deceased, the representative shall also present a certified copy of the death certificate or other satisfactory evidence of the death of the victim at the time a request is made. If the person is a representative of the victim and the victim is alive and not the subject of a conservatorship, the representative shall also present a written authorization, signed by the victim, making the person the victim's personal representative.

(d) This section shall apply to requests for domestic violence, sexual assault, stalking, human trafficking, or abuse of an elder or a dependent adult face sheets or incident reports, photographs, 911 recordings, and evidence made within five years from the date of completion of the incident report.

(e) This section shall be known and may be cited as the Access to Domestic Violence Reports Act of 1999.

(f) For purposes of this section, "victim" includes a minor who is 12 years of age or older.

(g) (1) For purposes of this section, if the victim is deceased, a "representative of the victim" means any of the following:

(A) The surviving spouse.

(B) A surviving child of the decedent who has attained 18 years of age.

(C) A domestic partner, as defined in subdivision (a) of Section 297.

(D) A surviving parent of the decedent.

(E) A surviving adult relative.

(F) The personal representative of the victim, as defined in Section 58 of the Probate Code, if one is appointed.

(G) The public administrator if one has been appointed.

(2) For purposes of this section, if the victim is not deceased, a "representative of the victim" means any of the following:

(A) A parent, guardian, or adult child of the victim, or an adult sibling of a victim 12 years of age or older, who shall present to law enforcement identification pursuant to subdivision (c). A guardian shall also present to law enforcement a copy of the letters of guardianship demonstrating that the person is the appointed guardian of the victim.

(B) An attorney for the victim, who shall present to law enforcement identification pursuant to subdivision (c) and written proof that the person is the attorney for the victim.

(C) A conservator of the victim who shall present to law enforcement identification pursuant to subdivision (c) and a copy of the letters of conservatorship demonstrating that the person is the appointed conservator of the victim.

(3) A representative of the victim does not include any person who has been convicted of murder in the first degree, as defined in Section 189 of the Penal Code, of the victim, or any person identified in the incident report face sheet as a suspect.[588]

6229. A minor, under 12 years of age, accompanied by a duly appointed and acting guardian ad litem, shall be permitted to appear in court without counsel for the limited purpose of requesting or opposing a request for a temporary restraining order or injunction, or both, under this division as provided in Section 374 of the Code of Civil Procedure.[216]

PART 3: EMERGENCY PROTECTIVE ORDERS

added by Stats. 1993, Ch. 219, Sec. 154

Chapter 1: General Provisions

6240. As used in this part:

(a) "Judicial officer" means a judge, commissioner, or referee designated under Section 6241.

(b) "Law enforcement officer" means one of the following officers who requests or enforces an emergency protective order under this part:

(1) A police officer.

(2) A sheriff's officer.

(3) A peace officer of the Department of the California Highway Patrol.

(4) A peace officer of the University of California Police Department.

(5) A peace officer of the California State University and College Police Departments.

(6) A peace officer of the Department of Parks and Recreation, as defined in subdivision (f) of Section 830.2 of the Penal Code.

(7) A peace officer of the Department of General Services of the City of Los Angeles, as defined in subdivision (c) of Section 830.31 of the Penal Code.

(8) A housing authority patrol officer, as defined in subdivision (d) of Section 830.31 of the Penal Code.

(9) A peace officer for a district attorney, as defined in Section 830.1 or 830.35 of the Penal Code.

(10) A parole officer, probation officer, or deputy probation officer, as defined in Section 830.5 of the Penal Code.

(11) A peace officer of a California Community College police department, as defined in subdivision (a) of Section 830.32.

(12) A peace officer employed by a police department of a school district, as defined in subdivision (b) of Section 830.32.

(c) "Abduct" means take, entice away, keep, withhold, or conceal.

6241. The presiding judge of the superior court in each county shall designate at least one judge, commissioner, or referee to be reasonably available to issue orally, by telephone or otherwise, emergency protective orders at all times whether or not the court is in session.

Chapter 2: Issuance and Effect of Emergency Protective Order

6250. A judicial officer may issue an ex parte emergency protective order where a law enforcement officer asserts reasonable grounds to believe any of the following:

(a) That a person is in immediate and present danger of domestic violence, based on the person's allegation of a recent incident of abuse or threat of abuse by the person against whom the order is sought.

(b) That a child is in immediate and present danger of abuse by a family or household member, based on an allegation of a recent incident of abuse or threat of abuse by the family or household member.

(c) That a child is in immediate and present danger of being abducted by a parent or relative, based on a reasonable belief that a person has an intent to abduct the child or flee with the child from the jurisdiction or based on an allegation of a recent threat to abduct the child or flee with the child from the jurisdiction.

(d) That an elder or dependent adult is in immediate and present danger of abuse as defined in Section 15610.07 of the Welfare and Institutions Code, based on an allegation of a recent incident of abuse or threat of abuse by the person against whom the order is sought, except that no emergency protective order shall be issued based solely on an allegation of financial abuse.[107]

6250.3. An emergency protective order is valid only if it is issued by a judicial officer after making the findings required by Section 6251 and pursuant to a specific request by a law enforcement officer.[129]

6250.5. A judicial officer may issue an ex parte emergency protective order to a peace officer defined in subdivisions (a) and (b) of Section 830.32 if the issuance of that order is consistent with an existing memorandum of understanding between the college or school police department where the peace officer is employed and the sheriff or police chief of the city in whose jurisdiction the peace officer's college or school is located and the peace officer asserts reasonable grounds to believe that there is a demonstrated threat to campus safety.

6251. An emergency protective order may be issued only if the judicial officer finds both of the following:

(a) That reasonable grounds have been asserted to believe that an immediate and present danger of domestic violence exists, that a child is in immediate and present danger of abuse or abduction, or that an elder or dependent adult is in immediate and present danger of abuse as defined in Section 15610.07 of the Welfare and Institutions Code.

(b) That an emergency protective order is necessary to prevent the occurrence or recurrence of domestic violence, child abuse, child abduction, or abuse of an elder or dependent adult.

6252. An emergency protective order may include any of the following specific orders, as appropriate:
(a) A protective order, as defined in Section 6218.
(b) An order determining the temporary care and control of any minor child of the endangered person and the person against whom the order is sought.
(c) An order authorized in Section 213.5 of the Welfare and Institutions Code, including provisions placing the temporary care and control of the endangered child and any other minor children in the family or household with the parent or guardian of the endangered child who is not a restrained party.
(d) An order determining the temporary care and control of any minor child who is in danger of being abducted.
(e) An order authorized by Section 15657.03 of the Welfare and Institutions Code.

6252.5. (a) The court shall order that any party enjoined pursuant to an order issued under this part be prohibited from taking any action to obtain the address or location of a protected party or a protected party's family members, caretakers, or guardian, unless there is good cause not to make that order.
(b) The Judicial Council shall promulgate forms necessary to effectuate this section.[124]

6253. An emergency protective order shall include all of the following:
(a) A statement of the grounds asserted for the order.
(b) The date and time the order expires.
(c) The address of the superior court for the district or county in which the endangered person or child in danger of being abducted resides.
(d) The following statements, which shall be printed in English and Spanish:
(1) "To the Protected Person: This order will last only until the date and time noted above. If you wish to seek continuing protection, you will have to apply for an order from the court, at the address noted above. You may seek the advice of an attorney as to any matter connected with your application for any future court orders. The attorney should be consulted promptly so that the attorney may assist you in making your application."
(2) "To the Restrained Person: This order will last until the date and time noted above. The protected party may, however, obtain a more permanent restraining order from the court. You may seek the advice of an attorney as to any matter connected with the application. The attorney should be consulted promptly so that the attorney may assist you in responding to the application."
(e) In the case of an endangered child, the following statement, which shall be printed in English and Spanish: "This order will last only until the date and time noted above. You may apply for a more permanent restraining order under Section 213.5 of the Welfare and Institutions Code from the court at the address noted above. You may seek

the advice of an attorney in connection with the application for a more permanent restraining order."

(f) In the case of a child in danger of being abducted, the following statement, which shall be printed in English and Spanish: "This order will last only until the date and time noted above. You may apply for a child custody order from the court, at the address noted above. You may seek the advice of an attorney as to any matter connected with the application. The attorney should be consulted promptly so that the attorney may assist you in responding to the application."

6254. The fact that the endangered person has left the household to avoid abuse does not affect the availability of an emergency protective order.

6255. An emergency protective order shall be issued without prejudice to any person.

6256. An emergency protective order expires at the earlier of the following times:

(a) The close of judicial business on the fifth court day following the day of its issuance.

(b) The seventh calendar day following the day of its issuance.

6257. If an emergency protective order concerns an endangered child, the child's parent or guardian who is not a restrained person, or a person having temporary custody of the endangered child, may apply to the court for a restraining order under Section 213.5 of the Welfare and Institutions Code.

Chapter 3: Issuance and Effect of Emergency Protective Order

6270. A law enforcement officer who requests an emergency protective order shall reduce the order to writing and sign it.

6271. A law enforcement officer who requests an emergency protective order shall do all of the following:

(a) Serve the order on the restrained person, if the restrained person can reasonably be located.

(b) Give a copy of the order to the protected person or, if the protected person is a minor child, to a parent or guardian of the endangered child who is not a restrained person, if the parent or guardian can reasonably be located, or to a person having temporary custody of the endangered child.

(c) File a copy of the order with the court as soon as practicable after issuance.

(d) Have the order entered into the computer database system for protective and restraining orders maintained by the Department of Justice.[267]

6272. (a) A law enforcement officer shall use every reasonable means to enforce an emergency protective order.

(b) A law enforcement officer who acts in good faith to enforce an emergency protective order is not civilly or criminally liable.

6274. A peace officer, as defined in Section 830.1 or 830.2 of the Penal Code, may seek an emergency protective order relating to stalking under Section 646.91 of the Penal Code if the requirements of that section are complied with.

6275. (a) A law enforcement officer

who responds to a situation in which the officer believes that there may be grounds for the issuance of an emergency protective order pursuant to Section 6250 of this code or Section 646.91 of the Penal Code, shall inform the person for whom an emergency protective order may be sought, or, if that person is a minor, the minor's parent or guardian, provided that the parent or guardian is not the person against whom the emergency protective order may be obtained, that the person may request the officer to request an emergency protective order pursuant to this part.
(b) Notwithstanding Section 6250, and pursuant to this part, an officer shall request an emergency protective order if the officer believes that the person requesting an emergency protective order is in immediate and present danger.[460]

PART 4: EMERGENCY PROTECTIVE ORDERS AND OTHER DOMESTIC VIOLENCE PREVENTION ORDERS

added by Stats. 1993, Ch. 219, Sec. 154

Chapter 1: General Provisions

6300. (a) An order may be issued under this part to restrain any person for the purpose specified in Section 6220, if an affidavit or testimony and any additional information provided to the court pursuant to Section 6306, shows, to the satisfaction of the court, reasonable proof of a past act or acts of abuse. The court may issue an order under this part based solely on the affidavit or testimony of the person requesting the restraining order.
(b) An ex parte restraining order issued pursuant to Article 1 (commencing with Section 6320) shall not be denied solely because the other party was not provided with notice.
(c) An ex parte request for a protective order, as defined in Section 6218, shall not be rejected for filing by the court clerk if it is submitted on mandatory Judicial Council forms, includes all of the forms required to issue an order, and identifies the party submitting the request and the party who is the subject of the requested order.[596]

6301. (a) An individual need not be a resident of the state to file a petition for an order under this part. A petition for an order under this part may be filed in any superior court in this state, consistent with Section 410.10 of the Code of Civil Procedure, which may include, but is not limited to:
(1) The county in which the petitioner resides or is temporarily located.
(2) The county in which the defendant resides.
(3) The county in which the offense occurred.
(4) Any other court that may have jurisdiction over the parties or the subject matter of the case.
(b) An order under this part may be granted to any person described in Section 6211, including a minor pursuant to subdivision (b) of Section 372 of the Code of Civil Procedure.
(c) The right to petition for relief shall not be denied because the petitioner has vacated the household to avoid abuse, and in the case of a marital relationship, notwithstanding that a petit-ion for dissolution of marriage, for nullity of marriage, or for legal separation of the parties has not been filed.
(d) The length of time since the most

recent act of abuse is not, by itself, determinative. The court shall consider the totality of the circumstances in determining whether to grant or deny a petition for relief.[596]

6301.5. (a) A minor or the minor's legal guardian may petition the court to have information regarding a minor that was obtained in connection with a request for a protective order pursuant to this division, including, but not limited to, the minor's name, address, and the circumstances surrounding the request for a protective order with respect to that minor, be kept confidential, except as provided in subdivision (d).

(b) The court may order the information specified in subdivision (a) be kept confidential if the court expressly finds all of the following:

(1) The minor's right to privacy overcomes the right of public access to the information.

(2) There is a substantial probability that the minor's interest will be prejudiced if the information is not kept confidential.

(3) The order to keep the information confidential is narrowly tailored.

(4) No less restrictive means exist to protect the minor's privacy.

(c) (1) If the request is granted, except as provided in subdivision (d), information regarding the minor shall be maintained in a confidential case file and shall not become part of the public file in the proceeding, any other proceeding initiated under the Family Code, or any other civil proceeding between the parties. Except as provided in paragraph (2), if the court determines that disclosure of confidential information has been made without a court order, the court may impose a sanction of up to one thousand dollars ($1,000). The minor who has alleged abuse as defined under this division shall not be sanctioned for disclosure of the confidential information. If the court imposes a sanction, the court shall first determine whether the person has, or is reasonably likely to have, the ability to pay.

(2) Confidential information may be disclosed without a court order pursuant to subdivision (d) only in the following circumstances:

(A) By the minor's legal guardian who petitioned to keep the information confidential pursuant to this section or the protected party in an order pursuant to this division, provided that the disclosure effectuates the purpose of this division specified in Section 6220 or is in the minor's best interest. A legal guardian or a protected party who makes a disclosure under this subparagraph is subject to the sanction in paragraph (1) only if the disclosure was malicious.

(B) By a person to whom confidential information is disclosed, provided that the disclosure effectuates the purpose of this division specified in Section 6220 or is in the best interest of the minor, no more information than necessary is disclosed, and a delay would be caused by first obtaining a court order to authorize the disclosure of the information. A person who makes a disclosure pursuant to this subparagraph is subject to the sanction in paragraph (1) if the person discloses the information in a manner that recklessly or maliciously disregards these requirements.

(d) (1) Confidential information shall be made available to both of the following:

(A) Law enforcement pursuant to Section 6380, to the extent necessary and only for the purpose of enforcing the protective order.

(B) The respondent to allow the respondent to comply with the order for confidentiality and to allow the respondent to comply with and respond to the protective order. A notice shall be provided to the respondent that identifies the specific information that has been made confidential and shall include a statement that disclosure is punishable by a monetary fine.

(2) At any time, the court on its own may authorize a disclosure of any portion of the confidential information to certain individuals or entities as necessary to effectuate the purpose of this division specified in Section 6220, including implementation of the protective order, or if it is in the best interest of the minor, including, but not limited to, disclosure to educational institutions, childcare providers, medical or mental health providers, professional or nonprofessional supervisors for visitation, the Department of Child Support Services, attorneys for the parties or the minor, judicial officers, court employees, child custody evaluators, family court mediators, and court reporters.

(3) The court may authorize a disclosure of any portion of the confidential information to any person that files a petition if the court determines disclosure would effectuate the purpose of this division specified in Section 6220 or if the court determines that disclosure is in the best interest of the minor. The party who petitioned the court to keep the information confidential pursuant to this section shall be served personally or by first-class mail with a copy of the petition and afforded an opportunity to object to the disclosure.

6302. A notice of hearing under this part shall notify the respondent that, if the respondent does not attend the hearing, the court may make orders against the respondent that could last up to five years.[461]

6303. (a) It is the function of a support person to provide moral and emotional support for a person who alleges to be a victim of domestic violence. The person who alleges to be a victim of domestic violence may select any individual to act as a support person. No certification, training, or other special qualification is required for an individual to act as a support person. The support person shall assist the person in feeling more confident that the person will not be injured or threatened by the other party during the proceedings where the person and the other party must be present in close proximity. The support person is not present as a legal adviser and shall not give legal advice.

(b) A support person shall be permitted to accompany either party to any proceeding to obtain a protective order, as defined in Section 6218. Where the party is not represented by an attorney, the support person may sit with the party at the table that is generally reserved for the party and the party's attorney.

(c) Notwithstanding any other law to the contrary, if a court has issued a protective order, a support person shall be permitted to accompany a party protected by the order during any mediation orientation or mediation session, including separate mediation sessions, held pursuant to a proceeding described in Section 3021. Family Court Services, and any agency charged with providing family court services, shall advise the party protected by the order of the right to have a support person during mediation. A mediator may exclude a support person from a mediation session if the support person participates in the mediation session, or acts as an advocate, or the presence of a particular support person is disruptive or disrupts the process of mediation. The presence of the support person does not waive the confidentiality of the mediation, and the support person is bound by the confidentiality of the mediation.

(d) In a proceeding subject to this section, a support person shall be permitted to accompany a party in court where there are allegations or threats of domestic violence and, where the party is not represented by an attorney, may sit with the party at the table that is generally reserved for the party and the party's attorney.

(e) This section does not preclude a court from exercising its discretion to remove a person from the courtroom when it would be in the interest of justice to do so, or when the court believes the person is prompting, swaying, or influencing the party protected by the order.[462]

6304. When making a protective order, as defined in Section 6218, where both parties are present in court, the court shall inform both the petitioner and the respondent of the terms of the order, including notice that the respondent is prohibited from owning, possessing, purchasing, or receiving or attempting to own, possess, purchase, or receive a firearm or ammunition, and including notice of the penalty for violation. Information provided shall include how any firearms or ammunition still in the restrained party's possession are to be relinquished, according to local procedures, and the process for submitting a receipt to the court showing proof of relinquishment.[500]

6305. (a) The court shall not issue a mutual order enjoining the parties from specific acts of abuse described in Section 6320 unless both of the following apply:

(1) Both parties personally appear and each party presents written evidence of abuse or domestic violence in an application for relief using a mandatory Judicial Council restraining order application form. For purposes of this paragraph, written evidence of abuse or domestic violence in a responsive pleading does not satisfy the party's obligation to present written evidence of abuse or domestic violence. By July 1, 2016, the Judicial Council shall modify forms as necessary to provide notice of this information.

(2) The court makes detailed findings of fact indicating that both parties acted as a primary aggressor and that neither party acted primarily in self-defense.

(b) For purposes of subdivision (a), in determining if both parties acted primarily as aggressors, the court shall consider the provisions concerning dominant aggressors set forth in paragraph (3) of subdivision (c) of Section 836 of the Penal Code.[328]

6306. (a) (1) Before a hearing on the issuance or denial of an order under this part, the court shall ensure that a search is or has been conducted to determine if the subject of the proposed order has a prior criminal conviction for a violent felony specified in Section 667.5 of the Penal Code or a serious felony specified in Section 1192.7 of the Penal Code; has a misdemeanor conviction involving domestic violence, weapons, or other violence; has an outstanding warrant; is currently on parole or probation; owns or possesses a firearm as reflected in the Department of Justice Automated Firearms System; or has a prior restraining order or a violation of a prior restraining order. The search shall be conducted of all records and databases readily available and reasonably accessible to the court, including, but not limited to, the following:

(A) The California Sex and Arson Registry (CSAR).

(B) The Supervised Release File.

(C) State summary criminal history information maintained by the Department of Justice pursuant to Section 11105 of the Penal Code.

(D) The Federal Bureau of Investigation's nationwide database.

(E) Locally maintained criminal history records or databases.

(F) The Department of Justice Automated Firearms System.

(2) However, a record or database need not be searched if the information available in that record or database can be obtained as a result of a search conducted in another record or database.

(3) If a court does not have electronic or other access to the Department of Justice Automated Firearms System and if there is no preexisting agreement between the court and a law enforcement agency that the law enforcement agency will conduct a search of the California Law Enforcement Telecommunications System in order to report to the court whether the subject of the proposed order owns or possesses a firearm, upon the request of the court, the sheriff shall access the California Law Enforcement Telecommunications System in order to search the Department of Justice Automated Firearms System for the purpose of determining whether the subject of the order owns or possesses firearms. The sheriff shall report the results of this search to the court.

(b) (1) Before deciding whether to issue an order under this part or when determining appropriate temporary custody and visitation orders, the court shall consider the following information obtained pursuant to a search conducted under subdivision (a): a conviction for a violent felony specified in Section 667.5 of the Penal Code or a serious felony specified in Section 1192.7 of the Penal Code; a misdemeanor conviction involving domestic violence, weapons, or other violence; an outstanding warrant; parole or probation status; a prior restraining order; and a violation of a prior restraining order.

(2) Information obtained as a result of the search that does not involve a conviction described in this subdivision shall not be considered by the court in making a determination

regarding the issuance of an order pursuant to this part. That information shall be destroyed and shall not become part of the public file in this or any other civil proceeding.

(c) (1) After issuing its ruling, the court shall advise the parties that they may request the information described in subdivision (b) upon which the court relied. The court shall admonish the party seeking the proposed order that it is unlawful, pursuant to Sections 11142 and 13303 of the Penal Code, to willfully release the information, except as authorized by law.

(2) Upon the request of either party to obtain the information described in subdivision (b) upon which the court relied, the court shall release the information to the parties or, upon either party's request, to the party's attorney in that proceeding.

(3) The party seeking the proposed order may release the information to the party's counsel, court personnel, and court-appointed mediators for the purpose of seeking judicial review of the court's order or for purposes of court proceedings under Section 213.5 of the Welfare and Institutions Code.

(d) Information obtained as a result of the search conducted pursuant to subdivision (a) and relied upon by the court shall be maintained in a confidential case file and shall not become part of the public file in the proceeding or any other civil proceeding. However, the contents of the confidential case file shall be disclosed to the court-appointed mediator assigned to the case or to a child custody evaluator appointed by the court pursuant to Section 3111 of this code or Section 730 of the Evidence Code. All court-appointed mediators and child custody evaluators appointed or contracted by the court pursuant to Section 3111 of this code or Section 730 of the Evidence Code who receive information from the search conducted pursuant to subdivision (a) shall be subject to, and shall comply with, the California Law Enforcement Telecommunications System policies, practices, and procedures adopted pursuant to Section 15160 of the Government Code.

(e) If the results of the search conducted pursuant to subdivision (a) indicate that an outstanding warrant exists against the subject of the order, the court shall order the clerk of the court to immediately notify, by the most effective means available, appropriate law enforcement officials of the issuance and contents of a protective order and of any other information obtained through the search that the court determines is appropriate. The law enforcement officials so notified shall take all actions necessary to execute any outstanding warrants or any other actions, with respect to the restrained person, as appropriate and as soon as practicable.

(f) If the results of the search conducted pursuant to subdivision (a) indicate that the subject of the order owns or possesses a firearm or if the court receives evidence of the subject's possession of a firearm or ammunition, the court shall make a written record as to whether the subject has relinquished the firearm or ammunition and provided proof of the require-ed storage, sale, or relinquishment of the firearm or ammunition. If evidence of compliance with firearms prohibitions is not provided pursuant to subdivision (c) of Section 6389, the court shall order the clerk of the court to immediately notify, by the most effective means available, appropriate law enforcement officials of the issuance and contents of a protective order, information about the firearm or ammunition, and of any other information obtained through the search that the court determines is appropriate. The law enforcement officials so notified shall take all actions necessary to obtain those and any other firearms or ammunition owned, possessed, or controlled by the restrained person and to address any violation of the order with respect to firearms or ammunition as appropriate and as soon as practicable.

(g) If the results of the search conducted pursuant to subdivision (a) indicate that the subject of the order is currently on parole or probation, the court shall order the clerk of the court to immediately notify, by the most effective means available, the appropriate parole or probation officer of the issuance and contents of a protective order issued by the court and of any other information obtained through the search that the court determines is appropriate. That officer shall take all actions necessary to revoke parole or probation, or any other actions, with respect to the restrained person, as appropriate and as soon as practicable.

(h) This section shall not delay the granting of an application for an order that may otherwise be granted without the information resulting from the database search. If the court finds that a protective order under this part should be granted on the basis of the affidavit presented with the petition, the court shall issue the protective order and shall then ensure that a search is conducted pursuant to subdivision (a) before the hearing.

(i) It is the intent of the Legislature that, except with regard to a search whether the subject of a proposed order owns or possesses a firearm, this section shall be implemented in those courts identified by the Judicial Council as having resources currently available for these purposes. This act shall be implemented in other courts to the extent that funds are appropriated for purposes of the act in the annual Budget Act.[589]

6306.5. (a) (1) Petitions seeking domestic violence restraining orders under Chapter 2 (commencing with Section 6320) and domestic violence temporary restraining orders under Part 4 (commencing with Section 240) of Division 2 may be submitted electronically in every trial court. Courts shall accept these filings consistent with the timeframe in Section 246.

(2) The notice of court date, copies of the request to mail on respondent, and the temporary restraining order, if granted, shall be remitted to the petitioner electronically.

(3) Notwithstanding paragraph (2), the petitioner may elect to receive documents by regular mail or to retrieve documents from the court.

(b) The Judicial Council shall develop or amend rules and forms as necessary to implement this section.

(c) There shall be no fee for any filings related to a petition submitted electronically in accordance with this section.

(d) This section shall become operative only upon an appropriation of funds for this purpose in the annual Budget Act or other statute.[498]

6306.6. (a) Information about access to self-help services regarding domestic violence restraining orders shall be prominently visible on the superior court's internet website.
(b) The Judicial Council shall develop or amend rules as necessary to implement this section.[499]

6307. (a) (1) (A) A court or court facility that receives petitions for domestic violence restraining orders under this part or domestic violence temporary restraining orders under Part 4 (commencing with Section 240) of Division 2 shall permit those petitions and any filings related to those petitions to be submitted electronically. The court or court facility shall, based on the time of receipt, act on these filings consistent with Section 246.
(B) Commencing January 1, 2027, petitions and filings submitted electronically pursuant to paragraph (1) shall be at no charge to the petitioner.
(2) The request, notice of the court date, copies of the request to serve on the respondent, and the temporary restraining order, if granted, shall be provided to the petitioner electronically, unless the petitioner notes, at the time of electronic filing, that these documents will be picked up from the court or court facility.
(b) (1) Information regarding electronic filing and access to the court's self-help center shall be prominently displayed on each court's homepage.
(2) Each self-help center shall maintain and make available information related to domestic violence restraining orders pursuant to this section.
(c) The Judicial Council may adopt or amend rules and forms to implement this section.[518]

6308. (a) A party, support person as defined in Section 6303, or witness may appear remotely at the hearing on a petition for a domestic violence restraining order. The superior court of each county shall develop local rules and instructions for remote appearances permitted under this section, which shall be posted on its internet website.
(b) Commencing January 1, 2027, there shall not be a fee for a party, support person as defined in Section 6303, or witness to appear remotely at the hearing.[519]

6309. (a) (1) The Legislature finds and declares all of the following:
(A) Domestic violence is an urgent public safety and public health crisis. More than one in three California women and one in seven men experience intimate partner physical violence, intimate partner sexual violence, or intimate partner stalking in their lifetimes. Sexual and gender minorities, including queer, gender nonbinary, intersex, and transgender persons, experience domestic violence at rates as high or higher than cisgender and heterosexual persons. Domestic violence accounts for more than 15 percent of all violent crimes in California and more than 10 percent of all California homicides.
(B) Domestic violence survivors are most at risk when attempting to leave an abusive relationship. Without effective intervention in domestic

abuse, the violence often increases in frequency and severity over time. Research has established that the civil domestic violence restraining order is the most effective legal remedy for intervening in and preventing future abuse.

(C) Domestic violence survivors who enter the family or civil court systems seeking protection often face ongoing abuse in the form of litigation abuse. Litigation abuse is the use of legal or bureaucratic procedures by abusive partners to continue to attack, harass, intimidate, coercively control, or maintain contact with their former partners through the litigation system by exerting power over them, forcing them to have contact, financially burdening them with excessive discovery and litigation, degrading and insulting them in legal papers, unduly delaying the court process and final resolution of important issues, or dissuading them from pursuing legal protection. Studies show that litigation abuse causes severe consequences for survivors, including economic hardship and psychological harm, and foregoing legal relief in part or in whole. Research also shows that judicial officers and court evaluators often misunderstand or overlook litigation abuse and its effects on survivors.

(2) It is the intent of the Legislature to accomplish the following:

(A) To promote the health and safety of domestic violence survivors and their children.

(B) To ensure that domestic violence survivors can seek and receive, without delay, the protection offered by the domestic violence restraining orders, which are remedial injunctive orders intended to offer expedited separation and protection from abuse.

(C) To provide for separation and to prevent future acts of domestic violence by streamlining any domestic violence restraining order discovery to expedite the adjudication of requests for restraining orders and prevent abusive litigation tactics that interfere with legislative intent to protect domestic violence victims.

(b) Consistent with the findings and declarations and statements of legislative intent in subdivision (a), discovery pursuant to the Civil Discovery Act (Title 4 (commencing with Section 2016.010) of Part 4 of the Code of Civil Procedure), is not permitted pursuant to this part except as set forth in this section.

(c) (1) A court may grant a request for discovery only upon a showing of good cause for the discovery by the party making the request.

(2) A party may make an oral or written request for discovery to the court at an evidentiary hearing pursuant to this part.

(3) A person shall not be required to make a written objection or response to a request for discovery but may express any objection or response orally or in writing or at the hearing.

(d) In determining whether to permit discovery in a proceeding pursuant to this part, the court shall consider all of the following:

(1) The importance and relevance of, and need for, the information sought to be obtained.

(2) The likelihood that the information may be acquired by

another permitted discovery method, or may be acquired by other methods including pleadings or examination at the hearing.

(3) The delay in completion of the hearing, which is entitled to calendar preference pursuant to Section 244, if the discovery is permitted.

(4) The potential, if any, that the discovery may induce trauma in any person involved in the proceeding.

(5) Whether one or more persons are subject to any restraining or protective orders.

(6) Any other factor that may affect the prompt and fair resolution of the proceeding.

(e) If a court finds good cause and grants a request for discovery pursuant to subdivision (c), the court may do either of the following:

(1) (A) Continue the commencement of hearing for a reasonable period to permit one or more methods of discovery.

(B) If the court continues the hearing to allow for discovery pursuant to subparagraph (A), the court shall extend, and may modify, any restraining order in place.

(2) Commence the hearing to receive evidence and then continue the hearing to permit one or more methods of discovery.

(f) The court shall limit and control any permitted discovery to the least intrusive methods as authorized pursuant to the Civil Discovery Act (Title 4 (commencing with Section 2016.010) of Part 4 of the Code of Civil Procedure) and the minimum number of items reasonably necessary to secure the requested information. The court shall specify the time for response to any permitted discovery after considering the items in subdivision (d).

(g) Nothing in this section is intended to take away rights afforded in the Domestic Violence Prevention Act. Nothing in this section is intended to infringe on the ability for abuse survivors to receive their police reports and evidence pursuant to Section 6228 or on parties' ability to discover their own business records without obtaining court permission, including medical records, phone records, or recordings of calls to 911, to provide corroborating proof.[573]

Chapter 2: Issuance of Orders

Article 1: Ex Parte Orders

6320. (a) The court may issue an ex parte order enjoining a party from molesting, attacking, striking, stalking, threatening, sexually assaulting, battering, credibly impersonating as described in Section 528.5 of the Penal Code, falsely personating as described in Section 529 of the Penal Code, harassing, telephoning, including, but not limited to, making annoying telephone calls as described in Section 653m of the Penal Code, destroying personal property, contacting, either directly or indirectly, by mail or otherwise, coming within a specified distance of, or disturbing the peace of the other party, and, in the discretion of the court, on a showing of good cause, of other named family or household members.

(b) On a showing of good cause, the court may include in a protective order a grant to the petitioner of the exclusive care, possession, or control of any animal owned, possessed, leased, kept, or held by either the petitioner or the respondent or a minor child residing in the residence or household of either the petitioner or the respondent. The court may order the respondent to stay away from the animal and forbid the respondent from taking, transferring, encumbering, concealing, molesting, attacking, striking, threatening, harming, or otherwise disposing of the animal.

(c) As used in subdivision (a), "disturbing the peace of the other party" refers to conduct that, based on the totality of the circumstances, destroys the mental or emotional calm of the other party. This conduct may be committed directly or indirectly, including through the use of a third party, and by any method or through any means including, but not limited to, telephone, online accounts, text messages, internet-connected devices, including connected devices as defined in Section 22948.30 of the Business and Professions Code, or other electronic technologies. This conduct includes, but is not limited to, coercive control, which is a pattern of behavior that in purpose or effect unreasonably interferes with a person's free will and personal liberty. Examples of coercive control include, but are not limited to, unreasonably engaging in any of the following:

(1) Isolating the other party from friends, relatives, or other sources of support.

(2) Depriving the other party of basic necessities.

(3) Controlling, regulating, or monitoring the other party's movements, communications, daily behavior, finances, economic resources, or access to services.

(4) Compelling the other party by force, threat of force, or intimidation, including threats based on actual or suspected immigration status, to engage in conduct from which the other party has a right to abstain or to abstain from conduct in which the other party has a right to engage.

(5) Engaging in reproductive coercion, which consists of control over the reproductive autonomy of another through force, threat of force, or intimidation, and may include, but is not limited to, unreasonably pressuring the other party to become pregnant, deliberately interfering with contraception use or access to reproductive health information, or using coercive tactics to control, or attempt to control, pregnancy outcomes.

(d) This section does not limit any remedies available under this act or any other provision of law.[491]

6320.5. (a) An order denying a petition for an ex parte order pursuant to Section 6320 shall include the reasons for denying the petition.

(b) An order denying a jurisdictionally adequate petition for an ex parte order, pursuant to Section 6320, shall provide the petitioner the right to a noticed hearing on the earliest date that the business of the court will permit, but not later than 21 days or, if good cause appears to the court, 25 days from the date of the order. The petitioner shall serve on the respondent, at least five days before the hearing, copies of all supporting papers filed with the court, including the application and affidavits.

(c) Notwithstanding subdivision (b), upon the denial of the ex parte order pursuant to Section 6320, the petitioner shall have the option of waiving the right to a noticed hearing.

However, this section does not preclude a petitioner who waives the right to a noticed hearing from refiling a new petition, without prejudice, at a later time.[463]

6321. (a) The court may issue an ex parte order excluding a party from the family dwelling, the dwelling of the other party, the common dwelling of both parties, or the dwelling of the person who has care, custody, and control of a child to be protected from domestic violence for the period of time and on the conditions the court determines, regardless of which party holds legal or equitable title or is the lessee of the dwelling.
(b) The court may issue an order under subdivision (a) only on a showing of all of the following:
(1) Facts sufficient for the court to ascertain that the party who will stay in the dwelling has a right under color of law to possession of the premises.
(2) That the party to be excluded has assaulted or threatens to assault the other party or any other person under the care, custody, and control of the other party, or any minor child of the parties or of the other party.
(3) That physical or emotional harm would otherwise result to the other party, to any person under the care, custody, and control of the other party, or to any minor child of the parties or of the other party.

6322. The court may issue an ex parte order enjoining a party from specified behavior that the court determines is necessary to effectuate orders under Section 6320 or 6321.

6322.5. (a) When relevant information is presented to the court at a noticed hearing that a restrained person has a firearm or ammunition, the court shall consider that information and determine, by a preponderance of the evidence, whether the person subject to a protective order has a firearm or ammunition in, or subject to, their immediate possession or control in violation of Section 6389.
(b) (1) In making the determination required pursuant to subdivision (a), the court may consider whether the restrained person filed a firearm relinquishment, storage, or sales receipt or if an exemption from the firearm prohibition was granted pursuant to subdivision (h) of Section 6389.
(2) The court may make the determination at a noticed hearing when a domestic violence protective order is issued, at a subsequent review hearing, or at any subsequent family or juvenile law hearing while the order remains in effect.
(3) If the court makes a determination that the restrained person has a firearm or ammunition in violation of Section 6389, the court shall make a written record of the determination and provide a copy to any party who is present at the hearing and, upon request, to any party not present at the hearing.
(c) (1) When presented with information pursuant to subdivision (a), the court may set a review hearing to determine whether there has been a violation of Section 6389.
(2) The review hearing shall be held within 10 court days after the noticed hearing at which the information was presented. If the restrained person is not present when the court sets the review hearing, the protected person shall provide notice of the review

hearing to the restrained person at least two court days before the review hearing, in accordance with Section 414.10 of the Code of Civil Procedure, by personal service or by mail to the restrained person's last known address.

(3) The court may, for good cause, extend the date of the review hearing for a reasonable period or remove it from the calendar.

(4) The court shall order the restrained person to appear at the hearing.

(5) The court may conduct the review hearing in the absence of the protected person.

(6) This section does not prohibit the court from permitting a party or witness to appear through technology that enables remote appearances, as determined by the court.

(d) The determination made pursuant to this section may be considered by the court in issuing an order to show cause for contempt pursuant to paragraph (5) of subdivision (a) of Section 1209 of the Code of Civil Procedure or an order for monetary sanctions pursuant to Section 177.5 of the Code of Civil Procedure.[501]

6322.7. (a) The court shall order that any party enjoined pursuant to an order issued under this part be prohibited from taking any action to obtain the address or location of any protected person, unless there is good cause not to make that order.

(b) The Judicial Council shall develop forms necessary to effectuate this section.[217]

6323. (a) Subject to Section 3064:

(1) The court may issue an ex parte order determining the temporary custody and visitation of a minor child, on the conditions the court determines, to a party who has established a parent and child relationship pursuant to paragraph (2). The parties shall inform the court if a custody or visitation order has already been issued in any other proceeding.

(2) (A) In making a determination of the best interest of the child, in order to limit the child's exposure to potential domestic violence, and to ensure the safety of all family members, if the party who has obtained the restraining order has established a parent and child relationship and the other party has not established that relationship, the court may award temporary sole legal and physical custody to the party to whom the restraining order was issued and may make an order of no visitation to the other party pending the establishment of a parent and child relationship between the child and the other party.

(B) A party may establish a parent and child relationship for purposes of subparagraph (A) only by offering proof of any of the following:

(i) The party gave birth to the child.

(ii) The child is conclusively presumed to be a child of the marriage between the parties, pursuant to Section 7540, or the party has been determined by a court to be a parent of the child, pursuant to Section 7541.

(iii) Legal adoption or pending legal adoption of the child by the party.

(iv) The party has signed a valid voluntary declaration of paternity, which has been in effect more than 60 days prior to the issuance of the restraining order, and that declaration has not been rescinded or set aside.

(v) A determination made by the juvenile court that there is a parent and child relationship between the party offering the proof and the child.

(vi) A determination of parentage made in a proceeding to determine custody or visitation in a case brought by the local child support agency pursuant to Chapter 2 (commencing with Section 17400) of Division 17.

(vii) The party has been determined to be the parent of the child through a proceeding under the Uniform Parentage Act (Part 3 (commencing with Section 7600) of Division 12).

(viii) Both parties stipulate, in writing or on the record, for purposes of this proceeding, that they are the parents of the child.

(b) (1) Except as provided in paragraph (2), the court shall not make a finding of paternity in this proceeding, and an order issued pursuant to this section shall be without prejudice in any other action brought to establish a parent and child relationship.

(2) The court may accept a stipulation of paternity by the parties and, if paternity is uncontested, enter a judgment establishing paternity, subject to the set-aside provisions in Section 7646.

(c) When making an order for custody or visitation pursuant to this section, the court's order shall specify the time, day, place, and manner of transfer of the child for custody or visitation to limit the child's exposure to potential domestic conflict or violence and to ensure the safety of all family members. If the court finds a party is staying in a place designated as a shelter for victims of domestic violence or other confidential location, the court's order for time, day, place, and manner of transfer of the child for custody or visitation shall be designed to prevent disclosure of the location of the shelter or other confidential location.

(d) When making an order for custody or visitation pursuant to this section, the court shall consider whether the best interest of the child, based upon the circumstances of the case, requires that a visitation or custody arrangement shall be limited to situations in which a third person, specified by the court, is present, or whether visitation or custody shall be suspended or denied.

(e) When determining whether visitation should be suspended, denied, or limited to situations in which a third person is present pursuant to subdivision (d), the court shall consider a determination made pursuant to Section 6322.5 that the party is a restrained person in possession or control of a firearm or ammunition in violation of Section 6389.[502]

6323.5. (a) For purposes of this section, the following definitions apply:

(1) "Discretionary services organization" includes any organization that provides nonessential services to children, such as recreational activities, entertainment, and summer camps. "Discretionary services organization" also includes a place of employment of a minor described in subdivision (b).

(2) "Essential care provider" includes a public or private school, health care facility, daycare facility, dental facility,

or other similar organization that frequently provides essential social, health, or care services to children.

(b) (1) Notwithstanding Section 3025, and in accordance with Section 6322, a court may include in an ex parte order a provision restraining a party from accessing records and information pertaining to the health care, education, daycare, recreational activities, or employment of a minor child of the parties.

(2) A parent or guardian may provide a copy of an order with a provision specified in paragraph (1) to an essential care provider or a discretionary services organization, or both.

(c) (1) (A) An essential care provider shall, on or before February 1, 2023, develop protocols relating to the provider's compliance with the order described in subdivision (b), including, at a minimum, designating the appropriate personnel responsible for receiving the protective order, establishing a means of ensuring that the restrained party is not able to access the records or information, and implementing a procedure for submission of a copy of an order and for providing the party that submits the copy of the order with documentation indicating when, and to whom, the copy of the order was submitted.

(B) A discretionary services organization that is provided an order described in subdivision (b), shall develop the protocols specified in paragraph (1) within 30 days of receipt of the first order.

(2) If an essential care provider or discretionary services organization is provided with a copy of an order described in subdivision (b), the essential care provider or discretionary services organization shall not release information or records pertaining to the child to the restrained party. This requirement applies regardless of whether the essential care provider or discretionary services organization has finalized the protocols described in paragraph (1).

(d) The Judicial Council shall develop or update any forms or rules of court that are necessary to implement this section.

(e) This section shall become operative on January 1, 2023.

6324. The court may issue an ex parte order determining the temporary use, possession, and control of real or personal property of the parties and the payment of any liens or encumbrances coming due during the period the order is in effect.

6325. The court may issue an ex parte order restraining a married person from specified acts in relation to community, quasi-community, and separate property as provided in Section 2045.

6325.5. (a) The court may issue an ex parte order restraining any party from cashing, borrowing against, canceling, transferring, disposing of, or changing the beneficiaries of any insurance or other coverage held for the benefit of the parties, or their child or children, if any, for whom support may be ordered, or both.

(b) This section shall become operative on July 1, 2014.[268]

6326. An ex parte order under this article shall be issued or denied on the same day that the application is submitted to the court, unless the application is filed too late in the day to permit effective review, in which case the order shall be issued or denied on the next day of judicial business in sufficient time for the order to be filed that day with the clerk of the court. A petition for an ex parte order pursuant to this article shall not be denied solely because the other party was not provided with notice.[371]

6327. Part 4 (commencing with Section 240) of Division 2 applies to the issuance of any ex parte order under this article, other than an order under Section 6322.5.

Article 2: Orders Issuable After Notice and Hearing

6340. (a) (1) The court may issue any of the orders described in Article 1 (commencing with Section 6320) after notice and a hearing. When determining whether to make any orders under this subdivision, the court shall consider whether failure to make any of these orders may jeopardize the safety of the petitioner and the child-ren for whom the custody or visitation orders are sought. If the court makes any order for custody, visitation, or support, that order shall survive the termination of any protective order. The Judicial Council shall provide notice of this provision on any Judicial Council forms related to this subdivision.

(2) (A) If at the time of a hearing with respect to an order issued pursuant to this part based on an ex parte temporary restraining order, the court determines that, after diligent effort, the petitioner has been unable to accomplish personal service, and that there is reason to believe that the restrained party is evading service, the court may permit an alternative method of service designed to give reasonable notice of the action to the respondent. Alternative methods of service include, but are not limited to, the following:

(i) Service by publication pursuant to the standards set forth in Section 415.50 of the Code of Civil Procedure.

(ii) Service by first-class mail sent to the respondent at the most current address for the respondent that is available to the court or delivering a copy of the pleadings and orders at the respondent's home or place of employment, pursuant to the standards set forth in Sections 415.20 to 415.40, inclusive, of the Code of Civil Procedure.

(B) If the court permits an alternative method of service under this paragraph, the court shall grant a continuance to allow for the alternative service pursuant to Section 245.

(b) The court shall, upon denying a petition under this part, provide a brief statement of the reasons for the decision in writing or on the record. A decision stating "denied" is insufficient.

(c) The court may issue an order described in Section 6321 excluding a person from a dwelling if the court finds that physical or emotional harm would otherwise result to the other party, to a person under the care, custody, and control of the other party, or to a minor child of the parties or of the other party.[372]

6341. (a) If the parties are married to

each other and no other child support order exists or if there is a presumption under Section 7611 that the respondent is the natural father of a minor child and the child is in the custody of the petitioner, after notice and a hearing, the court may, if requested by the petitioner, order a party to pay an amount necessary for the support and maintenance of the child if the order would otherwise be authorized in an action brought pursuant to Division 9 (commencing with Section 3500) or the Uniform Parentage Act (Part 3 (commencing with Section 7600) of Division 12). When determining whether to make any orders under this subdivision, the court shall consider whether failure to make any of these orders may jeopardize the safety of the petitioner and the children for whom child support is requested, including safety concerns related to the financial needs of the petitioner and the children. The Judicial Council shall provide notice of this provision on any Judicial Council forms related to this subdivision.

(b) An order issued pursuant to subdivision (a) of this section shall be without prejudice in an action brought pursuant to the Uniform Parentage Act (Part 3 (commencing with Section 7600) of Division 12).

(c) If the parties are married to each other and no spousal support order exists, after notice and a hearing, the court may order the respondent to pay spousal support in an amount, if any, that would otherwise be authorized in an action pursuant to Part 1 (commencing with Section 3500) or Part 3 (commencing with Section 4300) of Division 9. When determining whether to make any orders under this subdivision, the court shall consider whether failure to make any of these orders may jeopardize the safety of the petitioner, including safety concerns related to the financial needs of the petitioner. The Judicial Council shall provide notice of this provision on any Judicial Council forms related to this subdivision.

(d) An order issued pursuant to subdivision (c) shall be without prejudice in a proceeding for dissolution of marriage, nullity of marriage, or legal separation of the parties.[120]

6342. (a) After notice and a hearing, the court may issue any of the following orders:

(1) An order that restitution be paid to the petitioner for loss of earnings and out-of-pocket expenses, including, but not limited to, expenses for medical care and temporary housing, incurred as a direct result of the abuse inflicted by the respondent or any actual physical injuries sustained from the abuse.

(2) An order that restitution be paid by the petitioner for out-of-pocket expenses incurred by a party as a result of an ex parte order that is found by the court to have been issued on facts shown at a noticed hearing to be insufficient to support the order.

(3) An order that restitution be paid by the respondent to any public or private agency for the reasonable cost of providing services to the petitioner required as a direct result of the abuse inflicted by the respondent or any actual injuries sustained therefrom.

(b) An order for restitution under this section shall not include damages for pain and suffering.

6342.5. (a) After notice and a hearing, the court may issue an order determining the use, possession, and control of real or personal property of the parties during the period the order is in effect and the payment of any liens or encumbrances coming due during that period.

(b) The order described in subdivision (a) may include a finding that specific debts were incurred as the result of domestic violence and without the consent of a party. For purposes of this subdivision, the acts that may support this finding include, but are not limited to, the crimes proscribed by Section 530.5 of the Penal Code. This finding does not affect the priority of any lien or other security interest.

(c) The Judicial Council shall adopt appropriate forms and modify existing forms, as necessary, to effectuate this section.

(d) This section shall be operative on January 1, 2022.[487]

6343. (a) After notice and a hearing, the court may issue an order requiring the restrained party to participate in a batterer's program approved by the probation department as provided in Section 1203.097 of the Penal Code.

(b) (1) Commencing July 1, 2016, if the court orders a restrained party to participate in a batterer's program pursuant to subdivision (a), the restrained party shall do all of the following:

(A) Register for the program by the deadline ordered by the court. If no deadline is ordered by the court, the restrained party shall register no later than 30 days from the date the order was issued.

(B) At the time of enrollment, sign all necessary program consent forms for the program to release proof of enrollment, attendance records, and completion or termination reports to the court and the protected party, or the protected party's attorney. The court and the protected party may provide to the program a fax number or mailing address for purposes of receiving proof of enrollment, attendance records, and completion or termination reports.

(C) Provide the court and the protected party with the name, address, and telephone number of the program.

(2) By July 1, 2016, the Judicial Council shall revise or promulgate forms as necessary to effectuate this subdivision.

(c) The courts shall, in consultation with local domestic violence shelters and programs, develop a resource list of referrals to appropriate community domestic violence programs and services to be provided to each applicant for an order under this section.[464]

6344. (a) After notice and a hearing, a court, upon request, shall issue an order for the payment of attorney's fees and costs for a prevailing petitioner.

(b) After notice and a hearing, the court, upon request, may issue an order for the payment of attorney's fees and costs for a prevailing respondent only if the respondent establishes by a preponderance of the evidence that the petition or request is frivolous or solely intended to abuse, intimidate, or cause unnecessary delay.

(c) Before a court awards attorney's fees and costs pursuant to this section, the court shall first determine pursuant to Section 270 that the party ordered to pay has, or is reasonably likely to have, the ability to pay.[523]

6345. (a) In the discretion of the court, the personal conduct, stay-away, and residence exclusion orders contained in a court order issued after notice and a hearing under this article may have a duration of not more than five years, subject to termination or modification by further order of the court either on written stipulation filed with the court or on the motion of a party. These orders may be renewed, upon the request of a party, either for five or more years, or permanently, at the discretion of the court, without a showing of further abuse since the issuance of the original order. Renewals and subsequent renewals shall be subject to termination, modification, or subsequent renewal by further order of the court either on written stipulation filed with the court or on the motion of a party. The request for renewal may be brought at any time within the three months before the expiration of the orders.

(b) Notwithstanding subdivision (a), the duration of any orders, other than the protective orders described in subdivision (a), that are also contained in a court order issued after notice and a hearing under this article, including, but not limited to, orders for custody, visitation, support, and disposition of property, shall be governed by the law relating to those specific subjects.

(c) The failure to state the expiration date on the face of the form creates an order with a duration of three years from the date of issuance.

(d) If an action is filed for the purpose of terminating or modifying a protective order prior to the expiration date specified in the order by a party other than the protected party, the party who is protected by the order shall be given notice, pursuant to subdivision (b) of Section 1005 of the Code of Civil Procedure, of the proceeding by personal service or, if the protected party has satisfied the requirements of Chapter 3.1 (commencing with Section 6205) of Division 7 of Title 1 of the Government Code, by service on the Secretary of State. If the party who is protected by the order cannot be notified prior to the hearing for modification or termination of the protective order, the court shall deny the motion to modify or terminate the order without prejudice or continue the hearing until the party who is protected can be properly noticed and may, upon a showing of good cause, specify another method for service of process that is reasonably designed to afford actual notice to the protected party. The protected party may waive the right to notice if the protected party is physically present in court and does not challenge the sufficiency of the notice.

(e) On or before January 1, 2025, the Judicial Council shall create one or more specific forms for the purpose of requesting a modification of an existing restraining order.[575]

6346. The court may make appropriate custody and visitation orders pursuant to the Uniform Parentage Act (Part 3 (commencing with Section 7600) of Division 12) after notice and a hearing under this section when the party who has requested custody or visitation has not established a parent and child relationship under subparagraph (B) of paragraph (2) of subdivision (a) of

Section 6323, but has taken steps to establish that relationship by filing an action under the Uniform Parentage Act.

6347. (a) Commencing July 1, 2016, in order to ensure that the requesting party can maintain an existing wireless telephone number, and the wireless numbers of any minor children in the care of the requesting party, the court may issue an order, after notice and a hearing, directing a wireless telephone service provider to transfer the billing responsibility for and rights to the wireless telephone number or numbers to the requesting party, if the requesting party is not the accountholder.

(b) (1) The order transferring billing responsibility for and rights to the wireless telephone number or numbers to a requesting party shall be a separate order that is directed to the wireless telephone service provider. The order shall list the name and billing telephone number of the accountholder, the name and contact information of the person to whom the telephone number or numbers will be transferred, and each telephone number to be transferred to that person. The court shall ensure that the contact information of the requesting party is not provided to the accountholder in proceedings held pursuant to Division 10 (commencing with Section 6200).

(2) The order shall be served on the wireless service provider's agent for service of process listed with the Secretary of State.

(3) Where the wireless service provider cannot operationally or technically effectuate the order due to certain circumstances, including, but not limited to, any of the following, the wireless service provider shall notify the requesting party within 72 hours of receipt of the order:

(A) When the accountholder has already terminated the account.

(B) When differences in network technology prevent the functionality of a device on the network.

(C) When there are geographic or other limitations on network or service availability.

(c) (1) Upon transfer of billing responsibility for and rights to a wireless telephone number or numbers to a requesting party pursuant to subdivision (b) by a wireless telephone service provider, the requesting party shall assume all financial responsibility for the transferred wireless telephone number or numbers, monthly service costs, and costs for any mobile device associated with the wireless telephone number or numbers.

(2) This section shall not preclude a wireless service provider from applying any routine and customary requirements for account establishment to the requesting party as part of this transfer of billing responsibility for a wireless telephone number or numbers and any devices attached to that number or numbers, including, but not limited to, identification, financial information, and customer preferences.

(d) This section shall not affect the ability of the court to apportion the assets and debts of the parties as provided for in law, or the ability to determine the temporary use, possession, and control of personal property pursuant to Sections 6324 and 6340.

(e) No cause of action shall lie against any wireless telephone service

provider, its officers, employees, or agents, for actions taken in accordance with the terms of a court order issued pursuant to this section.
(f) The Judicial Council shall, on or before July 1, 2016, develop any forms or rules necessary to effectuate this section.[337]

Article 3: Orders Included in Judgement

6360. A judgment entered in a proceeding for dissolution of marriage, for nullity of marriage, for legal separation of the parties, in a proceeding brought pursuant to this division, or in an action brought pursuant to the Uniform Parentage Act (Part 3 (commencing with Section 7600) of Division 12) may include a protective order as defined in Section 6218.

6361. If an order is included in a judgment pursuant to this article, the judgment shall state on its face both of the following:
(a) Which provisions of the judgment are the orders.
(b) The date of expiration of the orders, which shall be not more than five years from the date the judgment is issued, unless extended by the court after notice and a hearing.[122]

Chapter 3: Registration and Enforcement of Orders

6380. (a) Each county, with the approval of the Department of Justice, shall, by July 1, 1996, develop a procedure, using existing systems, for the electronic transmission of data, as described in subdivision (b), to the Department of Justice. The data shall be electronically transmitted through the California Law Enforcement Telecommunications System (CLETS) of the Department of Justice by law enforcement personnel, or with the approval of the Department of Justice, court personnel, or another appropriate agency capable of maintaining and preserving the integrity of both the CLETS and the California Restraining and Protective Order System, as described in subdivision (e). Data entry is required to be entered only once under the requirements of this section, unless the order is served at a later time. A portion of all fees payable to the Department of Justice under subdivision (a) of Section 1203.097 of the Penal Code for the entry of the information required under this section, based upon the proportion of the costs incurred by the local agency and those incurred by the Department of Justice, shall be transferred to the local agency actually providing the data. All data with respect to criminal court protective orders issued, modified, extended, or terminated under Section 136.2 of the Penal Code, and all data filed with the court on the required Judicial Council forms with respect to protective orders, including their issuance, modification, extension, or termination, to which this division applies pursuant to Section 6221, shall be transmitted by the court or its designee within one business day to law enforcement personnel by either one of the following methods:
(1) Transmitting a physical copy of the order to a local law enforcement agency authorized by the Department of Justice to enter orders into CLETS.
(2) With the approval of the Department of Justice, entering the order into CLETS directly.

(b) Upon the issuance of a protective order to which this division applies pursuant to Section 6221, or the issuance of a temporary restraining order or injunction relating to harassment, unlawful violence, or the threat of violence pursuant to Section 527.6, 527.8, or 527.85 of the Code of Civil Procedure, or the issuance of a criminal court protective order under Section 136.2 of the Penal Code, or a retail crime restraining order under Section 490.8 of the Penal Code, or the issuance of a juvenile court restraining order related to domestic violence pursuant to Section 213.5, 304, or 362.4 of the Welfare and Institutions Code, or the issuance of a protective order pursuant to Section 15657.03 of the Welfare and Institutions Code, or upon registration with the court clerk of a domestic violence protective or restraining order issued by the tribunal of another state, as defined in Section 6401, and including any of the foregoing orders issued in connection with an order for modification of a custody or visitation order issued pursuant to a dissolution, legal separation, nullity, or paternity proceeding the Department of Justice shall be immediately notified of the contents of the order and the following information:

(1) The name, race, date of birth, and other personal descriptive information of the respondent as required by a form prescribed by the Department of Justice.

(2) The names of the protected persons.

(3) The date of issuance of the order.

(4) The duration or expiration date of the order.

(5) The terms and conditions of the protective order, including stay-away, no-contact, residency exclusion, custody, and visitation provisions of the order.

(6) The department or division number and the address of the court.

(7) Whether or not the order was served upon the respondent.

(8) The terms and conditions of any restrictions on the ownership or possession of firearms.

All available information shall be included; however, the inability to provide all categories of information shall not delay the entry of the information available.

(c) The information conveyed to the Department of Justice shall also indicate whether the respondent was present in court to be informed of the contents of the court order. The respondent's presence in court shall provide proof of service of notice of the terms of the protective order. The respondent's failure to appear shall also be included in the information provided to the Department of Justice.

(d) (1) Within one business day of service, a law enforcement officer who served a protective order shall submit the proof of service directly into the Department of Justice California Restraining and Protective Order System, including the officer's name and law enforcement agency, and shall transmit the original proof of service form to the issuing court.

(2) Within one business day of receipt of proof of service by a person other than a law enforcement officer, the clerk of the court shall submit the proof of service of a protective order directly into the Department of Justice California Restraining and Protective Order System, including

the name of the person who served the order. If the court is unable to provide this notification to the Department of Justice by electronic transmission, the court shall, within one business day of receipt, transmit a copy of the proof of service to a local law enforcement agency. The local law enforcement agency shall submit the proof of service directly into the Department of Justice California Restraining and Protective Order System within one business day of receipt from the court.

(e) The Department of Justice shall maintain a California Restraining and Protective Order System and shall make available to court clerks and law enforcement personnel, through computer access, all information regarding the protective and restraining orders and injunctions described in subdivision (b), whether or not served upon the respondent.

(f) If a court issues a modification, extension, or termination of a protective order, it shall be on forms adopted by the Judicial Council of California and that have been approved by the Department of Justice, and the transmitting agency for the county shall immediately notify the Department of Justice, by electronic transmission, of the terms of the modification, extension, or termination.

(g) The Judicial Council shall assist local courts charged with the responsibility for issuing protective orders by developing informational packets describing the general procedures for obtaining a domestic violence restraining order and indicating the appropriate Judicial Council forms. The informational packets shall include a design, that local courts shall complete, that describes local court procedures and maps to enable applicants to locate filing windows and appropriate courts, and shall also include information on how to return proofs of service, including mailing addresses and fax numbers. The court clerk shall provide a fee waiver form to all applicants for domestic violence protective orders. The court clerk shall provide all Judicial Council forms required by this chapter to applicants free of charge. The informational packet shall also contain a statement that the protective order is enforceable in any state, as defined in Section 6401, and general information about agencies in other jurisdictions that may be contacted regarding enforcement of an order issued by a court of this state.

(h) For the purposes of this part, "electronic transmission" shall include computer access through the California Law Enforcement Telecommunications System (CLETS).

(i) Only protective and restraining orders issued on forms adopted by the Judicial Council of California and that have been approved by the Department of Justice shall be transmitted to the Department of Justice. However, this provision does not apply to a valid protective or restraining order related to domestic or family violence issued by a tribunal of another state, as defined in Section 6401. Those orders shall, upon request, be registered pursuant to Section 6404.

(j) (1) All protective orders subject to transmittal to CLETS pursuant to this section are required to be so transmitted.

(2) This subdivision does not constitute a change in, but is declaratory of, existing law.[577]

6380.5. (a) This section shall be known, and may be cited, as Wyland's Law.
(b) Subject to an appropriation by the Legislature, the department may establish, or contract with a vendor to establish, an automated protected person information and notification system to provide a petitioner or protected person in a protective order case with automated access to information maintained in the California Restraining and Protective Order System about their case, which shall include all of the following:
(1) Whether the department has received a record of the protective order.
(2) If the protective order has been successfully served on the restrained person.
(3) Notwithstanding any other law, if the restrained person has violated the protective order by attempting to purchase or acquire a firearm or ammunition while the order is in effect.
(c) (1) Notwithstanding any other law, a record demonstrating whether the superior court has fulfilled its transmission obligations pursuant to subdivision (a) or (b) of Section 6380 is required to be open to public inspection and copying.
(2) Notwithstanding any other law, a record demonstrating receipt of information about a protective order that the department maintains is a public record that is not exempt from disclosure in response to a public record request made pursuant to the California Public Records Act (Division 10 (commencing with Section 7920.000) of Title 1 of the Government Code).
(3) Paragraph (2) of this subdivision does not constitute a change in, but is declaratory of, existing law.
(d) For purposes of this section, the following definitions apply:
(1) "Department" means the Department of Justice.
(2) "Protective order" includes all order types listed in Section 6380 and the reissuance, extension, modification, or termination of the order.[612]

6381. (a) Notwithstanding Section 6380 and subject to subdivision (b), an order issued under this part is enforceable in any place in this state.
(b) An order issued under this part is not enforceable by a law enforcement agency of a political subdivision unless that law enforcement agency has received a copy of the order, or the officer enforcing the order has been shown a copy of the order or has obtained information, through the California Restraining and Protective Order System maintained by the Department of Justice, of the contents of the order, as described in subdivision (b).
(c) The data contained in the California Restraining and Protective Order System shall be deemed to be original, self-authenticating, documentary evidence of the court orders. Oral notify-cation of the terms of the orders shall be sufficient notice for enforcement under subdivision (g) of Section 136.2 and Section 273.6 of the Penal Code.[465]

6382. Each appropriate law enforcement agency shall make

available to any law enforcement officer responding to the scene of reported domestic violence, through an existing system for verification, information as to the existence, terms, and current status of an order issued under this part.

6383. (a) A temporary restraining order, emergency protective order, or an order issued after hearing pursuant to this part shall, on request of the petitioner, be served on the respondent, whether or not the respondent has been taken into custody, either by a law enforcement officer, excluding those defined in subdivision (a) of Section 830.5 of the Penal Code, who is present at the scene of reported domestic violence involving the parties to the proceeding or who receives a request from the petitioner to provide service of the order.

(b) (1) The petitioner shall provide the officer with an endorsed copy of the order and a proof of service that the officer shall complete and transmit to the issuing court.

(2) Service shall be provided pursuant to Section 6389 of the Family Code.

(3) Notwithstanding any other law, a fee shall not be charged to the petitioner for service of an order described in subdivision (a).

(4) If a firearm is obtained at the scene of a domestic violence incident or during service as provided in this section, law enforcement shall enter, or cause to be entered, the firearm into the Department of Justice Automated Firearms System pursuant to Section 11108.2 of the Penal Code.

(c) It is a rebuttable presumption that the proof of service was signed on the date of service.

(d) Upon receiving information at the scene of a domestic violence incident that a protective order has been issued under this part, or that a person who has been taken into custody is the respondent to that order, if the protected person cannot produce an endorsed copy of the order, a law enforcement officer shall immediately inquire of the California Restraining and Protective Order System to verify the existence of the order.

(e) If the law enforcement officer determines that a protective order has been issued but not served, the officer shall immediately notify the respondent of the terms of the order and where a written copy of the order can be obtained, and the officer shall, at that time, also enforce the order. The law enforcement officer's verbal notice of the terms of the order shall constitute service of the order and is sufficient notice for the purposes of this section and for the purposes of Sections 273.6 and 29825 of the Penal Code.

(f) If a report is required under Section 13730 of the Penal Code, or if no report is required, then in the daily incident log, the officer shall provide the name and assignment of the officer notifying the respondent pursuant to subdivision (e) and the case number of the order.

(g) Upon service of the order outside of the court, a law enforcement officer shall advise the respondent to go to the local court to obtain a copy of the order containing the full terms and conditions of the order.

(h) (1) There shall be no civil liability on the part of, and no cause of action for false arrest or false imprisonment against, a peace officer who makes an arrest pursuant to a protective or restraining order that is regular upon its face, if the peace officer, in making the arrest, acts in good faith and has reasonable cause to believe that the person against whom the order is issued has notice of the order and has committed an act in violation of the order.

(2) If there is more than one order issued and one of the orders is an emergency protective order that has precedence in enforcement pursuant to paragraph (1) of subdivision (c) of Section 136.2 of the Penal Code, the peace officer shall enforce the emergency protective order. If there is more than one order issued, none of the orders issued is an emergency protective order that has precedence in enforcement, and one of the orders issued is a no-contact order, as described in Section 6320, the peace officer shall enforce the no-contact order. If there is more than one civil order regarding the same parties and neither an emergency protective order that has precedence in enforcement nor a no-contact order has been issued, the peace officer shall enforce the order that was issued last. If there are both civil and criminal orders regarding the same parties and neither an emergency protective order that has precedence in enforcement nor a no-contact order has been issued, the peace officer shall enforce the criminal order issued last, subject to the provisions of subdivisions (h) and (i) of Section 136.2 of the Penal Code. This section does not exonerate a peace officer from liability for the unreasonable use of force in the enforcement of the order. The immunities afforded by this section shall not affect the availability of any other immunity that may apply, including, but not limited to, Sections 820.2 and 820.4 of the Government Code.

(i) A peace officer listed in Section 18250 of the Penal Code shall take temporary custody of any firearm or other deadly weapon in plain sight or discovered pursuant to a consensual or otherwise lawful search as necessary for the protection of the peace officer or other persons present in any of the following circumstances:

(1) The peace officer is at the scene of a domestic violence incident involving a threat to human life or a physical assault.

(2) The peace officer is serving a protective order issued pursuant to this part.

(3) The peace officer is serving a gun violence restraining order issued pursuant to Division 3.2 (commencing with Section 18100) of Title 2 of Part 6 of the Penal Code.[559]

6384. (a) If a respondent named in an order issued under this part after a hearing has not been served personally with the order but has received actual notice of the existence and substance of the order through personal appearance in court to hear the terms of the order from the court, no additional proof of service is required for enforcement of the order.

If a respondent named in a temporary restraining order or emergency protective order is personally served with the order and notice of hearing with respect to a restraining order or protective order based on the temporary restraining order or emergency protective order, but the respondent does not appear at the hearing either in person or by counsel, and the terms and conditions of the restraining order or protective order issued at the hearing are identical to the temporary restraining or emergency protective order, except for the duration of the order, the restraining order or protective order issued at the hearing may be served on the respondent by first-class mail sent to the respondent at the most current address for the respondent that is available to the court.

(b) The Judicial Council forms for orders issued under this part shall contain a statement in substantially the following form:

"If you have been personally served with a temporary restraining order and notice of hearing, but you do not appear at the hearing either in person or by a lawyer, and a restraining order that is the same as this temporary restraining order except for the expiration date is issued at the hearing, a copy of the order will be served on you by mail at the following address:

If that address is not correct or you wish to verify that the temporary restraining order was converted to a restraining order at the hearing without substantive change and to find out the duration of that order, contact the clerk of the court."[218]

6385. (a) Proof of service of the protective order is not required for the purposes of Section 6380 if the order indicates on its face that both parties were personally present at the hearing at which the order was issued and that, for the purpose of Section 6384, no proof of service is required, or if the order was served by a law enforcement officer pursuant to Section 6383.

(b) The failure of the petitioner to provide the Department of Justice with the personal descriptive information regarding the person restrained does not invalidate the protective order.

(c) There is no civil liability on the part of, and no cause of action arises against, an employee of a local law enforcement agency, a court, or the Department of Justice, acting within the scope of employment, if a person described in Section 29825 of the Penal Code unlawfully purchases or receives or attempts to purchase or receive a firearm and a person is injured by that firearm or a person who is otherwise entitled to receive a firearm is denied a firearm and either wrongful action is due to a failure of a court to provide the notification provided for in this chapter.[211]

6386. (a) The court may, in its discretion, appoint counsel to represent the petitioner in a proceeding to enforce the terms of a protective order, as defined in Section 6218.

(b) In a proceeding in which private counsel was appointed by the court pursuant to subdivision (a), the court may order the respondent to pay reasonable attorney's fees and costs incurred by the petitioner.

6387. The court shall order the clerk of the court to provide to a petitioner, without cost, up to three certified, stamped, and endorsed copies of any order issued under this part, and of an extension, modification, or termination of the order.[219]

6388. A willful and knowing violation of a protective order, as defined in Section 6218, is a crime punishable as provided by Section 273.6 of the Penal

Code.

6389. (a) A person subject to a protective order, as defined in Section 6218, shall not own, possess, purchase, or receive a firearm or ammunition while that protective order is in effect. A person who owns, possesses, purchases, or receives, or attempts to purchase or receive, a firearm or ammunition while the protective order is in effect is punishable pursuant to Section 29825 of the Penal Code.

(b) On all forms providing notice that a protective order has been requested or granted, the Judicial Council shall include a notice that, upon service of the order, the respondent shall be ordered to relinquish possession or control of any firearms or ammunition and not to purchase or receive or attempt to purchase or receive any firearms or ammunition for a period not to exceed the duration of the restraining order.

(c) (1) Upon issuance of a protective order, as defined in Section 6218, the court shall order the respondent to relinquish any firearm or ammunition in the respondent's immediate possession or control or subject to the respondent's immediate possession or control.

(2) The relinquishment ordered pursuant to paragraph (1) shall occur by immediately surrendering the fire-arm or ammunition in a safe manner, upon request of a law enforcement officer, to the control of the officer, after being served with the protective order. A law enforcement officer serving a protective order that indicates that the respondent possesses weapons or ammunition shall request that the firearm or ammunition be immediately surrendered. Alternatively, if a request is not made by a law enforcement officer, the relinquishment shall occur within 24 hours of being served with the order, by either surrendering the firearm or ammunition in a safe manner to the control of local law enforcement officials, or by selling, transferring, or relinquishing for storage pursuant to Section 29830 of the Penal Code, the firearm or ammunition to a licensed gun deal-er, as specified in Article 1 (commencing with Section 26700) and Article 2 (commencing with Section 26800) of Chapter 2 of Division 6 of Title 4 of Part 6 of the Penal Code. The law enforcement officer or licensed gun dealer taking possession of the firearm or ammunition pursuant to this subdivision shall issue a receipt to the person relinquishing the firearm or ammunition at the time of relinquishment. A person ordered to relinquish a firearm or ammunition pursuant to this subdivision shall, within 48 hours after being served with the order, do both of the following:

(A) File, with the court that issued the protective order, the receipt showing the firearm or ammunition was surrendered to a local law enforcement agency or sold to a licensed gun dealer. Failure to timely file a receipt shall constitute a violation of the protective order.

(B) File a copy of the receipt described in subparagraph (A) with the law enforcement agency that served the protective order. Failure to timely file a copy of the receipt shall constitute a violation of the protective order.

(3) The forms for protective orders adopted by the Judicial Council and approved by the Department of

Justice shall require the petitioner to describe the number, types, and locations of any firearms or ammunition presently known by the petitioner to be possessed or controlled by the respondent.

(4) A court holding a hearing on this matter shall review the file to determine whether the receipt has been filed and inquire of the respondent whether they have complied with the requirement. Violations of the firearms prohibition of any restraining order under this section shall be reported to the prosecuting attorney in the jurisdiction where the order has been issued within two business days of the court hearing unless the restrained party provides a receipt showing compliance at a subsequent hearing or by direct filing with the clerk of the court.

(5) Every law enforcement agency in the state shall develop, adopt, and implement written policies and standards for law enforcement officers who request immediate relinquishment of firearms or ammunition.

(d) If the respondent declines to relinquish possession of a firearm or ammunition based on the assertion of the right against self-incrimination, as provided by the Fifth Amendment to the United States Constitution and Section 15 of Article I of the California Constitution, the court may grant use immunity for the act of relinquishing the firearm or ammunition required under this section.

(e) A local law enforcement agency may charge the respondent a fee for the storage of a firearm or ammunition pursuant to this section. This fee shall not exceed the actual cost incurred by the local law enforcement agency for the storage of the firearm or ammunition. For purposes of this subdivision, "actual cost" means expenses directly related to taking possession of a firearm or ammunition, storing the firearm or ammunition, and surrendering possession of the firearm or ammunition to a licensed dealer as defined in Section 26700 of the Penal Code or to the respondent.

(f) The restraining order requiring a person to relinquish a firearm or ammunition pursuant to subdivision (c) shall state on its face that the respondent is prohibited from owning, possessing, purchasing, or receiving a firearm or ammunition while the protective order is in effect and that the firearm or ammunition shall be relinquished to the local law enforcement agency for that jurisdiction or sold to a licensed gun dealer, and that proof of surrender or sale shall be filed with the court within a specified period of receipt of the order. The order shall also state on its face the expiration date for relinquishment. This section does not limit a respondent's right under existing law to petition the court at a later date for modification of the order.

(g) The restraining order requiring a person to relinquish a firearm or ammunition pursuant to subdivision (c) shall prohibit the person from possessing or controlling a firearm or ammunition for the duration of the order. At the expiration of the order, the local law enforcement agency shall return possession of the surrendered firearm or ammunition to the respondent, within five days after the expiration of the relinquishment order, unless the local law enforcement agency determines that (1) the firearm or ammunition has been stolen, (2) the respondent is prohibited from possessing a firearm or ammunition because the respondent is in a prohibited class for the possession of firearms or ammunition, as defined in Chapter 2 (commencing with Section 29800) and Chapter 3 (commencing with Section 29900) of Division 9 of Title 4 of Part 6 of the Penal Code, Section 30305 of the Penal Code, and Sections 8100 and 8103 of the Welfare and Institutions Code, or (3) another successive restraining order is issued against the respondent under this section. If the local law enforcement agency determines that the respondent is the legal owner of a firearm or ammunition deposited with the local law enforcement agency and is prohibited from possessing a firearm or ammunition, the respondent shall be entitled to sell or transfer the firearm or ammunition to a licensed dealer as defined in Section 26700 of the Penal Code. If the firearm or ammunition has been stolen, the firearm or ammunition shall be restored to the lawful owner upon the owner identifying the firearm and ammunition and providing proof of ownership.

(h) The court may, as part of the relinquishment order, grant an exemption from the relinquishment requirements of this section for a particular firearm or ammunition if the respondent is not otherwise prohibited from owning, possessing, controlling, or purchasing a firearm and ammunition under state or federal law and one of the following applies:

(1) (A) The respondent is currently employed as a sworn peace officer who is required, as a condition of continued employment, to carry a firearm, ammunition, or firearm and ammunition and the current employer is unable to reassign the peace officer to another position where use of a specified firearm or ammunition is unnecessary. In such a case, a court may allow the peace officer to continue to carry a specified firearm, ammunition, or firearm and ammunition, either on duty or off duty, if the court finds by a preponderance of the evidence, in writing or on the record, both of the following:

(i) The peace officer's personal safety depends on the ability to carry that specific firearm, ammunition, or firearm and ammunition outside of scheduled work hours.

(ii) The peace officer does not pose an additional threat of harm to a protected party or the public by having access to that specific firearm, ammunition, or firearm and ammunition, including whether the peace officer might use the firearm for a purpose other than as permitted under this paragraph.

(B) Prior to making this finding, the court shall require a mandatory psychological evaluation of the peace officer by a licensed mental health professional with domestic violence expertise. The court shall consider the results of an evaluation and may require the peace officer to enter into counseling or another remedial treatment program to deal with a propensity for domestic violence.

(2) (A) The respondent is not a peace officer but is required to carry a specific firearm, ammunition, or firearm and ammunition during scheduled

work hours as a condition of continued employment, the current employer is unable to reassign the respondent to another position where the firearm, ammunition, or firearm and ammunition is unnecessary. In such a case, a court may grant an exemption to allow the respondent to possess a specific firearm, ammunition, or firearm and ammunition only during scheduled work hours if the court finds by a preponderance of the evidence, in writing or on the record, that the respondent does not pose an additional threat of harm to a protected party or the public by having access to the specific firearm, ammunition, or firearm and ammunition only during scheduled work hours, including whether the respondent might utilize the firearm, ammunition, or firearm and ammunition for a purpose other than as permitted under this paragraph.

(B) To assist the court in making this determination, the court may order a psychological evaluation of the respondent by a licensed mental health professional with domestic violence expertise.

(C) If the court grants an exemption pursuant to this paragraph, the order shall provide that the specific firearm, ammunition, or firearm and ammunition shall be in the physical possession of the respondent only during scheduled work hours and that the exemption does not authorize the respondent to possess any other firearm or ammunition, or to possess the specific firearm, ammunition, or firearm and ammunition outside of scheduled work hours.

(i) (1) If an exemption is granted under subdivision (h) during the pendency of a temporary restraining order and the court subsequently issues a restraining order after hearing on the same application, the court shall review and make a finding, in writing or on the record, as to whether the exemption remains appropriate, based upon the criteria set forth in paragraph (1) or (2) of subdivision (h), as applicable, in light of the issuance of the order after hearing. This review and finding shall occur at the time the restraining order after hearing is issued.

(2) If an exemption is granted and the court subsequently renews the restraining order pursuant to Section 6345 at the request of a party, the court shall review and make a finding, in writing or on the record, as to whether the exemption remains appropriate, based upon the criteria set forth in paragraph (1) or (2) of subdivision (h), as applicable, in light of the renewal. This finding shall be made at the time the restraining order after hearing is renewed.

(3) The court may terminate or modify an exemption granted pursuant to this paragraph at any time if the respondent demonstrates a need to modify the specific firearm, ammunition, or firearm and ammunition authorized by the court pursuant to subdivision (h) or if the respondent no longer meets the requirements in this section or otherwise violates the restraining order.

(j) During the period of the relinquishment order, a respondent is entitled to make one sale of all firearms or ammunition that are in the possession of a local law enforcement agency pursuant to this section. A licensed gun dealer, who presents a local law enforcement agency with a bill of sale indicating that all firearms or ammunition owned by the respondent that are in the possession of the local law enforcement agency have been sold by the respondent to the licensed gun dealer, shall be given possession of those firearms or ammunition, at the location where a respondent's firearms or ammunition are stored, within five days of presenting the local law enforcement agency with a bill of sale.

(k) The disposition of any unclaimed property under this section shall be made pursuant to Section 1413 of the Penal Code.

(l) (1) The relinquishment of a firearm to a law enforcement agency pursuant to subdivision (g) shall not be subject to the requirements of Section 27545 of the Penal Code.

(2) The return of firearms and ammunition by a law enforcement agency pursuant to this section shall be governed by the applicable provisions of Chapter 2 (commencing with Section 33850) of Division 11 of Title 4 of Part 6 of the Penal Code.

(m) If the respondent notifies the court that the respondent owns a firearm or ammunition that is not in their immediate possession, the court may limit the order to exclude that firearm or ammunition if the judge is satisfied the respondent is unable to gain access to that firearm or ammunition while the protective order is in effect.

(n) A respondent to a protective order who violates an order issued pursuant to this section shall be punished under the provisions of Section 29825 of the Penal Code.

(o) This section shall become operative on January 1, 2026.[592]

PART 5: UNIFORM INTERSTATE ENFORCEMENT OF DOMESTIC VIOLENCE PROTECTION ORDERS ACT

added by Stats. 2001, Ch. 816, Sec. 3

6400. In this part: This part may be cited as the Uniform Interstate Enforcement of Domestic Violence Protection Orders Act.

6401. In this part:

(1) "Foreign protection order" means a protection order issued by a tribunal of another state.

(2) "Issuing state" means the state whose tribunal issues a protection order.

(3) "Mutual foreign protection order" means a foreign protection order that includes provisions in favor of both the protected individual seeking enforcement of the order and the respondent.

(4) "Protected individual" means an individual protected by a protection order.

(5) "Protection order" means an injunction or other order, issued by a tribunal under the domestic violence, family violence, or antistalking laws of the issuing state, to prevent an individual from engaging in violent or threatening acts against, harassment of, contact or communication with, or physical proximity to, another individual.

(6) "Respondent" means the individual against whom enforcement of a protection order is sought.

(7) "State" means a state of the United States, the District of Columbia,

Puerto Rico, the United States Virgin Islands, or any territory or insular possession subject to the jurisdiction of the United States. The term includes an Indian tribe or band, or any branch of the United States military, that has jurisdiction to issue protection orders.

(8) "Tribunal" means a court, agency, or other entity authorized by law to issue or modify a protection order.[97]

6402. (a) A person authorized by the law of this state to seek enforcement of a protection order may seek enforcement of a valid foreign protection order in a tribunal of this state. The tribunal shall enforce the terms of the order, including terms that provide relief that a tribunal of this state would lack power to provide but for this section. The tribunal shall enforce the order, whether the order was obtained by independent action or in another proceeding, if it is an order issued in response to a complaint, petition, or motion filed by or on behalf of an individual seeking protection. In a proceeding to enforce a foreign protection order, the tribunal shall follow the procedures of this state for the enforcement of protection orders.

(b) A tribunal of this state may not enforce a foreign protection order issued by a tribunal of a state that does not recognize the standing of a protected individual to seek enforcement of the order.

(c) A tribunal of this state shall enforce the provisions of a valid foreign protection order which govern custody and visitation, if the order was issued in accordance with the jurisdictional requirements governing the issuance of custody and visitation orders in the issuing state.

(d) A foreign protection order is valid if it meets all of the following criteria:

(1) Identifies the protected individual and the respondent.

(2) Is currently in effect.

(3) Was issued by a tribunal that had jurisdiction over the parties and subject matter under the law of the issuing state.

(4) Was issued after the respondent was given reasonable notice and had an opportunity to be heard before the tribunal issued the order or, in the case of an order ex parte, the respondent was given notice and has had or will have an opportunity to be heard within a reasonable time after the order was issued, in a manner consistent with the rights of the respondent to due process.

(e) A foreign protection order valid on its face is prima facie evidence of its validity.

(f) Absence of any of the criteria for validity of a foreign protection order is an affirmative defense in an action seeking enforcement of the order.

(g) A tribunal of this state may enforce provisions of a mutual foreign protection order which favor a respondent only if both of the following are true:

(1) The respondent filed a written pleading seeking a protection order from the tribunal of the issuing state.

(2) The tribunal of the issuing state made specific findings in favor of the respondent.[98]

6403. (a) A law enforcement officer of this state, upon determining that there is probable cause to believe that a valid foreign protection order exists and that the order has been violated, shall enforce the order as if it were the order of a tribunal of this state. Presentation of a protection order that identifies both the protected individual and the respondent and, on its face, is currently in effect constitutes, in and of itself, probable cause to believe that a valid foreign protection order exists. For the purposes of this section, the protection order may be inscribed on a tangible medium or may have been stored in an electronic or other medium if it is retrievable in perceivable form. Presentation of a certified copy of a protection order is not required for enforcement.

(b) If a foreign protection order is not presented, a law enforcement officer of this state may consider other information in determining whether there is probable cause to believe that a valid foreign protection order exists.

(c) If a law enforcement officer of this state determines that an otherwise valid foreign protection order cannot be enforced because the respondent has not been notified or served with the order, the officer shall inform the respondent of the order, make a reasonable effort to serve the order upon the respondent, and allow the respondent a reasonable opportunity to comply with the order before enforcing the order. Verbal notice of the terms of the order is sufficient notice for the purposes of this section.

(d) Registration or filing of an order in this state is not required for the enforcement of a valid foreign protection order pursuant to this part.

6404. (a) A foreign protection order shall, upon request of the person in possession of the order, be registered with a court of this state in order to be entered in the California Restraining and Protective Order System established under Section 6380. The Judicial Council shall adopt rules of court to do the following:

(1) Set forth the process whereby a person in possession of a foreign protection order may voluntarily register the order with a court of this state for entry into the California Restraining and Protective Order System.

(2) Require the sealing of foreign protection orders and provide access only to law enforcement, the person who registered the order upon written request with proof of identification, the defense after arraignment on criminal charges involving an alleged violation of the order, or upon further order of the court.

(b) A fee shall not be charged for the registration of a foreign protection order. The court clerk shall provide all Judicial Council forms required by this part to a person in possession of a foreign protection order free of charge.

6405. (a) There shall be no civil liability on the part of, and no cause of action for false arrest or false imprisonment against, a peace officer who makes an arrest pursuant to a foreign protection order that is regular upon its face, if the peace officer, in making the arrest, acts in good faith and has reasonable cause to believe that the person against whom the order is issued has notice of the order and has committed an act in violation of the order.

(b) If there is more than one order issued and one of the orders is an emergency protective order that has precedence in enforcement pursuant to paragraph (1) of subdivision (c) of Section 136.2 of the Penal Code, the peace officer shall enforce the emergency protective order. If there is more than one order issued, none of the orders issued is an emergency protective order that has precedence in enforcement, and one of the orders issued is a no-contact order, as described in Section 6320, the peace officer shall enforce the no-contact order. If there is more than one civil order regarding the same parties and neither an emergency protective order that has precedence in enforcement nor a no-contact order has been issued, the peace officer shall enforce the order that was issued last. If there are both civil and criminal orders regarding the same parties and neither an emergency protective order that has precedence in enforcement nor a no-contact order has been issued, the peace officer shall enforce the criminal order issued last.

(c) Nothing in this section shall be deemed to exonerate a peace officer from liability for the unreasonable use of force in the enforcement of the order. The immunities afforded by this section shall not affect the availability of any other immunity that may apply, including, but not limited to, Sections 820.2 and 820.4 of the Government Code.[269]

6406. A protected individual who pursues remedies under this part is not precluded from pursuing other legal or equitable remedies against the respondent.

6407. In applying and construing this part, consideration shall be given to the need to promote uniformity of the law with respect to its subject matter among states that also have adopted the act cited in Section 6400.

6408. If any provision of this part or its application to any person or circumstance is held invalid, the invalidity does not affect other provisions or applications of this part which can be given effect without the invalid provision or application, and to this end the provisions of this part are severable.

6409. This part applies to protection orders issued before January 1, 2002, and to continuing actions for enforcement of foreign protection orders commenced before January 1, 2002. A request for enforcement of a foreign protection order made on or after January 1, 2002, for violations of a foreign protection order occurring before January 1, 2002, is governed by this part.

PART 6: UNIFORM RECOGNITION AND ENFORCEMENT OF CANADIAN DOMESTIC VIOLENCE PROTECTION ORDERS ACT

added by Stats. 2017, Ch. 98, Sec. 1

6450. This part may be cited as the Uniform Recognition and Enforcement of Canadian Domestic Violence Protection Orders Act.[366]

6451. In this part:

(a) “Canadian domestic violence protection order” means a judgment or part of a judgment or order issued in English in a civil proceeding by a court of Canada under law of the issuing jurisdiction that relates to domestic violence and prohibits a respondent from doing any of the following:

(1) Being in physical proximity to a protected individual or following a protected individual.

(2) Directly or indirectly contacting or communicating with a protected individual or other individual described in the order.
(3) Being within a certain distance of a specified place or location associated with a protected individual.
(4) Molesting, annoying, harassing, or engaging in threatening conduct directed at a protected individual.
(b) "Domestic protection order" means an injunction or other order issued by a tribunal that relates to domestic or family violence laws to prevent an individual from engaging in violent or threatening acts against, harassment of, direct or indirect contact or communication with, or being in physical proximity to, another individual.
(c) "Issuing court" means the court that issues a Canadian domestic violence protection order.
(d) "Law enforcement officer" means an individual authorized by law of this state to enforce a domestic protection order.
(e) "Person" means an individual, estate, business or nonprofit entity, public corporation, government or governmental subdivision, agency, or instrumentality, or other legal entity.
(f) "Protected individual" means an individual protected by a Canadian domestic violence protection order.
(g) "Record" means information that is inscribed on a tangible medium or that is stored in an electronic or other medium and is retrievable in perceivable form.
(h) "Respondent" means an individual against whom a Canadian domestic violence protection order is issued.
(i) "State" means a state of the United States, the District of Columbia, Puerto Rico, the United States Virgin Islands, or any territory or insular possession subject to the jurisdiction of the United States. The term includes a federally recognized Indian tribe.
(j) "Tribunal" means a court, agency, or other entity authorized by law to establish, enforce, or modify a domestic protection order.[366]

6452. (a) If a law enforcement officer determines under subdivision (b) or (c) that there is probable cause to believe a valid Canadian domestic violence protection order exists and the order has been violated, the officer shall enforce the terms of the Canadian domestic violence protection order as if the terms were in an order of a tribunal of this state. Presentation to a law enforcement officer of a certified copy of a Canadian domestic violence protection order is not required for enforcement.
(b) Presentation to a law enforcement officer of a record of a Canadian domestic violence protection order that identifies both a protected individual and a respondent and on its face is in effect constitutes probable cause to believe that a valid order exists.
(c) If a record of a Canadian domestic violence protection order is not presented as provided in subdivision (b), a law enforcement officer may consider other information in determining whether there is probable cause to believe that a valid Canadian domestic violence protection order exists.
(d) If a law enforcement officer determines that an otherwise valid Canadian domestic violence protection order cannot be enforced because the respondent has not been notified of or

served with the order, the officer shall notify the protected individual that the officer will make reasonable efforts to contact the respondent, consistent with the safety of the protected individual. After notice to the protected individual and consistent with the safety of the individual, the officer shall make a reasonable effort to inform the respondent of the order, notify the respondent of the terms of the order, provide a record of the order, if available, to the respondent, and allow the respondent a reasonable opportunity to comply with the order before the officer enforces the order. Verbal notice of the terms of the order is sufficient for purposes of this subdivision.

(e) If a law enforcement officer determines that an individual is a protected individual, the officer shall inform the individual of available local victim services.[366]

6453. (a) A tribunal of this state may issue an order enforcing or refusing to enforce a Canadian domestic violence protection order on application of any of the following:

(1) A protected party or other person authorized by law of this state other than this part to seek enforcement of a domestic protection order.

(2) A respondent.

(b) In a proceeding under subdivision (a), the tribunal of this state shall follow the procedures of this state for enforcement of a domestic protection order. An order entered under this section is limited to the enforcement of the terms of the Canadian domestic violence protection order as described in subdivision (a) of Section 6451.

(c) A Canadian domestic violence protection order is enforceable under this section if all of the following apply:

(1) The order identifies a protected individual and a respondent.

(2) The order is valid and in effect.

(3) The issuing court had jurisdiction over the parties and the subject matter under law applicable in the issuing court.

(4) The order was issued after either of the following:

(A) The respondent was given reasonable notice and had an opportunity to be heard before the court issued the order.

(B) In the case of an ex parte order, the respondent was given reasonable notice and had or will have an opportunity to be heard within a reasonable time after the order was issued, in a manner consistent with the right of the respondent to due process.

(d) A Canadian domestic violence protection order valid on its face is prima facie evidence of its enforceability under this section.

(e) A claim that a Canadian domestic violence protection order does not comply with subdivision (c) is an affirmative defense in a proceeding seeking enforcement of the order. If the tribunal of this state determines that the order is not enforceable, the tribunal of this state shall issue an order that the Canadian domestic violence protection order is not enforceable under this section and Section 6452 and may not be registered under Section 6454.

(f) This section applies to enforcement of a provision of a Canadian domestic violence protection order against a party to the order in which each party is a protected individual and respondent only if both of the following apply:

(1) The party seeking enforcement of the order filed a pleading requesting the order from the issuing court.

(2) The court made detailed findings of fact indicating that both parties acted as a primary aggressor and that neither party acted primarily in self-defense.[366]

6454. (a) An individual may register a Canadian domestic violence protection order in this state. To register the order, the individual must present a certified copy of the order to a court of this state to be entered into the California Restraining and Protective Order System established under Section 6380, pursuant to procedures set forth in Section 6404.

(b) A fee shall not be charged for the registration of a Canadian domestic violence protection order under this section.

(c) Registration in this state or filing under law of this state other than this part of a Canadian domestic violence protection order is not required for its enforcement under this part.

6455. (a) There shall be no civil liability on the part of, and no cause of action for false arrest or false imprisonment against, a law enforcement officer who makes an arrest pursuant to a Canadian domestic violence protection order that is regular upon its face, if the law enforcement officer, in making the arrest, acts in good faith and has reasonable cause to believe that the person against whom the order is issued has notice of the order and has committed an act in violation of the order.

(b) Nothing in this section shall be deemed to exonerate a law enforcement officer from liability for the unreasonable use of force in the enforcement of the order. The immunities afforded by this section shall not affect the availability of any other immunity that may apply, including, but not limited to, Sections 820.2 and 820.4 of the Government Code.[366]

6456. An individual who seeks a remedy under this part may seek other legal or equitable remedies.[366]

6457. If there is more than one order issued and one of the orders is an emergency protective order that has precedence in enforcement pursuant to paragraph (1) of subdivision (c) of Section 136.2 of the Penal Code, the law enforcement officer shall enforce the emergency protective order. If there is more than one order issued, none of the orders issued is an emergency protective order that has precedence in enforcement, and one of the orders issued is a no-contact order, as described in Section 6320, the law enforcement officer shall enforce the no-contact order. If there is more than one civil order regarding the same parties and neither an emergency protective order that has precedence in enforcement nor a no-contact order has been issued, the law enforcement officer shall enforce the order that was issued last. If there are both civil and criminal orders regarding the same parties and neither an emergency protective order that has precedence in enforcement nor a no-contact order has been issued, the law enforcement officer shall enforce the criminal order issued last.[366]

6458. This part modifies, limits, or supersedes the federal Electronic

Signatures in Global and National Commerce Act (15 U.S.C. Sec. 7001 et seq.), but does not modify, limit, or supersede Section 101(c) of that act (15 U.S.C. Sec. 7001(c)), or authorize electronic delivery of any of the notices described in Section 103(b) of that act (15 U.S.C. Sec. 7003(b)).[366]

6459. This part applies to a Canadian domestic violence protection order issued before, on, or after January 1, 2018, and to a continuing action for enforcement of a Canadian domestic violence protection order commenced before, on, or after January 1, 2018. A request for enforcement of a Canadian domestic violence protection order made on or after January 1, 2018, for a violation of the order occurring before, on, or after January 1, 2018, is governed by this part.[366]

6460. If any provision of this part or its application to any person or circumstance is held invalid, the invalidity does not affect other provisions or applications of this part that can be given effect without the invalid provision or application, and to this end the provisions of this part are severable.[366]

DIVISION 11: MINORS

ENACTED BY STATS. 1992, CH. 162, SEC. 10.
SECTION 6500 – 7143

PART 1: AGE OF MAJORITY

enacted by Stats. 1992, Ch. 162, Sec. 10

6500. A minor is an individual who is under 18 years of age. The period of minority is calculated from the first minute of the day on which the individual is born to the same minute of the corresponding day completing the period of minority.[1]

6501. An adult is an individual who is 18 years of age or older.[1]

6502. (a) The use of or reference to the words "age of majority," "age of minority," "adult," "minor," or words of similar intent in any instrument, order, transfer, or governmental communication made in this state:

(1) Before March 4, 1972, makes reference to individuals 21 years of age and older, or younger than 21 years of age.

(2) On or after March 4, 1972, makes reference to individuals 18 years of age and older, or younger than 18 years of age.

(b) Nothing in subdivision (a) or in Chapter 1748 of the Statutes of 1971 prevents amendment of any court order, will, trust, contract, transfer, or instrument to refer to the 18-year-old age of majority if the court order, will, trust, contract, transfer, or instrument satisfies all of the following conditions:

(1) It was in existence on March 4, 1972.

(2) It is subject to amendment by law, and amendment is allowable or not prohibited by its terms.

(3) It is otherwise subject to the laws of this state.[1]

PART 1.5: CAREGIVERS

added by Stats. 1994, Ch. 98, Sec. 4

6550. (a) A caregiver's authorization affidavit that meets the requirements of this part authorizes a caregiver 18 years of age or older who completes items 1 to 4, inclusive, of the affidavit provided in Section 6552 and signs the affidavit to enroll a minor in school and consent to school-related medical care on behalf of the minor. A caregiver who is a relative and who completes items 1 to 8, inclusive, of the affidavit provided in Section 6552 and signs the affidavit shall have the same rights to authorize medical care and dental care for the minor that are given to guardians under Section 2353 of the Probate Code. The medical care authorized by this caregiver who is a relative may include mental health treatment subject to the limitations of Section 2356 of the Probate Code.

(b) The decision of a caregiver to consent to or to refuse medical or dental care for a minor shall be superseded by any contravening decision of the parent or other person having legal custody of the minor, provided the decision of the parent or other person having legal custody of the minor does not jeopardize the life, health, or safety of the minor.

(c) A person who acts in good faith

reliance on a caregiver's authorization affidavit to provide medical or dental care, without actual knowledge of facts contrary to those stated on the affidavit, is not subject to criminal liability or to civil liability to any person, and is not subject to professional disciplinary action, for that reliance if the applicable portions of the affidavit are completed. This subdivision applies even if medical or dental care is provided to a minor in contravention of the wishes of the parent or other person having legal custody of the minor as long as the person providing the medical or dental care has no actual knowledge of the wishes of the parent or other person having legal custody of the minor.

(d) A person who relies on the affidavit has no obligation to make any further inquiry or investigation.

(e) Nothing in this section relieves any individual from liability for violations of other provisions of law.

(f) If the minor stops living with the caregiver, the caregiver shall notify any school, health care provider, or health care service plan that has been given the affidavit. The affidavit is invalid after the school, health care provider, or health care service plan receives notice that the minor is no longer living with the caregiver.

(g) A caregiver's authorization affidavit shall be invalid, unless it substantially contains, in not less than 10-point boldface type or a reasonable equivalent thereof, the warning statement beginning with the word "warning" specified in Section 6552. The warning statement shall be enclosed in a box with 3-point rule lines.

(h) For purposes of this part, the following terms have the following meanings:

(1) "Person" includes an individual, corporation, partnership, association, the state, or any city, county, city and county, or other public entity or governmental subdivision or agency, or any other legal entity.

(2) "Relative" means a spouse, parent, stepparent, brother, sister, stepbrother, stepsister, half-brother, half-sister, uncle, aunt, niece, nephew, first cousin, or any person denoted by the prefix "grand" or "great," or the spouse of any of the persons specified in this definition, even after the marriage has been terminated by death or dissolution.

(3) "School-related medical care" means medical care, including immunizations, physical examinations, and medical examinations conducted in schools for pupils, that is required by state or local governmental authority as a condition for school enrollment or participation in local educational agency-related extracurricular activities.[604]

6552. The caregiver's authorization affidavit shall be in substantially the following form:

Caregiver's Authorization Affidavit

Use of this affidavit is authorized by Part 1.5 (commencing with Section 6550) of Division 11 of the California Family Code.

Instructions: Completion of items 1–4 and the signing of the affidavit is sufficient to authorize enrollment of a minor in school and authorize school-related medical care.

Completion of items 5–8 is additionally required to authorize any other medical care. Print clearly.

The minor named below lives in my home and I am 18 years of age or older.

1. Name of minor:.
2. Minor's birth date:.
3. My name (adult giving authorization):.
4. My home address:
5. I am a relative of the child (see back of this form for a definition of "relative").
6. Check one or both (for example, if one parent was advised and the other cannot be located):

☐ I have advised the parent(s) or other person(s) having legal custody of the minor of my intent to authorize medical care, and have received no objection.
☐ I am unable to contact the parent(s) or other person(s) having legal custody of the minor at this time, to notify them of my intended authorization.

7. My date of birth:.
8. My California driver's license or identification card number:.

Warning to Caregiver: Do not sign this form if any of the statements above are incorrect, or you will be committing a crime punishable by a fine, imprisonment, or both.

Warning to Local Educational Agencies and Health Care Service Providers: A seal or signature from a court is not required. This form is not required to be notarized.

I declare under penalty of perjury under the laws of the State of California that the foregoing is true and correct.
Dated: Signed:

Notices:

1. This declaration does not affect the rights of the minor's parents or legal guardian regarding the care, custody, and control of the minor, and does not mean that the caregiver has legal custody of the minor.
2. A person who relies on this affidavit has no obligation to make any further inquiry or investigation. Additional Information:

TO CAREGIVERS:

1. "Relative," for purposes of item 5, means an adult who is related to the child by blood, adoption, or affinity within the fifth degree of kinship, including stepparents, stepsiblings, and all relatives whose status is preceded by the words "great," "great-great," or "grand," or the spouse of any of these persons even if the marriage was terminated by death or dissolution.
2. The law may require you, if you are not a relative or a currently licensed, certified, or approved foster parent, to obtain resource family approval pursuant to Section 1517 of the Health and Safety Code or Section 16519.5 of the Welfare and Institutions Code in order to care for a minor. If you have any questions, please contact your local department of social services.
3. If the minor stops living with you, the affidavit is no longer valid. You are required to notify any school, health care provider, or health care service plan to which you have given this affidavit that the minor is no longer living with you and that, as a result, the affidavit is no longer valid.
4. If you do not have the information requested in item 8 (California driver's license or I.D., or government-issued consular card), provide another form of identification such as your social security number or Medi-Cal number.

TO SCHOOL OFFICIALS:

1. Section 48204 of the Education Code provides that this affidavit constitutes a sufficient basis for a determination of residency of the minor, without the requirement of a guardianship or other custody order, unless the school district determines from actual facts that the minor is not living with the caregiver.
2. The school district may require additional reasonable evidence that the caregiver lives at the address provided in item 4.
3. A seal or signature of the court is not required. This form is not required to be notarized.

TO HEALTH CARE PROVIDERS AND HEALTH CARE SERVICE PLANS:

1. When signed by a relative, this affidavit shall confer the same rights to authorize medical care and dental care for the minor that are given to guardians under Section 2353 of the Probate Code. The medical care authorized by a relative caregiver may include mental health treatment subject to the limitations of Section 2356 of the Probate Code.
2. A health care service provider who acts in good faith reliance upon a caregiver's authorization affidavit to provide medical or dental care, without actual knowledge of facts contrary to those stated on the affidavit, is not subject to criminal lia-

bility or to civil liability to any person, and is not subject to professional disciplinary action, for that reliance if the applicable portions of the form are completed. A seal or signature of the court is not required. This form is not required to be notarized.

3. This affidavit does not confer dependency for health care coverage purposes.[605]

PART 2: RIGHTS AND LIABILITIES; CIVIL ACTIONS AND PROCEEDINGS

enacted by Stats. 1992, Ch. 162, Sec. 10

6600. A minor is civilly liable for a wrong done by the minor, but is not liable in exemplary damages unless at the time of the act the minor was capable of knowing that the act was wrongful.[1]

6601. A minor may enforce the minor's rights by civil action or other legal proceedings in the same manner as an adult, except that a guardian must conduct the action or proceedings.[1]

6602. A contract for attorney's fees for services in litigation, made by or on behalf of a minor, is void unless the contract is approved, on petition by an interested person, by the court in which the litigation is pending or by the court having jurisdiction of the guardianship estate of the minor. If the contract is not approved and a judgment is recovered by or on behalf of the minor, the attorney's fees charge-able against the minor shall be fixed by the court rendering the judgment.[1]

PART 2.5: ONLINE PLATFORMS

added by Stats. 2024, Ch. 611, Sec. 1

6650. For the purposes of this part, all of the following definitions apply:

(a) "Age of majority" means 18 years of age or older.

(b) "Content" has the same meaning as defined in subdivision (b) of Section 22675 of the Business and Professions Code.

(c) "Family" means a group of persons related by blood or marriage, including civil partnerships, or whose close relationship with each other is considered equivalent to a family relationship by the individuals.

(d) "Minor" means an individual who is under 18 years of age.

(e) "Online platform" means any public-facing internet website, web application, or digital application, including a mobile application. "Online platform" includes a social media platform, as defined in Section 22675 of the Business and Professions Code, advertising network, mobile operating system, search engine, email service, or internet access service.

(f) "Reporting period" means a given month for which a parent, legal guardian, or family must set aside compensation for a minor pursuant to subdivision (a) of Section 6651.

(g) "Vlog" means content shared on an online platform in exchange for compensation.

(h) "Vlogger" means a parent, legal guardian, or family residing in California that creates image or video content that is performed in California in exchange for compensation. "Vlogger" does not include any person under 18 years of age who produces their own content.

(i) "Vlogging" means the act of sharing content on an online platform in exchange for compensation.[594]

6651. A minor is considered engaged in the work of vlogging when the following are met at any time during a given month:

(a) (1) At least 30 percent of the vlogger's compensated video content or the vlogger's compensated image content includes the likeness, name, or photograph of the minor.

(2) The percentage pursuant to paragraph (1) is measured by the amount of time the likeness, name, or photograph of the minor visually appears or is the subject of an oral narrative in a video segment, as compared to the total length of the segment.

(b) The number of views received per image or video segment on any online platform met the online platform's threshold for compensation or the vlogger received actual compensation for image or video content equal to or greater than ten cents ($0.10) per view.

(c) The vlogger received actual compensation for image or video content of at least one thousand two hundred fifty dollars ($1,250) in the month.[594]

6652. All vloggers whose content features a minor engaged in the work of vlogging, as described in subdivision (a) of Section 6651, shall maintain, and make available to the minor upon request, all of the following records:

(a) Documentary proof of the minor's age when they started vlogging, as described in subdivision (a) of Section 6651.

(b) The number of vlogs that generated compensation, as described in Section 6651 during each reporting period.

(c) The total number of minutes of the vlogs that the vlogger received compensation for during each reporting period.

(d) The total number of minutes each minor was included in, as described in paragraph (1) of subdivision (a) of Section 6651, vlogs during each reporting period.

(e) The total compensation generated from vlogs featuring the minor during the reporting period.

(f) The amount deposited for the reporting period into the trust account for the benefit of the minor engaged in vlogging pursuant to Section 6653. This amount shall be calculated by multiplying the percentage of total minutes in subdivision (c) in which the minor is featured in subdivision (d) by the total compensation in subdivision (e) multiplied by .65.[594]

6653. (a) A minor satisfying the requirements of subdivision (a) of Section 6651 shall be compensated by the vlogger, pursuant to the terms of this section. The vlogger shall set aside gross earnings on the image or video content meeting the requirements of Section 6651 in a trust account to be preserved for the benefit of the minor upon reaching the age of majority according to the following distribution:

(1) When only one minor meets the content threshold described in Section 6651, the minor shall receive a percentage of total gross earnings on any image or video segment, meeting the requirements of Section 6651, that is in proportion to the minor's appearances in vlogging content during an applicable reporting period.

(2) When more than one minor meets the content threshold described in Section 6651 and an image or video segment includes more than one of those minors, the percentage described in paragraph (1) for all minors in any segment shall be equally divided between the minors, regardless of the differences in percentage of content provided by the individual minors. Each minor shall have their own trust account.

(b) (1) The vlogger shall establish the trust within 60 business days after the minor first meets the criteria in subdivision (a) of Section 6651. The vlogger shall establish a trust for each qualifying minor.

(2) The vlogger shall establish the trust in California either with a financial institution that is and remains insured at all times by the Federal Deposit Insurance Corporation, the Securities Investor Protect-ion Corporation, or the National Credit Union Share Insurance Fund or their respective successors, or with a company that is and remains registered under the Investment Company Act of 1940. The trustee or trustees of the trust shall be the only individual, individuals, entity, or entities with the obligation or duty to ensure that the funds remain in trust, in an account or other savings plan insured in accordance with this section, or with a company that is and remains registered under the Investment Company Act of 1940 as authorized by this section.

(3) The vlogger shall, within 10 business days of establishing the trust, prepare a written statement, under penalty of perjury, that shall include the name, address, and telephone number of the financial institution, the name of the account, the number of the account, the name of the minor beneficiary, the name of the trustee or trustees of the account, and any additional information needed by the vlogger to deposit into the account the portion of the minor's gross earnings prescribed by subdivision (a). The trustee or trustees shall attach to the written statement a true and accurate photocopy of any information received from the financial institution confirming the creation of the account, such as an account agreement, account terms, passbook, or other similar writings.

(4) The funds in the account shall be available only to the beneficiary of the trust. The vlogger shall deposit the funds into the account no less than once every three months.

(5) Except as otherwise provided in this section, prior to the date on which the beneficiary of the trust attains the age of majority or the issuance of a declaration of emancipation of the minor pursuant to Section 7122, a withdrawal by the beneficiary or any other individual, individuals, entity, or entities shall not be made for the funds deposited in trust. Upon reaching the age of majority, the beneficiary may with-draw the funds on deposit in the trust only after providing a certified copy of the beneficiary's birth certificate to the financial institution where the trust is located.

(c) Upon application by the trustee or trustees, the trust funds shall be handled by the financial institution or company in which the trust is held in one or more of the following methods:

(1) The financial institution or company may transfer funds to another account or other savings plan at the same financial institution or company, provided that the funds transferred shall continue to be held in trust, and subject to this part.

(2) The financial institution or company may transfer funds to another financial institution or company, provided that the funds transferred shall continue to be held in trust, and subject to this part and that the transferring financial institution or company has provided written notice to the financial institution or company to which the funds will be transferred that the funds are subject to this section and written notice of the requirements of this part.

(3) The financial institution or company may use all or a part of the funds to purchase, in the name of and for the benefit of the minor, either of the following:

(A) Investment funds offered by a company registered under the Investment Company Act of 1940, provided that if the underlying investments are equity securities, the investment fund is a broad-based index fund or invests broadly across the domestic or a foreign regional economy, is not a sector fund, and has assets under management of at least two hundred fifty million dollars ($250,000,000).

(B) Government securities and bonds, certificates of deposit, money market instruments, money market accounts, or mutual funds investing solely in those government securities and bonds, certificates, instruments, and accounts that are available at the financial institution where the trust fund or other savings plan is held, provided that the funds shall continue to be held in trust and subject to this part, those purchases shall have a maturity date on or before the date upon which the minor will attain the age of majority, and any proceeds accruing from those purchases shall be redeposited into that account or accounts or used to further purchase any of those or similar securities, bonds, certificates, instruments, funds, or accounts.[594]

6654. If a vlogger knowingly violates this part or should have known they were in violation of this part, a minor satisfying the criteria described in subdivision (a) of Section 6651 may commence an action to enforce the provisions of this part. The court may award, to a minor who prevails in any action brought in accordance with this part, any of the following damages:

(a) Actual damages.

(b) Punitive damages.

(c) Cost of the action, including attorney's fees and litigation costs. [594]

6655. (a) This part does not affect a right or remedy available under any other law of the state.

(b) This part does not have any effect on a minor who produces their own content.[594]

6656. This part shall not apply to a contract for vlogging services between a minor and their parent or guardian only if a court approves the contract pursuant to subdivision (a) of Section 6751. In determining whether to approve such a contract, the court shall consider whether the terms of the contract are at least as beneficial to the minor as the compensation the minor would otherwise receive under this part.[594]

PART 3: CONTRACTS

enacted by Stats. 1992, Ch. 162, Sec. 10

Chapter 1: Capacity to Contract

6700. Except as provided in Section 6701, a minor may make a contract in the same manner as an adult, subject to the power of disaffirmance under Chapter 2 (commencing with Section 6710), and subject to Part 1 (commencing with Section 300) of Division 3 (validity of marriage).[1]

6701. A minor cannot do any of the following:
(a) Give a delegation of power.
(b) Make a contract relating to real property or any interest therein.
(c) Make a contract relating to any personal property not in the immediate possession or control of the minor.[1]

Chapter 2: Disaffirmance of Contracts

6710. Except as otherwise provided by statute, a contract of a minor may be disaffirmed by the minor before majority or within a reasonable time afterwards or, in case of the minor's death within that period, by the minor's heirs or personal representative.[1]

6711. A minor cannot disaffirm an obligation, otherwise valid, entered into by the minor under the express authority or direction of a statute.[1]

6712. A contract, otherwise valid, entered into during minority, may not be disaffirmed on that ground either during the actual minority of the person entering into the contract, or at any time thereafter, if all of the following requirements are satisfied:
(a) The contract is to pay the reasonable value of things necessary for the support of the minor or the minor's family.
(b) These things have been actually furnished to the minor or to the minor's family.
(c) The contract is entered into by the minor when not under the care of a parent or guardian able to provide for the minor or the minor's family.[1]

6713. If, before the contract of a minor is disaffirmed, goods the minor has sold are transferred to another purchaser who bought them in good faith for value and without notice of the transferor's defect of title, the minor cannot recover the goods from an innocent purchaser.[1]

Chapter 3: Contracts in Art, Entertainment, and Professional Sports

6750. (a) This chapter applies to the following types of contracts entered into between an unemancipated minor and a third party on or after January 1, 2000:

(1) A contract pursuant to which a minor is employed or agrees to render artistic or creative services, either directly or through a third party, including, but not limited to, a personal services corporation (loan-out company), or through a casting agency. "Artistic or creative services" includes, but is not limited to, services as an actor, actress, dancer, musician, comedian, singer, stuntperson, voice-over artist, content creator, or other performer or entertainer, or as a songwriter, musical producer or arranger, writer, director, producer, production executive, choreographer,

composer, conductor, or designer.

(2) A contract pursuant to which a minor agrees to purchase, or otherwise secure, sell, lease, license, or otherwise dispose of literary, musical, or dramatic properties, or use of a person's likeness, voice recording, performance, or story of or incidents in the person's life, either tangible or intangible, or any rights therein for use in motion pictures, television, the production of sound recordings in any format now known or hereafter devised, the legitimate or living stage, or otherwise in the entertainment field.

(3) A contract pursuant to which a minor is employed or agrees to render services as a participant or player in a sport.

(b) (1) If a minor is employed or agrees to render services directly for a person or entity, that person or entity shall be considered the minor's employer for purposes of this chapter.

(2) If a minor's services are being rendered through a third-party individual or personal services corporation (loan-out company), the person to whom or entity to which that third party is providing the minor's services shall be considered the minor's empl-oyer for purposes of this chapter.

(3) If a minor renders services as an extra, background performer, or in a similar capacity through an agency or service that provides one or more of those performers for a fee (casting agency), the agency or service shall be considered the minor's employer for the purposes of this chapter.

(c) For purposes of this chapter, the following definitions apply:

(1) "Content creator" means an individual who creates, posts, shares, or otherwise interacts with digital content on an online platform and engages in a direct contractual relationship with third parties. Content creators include, but are not limited to, vloggers, podcasters, social media influencers, and streamers.

(2) "Online platform" means any public-facing internet website, web application, or digital application, including, but not limited to, social media platforms as defined in Section 22675 of the Business and Professions Code, advertising networks, mobile applications, mobile operating systems, search engines, email services, and internet access services.

(d) (1) For purposes of this chapter, the minor's "gross earnings" means the total compensation payable to the minor under the contract or, if the minor's services are being rendered through a third-party individual or personal services corporation (loan-out company), the total compensation payable to that third party for the services of the minor.

(2) Notwithstanding paragraph (1), with respect to contracts pursuant to which a minor is employed or agrees to render services as a musician, singer, songwriter, musical producer, or arranger only, for purposes of this chapter, the minor's "gross earnings" means the total amount paid to the minor pursuant to the contract, including the payment of any advances to the minor pursuant to the contract, but excluding deductions to offset those advances or other expenses incurred by the employer pursuant to the contract, or, if the minor's services are being rendered through a third-party individual or personal services corporation (loan-

out company), the total amount payable to that third party for the services of the minor.[594]

6751. (a) A contract, otherwise valid, of a type described in Section 6750, entered into during minority, cannot be disaffirmed on that ground either during the minority of the person entering into the contract, or at any time thereafter, if the contract has been approved by the superior court in any county in which the minor resides or is employed or in which any party to the contract has its principal office in this state for the transaction of business.
(b) Approval of the court may be given on petition of any party to the contract, after such reasonable notice to all other parties to the contract as is fixed by the court, with opportunity to such other parties to appear and be heard.
(c) Approval of the court given under this section extends to the whole of the contract and all of its terms and provisions, including, but not limited to, any optional or conditional provisions contained in the contract for extension, prolongation, or termination of the term of the contract.
(d) For the purposes of any proceeding under this chapter, a parent or legal guardian, as the case may be, entitled to the physical custody, care, and control of the minor at the time of the proceeding shall be considered the minor's guardian ad litem for the proceeding, unless the court shall determine that appointment of a different individual as guardian ad litem is required in the best interests of the minor.

6752. (a) A parent or guardian entitled to the physical custody, care, and control of a minor who enters into a contract of a type described in Section 6750 shall provide a certified copy of the minor's birth certificate indicating the minor's minority to the other party or parties to the contract and in addition, in the case of a guardian, a certified copy of the court document appointing the person as the minor's legal guardian.
(b) (1) Notwithstanding any other statute, in an order approving a minor's contract of a type described in Section 6750, the court shall require that 15 percent of the minor's gross earnings pursuant to the contract be set aside by the minor's employer, except an employer of a minor for services as an extra, background performer, or in a similar capacity, as described in paragraph (3) of subdivision (b) of Section 6750. These amounts shall be held in trust, in an account or other savings plan, and preserved for the benefit of the minor in accordance with Section 6753.
(2) The court shall require that at least one parent or legal guardian, as the case may be, entitled to the physical custody, care, and control of the minor at the time the order is issued be appointed as trustee of the funds ordered to be set aside in trust for the benefit of the minor, unless the court shall determine that appointment of a different individual, individuals, entity, or entities as trustee or trustees is required in the best interest of the minor.
(3) Within 10 business days after commencement of employment, the trustee or trustees of the funds ordered to be set aside in trust shall provide the minor's employer with a true and accurate photocopy of the trustee's statement pursuant to

Section 6753. Upon presentation of the trustee's statement offered pursuant to this subdivision, the employer shall provide the parent or guardian with a written acknowledgment of receipt of the statement.

(4) The minor's employer shall deposit or disburse the 15 percent of the minor's gross earnings pursuant to the contract within 15 business days after receiving a true and accurate copy of the trustee's statement pursuant to subdivision (c) of Section 6753, a certified copy of the minor's birth certificate, and, in the case of a guardian, a certified copy of the court document appointing the person as the minor's guardian. Notwithstanding any other law, pending receipt of these documents, the minor's employer shall hold, for the benefit of the minor, the 15 percent of the minor's gross earnings pursuant to the contract. This paragraph does not apply to an employer of a minor for services as an extra, background performer, or in a similar capacity, as described in paragraph (3) of subdivision (b) of Section 6750.

(5) When making the initial deposit of funds, the minor's employer shall provide written notification to the financial institution or company that the funds are subject to Section 6753. Upon receipt of the court order, the minor's employer shall provide the financial institution with a copy of the order.

(6) Once the minor's employer deposits the set-aside funds pursuant to Section 6753, in trust, in an account or other savings plan, the minor's employer shall have no further obligation or duty to monitor or account for the funds. The trustee or trustees of the trust shall be the only individual, individuals, entity, or entities with the obligation or duty to monitor and account for those funds once they have been deposited by the minor's employer. The trustee or trustees shall do an annual accounting of the funds held in trust, in an account or other savings plan, in accordance with Sections 16062 and 16063 of the Probate Code.

(7) The court shall have continuing jurisdiction over the trust established pursuant to the order and may at any time, upon petition of the parent or legal guardian, the minor, through the minor's guardian ad litem, or the trustee or trustees, on good cause shown, order that the trust be amended or terminated, notwithstanding the provisions of the declaration of trust. An order amending or terminating a trust may be made only after reasonable notice to the beneficiary and, if the beneficiary is then a minor, to the parent or guardian, if any, and to the trustee or trustees of the funds with opportunity for all parties to appear and be heard.

(8) A parent or guardian entitled to the physical custody, care, and control of the minor shall promptly notify the minor's employer, in writing, of any change in facts that affect the employer's obligation or ability to set aside the funds in accordance with the order, including, but not limited to, a change of financial institution or account number, or the existence of a new or amended order issued pursuant to paragraph (7) amending or terminating the employer's obligations under this section. The written notification shall be accom-

panied by a true and accurate photocopy of the trustee's statement pursuant to Section 6753 and, if applicable, a true and accurate photocopy of the new or amended order.

(9) (A) If a parent, guardian, or trustee fails to provide the minor's employer with a true and accurate photocopy of the trustee's statement pursuant to Section 6753 within 180 days after the commencement of employment, the employer shall forward to The Actors' Fund of America 15 percent of the minor's gross earnings pursuant to the contract, together with the minor's name and, if known, the minor's social security number, birth date, last known address, telephone number, email address, dates of employment, and title of the project on which the minor was employed, and shall notify the parent, guardian, or trustee of that transfer by certified mail to the last known address. Upon receipt of those forwarded funds, The Actors' Fund of America shall become the trustee of those funds and the minor's employer shall have no further obligation or duty to monitor or account for the funds.

(B) The Actors' Fund of America shall make its best efforts to notify the parent, guardian, or trustee of their responsibilities to provide a true and accurate photocopy of the trustee's statement pursuant to Section 6753, and in the case of a guardian, a certified copy of the court document appointing the person as the minor's legal guardian. Within 15 business days after receiving those documents, The Actors' Fund of America shall deposit or disburse the funds as directed by the trustee's statement. When making that deposit or disbursal of the funds, The Actors' Fund of America shall provide to the financial institution notice that the funds are subject to Section 6753 and a copy of each applicable order, and shall thereafter have no further obligation or duty to monitor or account for the funds.

(C) The Actors' Fund of America shall notify each beneficiary of their entitlement to the funds that it holds for the beneficiary within 60 days after the date on which its records indicated that the beneficiary has attained 18 years of age or the date on which it received notice that the minor has been emancipated, by sending that notice to the last known address for the beneficiary or, if it has no specific separate address for the beneficiary, to the beneficiary's parent or guardian.

(c) (1) Notwithstanding any other statute, for any minor's contract of a type described in Section 6750 that is not being submitted for approval by the court pursuant to Section 6751, or for which the court has issued a final order denying approval, 15 percent of the minor's gross earnings pursuant to the contract shall be set aside by the minor's employer, except an employer of a minor for services as an extra, background performer, or in a similar capacity, as described in paragraph (3) of subdivision (b) of Section 6750. These amounts shall be held in trust, in an account or other savings plan, and preserved for the benefit of the minor in accordance with Section 6753. At least one parent or legal guardian, as the case may be, entitled to the physical custody, care, and control of the minor, shall be the trustee of the funds set aside for the benefit of the minor, unless the court, upon petition by the parent or legal guardian, the minor, through the minor's guardian ad litem, or the trustee or trustees of the trust, shall determine that appointment of a different individual, individuals, entity, or entities as trustee or trustees is required in the best interest of the minor.

(2) Within 10 business days of commencement after employment, a parent or guardian, as the case may be, entitled to the physical custody, care, and control of the minor shall provide the minor's employer with a true and accurate photocopy of the trustee's statement pursuant to Section 6753 and in addition, in the case of a guardian, a certified copy of the court document appointing the person as the minor's legal guardian. Upon presentation of the trustee's statement offered pursuant to this subdivision, the employer shall provide the parent or guardian with a written acknowledgment of receipt of the statement.

(3) The minor's employer shall deposit 15 percent of the minor's gross earnings pursuant to the contract within 15 business days of receiving the trustee's statement pursuant to Section 6753, or if the court denies approval of the contract, within 15 business days of receiving a final order denying approval of the contract. Notwithstanding any other statute, pending receipt of the trustee's statement or the final court order, the minor's employer shall hold for the benefit of the minor the 15 percent of the minor's gross earnings pursuant to the contract. When making the initial deposit of funds, the minor's employer shall provide written notification to the financial institution or company that the funds are subject to Section 6753. This paragraph does not apply to an employer of a minor for services as an extra, background performer, or in a similar capacity, as described in paragraph (3) of subdivision (b) of Section 6750.

(4) Once the minor's employer deposits the set-aside funds in trust, in an account or other savings plan pursuant to Section 6753, the minor's employer shall have no further obligation or duty to monitor or account for the funds. The trustee or trustees of the trust shall be the only individual, individuals, entity, or entities with the obligation or duty to monitor and account for those funds once they have been deposited by the minor's employer. The trustee or trustees shall do an annual accounting of the funds held in trust, in an account or other savings plan, in accordance with Sections 16062 and 16063 of the Probate Code.

(5) Upon petition of the parent or legal guardian, the minor, through the minor's guardian ad litem, or the trustee or trustees of the trust, to the superior court in a county in which the minor resides or in which the trust is established, the court may at any time, on good cause shown, order that the trust be amended or terminated, notwithstanding the provisions of the declaration of trust. An order amending or terminating a trust may be made only after reasonable notice to the beneficiary and, if the beneficiary is then a minor, to the parent or guardian, if any, and to the

trustee or trustees of the funds with opportunity for all parties to appear and be heard.

(6) A parent or guardian entitled to the physical custody, care, and control of the minor shall promptly notify the minor's employer in writing of any change in facts that affect the employer's obligation or ability to set aside funds for the benefit of the minor in accordance with this section, including, but not limited to, a change of financial institution or account number, or the existence of a new or amended order issued pursuant to paragraph (5) amending or terminating the employer's obligations under this section. The written notification shall be accompanied by a true and accurate photocopy of the trustee's statement and attachments pursuant to Section 6753 and, if applicable, a true and accurate photocopy of the new or amended order.

(7) (A) If a parent, guardian, or trustee fails to provide the minor's employer with a true and accurate photocopy of the trustee's statement pursuant to Section 6753, within 180 days after commencement of employment, the employer shall forward to The Actors' Fund of America the 15 percent of the minor's gross earnings pursuant to the contract, together with the minor's name and, if known, the minor's social security number, birth date, last known address, telephone number, email address, dates of employment, and the title of the project on which the minor was employed, and shall notify the parent, guardian, or trustee of that transfer by certified mail to the last known address. Upon receipt of those forwarded funds, The Actors' Fund of America shall become the trustee of those funds and the minor's employer shall have no further obligation or duty to monitor or account for the funds.

(B) The Actors' Fund of America shall make best efforts to notify the parent, guardian, or trustee of their responsibilities to provide a true and accurate photocopy of the trustee's statement pursuant to Section 6753 and in the case of a guardian, a certified copy of the court document appointing the person as the minor's legal guardian. After receiving those documents, The Actors' Fund of America shall deposit or disburse the funds as directed by the trustee's statement, and in accordance with Section 6753, within 15 business days. When making that deposit or disbursal of the funds, The Actors' Fund of America shall provide notice to the financial institution that the funds are subject to Section 6753, and shall thereafter have no further obligation or duty to monitor or account for the funds.

(C) The Actors' Fund of America shall notify each beneficiary of their entitlement to the funds that it holds for the beneficiary, within 60 days after the date on which its records indicate that the beneficiary has attained 18 years of age or the date on which it received notice that the minor has been emancipated, by sending that notice to the last known address that it has for the beneficiary, or to the beneficiary's parent or guardian, where it has no specific separate address for the beneficiary.

(d) Where a parent or guardian is entitled to the physical custody, care, and control of a minor who enters into a contract of a type described in Section 6750, the relationship between the parent or guardian and the minor is a fiduciary relationship that is governed by the law of trusts, whether or not a court has issued a formal order to that effect. The parent or guardian acting in a fiduciary relationship, shall, with the earnings and accumulations of the minor under the contract, pay all liabilities incurred by the minor under the contract, including, but not limited to, payments for taxes on all earnings, including taxes on the amounts set aside under subdivisions (b) and (c) of this section, and payments for personal or professional services rendered to the minor or the business related to the contract. This subdivision does not alter any other existing responsibilities of a parent or legal guardian to provide for the support of a minor child.

(e) (1) Except as otherwise provided in this subdivision, The Actors' Fund of America, as trustee of unclaimed set-aside funds, shall manage and administer those funds in the same manner as a trustee under the Probate Code. Notwithstanding the foregoing, The Actors' Fund of America is not required to open separate, segregated individual trust accounts for each beneficiary but may hold the set-aside funds in a single, segregated master account for all beneficiaries, provided it maintains accounting records for each beneficiary's interest in the master account.

(2) The Actors' Fund of America shall have the right to transfer funds from the master account, or from a beneficiary's segregated account to its general account in an amount equal to the beneficiary's balance. The Actors' Fund of America shall have the right to use those funds transferred to its general account to provide programs and services for young performers. This use of the funds does not limit or alter The Actors' Fund of America's obligation to disburse the set-aside funds to the beneficiary, or the beneficiary's parent, guardian, trustee, or estate pursuant to this chapter.

(3) (A) Upon receiving a certified copy of the beneficiary's birth certificate, or United States passport, and a true and accurate photocopy of the trustee's statement pursuant to Section 6753, The Actors' Fund of America shall transfer the beneficiary's balance to the trust account established for the beneficiary.

(B) The Actors' Fund of America shall disburse the set-aside funds to a beneficiary who has attained 18 years of age, after receiving proof of the beneficiary's identity and a certified copy of the beneficiary's birth certificate or United States passport, or to a beneficiary who has been emancipated, after receiving proof of the beneficiary's identity and appropriate documentation evidencing the beneficiary's emancipation.

(C) The Actors' Fund of America shall disburse the set-aside funds to the estate of a deceased beneficiary after receiving appropriate documentation evidencing the death of the beneficiary and the claimant's authority to collect those funds on behalf of the beneficiary.

(f) (1) The beneficiary of an account held by The Actors' Fund of America pursuant to this section shall be entitled to receive imputed interest on the balance in the account for the entire period during which the account is held at a rate equal to the lesser of the federal reserve rate in effect on the last business day of the prior calendar quarter or the national average money market rate as published in the New York Times on the last Sunday of the prior calendar quarter, adjusted quarterly.

(2) The Actors' Fund of America may assess and deduct from the balance in the beneficiary's account reasonable management, administrative, and investment expenses, including beneficiary-specific fees for initial setup, account notifications and account disbursements, and a reasonably allocable share of management, administrative, and investment expenses of the master account. Fees may not be charged to a beneficiary's account during the first year that the account is held by The Actors' Fund of America.

(3) Notwithstanding paragraph (2), the amount paid on any claim made by a beneficiary or the beneficiary's parent or guardian after The Actors' Fund of America receives and holds funds pursuant to this section may not be less than the amount of the funds received plus the imputed interest.

(g) Notwithstanding any provision of this chapter to the contrary, a minor's employer holding set-aside funds under this chapter, which funds remain unclaimed 180 days after the effective date hereof, shall forward those unclaimed funds to The Actors' Fund of America, along with the minor's name and, if known, the minor's social security number, birth date, last known address, telephone number, email address, dates of employment, and the title of the project on which the minor was employed, and shall notify the parent, guardian, or trustee of that transfer by certified mail to the last known address. Upon receipt of those forwarded funds by The Actors' Fund of America, the minor's employer shall have no further obligation or duty to monitor or account for the funds.

(h) All funds received by The Actors' Fund of America pursuant to this section shall be exempt from the application of the Unclaimed Property Law (Title 10 (commencing with Section 1300) of Part 3 of the Code of Civil Procedure), including, but not limited to, Section 1510 of the Code of Civil Procedure.

6753. (a) The trustee or trustees shall establish a trust account, that shall be known as a Coogan Trust Account, pursuant to this section at a bank, savings and loan institution, credit union, brokerage firm, or company registered under the Investment Company Act of 1940, that is located in the State of California, unless a similar trust has been previously established, for the purpose of preserving for the benefit of the minor the portion of the minor's gross earnings pursuant to paragraph (1) of subdivision (b) of Section 6752 or pursuant to paragraph (1) of subdivision (c) of Section 6752. The trustee or trustees shall establish the trust pursuant to this section within seven business days after the minor's contract is signed by the minor, the third-party individual or personal services corporation (loan-out company), and the employer.

(b) Except as otherwise provided in this section, prior to the date on which the beneficiary of the trust attains the age of 18 years or the issuance of a declaration of emancipation of the minor under Section 7122, no withdrawal by the beneficiary or any other individual, individuals, entity, or entities may be made of funds on deposit in trust without written order of the superior court pursuant to paragraph (7) of subdivision (b) or paragraph (5) of subdivision (c) of Section 6752. Upon reaching the age of 18 years, the beneficiary may withdraw the funds on deposit in trust only after providing a certified copy of the beneficiary's birth certificate to the financial institution where the trust is located.

(c) The trustee or trustees shall, within 10 business days after the minor's contract is signed by the minor, the third-party individual or personal services corporation (loan-out company), and the employer, prepare a written statement under penalty of perjury that shall include the name, address, and telephone number of the financial institution, the name of the account, the number of the account, the name of the minor beneficiary, the name of the trustee or trustees of the account, and any additional information needed by the minor's employer to deposit into the account the portion of the minor's gross earnings prescribed by paragraph (1) of subdivision (b) or paragraph (1) of subdivision (c) of Section 6752. The trustee or trustees shall attach to the written statement a true and accurate photocopy of any information received from the financial institution confirming the creation of the account, such as an account agreement, account terms, passbook, or other similar writings.

(d) The trust shall be established in California either with a financial institution that is and remains insured at all times by the Federal Deposit Insurance Corporation (FDIC), the Securities Investor Protection Corporation (SIPC), or the National Credit Union Share Insurance Fund (NCUSIF) or their respective successors, or with a company that is and remains registered under the Investment Company Act of 1940. The trustee or trustees of the trust shall be the only individual, individuals, entity, or entities with the obligation or duty to ensure that the funds remain in trust, in an account or other savings plan insured in accordance with this section, or with a company that is and remains registered under the Investment Company Act of 1940 as authorized by this section.

(e) Upon application by the trustee or trustees to the financial institution or company in which the trust is held, the trust funds shall be handled by the financial institution or company in one or more of the following methods:

(1) The financial institution or company may transfer funds to another account or other savings plan at the same financial institution or company, provided that the funds transferred shall continue to be held in trust, and subject to this chapter.

(2) The financial institution or company may transfer funds to another financial institution or company, provided that the funds transferred shall continue to be held in trust, and subject to this chapter and that the transferring financial institution or company has provided written notification to the financial institution or company to which the funds will be transferred that the funds are subject to this section and

written notice of the requirements of this chapter.

(3) The financial institution or company may use all or a part of the funds to purchase, in the name of and for the benefit of the minor, (A) investment funds offered by a company registered under the Investment Company Act of 1940, provided that if the underlying investments are equity securities, the investment fund is a broad-based index fund or invests broadly across the domestic or a foreign regional economy, is not a sector fund, and has assets under management of at least two hundred fifty million dollars ($250,000,000); or (B) government securities and bonds, certificates of deposit, money market instruments, money market accounts, or mutual funds investing solely in those government securities and bonds, certificates, instruments, and accounts, that are available at the financial institution where the trust fund or other savings plan is held, provided that the funds shall continue to be held in trust and subject to this chapter, those purchases shall have a maturity date on or before the date upon which the minor will attain the age of 18 years, and any proceeds accruing from those purchases shall be redeposited into that account or accounts or used to further purchase any of those or similar securities, bonds, certificates, instruments, funds, or accounts.[108]

PART 4: MEDICAL TREATMENT

enacted by Stats. 1992, Ch. 162, Sec. 10

Chapter 1: Definitions

6900. Unless the provision or context otherwise requires, the definitions in this chapter govern the construction of this part.[1]

6901. "Dental care" means X-ray examination, anesthetic, dental or surgical diagnosis or treatment, and hospital care by a dentist licensed under the Dental Practice Act.[1]

6902. "Medical care" means X-ray examination, anesthetic, medical or surgical diagnosis or treatment, and hospital care under the general or special supervision and upon the advice of or to be rendered by a physician and surgeon licensed under the Medical Practice Act. [1]

6903. "Parent or guardian" means either parent if both parents have legal custody, or the parent or person having legal custody, or the guardian, of a minor.[1]

6904. "Vision care" means the diagnosis, prevention, treatment, and management of disorders, diseases, and dysfunctions of the visual system and the provision of habilitative or rehabilitative optometric services by an optometrist licensed pursuant to Article 1 (commencing with Section 3000) of Chapter 7 of Division 2 of the Business and Professions Code.[545]

Chapter 2: Medical Treatment

6910. The parent, guardian, or caregiver of a minor who is a relative of the minor and who may authorize medical care and dental care under Section 6550, may authorize in writing an adult into whose care a minor has been entrusted to consent to medical care or dental care, or both, for the minor.

6911. (a) Upon application by a minor, the court may summarily grant consent for medical care or dental care or both for the minor if the court determines all of the following:

(1) The minor is 16 years of age or older and resides in this state.

(2) The consent of a parent or guardian is necessary to permit the medical care or dental care or both, and the minor has no parent or guardian available to give the consent.

(b) No fee may be charged for proceedings under this section.[1]

Chapter 3: Consent by Minor

6920. Subject to the limitations provided in this chapter, notwithstanding any other provision of law, a minor may consent to the matters provided in this chapter, and the consent of the minor's parent or guardian is not necessary. [1]

6921. A consent given by a minor under this chapter is not subject to disaffirmance because of minority.[1]

6922. (a) A minor may consent to the minor's medical care, vision care, or dental care if all of the following conditions are satisfied:

(1) The minor is 15 years of age or older.

(2) The minor is living separate and apart from the minor's parents or guardian, whether with or without the parent's or guardian's consent and regardless of the duration of the separate residence.

(3) The minor is managing the minor's own financial affairs, regardless of the source of the minor's income.

(b) The parents or guardian are not liable for medical care, vision care, or dental care provided pursuant to this section.

(c) A physician and surgeon, optometrist, or dentist may, with or without the consent of the minor patient, advise the minor's parent or guardian of the treatment given or needed if the physician and surgeon, optometrist, or dentist has reason to know, on the basis of the information given by the minor, the whereabouts of the parent or guardian.[546]

6924. (a) As used in this section:

(1) "Mental health treatment or counseling services" means the provision of mental health treatment or counseling on an outpatient basis by any of the following:

(A) A governmental agency.

(B) A person or agency having a contract with a governmental agency to provide the services.

(C) An agency that receives funding from community united funds.

(D) A runaway house or crisis resolution center.

(E) A professional person, as defined in paragraph (2).

(2) "Professional person" means either of the following:

(A) A professional person as defined in Section 124260 of the Health and Safety Code.

(B) The chief administrator of an agency referred to in paragraph (1) or (3).

(3) "Residential shelter services" means any of the following:

(A) The provision of residential and other support services to minors on a temporary or emergency basis in a facility that services only minors by a governmental agency, a person or agency having a contract with a governmental agency to provide these services, an agency that receives funding from community funds, or a licensed community care facility or crisis resolution center.

(B) The provision of other support services on a temporary or emergency basis by any professional person as defined in paragraph (2).

(b) A minor who is 12 years of age or older may consent to mental health treatment or counseling on an outpatient basis, or to residential shelter services, if the minor, in the opinion of the attending professional person, is mature enough to participate intelligently in the outpatient services or residential shelter services.

(c) A professional person offering residential shelter services, whether as an individual or as a representative of an entity specified in paragraph (3) of subdivision (a), shall make their best efforts to notify the parent or guardian of the provision of services.

(d) The mental health treatment or counseling of a minor authorized by this section shall include involvement of the minor's parent or guardian unless the professional person who is treating or counseling the minor, after consulting with the minor, determines that the involvement would be inappropriate. The professional person who is treating or counseling the minor shall state in the client record whether and when the person attempted to contact the minor's parent or guardian, and whether the attempt to contact was successful or unsuccessful, or the reason why, in the professional person's opinion, it would be inappropriate to contact the minor's parent or guardian.

(e) The minor's parents or guardian are not liable for payment for mental health treatment or counseling services provided pursuant to this section unless the parent or guardian participates in the mental health treatment or counseling, and then only for services rendered with the participation of the parent or guardian. The minor's parents or guardian are not liable for payment for any residential shelter services provided pursuant to this section unless the parent or guardian consented to the provision of those services.

(f) This section does not authorize a minor to receive convulsive therapy or psychosurgery as defined in subdivisions (f) and (g) of Section 5325 of the Welfare and Institutions Code, or psychotropic drugs without the consent of the minor's parent or guardian.

(g) This section shall become operative on July 1, 2024.[560]

6925. (a) A minor may consent to medical care related to the prevention or treatment of pregnancy.

(b) This section does not authorize a minor to be sterilized without the consent of the minor's parent or guardian.[603]

6926. (a) A minor who is 12 years of age or older and who may have come into contact with an infectious, contagious, or communicable disease may consent to medical care related to the diagnosis or treatment of the disease, if the disease or condition is one that is required by law or regulation adopted pursuant to law to

be reported to the local health officer, or is a related sexually transmitted disease, as may be determined by the State Public Health Officer.
(b) A minor who is 12 years of age or older may consent to medical care related to the prevention of a sexually transmitted disease.
(c) The minor's parents or guardian are not liable for payment for medical care provided pursuant to this section.[224]

6927. A minor who is 12 years of age or older and who is alleged to have been raped may consent to medical care related to the diagnosis or treatment of the condition and the collection of medical evidence with regard to the alleged rape.[1]

6928. (a) "Sexually assaulted" as used in this section includes, but is not limited to, conduct coming within Section 261, 286, or 287 of the Penal Code.
(b) A minor who is alleged to have been sexually assaulted may consent to medical care related to the diagnosis and treatment of the condition, and the collection of medical evidence with regard to the alleged sexual assault.
(c) The professional person providing medical treatment shall attempt to contact the minor's parent or guardian and shall note in the minor's treatment record the date and time the professional person attempted to contact the parent or guardian and whether the attempt was successful or unsuccessful. This subdivision does not apply if the professional person reasonably believes that the minor's parent or guardian committed the sexual assault on the minor.[376]

6929. (a) As used in this section:
(1) "Counseling" means the provision of counseling services by a provider under a contract with the state or a county to provide alcohol or drug abuse counseling services pursuant to Part 2 (commencing with Section 5600) of Division 5 of the Welfare and Institutions Code or pursuant to Division 10.5 (commencing with Section 11750) of the Health and Safety Code.
(2) "Drug or alcohol" includes, but is not limited to, any substance listed in any of the following:
(A) Section 380 or 381 of the Penal Code.
(B) Division 10 (commencing with Section 11000) of the Health and Safety Code.
(C) Subdivision (f) of Section 647 of the Penal Code.
(3) "LAAM" means levoalphacetylmethadol as specified in paragraph (10) of subdivision (c) of Section 11055 of the Health and Safety Code.
(4) "Professional person" means a physician and surgeon, registered nurse, psychologist, clinical social worker, professional clinical counselor, marriage and family therapist, registered marriage and family therapist intern when appropriately employed and supervised pursuant to Section 4980.43 of the Business and Professions Code, psychological assistant when appropriately employed and supervised pursuant to Section 2913 of the Business and Professions Code, associate clinical social worker when appropriately employed and supervised pursuant to Section 4996.18 of the Business and Professions Code, or registered clinical counselor intern when appropriately employed and supervised pursuant to Section 4999.42 of the Business and

Professions Code.

(b) A minor who is 12 years of age or older may consent to medical care and counseling relating to the diagnosis and treatment of a drug- or alcohol-related problem.

(c) The treatment plan of a minor authorized by this section shall include the involvement of the minor's parent or guardian, if appropriate, as determined by the professional person or treatment facility treating the minor. The professional person providing medical care or counseling to a minor shall state in the minor's treatment record whether and when the professional person attempted to contact the minor's parent or guardian, and whether the attempt to contact the parent or guardian was successful or unsuccessful, or the reason why, in the opinion of the professional person, it would not be appropriate to contact the minor's parent or guardian.

(d) The minor's parent or guardian is not liable for payment for care provided to a minor pursuant to this section, except that if the minor's parent or guardian participates in a counseling program pursuant to this section, the parent or guardian is liable for the cost of the services provided to the minor and the parent or guardian.

(e) (1) This section does not authorize a minor to receive replacement narcotic therapy, in a program licensed pursuant to Article 1 (commencing with Section 11839) of Chapter 10 of Part 2 of Division 10.5 of the Health and Safety Code, without the consent of the minor's parent or guardian.

(2) Notwithstanding paragraph (1), a minor 16 years of age or older may consent to receive medications for opioid use disorder from a licensed narcotic treatment program as replacement narcotic therapy without the consent of the minor's parent or guardian only if, and to the extent, expressly permitted by federal law.

(f) It is the intent of the Legislature that the state shall respect the right of a parent or legal guardian to seek medical care and counseling for a drug- or alcohol-related problem of a minor child when the child does not consent to the medical care and counseling, and nothing in this section shall be construed to restrict or eliminate this right.

(g) Notwithstanding any other law, when a parent or legal guardian has sought the medical care and counseling for a drug- or alcohol-related problem of a minor child, the physician and surgeon shall disclose medical information concerning the care to the minor's parent or legal guardian upon the parent's or guardian's request, even if the minor child does not consent to disclosure, without liability for the disclosure.[561]

6929.1. Notwithstanding any other law, a minor 16 years of age or older may consent to opioid use disorder treatment that uses buprenorphine at a physician's office, clinic, or health facility, by a licensed physician and surgeon or other health care provider acting within the scope of their practice, whether or not the minor also has the consent of their parent or guardian.[562]

6930. (a) A minor who is 12 years of age or older and who states that the minor is injured as a result of intimate partner violence may consent to medical care related to the diagnosis or treatment of the injury and the collection of medical evidence with regard to the alleged intimate partner violence.

(b) (1) For purposes of this section, "intimate partner violence" means an intentional or reckless infliction of bodily harm that is perpetrated by a person with whom the minor has or has had a sexual, dating, or spousal relationship.

(2) This section does not apply when a minor is an alleged victim of rape, as defined in Section 261 of the Penal Code, in which case Section 6927 shall apply, and does not apply when a minor is alleged to have been sexually assaulted, as described in Section 6928, in which case that section shall apply.

(c) If the health practitioner providing treatment believes that the injuries described in subdivision (a) require a report pursuant to Section 11160 of the Penal Code, the health practitioner shall do both of the following:

(1) Inform the minor that the report will be made.

(2) Attempt to contact the minor's parent or guardian and inform them of the report. The health practitioner shall note in the minor's treatment record the date and time of the attempt to contact the parent or guardian and whether the attempt was successful or unsuccessful. This paragraph does not apply if the health practitioner reasonably believes that the minor's parent or guardian committed the intimate partner violence on the minor.[497]

PART 5: ENLISTMENT IN ARMED FORCES

enacted by Stats. 1992, Ch. 162, Sec. 10

6950. (a) Upon application by a minor, the court may summarily grant consent for enlistment by the minor in the armed forces of the United States if the court determines all of the following:

(1) The minor is 16 years of age or older and resides in this state.

(2) The consent of a parent or guardian is necessary to permit the enlistment, and the minor has no parent or guardian available to give the consent.

(b) No fee may be charged for proceedings under this section.[1]

PART 6: EMANCIPATION OF MINORS LAW

enacted by Stats. 1992, Ch. 162, Sec. 10

Chapter 1: General Provisions

7000. This part may be cited as the Emancipation of Minors Law.[1]

7001. It is the purpose of this part to provide a clear statement defining emancipation and its consequences and to permit an emancipated minor to obtain a court declaration of the minor's status. This part is not intended to affect the status of minors who may become emancipated under the decisional case law that was in effect before the enactment of Chapter 1059 of the Statutes of 1978.[1]

7002. A person under the age of 18 years is an emancipated minor if any of the following conditions is satisfied:

(a) The person has entered into a valid marriage, or has established a valid domestic partnership, regardless of whether the marriage or the domestic partnership has been dissolved.

(b) The person is on active duty with the Armed Forces of the United States.

(c) The person has received a declaration of emancipation pursuant to Section 7122.[385]

Chapter 2: Effect of Emancipation

7050. An emancipated minor shall be considered as being an adult for the following purposes:

(a) The minor's right to support by the minor's parents.

(b) The right of the minor's parents to the minor's earnings and to control the minor.

(c) The application of Sections 300 and 601 of the Welfare and Institutions Code.

(d) Ending all vicarious or imputed liability of the minor's parents or guardian for the minor's torts. Nothing in this section affects any liability of a parent, guardian, spouse, or employer imposed by the Vehicle Code, or any vicarious liability that arises from an agency relationship.

(e) The minor's capacity to do any of the following:

(1) Consent to medical, dental, or psychiatric care, without parental consent, knowledge, or liability.

(2) Enter into a binding contract or give a delegation of power.

(3) Buy, sell, lease, encumber, exchange, or transfer an interest in real or personal property, including, but not limited to, shares of stock in a domestic or foreign corporation or a membership in a nonprofit corporation.

(4) Sue or be sued in the minor's own name.

(5) Compromise, settle, arbitrate, or otherwise adjust a claim, action, or proceeding by or against the minor.

(6) Make or revoke a will.

(7) Make a gift, outright or in trust.

(8) Convey or release contingent or expectant interests in property, including marital property rights and any right of survivorship incident to joint tenancy, and consent to a transfer, encumbrance, or gift of marital property.

(9) Exercise or release the minor's powers as done of a power of appointment unless the creating instrument otherwise provides.

(10) Create for the minor's own benefit or for the benefit of others a revocable or irrevocable trust.

(11) Revoke a revocable trust.

(12) Elect to take under or against a will.

(13) Renounce or disclaim any interest acquired by testate or intestate succession or by inter vivo transfer, including exercise of the right to surrender the right to revoke a revocable trust.

(14) Make an election referred to in Section 13502 of, or an election and agreement referred to in Section 13503 of, the Probate Code.

(15) Establish the minor's own residence.

(16) Apply for a work permit pursuant to Section 49110 of the Education Code without the request of the minor's parents.

(17) Enroll in a school or college.[1]

7051. An insurance contract entered into by an emancipated minor has the same effect as if it were entered into by an adult and, with respect to that contract, the minor has the same rights, duties, and liabilities as an adult.[1]

7052. With respect to shares of stock in a domestic or foreign corporation held by an emancipated minor, a membership in a nonprofit corporation held by an emancipated minor, or other property held by an emancipated minor, the minor may do all of the following:
(a) Vote in person, and give proxies to exercise any voting rights, with respect to the shares, membership, or property.
(b) Waive notice of any meeting or give consent to the holding of any meeting.
(c) Authorize, ratify, approve, or confirm any action that could be taken by shareholders, members, or property owners.[1]

Chapter 3: Court Declaration of Emancipation

Article 1: General Provisions

7110. It is the intent of the Legislature that proceedings under this part be as simple and inexpensive as possible. To that end, the Judicial Council is requested to prepare and distribute to the clerks of the superior courts appropriate forms for the proceedings that are suitable for use by minors acting as their own counsel.[1]

7111. The issuance of a declaration of emancipation does not entitle the minor to any benefits under Division 9 (commencing with Section 10000) of the Welfare and Institutions Code which would not otherwise accrue to an emancipated minor.[1]

Article 2: Procedure for Declaration

7120. (a) A minor may petition the superior court of the county in which the minor resides or is temporarily domiciled for a declaration of emancipation.
(b) The petition shall set forth with specificity all of the following facts:
(1) The minor is at least 14 years of age.
(2) The minor willingly lives separate and apart from the minor's parents or guardian with the consent or acquiescence of the minor's parents or guardian.
(3) The minor is managing their own financial affairs. As evidence of this, the minor shall complete and attach a declaration of income and expenses as provided in Judicial Council form FL-150.
(4) The source of the minor's income is not derived from any activity declared to be a crime by the laws of this state or the laws of the United States.

7121. (a) Before the petition for a declaration of emancipation is heard, notice the court determines is reasonable shall be given to the minor's parents, guardian, or other person entitled to the custody of the minor, or proof shall be made to the court that their addresses are unknown or that for other reasons the notice cannot be given.
(b) The clerk of the court shall also notify the local child support agency of the county in which the matter is to be heard of the proceeding. If the minor is a ward of the court, notice shall be given to the probation department. If the child is a dependent child of the court, notice shall be given to the county welfare department.
(c) The notice shall include a form whereby the minor's parents, guardian, or other person entitled to the custody of the minor may give their written

consent to the petitioner's emancipation. The notice shall include a warning that a court may void or rescind the declaration of emancipation and the parents may become liable for support and medical insurance coverage pursuant to Chapter 2 (commencing with Section 4000) of Part 2 of Division 9 and Sections 17400, 17402, 17404, and 17422.[102]

7122. (a) The court shall sustain the petition if it finds that the minor is a person described by Section 7120 and that emancipation would not be contrary to the minor's best interest.
(b) If the petition is sustained, the court shall forthwith issue a declaration of emancipation, which shall be filed by the clerk of the court.
(c) A declaration is conclusive evidence that the minor is emancipated.[86]

7123. (a) If the petition is denied, the minor has a right to file a petition for a writ of mandate.
(b) If the petition is sustained, the parents or guardian have a right to file a petition for a writ of mandate if they have appeared in the proceeding and opposed the granting of the petition.[1]

Article 3: Voiding or Rescinding Declaration

7130. (a) A declaration of emancipation obtained by fraud or by the withholding of material information is voidable.
(b) A declaration of emancipation of a minor who is indigent and has no means of support is subject to rescission.[1]

7131. A petition to void a declaration of emancipation on the ground that the declaration was obtained by fraud or by the withholding of material information may be filed by any person or by any public or private agency. The petition shall be filed in the court that made the declaration.[1]

7132. (a) A petition to rescind a declaration of emancipation on the ground that the minor is indigent and has no means of support may be filed by the minor declared emancipated, by the minor's conservator, or by the district attorney of the county in which the minor resides. The petition shall be filed in the county in which the minor or the conservator resides.
(b) The minor may be considered indigent if the minor's only source of income is from public assistance benefits. The court shall consider the impact of the rescission of the declaration of emancipation on the minor and shall find the rescission of the declaration of emancipation will not be contrary to the best interest of the minor before granting the order to rescind.[32]

7133. (a) Before a petition under this article is heard, notice the court determines is reasonable shall be given to the minor's parents or guardian, or proof shall be made to the court that their addresses are unknown or that for other reasons the notice cannot be given.
(b) The notice to parents shall state that if the declaration of emancipation is voided or rescinded, the parents may be liable to provide support and medical insurance coverage for the child pursuant to Chapter 2 (commencing with Section 4000) of Part 2 of Division 9 of this code and Sections 11350, 11350.1, 11475.1, and 11490 of the Welfare and Institutions Code.

(c) No liability accrues to a parent or guardian not given actual notice, as a result of voiding or rescinding the declaration of emancipation, until that parent or guardian is given actual notice.[33]

7134. If the petition is sustained, the court shall forthwith issue an order voiding or rescinding the declaration of emancipation, which shall be filed by the clerk of the court.[87]

7135. Voiding or rescission of the declaration of emancipation does not alter any contractual obligation or right or any property right or interest that arose during the period that the declaration was in effect.[1]

Article 4: Identification Cards and Information

7140. On application of a minor declared emancipated under this chapter, the Department of Motor Vehicles shall enter identifying information in its law enforcement computer network, and the fact of emancipation shall be stated on the department's identification card issued to the emancipated minor.[1]

7141. A person who, in good faith, has examined a minor's identification card and relies on a minor's representation that the minor is emancipated, has the same rights and obligations as if the minor were in fact emancipated at the time of the representation.[1]

7142. No public entity or employee is liable for any loss or injury resulting directly or indirectly from false or inaccurate information contained in the Department of Motor Vehicles records system or identification cards as provided in this part.[1]

7143. If a declaration of emancipation is voided or rescinded, notice shall be sent immediately to the Department of Motor Vehicles which shall remove the information relating to emancipation in its law enforcement computer network. Any identification card issued stating emancipation shall be invalidated.[1]

DIVISION 12: PARENT AND CHILD RELATIONSHIP

ENACTED BY STATS. 1992, CH. 162, SEC. 10.
SECTION 7500 – 7962

PART 1: EMANCIPATION OF MINORS LAW

amended by Stats. 1993, Ch. 219, Sec. 160

7500. (a) The mother of an unemancipated minor child, and the father, if presumed to be the father under Section 7611, are equally entitled to the services and earnings of the child.
(b) If one parent is dead, is unable or refuses to take custody, or has abandoned the child, the other parent is entitled to the services and earnings of the child.
(c) This section shall not apply to any services or earnings of an unemancipated minor child related to a contract of a type described in Section 6750.

7501. (a) A parent entitled to the custody of a child has a right to change the residence of the child, subject to the power of the court to restrain a removal that would prejudice the rights or welfare of the child.
(b) It is the intent of the Legislature to affirm the decision in *In re Marriage of Burgess* (1996) 13 Cal. 4th 25, and to declare that ruling to be the public policy and law of this state.[109]

7502. The parent, as such, has no control over the property of the child.[36]

7503. The employer of a minor shall pay the earnings of the minor to the minor until the parent or guardian entitled to the earnings gives the employer notice that the parent or guardian claims the earnings.[37]

7504. The parent, whether solvent or insolvent, may relinquish to the child the right of controlling the child and receiving the child's earnings. Abandonment by the parent is presumptive evidence of that relinquishment.[38]

7505. The authority of a parent ceases on any of the following:
(a) The appointment, by a court, of a guardian of the person of the child.
(b) The marriage of the child.
(c) The child attaining the age of majority.[39]

7506. Where a child, after attaining the age of majority, continues to serve and to be supported by the parent, neither party is entitled to compensation, in the absence of an agreement for the compensation.[40]

7507. The abuse of parental authority is the subject of judicial cognizance in a civil action brought by the child, or by the child's relative within the third degree, or by the supervisors of the county where the child resides; and when the abuse is established, the child may be freed from the dominion of the parent, and the duty of support and education enforced.[41]

PART 2: PRESUMPTION CONCERNING CHILD OF MARRIAGE AND GENETIC TESTING TO DETERMINE PARENTAGE

Heading of Part 2 amended by Stats. 2018, Ch. 876, Sec. 3

Chapter 1: Child of Wife Cohabiting with Husband

7540. (a) Except as provided in Section 7541, the child of spouses who cohabited at the time of conception and birth is conclusively presumed to be a child of the marriage.
(b) The conclusive marital presumption in subdivision (a) does not apply if the court determines that the husband of the woman who gave birth was impotent or sterile at the time of conception and that the child was not conceived through assisted reproduction.[389]

7541. (a) If the court finds that the spouse who is a presumed parent under Section 7540 is not a genetic parent of the child pursuant to Chapter 2 (commencing with Section 7550), the question of parentage shall be resolved in accordance with all other applicable provisions of this division, including, but not limited to, Section 7612.
(b) An action to challenge the parentage of the spouse who is a presumed parent under Section 7540 shall be filed and served not later than two years from the child's date of birth and may only be filed by any of the following:
(1) By either spouse.
(2) By a person who is a presumed parent under Section 7611 or by the child, through or by the child's guardian ad litem, to establish the parentage of the person who is a presumed parent under Section 7611.
(c) The petition or motion to challenge a presumption under Section 7540 pursuant to this section shall be supported by a declaration under oath submitted by the moving party stating the factual basis for placing the issue of parentage before the court.
(d) Genetic testing may not be used to challenge parentage, in either of the following cases:
(1) A case that reached final judgment of parentage on or before September 30, 1980.
(2) A case challenging the parentage of a spouse who is a parent pursuant to Section 7962 or subdivision (a) of Section 7613, except to resolve a dispute regarding whether the child was conceived through assisted reproduction.

Chapter 2: Genetic Testing to Determine Parentage

7550. This chapter shall govern both of the following:
(a) The genetic testing of a person who either voluntarily submits to genetic testing or is ordered to submit to genetic testing pursuant to an order of a court or local child support agency.
(b) The use of genetic testing in a proceeding to determine parentage.[390]

7550.5. The following definitions shall apply to this chapter:
(a) "Combined relationship index" means the product of all tested relationship indices.
(b) "Ethnic or racial group" means, for the purpose of genetic testing, a recognized group that a person identifies as

the person's ancestry, or part of the ancestry, or that is identified by other information.

(c) "Genetic testing" means any genetic testing that complies with Section 7552.

(d) "Hypothesized genetic relationship" means an asserted genetic relationship between a person and a child.

(e) "Probability of parentage" means, for the ethnic or racial group to which a person alleged to be a parent belongs, the probability that a hypothesized genetic relationship is supported, compared to the probability that a genetic relationship is supported between the child and a random person of the ethnic or racial group used in the hypothesized genetic relationship, expressed as a percentage incorporating the combined relationship index and a prior probability.

(f) "Relationship index" means a likelihood ratio that compares the probability of a genetic marker given a hypothesized genetic relationship and the probability of the genetic marker given a genetic relationship between the child and a random person of the ethnic or racial group used in the hypothesized genetic relationship.[391]

7551. (a) Except as provided in subdivisions (b) and (c), in a civil action or proceeding in which parentage is a relevant fact, the court may, upon its own initiative or upon suggestion made by or on behalf of any person who is involved, and shall upon motion of any party to the action or proceeding made at a time so as not to delay the proceedings unduly, order the woman who gave birth, the child, and the alleged genetic parent to submit to genetic testing.

(b) (1) Genetic testing shall not be used for any of the following purposes:

(A) To challenge the parentage of a person who is a parent pursuant to subdivision (a) of Section 7613, except to resolve a dispute whether the child was conceived through assisted reproduction.

(B) To challenge the parentage of a person who is a parent pursuant to Section 7962, except to resolve a dispute whether the gestational carrier surrogate is a genetic parent.

(C) To establish the parentage of a person who is a donor pursuant to Section 7613, except to resolve a dispute whether the child was conceived through assisted reproduction.

(2) If the child has a presumed parent pursuant to Section 7540, a motion for genetic testing is governed by Section 7541.

(3) If the child has a parent whose parentage has been previously established in a judgment, a request for genetic testing shall be governed by Section 7647.7.

(4) A court shall not order genetic testing if the genetic testing would be used to establish the parentage of a person who is prohibited under this division from establishing parentage based on evidence of genetic testing.

(c) A court shall not order in utero genetic testing.

(d) In any case under this division in which genetic testing is ordered, the following shall apply:

(1) If a party refuses to submit to genetic testing, the court may resolve the question of parentage against that party or enforce its order if the rights of others and the interests of justice so require.

(2) The refusal of a party to submit to

genetic testing is admissible in evidence in any proceeding to determine parentage.

(3) If two or more persons are subject to court-ordered genetic testing, the court may order that the testing be completed concurrently or sequentially.

(4) Genetic testing of a woman who gave birth to a child is not a condition precedent to the testing of the child and a person whose genetic parentage of the child is being determined. If the woman is unavailable for genetic testing, the court may order genetic testing of the child and each person whose genetic parentage of the child is at issue.

(5) An order under this division for genetic testing is enforceable by contempt.[564]

7551.5. All hospitals, local child support agencies, welfare offices, and family courts shall facilitate genetic tests for purposes of enforcement of this chapter. This may include having a health care professional available for purposes of extracting samples to be used for genetic testing.[75]

7552. (a) Genetic testing shall be of a type reasonably relied on by experts in the field of genetic testing and performed in a testing laboratory accredited by either of the following:

(1) The AABB, formerly known as the American Association of Blood Banks, or a successor organization.

(2) An accrediting body designated by the Secretary of the United States Department of Health and Human Services.

(b) A specimen used in genetic testing may consist of a sample or a combination of samples of blood, buccal cells, bone, hair, or other body tissue or fluid. The specimen used in the testing need not be of the same kind for each person undergoing genetic testing.

(c) Based on the ethnic or racial group of a person undergoing genetic testing, a testing laboratory shall determine the databases from which to select frequencies for use in calculating a relationship index. If a person or a local child support agency object to the laboratory's choice, the following rules shall apply:

(1) Not later than 30 days after receipt of the report of the test, the objecting person or local child support agency may request the court to require the laboratory to recalculate the relationship index using an ethnic or racial group different from that used by the laboratory.

(2) The person or local child support agency objecting to the choice of laboratories under this subdivision shall do either of the following:

(A) If the requested frequencies are not available to the laboratory for the ethnic or racial group requested, provide the requested frequencies compiled in a manner recognized by accrediting bodies.

(B) Engage another laboratory to perform the calculations.

(3) The laboratory may use its own statistical estimate if there is a question of which ethnic or racial group is appropriate. The laboratory shall calculate the frequencies using statistics, if available, for any other ethnic or racial group requested.

(d) If, after recalculation of the relationship index pursuant to subdivision (c) using a different ethnic or racial group, genetic testing does not identify a person as a genetic parent of the child, the court may require a person who has been tested to submit to additional genetic testing to identify a genetic parent.[392]

7552.5. (a) A copy of the results of all genetic testing performed under Section 7551 or 7558 shall be served upon all parties, by any method of service authorized under Chapter 5 (commencing with Section 1010) of Title 14 of Part 2 of the Code of Civil Procedure except personal service, no later than 20 days prior to a hearing in which the genetic test results may be admitted into evidence. The genetic test results shall be accompanied by a declaration under penalty of perjury of the custodian of records or other qualified employee of the laboratory that conducted the genetic tests, stating in substance each of the following:

(1) The declarant is the duly authorized custodian of the records or other qualified employee of the laboratory, and has authority to certify the records.

(2) A statement that establishes in detail the chain of custody of all genetic samples collected, including the date on which the genetic sample was collected, the identity of each person from whom a genetic sample was collected, the identity of the person who performed or witnessed the collecting of the genetic samples and packaged them for transmission to the laboratory, the date on which the genetic samples were received by the laboratory, the identity of the person who unpacked the samples and forwarded them to the person who performed the laboratory analysis of the genetic sample, and the identification and qualifications of all persons who performed the laboratory analysis and published the results.

(3) A statement that establishes that the procedures used by the laboratory to conduct the tests for which the test results are attached are used in the laboratory's ordinary course of business to ensure accuracy and proper identification of genetic samples.

(4) The genetic test results were prepared at or near the time of completion of the genetic tests by personnel of the business qualified to perform genetic tests in the ordinary course of business.

(b) The genetic test results shall be admitted into evidence at the hearing or trial to establish parentage, without the need for foundation testimony of authenticity and accuracy, unless a written objection to the genetic test results is filed with the court and served on all other parties, by a party no later than five days prior to the hearing or trial in which parentage is at issue.

(c) If a written objection is filed with the court and served on all parties within the time specified in subdivision (b), experts appointed by the court shall be called by the court as witnesses to testify to their findings and are subject to cross-examination by the parties.[393]

7553. (a) The compensation of each expert witness appointed by the court shall be fixed at a reasonable amount. It shall be paid as the court shall order. Except as provided in subdivision (b), the court may order that it be paid by the parties in the proportions and at the times the court prescribes, or that the proportion of any party be paid by the county, and that, after payment by the parties or the county or both, all or part or none of it be taxed as costs in the action or proceeding.

(b) If the expert witness is appointed for the court's needs, the compensation shall be paid by the court.[262]

7554. (a) If the woman who gave birth to the child is the only other person who is a parent or has a claim to parentage of the child under this division, the court shall find the person who is the alleged father or genetic parent who is not a donor under Section 7613 to be a parent of the child if the person meets any of the following:

(1) Is identified pursuant to Section 7555 as a genetic parent of the child and the identification is not successfully challenged.

(2) Admits parentage in a pleading, when making an appearance, or during a hearing, the court accepts the admission, and the court determines that the person is a genetic parent of the child.

(3) Declines to submit to genetic testing ordered by the court or a local child support agency, in which case, the court may find that the person is a parent of the child even if the person denies a genetic relationship with the child.

(4) Is in default after service of process and the court determines the person to be a genetic parent of the child.

(5) Is neither identified nor excluded as a genetic parent by genetic testing and, based on other evidence, the court determines the person to be a genetic parent of the child.

(b) If more than one person other than the woman who gave birth asserts a claim under this division to be the child's parent, parentage shall be determined under provisions of this division.

7555. (a) Subject to a challenge under subdivision (b), a person is identified under this part as a genetic parent of a child if genetic testing complies with this part and the results of the testing disclose both of the following:

(1) The person has at least a 99 percent probability of parentage, using a prior probability of 0.50, as calculated by using the combined relationship index obtained in the testing.

(2) A combined relationship index of at least 100 to 1.

(b) A person identified pursuant to subdivision (a) as a genetic parent of the child may challenge the genetic testing results only by other genetic testing satisfying the requirements of this chapter that either excludes the person as a genetic parent of the child or identifies another person as a possible genetic parent of the child other than the woman who gave birth to the child or the person challenging parentage.

(c) If more than one person, other than the woman who gave birth to the child, is identified by genetic testing as a possible genetic parent of the child, the court shall order each person to submit to further genetic testing to identify a genetic parent.[394]

7556. This part applies to criminal actions subject to the following limitations and provisions:

(a) An order for genetic testing shall be made only upon application of a party or on the court's initiative.

(b) The compensation of the experts, other than an expert witness appointed by the court for the court's needs, shall be paid by the county under order of court. The compensation of an expert witness appointed for the court's needs shall be paid by the court.

(c) The court may direct a verdict of

acquittal if the person is found not to be a genetic parent pursuant to Section 7555, otherwise the case shall be submitted for determination upon all the evidence.[395]

7557. Nothing in this part prevents a party to an action or proceeding from producing other expert evidence on the matter covered by this part; but, where other expert witnesses are called by a party to the action or proceeding, their fees shall be paid by the party calling them and only ordinary witness fees shall be taxed as costs in the action or proceeding.[1]

7558. (a) This section applies only to cases where support enforcement services are being provided by the local child support agency pursuant to Section 17400.

(b) In any civil action or proceeding in which parentage is a relevant fact, and in which the issue of parentage is contested, the local child support agency may issue an administrative order requiring the mother, child, and the alleged father to submit to genetic testing if any of the following conditions exist:

(1) The person alleging parentage has signed a statement under penalty of perjury that sets forth facts that establish a reasonable possibility that the person is the child's genetic parent.

(2) The person denying parentage has signed a statement under penalty of perjury that sets forth facts that establish a reasonable possibility that the person is not a genetic parent of the child.

(3) The alleged father has filed an answer in the action or proceeding in which parentage is a relevant fact and has requested that genetic tests be performed.

(4) The woman who gave birth to the child and the alleged father agree in writing to submit to genetic tests.

(c) Notwithstanding subdivision (b), the local child support agency may not order a person to submit to genetic tests in any of the following instances:

(1) The person has been found to have good cause for failure to cooperate in the determination of parentage pursuant to Section 11477 of the Welfare and Institutions Code.

(2) A case in which more than one person other than the woman who gave birth asserts a claim under this division to be the child's parent.

(3) A case involving a child conceived through assisted reproduction.

(d) The local child support agency shall pay the costs of any genetic tests that are ordered under subdivision (b), subject to the county obtaining a court order for reimbursement from the alleged father if parentage is established pursuant to Section 7553.

(e) This section does not prohibit a person who has been ordered by the local child support agency to submit to genetic tests pursuant to this section from filing a notice of motion with the court in the action or proceeding in which parentage is a relevant fact seeking relief from the local child support agency's order to submit to genetic tests. In that event, the court shall resolve the issue of whether genetic tests should be ordered as provided in Section 7551. When a person refuses to submit to the tests after receipt of the administrative order pursuant to this section and fails to seek relief from the court from the administrative order either prior to the scheduled tests or within 10 days after the tests are scheduled, the court may resolve the question of parentage against that person or enforce the administrative order if the rights of others or the interest of justice so require. Except as provided in subdivision (c), a person's refusal to submit to tests ordered by the local child support agency is admissible in evidence in any proceeding to determine parentage if a notice of motion is not filed within the timeframes specified in this subdivision.

(f) If the original test result is contested, the local child support agency shall order an additional test only upon request and advance payment of the contestant.

(g) The local child support agency shall not order in utero genetic testing.

(h) The local child support agency shall administer this section consistent with federal law.[396]

7559. Payment of the cost of initial genetic testing shall be made in advance when agreed to by the parties or ordered by the court pursuant to Section 7640.[397]

7560. The court or local child support agency shall order additional genetic testing upon the request of a person who contests the results of the initial testing under Section 7555.[398]

7562. If a person seeking genetic testing demonstrates good cause, the court may order genetic testing of a deceased person.[399]

Chapter 3: Establishment of Parentage by Voluntary Declaration

7570. (a) The Legislature hereby finds and declares as follows:

(1) There is a compelling state interest in establishing parentage for all children. Establishing parentage is the first step toward a child support award, which, in turn, provides children with equal rights and access to benefits, including, but not limited to, social security, health insurance, survivors' benefits, military benefits, and inheritance rights.

(2) A simple administrative system allowing for establishment of voluntary parentage will result in a significant increase in the ease of establishing parentage, a significant increase in parentage establishment, an increase in the number of children who have greater access to child support and other benefits, and a significant decrease in the time and money required to establish parentage due to the removal of the need for a lengthy and expensive court process to determine and establish parentage and is in the public interest.

(b) This section shall become operative on January 1, 2020.

7571. (a) On and after January 1, 1995, upon the event of a live birth, prior to an unmarried mother or a mother who gave birth to a child conceived through assisted reproduction leaving a hospital, the person responsible for registering live births under Section 102405 of the Health and Safety Code shall provide to the woman giving birth and shall attempt to provide, at the place of birth, to the person identified by the woman giving birth as either the only possible genetic parent other than the woman who gave birth or the intended parent of a child conceived through assisted reproduction, a voluntary declaration of parentage together with the written materials described in Section 7572. Staff in the hospital shall witness the signatures of parents signing a voluntary declaration of parentage and shall forward the signed declaration to the Department of Child Support Services within 20 days of the date the declaration was signed. A copy of the declaration shall be made available to each of the attesting parents.

(b) A health care provider shall not be subject to civil, criminal, or administrative liability for a negligent act or omission relative to the accuracy of the information provided or for filing the declaration with the appropriate state or local agencies.

(c) The local child support agency shall pay the sum of ten dollars ($10) to birthing hospitals and other entities that provide prenatal services for each completed declaration of parentage that is filed with the Department of Child Support Services, provided that the local child support agency and the hospital or other entity providing prenatal services has entered into a written agreement that specifies the terms and conditions for the payment as required by federal law.

(d) If the declaration is not registered by the person responsible for registering live births at the hospital, it may be completed by the attesting parents, notarized, and mailed to the Department of Child Support Services at any time after the child's birth.

(e) Prenatal clinics shall offer prospective parents the opportunity to sign a voluntary declaration of parentage. In order to be paid for their services as provided in subdivision (c), prenatal clinics must ensure that the form is witnessed and forwarded to the Department of Child Support Services within 20 days of the date the declaration was signed.

(f) Declarations shall be made available without charge at all local child support agency offices, offices of local registrars of births and deaths, courts, and county welfare departments within this state. Staff in these offices shall witness the signatures of parents wishing to sign a voluntary declaration of parentage and shall be responsible for forwarding the signed declaration to the Department of Child Support Services within 20 days of the date the declaration was signed.

(g) The Department of Child Support Services, at its option, may pay the sum of ten dollars ($10) to local registrars of births and deaths, county welfare departments, or courts for each completed declaration of parentage that is witnessed by staff in these offices and filed with the Department of Child Support Services. In order to receive payment, the Department of Child Support Services and the entity shall enter into a written agreement that specifies the terms and conditions for payment as required by federal law. The Department of Child Support Services shall study the effect of the ten-dollar ($10) payment on obtaining completed voluntary declaration of parentage forms.

(h) The Department of Child Support Services and local child support agencies shall publicize the availability of the declarations. The local child support agency shall make the declaration, together with the written materials described in subdivision (a) of Section 7572, available upon request to any parent and any agency or organization that is required to offer parents the opportunity to sign a voluntary declaration of parentage. The local child support agency shall also provide qualified staff to answer parents' questions regarding the declaration and the process of establishing parentage.

(i) Copies of the declaration and any rescissions filed with the Department of Child Support Services shall be made available only to the parents, the child, the local child support agency, the county welfare department, the county counsel, the State Department of Public Health, and the courts.

(j) Publicly funded or licensed health clinics, pediatric offices, Head Start programs, child care centers, social services providers, prisons, and schools may offer parents the opportunity to sign a voluntary declaration of parentage. In order to be paid for their services as provided in subdivision (c), publicly funded or licensed health clinics, pediatric offices, Head Start programs, child care centers, social services providers, prisons, and schools shall ensure that the form is witnessed and forwarded to the Department of Child Support Services.

(k) An agency or organization required to offer parents the opportunity to sign a voluntary declaration of parentage shall also identify parents who are willing to sign but were unavailable when the child was born. The organization shall then contact these parents within 10 days and again offer the parent the opportunity to sign a voluntary declaration of parentage.

(l) This section shall become operative on January 1, 2020.[542]

7572. (a) The Department of Child Support Services, in consultation with the State Department of Health Care Services, the California Association of Hospitals and Health Systems, and other affected health provider organizations, shall work cooperatively to develop written materials to assist providers and parents in complying with this chapter. These written materials shall be updated periodically by the Department of Child Support Services to reflect changes in law, procedures, or public need.

(b) The written materials for unmarried parents or parents of a child conceived through assisted reproduction that shall be attached to the form specified in Section 7574 and shall contain the following information:

(1) A signed voluntary declaration of parentage that is filed with the Department of Child Support Services legally establishes parentage.

(2) The legal rights and obligations of both parents and the child that result from the establishment of parentage.

(3) An alleged father's constitutional rights to have the issue of parentage decided by a court; to notice of any hearing on the issue of parentage; to have an opportunity to present the alleged father's case to the court, including the right to present and cross-examine witnesses; to be represented by an attorney; and to have an attorney appointed if the alleged father cannot afford one in a parentage action filed by a local child support agency.

(4) That by signing the voluntary declaration of parentage, the father is voluntarily waiving the father's constitutional rights.

(c) Parents shall also be given oral notice of the rights and responsibilities specified in subdivision (b). Oral notice may be accomplished through the use of audio- or video-recorded programs developed by the Department of Child Support Services to the extent permitted by federal law.

(d) The Department of Child Support Services shall, free of charge, make available to hospitals, clinics, and other places of birth all informational and training materials for the program under this chapter, as well as the declaration of parentage form. The Department of Child Support Services shall make training available to every participating hospital, clinic, local registrar of births and deaths, and other place of birth no later than June 30, 1999.

(e) The Department of Child Support Services may adopt regulations, including emergency regulations, necessary to implement this chapter.[543]

7573. (a) The following persons may sign a voluntary declaration of parentage to establish the parentage of the child:

(1) An unmarried woman who gave birth to the child and another person who is a genetic parent.

(2) A married or unmarried woman who gave birth to the child and another person who is a parent under Section 7613 of a child conceived through assisted reproduction.

(b) A voluntary declaration of parentage shall be in a record signed by the woman who gave birth to the child and by either the only possible genetic parent other than the woman who gave birth or the intended parent of a child conceived through assisted reproduction, and the signatures shall be attested by a notary or witnessed.

(c) Except as provided by Section 7580, a voluntary declaration of parentage takes effect on the filing of the document with the Department of Child Support Services.

(d) Except as provided in Sections 7573.5, 7575, 7576, 7577, and 7580, a completed voluntary declaration of parentage that complies with this chapter and that has been filed with the Department of Child Support Services is equivalent to a judgment of parentage of the child and confers on the declarant all rights and duties of a parent.

(e) The court shall give full faith and credit to a voluntary declaration of parentage effective in another state if the declaration was in a signed record and otherwise complies with the law of the other state.

(f) This section shall become operative on January 1, 2020.

7573.5. (a) A voluntary declaration of parentage is void if, at the time of signing, any of the following are true:

(1) A person other than the woman who gave birth to the child or a person seeking to establish parentage through a voluntary declaration of parentage is a presumed parent under Section 7540 or subdivision (a), (b), or (c) of Section 7611.

(2) A court has entered a judgment of parentage of the child.

(3) Another person has signed a valid voluntary declaration of parentage.

(4) The child has a parent under Section 7613 or 7962 other than the signatories.

(5) The person seeking to establish parentage is a donor pursuant to Section 7613.

(6) The person seeking to establish parentage asserts that the person is a parent under Section 7613 and the child was not conceived through assisted reproduction.

(b) In an action in which a party is seeking a determination that a voluntary declaration of parentage is void under this section, notice shall be provided pursuant to Section 7635.[565]

7574. (a) The voluntary declaration of parentage shall be executed on a form developed by the Department of Child Support Services in consultation with the State Department of Public Health and groups addressing child support, child custody, assisted reproduction issues, and lesbian, gay, bisexual, and transgender rights.

(b) The form described in subdivision (a) shall contain, at a minimum, all of the following:

(1) The name and the signature of the woman who gave birth to the child.

(2) The name and the signature of the person seeking to establish parentage.

(3) The name of the child.

(4) The date of birth of the child.

(5) For a voluntary declaration of parentage signed pursuant to paragraph (1) of subdivision (a) of Section 7573, all of the following:

(A) A statement by the woman who gave birth that the woman is unmarried and understands the written materials described in Section 7572, that the person who is signing the voluntary declaration of parentage is the only possible genetic parent other than the woman who gave birth, that the woman who gave birth consents to the establishment of parentage by the genetic parent signing the voluntary declaration of parentage, and that the woman who gave birth understands that a challenge by a signatory to a valid declaration of parentage is permitted only under limited circumstances and is barred two years after the effective date of the declaration.

(B) A statement by the person signing the voluntary declaration of parentage that the person has read and understands the written materials described in Section 7572, understands that by signing the voluntary declaration of parentage the person is waiving rights as described in the written materials, that the person is the genetic parent of the child, that the person consents to the establishment of parentage by signing the voluntary declaration of parentage, that the person is assuming all the rights and responsibilities of a parent and wishes to be named on the child's birth certificate, and that the person understands that a challenge by a signatory to a valid declaration of parentage is permitted only under limited circumstances and is barred two years after the effective date of the declaration.

(6) For a voluntary declaration of parentage signed pursuant to paragraph (2) of subdivision (a) of Section 7573, all of the following:

(A) A statement by the woman ho gave birth that the woman has read and understands the written materials described in Section 7572, that the person who is signing the voluntary declaration of parentage is the intended parent of a child conceived through assisted reproduction, that the woman who gave birth consents to the establishment of parentage by the other person signing the voluntary declaration of parentage, and that the woman who gave birth understands that a challenge by a signatory to a valid declaration of parentage is permitted only under limited circumstances and is barred two years after the effective date of the declaration.

(B) A statement that the person seeking to establish parentage has read and understands the written materials described in Section 7572, understands that by signing the voluntary declaration of parentage the person is waiving rights as described in the written materials, that the person is the intended parent of the child conceived through assisted reproduction, that the person consents to the establishment of parentage by signing the voluntary declaration of parentage, that the person is assuming all the rights and responsibilities of a parent and wishes to be named on the child's birth certificate, and that the person understands that a challenge by a signatory to a valid declaration of parentage is permitted only under limited circumstances and is barred two years after the effective date of the declaration.

(7) The name and the signature of the person who witnesses the signing of the declaration.

7575. (a) Either parent may rescind the voluntary declaration of parentage by filing a rescission form with the Department of Child Support Services within 60 days of the date of execution of the declaration by the attesting parents, whichever signature is later, unless a court order for custody, visitation, or child support has been entered in an action in which the signatory seeking to rescind was a party. The Department of Child Support Services shall develop a form to be used by parents to rescind the declaration of parentage and instructions on how to complete and file the rescission with the Department of Child Support Services. The form shall include a declaration under penalty of perjury completed by the person filing the rescission form that certifies that a copy of the rescission form was sent by any form of mail requiring a return receipt to the other person who signed the voluntary declaration of parentage. A copy of the return receipt shall be attached to the rescission form when filed with the Department of Child Support Services. The form and instructions shall be written in simple, easy to understand language and shall be made available at the local family support office and the office of local registrar of births and deaths. The department shall, upon written request, provide to a court or commissioner a copy of any rescission form filed with the department that is relevant to proceedings before the court or commissioner.

(b) This section shall become operative on January 1, 2020.

7576. (a) After the period for rescission provided in Section 7575 expires, but not later than two years after the effective date provided in subdivision (c) of Section 7573 of a voluntary declaration of parentage, a signatory of the voluntary declaration of parentage may commence a proceeding to challenge the declaration on the basis of fraud, duress, or material mistake of fact.

(b) The limitations period provided in subdivision (a) shall not apply if the voluntary declaration of parentage is void under Section 7573.5.

(c) This section shall become operative on January 1, 2020.

7577. The following rules apply in an action to challenge a valid voluntary declaration of parentage brought by a person who is not a signatory to the declaration. This section does not apply to a voluntary declaration of parentage that is void under Section 7573.5.

(a) A person has standing under this section if the person is an alleged genetic parent who is not a donor under Section 7613, is a presumed parent under Section 7611, or any person who has standing under Section 7630.

(b) The petition challenging a voluntary declaration of parentage pursuant to this section shall be supported by a declaration under oath alleging specific facts to support standing under this section.

(c) If the court holds a hearing to determine standing, the hearing shall be held on an expedited basis. If the person challenging the voluntary declaration of parentage is an alleged genetic parent, genetic testing shall be ordered on an expedited basis.

(d) The action shall be filed not later than two years after the effective date of the declaration. This limitations period does not apply if the voluntary declaration of parentage is void under Section 7573.5.

(e) Notice shall be provided to the signatories of the declaration and to any person entitled to notice under Section 7635. A person who asserts a claim to parentage under this division shall be joined in the action.

(f) With respect to whether the voluntary declaration of parentage should be set aside, the person petitioning to set aside the voluntary declaration of parentage shall have the burden of proof by a preponderance of the evidence.

(g) The court may grant the petition to set aside the voluntary declaration of parentage only if the court finds that setting aside the voluntary declaration of parentage is in the best interest of the child, based on consideration of all of the following factors:

(1) The age of the child.

(2) The length of time since the effective date of the voluntary declaration of parentage.

(3) The nature, duration, and quality of any relationship between the person who signed the voluntary declaration of parentage and the child, including the duration and frequency of any time periods during which the child and the person resided in the same household or enjoyed a parent and child relationship.

(4) The request of the person who signed the voluntary declaration of parentage that the parent and child relationship continue.

(5) If the person challenges a voluntary declaration of parentage signed pursuant to paragraph (1) of subdivision (a) of Section 7573, the court shall additionally consider all of the following:

(A) Notice by the genetic parent of the child that the genetic parent does not oppose preservation of the relationship between the person who signed the declaration of parentage and the child.

(B) Whether any conduct of the person who signed the voluntary declaration has impaired the ability to ascertain the identity of, or obtain support from, the genetic parent.

(6) Additional factors deemed by the court to be relevant to its determination of the best interest of the child.

(h) If the voluntary declaration of parentage is challenged by a person who is presumed to be a parent under subdivision (d) of Section 7611, the court's ruling on the petition to set aside the voluntary declaration of parentage shall, in addition to the factors under subdivision (g), also take into account the nature, duration, and quality of the relationship between the petitioning party and the child and the benefit or detriment to the child of continuing that relationship.

(i) If the court denies the petition to set aside the voluntary declaration of parentage, the court shall state on the record the basis for the denial of the action and any supporting facts.

(j) (1) If the court grants the petition to set aside the voluntary declaration of parentage, the court shall adjudicate parentage pursuant to Section 7612.

(2) An order for custody, visitation, or child support shall remain in effect until the court determines that the voluntary declaration of parentage should be set aside, subject to the court's power to modify the orders as otherwise provided by law.

(k) This section does not prejudice or bar the rights of a person who is not a signatory and has standing under subdivision (a) to file an action or motion to set aside the voluntary declaration of parentage on any of the grounds described in, and within the time limits specified in, Section 473 of the Code of Civil Procedure. If the action or motion to set aside a judgment is required to be filed within a specified time period under Section 473 of the Code of Civil Procedure, the period within which the action or motion to set aside the voluntary declaration of parentage must be filed shall commence on the date that the court makes an initial order for custody, visitation, or child support based upon a voluntary declaration of parentage.

(l) This section does not restrict a court from acting as a court of equity.

(m) The Judicial Council shall develop the forms and procedures necessary to effectuate this section.

7578. (a) Every signatory to a voluntary declaration of parentage shall be made a party to a proceeding to challenge the declaration.

(b) By signing a voluntary declaration, a signatory submits to personal jurisdiction in this state in a proceeding to challenge the declaration, effective on the filing of the declaration with the Department of Child Support Services.

(c) The court shall not suspend the legal responsibilities arising from a voluntary declaration of parentage, including the duty to pay child support, during the pendency of a proceeding to challenge the voluntary declaration of parentage, unless the party challenging the declaration shows good cause.

(d) A party challenging a voluntary declaration of parentage has the burden of proof by a preponderance of the evidence.

(e) If the judgment or order of the court is at variance with the child's birth certificate, the court shall order that a new birth certificate be issued as prescribed in Article 2 (commencing with Section 102725) of Chapter 5 of Part 1 of Division 102 of the Health and Safety Code.

(f) This section shall become operative on January 1, 2020.

7580. (a) Notwithstanding subdivision (c) of Section 7573, a voluntary declaration of parentage that is signed by a minor parent does not establish parentage until 60 days after both signatories have reached 18 years of age or are emancipated, whichever first occurs.

(b) A person who signs a voluntary declaration of parentage as a minor may rescind the voluntary declaration of parentage at any time up to 60 days after the signatory reaches 18 years of age or becomes emancipated, whichever first occurs.
(c) A voluntary declaration of parentage signed by a minor creates a rebuttable presumption for or against parentage until the date that it establishes parentage as specified in subdivision (a).
(d) A voluntary declaration of parentage signed by a minor shall be admissible as evidence in a civil action to establish parentage of the minor named in the voluntary declaration.
(e) A voluntary declaration of parentage that is signed by a minor shall not be admissible as evidence in a criminal prosecution for violation of Section 261.5 of the Penal Code.

7581. The following provisions shall apply for voluntary declarations signed on or before December 31, 1996.
(a) Except as provided in subdivision (d), the child of a woman and a man executing a declaration of paternity under this chapter is conclusively presumed to be the man's child. The presumption under this section has the same force and effect as the presumption under Section 7540.
(b) A voluntary declaration of paternity shall be recognized as the basis for the establishment of an order for child custody or support.
(c) In an action to rebut the presumption created by this section, a voluntary declaration of paternity shall be admissible as evidence to determine paternity of the child named in the voluntary declaration of paternity.
(d) The presumption established by this section may be rebutted by any person by requesting genetic testing pursuant to Chapter 2 (commencing with Section 7550). The notice of motion for genetic testing pursuant to this section shall be supported by a declaration under oath submitted by the moving party stating the factual basis for placing the issue of paternity before the court. The notice of motion for genetic testing shall be made within three years from the date of execution of the declaration by the attesting father, or by the attesting mother, whichever signature is later. The two-year statute of limitations specified in subdivision (b) of Section 7541 is inapplicable for purposes of this section.
(e) A presumption under this section shall override all statutory presumptions of paternity, except a presumption arising under Section 7540, a claim made pursuant to Section 7555, or as provided in Section 7612.
(f) This section shall become operative on January 1, 2020.

PART 3: UNIFORM PARENTAGE ACT

enacted by Stats. 1992, Ch. 162, Sec. 10

Chapter 1: General Provisions

7600. This part may be cited as the Uniform Parentage Act.[1]

7601. (a) "Natural parent" as used in this code means a nonadoptive parent established under this part, whether biologically related to the child or not.
(b) "Parent and child relationship" as used in this part means the legal relationship existing between a child and the child's natural or adoptive parents incident to which the law confers or imposes rights, privileges, duties, and

obligations. The term includes the mother and child relationship and the father and child relationship.

(c) This part does not preclude a finding that a child has a parent and child relationship with more than two parents.

(d) For purposes of state law, administrative regulations, court rules, government policies, common law, and any other provision or source of law governing the rights, protections, benefits, responsibilities, obligations, and duties of parents, any reference to two parents shall be interpreted to apply to every parent of a child where that child has been found to have more than two parents under this part.[279]

7602. The parent and child relationship extends equally to every child and to every parent, regardless of the marital status of the parents.[1]

7603. Section 3140 is applicable to proceedings pursuant to this part.[1]

7604. A court may order pendente lite relief consisting of a custody or visitation order pursuant to Part 2 (commencing with Section 3020) of Division 8, if the court finds both of the following:

(a) A parent and child relationship exists pursuant to Section 7540 or 7541.

(b) The custody or visitation order would be in the best interest of the child.[400]

7604.5. Notwithstanding any other provision of law, bills for pregnancy, childbirth, and genetic testing shall be admissible as evidence without third-party foundation testimony and shall constitute prima facie evidence of costs incurred for those services.

7605. (a) In any proceeding to establish physical or legal custody of a child or a visitation order under this part, and in any proceeding subsequent to entry of a related judgment, the court shall ensure that each party has access to legal representation to preserve each party's rights by ordering, if necessary based on the income and needs assessments, one party, except a government entity, to pay to the other party, or to the other party's attorney, whatever amount is reasonably necessary for attorney's fees and for the cost of maintaining or defending the proceeding during the pendency of the proceeding.

(b) When a request for attorney's fees and costs is made under this section, the court shall make findings on whether an award of attorney's fees and costs is appropriate, whether there is a disparity in access to funds to retain counsel, and whether one party is able to pay for legal representation of both parties. If the findings demonstrate disparity in access and ability to pay, the court shall make an order awarding attorney's fees and costs. A party who lacks the financial ability to hire an attorney may request, as an in pro per litigant, that the court order the other party, if that other party has the financial ability, to pay a reasonable amount to allow the unrepresented party to retain an attorney in a timely manner before proceedings in the matter go forward.

(c) Attorney's fees and costs within this section may be awarded for legal services rendered or costs incurred before or after the commencement of the proceeding.

(d) The court shall augment or modify the original award for attorney's fees and costs as may be reasonably necessary for the prosecution or defense of a proceeding described in subdivision (a), or any proceeding related thereto, including after any appeal has been concluded.

(e) Except as provided in subdivision (f), an application for a temporary order making, augmenting, or modifying an award of attorney's fees, including a reasonable retainer to hire an attorney, or costs, or both, shall be made by motion on notice or by an order to show cause during the pendency of any proceeding described in subdivision (a).

(f) The court shall rule on an application for fees under this section within 15 days of the hearing on the motion or order to show cause. An order described in subdivision (a) may be made without notice by an oral motion in open court at either of the following times:

(1) At the time of the hearing of the cause on the merits.

(2) At any time before entry of judgment against a party whose default has been entered pursuant to Section 585 or 586 of the Code of Civil Procedure. The court shall rule on any motion made pursuant to this subdivision within 15 days and prior to the entry of any judgment.[252]

7606. As used in this part, the following definitions shall apply:

(a) "Assisted reproduction" means conception by any means other than sexual intercourse.

(b) "Assisted reproduction agreement" means a written contract that includes a person who intends to be the legal parent of a child or children born through assisted reproduction and that defines the terms of the relationship between the parties to the contract.[141]

Chapter 2: Establishing Parent and Child Relationship

7610. The parent and child relationship may be established as follows:

(a) Between a child and the natural parent, it may be established by proof of having given birth to the child, or under this part.

(b) Between a child and an adoptive parent, it may be established by proof of adoption.[271]

7611. A person is presumed to be the natural parent of a child if the person meets the conditions provided in Chapter 1 (commencing with Section 7540) or Chapter 3 (commencing with Section 7570) of Part 2 or in any of the following subdivisions:

(a) The presumed parent and the child's natural mother are, or have been, married to each other and the child is born during the marriage, or within 300 days after the marriage is terminated by death, annulment, declaration of invalidity, or divorce, or after a judgment of separation is entered by a court.

(b) Before the child's birth, the presumed parent and the child's natural mother have attempted to marry each other by a marriage solemnized in apparent compliance with law, although the attempted marriage is or could be declared invalid, and either of the following is true:

(1) If the attempted marriage could be declared invalid only by a court, the child is born during the attempted marriage, or within 300 days after its termination by death, annulment, declaration of invalidity, or divorce.

(2) If the attempted marriage is invalid without a court order, the child is born within 300 days after the

termination of cohabitation.

(c) After the child's birth, the presumed parent and the child's natural mother have married, or attempted to marry, each other by a marriage solemnized in apparent compliance with law, although the attempted marriage is or could be declared invalid, and either of the following is true:

(1) With the presumed parent's consent, the presumed parent is named as the child's parent on the child's birth certificate.

(2) The presumed parent is obligated to support the child under a written voluntary promise or by court order.

(d) The presumed parent receives the child into their home and openly holds out the child as their natural child.

(e) The child is in utero after the death of the decedent and the conditions set forth in Section 249.5 of the Probate Code are satisfied.

7611.5. Where Section 7611 does not apply, a man shall not be presumed to be the natural father of a child if either of the following is true:

(a) The child was conceived as a result of an act in violation of Section 261 of the Penal Code and the father was convicted of that violation.

(b) The child was conceived as a result of an act in violation of Section 261.5 of the Penal Code, the father was convicted of that violation, and the mother was under the age of 15 years and the father was 21 years of age or older at the time of conception.[42]

7612. (a) Except as provided in Chapter 1 (commencing with Section 7540) and Chapter 3 (commencing with Section 7570) of Part 2, a presumption under Section 7611 is a rebuttable presumption affecting the burden of proof and may be rebutted in an appropriate action only by clear and convincing evidence.

(b) If two or more presumptions arise under Section 7611 that conflict with each other, or if one or more presumptions under Section 7611 conflict with a claim by a person identified as a genetic parent pursuant to Section 7555, the presumption that on the facts is founded on the weightier considerations of policy and logic controls. If one of the presumed parents is also a presumed parent under Section 7540, the presumption arising under Section 7540 may only be rebutted pursuant to Section 7541.

(c) In an appropriate action, a court may find that more than two persons with a claim to parentage under this division are parents if the court finds that recognizing only two parents would be detrimental to the child. In determining detriment to the child, the court shall consider all relevant factors, including, but not limited to, the harm of removing the child from a stable placement with a parent who has fulfilled the child's physical needs and the child's psychological needs for care and affection, and who has assumed that role for a substantial period of time. A finding of detriment to the child does not require a finding of unfitness of any of the parents or persons with a claim to parentage.

(d) Unless a court orders otherwise after making the determination specified in subdivision (c), a presumption under Section 7611 is rebutted by a judgment establishing parentage of the child by another person.

(e) A person's offer or refusal to sign a voluntary declaration of parentage may be considered as a factor, but shall not be determinative, as to the issue of legal parentage in a proceeding regarding the establishment or termination of parental rights.

(f) This section shall become operative on January 1, 2020.

7613. (a) (1) If a woman conceives through assisted reproduction with semen or ova or both donated by a donor who is not the woman's spouse, with the consent of another intended parent, that intended parent is treated in law as if that intended parent is the natural parent of a child thereby conceived. The other intended parent's consent shall be in writing and signed by the other intended parent and the woman conceiving through assisted reproduction.

(2) Failure to consent in writing, a required by paragraph (1), does not preclude the court from finding that the intended parent consented if the court finds by clear and convincing evidence that, prior to the conception of the child, the woman and the intended parent had an oral agreement that the woman and the intended parent would both be parents of the child.

(b) (1) The donor of semen provided to a licensed physician and surgeon or to a licensed sperm bank for use in assisted reproduction by a woman other than the donor's spouse is treated in law as if the donor is not the natural parent of a child thereby conceived, unless the donor and the woman signed a written agreement before the conception of the child, that the donor would be a parent.

(2) If the semen is not provided to a licensed physician and surgeon or a licensed sperm bank as specified in paragraph (1), the donor of semen for use in assisted reproduction by a woman other than the donor's spouse is treated in law as if the donor is not the natural parent of a child thereby conceived if either of the following are met:

(A) The donor and the woman signed a written agreement before conception that the donor would not be a parent.

(B) A court finds by clear and convincing evidence that the child was conceived through assisted reproduction and that, prior to the conception of the child, the woman and the donor had an oral agreement that the donor would not be a parent.

(c) A person providing ova for use in assisted reproduction by a person other than the provider's spouse or nonmarital partner is treated in law as if the provider is not the natural parent of a child thereby conceived unless the court finds satisfactory evidence that the provider of the ova, and each recipient, intended for that provider to have parental rights.

(d) (1) A provider of an embryo for use in assisted reproduction to an intended parent who is not the provider's spouse or nonmarital partner is treated in law as if the provider is not the natural parent of a child thereby conceived unless the court finds satisfactory evidence that the provider and the intended parent intended for the provider to be a parent.

(2) If the provider of ova, semen, or embryos is not the original source of the ova or sperm, each original provider's written consent to the donation is required unless that person has executed a writing to consent to the donation, or to waive

or relinquish their right to the genetic material, or as otherwise ordered by a court of law.

(e) (1) Notwithstanding any other law, persons who are not married to one another and who share legal control over the disposition of embryos shall not be prevented from entering into a written agreement whereby one person renounces all legal interest in the embryos, with the specific intent that the person renouncing all legal interest shall not be a legal parent of any child conceived with use of the embryos, despite any prior oral or written agreements, or legal judgments to the contrary. After that interest has been renounced in a writing signed by all persons with legal interest in or control over disposition of the embryos, the renouncing person shall be treated in law as a donor, and not a legal parent. Upon execution of that agreement, the person who retains legal interest in and control over disposition of the embryos shall have the sole right to determine the use and disposition of the embryos, including the right to attempt conception of a child, subject to any limitation pursuant to paragraph (2) of subdivision (d). Either party may file the agreement with the court, and the court shall issue an order establishing the nonparentage of the donor.

(2) If persons who share legal control over and interest in one or more embryos are married to one another at the time of signing the agreement, the agreement shall only become legally binding upon the court's entry of a final decree of dissolution that incorporates the agreement, after which the presumptions pursuant to Section 7540 or subdivisions (a), (b), or (c) of Section 7611 shall not apply.[566]

7613.5. (a) An intended parent may, but is not required to, use the forms set forth in this section to demonstrate the intent to be a legal parent of a child conceived through assisted reproduction. These forms shall satisfy the writing requirement specified in Section 7613, and are designed to provide clarity regarding the intentions, at the time of conception, of intended parents using assisted reproduction. These forms do not affect any presumptions of parentage based on Section 7611, and do not preclude a court from considering any other claims to parentage under California statute or case law.

(b) These forms apply only in very limited circumstances. Please read the forms carefully to see if you qualify for use of the forms.

(c) These forms do not apply to assisted reproduction agreements for gestational carriers or surrogacy agreements.

(d) This section does not require the use of one of these forms to satisfy the writing requirement of Section 7613.

(e) The following are the optional California Statutory Forms for Assisted Reproduction:

California Statutory Forms for Assisted Reproduction, Form 1:

Two Married or Unmarried People Using Assisted Reproduction to Conceive a Child

Use this form if: You and another intended parent, who may be your spouse or registered domestic partner, are conceiving a child through assisted reproduction using sperm and/or egg donation; and one of you will be giving birth.

WARNING: Signing this form does not terminate the parentage claim of a sperm donor. A sperm donor's claim to parentage is terminated if the sperm is provided to a licensed physician and surgeon or to a licensed sperm bank prior to insemination, or if you conceive without having sexual intercourse and you have a written agreement signed by you and the donor that you will conceive using assisted reproduction and do not intend for the donor to be a parent, as required by Section 7613(b) of the Family Code.

The laws about parentage of a child are complicated. You are strongly encouraged to consult with an attorney about your rights. Even if you do not fill out this form, a spouse or domestic partner of the parent giving birth is presumed to be a legal parent of any child born during the marriage or domestic partnership.

This form demonstrates your intent to be parents of the child you plan to conceive through assisted reproduction using sperm and/or egg donation.

I, ____________________ (print name of person not giving birth), intend to be a parent of a child that ____________________ (print name of person giving birth) will or has conceived through assisted reproduction using sperm and/or egg donation. I consent to the use of assisted reproduction by the person who will give birth. I INTEND to be a parent of the child conceived.

SIGNATURES
Intended parent who will give birth: __________________ (print name)
__________________________ (signature) ____________(date)
Intended parent who will not give birth: _____________ (print name)
__________________________ (signature) ____________(date)

NOTARY ACKNOWLEDGMENT

State of California

County of) _____

On before me, (insert name and title of the officer)

personally appeared ,

who proved to me on the basis of satisfactory evidence to be the person(s) whose name(s) is/are subscribed to the within instrument and acknowledged to me that he/she/they executed the same in his/her/their authorized capacity, and that by his/her/their signature(s) on the instrument the person(s), or the entity upon behalf of which the person(s) acted, executed the instrument.

I certify under PENALTY OF PERJURY under the laws of the State of California that the foregoing paragraph is true and correct.

WITNESS my hand and official seal.

Signature(Seal)

California Statutory Forms for Assisted Reproduction, Form 2:

Unmarried, Intended Parents Using Intended Parent's Sperm to Conceive a Child

Use this form if: (1) Neither you or the other person are married or in a registered domestic partnership (including a registered domestic partnership or civil union from another state); (2) one of you will give birth to a child conceived through assisted reproduction using the intended parent's sperm; and (3) you both intend to be parents of that child.

Do not use this form if you are conceiving using a surrogate.

WARNING: If you do not sign this form, or a similar agreement, you may be treated as a sperm donor if you conceive without having sexual intercourse according to Section 7613(b) of the Family Code.

The laws about parentage of a child are complicated. You are strongly encouraged to consult with an attorney about your rights.

This form demonstrates your intent to be parents of the child you plan to conceive through assisted reproduction using sperm donation.

I, ____________________ (print name of parent giving birth), plan to use assisted reproduction with another intended parent who is providing sperm to conceive the child. I am not married and am not in a registered domestic partnership (including a registered domestic partnership or civil union from another jurisdiction), and I INTEND for the person providing sperm to be a parent of the child to be conceived.

I, ____________________ (print name of parent providing sperm), plan to use assisted reproduction to conceive a child using my sperm with the parent giving birth. I am not married and am not in a registered domestic partnership (including a registered domestic partnership or civil union from another jurisdiction), and I INTEND to be a parent of the child to be conceived.

SIGNATURES

Intended parent giving birth: ____________________ (print name)

__________________________ (signature) ____________(date)

Intended parent providing sperm: ____________ (print name)

__________________________ (signature) ____________(date)

NOTARY ACKNOWLEDGMENT

State of California

County of) _____

On before me, (insert name and title of the officer)

personally appeared ,

who proved to me on the basis of satisfactory evidence to be the person(s) whose name(s) is/are subscribed to the within instrument and acknowledged to me that he/she/they executed the same in his/her/their authorized capacity, and that by his/her/their signature(s) on the instrument the person(s), or the entity upon behalf of which the person(s) acted, executed the instrument.

I certify under PENALTY OF PERJURY under the laws of the State of California that the foregoing paragraph is true and correct.

WITNESS my hand and official seal.

Signature(Seal)

California Statutory Forms for Assisted Reproduction, Form 3:

Intended Parents Conceiving a Child Using Eggs from One Parent and the Other Parent Will Give Birth

Use this form if: You are conceiving a child using the eggs from one of you and the other person will give birth to the child; (2) and you both intend to be parents to that child.

Do not use this form if you are conceiving using a surrogate.

WARNING: Signing this form does not terminate the parentage claim of a sperm donor. A sperm donor's claim to parentage is terminated if the sperm is provided to a licensed physician and surgeon or to a licensed sperm bank prior to insemination, or if you conceive without having sexual intercourse and you have a written agreement signed by you and the donor that you will conceive using assisted reproduction and do not intend for the donor to be a parent, as required by Section 7613(b) of the Family Code.

The laws about parentage of a child are complicated. You are strongly encouraged to consult with an attorney about your rights.

This form demonstrates your intent to be parents of the child you plan to conceive through assisted reproduction using eggs from one parent and the other parent will give birth to the child.

I, ____________________ (print name of parent giving birth), plan to use assisted reproduction to conceive and give birth to a child with another person who will provide eggs to conceive the child. I INTEND for the person providing eggs to be a parent of the child to be conceived.

I, ____________________ (print name of parent providing eggs), plan to use assisted reproduction to conceive a child with another person who will give birth to the child conceived using my eggs. I INTEND to be a parent of the child to be conceived.

SIGNATURES
Intended parent giving birth: ____________________ (print name)
________________________ (signature) ____________(date)
Intended parent providing eggs: ____________ (print name)
________________________ (signature) ___________(date)

NOTARY ACKNOWLEDGMENT

State of California

County of) _____

On before me, (insert name and title of the officer)

personally appeared ,

who proved to me on the basis of satisfactory evidence to be the person(s) whose name(s) is/are subscribed to the within instrument and acknowledged to me that he/she/they executed the same in his/her/their authorized capacity, and that by his/her/their signature(s) on the instrument the person(s), or the entity upon behalf of which the person(s) acted, executed the instrument.

I certify under PENALTY OF PERJURY under the laws of the State of California that the foregoing paragraph is true and correct.

WITNESS my hand and official seal.

Signature(Seal)

California Statutory Forms for Assisted Reproduction, Form 4:

Intended Parent(s) Using a Known Sperm and/or Egg Donor(s) to Conceive a Child

Use this form if: You are using a known sperm and/or egg donor(s), or embryo donation, to conceive a child and you do not intend for the donor(s) to be a parent.

Do not use this form if you are conceiving using a surrogate.

If you do not sign this form or a similar agreement, your sperm donor may be treated as a parent unless the sperm is provided to a licensed physician and surgeon or to a licensed sperm bank prior to insemination, or a court finds by clear and convincing evidence that you planned to conceive through assisted reproduction and did not intend for the donor to be a parent, as required by Section 7613(b) of the Family Code. If you do not sign this form or a similar agreement, your egg donor may be treated as a parent unless a court finds that there is satisfactory evidence that you planned to conceive through assisted reproduction and did not intend for the donor to be a parent, as required by Section 7613(c) of the Family Code.

The laws about parentage of a child are complicated. You are strongly encouraged to consult with an attorney about your rights.

This form demonstrates your intent that your sperm and/or egg or embryo donor(s) will not be a parent or parents of the child you plan to conceive through assisted reproduction.

I, ____________________ (print name of parent giving birth), plan to use assisted reproduction to conceive using a sperm and/or egg donor(s) or embryo donation, and I DO NOT INTEND for the sperm and/or egg or embryo donor(s) to be a parent of the child to be conceived.

(If applicable) I, ____________________ (print name of sperm donor), plan to donate my sperm to____________________ (print name of parent giving birth and second parent if applicable). I am not married to and am not in a registered domestic partnership (including a registered domestic partnership or a civil union from another jurisdiction) with ____________________ (print name of parent giving birth), and I DO NOT INTEND to be a parent of the child to be conceived.

(If applicable) I, ____________________ (print name of egg donor), plan to donate my ova to____________________ (print name of parent giving birth and second parent if applicable). I am not married to and am not in a registered domestic partnership (including a registered domestic partnership or a civil union from another jurisdiction) with ____________________ (print name of parent giving birth), or any intimate and nonmarital relationship with ____________________ (print name of parent giving birth) and I DO NOT INTEND to be a parent of the child to be conceived.

(If applicable) I, ____________________ (print name of intended parent not giving birth), INTEND to be a parent of the child that____________________ (print name of parent giving birth) will conceive through assisted reproduction using sperm and/or egg donation and I DO NOT INTEND for the sperm and/or egg or embryo donor(s) to be a parent. I consent to the use of assisted reproduction by the person who will give birth.

SIGNATURES

Intended parent giving birth: ____________________ (print name)

__________________________ (signature) ____________(date)

(If applicable) Sperm Donor: ____________________ (print name)

__________________________ (signature) ____________(date)

(If applicable) Egg Donor: ____________________ (print name)

__________________________ (signature) ____________(date)

(If applicable) Intended parent not giving birth: ____________ (print name)

__________________________ (signature) ____________(date)

NOTARY ACKNOWLEDGMENT

State of California

County of) _____

On before me, (insert name and title of the officer)

personally appeared ,

who proved to me on the basis of satisfactory evidence to be the person(s) whose name(s) is/are subscribed to the within instrument and acknowledged to me that he/she/they executed the same in his/her/their authorized capacity, and that by his/her/their signature(s) on the instrument the person(s), or the entity upon behalf of which the person(s) acted, executed the instrument.

I certify under PENALTY OF PERJURY under the laws of the State of California that the foregoing paragraph is true and correct.

WITNESS my hand and official seal.

Signature(Seal)

7614. (a) A promise in writing to furnish support for a child, growing out of a presumed parent or alleged father and child relationship, does not require consideration and, subject to Section 7632, is enforceable according to its terms.

(b) In the best interest of the child or the other parent, the court may, and upon the promisor's request shall, order the promise to be kept in confidence and designate a person or agency to receive and disburse on behalf of the child all amounts paid in performance of the promise.[272]

Chapter 3: Jurisdiction and Venue

7620. (a) A person who has sexual intercourse or causes conception with the intent to become a legal parent by assisted reproduction in this state, or who enters into an assisted reproduction agreement for gestational carriers in this state, thereby submits to the jurisdiction of the courts of this state as to an action brought under this part with respect to a child who may have been conceived by that act of intercourse or assisted reproduction, or who may have been conceived as a result of that assisted reproduction agreement.

(b) If a child is conceived pursuant to an assisted reproduction agreement for gestational carriers, as defined in Section 7960 and as described in Section 7962, the courts of this state shall have jurisdiction over a proceeding to determine parentage of the child if any of the following conditions is satisfied:

(1) One or more of the parties to the assisted reproduction agreement for gestational carriers resides in this state, or resided in this state at the time the assisted reproduction agreement for gestational carriers was executed.

(2) The medical procedures leading to conception, including in vitro fertilization or embryo transfer, or both, were carried out in this state.

(3) The child is born in this state.

(c) An action under this part shall be brought in one of the following:

(1) The county in which the child resides or is found.

(2) If the child is the subject of a pending or proposed adoption, any county in which a licensed California adoption agency to which the child has been relinquished or is proposed to be relinquished maintains an office.

(3) If the child is the subject of a pending or proposed adoption, the county in which an office of the department or a public adoption agency investigating the petition is located.

(4) If the parent is deceased, the county in which proceedings for probate of the estate of the parent of the child have been or could be commenced.

(5) If the child was conceived pursuant to an assisted reproduction agreement for gestational carriers, any county described in subdivision (e) of Section 7962.[351]

Chapter 4: Determination of parent and Child Relationship

Article 1: Determination of Parent and Child Relationship

7630. (a) A child, the child's natural mother, a person presumed to be the child's parent under subdivision (a), (b), or (c) of Section 7611, a person seeking to be adjudicated as a parent or donor under Section 7613, an adoption agency to whom the child has been relinquished, or a prospective adoptive parent of the child may bring an action as follows:

(1) At any time for the purpose of declaring the existence of the parent and child relationship presumed under subdivision (a), (b), or (c) of Section 7611, or established pursuant to Section 7613.

(2) For the purpose of declaring the nonexistence of the parent and child relationship presumed under subdivision (a), (b), or (c) of Section 7611 only if the action is brought within a reasonable time after obtaining knowledge of relevant facts. After the presumption has been rebutted, parentage of the child by another person may be determined in the same action, if that person has been made a party.

(3) At any time for the purpose of declaring the nonexistence of the parent and child relationship of a donor under Section 7613.

(b) Any interested party may bring an action at any time for the purpose of determining the existence or nonexistence of the parent and child relationship presumed under subdivision (d) or (e) of Section 7611.

(c) Except as to cases coming within Chapter 1 (commencing with Section 7540) of Part 2 or when paragraph (2) of subdivision (a) applies, an action to determine parentage may be brought by the child, a personal representative of the child, the Department of Child Support Services, a presumed parent or the personal representative or a parent of that presumed parent if that parent has died or is a minor, or, when the natural mother is the only presumed parent or an action under Section 300 of the Welfare and Institutions Code or adoption is pending, a man alleged or claiming to be the father or the personal representative or a parent of the alleged father if the alleged father has died or is a minor.

(d) (1) If a proceeding has been filed under Chapter 2 (commencing with Section 7820) of Part 4, an action under subdivision (a) or (b) shall be consolidated with that proceeding. The parental rights of the presumed parent shall be determined as set forth in Sections 7820 to 7829, inclusive.

(2) If a proceeding pursuant to Section 7662 has been filed under Chapter 5 (commencing with Section 7660), an action under subdivision (c) shall be consolidated with that proceeding. The parental rights of the alleged father shall be determined as set forth in Section 7664.

(3) The consolidated action under paragraph (1) or (2) shall be heard in the court in which the proceeding under Section 7662 or Chapter 2 (commencing with Section 7820) of Part 4 is filed, unless the court finds, by clear and convincing evidence, that transferring the action to the other court poses a substantial hardship to the petitioner. Mere inconvenience does not constitute a sufficient basis for a finding of substantial hardship. If the court determines there is a substantial hardship, the consolidated action shall be heard in the court in which the parentage action is filed.

(e) (1) If a prospective adoptive parent who has physical custody of the child, a licensed California adoption agency that has legal custody of the child or to which the mother proposes to relinquish the child for adoption, or a person whom the mother has designated as the prospective adoptive parent in a written statement executed before a hospital social worker, an adoption service provider, an adoption agency representative, or a notary public, has not been joined as a party to an action to determine the existence of a parent and child relationship under subdivision (a), (b), or (c), or an action for custody by a person claiming to be a parent under this division, the court shall join the prospective adoptive parent or licensed California adoption agency as a party upon application or on its own motion, without the necessity of a motion for joinder. A joined party shall not be required to pay a fee in connection with this action.

(2) If a person brings an action to determine parentage and custody of a child who the person has reason to believe is in the physical or legal custody of an adoption agency, or of one or more persons other than the child's parent who are prospective adoptive parents, the person shall serve the entire pleading on, and give notice of all proceedings to, the adoption agency or the prospective adoptive parents, or both.

(f) A party to an assisted reproduction agreement may bring an action at any time to establish a parent and child relationship consistent with the intent expressed in that assisted reproduction agreement.

(g) (1) In an action to determine the existence of the parent and child relationship brought pursuant to subdivision (b), if the child's other parent has died and there are no existing court orders or pending court actions involving custody or guardianship of the child, then the persons having physical custody of the child shall be served with notice of the proceeding at least 15 days prior to the hearing, either by mail or in a manner authorized by the court. If a person identified as having physical custody of the child cannot be located, the court shall prescribe the manner of giving notice.

(2) If known to the person bringing the parentage action, relatives within the second degree of the child shall be given notice of the proceeding at least 15 days prior to the hearing, either by mail or in a manner authorized by the court. If a person identified as a relative of the second degree of the child cannot be located, or the relative's whereabouts are unknown or cannot be ascertained, the court shall prescribe the manner of giving notice, or shall dispense with giving notice to that person.

(3) Proof of notice pursuant to this subdivision shall be filed with the court before the proceeding to determine the existence of the parent and child relationship is heard.[490]

7632. Regardless of its terms, an agreement between an alleged father or a presumed parent and the other parent or child does not bar an action under this chapter.[273]

7633. An action under this chapter may be brought, an order or judgment may be entered before the birth of the child, and enforcement of that order or judgment shall be stayed until the birth of the child.[142]

7634. (a) The local child support agency may, in the local child support agency's discretion, bring an action under this chapter in any case in which the local child support agency believes it to be appropriate.

(b) The Department of Child Support

Services may review the current practices of service of process used by the local child support agencies pursuant to subdivision (a), and may develop methods to increase the number of persons served using personal delivery.

7635. (a) The child may, if under the age of 12 years, and shall, if 12 years of age or older, be made a party to the action. If the child is a minor and a party to the action, the child shall be represented by a guardian ad litem appointed by the court. The guardian ad litem need not be represented by counsel if the guardian ad litem is a relative of the child.
(b) A natural parent, each person presumed to be a parent under Section 7611 or 7540, each person who is a parent of the child under Section 7613 or 7962, and each person alleged to be the genetic parent unless precluded under this division from establishing parentage based on genetic testing, shall be given notice of the action in the manner prescribed in Section 7666 and an opportunity to be heard, and shall be made a party if they request to be joined. Appointment of a guardian ad litem shall not be required for a minor who is a parent of the child who is the subject of the petition to establish parental relationship, unless the minor parent is unable to understand the nature of the proceedings or to assist counsel in preparing the case.
(c) The court may align the parties.
(d) In any initial or subsequent proceeding under this chapter where custody of, or visitation with, a minor child is in issue, the court may, if it determines it would be in the best interest of the minor child, appoint private counsel to represent the interests of the minor child pursuant to Chapter 10 (commencing with Section 3150) of Part 2 of Division 8.[401]

7635.5. In any action brought pursuant to this article, if the alleged father is present in court for the action, the court shall inform the alleged father of the alleged father's right to have genetic testing performed to determine the biological parentage of the child. The court shall further inform the alleged father of the alleged father's right to move to set aside or vacate a judgment of parentage pursuant to Section 7646 within two years of the date notice of the action to establish parentage is received, and that after that time has expired the alleged father may not move to set aside or vacate the judgment of parentage, regardless of whether genetic testing shows the alleged father not to be the biological father of the child.

7636. The judgment or order of the court determining the existence or nonexistence of the parent and child relationship is determinative for all purposes except for actions brought pursuant to Section 270 of the Penal Code.[1]

7637. The judgment or order may contain any other provision directed against the appropriate party to the proceeding, concerning the duty of support, the custody and guardianship of the child, visitation privileges with the child, the furnishing of bond or other security for the payment of the judgment, or any other matter in the best interest of the child. The judgment or order may direct the parent to pay the reasonable expenses of the mother's pregnancy and confinement.[274]

7638. The procedure in an action under this part to change the name of a minor or adult child for whom a parent and child relationship is established pursuant to Section 7636, upon application in accordance with Title 8 (commencing with Section 1275) of Part 3 of the Code of Civil Procedure shall conform to those provisions, except that the application for the change of name may be included with the petition filed under this part and except as provided in Sections 1277 and 1278 of the Code of Civil Procedure.[1]

7639. If the judgment or order of the court is at variance with the child's birth certificate, the court shall order that a new birth certificate be issued as prescribed in Article 2 (commencing with Section 102725) of Chapter 5 of Part 1 of Division 102 of the Health and Safety Code.

7640. The court may order reasonable fees of counsel, experts, and the child's guardian ad litem, and other costs of the action and pretrial proceedings, including genetic testing, to be paid by the parties, excluding any governmental entity, in proportions and at times determined by the court. The court may apply the standards set forth in Sections 2032 and 7605 in making this determination.[402]

7641. (a) If there is a voluntary declaration of paternity in place, or parentage or a duty of support has been acknowledged or adjudicated under this part or under prior law, the obligation of the parent may be enforced in the same or other proceedings by any of the following:

(1) The other parent.

(2) The child.

(3) The public authority that has furnished or may furnish the reasonable expenses of pregnancy, confinement, education, support, or funeral.

(4) Any other person, including a private agency, to the extent the person has furnished or is furnishing these expenses.

(b) The court may order support payments to be made to any of the following:

(1) The other parent.

(2) The clerk of the court.

(3) A person, corporation, or agency designated to administer the payments for the benefit of the child under the supervision of the court.

(c) Willful failure to obey the judgment or order of the court is a civil contempt of the court. All remedies for the enforcement of judgments, including imprisonment for contempt, apply.[275]

7642. The court has continuing jurisdiction to modify or set aside a judgment or order made under this part. A judgment or order relating to an adoption may only be modified or set aside in the same manner and under the same conditions as an order of adoption may be modified or set aside under Section 9100 or 9102.

7643. (a) Notwithstanding any other law concerning public hearings and records, a hearing or trial held under this part may be held in closed court without admittance of any person other than those necessary to the action or proceeding. Except as provided in subdivision (b), all papers and records, other than the final judgment, pertaining to the action or proceeding, whether part of the permanent record of the court or of a file in a public agency or elsewhere, are subject to inspection and copying only in exceptional cases upon an order of the court for good cause shown.

(b) (1) Papers and records pertaining to the action or proceeding that are part of the permanent record of the court are subject to inspection and copying by the parties to the action, their attorneys, and by agents acting pursuant to written authorization from the parties to the action or their attorneys. An attorney shall obtain the consent of the party to the action before authorizing an agent to inspect and copy the permanent record. An attorney shall also state on the written authorization that the attorney has obtained the consent of the party to authorize an agent to inspect and copy the permanent record.

(2) For purposes of establishing parentage and establishing and enforcing child support orders, papers and records pertaining to the action or proceeding that are part of the permanent record of the court are subject to inspection and copying by any local child support agency, as defined in subdivision (h) of Section 17000.

(c) This section applies only to actions filed before January 1, 2023.[520]

7643.5. (a) Notwithstanding any other law concerning public hearings and records, a hearing or trial held under this part for an action filed on or after January 1, 2023, under Section 7613, subdivision (f) of Section 7630, or Part 7 (commencing with Section 7960), may be held in closed court without admittance of any person other than those necessary to the action or proceeding. Except as provided in subdivision (b), all papers and records, other than the final judgment, pertaining to the action or proceeding, whether part of the permanent record of the court or of a file in a public agency or elsewhere, are subject to inspection and copying only in exceptional cases upon an order of the court for good cause shown.

(b) (1) Papers and records pertaining to the action or proceeding that are part of the permanent record of the court are subject to inspection and copying by the parties to the action, their attorneys, and by agents acting pursuant to written authorization from the parties to the action or their attorneys. An attorney shall obtain the consent of the party to the action before authorizing an agent to inspect and copy the permanent record. An attorney shall also state on the written authorization that the attorney has obtained the consent of the party to authorize an agent to inspect and copy the permanent record.

(2) For purposes of establishing parentage and establishing and enforcing child support orders, papers and records pertaining to the action or proceeding that are part of the permanent record of the court are subject to inspection and copying by any local child support agency, as defined in subdivision (h) of Section 17000.

(c) On or before January 1, 2023, the Judicial Council shall create a new form or modify an existing form, as it deems appropriate, that requires a party initiating an action or proceeding filed under Section 7613, subdivision (f) of Section 7630, or Part 7 (commencing with Section 7960) to designate the action or proceeding as filed under the identified statutory provision.

(d) Notwithstanding Section 4, this section shall apply to all actions filed before January 1, 2023.[521]

7644. (a) Notwithstanding any other law, an action for child custody and support and for other relief as provided in Section 7637 may be filed based upon a voluntary declaration of parentage as provided in Chapter 3 (commencing with Section 7570) of Part 2.
(b) Except as provided in Section 7581, the voluntary declaration of parentage shall be given the same force and effect as a judgment of parentage entered by a court of competent jurisdiction. The court shall make appropriate orders as specified in Section 7637 based upon the voluntary declaration of parentage unless evidence is presented that the voluntary declaration of parentage has been rescinded by the parties, set aside as provided in Section 7575, 7576, or 7577, or is void under Section 7573.5.
(c) The Judicial Council shall develop the forms and procedures necessary to implement this section.
(d) This section shall become operative on January 1, 2020.

Article 1.5: Setting Aside or Vacating Judgement of Parentage

7645. For purposes of this article, the following definitions shall apply:
(a) "Child" means the child of a previously established father or mother, as determined by the superior court in a judgment that is the subject of a motion brought pursuant to this article, or as a matter of law.
(b) "Judgment" means a judgment, order, or decree entered in a court of this state that establishes parentage, including a determination of parentage made pursuant to a petition filed under Section 300, 601, or 602 of the Welfare and Institutions Code. For purposes of this article, "judgment" does not include a judgment in any action for marital dissolution, legal separation, or nullity.
(c) "Previously established father" means a person identified as the father of a child in a judgment that is the subject of a motion brought pursuant to this article.
(d) "Previously established mother" means a person identified as the mother of a child in a judgment that is the subject of a motion brought pursuant to this article.[403]

7646. (a) Notwithstanding any other law, a judgment establishing parentage may be set aside or vacated upon a motion by a previously established parent, the child, or the legal representative of any of these persons if genetic testing indicates that the previously established father of a child is not the genetic father of the child. The motion shall be brought within one of the following time periods:
(1) Within a two-year period commencing with the date on which the previously established father knew or should have known of a judgment that established the father's parentage of the child or commencing with the date the previously established father knew or should have known of the existence of an action to adjudicate the issue of parentage, whichever is first, except as provided in paragraph (2).
(2) In the case of a previously established father who is the legal father as a result of a default judgment as of the effective date of this section, within a two-year period from January 1, 2005,

to December 31, 2006, inclusive.

(b) Subdivision (a) does not apply if the child is presumed to be a child of a marriage pursuant to Section 7540, the previously established parent is a parent under Section 7613 or 7962, or the action is barred by paragraph (2) of subdivision (a) of Section 7630.

(c) Reconsideration of a motion brought under paragraph (3) of subdivision (a) may be requested and granted if the following requirements are met:

(1) The motion was filed with the court between September 24, 2006, and December 31, 2006, inclusive.

(2) The motion was denied solely on the basis that it was untimely.

(3) The request for reconsideration of the motion is filed on or before December 31, 2009.

7647. (a) A court may grant a motion to set aside or vacate a judgment establishing parentage only if all of the following conditions are met:

(1) The motion is filed in a court of proper venue.

(2) The motion contains, at a minimum, all of the following information, if known:

(A) The legal name, age, county of residence, and residence address of the child.

(B) The names, mailing addresses, and counties of residence, or, if deceased, the date and place of death, of the following persons:

(i) The previously established parents and the alleged father of the child.

(ii) The guardian of the child, if any.

(iii) Any person who has physical custody of the child.

(iv) The guardian ad litem of the child, if any, as appointed pursuant to Section 7647.5.

(C) A declaration that the person filing the motion believes that the previously established father is not the genetic father of the child, the specific reasons for this belief, and a declaration that the person desires that the motion be granted. The moving party is not required to present evidence of genetic testing indicating that the previously established father is not the genetic father of the child in order to bring this motion pursuant to Section 7646.

(D) A declaration that the marital presumption set forth in Section 7540 does not apply and that an action is not barred under paragraph (2) of subdivision (a) of Section 7630.

(3) The court finds that the previously established father is not a genetic parent pursuant to Section 7555.

(b) The motion shall include a proof of service upon the following persons, excluding the person bringing the motion:

(1) The parties to the action resulting in the judgment of parentage.

(2) The local child support agency, if services are being provided to the child pursuant to Title IV-D or IV-E of the Social Security Act (42 U.S.C. Sec. 651 et seq. and 42 U.S.C. Sec. 670 et seq.).

(3) The child's guardian ad litem, if any.[404]

7647.5. A guardian ad litem may be appointed for the child to represent the best interests of the child in an action brought pursuant to this article.

7647.7. Any genetic testing used to support the motion to set aside or vacate shall be conducted in accordance with Section 7552. The court shall, at the request of any person authorized to make a motion pursuant to this article, or may upon its own motion, order genetic testing to assist the court in making a determination whether the previously established father is the genetic father of the child.[405]

7648. The court may deny the motion to set aside or vacate a judgment establishing parentage if it determines that denial of the motion is in the best interest of the child, after consideration of the following factors:
(a) The age of the child.
(b) The length of time since the entry of the judgment establishing parentage.
(c) The nature, duration, and quality of any relationship between the previously established father and the child, including the duration and frequency of any time periods during which the child and the previously established father resided in the same household or enjoyed a parent and child relationship.
(d) The request of the previously established father that the parent and child relationship continue.
(e) Notice by the biological father of the child that the biological father does not oppose preservation of the relationship between the previously established father and the child.
(f) The benefit or detriment to the child in establishing the genetic father as the parent of the child.
(g) Whether the conduct of the previously established father has impaired the ability to ascertain the identity of, or get support from, the biological father.
(h) Additional factors deemed by the court to be relevant to its determination of the best interest of the child.

7648.1. If the court denies a motion pursuant to Section 7648, the court shall state on the record the basis for the denial of that motion and any supporting facts.

7648.2. (a) This section applies only to cases where support enforcement services are being provided by a local child support agency pursuant to Section 17400.
(b) Upon receipt of any motion brought pursuant to Section 7646, the local child support agency may issue an administrative order requiring the mother, child, and the previously established father to submit to genetic testing if all of the conditions of paragraphs (1) and (2) of subdivision (a) of Section 7647 are satisfied.
(c) The local child support agency shall pay the costs of any genetic tests that are ordered under subdivision (b) or are ordered by a court for cases in which the local child support agency is providing services under Title IV-D of the Social Security Act (42 U.S.C. Sec. 651 et seq.).
(d) Nothing in this section prohibits any person who has been ordered by a local child support agency to submit to genetic tests pursuant to this section from filing a notice of motion with the court seeking relief from the local child support agency's order to submit to genetic tests. In that event, the court shall resolve the issue of whether genetic tests should be ordered as provided in Section 7647.7. If any person refuses to submit to the tests after receipt of the administrative order pursuant to this section and fails to seek relief from the court from the administrative order either prior to the scheduled tests or within 10 days after the tests are scheduled, the court may

resolve the question of paternity against that person or enforce the administrative order if the rights of others or the interest of justice so require.

7648.3. A court may not issue an order setting aside or vacating a judgment establishing paternity pursuant to this article under any of the following circumstances:
(a) The judgment was made or entered by a tribunal of another state, even if the enforcement of that judgment is sought in this state.
(b) The judgment was made or entered in these state and genetic tests were conducted prior to the entry of the judgment which did not exclude the previously established father as the biological father of the child.

7648.4. Notwithstanding any other provision of law, if the court grants a motion to set aside or vacate a paternity judgment pursuant to this article, the court shall vacate any order for child support and arrearages issued on the basis of that previous judgment of paternity. The previously established father has no right of reimbursement for any amount of support paid prior to the granting of the motion.

7648.8. This article does not establish a basis for termination of any adoption, and does not affect any obligation of an adoptive parent to an adoptive child.

7648.9. This article does not establish a basis for setting aside or vacating a judgment establishing paternity with regard to a child conceived by assisted reproduction pursuant to Section 7613 or a child conceived pursuant to a surrogacy agreement.[276]

7649. This article does not limit the rights and remedies available under any other law with regard to setting aside or vacating a judgment of parentage.[406]

7649.5. Notwithstanding any other provision of this article, a distribution from the estate of a decedent or payment made by a trustee, insurance company, pension fund, or any other person or entity that was made in good faith reliance on a judgment establishing paternity that is final for purposes of direct appeal, may not be set aside or subject to direct or collateral attack because of the entry of an order setting aside or vacating a judgment under this article. An estate, trust, personal representative, trustee, or any other person or entity that made that distribution or payment may not incur any liability to any person because of the distribution or payment or because of the entry of an order under this article.

Article 2: Determination of Mother and Child Relationship

7650. (a) Any interested person may bring an action to determine the existence or nonexistence of a mother and child relationship. Insofar as practicable, the provisions of this division applicable to the father and child relationship apply.
(b) A woman is presumed to be the natural mother of a child if the child is in utero after the death of the decedent and the conditions set forth in Section 249.5 of the Probate Code are satisfied.[407]

Chapter 5: Termination of Parental Rights in Adoption Proceedings

7660. If a mother relinquishes for or consents to, or proposes to relinquish for or consent to, the adoption of a child who has a presumed parent under Section 7611, the presumed parent shall be given notice of the adoption proceeding and have the rights provided under Part 2 (commencing with Section 8600) of Division 13, unless that parent's relationship to the child has been previously terminated or determined by a court not to exist or the presumed parent has voluntarily relinquished for or consented to the adoption of the child.

7660.5. Notwithstanding any other provision of law, a presumed father may waive the right to notice of any adoption proceeding by executing a form developed by the department before an authorized representative of the department, an authorized representative of a licensed public or private adoption agency, or a notary public or other person authorized to perform notarial acts. The waiver of notice form may be validly executed before or after the birth of the child, and once signed no notice, relinquishment for, or consent to adoption of the child shall be required from the father for the adoption to proceed. This shall be a voluntary and informed waiver without undue influence. If the child is an Indian child as defined under the Indian Child Welfare Act (ICWA), any waiver of consent by an Indian presumed father shall be executed in accordance with the requirements for voluntary adoptions set forth in Section 1913 of Title 25 of the United States Code. The waiver shall not affect the rights of any known federally recognized Indian tribe or tribes from which the child or the presumed father may be descended to notification of, or participation in, adoption proceedings as provided by the ICWA. Notice that the waiver has been executed shall be given to any known federally recognized Indian tribe or tribes from which the child or the presumed father may be descended, as required by the ICWA.[186]

7661. If the other parent relinquishes for or consents to, or proposes to relinquish for or consent to, the adoption of a child, the mother shall be given notice of the adoption proceeding and have the rights provided under Part 2 (commencing with Section 8600) of Division 13, unless the mother's relationship to the child has been previously terminated by a court or the mother has voluntarily relinquished for or consented to the adoption of the child.

7662. (a) If a mother relinquishes for or consents to, or proposes to relinquish for or consent to, the adoption of a child, or if a child otherwise becomes the subject of an adoption proceeding, the agency or person to whom the child has been or is to be relinquished, or the mother or the person having physical or legal custody of the child, or the prospective adoptive parent, shall file a petition to terminate the parental rights of the alleged father, unless one of the following occurs:

(1) The alleged father's relationship to the child has been previously terminated or determined not to exist by a court.

(2) The alleged father has been served as prescribed in Section 7666 with a written notice alleging that the alleged father is or could be the biological father of the child to be adopted or placed for adoption and has failed to

bring an action for the purpose of declaring the existence of the father and child relationship pursuant to subdivision (c) of Section 7630 within 30 days of service of the notice or the birth of the child, whichever is later.

(3) The alleged father has executed a written form developed by the department to waive notice, to deny parentage, relinquish the child for adoption, or consent to the adoption of the child.

(b) The alleged father may validly execute a waiver or denial of parentage before or after the birth of the child, and, once signed, no notice of, relinquishment for, or consent to adoption of the child shall be required from the alleged father for the adoption to proceed.

(c) Except as provided in this subdivision and subdivision (d), all proceedings affecting a child, including proceedings under Divisions 8 (commencing with Section 3000) to 11 (commencing with Section 6500), inclusive, Part 1 (commencing with Section 7500) to Part 3 (commencing with Section 7600), inclusive, of this division, and Part 1 (commencing with Section 1400), Part 2 (commencing with Section 1500), and Part 4 (commencing with Section 2100) of Division 4 of the Probate Code, and any motion or petition for custody or visitation filed in a proceeding under this part, shall be stayed. The petition to terminate parental rights under this section is the only matter that may be heard during the stay until the court issues a final ruling on the petition.

(d) This section does not limit the jurisdiction of the court pursuant to Part 3 (commencing with Section 6240) and Part 4 (commencing with Section 6300) of Division 10 with respect to domestic violence orders, or pursuant to Article 6 (commencing with Section 300) of Chapter 2 of Part 1 of Division 2 of the Welfare and Institutions Code with respect to dependency proceedings.

7663. (a) In an effort to identify all alleged fathers and presumed parents, the court shall cause inquiry to be made of the mother and any other appropriate person by one of the following:

(1) The State Department of Social Services.

(2) A licensed county adoption agency.

(3) The licensed adoption agency to which the child is to be relinquished.

(4) In the case of a stepparent adoption, the licensed clinical social worker, licensed marriage and family therapist, or licensed professional clinical counselor who is performing the investigation pursuant to Section 9001, if applicable. In the case of a stepparent adoption in which a licensed clinical social worker, licensed marriage and family therapist, or licensed professional clinical counselor is not performing the investigation pursuant to Section 9001, the board of supervisors may assign those inquiries to a licensed county adoption agency, the county department designated by the board of supervisors to administer the public social services program, or the county probation department.

(b) The inquiry shall include all of the following:

(1) Whether the mother was married at the time of conception of the child or at any time thereafter.

(2) Whether the mother was

cohabiting with a man at the time of conception or birth of the child.
(3) Whether the mother has received support payments or promises of support with respect to the child or in connection with the pregnancy.
(4) Whether any person has formally or informally acknowledged or declared possible parentage of the child.
(5) The names and whereabouts, if known, of every person presumed or alleged to be the parent of the child, and the efforts made to give notice of the proposed adoption to each person identified.
(c) The agency that completes the inquiry shall file a written report of the findings with the court.

7664. (a) If, after the inquiry, the biological father is identified to the satisfaction of the court, or if more than one man is identified as a possible biological father, notice of the proceeding shall be given in accordance with Section 7666. If an alleged biological father fails to appear or, if appearing, fails to claim parental rights, those parental rights with reference to the child shall be terminated.
(b) If the biological father or a man claiming to be the biological father claims parental rights, the court shall determine biological parentage. The court shall then determine if it is in the best interest of the child that the biological father retain parental rights, or that an adoption of the child be allowed to proceed. The court, in making that determination, may consider all relevant evidence, including the efforts made by the biological father to obtain custody, the age and prior placement of the child, and the effects of a change of placement on the child.
(c) If the court finds that it is in the best interest of the child that the biological father should be allowed to retain parental rights, the court shall order that the biological father's consent is necessary for an adoption. If the court finds that the man claiming parental rights is not the biological father, or that if the man is the biological father it is in the child's best interest that an adoption be allowed to proceed, the court shall order that the consent of that man is not required for an adoption. This finding terminates all parental rights and responsibilities with respect to the child.

7665. If, after the inquiry, the court is unable to identify the biological father or any possible biological father and no person has appeared claiming to be the biological father and claiming custodial rights, the court shall enter an order terminating the unknown biological father's parental rights with reference to the child.[277]

7666. (a) Except as provided in subdivision (b), notice of the proceeding shall be given to every person identified as the biological father or a possible biological father in accordance with the Code of Civil Procedure for the service of process in a civil action in this state at least 10 days before the date of the proceeding, except that publication or posting of the notice of the proceeding is not required, and service on the parent or guardian of a biological father or possible biological father who is a minor is not required unless the minor has previously provided written authorization to serve the minor's parent or guardian. Proof of giving the notice shall be filed with the court before the petition is heard.

(b) Notice to a man identified as or alleged to be the biological father is not required, and the court shall issue an order dispensing with that notice under any of the following circumstances:

(1) The relationship to the child has been previously terminated or determined not to exist by a court.

(2) The alleged father has executed a written form to waive notice, deny parentage, relinquish the child for adoption, or consent to the adoption of the child.

(3) The whereabouts or identity of the alleged father are unknown or cannot be ascertained.

(4) The alleged father has been served with written notice of alleged parentage and the proposed adoption, and has failed to bring an action pursuant to subdivision (c) of Section 7630 within 30 days of service of the notice or the birth of the child, whichever is later.

7667. (a) Notwithstanding any other law, an action to terminate the parental rights of an alleged father of a child as specified in this part shall be set for hearing not more than 45 days after filing of the petition, except as provided in subdivision (c).

(b) The matter so set shall have precedence over all other civil matters on the date set for trial, except an action to terminate parental rights pursuant to Part 4 (commencing with Section 7800).

(c) The court may dispense with a hearing and issue an ex parte order terminating parental rights if any of the following applies:

(1) The identity or whereabouts of the alleged father are unknown.

(2) The alleged father has validly executed a waiver of the right to notice or a denial of parentage.

(3) The alleged father has been served with written notice of alleged parentage and the proposed adoption, and has failed to bring an action pursuant to subdivision (c) of Section 7630 within 30 days of service of the notice or the birth of the child, whichever is later.

7668. (a) The court may continue the proceedings for not more than 30 days as necessary to appoint counsel and to enable counsel to prepare for the case adequately or for other good cause.

(b) In order to obtain an order for a continuance of the hearing, written notice shall be filed within two court days of the date set for the hearing, together with affidavits or declarations detailing specific facts showing that a continuance is necessary, unless the court for good cause entertains an oral motion for continuance.

(c) Continuances shall be granted only upon a showing of good cause. Neither a stipulation between counsel nor the convenience of the parties is in and of itself a good cause.

(d) A continuance shall be granted only for that period of time shown to be necessary by the evidence considered at the hearing on the motion. If a continuance is granted, the facts proven which require the continuance shall be entered upon the minutes of the court.[1]

7669. (a) An order requiring or dispensing with an alleged father's consent for the adoption of a child may be appealed from in the same manner as an order of the juvenile court declaring a person to be a ward of the juvenile court and is conclusive and binding upon the alleged father.

(b) After making the order, the court has no power to set aside, change, or modify that order.

(c) Nothing in this section limits the right to appeal from the order and judgment.[278]

7670. There shall be no filing fee charged for a petition filed pursuant to Section 7662.[1]

7671. A single petition may be filed pursuant to Section 7662 to terminate the parental rights of the alleged father or fathers of two or more biological siblings or to terminate the parental rights of two or more alleged fathers of the same child. A petition filed in accordance with this section may be granted in whole or in part in accordance with the procedures set forth in this chapter. The court shall retain discretion to bifurcate any case in which the petition was filed in accordance with this section, and shall do so whenever it is necessary to protect the interests of a party or a child who is the subject of the proceeding.[316]

Chapter 6: Protective and Restraining Orders

Article 1: Orders in Summons

7700. In addition to the contents required by Section 412.20 of the Code of Civil Procedure, in a proceeding under this part the summons shall contain a temporary restraining order restraining all parties, without the prior written consent of the other party or an order of the court, from removing from the state any minor child for whom the proceeding seeks to establish a parent and child relationship.

Article 2: Ex Parte Orders

7710. During the pendency of a proceeding under this part, on application of a party in the manner provided by Part 4 (commencing with Section 240) of Division 2, the court may issue ex parte a protective order as defined in Section 6218 and any other order as provided in Article 1 (commencing with Section 6320) of Chapter 2 of Part 4 of Division 10.

Article 3: Orders After Notice and Hearing

7720. (a) After notice and a hearing, the court may issue a protective order as defined in Section 6218 and any other restraining order as provided in Article 2 (commencing with Section 6340) of Chapter 2 of Part 4 of Division 10.

(b) The court may not issue a mutual protective order pursuant to subdivision (a) unless it meets the requirements of Section 6305.

Article 4: Orders Included in Judgement

7730. A judgment entered in a proceeding under this part may include a protective order as defined in Section 6218 and any other restraining order as provided in Article 3 (commencing with Section 6360) of Chapter 2 of Part 4 of Division 10.

PART 4: FREEDOM FROM PARENTAL CUSTODY AND CONTROL

enacted by Stats. 1992, Ch. 162, Sec. 10

Chapter 1: General Provisions

7800. The purpose of this part is to serve the welfare and best interest of a child by providing the stability and security of an adoptive home when those conditions are otherwise missing from the child's life.[1]

7801. This part shall be liberally construed to serve and protect the interests and welfare of the child.[1]

7802. A proceeding may be brought under this part for the purpose of having a minor child declared free from the custody and control of either or both parents.[1]

7803. A declaration of freedom from parental custody and control pursuant to this part terminates all parental rights and responsibilities with regard to the child.[1]

7804. In a proceeding under this part, the court may appoint a suitable party to act in behalf of the child and may order such further notice of the proceedings to be given as the court deems proper.[1]

7805. (a) A petition filed in a proceeding under this part, or a report of the probation officer or county department designated by the board of supervisors to administer the public social services program filed in a proceeding under this part, may be inspected only by the following persons:

(1) Court personnel.

(2) The child who is the subject of the proceeding.

(3) The parents or guardian of the child.

(4) The attorneys for the parties.

(5) Any other person designated by the judge.

(b) In a proceeding before the court of appeal or Supreme Court to review a judgment or order entered in a proceeding under this part, the court record and briefs filed by the parties may be inspected only by the following persons:

(1) Court personnel.

(2) A party to the proceeding.

(3) The attorneys for the parties.

(4) Any other person designated by the presiding judge of the court before which the matter is pending.

(c) Notwithstanding any other provision of law, if it is believed that the welfare of the child will be promoted thereby, the court and the probation officer may furnish information, pertaining to a petition under this part, to any of the following:

(1) The State Department of Social Services.

(2) A county welfare department.

(3) A public welfare agency.

(4) A private welfare agency licensed by the State Department of Social Services.[1]

7806. There shall be no filing fee charged for a proceeding brought under this part.[1]

7807. (a) Sections 3020, 3022, 3040 to 3043, inclusive, and 3409 do not apply in a proceeding under this part.

(b) Except as provided in this subdivision and subdivision (c), all proceedings affecting a child, including proceedings under Divisions 8 (commencing with Section 3000) to 11 (commencing with Section 6500), inclusive, Part 1 (commencing with Section 7500) to Part 3 (commencing with Section 7600), inclusive, of this division, and Part 1 (commencing with Section 1400), Part 2 (commencing with Section 1500), and Part 4 (commencing with Section 2100) of Division 4 of the Probate Code, and any motion or petition for custody or

visitation filed in a proceeding under this part, shall be stayed. The petition to free the minor from parental custody and control under this section is the only matter that may be heard during the stay until the court issues a final ruling on the petition.
(c) This section does not limit the jurisdiction of the court pursuant to Part 3 (commencing with Section 6240) and Part 4 (commencing with Section 6300) of Division 10 with respect to domestic violence orders, or pursuant to Article 6 (commencing with Section 300) of Chapter 2 of Part 1 of Division 2 of the Welfare and Institutions Code with respect to dependency proceedings.[317]

7808. This part does not apply to a minor adjudged a dependent child of the juvenile court pursuant to subdivision (c) of Section 360 of the Welfare and Institutions Code on and after January 1, 1989, during the period in which the minor is a dependent child of the court. For those minors, the exclusive means for the termination of parental rights are provided in the following statutes:
(a) Section 366.26 of the Welfare and Institutions Code.
(b) Sections 8604 to 8606, inclusive, and 8700 of this code.
(c) Chapter 5 (commencing with Section 7660) of Part 3 of this division of this code.

Chapter 2: Circumstances Where Proceeding May Be Brought

7820. A proceeding may be brought under this part for the purpose of having a child under the age of 18 years declared free from the custody and control of either or both parents if the child comes within any of the descriptions set out in this chapter.[1]

7821. A finding pursuant to this chapter shall be supported by clear and convincing evidence, except as otherwise provided.[144]

7822. (a) A proceeding under this part may be brought if any of the following occur:
(1) The child has been left without provision for the child's identification by the child's parent or parents.
(2) The child has been left by both parents or the sole parent in the care and custody of another person for a period of six months without any provision for the child's support, or without communication from the parent or parents, with the intent on the part of the parent or parents to abandon the child.
(3) One parent has left the child in the care and custody of the other parent for a period of one year without any provision for the child's support, or without communication from the parent, with the intent on the part of the parent to abandon the child.
(b) The failure to provide identification, failure to provide support, or failure to communicate is presumptive evidence of the intent to abandon. If the parent or parents have made only token efforts to support or communicate with the child, the court may declare the child abandoned by the parent or parents. In the event that a guardian has been appointed for the child, the court may still declare the child abandoned if the parent or parents have failed to communicate with or support the child within the meaning of this section.
(c) If the child has been left without

provision for the child's identification and the whereabouts of the parents are unknown, a petition may be filed after the 120th day following the discovery of the child and citation by publication may be commenced. The petition may not be heard until after the 180th day following the discovery of the child.

(d) If the parent has agreed for the child to be in the physical custody of another person or persons for adoption and has not signed an adoption placement agreement pursuant to Section 8801.3, a consent to adoption pursuant to Section 8814, or a relinquishment to a licensed adoption agency pursuant to Section 8700, evidence of the adoptive placement shall not in itself preclude the court from finding an intent on the part of that parent to abandon the child. If the parent has placed the child for adoption pursuant to Section 8801.3, consented to adoption pursuant to Section 8814, or relinquished the child to a licensed adoption agency pursuant to Section 8700, and has then either revoked the consent or rescinded the relinquishment, but has not taken reasonable action to obtain custody of the child, evidence of the adoptive placement shall not in itself preclude the court from finding an intent on the part of that parent to abandon the child.

(e) Notwithstanding subdivisions (a), (b), (c), and (d), if the parent of an Indian child has transferred physical care, custody, and control of the child to an Indian custodian, that action shall not be deemed to constitute an abandonment of the child, unless the parent manifests the intent to abandon the child by either of the following:

(1) Failing to resume physical care, custody, and control of the child upon the request of the Indian custodian provided that, if the Indian custodian is unable to make a request because the parent has failed to keep the Indian custodian apprised of the parent's whereabouts and the Indian custodian has made reasonable efforts to determine the whereabouts of the parent without success, there may be evidence of intent to abandon.

(2) Failing to substantially comply with any obligations assumed by the parent in the agreement with the Indian custodian despite the Indian custodian's objection to the noncompliance.

7823. (a) A proceeding under this part may be brought if all of the following requirements are satisfied:

(1) The child has been neglected or cruelly treated by either or both parents. A finding that a parent committed severe sexual abuse, as described in paragraph (6) of subdivision (b) of Section 361.5 of the Welfare and Institutions Code, against the child shall be prima facie evidence that the parent has neglected or cruelly treated the child within the meaning of this subdivision.

(2) The child has been a dependent child of the juvenile court under any subdivision of Section 300 of the Welfare and Institutions Code and the parent or parents have been deprived of the child's custody for one year before the filing of a petition pursuant to this part.

(b) Physical custody by the parent or parents for insubstantial periods of time does not interrupt the running of the one-year period.[370]

7824. (a) "Disability" as used in this section means any physical or mental incapacity which renders the parent or parents unable to care for and control the child adequately.

(b) A proceeding under this part may be brought where all of the following requirements are satisfied:

(1) The child is one whose parent or parents (A) suffer a disability because of the habitual use of alcohol, or any of the controlled substances specified in Schedules I to V, inclusive, of Division 10 (commencing with Section 11000) of the Health and Safety Code, except when these controlled substances are used as part of a medically prescribed plan, or (B) are morally depraved.

(2) The child has been a dependent child of the juvenile court, and the parent or parents have been deprived of the child's custody continuously for one year immediately before the filing of a petition pursuant to this part.

(c) Physical custody by the parent or parents for insubstantial periods of time does not interrupt the running of the one-year period.[1]

7825. (a) A proceeding under this part may be brought where both of the following requirements are satisfied:

(1) The child is one whose parent or parents are convicted of a felony.

(2) The facts of the crime of which the parent or parents were convicted are of such a nature so as to prove the unfitness of the parent or parents to have the future custody and control of the child. In making a determination pursuant to this section, the court may consider the parent's criminal record prior to the felony conviction to the extent that the criminal record demonstrates a pattern of behavior substantially related to the welfare of the child or the parent's ability to exercise custody and control regarding the child.

(b) The mother of a child may bring a proceeding under this part against the father of the child, where the child was conceived as a result of an act in violation of Section 261 of the Penal Code, and where the father was convicted of that violation. For purposes of this subdivision, there is a conclusive presumption that the father is unfit to have custody or control of the child.

7826. A proceeding under this part may be brought where both of the following requirements are satisfied:

(a) The child is one whose parent or parents have been declared by a court of competent jurisdiction, wherever situated, to be developmentally disabled or mentally ill.

(b) In the state or country in which the parent or parents reside or are hospitalized, the Director of State Hospitals or the Director of Developmental Services, or their equivalent, if any, and the executive director of the hospital, if any, of which the parent or parents are inmates or patients, certify that the parent or parents so declared to be developmentally disabled or mentally ill will not be capable of supporting or controlling the child in a proper manner.[250]

7827. (a) "Mentally disabled" as used in this section means that a parent or parents suffer a mental incapacity or disorder that renders the parent or parents unable to care for and control the child adequately.

(b) A proceeding under this part may be brought if the child is one whose parent or parents are mentally disabled and are likely to remain so in the foreseeable future.

(c) Except as provided in subdivision (d), the evidence of any two experts, each of whom shall be a physician and surgeon, certified either by the American Board of Psychiatry and Neurology or under Section 6750 of the Welfare and Institutions Code, a licensed psychologist who has a doctoral degree in psychology and at least five years of postgraduate experience in the diagnosis and treatment of emotional and mental disorders, is required to support a finding under this section. In addition to this requirement, the court shall have the discretion to call a licensed marriage and family therapist, a licensed professional clinical counselor, or a licensed clinical social worker, either of whom shall have at least five years of relevant post licensure experience, in circumstances in which the court determines that this testimony is in the best interest of the child and is warranted by the circumstances of the particular family or parenting issues involved. However, the court may not call a licensed marriage and family therapist, licensed professional clinical counselor, or licensed clinical social worker pursuant to this section who is the adoption service provider, as defined in Section 8502, of the child who is the subject of the petition to terminate parental rights.

(d) If the parent or parents reside in another state or in a foreign country, the evidence required by this section may be supplied by the affidavits of two experts, each of whom shall be either of the following:

(1) A physician and surgeon who is a resident of that state or foreign country, and who has been certified by a medical organization or society of that state or foreign country to practice psychiatric or neurological medicine.

(2) A licensed psychologist who has a doctoral degree in psychology and at least five years of postgraduate experience in the diagnosis and treatment of emotional and mental disorders and who is licensed in that state or authorized to practice in that country.

(e) If the rights of a parent are sought to be terminated pursuant to this section, and the parent does not have an attorney, the court shall appoint an attorney for the parent pursuant to Article 4 (commencing with Section 7860) of Chapter 3, whether or not a request for the appointment is made by the parent.[373]

Chapter 3: Procedure

Article 1: Authorized Petitioners

7840. (a) A petition may be filed under this part for an order or judgment declaring a child free from the custody and control of either or both parents by any of the following:

(1) The State Department of Social Services, a county welfare department, a licensed private or public adoption agency, a county adoption department, or a county probation department which is planning adoptive placement of the child with a licensed adoption agency.

(2) The State Department of Social Services acting as an adoption agency in counties which are not served by a county adoption agency.

(b) The fact that a child is in a foster care home subject to the requirements of Chapter 3 (commencing with Section 1500) of Division 2 of the Health and Safety Code does not prevent the filing of a petition under subdivision (a).

(c) The county counsel or, if there is no county counsel, the district attorney of the county specified in Section 7845 shall, in a proper case, institute the proceeding upon the request of any of the state or county agencies mentioned in subdivision (a). The proceeding shall be instituted pursuant to this part within 30 days of the request.

(d) If, at the time of the filing of a petition by a department or agency specified in subdivision (a), the child is in the custody of the petitioner, the petitioner may continue to have custody of the child pending the hearing on the petition unless the court, in its discretion, makes such other order regarding custody pending the hearing as it finds will best serve and protect the interest and welfare of the child.[1]

7841. (a) An interested person may file a petition under this part for an order or judgment declaring a child free from the custody and control of either or both parents.

(b) For purposes of this section, an "interested person" is one who has a direct interest in the action, and includes, but is not limited to, a person who has filed, or who intends to file within a period of 6 months, an adoption petition under Section 8714, 8802, or 9000, or a licensed adoption agency to whom the child has been relinquished by the other parent.[170]

7842. A single petition may be filed under this part to free a child, or more than one child if the children are biological siblings, from the custody and control of both parents. A petition filed in accordance with this section may be granted in whole or in part in accordance with the procedures set forth in this chapter. The court shall retain discretion to bifurcate any case in which the petition was filed in accordance with this section, and shall do so whenever it is necessary to protect the interests of a party or a child who is the subject of the proceeding.[318]

Article 2: Venue

7845. The petition shall be filed in any of the following:

(a) The county in which a minor described in Chapter 2 (commencing with Section 7820) resides or is found.

(b) The county in which any of the acts which are set forth in Chapter 2 (commencing with Section 7820) are alleged to have occurred.

(c) The county in which a petition for the adoption of the child has been filed or the adoption agency to which the child has been relinquished or proposed to be relinquished has an office.[192]

Article 3: Investigation and Report

7850. Upon the filing of a petition under Section 7841, the clerk of the court shall, in accordance with the direction of the court, immediately notify the juvenile probation officer, qualified court investigator, licensed clinical social worker, licensed marriage and family therapist, licensed professional clinical counselor, or the county department designated by the board of supervisors to administer the public social services program, who shall immediately investigate the circumstances of the child and the circumstances which are alleged to bring the child within any provision of Chapter 2 (commencing with Section 7820).[374]

7851. (a) The juvenile probation officer, qualified court investigator, licensed clinical social worker, licensed marriage and family therapist, licensed professional clinical counselor, or the county department shall render to the court a written report of the investigation with a recommendation of the proper disposition to be made in the proceeding in the best interest of the child.
(b) The report shall include all of the following:
(1) A statement that the person making the report explained to the child the nature of the proceeding to end parental custody and control.
(2) A statement of the child's feelings and thoughts concerning the pending proceeding.
(3) A statement of the child's attitude towards the child's parent or parents and particularly whether or not the child would prefer living with the parent or parents.
(4) A statement that the child was informed of the child's right to attend the hearing on the petition and the child's feelings concerning attending the hearing.
(c) If the age, or the physical, emotional, or other condition of the child precludes the child's meaningful response to the explanations, inquiries, and information required by subdivision (b), a description of the condition shall satisfy the requirement of that subdivision.
(d) The court shall receive the report in evidence and shall read and consider its contents in rendering the court's judgment.

7851.5. The petitioner shall be liable for all reasonable costs incurred in connection with the termination of parental rights, including, but not limited to, costs incurred for the investigation required by this article. However, public agencies and nonprofit organizations are exempt from payment of the costs of the investigation. The liability of a petitioner for costs under this section shall not exceed nine hundred dollars ($900). The court may defer, waive, or reduce the costs when the payment would cause an economic hardship which would be detrimental to the welfare of the child.[56]

7852. "Qualified court investigator," as used in this article, has the meaning provided by Section 8543.

Article 4: Appointment of Counsel

7860. At the beginning of the proceeding on a petition filed pursuant to this part, counsel shall be appointed as provided in this article. The public defender or private counsel may be appointed as counsel pursuant to this article. The same counsel shall not be appointed to represent both the child and the child's parent.[1]

7861. The court shall consider whether the interests of the child require the appointment of counsel. If the court finds that the interests of the child require representation by counsel, the court shall appoint counsel to represent the child, whether or not the child is able to afford counsel. The child shall not be present in court unless the child so requests or the court so orders.[1]

7862. If a parent appears without counsel and is unable to afford counsel, the court shall appoint counsel for the parent, unless that representation is knowingly and intelligently waived.[1]

7863. Private counsel appointed under this article shall receive a reasonable sum for compensation and expenses, the amount of which shall be determined by the court. The amount so determined shall be paid by the real parties in interest, other than the child, in proportions the court deems just. However, if the court finds that any of the real parties in interest are unable to afford counsel, the amount shall be paid out of the general fund of the county.[1]

7864. The court may continue the proceeding for not to exceed 30 days as necessary to appoint counsel and to enable counsel to become acquainted with the case.[1]

Article 5: Time for Hearing; Continuance

7870. (a) It is the public policy of this state that judicial proceedings to declare a child free from parental custody and control shall be fully determined as expeditiously as possible.
(b) Notwithstanding any other provision of law, a proceeding to declare a child free from parental custody and control pursuant to this part shall be set for hearing not more than 45 days after the filing of the petition. If, at the time set for hearing, or at any continuance thereof, service has been completed and no interested person appears to contest, the court may issue an order based on the verified pleadings and any other evidence as may be submitted. If any interested person appears to contest the matter, the court shall set the matter for trial. The matter so set has precedence over all other civil matters on the date set for trial.
(c) The court may continue the proceeding as provided in Section 7864 or Section 7871.[263]

7871. (a) A continuance may be granted only upon a showing of good cause. Neither a stipulation between counsel nor the convenience of the parties is in and of itself a good cause.
(b) Unless the court for good cause entertains an oral motion for continuance, written notice of a motion for a continuance of the hearing shall be filed within two court days of the date set for the hearing, together with affidavits or declarations detailing specific facts showing that a continuance is necessary.
(c) A continuance shall be granted only for that period of time shown to be necessary by the evidence considered at the hearing on the motion. Whenever a continuance is granted, the facts proven which require the continuance shall be entered upon the minutes of the court.[1]

Article 6: Notice of Proceeding and Attendance at Hearing

7880. (a) Upon the filing of the petition, a citation shall issue requiring any person having the custody or control of the child, or the person with whom the child is, to appear at a time and place stated in the citation.
(b) The citation shall also require the person to appear with the child except that, if the child is under the age of 10 years, appearance with the child is required only upon order of the court after necessity has been shown.
(c) Service of the citation shall be made in the manner prescribed by law for service of civil process at least 10 days

before the time stated in the citation for the appearance. The party or attorney responsible for serving the citation shall do so in a timely manner in order to maximize the response time available to the party being served.[264]

7881. (a) Notice of the proceeding shall be given by service of a citation on the father or mother of the child, if the place of residence of the father or mother is known to the petitioner. If the place of residence of the father or mother is not known to the petitioner, then the citation shall be served on the grandparents and adult brothers, sisters, uncles, aunts, and first cousins of the child, if there are any and if their residences and relationships to the child are known to the petitioner.
(b) The citation shall advise the person or persons that they may appear at the time and place stated in the citation. The citation shall also advise the person or persons of the rights and procedures set forth in Article 4 (commencing with Section 7860). If the petition is filed for the purpose of freeing the child for placement for adoption, the citation shall so state.
(c) The citation shall be served in the manner provided by law for the service of a summons in a civil action, other than by publication. If one parent has relinquished the child for the purpose of adoption, or has signed a consent for adoption as provided in Sections 8700, 8814, or 9003, notice as provided in this section need not be given to the parent who has signed the relinquishment or consent.
(d) Service of the citations required by this section shall be made at least 10 days before the time stated in the citation for the appearance.[1]

7882. (a) If the parent of the child or a person alleged to be or claiming to be the parent cannot, with reasonable diligence, be served as provided for in Section 7881, or if the parent's place of residence is not known to the petitioner, the petitioner or the petitioner's agent or attorney shall make and file an affidavit stating the name of the parent or alleged parent and their place of residence, if known to the petitioner, and the name of the parent or alleged parent whose place of residence is unknown to the petitioner.
(b) Upon the filing of the affidavit, the court shall make an order that (1) the service shall be made by the publication of a citation requiring the parent or alleged parent to appear at the time and place stated in the citation and (2) the citation shall be published pursuant to Section 6064 of the Government Code in a newspaper to be named and designated in the order as most likely to give notice to the parent or alleged parent to be served.
(c) In case of publication where the residence of a parent or alleged parent is known, the court shall also direct a copy of the citation to be forthwith served upon that parent or alleged parent by mail by deposit in the post office properly addressed and with the postage thereon fully prepaid, directed to that parent or alleged parent at the place of residence. When publication is ordered, service of a copy of the citation in the manner provided for in Section 7881 is equivalent to publication and deposit in the post office.
(d) If one or both of the parents of the child are unknown or if the names of one or both of the child's parents are uncertain, that fact shall be set forth in the affidavit and the court shall order

the citation to be directed to either or both of the child's parents, naming and otherwise describing the child, and to all persons claiming to be a parent of the child.

(e) Service is complete at the expiration of the time prescribed by the order for publication or when service is made as provided for in Section 7881, whichever event first occurs.

7883. If a person personally served with a citation within this state as provided in Section 7880 fails without reasonable cause to appear and abide by the order of the court, or to bring the child before the court if so required in the citation, the failure constitutes a contempt of court.[1]

7884. (a) Unless requested by the child concerning whom the petition has been filed and any parent or guardian present, the public shall not be admitted to a proceeding under this part.

(b) Notwithstanding subdivision (a), the judge may admit those persons the judge determines have a direct and legitimate interest in the particular case or in the work of the court.[1]

Article 7: Hearing and Subsequent Proceedings

7890. In a proceeding under this part, the court shall consider the wishes of the child, bearing in mind the age of the child, and shall act in the best interest of the child.[1]

7891. (a) Except as otherwise provided in this section, if the child who is the subject of the petition is 10 years of age or older, the child shall be heard by the court in chambers on at least the following matters:

(1) The feelings and thoughts of the child concerning the custody proceeding about to take place.

(2) The feelings and thoughts of the child about the child's parent or parents.

(3) The child's preference as to custody, according to Section 3042.

(b) The court shall inform the child of the child's right to attend the hearing. However, counsel for the child may waive the hearing in chambers by the court.

(c) This section does not apply if the child is confined because of illness or other incapacity to an institution or residence and is therefore unable to attend.

7892. (a) The testimony of the child may be taken in chambers and outside the presence of the child's parent or parents if the child's parent or parents are represented by counsel, the counsel is present, and any of the following circumstances exist:

(1) The court determines that testimony in chambers is necessary to ensure truthful testimony.

(2) The child is likely to be intimidated by a formal courtroom setting.

(3) The child is afraid to testify in front of the child's parent or parents.

(b) The testimony of a child also may be taken in chambers and outside the presence of the guardian or guardians of a child under the circumstances specified in subdivision (a).

(c) A finding pursuant to this section shall be supported by clear and convincing evidence.

(d) After testimony in chambers, the parent or parents of the child may elect to have the court reporter read back the testimony or have the testimony summarized by counsel for the parent or parents.[1]

7892.5. The court shall not declare an Indian child free from the custody or control of a parent, unless both of the following apply:
(a) The court finds, supported by clear and convincing evidence, that active efforts were made in accordance with Section 361.7 of the Welfare and Institutions Code.
(b) The court finds, supported by evidence beyond a reasonable doubt, including testimony of one or more "qualified expert witnesses" as described in Section 224.5 of the Welfare and Institutions Code, that the continued custody of the child by the parent is likely to result in serious emotional or physical damage to the child.
(c) This section shall only apply to proceedings involving an Indian child.[145]

7893. (a) If the court, by order or judgment, declares a child free from the custody and control of both parents under this part, or one parent if the other no longer has custody and control, the court shall at the same time take one of the following actions:
(1) Appoint a guardian for the child.
(2) At the request of the State Department of Social Services or a licensed adoption agency, or where the court finds it is in the child's best interest, refer the child to a licensed adoption agency for adoptive placement by the agency.
(b) When the court refers the child to a licensed adoption agency for adoptive placement by the agency:
(1) The agency is responsible for the care of the child and is entitled to the exclusive custody and control of the child at all times until a petition for adoption has been granted.
(2) After the referral, no petition for guardianship may be filed without the consent of the agency.
(3) No petition for adoption may be heard until the appellate rights of the natural parents have been exhausted.[1]

7894. (a) An order and judgment of the court declaring a child free from the custody and control of a parent or parents under this part is conclusive and binding upon the child, upon the parent or parents, and upon all other persons who have been served with citations by publication or otherwise as provided in this part.
(b) After making the order and judgment, the court has no power to set aside, change, or modify it.
(c) Nothing in this section limits the right to appeal from the order and judgment. [1]

7895. (a) Upon appeal from a judgment freeing a child who is a dependent child of the juvenile court from parental custody and control, the appellate court shall appoint counsel for the appellant as provided by this section.
(b) Upon motion by the appellant and a finding that the appellant is unable to afford counsel, the appellate court shall appoint counsel for the indigent appellant, and appellant's counsel shall be provided a free copy of the reporter's and clerk's transcript. All of those costs are a charge against the court.
(c) The reporter's and clerk's transcripts shall be prepared and transmitted immediately after filing of the notice of appeal, at court expense and without advance payment of fees. If the appellant is able to afford counsel, the court may seek reimbursement from the appellant for the cost of the transcripts under subdivision (c) of

Section 68511.3 of the Government Code as though the appellant had been granted permission to proceed in forma pauperis.

PART 5: INTERSTATE COMPACT ON PLACEMENT OF CHILDREN

enacted by Stats. 1992, Ch. 162, Sec. 10

7900. The Interstate Compact on Placement of Children as set forth in Section 7901 is hereby adopted and entered into with all other jurisdictions joining therein.[1]

7901. The provisions of the interstate compact referred to in Section 7900 are as follows:

INTERSTATE COMPACT ON THE PLACEMENT OF CHILDREN

Article 1: Purpose and Policy

It is the purpose and policy of the party states to cooperate with each other in the interstate placement of children to the end that:

(a) Each child requiring placement shall receive the maximum opportunity to be placed in a suitable environment and with persons or institutions having appropriate qualifications and facilities to provide a necessary and desirable degree and type of care.

(b) The appropriate authorities in a state where a child is to be placed may have full opportunity to ascertain the circumstances of the proposed placement, thereby promoting full compliance with applicable requirements for the protection of the child.

(c) The proper authorities of the state from which the placement is made may obtain the most complete information on the basis on which to evaluate a projected placement before it is made.

(d) Appropriate jurisdictional arrangements for the care of children will be promoted.

Article 2: Definitions

As used in this compact:

(a) "Child" means a person who, by reason of minority, is legally subject to parental, guardianship, or similar control.

(b) "Sending agency" means a party state, or officer or employee thereof; subdivision of a party state, or officer or employee thereof; a court of a party state; a person, corporation, association, charitable agency, or other entity that sends, brings, or causes to be sent or brought any child to another party state.

(c) "Receiving state" means the state to which a child is sent, brought, or caused to be sent or brought, whether by public authorities or private persons or agencies, and whether for placement with state or local public authorities or for placement with private agencies or persons.

(d) "Placement" means the arrangement for the care of a child in a family free or boarding home or in a child-caring agency or institution, but does not include any institution caring for persons with developmental disabilities or mental health disorders or any institution primarily educational in character, and any hospital or other medical facility.

Article 3: Conditions for Placement

(a) A sending agency shall not send, bring, or cause to be sent or brought into any other party state any child for placement in foster care or as a preliminary to a possible adoption unless the sending agency complies with each and every requirement set forth in this article and with the applicable laws of the receiving state governing the placement of children therein.

(b) Before sending, bringing, or causing any child to be sent or brought into a receiving state for placement in foster care or as a preliminary to a possible adoption, the sending agency shall furnish the appropriate public authorities in the receiving state written notice of the intention to send, bring, or place the child in the receiving state. The notice shall contain:

(1) The name, date, and place of birth of the child.

(2) The identity and address or addresses of the parents or legal guardian.

(3) The name and address of the person, agency, or institution to or with which the sending agency proposes to send, bring, or place the child.

(4) A full statement of the reasons for the proposed action and evidence of the authority pursuant to which the placement is proposed to be made.

(c) Any public officer or agency in a receiving state that receives notice pursuant to paragraph (b) of this article may request of the sending agency, or any other appropriate officer or agency of or in the sending agency's state, and shall be entitled to receive therefrom, supporting or additional information it deems necessary under the circumstances to carry out the purpose and policy of this compact.

(d) The child shall not be sent, brought, or caused to be sent or brought into the receiving state until the appropriate public authorities in the receiving state notify the sending agency, in writing, to the effect that the proposed placement does not appear to be contrary to the interest of the child.

Article 4. Penalty for Illegal Placement

The sending, bringing, or causing to be sent or brought into any receiving state of a child in violation of the terms of this compact shall constitute a violation of the laws respecting the placement of children of both the state in which the sending agency is located or from which it sends or brings the child and of the receiving state. A violation may be punished or subjected to penalty in either jurisdiction in accordance with its laws. In addition to liability for any punishment or penalty, any violation shall constitute full and sufficient grounds for the suspension or revocation of any license, permit, or other legal authorization held by the sending agency that empowers or allows it to place or care for children.

Article 5: Continuing Jurisdiction

(a) The sending agency shall retain jurisdiction over the child sufficient to determine all matters in relation to the custody, supervision, care, treatment, and disposition of the child that it would have had if the child had remained in the sending agency's state, until the child is adopted, reaches majority, becomes self-supporting, or is discharged with the concurrence of the appropriate authority in the receiving state. That jurisdiction shall also include the power to effect or cause the return of the child or the child's transfer to another location and custody pursuant to law. The sending agency shall continue to have financial responsibility for support and maintenance of the child during the period of the placement. Nothing contained herein shall defeat a claim of jurisdiction by a receiving state sufficient to deal with an act of delinquency or crime committed therein.

(b) When the sending agency is a public agency, it may enter into an agreement with an authorized public or private agency in the receiving state providing for the performance of one or more services in respect of that case by the latter as agent for the sending agency.

(c) This compact shall not be construed to prevent a private charitable agency authorized to place children in the receiving state from performing services or acting as agent in that state for a private charitable agency of the sending state or to prevent the agency in the receiving state from discharging financial responsibility for the support and maintenance of a child who has been placed on behalf of the sending agency without relieving the responsibility set forth in paragraph (a) of this article.

Article 6: Institutional Care of Delinquent Children

A child adjudicated delinquent may be placed in an institution in another party jurisdiction pursuant to this compact but that placement shall not be made unless the child is given a court hearing on notice to the parent or guardian with opportunity to be heard, before being sent to the other party jurisdiction for institutional care and the court finds that both of the following exist:

(a) Equivalent facilities for the child are not available in the sending agency's jurisdiction.

(b) Institutional care in the other jurisdiction is in the best interest of the child and will not produce undue hardship.

Article 7: Compact Administrator

The executive head of each jurisdiction party to this compact shall designate an officer who shall be general coordinator of activities under this compact in that jurisdiction and who, acting jointly with like officers of other party jurisdictions, shall have power to promulgate rules and regulations to carry out more effectively the terms and provisions of this compact.

Article 8: Limitations

This compact shall not apply to:

(a) The sending or bringing of a child into a receiving state by the child's parent, stepparent, grandparent, adult brother or sister, adult uncle or aunt, or the child's guardian and leaving the child with any such relative or nonagency guardian in the receiving state.

(b) Any placement, sending, or bringing of a child into a receiving state pursuant to any other interstate compact to which both the state from which the child is sent or brought and the receiving state are party, or to any other agreement between those states that has the force of law.

Article 9: Enactment and Withdrawal

This compact shall be open to joinder by any state, territory, or possession of the United States, the District of Columbia, the Commonwealth of Puerto Rico, and, with the consent of Congress, the government of Canada or any province thereof. It shall become effective with respect to any of these jurisdictions when that jurisdiction has enacted the same into law. Withdrawal from this compact shall be by the enactment of a statute repealing the same, but shall not take effect until two years after the effective date of the statute and until written notice of the withdrawal has been given by the withdrawing state to the Governor of each other party jurisdiction. Withdrawal of a party state shall not affect the rights, duties, and obligations under this compact of any sending agency therein with respect to a placement made before the effective date of withdrawal.

Article 10: Construction and Severability

The provisions of this compact shall be liberally construed to effectuate the purposes thereof. The provisions of this compact shall be severable and if any phrase, clause, sentence, or provision of this compact is declared to be contrary to the constitution of any party state or of the United States or the applicability thereof to any government, agency, person, or circumstance is held invalid, the validity of the remainder of this com-pact and the applicability thereof to any government, agency, person, or circumstance shall not be affected thereby. If this compact shall be held contrary to the constitution of any state party thereto, the compact shall remain in full force and effect as to the remaining states and in full force and effect as to the state affected as to all severable matters.

7901.1. (a) Within 60 days of receipt of a request from another state to conduct a study of a home environment for purposes of assessing the safety and suitability of placing a child in the home, a county child welfare agency shall, directly or by contract, do both of the following:

(1) Conduct and complete the study.

(2) Return a report to the requesting state on the results of the study. The report shall address the extent to which placement in the home would meet the needs of the child.

(b) Except as provided in subdivision (c), in the case of a home study commenced on or before September 30, 2008, if the agency fails to comply with subdivision (a) within the 60-day period as a result of circumstances beyond the control of the agency, the agency shall have 75 days to comply with subdivision (a). The agency shall document the circumstances involved and certify that completing the home study is in the best interests of the child. For purposes of this subdivision, "circumstances beyond the control of the agency" include, but are not limited to, the failure of a federal agency to provide the results of a background check or the failure of any entity to provide completed medical forms, if the background check or records were requested by the agency at least 45 days before the end of the 60-day period.

(c) Subdivision (b) shall not be construed to require the agency to have completed, within the applicable period, the parts of the home study involving the education and training of the prospective foster or adoptive parents.

(d) The agency shall treat any report described in subdivision (a) that is received from another state, an Indian tribe, or a private agency under contract with another state, as meeting any requirements imposed by the state for

the completion of a home study before placing a child in the home, unless, within 14 days after receipt of the report, the agency determines, based on grounds that are specific to the content of the report, that making a decision in reliance on the report would be contrary to the welfare of the child.
(e) A county is not restricted from contracting with a private agency for the conduct of a home study described in subdivision (a).
(f) The department shall work with counties to identify barriers to meeting the timeframes specified in this section and to develop recommendations to reduce or eliminate those barriers.[178]

7902. Financial responsibility for a child placed pursuant to the Interstate Compact on the Placement of Children shall be determined in accordance with Article 5 of the compact in the first instance. However, in the event of partial or complete default of performance thereunder, the provisions of other state laws also may be invoked.[1]

7903. The phrase "appropriate public authorities" as used in Article 3 of the Interstate Compact on the Placement of Children means, with reference to this state, the State Department of Social Services, and that department shall receive and act with reference to notices required by Article 3 of the compact.[1]

7904. The phrase "appropriate authority in receiving state" as used in paragraph (a) of Article 5 of the Interstate Compact on the Placement of Children, with reference to this state, means the State Department of Social Services.[1]

7905. The officers and agencies of this state and its subdivisions having authority to place children are hereby empowered to enter into agreements with appropriate officers or agencies of or in other party states pursuant to paragraph (b) of Article 5 of the Interstate Compact on the Placement of Children. Any such agreement which contains a financial commitment or imposes a financial obligation on this state or subdivision or agency thereof is not binding unless it has the approval in writing of the Controller in the case of the state and of the chief local fiscal officer in the case of a subdivision of the state.[1]

7906. Any requirements for visitation, inspection, or supervision of children, homes, institutions, or other agencies in another party state which may apply under the law of this state shall be deemed to be met if performed pursuant to an agreement entered into by appropriate officers or agencies of this state or a subdivision thereof as contemplated by paragraph (b) of Article 5 of the Interstate Compact on the Placement of Children. [1]

7906.5. (a) Within 60 days after an officer or agency of this state, or its political subdivision, receives a request from another state to conduct a study of a home environment for purposes of assessing the safety and suitability of placing a child, who is in the custody of the requesting state, in the home, the county child welfare agency shall, directly or indirectly, do both of the following:
(1) Conduct and complete the home study.
(2) Return to the requesting state a report on the results of the home study, which shall address the extent

to which placement in the home would meet the needs of the child.

(b) A licensed private adoption agency may agree to provide the services listed in subdivision (a), and upon that agreement, shall comply with the requirements of paragraphs (1) and (2) of subdivision (a).

(c) Notwithstanding subdivision (a), in the case of a home study commenced on or before September 30, 2008, if the county fails to comply with subdivision (a) within the 60-day period as a result of circumstances beyond the control of the state, including, but not limited to, failure by a federal agency to provide the results of a background check or failure of any entity to provide completed medical forms requested by the state at least 45 days before the end of the 60-day period, the county shall have 75 days to comply with subdivision (a) if the county documents the circumstances involved and certifies that completing the home study is in the best interest of the child.

(d) Nothing in this section shall be construed to require the county to have completed, within the applicable period, those portions of the home study concerning the education and training of the prospective foster parent or adoptive parent.

(e) The county shall treat any report described in subdivision (a) that is received from another state, an Indian tribe, or a private agency under contract with another state, as meeting any requirements imposed by the state for the completion of a home study before placing a child in the home, unless, within 14 days after receipt of the report, the county determines, based on grounds that are specific to the content of the report, that making a decision in reliance on the report would be contrary to the welfare of the child.

(f) A county is not restricted from contracting with a private agency for the conduct of a home study described in subdivision (a).[179]

7907. No provision of law restricting out-of-state placement of children for adoption shall apply to placements made pursuant to the Interstate Compact on the Placement of Children.[1]

7907.3. The Interstate Compact on the Placement of Children shall not apply to any placement, sending, or bringing of an Indian child into another state pursuant to a transfer of jurisdiction to a tribal court under Section 1911 of the Indian Child Welfare Act (25 U.S.C. Sec. 1901 et seq.).[146]

7907.5. (a) A child who is born in this state and placed for adoption in this state with a resident of this state is not subject to the provisions of the Interstate Compact on the Placement of Children.

(b) A child who is born in this state and placed for adoption with a person who is not a resident of this state is subject to the provisions of the Interstate Compact on the Placement of Children, regardless of whether the adoption petition is filed in this state. In interstate placements, this state shall be deemed the sending state for any child born in the state.

7908. A court having jurisdiction to place children adjudged wards of the court may place a ward in an out-of-state facility, as defined in subdivision (b) of Section 7910, pursuant to Section 727.1 of the Welfare and Institutions Code and Article 6 of the Interstate Compact on the Placement of

Children and shall retain jurisdiction as provided in Article 5 of the compact.[480]

7908.5. For the purposes of an interstate adoption placement, the term "jurisdiction" as used in Article 5 of the Interstate Compact on the Placement of Children means "jurisdiction over or legal responsibility for the child." It is the intent of the Legislature that this section make a technical clarification to the Interstate Compact on the Placement of Children and not a substantive change.[83]

7909. "Executive head" as used in Article 7 of the Interstate Compact on the Placement of Children means the Governor. The Governor shall appoint a compact administrator in accordance with the terms of Article 7 of the compact.[1]

7910. (a) Approval of an interstate placement of a child for adoption shall not be granted by the Compact Administrator if the placement is in violation of either Section 8801 of this code or Section 273 of the Penal Code.

(b) (1) The Compact Administrator shall not submit to a receiving state a request to place a dependent or ward for whom a county child welfare agency or county probation department has placement and care responsibility in an out-of-state residential facility, unless the requirements of Section 7911.1 of this code and Section 361.21 of, or subdivision (b) of Section 727.1 of, the Welfare and Institutions Code are met.

(2) For the purpose of this section, an "out-of-state residential facility" is a facility that is located in a state outside of California, is licensed or otherwise approved by the applicable state or tribal authority, and provides an integrated program of specialized and intensive care and supervision, services and supports, treatment, and short-term, 24-hour, trauma-informed care and supervision to children. An out-of-state residential facility may be called another name, including a group home, a residential treatment facility, or a residential care treatment facility.[481]

7911. (a) The Legislature finds and declares all of the following:

(1) The health and safety of California children placed by a county child welfare agency or probation department out of state pursuant to the provisions of the Interstate Compact on the Placement of Children are a matter of statewide concern.

(2) The State Department of Social Services has full authority to require any placement of a child in an out-of-state residential facility by a county child welfare agency or county probation department be approved on a child-specific basis after the county has exhausted in-state placement and services options that meet the needs of the child and participated in the department's technical assistance program. Before the juvenile court approves the placement pursuant to Section 361.21 of, or subdivision (b) of Section 727.1 of, the Welfare and Institutions Code, the State Department of Social Services shall certify the out-of-state residential facility pursuant to Section 7911.1. Before processing an application for out-of-state placement in a residential facility pursuant to the Interstate Compact on the Placement of Children, the Compact Administrator shall verify that the placement was approved by

the juvenile court and that it has been certified by the department.

(3) The Legislature further finds and declares that certification of facilities licensed under a separate state's licensing standards has not been sufficient to ensure that the stringent California short-term residential therapeutic programs requirements are maintained to safeguard the health, safety, and well-being of California's foster children and youth. Further research demonstrates that dependents and wards in foster care placements are generally better served when they are able to maintain and develop local community supports closer to their families and communities.

(b) (1) On and after July 1, 2021, foster care placements by county child welfare agencies or probation departments into out-of-state residential facilities shall not be made, except in the limited circumstances authorized by Section 361.21 of, or subdivision (b) of Section 727.1 of, the Welfare and Institutions Code, as applicable. Unless placement of a child in an out-of-state residential facility does not require certification pursuant to subdivision (h) of Section 7911.1, the Compact Administrator shall not seek approval of placement in an out-of-state residential facility from the receiving state unless all of the following criteria are met:

(A) The Compact Administrator has received from the county placing agency documentation that it has complied with the requirements of Section 16010.9 of the Welfare and Institutions Code.

(B) The Compact Administrator has received documentation that the out-of-state residential facility has been certified by the State Department of Social Services, including documentation that the director of the State Department of Social Services has approved the certification.

(C) The Compact Administrator has received a copy of the juvenile court order authorizing placement of the child in the out-of-state residential facility pursuant to Section 361.21 or 727.1 of the Welfare and Institutions Code.

(2) On and after July 1, 2022, county child welfare agencies or probation departments shall not make new placements in out-of-state residential facilities, except for placements described in subdivision (h) of Section 7911.1.

(c) Notwithstanding any other law, on and after July 1, 2022, the State Department of Social Services shall not certify any new out-of-state residential facilities for placement by county child welfare agencies or probation departments. On and after July 1, 2022, the Compact Administrator shall not seek approval of any new placements by county child welfare agencies or probation departments in out-of-state residential facilities.

(d) The state shall decertify all out-of-state residential facilities for placement by county child welfare agencies or probation departments on January 1, 2023, and ensure that all children and youth placed in out of state residential facilities have been returned to California by that date.

(e) This section is declaratory of existing law with respect to the Governor's designation of the State Department of Social Services to act as the Compact Administrator and of that department to act as the single state agency charged with supervision of public social services under Section 10600 of the Welfare and Institutions Code.[482]

7911.1. (a) Notwithstanding any other law, the State Department of Social Services or its designee shall investigate any threat to the health and safety of children placed by a California county child welfare agency or probation department in an out-of-state residential facility, as defined in subdivision (b) of Section 7910, pursuant to the provisions of the Interstate Compact on the Placement of Children. This authority shall include the authority to interview children or staff in private or review their file at the out-of-state residential facility or wherever the child or files may be at the time of the investigation. Notwithstanding any other law, the State Department of Social Services or its designee shall require certified out-of-state residential facilities to comply with the reporting requirements applicable to short-term residential therapeutic programs licensed in California for each child in care, regardless of whether or not the child is a California placement, by submitting a copy of the required reports to the Compact Administrator within regulatory timeframes. The Compact Administrator, within one business day of receiving a serious incident report from a certified out-of-state residential facility, shall verbally notify any county child welfare agency or probation department with a child placed at the certified out-of-state residential facility of the serious incident report. The Compact Administrator, within five business days of receiving a written serious incident report from a certified out-of-state residential facility, shall forward a copy of the written serious incident report to any county child welfare agency or probation department with a child placed at the certified out-of-state residential facility.

(b) Any contract, memorandum of understanding, or agreement entered into pursuant to paragraph (b) of Article 5 of the Interstate Compact on the Placement of Children regarding the placement of a child out of state by a California county social services agency or probation department shall include the language set forth in subdivision (a).

(c) Upon receipt of a request from a county child welfare agency or probation department for a child-specific certification of a placement in an out-of-state residential facility, the State Department of Social Services or its designee shall expedite the review of the request in order to determine any additional information needed, shall communicate with the requesting county agency regarding its review including regular status updates, and shall, in a timely manner, determine whether it will issue a child-specific certification to the out-of-state residential facility pursuant to this section.

(1) The licensing standards applicable to an out-of-state residential facility certified by the department shall be those required of short-term residential therapeutic programs operated in this state.

(2) Before issuing a child-specific certification to the out-of-state residential facility, the department shall do all of the following:

(A) Review documentation provided by the county placing agency pursuant to subdivision (e) of Section 16010.9 of the Welfare and Institutions Code.

(B) Perform an on-site inspection of the out-of-state residential facility's physical site.

(C) At a minimum, review all of the following sections of the out-of-state residential facility's program statement:

(i) Core Services and Supports.

(ii) Trauma Informed Interventions and Treatment Practices.

(iii) Personal Rights.

(iv) House Rules.

(v) Discipline Policies and Procedures.

(vi) Emergency Intervention Plan (Including Runaway Plan).

(D) Review the out-of-state residential facility's serious incident reports.

(E) Review the out-of-state residential facility's current license. In order for the out-of-state residential facility to receive a certification, the out-of-state residential facility shall have a current license, or an equivalent approval, in good standing issued by the appropriate authority or authorities of the state in which it is operating.

(F) Review the out-of-state residential facility's licensing history, including any substantiated complaints.

(G) Review the documentation provided by the State Department of Health Care Services pursuant to subdivision (d).

(H) Obtain approval from the director of the department of the child-specific certification for the out-of-state residential facility. Director approval may be given after all of the requirements of subparagraphs (A) to (G), inclusive, have been satisfied.

(3) The department shall not issue a child-specific certification to the out-of-state residential facility if the out-of-state residential facility fails to cooperate during the certification process, including failing to provide any of the documentation listed in paragraph (2).

(4) If all the requirements of paragraph (2) have been satisfied, the department shall certify the out-of-state residential facility pursuant to this section. The department shall provide written documentation of this certification to the county placing agency.

(5) The child-specific certification is discontinued, effective immediately, upon the child transitioning out of the out-of-state residential facility's program.

(d) The licensing standards applicable to out-of-state residential facilities certified by the department, as described in subdivision (c), shall include the licensing standards for mental health program approval described in Section 1562.01 of the Health and Safety Code. These standards shall be satisfied if the State Department of Health Care Services determines that the out-of-state residential facility has an equivalent mental health program approval in the state in which it is operating. Upon receipt of a request for the State Department of Health Care Services to determine whether an out-of-state residential facility has an equivalent mental health program approval in the state in which it is operation, the State Department of Health Care Services shall expedite the review of the request in order to determine any additional information needed, shall communicate with the requesting county agency regarding its review including regular status updates, and shall, in a timely manner, make its determination. If an out-of-state residential facility cannot satisfy the licensing standards for an equivalent mental health program approval, the department shall not certify the facility.

(e) Failure by an out-of-state residential facility to make children or staff available as required by subdivision (a) for a private interview or make files available for review shall be grounds to deny or discontinue the certification.

(f) Certifications made pursuant to this section shall be reviewed as often as necessary to ensure the health and safety of children in care. At a minimum, certifications made pursuant to this section shall be reviewed semiannually. The department shall complete a full review of the facility's program statement semiannually.

(g) (1) The department may deny or discontinue the certification of the out-of-state residential facility if the department makes a finding that the out-of-state residential facility is not operating in compliance with the requirements of this section. The department shall engage with counties that have one or more youth at a facility proposed for decertification to allow for a transition to occur, to the extent possible while ensuring the youths' safety and well-being.

(2) If the out-of-state residential facility disagrees with any decision by the department to deny or discontinue the certification, the out-of-state residential facility may appeal the decision immediately upon receipt of the notice of decertification. If the out-of-state residential facility decides to appeal the decision, the appeal shall be submitted to the department not later than 30 calendar days after the out-of-state residential facility receives the decision. The out-of-state residential facility's appeal shall be in writing and include all information, including supporting documents, that forms the basis of the appeal. The department shall issue a final determination not later than 30 calendar days after receipt of the appeal. If the out-of-state residential facility disagrees with the department's determination, the out-of-state residential facility may file a writ pursuant to paragraph (3). If the out-of-state residential facility decides to file a writ, the writ shall be filed not later than 30 calendar days after the out-of-state residential facility receives the final determination.

(3) Any judicial proceeding to contest the department's determination as to the status of the out-of-state residential facility's certificate shall be held in California pursuant to Section 1085 of the Code of Civil Procedure.

(h) The certification requirements of this section shall not impact any of the following:

(1) Placement of emotionally disturbed children made pursuant to an individualized education program developed pursuant to the federal Individuals with Disabilities Education Act (20 U.S.C. Sec. 1400 et seq.) if the placement is not funded with federal or state foster care funds.

(2) Placement of Indian children, as defined by the Indian Child Welfare Act of 1978 (25 U.S.C. Sec. 1901 et. seq.) and Section 224.1 of the Welfare and Institutions Code.

(i) Failure by an out-of-state residential facility to obtain or maintain its certification, as required by this section, shall preclude the use of any public funds, whether county, state, or federal, in the payment for the placement of any child in that out-of-state residential facility pursuant to the Interstate Compact on the Placement of Children.

(j) Notwithstanding the rulemaking provisions of the Administrative Procedure Act (Chapter 3.5 (commencing with Section 11340) of Part 1 of Division 3 of Title 2 of the Government Code), the State Department of Social Services and the State Department of Health Care Services may implement, interpret, or make specific this section by means of all-county letters, written directives, interim licensing standards, or similar written instructions from the department until regulations are adopted. These all-county letters, written directives, interim licensing standards, or similar written instructions shall have the same force and effect as regulations until the adoption of regulations.[483]

7912. (a) The Legislature finds and declares that the health and safety of children placed in out-of-state residential facilities pursuant to the Interstate Compact on the Placement of Children is a matter of statewide concern. The Legislature therefore affirms its intention that children placed by a county child welfare agency or probation department in out-of-state residential facilities be accorded the same personal rights and safeguards of a child placed in a California licensed short-term residential therapeutic program. This section is in clarification of existing law.

(b) (1) On or before September 1, 2021, and each month thereafter, the department shall report to the relevant policy and fiscal committees of the Legislature the number of children placed by a county child welfare agency or probation department in out-of-state residential facilities pursuant to the Interstate Compact on the Placement of Children.

(2) On or before January 1, 2022, and every six months thereafter until facilities are decertified and all children returned to California on or before January 1, 2023, the department, in consultation with the counties, shall report to the relevant policy and fiscal committees of the Legislature on the capacity for serving all child welfare and probation-supervised foster children within California or in home-based settings outside of the state. The report shall also include all of the following data, as applicable:

(A) The number of children served by out-of-state residential facilities, disaggregated by child welfare services agency and probation department supervision.

(B) Data measures related to ongoing transition planning efforts, including child and family team meetings, child-specific recruitment and family finding activities, and multiagency care coordination efforts that occurred for each child before and during placement in the out-of-state residential facility.

(C) The lengths of stay of each child placed in an out-of-state residential facility by a California child welfare agency or probation department.

(D) The total number of all serious incident reports received regarding out-of-state residential facilities, and descriptions of the types of incidents reported.

(E) The total number of serious incident reports received regarding California children placed in out-of-state residential facilities, and descriptions of the types of incidents reported.

(3) Reports made pursuant to this subdivision shall not include any demographic data that would permit identification of any child or nonminor dependent.[484]

7913. (a) When a full service licensed private adoption agency has provided adoption-related services to a birth parent or prospective adoptive parent, that agency is delegated the authority to determine whether the placement shall or shall not be made pursuant to the Interstate Compact on the Placement of Children, and to sign the compact forms documenting that determination and date of placement.

(b) For children entering California in independent adoptions, prior to making a determination regarding placement and as soon as feasible, the private adoption agency shall notify the appropriate district office or delegated county adoption agency of the matter and verify that the preplacement interview of the prospective adoptive parent or parents has been completed.

(c) This section shall not apply to a child who is a dependent of the court or a child subject to a petition filed under Section 300 of the Welfare and Institutions Code.[221]

PART 6: FOSTER CARE PLACEMENT CONSIDERATIONS

repealed and added by Stats. 1995, Ch. 884, Sec. 2

7950. (a) With full consideration for the proximity of the natural parents to the placement so as to facilitate visitation and family reunification, when a placement in foster care is being made, the following considerations shall be used:

(1) Placement shall, if possible, be made in the home of a relative, unless the placement would not be in the best interest of the child. Diligent efforts shall be made by an agency or entity to which this subdivision applies, to locate an appropriate relative as defined in paragraph (2) of subdivision (h) of Section 319 of the Welfare and Institutions Code. At a permanency hearing in which the court terminates reunification services, or at a postpermanency hearing for a child not placed for adoption, the court shall find that the agency or entity to which this subdivision applies has made diligent efforts to locate an appropriate relative and that each relative whose name has been submitted to the agency or entity as a possible caretaker, either by the relative or by other persons, has been evaluated as an appropriate placement resource.

(2) An agency or entity that receives state assistance and is involved in foster care placements shall not do either of the following:

(A) Deny a person the opportunity to become a foster parent on the basis of the race, color, or national origin of the person or the child involved.

(B) Delay or deny the placement of a child into foster care on the basis of the race, color, or national origin of the foster parent or the child involved.

(b) Subdivision (a) does not affect the application of the Indian Child Welfare Act of 1978 (25 U.S.C. Sec.

1901 et seq.).

(c) This section does not preclude a search for an appropriate relative being conducted simultaneously with a search for a foster family.[600]

7951. This part does not apply in determining the foster care setting in which the child may be placed for a period not intended to exceed 30 days.

7952. A minor 10 years of age or older being considered for placement in a foster home has the right to make a brief statement to the court making a decision on placement. The court may disregard any preferences expressed by the minor. The minor's right to make a statement is not limited to the initial placement, but continues for any proceedings concerning continued placement or a decision to return to parental custody.

PART 7: SURROGACY AND DONOR FACILITATORS, ASSISTED REPRODUCTION AGREEMENTS FOR GESTATIONAL CARRIERS, AND OOCYTE DONATIONS

amended by Stats. 2015, Ch. 91, Sec. 2

7960. For purposes of this part, the following terms have the following meanings:

(a) "Assisted reproduction agreement" has the same meaning as defined in subdivision (b) of Section 7606.

(b) "Fund management agreement" means the agreement between the intended parents and the surrogacy or donor facilitator relating to the fee or other valuable consideration for services rendered or that will be rendered by the surrogacy or donor facilitator.

(c) "Intended parent" means an individual, married or unmarried, who manifests the intent to be legally bound as the parent of a child resulting from assisted reproduction.

(d) "Nonattorney surrogacy or donor facilitator" means a surrogacy or donor practitioner who is not an attorney in good standing licensed to practice law in this state.

(e) "Surrogacy or donor facilitator" means a person or organization that engages in either of the following activities:

(1) Advertising for the purpose of soliciting parties to an assisted reproduction agreement or for the donation of oocytes for use by a person other than the provider of the oocytes, or acting as an intermediary between the parties to an assisted reproduction agreement or oocyte donation.

(2) Charging a fee or other valuable consideration for services rendered relating to an assisted reproduction agreement or oocyte donation.

(f) "Surrogate" means a woman who bears and carries a child for another through medically assisted reproduction and pursuant to a written agreement, as set forth in Sections 7606 and 7962. Within the definition of surrogate are two different and distinct types:

(1) "Traditional surrogate" means a woman who agrees to gestate an embryo, in which the woman is the gamete donor and the embryo was created using the sperm of the intended father or a donor arranged by the intended parent or parents.

(2) "Gestational carrier" means a woman who is not an intended parent

and who agrees to gestate a genetically unrelated embryo pursuant to an assisted reproduction agreement.

(g) "Donor" means a woman who provides oocytes for use by another for the purpose of assisting the recipient of the oocytes in having a child or children.

7961. (a) A nonattorney surrogacy or donor facilitator shall direct the client to deposit all client funds into either of the following:

(1) An independent, bonded escrow depository maintained by a licensed, independent, bonded escrow company.

(2) A trust account maintained by an attorney.

(b) For purposes of this section, a nonattorney surrogacy or donor facilitator may not have a financial interest in any escrow company holding client funds. A nonattorney surrogacy or donor facilitator and any of its directors or employees shall not be an agent of any escrow company holding client funds.

(c) Client funds may only be disbursed by the attorney or escrow agent as set forth in the assisted reproduction agreement and fund management agreement.

(d) This section shall not apply to funds that are both of the following:

(1) Not provided for in the fund management agreement.

(2) Paid directly to a medical doctor for medical services or a psychologist for psychological services.[329]

7962. (a) An assisted reproduction agreement for gestational carriers shall contain, but shall not be limited to, all of the following information:

(1) The date on which the assisted reproduction agreement for gestational carriers was executed.

(2) The persons from which the gametes originated, unless donated gametes were used, in which case the assisted reproduction agreement does not need to specify the name of the donor but shall specify whether the donated gamete or gametes were eggs, sperm, or embryos, or all.

(3) The identity of the intended parent or parents.

(4) Disclosure of how the intended parents will cover the medical expenses of the gestational carrier and of the newborn or newborns. If health care coverage is used to cover those medical expenses, the disclosure shall include a review of the health care policy provisions related to coverage for surrogate pregnancy, including any possible liability of the gestational carrier, third-party liability liens or other insurance coverage, and any notice requirements that could affect coverage or liability of the gestational carrier. The review and disclosure do not constitute legal advice. If coverage of liability is uncertain, a statement of that fact shall be sufficient to meet the requirements of this section.

(b) Prior to executing the written assisted reproduction agreement for gestational carriers, a surrogate and the intended parent or intended parents shall be represented by separate independent licensed attorneys of their choosing.

(c) The assisted reproduction agreement for gestational carriers shall be executed by the parties and the signatures on the assisted reproduction agreement for gestational carriers shall be notarized or witnessed by an equivalent method of affirmation as required in the jurisdiction where the assisted reproduction agreement for gestational carriers is executed.

(d) The parties to an assisted reproduction agreement for gestational carriers shall not undergo an embryo transfer procedure, or commence injectable medication in preparation for an embryo transfer for assisted reproduction purposes, until the assisted reproduction agreement for gestational carriers has been fully executed as required by subdivisions (b) and (c) of this section.

(e) An action to establish the parent and child relationship between the intended parent or parents and the child as to a child conceived pursuant to an assisted reproduction agreement for gestational carriers may be filed before the child's birth and may be filed in the county where the child is anticipated to be born, the county where the intended parent or intended parents reside, the county where the surrogate resides, the county where the assisted reproduction agreement for gestational carriers is executed, or the county where medical procedures pursuant to the agreement are to be performed. A copy of the assisted reproduction agreement for gestational carriers shall be lodged in the court action filed for the purpose of establishing the parent and child relationship. The parties to the assisted reproduction agreement for gestational carriers shall attest, under penalty of perjury, and to the best of their knowledge and belief, as to the parties' compliance with this section in entering into the assisted reproduction agreement for gestational carriers. Submitting those declarations shall not constitute a waiver, under Section 912 of the Evidence Code, of the lawyer-client privilege described in Article 3 (commencing with Section 950) of Chapter 4 of Division 8 of the Evidence Code.

(f) (1) A notarized assisted reproduction agreement for gestational carriers signed by all the parties, with the attached declarations of independent attorneys, and lodged with the superior court in accordance with this section, shall rebut any presumptions contained within Part 2 (commencing with Section 7540), subdivision (a) of Section 7610, and Sections 7611 and 7613, as to the gestational carrier surrogate, or the gestational carrier surrogate's spouse or partner, being a parent of the child or children.

(2) Upon petition of any party to a properly executed assisted reproduction agreement for gestational carriers, the court shall issue a judgment or order establishing a parent and child relationship, whether pursuant to Section 7630 or otherwise. The judgment or order may be issued before or after the child's or children's birth subject to the limitations of Section 7633. Subject to proof of compliance with this section, the judgment or order shall establish the parent and child relationship of the intended parent or intended parents identified in the surrogacy agreement and shall establish that the surrogate, and the surrogate's spouse or partner, is not a parent of, and has no parental rights or duties with respect to, the child or children. The judgment or order shall be issued forthwith and without further hearing or evidence, unless the court or a party to the assisted reproduction agreement for gestational carriers has a good faith, reasonable belief that the

assisted reproduction agreement for gestational carriers or attorney declarations were not executed in accordance with this section. Upon motion by a party to the assisted reproduction agreement for gestational carriers, the matter shall be scheduled for hearing before a judgment or order is issued. This section does not prevent a court from finding and declaring that the intended parent is, or intended parents are, the parent or parents of the child where compliance with this section has not been met; however, the court shall require sufficient proof entitling the parties to the relief sought.

(g) The petition, relinquishment or consent, agreement, order, report to the court from any investigating agency, and any power of attorney and deposition filed in the office of the clerk of the court pursuant to this part shall not be open to inspection by any person other than the parties to the proceeding and their attorneys and the State Department of Social Services, except upon the written authority of a judge of the superior court. A judge of the superior court shall not authorize anyone to inspect the petition, relinquishment or consent, agreement, order, report to the court from any investigating agency, or power of attorney or deposition, or any portion of those documents, except in exceptional circumstances and where necessary. The petitioner may be required to pay the expense of preparing the copies of the documents to be inspected.

(h) Upon the written request of any party to the proceeding and the order of any judge of the superior court, the clerk of the court shall not provide any documents referred to in subdivision (g) for inspection or copying to any other person, unless the name of the gestational carrier or any information tending to identify the gestational carrier is deleted from the documents or copies thereof.

(i) An assisted reproduction agreement for gestational carriers executed in accordance with this section is presumptively valid and shall not be rescinded or revoked without a court order. For purposes of this part, any failure to comply with the requirements of this section shall rebut the presumption of the validity of the assisted reproduction agreement for gestational carriers.

DIVISION 13: ADOPTION

ENACTED BY STATS. 1992, CH. 162, SEC. 10.
SECTION 8500-9340

PART 1: DEFINITIONS

enacted by Stats. 1992, Ch. 162, Sec. 10

8502. (a) "Adoption service provider" means any of the following:

(1) A licensed private adoption agency.

(2) An individual who has presented satisfactory evidence to the department that the individual is a licensed clinical social worker who also has a minimum of five years of experience providing professional social work services while employed by a licensed California adoption agency or the department.

(3) In a state other than California, or a country other than the United States, an adoption agency licensed or otherwise approved under the laws of that state or country, or an individual who is licensed or otherwise certified as a clinical social worker under the laws of that state or country.

(4) An individual who has presented satisfactory evidence to the department that the individual is a licensed marriage and family therapist who has a minimum of five years of experience providing professional adoption casework services while employed by a licensed California adoption agency or the department. The department shall review the qualifications of each individual to determine if the individual has performed professional adoption casework services for five years as required by this section while employed by a licensed California adoption agency or the department.

(5) An individual who has presented satisfactory evidence to the department that the individual is a licensed professional clinical counselor who has a minimum of five years' experience providing professional adoption casework services while employed by a licensed California adoption agency or the department. The department shall review the credentials of each individual to determine if the individual has performed professional adoption casework services as required by this paragraph.

(b) If, in the case of a birth parent located in California, at least three adoption service providers are not reasonably available, or, in the case of a birth parent located outside of California or outside of the United States who has contacted at least three potential adoption service providers and been unsuccessful in obtaining the services of an adoption service provider who is reasonably available and willing to provide services, independent legal counsel for the birth parent may serve as an adoption service provider pursuant to subdivision (e) of Section 8801.5. "Reasonably available" means that an adoption service provider is all of the following:

(1) Available within five days for an advisement of rights pursuant to Section 8801.5, or within 24 hours for the signing of the placement agreement

pursuant to paragraph (3) of subdivision (b) of Section 8801.3.

(2) Within 100 miles of the birth mother.

(3) Available for a cost not exceeding five hundred dollars ($500) to make an advisement of rights and to witness the signing of the placement agreement.

(c) If an attorney acts as an adoption service provider, the fee to make an advisement of rights and to witness the signing of the placement agreement shall not exceed five hundred dollars ($500).

8503. "Adoptive parent" means a person who has obtained an order of adoption of a minor child or, in the case of an adult adoption, an adult.[1]

8506. "Agency adoption" means the adoption of a minor, other than an intercountry adoption, in which the department, county adoption agency, or licensed adoption agency is a party to, or joins in, the adoption petition.[226]

8509. "Applicant" means a person who has submitted a written application to adopt a child from the department, county adoption agency, or licensed adoption agency and who is being considered by the adoption agency for the adoptive placement of a child.[227]

8512. "Birth parent" means the biological parent or, in the case of a person previously adopted, the adoptive parent.[1]

8513. "County adoption agency" means an adoption agency operated by a county or consortium of counties.[228]

8514. "Days" means calendar days, unless otherwise specified.

8515. "Delegated county adoption agency" means a county adoption agency that has agreed to provide the services described in Chapter 3 (commencing with Section 8800) of Part 2.[229]

8518. "Department" means the State Department of Social Services.[1]

8521. (a) "Full-service adoption agency" means a licensed or authorized entity engaged in the business of providing adoption services, that does all of the following:

(1) Assumes care, custody, and control of a child through relinquishment of the child to the agency or involuntary termination of parental rights to the child.

(2) Assesses the birth parents, prospective adoptive parents, or child.

(3) Places children for adoption.

(4) Supervises adoptive placements.

(5) Recruits prospective adoptive parents, locates children for adoption, or acts as an intermediary between the parties to an adoption.

(b) Private full-service adoption agencies shall be organized and operated on a nonprofit basis. As a condition of licensure to provide intercountry adoption services, a private full-service adoption agency shall be accredited by the Council on Accreditation, or supervised by an accredited primary provider, or acting as an exempted provider, in compliance with Subpart F (commencing with Section 96.29) of Part 96 of Title 22 of the Code of Federal Regulations.[530]

8524. "Independent adoption" means the adoption of a child in which neither the department, county adoption agency, nor agency licensed by the department is a party to, or joins in, the adoption petition.[230]

8527. "Intercountry adoption" means the adoption of a foreign-born child for whom federal law makes a special immigration visa available. Intercountry adoption includes completion of the adoption in the child's native country or completion of the adoption in this state.[1]

8530. "Licensed adoption agency" means any agency licensed by the department to provide the adoption services specified in paragraphs (9) and (10) of subdivision (a) of Section 1502 of the Health and Safety Code.[531]

8533. (a) "Noncustodial adoption agency" means any licensed entity engaged in the business of providing adoption services, which does all of the following:

(1) Assesses the prospective adoptive parents.

(2) Cooperatively matches children freed for adoption, who are under the care, custody, and control of a licensed adoption agency, for adoption, with assessed and approved prospective adoptive parents.

(3) Cooperatively supervises adoptive placements with a full-service adoption agency, but does not disrupt a placement or remove a child from a placement.

(4) Recruits prospective adoptive parents, locates children for an adoption, or acts as an intermediary between the parties to an adoption.

(b) Private noncustodial adoption agencies shall be organized and operated on a nonprofit basis. As a condition of licensure to provide intercountry adoption services, a noncustodial adoption agency shall be accredited by the Council on Accreditation, or supervised by an accredited primary provider, or acting as an exempted provider, in compliance with Subpart F (commencing with Section 96.29) of Part 96 of Title 22 of the Code of Federal Regulations.[532]

8539. "Place for adoption" means, in the case of an independent adoption, the selection of a prospective adoptive parent or parents for a child by the birth parent or parents and the completion of an adoptive placement agreement on a form prescribed by the department by the birth parent or parents placing the child with prospective adoptive parents.

This section shall become operative on January 1, 1995.

8542. "Prospective adoptive parent" means a person who has filed or intends to file a petition under Part 2 (commencing with Section 8600) to adopt a child who has been or who is to be placed in the person's physical care or a petition under Part 3 (commencing with Section 9300) to adopt an adult.[1]

8543. "Qualified court investigator" means a superior court investigator with the same minimum qualifications as a probation officer or county welfare worker designated to conduct stepparent adoption investigations in stepparent adoption proceedings and proceedings to declare a minor free from parental custody and control.

8545. "Special needs child" means a child for whom all of the following are true:

(a) It has been determined that the child cannot or should not be returned to the parent's home, as evidenced by

a petition for termination of parental rights, a court order terminating parental rights, or a signed relinquishment.
(b) The child has at least one of the following characteristics that is a barrier to adoption:
(1) Adoptive placement without financial assistance is unlikely because of membership in a sibling group that should remain intact, or by virtue of race, ethnicity, color, language, age of three years or older, or parental background of a medical or behavioral nature that can be determined to adversely affect the development of the child.
(2) Adoptive placement without financial assistance is unlikely because the child has a mental, physical, emotional, or medical disability that has been certified by a licensed professional competent to make an assessment and operating within the scope of that person's profession. This paragraph shall also apply to children with a developmental disability as defined in subdivision
(a) of Section 4512 of the Welfare and Institutions Code, including those determined to require out-of-home nonmedical care as described in Section 11464 of the Welfare and Institutions Code.
(c) The need for adoption subsidy is evidenced by an unsuccessful search for an adoptive home to take the child without financial assistance, as documented in the case file of the prospective adoptive child. The requirement for this search shall be waived when it would be against the best interest of the child because of the existence of significant emotional ties with prospective adoptive parents while in the care of these persons as a foster child.

8548. "Stepparent adoption" means an adoption of a child by a stepparent where one birth parent retains custody and control of the child.[1]

PART 2: ADOPTION OF UNMARRIED MINORS

enacted by Stats. 1992, Ch. 162, Sec. 10

Chapter 1: General Provisions

8600. An unmarried minor may be adopted by an adult as provided in this part.[1]

8600.5. Tribal customary adoption as defined in Section 366.24 of the Welfare and Institutions Code and as applied to Indian Children who are dependents of the court, does not apply to this part.[231]

8601. (a) Except as otherwise provided in subdivision (b), a prospective adoptive parent or parents shall be at least 10 years older than the child.
(b) If the court is satisfied that the adoption of a child by a stepparent, or by a sister, brother, aunt, uncle, or first cousin and, if that person is married, by that person and that person's spouse, is in the best interest of the parties and is in the public interest, it may approve the adoption without regard to the ages of the child and the prospective adoptive parent or parents.[1]

8601.5. (a) A court may issue an order of adoption and declare that it shall be entered nunc pro tunc when it will serve public policy and the best interests of the child, such as cases where adoption finalization has been delayed beyond the child's 18th

birthday due to factors beyond the control of the prospective adoptive family and the proposed adoptee.
(b) The request for nunc pro tunc entry of the order shall be stated in the adoption request or an amendment thereto, and shall set forth specific facts in support thereof.
(c) To the extent that a child's eligibility for any publicly funded benefit program is or could be altered by the entry of an order of adoption, the change in eligibility shall not be determined as of the nunc pro tunc date, but shall be determined as of the date of the adoption finalization hearing.
(d) The nunc pro tunc date shall not precede the date upon which the parental rights of the birth parent or parents were initially terminated, whether voluntarily or involuntarily.[222]

8602. The consent of a child, if over the age of 12 years, is necessary to the child's adoption.[1]

8603. (a) A married person, not lawfully separated from the person's spouse, shall not adopt a child without the consent of the spouse, provided that the spouse is capable of giving that consent.
(b) The consent of the spouse shall not establish any parental rights or responsibilities on the part of the consenting spouse unless that person has consented to adopt the child in a writing filed with the court and is named in the final decree as an adoptive parent. The court shall not name the consenting spouse as an adoptive parent in the final decree unless the consenting spouse has filed a written consent to adopt the child with the court and has an approved adoption home study.
(c) The court may dispense with the consent of a spouse who cannot be located after diligent search, or a spouse determined by the court to lack the capacity to consent. A spouse for whom consent was dispensed shall not be named as an adoptive parent in the final decree.

8604. (a) Except as provided in subdivision (b), a child having a presumed father under Section 7611 shall not be adopted without the consent of the child's birth parents, if living. The consent of a presumed father is not required for the child's adoption unless the person became a presumed father as described in Chapter 1 (commencing with Section 7540) or Chapter 3 (commencing with Section 7570) of Part 2 of Division 12, or subdivision (a), (b), or (c) of Section 7611 before the mother's relinquishment or consent becomes irrevocable or before the mother's parental rights have been terminated.
(b) If one birth parent has been awarded custody by judicial order, or has custody by agreement of both parents, and the other birth parent for a period of one year willfully fails to communicate with, and to pay for, the care, support, and education of the child when able to do so, then the birth parent having sole custody may consent to the adoption, but only after the birth parent not having custody has been served with a copy of a citation in the manner provided by law for the service of a summons in a civil action that requires the birth parent not having custody to appear at the time and place set for the appearance in court under Section 8718, 8823, 8913, or 9007.
(c) Failure of a birth parent to pay for

the care, support, and education of the child for the period of one year or failure of a birth parent to communicate with the child for the period of one year is prima facie evidence that the failure was willful and without lawful excuse. If the birth parent or parents have made only token efforts to support or communicate with the child, the court may disregard those token efforts.

(d) (1) If the birth mother of a child for whom there is not a presumed father leaves the child in the physical care of a licensed private adoption agency, in the physical care of a prospective adoptive parent who has an approved preplacement evaluation or private agency adoption home study, or in the hospital after designating a licensed private adoption agency or an approved prospective adoptive parent in a signed document, completed with a hospital social worker, adoption service provider, licensed private adoption agency worker, notary, or attorney, but fails to sign a placement agreement, consent, or relinquishment for adoption, the approved prospective adoptive parent or the licensed private adoption agency may apply for, and the court may issue, a temporary custody order placing the child in the care and custody of the applicant.

(2) A temporary custody order issued pursuant to this subdivision shall include all of the following:

(A) A requirement that the applicant keep the court informed of the child's residence at all times.

(B) A requirement that the child shall not be removed from the state or concealed within the state.

(C) The expiration date of the order, which shall not be more than six months after the order is issued.

(3) A temporary custody order issued pursuant to this subdivision may be voided upon the birth mother's request to have the child returned to the birth mother's care and custody.

8605. A child not having a presumed father under Section 7611 may not be adopted without the consent of the child's mother, if living.[1]

8606. Notwithstanding Sections 8604 and 8605, the consent of a birth parent is not necessary in the following cases:

(a) Where the birth parent has been judicially deprived of the custody and control of the child (1) by a court order declaring the child to be free from the custody and control of either or both birth parents pursuant to Part 4 (commencing with Section 7800) of Division 12 of this code, or Section 366.25 or 366.26 of the Welfare and Institutions Code, or (2) by a similar order of a court of another jurisdiction, pursuant to a law of that jurisdiction authorizing the order.

(b) Where the birth parent has, in a judicial proceeding in another jurisdiction, voluntarily surrendered the right to the custody and control of the child pursuant to a law of that jurisdiction providing for the surrender.

(c) Where the birth parent has deserted the child without provision for identification of the child.

(d) Where the birth parent has relinquished the child for adoption as provided in Section 8700.

(e) Where the birth parent has relinquished the child for adoption to a licensed or authorized child-placing agency in another jurisdiction pursuant to the law of that jurisdiction.[1]

8606.5. (a) Notwithstanding any other

section in this part, and in accordance with Section 1913 of the Indian Child Welfare Act (25 U.S.C. Sec. 1901 et seq.), consent to adoption given by an Indian child's parent is not valid unless both of the following occur:

(1) The consent is executed in writing at least 10 days after the child's birth and recorded before a judge.

(2) The judge certifies that the terms and consequences of the consent were fully explained in detail in English and were fully understood by the parent or that they were interpreted into a language that the parent understood.

(b) The parent of an Indian child may withdraw consent to adoption for any reason at any time prior to the entry of a final decree of adoption and the child shall be returned to the parent.

(c) After the entry of a final decree of adoption of an Indian child, the Indian child's parent may withdraw consent to the adoption upon the grounds that consent was obtained through fraud or duress and may petition the court to vacate the decree. Upon a finding that consent was obtained through fraud or duress, the court shall vacate the decree and return the child to the parent, provided that no adoption that has been effective for at least two years may be invalidated unless otherwise permitted under state law.

8607. All forms adopted by the department authorizing the release of an infant from a health facility to the custody of persons other than the person entitled to custody of the child pursuant to Section 3010 and authorizing these other persons to obtain medical care for the infant shall contain a statement in boldface type delineating the various types of adoptions available, the birth parents' rights with regard thereto, including, but not limited to, rights with regard to revocation of consent to adoption, and a statement regarding the authority of the court under Part 4 (commencing with Section 7800) of Division 12 to declare the child abandoned by the birth parent or parents.[1]

8608. (a) The department shall adopt regulations specifying the form and content of the reports required by Sections 8706, 8817, and 8909. In addition to any other material that may be required by the department, the form shall include inquiries designed to elicit information on any illness, disease, or defect of a genetic or hereditary nature.

(b) All county adoption agencies and licensed adoption agencies shall cooperate with and assist the department in devising a plan that will effectuate the effective and discreet transmission to adoptees or prospective adoptive parents of pertinent medical information reported to the department, county adoption agency, or licensed adoption agency, upon the request of the person reporting the medical information.[232]

8609. (a) Any person or organization that advertises in any periodical or newspaper, by radio, or other public medium, that the person or organization will place children for adoption, or accept, supply, provide, or obtain children for adoption, or that causes any advertisement to be published in or by any public medium soliciting, requesting, or asking for any child or children for adoption, is guilty of a misdemeanor, unless one of the following conditions apply:

(1) The person or organization holds

a valid and unrevoked license to operate as a licensed adoption agency, as defined in Section 8530, and is authorized to place children for adoption.

(2) The person or organization is exempt from licensure pursuant to subdivision (w) or (x) of Section 1505 of the Health and Safety Code.

(b) Any person, organization, association, or corporation that seeks to place any child for adoption is guilty of a misdemeanor, unless one of the following conditions applies:

(1) The person, organization, or corporation holds a valid and unrevoked license to operate as a licensed adoption agency, as defined in Section 8530, and is authorized to place children for adoption.

(2) The person, organization, or corporation is exempt from licensure pursuant to subdivision (w) or (x) of Section 1505 of the Health and Safety Code.

(3) The person is the legal parent.

(c) Any person or organization that performs any of the functions of an adoption agency or holds itself out as performing any of the functions of an adoption agency, as described in paragraphs (9) and (10) of subdivision (a) of Section 1502 of the Health and Safety Code, without a valid and unrevoked license issued by the department shall be deemed an unlicensed adoption agency, as referenced in paragraph (6) of subdivision (a) of Section 1503.5 of Health and Safety Code, unless otherwise permitted under California law.[537]

8609.5. An adoption request for the adoption or readoption of a nondependent minor may be filed with the court in the county in which one of the following applies:

(a) The petitioner resides.

(b) The child was born or resides at the time of filing.

(c) An office of the agency that placed the child or is filing the petition for adoption is located.

(d) An office of the department or a public adoption agency that is investigating the petition is located.

(e) The county in which a placing birth parent or parents resided when the adoptive placement agreement, consent, or relinquishment was signed.

(f) The county in which a placing birth parent or parents resided when the petition was filed.

(g) The county in which the child was freed for adoption.[510]

8610. (a) The petitioners in a proceeding for adoption of a child shall file with the court a full accounting report of all disbursements of anything of value made or agreed to be made by them or on their behalf in connection with the birth of the child, the placement of the child with the petitioners, any medical or hospital care received by the child's birth mother or by the child in connection with the child's birth, any other expenses of either birth parent, or the adoption. The accounting report shall be made under penalty of perjury and shall be submitted to the court on or before the date set for the hearing on the adoption petition, unless the court grants an extension of time.

(b) The accounting report shall be itemized in detail and shall show the services relating to the adoption or to the placement of the child for adoption that were received by the petitioners, by either birth parent, or by the child. The report shall also

include the dates of each payment, the names and addresses of each attorney, physician and surgeon, hospital, licensed adoption agency, or any other person or organization that received payment.
(c) This section does not apply to an adoption by a stepparent if at least one legal parent retains custody and control of the child.[538]

8611. All court hearings in an adoption proceeding shall be held in private, and the court shall exclude all persons except the officers of the court, the parties, their witnesses, counsel, and representatives of the agencies present to perform their official duties under the law governing adoptions.[1]

8612. (a) The court shall examine all persons appearing before it pursuant to this part. The examination of each person shall be conducted separately but within the physical presence of every other person unless the court, in its discretion, orders otherwise.
(b) The prospective adoptive parent or parents shall execute and acknowledge an agreement in writing that the child will be treated in all respects as their lawful child.
(c) If satisfied that the interest of the child will be promoted by the adoption, the court may make and enter an order of adoption of the child by the prospective adoptive parent or parents.[1]

8613. (a) If the prospective adoptive parent is commissioned or enlisted in the military service, or auxiliary thereof, of the United States, or of any of its allies, or is engaged in service on behalf of any governmental entity of the United States, or in the American Red Cross, or in any other recognized charitable or religious organization, so that it is impossible or impracticable, because of the prospective adoptive parent's absence from this state, or otherwise, to make an appearance in person, and the circumstances are established by satisfactory evidence, the appearance may be made for the prospective adoptive parent by counsel, commissioned and empowered in writing for that purpose. The power of attorney may be incorporated in the adoption petition.
(b) Where the prospective adoptive parent is permitted to appear by counsel, the agreement may be executed and acknowledged by the counsel, or may be executed by the absent party before a notary public, or any other person authorized to take acknowledgments including the persons authorized by Sections 1183 and 1183.5 of the Civil Code.
(c) Where the prospective adoptive parent is permitted to appear by counsel, or otherwise, the court may, in its discretion, cause an examination of the prospective adoptive parent, other interested person, or witness to be made upon deposition, as it deems necessary. The deposition shall be taken upon commission, as prescribed by the Code of Civil Procedure, and the expense thereof shall be borne by the petitioner.
(d) The petition, relinquishment or consent, agreement, order, report to the court from any investigating agency, and any power of attorney and deposition shall be filed in the office of the clerk of the court.
(e) The provisions of this section permitting an appearance through counsel are equally applicable to the spouse of

a prospective adoptive parent who resides with the prospective adoptive parent outside this state.

(f) Where, pursuant to this section, neither prospective adoptive parent need appear before the court, the child proposed to be adopted need not appear. If the law otherwise requires that the child execute any document during the course of the hearing, the child may do so through counsel.

(g) Where none of the parties appears, the court may not make an order of adoption until after a report has been filed with the court pursuant to Section 8715, 8807, 8914, or 9001.[88]

8613.5. (a) (1) If it is impossible or impracticable for either prospective adoptive parent to make an appearance in person, and the circumstances are established by clear and convincing documentary evidence, the court may, in its discretion, do either of the following:

(A) Waive the personal appearance of the prospective adoptive parent. The appearance may be made for the prospective adoptive parent by counsel, commissioned and empowered in writing for that purpose. The power of attorney may be incorporated in the adoption petition.

(B) Authorize the prospective adoptive parent to appear by telephone, videoconference, or other remote electronic means that the court deems reasonable, prudent, and reliable.

(2) For purposes of this section, if the circumstances that make an appearance in person by a prospective adoptive parent impossible or impracticable are temporary in nature or of a short duration, the court shall not waive the personal appearance of that prospective adoptive parent.

(b) If the prospective adoptive parent is permitted to appear by counsel, the agreement may be executed and acknowledged by the counsel, or may be executed by the absent party before a notary public, or any other person authorized to take acknowledgments including the persons authorized by Sections 1183 and 1183.5 of the Civil Code.

(c) If the prospective adoptive parent is permitted to appear by counsel, or otherwise, the court may, in its discretion, cause an examination of the prospective adoptive parent, other interested person, or witness to be made upon deposition, as it deems necessary. The deposition shall be taken upon commission, as prescribed by the Code of Civil Procedure, and the expense thereof shall be borne by the petitioner.

(d) The petition, relinquishment or consent, agreement, order, report to the court from any investigating agency, and any power of attorney and deposition shall be filed in the office of the clerk of the court.

(e) The provisions of this section permitting an appearance by counsel or electronically pursuant to subparagraph (B) of paragraph (1) of subdivision (a) are equally applicable to the spouse of a prospective adoptive parent who resides with the prospective adoptive parent outside this state.

(f) If, pursuant to this section, neither prospective adoptive parent need appear before the court, the child proposed to be adopted need not appear. If the law otherwise requires that the child execute any document during the course of the hearing, the child may do so through counsel.

(g) If none of the parties appear, the court may not make an order of adoption until after a report has been filed with the court pursuant to Section 8715, 8807, 8914, or 9001.[319]

8613.7. On and after January 1, 2014, the court shall provide to any petitioner for adoption pursuant to this part a notice informing the petitioner that they may be eligible for reduced-cost coverage through the California Health Benefit Exchange established under Title 22 (commencing with Section 100500) of the Government Code or no-cost coverage through Medi-Cal. The notice shall include information on obtaining coverage pursuant to those programs, and shall be developed by the California Health Benefit Exchange.

8614. Upon the request of the adoptive parents or the adopted child, a clerk of the superior court may issue a certificate of adoption that states the date and place of adoption, the birthday of the child, the names of the adoptive parents, and the name the child has taken. Unless the child has been adopted by a stepparent or by a relative, as defined in subdivision (c) of Section 8616.5, the certificate shall not state the name of the birth parents of the child.[99]

8615. (a) Notwithstanding any other law, an action may be brought in the county in which the petitioner resides for the purpose of obtaining for a child adopted by the petitioner a new birth certificate specifying that a deceased spouse of the petitioner who was in the home at the time of the initial placement of the child is a parent of the child.

(b) In an adoption proceeding, the petitioner may request that the new birth certificate specify that a deceased spouse of the petitioner who was in the home at the time of the initial placement of the child is a parent of the child.

(c) The inclusion of the name of a deceased person in a birth certificate issued pursuant to a court order under this section does not affect any matter of testate or intestate succession, and is not competent evidence on the issue of the relationship between the adopted child and the deceased person in any action or proceeding.[1]

8616. After adoption, the adopted child and the adoptive parents shall sustain towards each other the legal relationship of parent and child and have all the rights and are subject to all the duties of that relationship.[1]

8616.5. (a) The Legislature finds and declares that some adoptive children may benefit from either direct or indirect contact with birth relatives, including the birth parent or parents or any siblings, or an Indian tribe, after being adopted. Postadoption contact agreements are intended to ensure children of an achievable level of continuing contact when contact is beneficial to the children and the agreements are voluntarily executed by birth relatives, including the birth parent or parents or any siblings, or an Indian tribe, and adoptive parents. Nothing in this section requires all of the listed parties to participate in the development of a postadoption contact agreement in order for the agreement to be executed.

(b) (1) Nothing in the adoption laws of this state shall be construed to prevent the adopting parent or parents, the birth relatives, including the birth parent or parents or any siblings, or an Indian tribe, and the child from voluntarily executing a written agreement to permit continuing contact between the birth relatives, including the birth parent or parents or any siblings, or an Indian tribe, and the child if the agreement is found by the court to have been executed voluntarily and to be in the best interests of the child at the time the adoption petition is granted.

(2) The terms of a postadoption contact agreement executed under this section shall be limited to, but need not include, all of the following:

(A) Provisions for visitation between the child and a birth parent or parents and other birth relatives, including siblings, and the child's Indian tribe if the case is governed by the federal Indian Child Welfare Act of 1978 (25 U.S.C. Sec. 1901 et seq.).

(B) Provisions for future contact between a birth parent or parents or other birth relatives, including siblings, or both, and the child or an adoptive parent, or both, and in cases governed by the Indian Child Welfare Act, the child's Indian tribe.

(C) Provisions for the sharing of information about the child in the future.

(3) The terms of a postadoption contact agreement with birth relatives, including siblings, other than the child's birth parent or parents shall be limited to the sharing of information about the child, unless the child has a preexisting relationship with the birth relative.

(c) At the time an adoption decree is entered pursuant to a petition filed pursuant to Section 8714, 8714.5, 8802, 8912, or 9000, the court entering the decree may grant postadoption privileges if an agreement for those privileges has been executed, including agreements executed pursuant to subdivision (f) of Section 8620. The hearing to grant the adoption petition and issue an order of adoption may be continued as necessary to permit parties who are in the process of negotiating a postadoption agreement to reach a final agreement.

(d) The child who is the subject of the adoption petition shall be considered a party to the postadoption contact agreement. The written consent to the terms and conditions of the postadoption contact agreement and any subsequent modifications of the agreement by a child who is 12 years of age or older is a necessary condition to the granting of privileges regarding visitation, contact, or sharing of information about the child, unless the court finds by a preponderance of the evidence that the agreement, as written, is in the best interests of the child. A child who has been found to come within Section 300 of the Welfare and Institutions Code or who is the subject of a petition for jurisdiction of the juvenile court under Section 300 of the Welfare and Institutions Code shall be represented by an attorney for purposes of consent to the postadoption contact agreement.

(e) A postadoption contact agreement shall contain the following warnings in bold type:

(1) After the adoption petition has been granted by the court, the adoption cannot be set aside due to the failure of an adopting parent, a birth parent, a birth relative, including a sibling, an Indian tribe, or the child to follow the terms of this agreement

or a later change to this agreement.

(2) A disagreement between the parties or litigation brought to enforce or modify the agreement shall not affect the validity of the adoption and shall not serve as a basis for orders affecting the custody of the child.

(3) A court will not act on a petition to change or enforce this agreement unless the petitioner has participated, or attempted to participate, in good faith in mediation or other appropriate dispute resolution proceedings to resolve the dispute.

(f) Upon the granting of the adoption petition and the issuing of the order of adoption of a child who is a dependent of the juvenile court, juvenile court dependency jurisdiction shall be terminated. Enforcement of the postadoption contact agreement shall be under the continuing jurisdiction of the court granting the petition of adoption. The court may not order compliance with the agreement absent a finding that the party seeking the enforcement participated, or attempted to participate, in good faith in mediation or other appropriate dispute resolution proceedings regarding the conflict, prior to the filing of the enforcement action, and that the enforcement is in the best interests of the child. Documentary evidence or offers of proof may serve as the basis for the court's decision regarding enforcement. No testimony or evidentiary hearing shall be required. The court shall not order further investigation or evaluation by a public or private agency or individual absent a finding by clear and convincing evidence that the best interests of the child may be protected or advanced only by that inquiry and that the inquiry will not disturb the stability of the child's home to the detriment of the child.

(g) The court may not award monetary damages as a result of the filing of the civil action pursuant to subdivision (e).

(h) A postadoption contact agreement may be modified or terminated only if either of the following occurs:

(1) All parties, including the child if the child is 12 years of age or older at the time of the requested termination or modification, have signed a modified postadoption contact agreement and the agreement is filed with the court that granted the petition of adoption.

(2) The court finds all of the following:

(A) The termination or modification is necessary to serve the best interests of the child.

(B) There has been a substantial change of circumstances since the original agreement was executed and approved by the court.

(C) The party seeking the termination or modification has participated, or attempted to participate, in good faith in mediation or other appropriate dispute resolution proceedings prior to seeking court approval of the proposed termination or modification.

Documentary evidence or offers of proof may serve as the basis for the court's decision. No testimony or evidentiary hearing shall be required. The court shall not order further investigation or evaluation by a public or private agency or individual absent a finding by clear and convincing evidence that the best interests of the child may be protected or advanced only by that inquiry and that the inquiry will not disturb the stability of the child's home to the detriment of the child.

(i) All costs and fees of mediation or other appropriate dispute resolution proceedings shall be borne by each party, excluding the child. All costs and fees of litigation shall be borne by the party filing the action to modify or enforce the agreement when no party has been found by the court as failing to comply with an existing post-adoption contact agreement. Otherwise, a party, other than the child, found by the court as failing to comply without good cause with an existing agreement shall bear all the costs and fees of litigation.

(j) The Judicial Council shall adopt rules of court and forms for motions to enforce, terminate, or modify post-adoption contact agreements.

(k) The court shall not set aside a decree of adoption, rescind a relinquishment, or modify an order to terminate parental rights or any other prior court order because of the failure of a birth parent, adoptive parent, birth relative, including a sibling, an Indian tribe, or the child to comply with any of the original terms of, or subsequent modifications to, the postadoption contact agreement, except as follows:

(1) Prior to issuing the order of adoption, in an adoption involving an Indian child, the court may, upon a petition of the birth parent, birth relative, including a sibling, or an Indian tribe, order the parties to engage in family mediation services for the purpose of reaching a postadoption contact agreement if the prospective adoptive parent fails to negotiate in good faith to execute a postadoption contact agreement, after having agreed to enter into negotiations, provided that the failure of the parties to reach an agreement is not in and of itself proof of bad faith.

(2) Prior to issuing the order of adoption, if the parties fail to negotiate in good faith to execute a postadoption contact agreement during the negotiations entered into pursuant to, and in accordance with, paragraph (1), the court may modify prior orders or issue new orders as necessary to ensure the best interest of the Indian child is met, including, but not limited to, requiring parties to engage in further family mediation services for the purpose of reaching a postadoption contact agreement, initiating guardianship proceeding in lieu of adoption, or authorizing a change of adoptive placement for the child.

(l) As used in this section, "sibling" means a person related to the identified child by blood, adoption, or affinity through a common legal or biological parent.

(m) (1) In every adoption, each petitioner shall inform the court in writing, on ADOPT-200, whether that petitioner has entered, or has agreed to enter into a postadoption contact agreement with any person or persons.

(2) (A) If a postadoption contact agreement has been entered into, the terms of the agreement shall be set forth on or attached to ADOPT-310 and that form shall be signed by all adult parties to the agreement, and if applicable pursuant to subdivision (d), by the child who is the subject of the adoption.

(B) Prior to finalization of the adoption, the petitioner shall file this form and any attachments with the court. The petitioner shall provide a file-marked copy of the form to all signatories to the agreement, and to any licensed adoption agency that placed the child for adoption or consented to the adoption, within 30 days of the petitioner's receipt of the file-marked copy.[576]

8617. (a) Except as provided in subdivision (b), the existing parent or parents of an adopted child are, from the time of the adoption, relieved of all parental duties towards, and all responsibility for, the adopted child, and have no right over the child.
(b) The termination of the parental duties and responsibilities of the existing parent or parents under subdivision (a) may be waived if both the existing parent or parents and the prospective adoptive parent or parents sign a waiver at any time prior to the finalization of the adoption. The waiver shall be filed with the court.
(c) This section applies to all adoptions except intercountry adoptions governed by Chapter 4 (commencing with Section 8900).

8618. A child adopted pursuant to this part may take the family name of the adoptive parent.[1]

8619. The department shall adopt rules and regulations it determines are reasonably necessary to ensure that the birth parent or parents of Indian ancestry, seeking to relinquish a child for adoption, provide sufficient information to the department, county adoption agency, or licensed adoption agency so that a certificate of degree of Indian blood can be obtained from the Bureau of Indian Affairs. The department shall immediately request a certificate of degree of Indian blood from the Bureau of Indian Affairs upon obtaining the information. A copy of all documents pertaining to the degree of Indian blood and tribal enrollment, including a copy of the certificate of degree of Indian blood, shall become a permanent record in the adoption files and shall be housed in a central location and made available to authorized personnel from the Bureau of Indian Affairs when required to determine the adopted person's eligibility to receive services or benefits because of the adopted person's status as an Indian. This information shall be made available to the adopted person upon reaching the age of majority.[233]

8619.5. Whenever a final decree of adoption of an Indian child has been vacated or set aside or the adoptive parent voluntary consents to termination of parental rights to the child, a biological parent or prior Indian custodian may petition for return of custody and the court shall grant that petition unless there is a showing, in a proceeding subject to the provisions of Section 1912 of the Indian Child Welfare Act (25 U.S.C. Sec. 1901 et seq.), that the return of custody is not in the best interest of the child.

8620. (a) (1) If a parent is seeking to relinquish a child pursuant to Section 8700 or execute an adoption placement agreement pursuant to Section 8801.3, the department, county adoption agency, licensed adoption agency, or adoption service provider, as applicable, shall ask the child and the child's parent or custodian whether the child is, or may be, a member of, or eligible for membership in an Indian tribe or whether the child has been identified as a member of an Indian organization. The department, county adoption agency, licensed adoption agency, or adoption service provider, as applicable, shall complete the forms provided for this purpose by the department and shall make this completed form a part of the file.

(2) If there is any oral or written information that indicates that the child is, or may be, an Indian child, the department, county adoption agency, licensed adoption agency, or adoption service provider, as applicable, shall obtain the following information:

(A) The name of the child involved, and the actual date and place of birth of the child.

(B) The name, address, date of birth, and tribal affiliation of the birth parents, maternal and paternal grandparents, and maternal and paternal great-grandparents of the child.

(C) The name and address of extended family members of the child who have a tribal affiliation.

(D) The name and address of the Indian tribes or Indian organizations of which the child is, or may be, a member.

(E) A statement of the reasons why the child is, or may be, an Indian.

(3) (A) The department, county adoption agency, licensed adoption agency, attorney for the prospective adoptive parents, or adoption service provider shall send a notice, which shall include information obtained pursuant to paragraph (2) and a request for confirmation of the child's Indian status, to any parent and any custodian of the child, and to any Indian tribe of which the child is, or may be, a member or eligible for membership. If any of the information required under paragraph (2) cannot be obtained, the notice shall indicate that fact.

(B) The notice sent pursuant to subparagraph (A) shall describe the nature of the proceeding and advise the recipient of the Indian tribe's right to intervene in the proceeding on its own behalf or on behalf of a tribal member relative of the child.

(b) The department shall adopt regulations to ensure that if a child who is being voluntarily relinquished for adoption, pursuant to Section 8700, is an Indian child, the parent of the child shall be advised of the right to withdraw consent and thereby rescind the relinquishment of an Indian child for any reason at any time prior to entry of a final decree of termination of parental rights or adoption, pursuant to Section 1913 of Title 25 of the United States Code.

(c) If a child who is the subject of an adoption proceeding after being relinquished for adoption pursuant to Section 8700, is an Indian child, the child's Indian tribe may intervene in that proceeding on behalf of a tribal member relative of the child.

(d) Any notice sent under this section shall comply with Section 180.

(e) If all prior notices required by this section have been provided to an Indian tribe, the Indian tribe receiving those prior notices is encouraged to provide notice to the department and to the licensed adoption agency, county adoption agency, or adoption service provider, not later than five calendar days prior to the date of the hearing to determine whether or not the final adoption order is to be granted, indicating whether or not it intends to intervene in the proceeding required by this section, either on its own behalf or on behalf of a tribal member who is a relative of the child.

(f) The Legislature finds and declares that some adoptive children may benefit from either direct or indirect contact with an Indian tribe. The adoption laws of this state shall not be construed to prevent the adopting parent or parents, the birth relatives, including the birth parent or parents, an Indian tribe, and the child, from voluntarily entering into a written agreement to permit continuing contact between the Indian tribe and the child, if the agreement is found by the court to have been entered into voluntarily and to be in the best interest of the child at the time the adoption petition is granted.

(g) With respect to giving notice to Indian tribes in the case of voluntary placements of Indian children pursuant to this section, a person, other than a birth parent of the child, shall be subject to a civil penalty if that person knowingly and willfully:

(1) Falsifies, conceals, or covers up by trick, scheme, or device, a material fact concerning whether the child is an Indian child or the parent is an Indian.

(2) Makes a false, fictitious, or fraudulent statement, omission, or representation.

(3) Falsifies a written document knowing that the document contains a false, fictitious, or fraudulent statement or entry relating to a material fact.

(4) Assists a person in physically removing a child from the State of California in order to obstruct the application of notification.

(h) Civil penalties for a violation of subdivision (g) by a person other than a birth parent of the child are as follows:

(1) For the initial violation, a person shall be fined not more than ten thousand dollars ($10,000).

(2) For any subsequent violation, a person shall be fined not more than twenty thousand dollars ($20,000).

8621. (a) The department shall adopt regulations regarding the provision of adoption services by the department, county adoption agencies, licensed adoption agencies, and other adoption service providers authorized pursuant to this division and shall monitor the provision of those services by county adoption agencies, licensed adoption agencies, and other adoption service providers as provided by law. The department shall report any violations of these regulations to the appropriate licensing authority.

(b) Notwithstanding the rulemaking provisions of the Administrative Procedure Act (Chapter 3.5 (commencing with Section 11340) of Part 1 of Division 3 of Title 2 of the Government Code), the State Department of Social Services may implement, interpret, or make specific the changes made to this chapter by the act adding this subdivision by means of all-county letters, written directives, interim licensing standards, or similar written instructions from the department until regulations are adopted. These all-county letters, written directives, interim licensing standards, or similar written instructions shall have the same force and effect as regulations until the adoption of regulations.[533]

8622. A licensed private adoption agency whose services are limited to a particular target population shall inform all birth parents and prospective adoptive parents of its service limitations before commencing any services, signing any documents or agreements, or accepting any fees.

This section shall become operative on January 1, 1995.

8623. Notwithstanding any other law, all adoption facilitators registered with the department on its statewide registry as of July 1, 2023, shall cease operation in this state on or before December 31, 2023. An adoption facilitator that continues to operate on or after January 1, 2024, shall be deemed an unlicensed adoption agency as referenced in paragraph (6) of subdivision (a) of Section 1503.5 of the Health and Safety Code.[535]

8624. (a) A person aggrieved by a violation of Section 8609 may bring a civil action for damages, rescission, injunctive relief, or any other civil or equitable remedy. Operation of an unlicensed adoption agency, as referenced in paragraph (6) of subdivision (a) of Section 1503.5 of the Health and Safety Code, shall be an act of unfair competition and an unfair business practice within the meaning of Chapter 5 (commencing with Section 17200) of Part 2 of Division 7 of the Business and Professions Code.

(b) If the court finds that a person has violated Section 8609, it shall award actual damages plus an amount equal to treble the amount of the actual damages or two thousand five hundred dollars ($2,500) per violation, whichever is greater.

(c) In a civil action under this section, a prevailing party may recover reasonable attorney's fees and costs.

(d) The Attorney General, a district attorney, or a city attorney may bring a civil action for injunctive relief, restitution, or other equitable relief against an unlicensed adoption agency as referenced in paragraph (6) of subdivision (a) of Section 1503.5 of the Health and Safety Code pursuant to this section in the name of the people of the State of California.

(e) Any other interested person who, based upon information or belief, claims a violation of Section 8609 has been committed may bring a civil action for injunctive relief on behalf of the general public. This section authorizes a referral by the department to the appropriate law enforcement entities consistent with these provisions.[535]

8625. (a) The department shall create a section on its internet website dedicated to educating the public on unlicensed adoption agencies. The section shall include both of the following:

(1) A statement informing the public that, as of January 1, 2024, operating as an "adoption facilitator" in the state is prohibited. The statement shall include common practices and services undertaken by adoption facilitators. The statement shall also inform the public that only the authorized persons or organizations specified in Section 8609 may engage in the practices described in that section.

(2) A listing of all persons or organizations on the department's adoption facilitator registry as of December 31, 2023.

(b) The department shall individually notify each adoption facilitator on the registry as July 1, 2023, that operations must cease pursuant to Section 8623. The notice shall also require each adoption facilitator to comply with both of the following:

(1) Publish the statement described in subdivision (a) on any internet website operated by the adoption facilitator.

(2) Provide written notice to any individuals under contract indicating that the adoption facilitator must cease operation on or before December 31, 2023. This written notice must also include information on licensed entities that can provide adoption services and any additional information the department deems necessary.[536]

8626. Notwithstanding any other law, an adoption order issued pursuant to this part shall include the names of the adoptive parent or parents and any existing parent or parents who will maintain their parental rights after the finalization of the adoption. A failure to include an existing parent or parents on the adoption order in compliance with this section shall not be construed to terminate the parental rights and responsibilities otherwise maintained under existing law by an existing parent or parents.[608]

Chapter 2: Agency Adoptions

8700. (a) Either birth parent may relinquish a child to the department, county adoption agency, or licensed adoption agency for adoption by a written statement signed before two subscribing witnesses and acknowledged before an authorized official of the department, county adoption agency, or licensed adoption agency. The relinquishment, when reciting that the person making it is entitled to the sole custody of the child and acknowledged before the officer, is prima facie evidence of the right of the person making it to the sole custody of the child and the person's sole right to relinquish.

(b) A relinquishing parent who is a minor has the right to relinquish a child for adoption to the department, county adoption agency, or licensed adoption agency, and the relinquishment is not subject to revocation by the relinquishing parent by reason of the minority, or because the parent or guardian of the relinquishing minor parent was not served with notice that the relinquishing minor parent relinquished the child for adoption, unless the relinquishing minor parent has previously provided written authorization to serve the relinquishing minor's parent or guardian with that notice.

(c) If a parent resides outside this state and the other parent has relinquished the child for adoption pursuant to subdivision (a) or (d), the parent residing out of state may relinquish the child by a written statement signed before a notary on a form prescribed by the department, and previously signed by an authorized official of the department, county adoption agency, or licensed adoption agency that signifies the willingness of the department, county adoption agency, or licensed adoption agency to accept the relinquishment.

(d) If a parent and child reside outside this state and the other parent has not relinquished the child for adoption to the department, county adoption agency, or licensed adoption agency, the parent residing out of state may relinquish the child to the department, county adoption agency, or licensed adoption agency by a written statement signed by the relinquishing parent, after the following requirements have been satisfied:

(1) Prior to signing the relinquishment, the relinquishing parent shall have received, from a representative of an agency licensed or otherwise approved to provide adoption services under the laws of the relinquishing parent's state of residence, the same counseling and advisement services as if the relinquishing parent resided in this state.

(2) The relinquishment shall be signed before a representative of an agency licensed or otherwise approved to provide adoption services under the laws of the relinquishing parent's state of residence whenever possible or before a licensed social worker on a form prescribed by the department, and previously signed by an authorized official of the department, county adoption agency, or licensed adoption agency, that signifies the willingness of the department, county adoption agency, or licensed adoption agency to accept the relinquishment.

(e) (1) The relinquishment authorized by this section has no effect until a certified copy is sent to, and filed with, the department. The county adoption agency or licensed adoption agency shall send that copy by certified mail, return receipt requested, or by overnight courier or messenger, with proof of delivery, to the department no earlier than the end of the business day following the signing thereof. The agency shall inform the birth parent that during this time period the birth parent may request that the relinquishment be withdrawn and that, if the birth parent makes the request, the relinquishment shall be withdrawn. The relinquishment shall be final 10 business days after receipt of the filing by the department, unless any of the following applies:

(A) The department sends written acknowledgment of receipt of the relinquishment prior to the expiration of that 10-day period, at which time the relinquishment shall be final.

(B) A longer period of time is necessary due to a pending court action or some other cause beyond control of the department.

(C) The birth parent signs a waiver of right to revoke relinquishment pursuant to Section 8700.5, in which case the relinquishment shall become final as provided in that section.

(2) After the relinquishment is final, it may be rescinded only by the mutual consent of the department, county adoption agency, or licensed adoption agency to which the child was relinquished and the birth parent or parents relinquishing the child.

(f) The relinquishing parent may name in the relinquishment the person or persons with whom the relinquishing parent intends that placement of the child for adoption be made by the department, county adoption agency, or licensed adoption agency.

(g) Notwithstanding subdivision (e), if the relinquishment names the person or persons with whom placement by the department, county adoption agency, or licensed adoption agency is intended and the child is not placed in the home of the named person or persons or the child is removed from the home prior to the granting of the adoption, the department, county adoption agency, or licensed adoption agency shall mail a notice by certified mail, return receipt requested, to the birth parent signing the relinquishment within 72 hours of the decision not to place the child for adoption or the decision to remove the child from the home.

(h) The relinquishing parent has 30 days from the date on which the notice described in subdivision (g) was mailed to rescind the relinquishment.

(1) If the relinquishing parent requests rescission during the 30-day period, the department, county adoption agency, or licensed adoption agency shall rescind the relinquishment.

(2) If the relinquishing parent does not request rescission during the 30-day period, the department, county adoption agency, or licensed adoption agency shall select adoptive parents for the child.

(3) If the relinquishing parent and the department, county adoption agency, or licensed adoption agency wish to identify a different person or persons during the 30-day period with whom the child is intended to be placed, the initial relinquishment shall be rescinded and a new relinquishment identifying the person or persons completed.

(i) Subject to the requirements of subdivision (b) of Section 361 of the Welfare and Institutions Code, a parent may sign a relinquishment of a child described in paragraph (1) of subdivision (b) of Section 361 of the Welfare and Institutions Code. If the relinquishment is to a licensed private adoption agency, the parent shall be advised, in writing, that the relinquishment shall have no effect and will be not be filed with, or acknowledged by, the department, unless the court approves the relinquishment pursuant to paragraph (3) of subdivision (b) of Section 361 of the Welfare and Institutions Code. If the court issues an order approving the relinquishment, the licensed private adoption agency shall file the relinquishment and the order with the department. If the court denies the relinquishment, the licensed private adoption agency shall void the relinquishment and inform the parent of that fact.

(j) The filing of the relinquishment with the department terminates all parental rights and responsibilities with regard to the child, except as provided in subdivisions (g) and (h).

(k) The department shall adopt regulations to administer the provisions of this section.

8700.5. (a) A relinquishing birth parent may elect to sign a waiver of the right to revoke relinquishment in the presence of any of the following:

(1) A representative of the department or the delegated county adoption agency, or any public adoption agency of another state.

(2) A judicial officer of a court of record, within or outside of California, if the birth parent is represented by independent legal counsel.

(3) An authorized representative of a licensed private adoption agency within or outside of California, including a representative of the adoption agency that witnessed or accepted the relinquishment, if the birth parent is represented by independent legal counsel.

(b) The waiver of the right to revoke relinquishment may not be signed until the department, delegated county adoption agency, or public adoption agency of another state has completed an interview, unless the waiver is signed in the presence of a judicial officer of a court of record of any state or an authorized representative of a private adoption agency licensed within or outside of California. If the waiver is signed in the presence of a judicial officer, the interview and witnessing of the signing of the waiver shall be conducted by the judicial officer. If the waiver is signed in the presence of an authorized representative of a licensed adoption agency, the interview shall be conducted by the independent legal counsel for the birth parent or parents, who shall:

(1) Review the waiver with the birth parent or parents.

(2) Counsel the birth parent or parents about the nature of the intended waiver.

(3) Sign and deliver to the birth parent or parents and the licensed adoption agency a certificate in substantially the following form:

"I, (name of attorney), have counseled my client, (name of client), about the nature and legal effect of the waiver of the right to revoke the relinquishment for adoption. I am so disassociated from the interest of the prospective adoptive parent(s) and the licensed adoption agency as to be in a position to advise my client impartially and confidentially as to the consequences of the waiver. My client is aware that California law provides an indeterminate period, usually 2 to 10 business days, during which a birth parent may revoke a relinquishment for adoption. On the basis of this counsel, I conclude that it is the intent of my client to waive the right to revoke, and to make a permanent and irrevocable relinquishment for adoption. My client understands that upon signing this waiver, my client will not be able to regain custody of the child unless the prospective adoptive parent or parents agree to withdraw the petition for adoption or the court denies the adoption petition."

(c) If the placing birth parent signs the waiver in front of a judicial officer or the department, the relinquishment shall become final and irrevocable at the time the waiver is signed. If the waiver is signed in the presence of an authorized representative of a private licensed adoption agency, the relinquishment shall become final and irrevocable at the close of the next business day after the relinquishment was signed, or at the close of the next business day after expiration of any holding period specified in writing, whichever is later.

(d) The licensed adoption agency shall submit the waiver and certificate to the department with the relinquishment, unless the relinquishment was submitted to the department before the waiver was signed, in which case the waiver and certificate shall be submitted to the department no later than two business days after signing.

(e) A waiver executed pursuant to this section shall be void if any of the following occur:

(1) The relinquishment is determined to be invalid.

(2) The relinquishment is revoked during any holding period specified in writing.

(3) The relinquishment is rescinded pursuant to Section 8700.

(f) This section does not limit the birth parent's right to rescind the relinquishment pursuant to Section 8700.

8701. At or before the time a relinquishment is signed, the

department, county adoption agency, or licensed adoption agency shall advise the birth parent signing the relinquishment, verbally and in writing, that the birth parent may, at any time in the future, request from the department, county adoption agency, or licensed adoption agency all known information about the status of the child's adoption, except for personal, identifying information about the adoptive family. The birth parent shall be advised that this information includes, but is not limited to, all of the following:

(a) Whether the child has been placed for adoption.

(b) The approximate date that an adoption was completed.

(c) If the adoption was not completed or was vacated, for any reason, whether adoptive placement of the child is again being considered.[234]

8702. (a) The department shall adopt a statement to be presented to the birth parents at the time a relinquishment is signed and to prospective adoptive parents at the time of the home study. The statement shall, in a clear and concise manner and in words calculated to ensure the confidence of the birth parents in the integrity of the adoption process, communicate to the birth parents of a child who is the subject of an adoption petition all of the following facts:

(1) It is in the child's best interest that the birth parent keep the department, county adoption agency, or licensed adoption agency to whom the child was relinquished for adoption informed of any health problems that the parent develops that could affect the child.

(2) It is extremely important that the birth parent keep an address current with the department, county adoption agency, or licensed adoption agency to whom the child was relinquished for adoption in order to permit a response to inquiries concerning medical or social history.

(3) Section 9203 of the Family Code authorizes a person who has been adopted and who attains the age of 21 years to request the department, county adoption agency, or the licensed adoption agency to disclose the name and address of the adoptee's birth parents. Consequently, it is of the utmost importance that the birth parent indicate whether to allow this disclosure by checking the appropriate box provided on the form.

(4) The birth parent may change the decision whether to permit disclosure of the birth parent's name and address, at any time, by sending a notarized letter to that effect, by certified mail, return receipt requested, to the department, county adoption agency, or to the licensed adoption agency that joined in the adoption petition.

(5) The relinquishment will be filed in the office of the clerk of the court in which the adoption takes place. The file is not open to inspection by any persons other than the parties to the adoption proceeding, their attorneys, and the department, except upon order of a judge of the superior court.

(b) The department shall adopt a form to be signed by the birth parents at the time the relinquishment is signed, which shall provide as follows:

"Section 9203 of the Family Code authorizes a person who has been adopted and who attains the age of 21 years to make a request to the State

Department of Social Services, county adoption agency, or licensed adoption agency that joined in the adoption petition, for the name and address of the adoptee's birth parents. Indicate by checking one of the boxes below whether or not you wish your name and address to be disclosed:

□ YES

□ NO

□ UNCERTAIN AT THIS TIME; WILL NOTIFY AGENCY AT LATER DATE." [235]

8703. When the parental rights of a birth parent are terminated pursuant to Chapter 5 (commencing with Section 7660) of Part 3 of Division 12 or Part 4 (commencing with Section 7800) of Division 12, or pursuant to Section 366.25 or 366.26 of the Welfare and Institutions Code, the department, county adoption agency, or licensed adoption agency responsible for the adoptive placement of the child shall send a written notice to the birth parent, if the birth parent's address is known, that contains the following statement:

(a) "You are encouraged to keep the department or this agency informed of your current address in order to permit a response to any inquiry concerning medical or social history made by or on behalf of the child who was the subject of the court action terminating parental rights.

(b) Section 9203 of the Family Code authorizes a person who has been adopted and who attains the age of 21 years to make a request to the State Department of Social Services, county adoption agency, or licensed adoption agency, that joined in the adoption petition, for the name and address of the adoptee's birth parents. Indicate by checking one of the boxes below whether or not you wish your name and address to be disclosed:

□ YES

□ NO

□ UNCERTAIN AT THIS TIME; WILL NOTIFY AGENCY AT LATER DATE." [236]

8704. (a) The department, county adoption agency, or licensed adoption agency to which a child has been freed for adoption by either relinquishment or termination of parental rights is responsible for the care of the child, and is entitled to the exclusive custody and control of the child until an order of adoption is granted. Any placement for temporary care, or for adoption, made by the department, county adoption agency, or licensed adoption agency may be terminated in its discretion at any time before the granting of an order of adoption. In the event of termination of any placement for temporary care or for adoption, the child shall be returned promptly to the physical custody of the department, county adoption agency, or licensed adoption agency.

(b) No petition may be filed to adopt a child relinquished to the department, county adoption agency, or licensed adoption agency or a child declared free from the custody and control of either or both birth parents and referred to the department, county adoption agency, or licensed adoption agency for adoptive placement, except by the prospective adoptive parents with whom the child has been placed for adoption by the department, county adoption agency, or licensed adoption agency. After the adoption petition has been filed, the department, county adoption agency, or licensed adoption agency may remove the child from the prospective adoptive parents only with the approval of the court, upon motion by the department, county adoption agency, or licensed adoption agency after notice to the prospective adoptive parents, supported by an affidavit or affidavits stating the grounds on which removal is sought. If the department, county adoption agency, or licensed adoption agency refuses to consent to the adoption of a child by the person or persons with whom the department, county adoption agency, or licensed adoption agency placed the child for adoption, the court may nevertheless order the adoption if it finds that the refusal to consent is not in the child's best interest.[237]

8704.5. (a) A foster care license or certification or resource family approval shall not be required for placement of a nondependent child who is relinquished for adoption to a licensed private adoption agency, if the child is placed in the care of prospective adoptive parents who have an approved adoption home study that meets the criteria established by the department for home studies conducted within the state.
(b) During a preadoptive placement made pursuant to subdivision (a), the licensed private adoption agency shall conduct in-home supervisory visits no less than once every 30 days, until the child has been legally freed and formally placed for adoption.[367]

8705. (a) Where a child is in the custody of a public agency or licensed adoption agency, if it is established that the persons whose consent to the adoption is required by law are deceased, an action may be brought by the department, county adoption agency, or licensed adoption agency requesting the court to make an order establishing that the requesting agency has the right to custody and control of the child and the authority to place the child for adoption. The department, county adoption agency, or licensed adoption agency bringing the action shall give notice in the form prescribed by the court to all known relatives of the child up to and including the third degree of lineal or collateral consanguinity.
(b) This section does not apply where a guardian of the person of the child has been appointed pursuant to nomination by a will.[238]

8706. (a) An agency may not place a child for adoption unless a written report on the child's medical background and, if available, the medical background of the child's biological parents so far as ascertainable, has been submitted to the prospective adoptive parents and they have acknowledged in writing the receipt of the report.
(b) The report on the child's background shall contain all known diagnostic information, including current medical reports on the child, psychological evaluations, and scholastic information, as well as all known information regarding the child's developmental history and family life.
(c) (1) The biological parents may provide a blood sample at a clinic or hospital approved by the State Department of Health Services. The biological parents' failure to provide a blood sample shall not affect the adoption of the child.

(2) The blood sample shall be stored at a laboratory under contract with the State Department of Health Services for a period of 30 years following the adoption of the child.

(3) The purpose of the stored sample of blood is to provide a blood sample from which DNA testing can be done at a later date after entry of the order of adoption at the request of the adoptive parents or the adopted child. The cost of drawing and storing the blood samples shall be paid for by a separate fee in addition to the fee required under Section 8716. The amount of this additional fee shall be based on the cost of drawing and storing the blood samples but at no time shall the additional fee be more than one hundred dollars ($100).

(d) (1) The blood sample shall be stored and released in such a manner as to not identify any party to the adoption.

(2) Any results of the DNA testing shall be stored and released in such a manner as to not identify any party to the adoption.

8707. (a) The department shall establish a statewide photo-listing service to serve all county adoption agencies and licensed adoption agencies in the state as a means of recruiting adoptive families. The department shall adopt regulations governing the operations of the photo-listing service and shall establish procedures for monitoring compliance with this section.

(b) The photo-listing service shall maintain child specific information that, except as provided in this section, contains a photograph and description of each child who has been legally freed for adoption and whose case plan goal is adoption. Registration of children with the photo-listing service and notification by the licensed adoption agency of changes in a child's photo-listing status shall be reflected in the photo-listing service within 30 working days of receipt of the registration or notification.

(c) The photo-listing service shall be provided to all county adoption agencies, licensed adoption agencies, adoption support groups, and state, regional, and national photo-listings and exchanges requesting copies of the photo-listing service.

(d) All children legally freed for adoption whose case plan goal is adoption shall be photo-listed, unless deferred as provided in subdivision (e) or (f). Adoption agencies shall send a recent photograph and description of each legally freed child to the photo-listing service within 15 working days of the time a child is legally freed for adoption. When adoption has become the case plan goal for a particular child, the adoption agency may photo-list that child before the child becomes legally freed for adoption.

(e) A child shall be deferred from the photo-listing service when the child's foster parents or other identified individuals who have applied to adopt the child are meeting the county adoption agency's or licensed adoption agency's requests for required documen-tation and are cooperating in the completion of a home study being conducted by the agency.

(f) A child who is 12 years old or older may be deferred from the photo-listing service if the child does not consent to being adopted.

(g) Within 15 working days following a one-year period in which a child is listed in the photo-listing service, the county adoption agency or licensed adoption agency shall submit a revised description and photograph of the child.

(h) County adoption agencies and licensed adoption agencies shall notify the photo-listing service, by telephone, of any adoptive placements or of significant changes in a child's photo-listing status within two working days of the change.

(i) The department shall establish procedures for semiannual review of the photo-listing status of all legally freed children whose case plan goal is adoption, including those who are registered with the photo-listing service and those whose registration has been deferred.[239]

8707.1. (a) The agency responsible for recruitment of potential adoptive parents shall make diligent efforts to recruit individuals who reflect the ethnic, racial, and cultural diversity of children for whom adoptive homes are needed.

(b) This section shall not be construed to affect the application of the federal Indian Child Welfare Act.[324]

8708. (a) The adoption agency to which a child has been freed for adoption by either relinquishment or termination of parental rights shall not do any of the following:

(1) Deny to any person the opportunity to become an adoptive parent on the basis of the race, color, or national origin of the person or the child involved.

(2) Delay or deny the placement of a child for adoption on the basis of the race, color, or national origin of the adoptive parent or the child involved.

(3) Delay or deny the placement of a child for adoption solely because the prospective, approved adoptive family resides outside the jurisdiction of the department, county adoption agency, or licensed adoption agency. For purposes of this paragraph, an approved adoptive family means a family approved pursuant to the California adoptive applicant assessment standards or approved as a resource family pursuant to Section 1517 of the Health and Safety Code or Section 16519.5 of the Welfare and Institutions Code. If the adoptive applicant assessment was conducted in another state according to that state's standards, the California placing agency shall determine whether the standards of the other state substantially meet the standards and criteria established in California adoption regulations.

(b) This section shall not be construed to affect the application of the federal Indian Child Welfare Act (25 U.S.C. Sec. 1901 and following).[368]

8709. (a) The department, county adoption agency, or licensed adoption agency to which a child has been freed for adoption by either relinquishment or termination of parental rights may consider the child's religious background in determining an appropriate placement.

(b) This section shall not be construed to affect the application of the federal Indian Child Welfare Act (25 U.S.C. Sec. 1901 and following).[240]

8710. (a) If a child is being considered for adoption, the department, county adoption agency, or licensed adoption agency shall first consider adoptive placement in the home of a relative or, in the case of an Indian child, according to the placement preferences and standards set out in subdivisions (c), (d), (e), (f), (g), (h), and (i) of Section 361.31 of the Welfare and Institutions Code. However, if the birth parent refuses to consider a relative or sibling placement, if a relative is not available, if placement with an available relative is not in the child's best interest, or if placement would permanently separate the child from other siblings who are being considered for adoption or who are in foster care and an alternative placement would not require the permanent separation, the foster parent or parents of the child shall be considered with respect to the child along with all other prospective adoptive parents where all of the following conditions are present:

(1) The child has been in foster care with the foster parent or parents for a period of more than four months.

(2) The child has substantial emotional ties to the foster parent or parents.

(3) The child's removal from the foster home would be seriously detrimental to the child's well-being.

(4) The foster parent or parents have made a written request to be considered to adopt the child.

(b) In the case of an Indian child whose foster parent or parents or other prospective adoptive parents do not fall within the placement preferences established in subdivision (c) or (d) of Section 361.31 of the Welfare and Institutions Code, the foster parent or parents or other prospective adoptive parents shall only be considered if the court finds, supported by clear and convincing evidence, that good cause exists to deviate from these placement preferences.

(c) This section does not apply to a child who has been adjudged a dependent of the juvenile court pursuant to Section 300 of the Welfare and Institutions Code.

(d) Upon a request to move a child from a prospective adoptive home for the purpose of placement with siblings or other relatives, the court shall consider the best interests of the child.[241]

8710.1. If there is not an adoptive placement plan for a child with an approved adoptive family, as defined in subdivision (c) of Section 8708, within the department's, county adoption agency's, or licensed adoption agency's jurisdiction, then the department, county adoption agency, or licensed adoption agency shall register the child with the exchange system described in Section 8710.2.[242]

8710.2. In order to preclude the delays or denials described in paragraph (3) of subdivision (a) of Section 8708, the department shall establish a statewide exchange system that interjurisdictionally matches waiting children and approved adoptive families. The department may create a new statewide exchange system, modify an existing statewide exchange system, such as the photo-listing service described in Section 8707, or designate an existing exchange system, such as the Adoption Exchange Enhancement Program, as the statewide exchange system for purposes of this section.

8710.3. If the department, county adoption agency, or licensed adoption agency has approved a family for adoption pursuant to subdivision (c) of Section 8708 and that family may be appropriate for placement of a child

who has been adjudged a dependent child of the juvenile court, the department, county adoption agency, or licensed adoption agency shall register the family with the statewide exchange system established pursuant to Section 8710.2, except in either of the following circumstances:
(a) The family refuses to consent to the registration.
(b) A specific child or children have already been identified for adoptive placement with the family.[243]

8710.4. (a) The department shall ensure that information regarding families and children registered with the statewide exchange system described in Section 8710.2 is accessible by licensed adoption agency personnel throughout the state. Provision shall be made for secure Internet, telephone, and facsimile access by authorized licensed adoption agency personnel.
(b) Information regarding children maintained by the statewide exchange system described in Section 8710.2 shall be confidential and shall not be disclosed to any parties other than authorized adoption agency personnel, except when consent to disclosure has been received in writing from the birth parents or the court that has jurisdiction.

8711. Sections 8708 to 8710.4, inclusive, apply only in determining the placement of a child who has been relinquished for adoption or has been declared free from the custody and control of the birth parents.

8711.5. The department shall adopt regulations to administer the provisions of Sections 8708 to 8711, inclusive.[58]

8712. (a) (1) The department, county adoption agency, or licensed adoption agency shall require each person who files an application for adoption to be fingerprinted and shall secure from an appropriate law enforcement agency any criminal record of that person to determine whether the person has ever been convicted of a crime other than a minor traffic violation. The department, county adoption agency, or licensed adoption agency may also secure the person's full criminal record, if any, with the exception of any convictions for which relief has been granted pursuant to Section 1203.49 of the Penal Code. A federal-level criminal offender record request to the Department of Justice shall be submitted with fingerprint images and related information required by the Department of Justice for the purposes of obtaining information as to the existence and content of a record of an out-of-state or federal conviction or arrest of a person or information regarding any out-of-state or federal crimes or arrests for which the Department of Justice establishes that the person is free on bail, or on their own recognizance pending trial or appeal. The Department of Justice shall forward to the Federal Bureau of Investigation any requests for federal summary criminal history information received pursuant to this section. The Department of Justice shall review the information returned from the Federal Bureau of Investigation and shall compile and disseminate a response to the department, county adoption agency, or licensed adoption agency.
(2) The department, county adoption agency, or licensed adoption agency

may obtain arrest or conviction records or reports from any law enforcement agency as necessary to the performance of its duties, as provided in this section.

(b) Notwithstanding subdivision (c), the criminal record, if any, shall be taken into consideration when evaluating the prospective adoptive parent, and an assessment of the effects of any criminal history on the ability of the prospective adoptive parent to provide adequate and proper care and guidance to the child shall be included in the report to the court.

(c) The department, county adoption agency, or licensed adoption agency shall not give final approval for an adoptive placement in any home in which the prospective adoptive parent or any adult living in the prospective adoptive home has been convicted of an offense for which an exemption cannot be granted pursuant to subparagraph (A) of paragraph (2) of subdivision (g) of Section 1522 of the Health and Safety Code.

(d) Any fee charged by a law enforcement agency for fingerprinting or for checking or obtaining the criminal record of the applicant shall be paid by the applicant. The department, county adoption agency, or licensed adoption agency may defer, waive, or reduce the fee when its payment would cause economic hardship to prospective adoptive parents detrimental to the welfare of the adopted child, when the child has been in the foster care of the prospective adoptive parents for at least one year, or if necessary for the placement of a special-needs child.

8713. (a) In no event may a child who has been freed for adoption be removed from the county in which the child was placed, by any person who has not petitioned to adopt the child, without first obtaining the written consent of the department, county adoption agency, or licensed adoption agency responsible for the child.

(b) During the pendency of an adoption proceeding:

(1) The child proposed to be adopted shall not be concealed from the agency that is investigating the adoption or from the court with jurisdiction over the adoption proceeding.

(2) The child shall not be removed from the county of the petitioner's residence at the time of placement, unless the petitioners or other interested persons first obtain permission for the removal from the court, after giving advance written notice of intent to obtain the court's permission to the department, county adoption agency, or licensed adoption agency responsible for the child. Upon proof of giving notice, permission may be granted by the court if, within a period of 15 days after the date of giving notice, no objections are filed with the court by the department, county adoption agency, or licensed adoption agency responsible for the child. If the department, county adoption agency, or licensed adoption agency files objections within the 15-day period, upon the request of the petitioners the court shall immediately set the matter for hearing and give to the objector, the petitioners, and the party or parties requesting permission for the removal reasonable notice of the hearing by certified mail, return receipt requested, to the address of each as shown in the records of the adoption proceeding. Upon a finding that

the objections are without good cause, the court may grant the requested permission for removal of the child, subject to any limitations that appear to be in the child's best interest.

(c) This section does not apply in any of the following situations:

(1) When the child is absent for a period of not more than 30 days from the county of the petitioner's residence at the time of placement, unless a notice of recommendation of denial of petition has been personally served on the petitioners or the court has issued an order prohibiting the child's removal from the county of the petitioner's residence at the time of placement, pending consideration of any of the following:

(A) The suitability of the petitioners.

(B) The care provided the child.

(C) The availability of the legally required agency consents to the adoption.

(2) Where the child has been returned to and remains in the custody and control of the child's birth parent or parents.

(3) Where written consent for the removal of the child is obtained from the department, county adoption agency, or licensed adoption agency responsible for the child.

(d) A violation of this section is a violation of Section 280 of the Penal Code.

(e) Neither this section nor Section 280 of the Penal Code may be construed to render lawful any act that is unlawful under any other applicable law.[511]

8714. (a) A person desiring to adopt a nondependent child may for that purpose file an adoption request in a county authorized by Section 8609.5. A person desiring to adopt a child who has been adjudged to be a dependent of the juvenile court pursuant to Section 300 of the Welfare and Institutions Code, freed for adoption by the juvenile court, and placed for adoption with the petitioner, may file the adoption request either in the county where the petitioner resides or in the county where the child was freed for adoption.

(b) The court clerk shall immediately notify the department at Sacramento in writing of the pendency of the proceeding and of any subsequent action taken.

(c) If the petitioner has entered into a postadoption contact agreement as set forth in Section 8616.5, the petitioner shall file the agreement, signed by the participating parties, with the court before the adoption is finalized.

(d) The caption of the adoption petition shall contain the names of the petitioners, but not the child's name. The petition shall state the child's sex and date of birth. The name the child had before adoption shall appear in the joinder signed by the licensed adoption agency.

(e) If the child is the subject of a guardianship petition, the adoption petition shall so state and shall include the caption and docket number or have attached a copy of the letters of the guardianship or temporary guardianship. The petitioners shall notify the court of any petition for guardianship or temporary guardianship filed after the adoption petition. The guardianship proceeding shall be consolidated with the adoption proceeding.

(f) The order of adoption shall contain the child's adopted name and the name the child had before adoption.[567]

8714.5. (a) The Legislature finds and declares the following:

(1) It is the intent of the Legislature to expedite legal permanency for children who cannot return to their parents and to remove barriers to adoption by relatives of children who are already in the dependency system or who are at risk of entering the dependency system.

(2) This goal will be achieved by empowering families, including extended families, to care for their own children safely and permanently whenever possible, by preserving existing family relationships, thereby causing the least amount of disruption to the child and the family, and by recognizing the importance of sibling and half-sibling relationships.

(b) A relative desiring to adopt a child may for that purpose file a petition in the county in which the petitioner resides. Where a child has been adjudged to be a dependent of the juvenile court pursuant to Section 300 of the Welfare and Institutions Code, and thereafter has been freed for adoption by the juvenile court, the petition may be filed either in the county where the petitioner resides or in the county where the child was freed for adoption.

(c) Upon the filing of a petition for adoption by a relative, the clerk of the court shall immediately notify the State Department of Social Services in Sacramento in writing of the pendency of the proceeding and of any subsequent action taken.

(d) If the adopting relative has entered into a postadoption contact agreement with the birth parent as set forth in Section 8616.5 the agreement, signed by the participating parties, shall be attached to and filed with the petition for adoption under subdivision (b).

(e) The caption of the adoption petition shall contain the name of the relative petitioner. The petition shall state the child's name, sex, and date of birth.

(f) If the child is the subject of a guardianship petition, the adoption petition shall so state and shall include the caption and docket number or have attached a copy of the letters of the guardianship or temporary guardianship. The petitioner shall notify the court of any petition for adoption. The guardianship proceeding shall be consolidated with the adoption proceeding, and the consolidated case shall be heard and decided in the court in which the adoption is pending.

(g) The order of adoption shall contain the child's adopted name and, if requested by the adopting relative, or if requested by the child who is 12 years of age or older, the name the child had before adoption.

(h) For purposes of this section, "relative" means an adult who is related to the child or the child's half-sibling by blood or affinity, including all relatives whose status is preceded by the words "step," "great," "great-great," or "grand," or the spouse of any of these persons, even if the marriage was terminated by death or dissolution.[187]

8715. (a) The department, county adoption agency, or licensed adoption agency, whichever is a party to, or joins in, the petition, shall submit a full report of the facts of the case to the court.

(b) If the child has been adjudged to be a dependent of the juvenile court pursuant to Section 300 of the Welfare and Institutions Code, and has

thereafter been freed for adoption by the juvenile court, the report required by this section shall describe whether the requirements of subdivision (e) of Section 16002 of the Welfare and Institutions Code have been completed and what, if any, plan exists for facilitation of postadoptive contact between the child who is the subject of the adoption petition and the child's siblings and half siblings.
(c) If a petition for adoption has been filed with a postadoption contact agreement pursuant to Section 8616.5, the report shall address whether the postadoption contact agreement has been entered into voluntarily, and whether it is in the best interest of the child who is the subject of the petition.
(d) The department may also submit a report in those cases in which a county adoption agency, or licensed adoption agency is a party or joins in the adoption petition.
(e) If a petitioner is a resident of a state other than California, an updated and current home study report, conducted and approved by a licensed adoption agency or other authorized resource in the state in which the petitioner resides, shall be reviewed and endorsed by the department, county adoption agency, or licensed adoption agency, if the standards and criteria established for a home study report in the other state are substantially commensurate with the home study standards and criteria established in California adoption regulations.

8716. Where a petition is filed for the adoption of a child who has been placed for adoption by a county adoption agency, licensed county adoption agency, or the department, the county adoption agency, licensed adoption agency, or department may, at the time of filing a favorable report with the court, require the petitioners to pay to the agency, as agent of the state, or to the department, a fee of five hundred dollars ($500). The county adoption agency, licensed adoption agency, or department may defer, waive, or reduce the fee if its payment would cause economic hardship to the prospective adoptive parents detrimental to the welfare of the adopted child, if the child has been in the foster care of the prospective adoptive parents for at least one year, or if necessary for the placement of a special-needs child.[244]

8717. When any report or findings are submitted to the court by the department, county adoption agency, or licensed adoption agency, a copy of the report or findings, whether favorable or unfavorable, shall be given to the petitioner's attorney in the proceeding, if the petitioner has an attorney of record, or to the petitioner.[245]

8718. The prospective adoptive parents and the child proposed to be adopted shall appear before the court pursuant to Sections 8612 and 8613. [1]

8719. If the petitioners move to withdraw the adoption petition or to dismiss the proceeding, the court clerk shall immediately notify the department at Sacramento of the action.[1]

8720. (a) If the department, county adoption agency, or licensed adoption agency finds that the home of the petitioners is not suitable for the child or that the required agency consents are not available and the department, county adoption agency, or licensed adoption agency recommends that the petition be denied, or if the petitioners desire to withdraw the petition and the department, county adoption agency, or licensed adoption agency recommends that the petition be denied, the clerk upon receipt of the report of the department, county adoption agency, or licensed adoption agency shall immediately refer it to the court for review.

(b) Upon receipt of the report, the court shall set a date for a hearing of the petition and shall give reasonable notice of the hearing to the department, county adoption agency, or licensed adoption agency, the petitioners, and, if necessary, the birth parents, by certified mail, return receipt requested, to the address of each as shown in the proceeding.

(c) The department, county adoption agency, or licensed adoption agency shall appear to represent the child.[246]

Chapter 2.5: Adoptions by Relative Caregivers or Foster Parents

8730. (a) Subject to the requirements of subdivision (b), the department, county adoption agency, or licensed adoption agency may provide an abbreviated home study assessment for any of the following:

(1) A licensed or certified foster parent with whom the child has lived for a minimum of six months.

(2) An approved relative caregiver or nonrelated extended family member with whom the child has had an ongoing and significant relationship.

(3) A court-appointed relative guardian of the child who has been investigated and approved pursuant to the guardianship investigation process and has had physical custody of the child for at least one year.

(4) A prospective adoptive parent who has completed an agency-supervised adoption within the last two years.

(b) Unless otherwise ordered by a court with jurisdiction over the child, home study assessments completed pursuant to subdivision (a) shall include, at minimum, all of the following:

(1) A criminal records check, as required by all applicable state and federal statutes and regulations.

(2) A determination that the applicant has sufficient financial stability to support the child and ensure that an adoption assistance program payment or other government assistance to which the child is entitled is used exclusively to meet the child's needs. In making this determination, the experience of the applicant only while the child was in the applicant's care shall be considered. For purposes of this section, the applicant shall be required to provide verification of employment records or income or both.

(3) A determination that the applicant has not abused or neglected the child while the child has been in the applicant's care and has fostered the healthy growth and development of the child. This determination shall include a review of the disciplinary practices of the applicant to ensure that the practices are age appropriate and do not physically or emotionally endanger the child.

(4) A determination that the applicant is not likely to abuse or neglect the child in the future and that the applicant can protect the child, ensure necessary care and supervision, and foster the child's healthy growth and development.

(5) A determination that the applicant can address issues that may affect the child's well-being, including, but not limited to, the child's physical health, mental health, and educational needs.
(6) An interview with the applicant, an interview with each individual residing in the home, and an interview with the child to be adopted.
(7) A review by the department, county adoption agency, or licensed adoption agency of all previous guardianship investigation reports, home study assessments, and preplacement evaluations of each applicant. Notwithstanding any other law regarding the confidential nature of these reports, upon the written request of the department, county adoption agency, or licensed adoption agency that is accompanied by a signed release from the applicant, the department, county adoption agency, or licensed adoption agency may receive a copy of any of these reports from a court, investigating agency, or other person or entity in possession of the report. The department, county adoption agency, or licensed adoption agency shall document attempts to obtain the report and, if applicable, the reason the report is unavailable.
(c) The department may promulgate regulations as necessary or appropriate to implement this section.
(d) This section does not apply to independent adoptions filed pursuant to Chapter 3 (commencing with Section 8800).

8731. If the prospective adoptive parent of a child is a foster parent, the assessment or home study described in Section 8730 shall not be initiated until the child to be adopted has resided in the home of the foster parent for at least six months.

8732. A report of a medical examination of the foster parent with whom the child has lived for a minimum of six months or the relative caregiver who has had an ongoing and significant relationship with the child shall be included in the assessment of each applicant unless the department, county adoption agency, or licensed adoption agency determines that, based on other available information, this report is unnecessary.

8733. The department, county adoption agency, or licensed adoption agency shall require the adoptive parent to be provided with information related to the specific needs of the child to be adopted, that, as determined by the licensed adoption agency, may include information regarding the following: issues surrounding birth parents, the effects of abuse and neglect on children, cultural and racial issues, sexuality, contingency planning for children in the event of the parents' death or disability, financial assistance for adopted children, common childhood disabilities, including, but not limited to, emotional disturbances, attention deficit disorder, learning disabilities, speech and hearing impairment, and dyslexia, the importance of sibling and half-sibling relationships, and other issues related to adoption and child development and the availability of counseling to deal with these issues. [247]

8734. The department shall encourage adoption agencies to make adoption training programs available to prospective adoptive families.

8735. The department shall adopt regulations requiring county adoption agencies and licensed adoption agencies to inform the agency responsible for the foster care placement when a relative caregiver or foster parent has been denied approval to adopt based on an inability of the relative caregiver or foster parent to provide for the mental and emotional health, safety, and security of the child and to recommend either that the relative caregiver or foster parent be provided with additional support and supervision or that the child be removed from the home of the relative caregiver or foster parent. [248]

8736. The requirements of this chapter shall not be used as basis for removing a child who has been placed with a relative caregiver or foster parent prior to January 1, 1999, unless the noncompliance with the standards described therein present a danger to the health, safety, or emotional well-being of the child.

Chapter 3: Independent Adoptions

8800. (a) The Legislature finds and declares that an attorney's ability to effectively represent a client may be seriously impaired when conflict of interest deprives the client of the attorney's undivided loyalty and effort. The Legislature further finds and declares that the relation between attorney and client is a fiduciary relation of the very highest character, and binds the attorney to the most conscientious fidelity.

(b) The Legislature finds that Rule 2-111(A)(2) of the State Bar Rules of Professional Conduct provides that an attorney shall not withdraw from employment until the attorney has taken reasonable steps to avoid foreseeable prejudice to the rights of the client, including giving due notice to the client, allowing time for employment of other counsel, delivering to the client all papers and property to which the client is entitled, and complying with applicable laws and rules.

(c) The Legislature declares that in an independent adoption proceeding, whether or not written consent is obtained, multiple representation by an attorney should be avoided whenever a birth parent displays the slightest reason for the attorney to believe any controversy might arise. The Legislature finds and declares that it is the duty of the attorney, when a conflict of interest occurs, to withdraw promptly from any case, advise the parties to retain independent counsel, refrain from taking positions in opposition to any of these former clients, and thereafter maintain an impartial, fair, and open attitude toward the new attorneys.

(d) Notwithstanding any other law, it is unethical for an attorney to undertake the representation of both the prospective adoptive parents and the birth parents of a child in any negotiations or proceedings in connection with an adoption unless a written consent is obtained from both parties. The written consent shall include all of the following:

(1) A notice to the birth parents, in the form specified in this section, of their right to have an independent attorney advise and represent them in the adoption proceeding and that the prospective adoptive parents may be required to pay the reasonable

attorney's fees up to a maximum of five hundred dollars ($500) for that representation, unless a higher fee is agreed to by the parties.

(2) A notice to the birth parents that they may waive their right to an independent attorney and may be represented by the attorney representing the prospective adoptive parents.

(3) A waiver by the birth parents of representation by an independent attorney.

(4) An agreement that the attorney representing the prospective adoptive parents shall represent the birth parents.

(e) Upon the petition or motion of any party, or upon motion of the court, the court may appoint an attorney to represent a child's birth parent or parents in negotiations or proceedings in connection with the child's adoption.

(f) The birth parent or parents may have an attorney, other than the attorney representing the interests of the prospective adoptive parents, to advise them fully of the adoption procedures and of their legal rights. The birth parent or parents also may retain an attorney to represent them in negotiations or proceedings in connection with the child's adoption. The court may award attorney's fees and costs for just cause and based upon the ability of the parties to pay those fees and costs.

(g) In the initial communication between the attorney retained by or representing the prospective adoptive parents and the birth parents, or as soon thereafter as reasonable, but before any written consent for dual representation, the attorney shall advise the birth parents of their rights regarding an independent attorney and that it is possible to waive the independent attorney.

(h) The attorney retained by or representing the prospective adoptive parents shall inform the prospective adoptive parents in writing that the birth parent or parents can revoke consent to the adoption pursuant to Section 8814.5 and that any moneys expended in negotiations or proceedings in connection with the child's adoption are not reimbursable. The prospective adoptive parents shall sign a statement to indicate their understanding of this information.

(i) Written consent to dual representation shall be filed with the court before the filing of the birth parent's consent to adoption.

8801. (a) The selection of a prospective adoptive parent or parents shall be personally made by the child's birth parent or parents and may not be delegated to an agent. The act of selection by the birth parent or parents shall be based upon personal knowledge of the prospective adoptive parent or parents.

(b) "Personal knowledge" as used in this section includes, but is not limited to, substantially correct knowledge of all of the following regarding the prospective adoptive parents: their full legal names, ages, religion, race or ethnicity, length of current marriage and number of previous marriages, employment, whether other children or adults reside in their home, whether there are other children who do not reside in their home and the child support obligation for these children and any failure to meet these obligations, any health conditions curtailing their normal daily activities or reducing their normal life expectancies, any convictions for crimes other than minor traffic violations, any removals of children from their care due to child abuse or neglect, and their general area of residence or, upon request, their address.

8801.3. A child shall not be considered to have been placed for adoption unless each of the following is true:

(a) Each birth parent placing the child for adoption has been advised of their rights, and if desired, has been counseled pursuant to Section 8801.5.

(b) The adoption service provider, each prospective adoptive parent, and each birth parent placing the child have signed an adoption placement agreement on a form prescribed by the department. The signing of the agreement shall satisfy all of the following requirements:

(1) Each birth parent shall have been advised of their rights pursuant to Section 8801.5 at least 10 days before signing the agreement, unless the adoption service provider finds exigent circumstances that shall be set forth in the adoption placement agreement.

(2) The agreement may not be signed by either the birth parents or the prospective adoptive parents until the time of discharge of the birth mother from the hospital. However, if the birth mother remains hospitalized for a period longer than the hospitalization of the child, the agreement may be signed by all parties at the time of or after the child's discharge from the hospital but prior to the birth mother's discharge from the hospital if the birth mother's competency to sign is verified by the attending physician and surgeon before signing the agreement.

(3) The birth parents and prospective adoptive parents shall sign the agreement in the presence of an adoption service provider.

(4) The adoption service provider who witnesses the signatures shall keep the original of the adoption placement agreement and immediately forward it and supporting documentation as required by the department to the department or delegated county adoption agency.

(5) The child is not deemed to be placed for adoption with the prospective adoptive parents until the adoption placement agreement has been signed and witnessed.

(6) If the birth parent is not located in this state or country, the adoption placement agreement shall be signed before an adoption service provider or, for purposes of identification of the birth parent only, before a notary or other person authorized to perform notarial acts in the state or country in which the birth parent is located. This paragraph is not applicable to intercountry adoptions, as defined in Section 8527, which shall be governed by Chapter 4 (commencing with Section 8900).

(c) The adoption placement agreement form shall include all of the following:

(1) A statement that the birth parent received the advisement of rights and the date upon which it was received.

(2) A statement that the birth parent understands that the placement is for the purpose of adoption and that if the birth parent takes no further action, on the 31st day after signing the adoption placement agreement, the agreement shall become a permanent and irrevocable consent to the adoption.

(3) A statement that the birth parent signs the agreement having personal knowledge of certain facts regarding the prospective adoptive parents as provided in Section 8801.

(4) A statement that the adoptive parents have been informed of the basic health and social history of the birth parents.

(5) A consent to the adoption that may be revoked as provided by Section 8814.5.

(d) The adoption placement agreement shall also meet the requirements of the Interstate Compact on the Placement of Children in Section 7901.

8801.5. (a) Each birth parent placing a child for adoption shall be advised of their rights by an adoption service provider.

(b) The birth parent shall be advised of their rights in a face-to-face meeting in which the birth parent may ask questions and have questions answered, as provided by Section 8801.3.

(c) The department shall prescribe the format and process for advising birth parents of their rights, the content of which shall include, but not be limited to, the following:

(1) The alternatives to adoption.

(2) The alternative types of adoption, including a description of the full procedures and timeframes involved in each type.

(3) The full rights and responsibilities of the birth parent with respect to adoption, including the need to keep the department informed of the birth parent's current address in case of a medical emergency requiring contact and of providing a full health history.

(4) The right to separate legal counsel paid for by the prospective adoptive parents upon the request of the birth parent, as provided for by Section 8800.

(5) The right to a minimum of three separate counseling sessions, each to be held on different days, to be paid for by the prospective adoptive parents upon the request of the birth parents, as provided for by subdivision (d).

(d) Each person advised pursuant to this section shall be offered at least three separate counseling sessions, to be held on different days. Each counseling session shall be not less than 50 minutes in duration. The counseling may be provided by the adoption service provider who informs the birth parent of their rights, or by another adoption service provider, or by a licensed psychotherapist, as defined by Section 1010 of the Evidence Code, as elected by the person, and after having been informed of these choices.

(e) The counselor owes a duty of care to the birth parent being counseled, similar to the duty of care established by a psychotherapist-patient relationship, regardless of who pays the fees of the counselor. A counselor shall not have a contractual relationship with the adoptive parents, an attorney for the adoptive parents, or any other individual or an organization performing any type of services for the adoptive parents and for which the adoptive parents are paying a fee, except as relates to payment of the birth parents' fee.

(f) The advisement and counseling fees shall be paid by the prospective adoptive parents at the request of the birth parent.

(g) Failure to fulfill the duties specified in this section shall not be construed as a basis for setting aside the consent or the adoption, but may give rise to a cause of action for malpractice or negligence against those professionals or agencies serving as adoption service providers that are responsible for fulfilling the duties.

8801.7. (a) An adoption service provider shall also witness the signature of the adoption placement agreement and offer to interview the birth parent after the placement of the child with prospective adoptive parents. The interview shall occur within 10 working days after the placement of the child for adoption and shall include a consideration of any concerns or problems the birth parent has with the placement, a readvisement of the rights of the birth parent, and the taking of the health and social history of the birth parent, if not taken previously.

(b) The adoption service provider shall immediately notify the department or delegated county adoption agency if the birth parent is not interviewed as provided in subdivision (a) or if there are any concerns regarding the placement. If the birth parent wishes to revoke the consent, the adoption service provider shall assist the birth parent in obtaining the return of the child.

(c) The adoption service provider owes a very high duty of care to the birth parent being advised, regardless of who pays the provider's fees. The duty of care specifically does not include a duty to investigate information provided by the birth parents, prospective adoptive parents, or their attorneys or agents. No adoption service provider shall have a contractual relationship with prospective adoptive parents, an attorney or representative for prospective adoptive parents, or any individual or organization providing services of any type to prospective adoptive parents for which the adoptive parents are paying a fee, except as relates to the payment of the fees for the advising and counseling of the birth parents.

(d) This section shall become operative on January 1, 1995.

8802. (a) Any of the following adult persons who desire to adopt a child may, for that purpose, file an adoption request in a county authorized by Section 8609.5:

(1) A person who is related to the child or the child's half sibling by blood or affinity, including all relatives whose status is preceded by the words "step," "great," "great-great," or "grand," or the spouse of any of these persons, even if the marriage was terminated by death or dissolution.

(2) A person named in the will of a deceased parent as an intended adoptive parent where the child has no other parent.

(3) A person with whom a child has been placed for adoption, in which case a copy of the independent adoption placement agreement shall be attached to the petition.

(4) A person who has been the child's legal guardian for more than one year. However, if the guardian was nominated by a parent for a purpose other than adoption and for a specified time period, or if the guardianship was established pursuant to Section 360 of the Welfare and Institutions Code, the guardianship shall have been in existence for at least three years, unless parental rights have already

been terminated.

(5) If the child is alleged to have been abandoned pursuant to Section 7822, a person who has been the child's legal guardian for more than six months. The legal guardian may file a petition pursuant to Section 7822 in the same court and concurrently with the adoption request.

(6) A person named in a court order terminating parental rights as the child's legal guardian or prospective adoptive parent.

(b) The court clerk shall immediately notify the department in Sacramento in writing of the pendency of the proceeding and of any subsequent action taken.

(c) The adoption request shall contain an allegation that the petitioners will file promptly with the department or delegated county adoption agency information required by the department in the investigation of the proposed adoption. The omission of the allegation from the adoption request does not affect the jurisdiction of the court to proceed or the validity of an adoption order or other order based on the adoption request.

(d) The caption of the adoption request shall contain the names of the petitioners, but not the child's name. The body of the adoption request shall state the child's sex and date of birth and the name the child had before adoption.

(e) If the child is the subject of a guardianship petition, the adoption request shall so state and shall include the caption and docket number or have attached a copy of the letters of the guardianship or temporary guardianship. The petitioners shall notify the court of any petition for guardianship or temporary guardianship filed after the adoption request. The guardianship proceeding shall be consolidated with the adoption proceeding, and the consolidated case shall be heard and decided in the court in which the adoption is pending.

(f) If the petitioner has entered into a postadoption contact agreement as set forth in Section 8616.5, the petitioner shall file the agreement, signed by the participating parties, with the court before the adoption is finalized.

(g) The order of adoption shall contain the child's adopted name and the name the child had before adoption.[568]

8803. (a) During the pendency of an adoption proceeding:

(1) The child proposed to be adopted shall not be concealed from the agency that is investigating the adoption, or from the court with jurisdiction over the adoption proceeding.

(2) The child shall not be removed from the county of the petitioner's residence at the time of placement, unless the petitioners or other interested persons first obtain permission for the removal from the court, after giving advance written notice of intent to obtain the court's permission to the department or delegated county adoption agency responsible for the investigation of the proposed adoption. Upon proof of giving notice, permission may be granted by the court if, within a period of 15 days after the date of giving notice, no objections are filed with the court by the department or delegated county adoption agency. If the department or delegated county adoption agency files objections within the 15-day period, upon the request of the petitioners the court

shall immediately set the matter for hearing and give to the objector, the petitioners, and the party or parties requesting permission for the removal reasonable notice of the hearing by certified mail, return receipt requested, to the address of each as shown in the records of the adoption proceeding. Upon a finding that the objections are without good cause, the court may grant the requested permission for removal of the child, subject to any limitations that appear to be in the child's best interest.

(b) This section does not apply in any of the following situations:

(1) When the child is absent for a period of not more than 30 days from the county of the petitioner's residence at the time of placement, unless a notice of recommendation of denial of petition has been personally served on the petitioners or the court has issued an order prohibiting the child's removal from the county of the petitioner's residence at the time of placement, pending consideration of any of the following:

(A) The suitability of the petitioners.

(B) The care provided the child.

(C) The availability of the legally required consents to the adoption.

(2) Where the child has been returned to and remains in the custody and control of the child's birth parent or parents.

(c) A violation of this section is a violation of Section 280 of the Penal Code.

(d) Neither this section nor Section 280 of the Penal Code may be construed to render lawful any act that is unlawful under any other applicable law.[512]

8804. (a) Whenever the petitioners move to withdraw the petition for the adoption or to dismiss the proceeding, the clerk of the court in which the proceeding is pending shall immediately notify the department at Sacramento of the action. The department or the delegated county adoption agency shall file a full report with the court recommending a suitable plan for the child in every case where the petitioners move to withdraw the petition for the adoption or where the department or delegated county adoption agency recommends that the petition for adoption be denied and shall appear before the court for the purpose of representing the child.

(b) Notwithstanding the withdrawal or dismissal of the petition, the court may retain jurisdiction over the child for the purposes of making any order for the child's custody that the court deems to be in the child's best interest.

(c) If a birth parent who did not place a child for adoption as specified in Section 8801.3 has refused to give the required consent, or a birth parent revokes consent as specified in Section 8814.5, the child shall be restored to the care and custody of the birth parent or parents, unless the court orders otherwise, subject to Section 3041.[320]

8805. At the hearing, if the court sustains the recommendation of the department or delegated county adoption agency that the child be removed from the home of the petitioners because the department or agency recommends denial or if the petitioners move to withdraw the petition or if the court dismisses the petition and does not return the child to the birth parents, the court shall commit the child to the care of the department or delegated county adoption agency, whichever made the recommendation, for the department or agency to arrange adoptive placement or to make a suitable plan. In those counties not served by a delegated county adoption agency, the county welfare department shall act as the agent of the department and shall provide care for the child in accordance with rules and regulations established by the department.[1]

8806. The department or delegated county adoption agency shall accept the consent of the birth parents to the adoption of the child by the petitioners and, before filing its report with the court, shall ascertain whether the child is a proper subject for adoption and whether the proposed home is suitable for the child.[1]

8807. (a) Except as provided in subdivisions (b) and (c), within 180 days after receiving 50 percent of the fee, the department or delegated county adoption agency shall investigate the proposed independent adoption and, after the remaining balance of the fee is paid, submit to the court a full report of the facts disclosed by its inquiry with a recommendation regarding the granting of the petition. If the petitioners have a valid preplacement evaluation or a valid private agency adoption home study, as described in paragraph (2) of subdivision (a) of Section 8810, and no new information has been discovered and no new event has occurred subsequent to the approval of the evaluation or home study that creates a reasonable belief that further investigation is necessary, the department or delegated county adoption agency may elect not to reinvestigate any matters covered in the evaluation or home study, except that the department shall complete all background clearances required by law.

(b) If the investigation establishes that there is a serious question concerning the suitability of the petitioners, the care provided to the child, or the availability of the consent to adoption, the report shall be filed immediately.

(c) In its discretion, the court may allow additional time for the filing of the report, after at least five days' notice to the petitioner or petitioners and an opportunity for the petitioner or petitioners to be heard with respect to the request for additional time.

(d) If a petitioner is a resident of a state other than California, an updated and current home study report, conducted and approved by a licensed adoption agency or other authorized resource in the state in which the petitioner resides, shall be reviewed and endorsed by the department or delegated county adoption agency, if the standards and criteria established for a home study report in the other state are substantially commensurate with the home study standards and criteria established in California adoption regulations. If the home study report is not substantially commensurate with California standards or is otherwise missing required information, petitioners shall be responsible for providing any additional documentation or information necessary for the department or the delegated county adoption agency to complete the independent adoption investigation.[321]

8808. (a) The department or delegated county adoption agency shall interview the petitioners within 45 working days, excluding legal holidays, after the department or delegated county adoption agency receives 50 percent of the investigation fee together with a stamped file copy of the adoption petition.

(b) The department or delegated county adoption agency shall interview all persons from whom consent is required and whose addresses are known. The interview with the placing parent or parents shall include, but not be limited to, discussion of any concerns or problems that the parent has with the placement and, if the placing parent was not interviewed as provided in Section 8801.7, the content required in that interview. At the interview, the agency shall give the parent an opportunity to sign either a statement revoking the consent, or a waiver of the right to revoke consent, as provided in Section 8814.5, unless the parent has already signed a waiver or the time period allowed to revoke consent has expired.

(c) In order to facilitate the interview described in this section, within five business days of filing the petition, the petitioners shall provide the department or delegated county adoption agency a stamped file copy of the petition together with 50 percent of the fee, a copy of any valid preplacement evaluation or any valid private agency adoption home study, as described in paragraph (2) of subdivision (a) of Section 8810, and the names, addresses, and telephone numbers of all parties to be interviewed, if known.[322]

8810. (a) Except as otherwise provided in this section, whenever a petition is filed under this chapter for the adoption of a child, the petitioner shall pay a nonrefundable fee to the department or to the delegated county adoption agency for the cost of investigating the adoption petition. Fifty percent of the payment shall be made to the department or delegated county adoption agency at the time the adoption petition is filed, and the remaining balance shall be paid no later than the date determined by the department or the delegated county adoption agency in an amount as follows:

(1) For petitions filed on and after October 1, 2008, four thousand five hundred dollars ($4,500).

(2) For petitioners who have a valid preplacement evaluation less than one year old pursuant to Section 8811.5, or a valid private agency adoption home study less than two years old at the time of filing a petition, one thousand five hundred fifty dollars ($1,550) for a postplacement evaluation pursuant to Sections 8806 and 8807.

(b) Revenues produced by fees collected by the department pursuant to subdivision (a) shall be used, when appropriated by the Legislature, to fund only the direct costs associated with the state program for independent adoptions. Revenues produced by fees collected by the delegated county adoption agency pursuant to subdivision (a) shall be used by the county to fund the county program for independent adoptions.

(c) The department or delegated county adoption agency may reduce the fee to no less than five hundred dollars ($500) when the prospective adoptive parents are lower income, according to the income limits published by the Department of Housing and Community Development, and when making the required payment would be detrimental to the welfare of an adopted child. The department shall develop additional guidelines regarding income and assets to determine the financial criteria for reduction of the fee under this subdivision.

8811. (a) The department or delegated county adoption agency shall require each person who files an adoption petition to be fingerprinted and shall secure from an appropriate law enforcement agency any criminal record of that person to determine if the person has ever been convicted of a crime other than a minor traffic violation. The department or delegated county adoption agency may also secure the person's full criminal record, if any, with the exception of any convictions for which relief has been granted pursuant to Section 1203.49 of the Penal Code. Any federal-level criminal offender record requests to the Department of Justice shall be submitted with fingerprint images and related information required by the Department of Justice for the purposes of obtaining information as to the existence and content of a record of an out-of-state or federal conviction or arrest of a person or information regarding any out-of-state or federal crimes or arrests for which the Department of Justice establishes that the person is free on bail, or on their own recognizance pending trial or appeal. The Department of Justice shall forward to the Federal Bureau of Investigation any requests for federal summary criminal history information received pursuant to this section. The Department of Justice shall review the information returned from the Federal Bureau of Investigation and shall compile and disseminate a response to the department or delegated county adoption agency.

(b) Notwithstanding subdivision (c), the criminal record, if any, shall be taken into consideration when evaluating the prospective adoptive parent, and an assessment of the effects of any criminal history on the ability of the prospective adoptive parent to provide adequate and proper care and guidance to the child shall be included in the report to the court.

(c) (1) The department or a delegated county adoption agency shall not give final approval for an adoptive placement in any home in which the prospective adoptive parent or any adult living in the prospective adoptive home has either of the following:

(A) A felony conviction for child abuse or neglect, spousal abuse, crimes against a child, including child pornography, or for a crime involving violence, including rape, sexual assault, or homicide, but not including other physical assault and battery. For purposes of this subdivision, crimes involving violence means those violent crimes contained in clause (i) of subparagraph (A), and subparagraph (B), of paragraph (1) of subdivision (g) of Section 1522 of the Health and Safety Code.

(B) A felony conviction that occurred within the last five years for physical assault, battery, or a drug- or alcohol-related offense.

(2) This subdivision shall become operative on October 1, 2008, and shall remain operative only to the extent that compliance with its provisions is required by federal law as a condition of receiving funding under Title IV-E of the federal Social Security Act (42 U.S.C. Sec. 670 et seq.).

(d) A fee charged by a law enforcement agency for fingerprinting or for checking or obtaining the criminal record of the petitioner shall be paid by the petitioner. The department or delegated county adoption agency may defer, waive, or reduce the fee if its payment would cause economic hardship to the prospective adoptive parents detrimental to the welfare of the adopted child, if the child has been in the foster care of the prospective adoptive parents for at least one year, or if necessary for the placement of a special-needs child.

8811.5. (a) A licensed private or public adoption agency of the state of the petitioners' residency may certify prospective adoptive parents by a preplacement evaluation that contains a finding that an individual is suited to be an adoptive parent.
(b) The preplacement evaluation shall include an investigation pursuant to standards included in the regulations governing independent adoption investigations established by the department. Fees for the investigation shall be commensurate with those fees charged for a comparable investigation conducted by the department or by a delegated licensed county adoption agency.
(c) The preplacement evaluation, whether it is conducted for the purpose of initially certifying prospective adoptive parents or for renewing that certification, shall be completed no more than one year prior to the signing of an adoption placement agreement. The cost for renewal of that certification shall be in proportion to the extent of the work required to prepare the renewal that is attributable to changes in family circumstances.

8812. Any request by a birth parent or birth parents for payment by the prospective adoptive parents of attorney's fees, medical fees and expenses, counseling fees, or living expenses of the birth mother shall be in writing. The birth parent or parents shall, by first-class mail or other agreed upon means to ensure receipt, provide the prospective adoptive parents written receipts for any money provided to the birth parent or birth parents. The prospective adoptive parents shall provide the receipts to the court when the accounting report required pursuant to Section 8610 is filed.

8813. At or before the time a consent to adoption is signed, the department or delegated county adoption agency shall advise the birth parent signing the consent, verbally and in writing, that the birth parent may, at any time in the future, request from the department or agency, all known information about the status of the child's adoption, except for personal, identifying information about the adoptive family. The birth parent shall be advised that this information includes, but is not limited to, all of the following:
(a) Whether the child has been placed for adoption.
(b) The approximate date that an adoption was completed.
(c) If the adoption was not completed or was vacated, for any reason, whether adoptive placement of the child is again being considered.[1]

8814. (a) Except as provided in Section 7662, the consent of the birth parent or parents who did not place the child for adoption, as described in Section 8801.3, to the adoption shall be signed in the presence of an agent of the department or of a delegated county adoption agency on a form prescribed by the department. The consent shall be filed with the clerk of the appropriate superior court.

(b) The consent described in subdivision (a), when reciting that the person giving it is entitled to the sole custody of the child and when acknowledged before that agent, is prima facie evidence of the right of the person making it to the sole custody of the child and that person's sole right to consent.

(c) If the birth parent described in subdivision (a) is located outside this state for an extended period of time unrelated to the adoption at the time of signing the consent, the consent may be signed before a notary or other person authorized to perform notarial acts, and in that case the consent of the department or of the delegated county adoption agency is also necessary.

(d) A birth parent who is a minor has the right to sign a consent for the adoption of the birth parent's child and the consent is not subject to revocation by the birth parent by reason of minority, or because the parent or guardian of the consenting minor parent was not served with notice that the minor parent consented to the adoption, unless the minor parent has previously provided written authorization to serve the minor parent's parent or guardian with that notice.

8814.5. (a) After a consent to the adoption is signed by the birth parent or parents pursuant to Section 8801.3 or 8814, the birth parent or parents signing the consent shall have 30 days to take one of the following actions:

(1) Sign and deliver to the department or delegated county adoption agency a written statement revoking the consent and requesting the child to be returned to the birth parent or parents. After revoking consent, in cases where the birth parent or parents have not regained custody, or the birth parent or parents have failed to make efforts to exercise their rights under subdivision (b) of Section 8815, a written notarized statement reinstating the original consent may be signed and delivered to the department or delegated county adoption agency, in which case the revocation of consent shall be void and the remainder of the original 30-day period shall commence. After revoking consent, in cases in which the birth parent or parents have regained custody or made efforts to exercise their rights under subdivision (b) of Section 8815 by requesting the return of the child, upon the delivery of a written notarized statement reinstating the original consent to the department or delegated county adoption agency, the revocation of consent shall be void and a new 30-day period shall commence. The birth mother shall be informed of the operational timelines associated with this section at the time of signing of the statement reinstating the original consent.

(2) (A) Sign a waiver of the right to revoke consent on a form prescribed by the department in the presence of any of the following:

(i) A representative of the department or delegated county adoption agency.

(ii) A judicial officer of a court of record if the birth parent is represented by independent legal counsel.

(iii) An adoption service provider, including, but not limited to, the adoption service provider who advised the birth mother and witnessed the signing of the consent, if the birth parent or parents are represented by independent legal counsel. The adoption service provider shall ensure that the waiver is delivered to the department, the petitioners, or their counsel no earlier than the end of the business day following the signing of the waiver. The adoption service provider shall inform the birth parent that during this time period the birth parent may request that the waiver be withdrawn and that, if that request is made, the waiver shall be withdrawn.

(B) An adoption service provider may assist the birth parent or parents in any activity where the primary purpose of that activity is to facilitate the signing of the waiver with the department, a delegated county agency, or a judicial officer. The adoption service provider or another person designated by the birth parent or parents may also be present at any interview conducted pursuant to this section to provide support to the birth parent or parents, except when the interview is conducted by independent legal counsel for the birth parent or parents.

(C) The waiver of the right to revoke consent may not be signed until an interview has been completed by the department or delegated county adoption agency unless the waiver of the right to revoke consent is signed in the presence of a judicial officer of a court of record or an adoption service provider as specified in this section. If the waiver is signed in the presence of a judicial officer, the interview and the witnessing of the signing of the waiver shall be conducted by the judicial officer. If the waiver is signed in the presence of an adoption service provider, the interview shall be conducted by the independent legal counsel for the birth parent or parents. If the waiver is to be signed in the presence of an adoption service provider, prior to the waiver being signed the waiver shall be reviewed by the independent legal counsel who (i) counsels the birth parent or parents about the nature of the intended waiver and (ii) signs and delivers to the birth parent or parents and the department a certificate in substantially the following form:

I, (name of attorney), have counseled my client, (name of client), on the nature and legal effect of the waiver of right to revoke consent to adoption. I am so disassociated from the interest of the petitioner(s)/prospective adoptive parent(s) as to be in a position to advise my client impartially and confidentially as to the consequences of the waiver. (Name of client) is aware that California law provides for a 30-day period during which a birth parent may revoke consent to adoption. On the basis of this counsel, I conclude that it is the intent of (name of client) to waive the right to revoke, and make a permanent and irrevocable consent to adoption. (Name of client) understands that they will not be able to regain custody of the child unless the petitioner(s)/prospective adoptive parent(s) agree(s) to withdraw their petition for adoption or the court denies the adoption petition.

(D) Within 10 working days of a request made after the department or the delegated county adoption agency has received a copy of the petition for the adoption and the names and addresses of the persons to be interviewed, the department or the delegated county adoption agency shall interview, at the department or agency office, any birth parent requesting to be interviewed.

(E) Notwithstanding subparagraphs (A) and (C), the interview, and the witnessing of the signing of a waiver of the right to revoke consent of a birth parent residing outside of California or located outside of California for an extended period of time unrelated to the adoption may be conducted in the state where the birth parent is located, by any of the following:

(i) A representative of a public adoption agency in that state.

(ii) A judicial officer in that state where the birth parent is represented by independent legal counsel.

(iii) An adoption service provider.

(3) Allow the consent to become a permanent consent on the 31st day after signing.

(b) The consent may not be revoked after a waiver of the right to revoke consent has been signed or after 30 days, beginning on the date the consent was signed or as provided in paragraph (1) of subdivision (a), whichever occurs first.

8815. (a) Once the revocable consent to adoption has become permanent as provided in Section 8814.5, the consent to the adoption by the prospective adoptive parents may not be withdrawn.

(b) Before the time when the revocable consent becomes permanent as provided in Section 8814.5, the birth parent or parents may request return of the child. In that case the child shall immediately be returned to the requesting birth parent or parents, unless a court orders otherwise.

(c) If the person or persons with whom the child has been placed have concerns that the birth parent or parents requesting return of the child are unfit or present a danger of harm to the child, that person or those persons may report their concerns to the appropriate child welfare agency. These concerns shall not be a basis for failure to immediately return the child, unless a court orders otherwise.[323]

8816. In an independent adoption where the consent of the birth parent or parents is not necessary, the department or delegated county adoption agency shall, before the hearing of the petition, file its consent to the adoption with the clerk of the court in which the petition is filed. The consent may not be given unless the child's welfare will be promoted by the adoption.[1]

8817. (a) A written report on the child's medical background, and if available, the medical background of the child's biological parents so far as ascertainable, shall be made by the department or delegated county adoption agency as part of the study required by Section 8806.

(b) The report on the child's background shall contain all known diagnostic information, including current medical reports on the child, psychological evaluations, and scholastic information, as well as all known information regarding the child's developmental history and family life.

(c) The report shall be submitted to the prospective adoptive parents who shall acknowledge its receipt in writing.

(d) (1) The biological parents may provide a blood sample at a clinic or hospital approved by the State Department of Health Services. The biological parents' failure to provide a blood sample shall not affect the adoption of the child.

(2) The blood sample shall be stored at a laboratory under contract with the State Department of Health Services for a period of 30 years following the adoption of the child.

(3) The purpose of the stored sample of blood is to provide a blood sample from which DNA testing can be done at a later date after entry of the order of adoption at the request of the adoptive parents or the adopted child. The cost of drawing and storing the blood samples shall be paid for by a separate fee in addition to the fee required under Section 8810. The amount of this additional fee shall be based on the cost of drawing and storing the blood samples but at no time shall the additional fee be more than one hundred dollars ($100).

(e) (1) The blood sample shall be stored and released in such a manner as to not identify any party to the adoption.

(2) Any results of the DNA testing shall be stored and released in such a manner as to not identify any party to the adoption.

8818. (a) The department shall adopt a statement to be presented to the birth parents at the time the consent to adoption is signed and to prospective adoptive parents at the time of the home study. The statement shall, in a clear and concise manner and in words calculated to ensure the confidence of the birth parents in the integrity of the adoption process, communicate to the birth parent of a child who is the subject of an adoption petition all of the following facts:

(1) It is in the child's best interest that the birth parents keep the department informed of any health problems that the parent develops that could affect the child.

(2) It is extremely important that the birth parent keep an address current with the department in order to permit a response to inquiries concerning medical or social history.

(3) Section 9203 of the Family Code authorizes a person who has been adopted and who attains the age of 21 years to request the department to disclose the name and address of the adoptee's birth parents. Consequently, it is of the utmost importance that the birth parent indicate whether to allow this disclosure by checking the appropriate box provided on the form.

(4) The birth parent may change the decision whether to permit disclosure of the birth parent's name and address, at any time, by sending a notarized letter to that effect, by certified mail, return receipt requested, to the department.

(5) The consent will be filed in the office of the clerk of the court in which the adoption takes place. The file is not open to inspection by any persons other than the parties to the adoption proceeding, their attorneys, and the

department, except upon order of a judge of the superior court.

(b) The department shall adopt a form to be signed by the birth parents at the time the consent to adoption is signed, which shall provide as follows:

"Section 9203 of the Family Code authorizes a person who has been adopted and who attains the age of 21 years to make a request to the State Department of Social Services, or the licensed adoption agency that joined in the adoption petition, for the name and address of the adoptee's birth parents. Indicate by checking one of the boxes below whether or not you wish your name and address to be disclosed:

□ YES

□ NO

□ UNCERTAIN AT THIS TIME; WILL NOTIFY AGENCY AT LATER DATE."[89]

8819. When the parental rights of a birth parent are terminated pursuant to Chapter 5 (commencing with Section 7660) of Part 3 of Division 12 or Part 4 (commencing with Section 7800) of Division 12, the department or delegated county adoption agency shall send a written notice to the birth parent, if the birth parent's address is known, that contains the following statement:

"You are encouraged to keep the department or this agency informed of your current address in order to permit a response to any inquiry concerning medical or social history made by or on behalf of the child who was the subject of the court action terminating parental rights."[1]

8820. (a) The birth parent or parents or the petitioner may appeal in either of the following cases:

(1) If for a period of 180 days from the date of paying 50 percent of the fee, or upon the expiration of any extension of the period granted by the court, the department or delegated county adoption agency fails or refuses to accept the consent of the birth parent or parents to the adoption.

(2) In a case where the consent of the department or delegated county adoption agency is required by this chapter, if the department or agency fails or refuses to file or give its consent to the adoption after full payment has been received.

(b) The appeal shall be filed in the court in which the adoption petition is filed. The court clerk shall immediately notify the department or delegated county adoption agency of the appeal and the department or agency shall, within 10 days, file a report of its findings and the reasons for its failure or refusal to consent to the adoption or to accept the consent of the birth parent or parents.

(c) After the filing of the report by the department or delegated county adoption agency, the court may, if it deems that the welfare of the child will be promoted by that adoption, allow the signing of the consent by the birth parent or parents in open court or, if the appeal is from the refusal of the department or delegated county adoption agency to consent thereto, grant the petition without the consent.

(d) This section shall become operative on October 1, 2008.[185]

8821. When any report or findings are submitted to the court by the department or a delegated county adoption agency, a copy of the report or findings, whether favorable or unfavorable, shall be given to the petitioner's attorney in the proceeding, if the petitioner has an attorney of record, or to the petitioner.[1]

8822. (a) If the findings of the department or delegated county adoption agency are that the home of the petitioners is not suitable for the child or that the required consents are not available and the department or agency recommends that the petition be denied, or if the petitioners desire to withdraw the petition and the department or agency recommends that the petition be denied, the clerk upon receipt of the report of the department or agency shall immediately refer it to the court for review.
(b) Upon receipt of the report, the court shall set a date for a hearing of the petition and shall give reasonable notice of the hearing to the department or delegated county adoption agency, the petitioners, and the birth parents by certified mail, return receipt requested, to the address of each as shown in the proceeding.
(c) The department or delegated county adoption agency shall appear to represent the child.[1]

8823. The prospective adoptive parents and the child proposed to be adopted shall appear before the court pursuant to Sections 8612 and 8613.[1]

Chapter 4: Intercountry Adoptions

8900. (a) Intercountry adoption services described in this chapter shall be exclusively provided by private adoption agencies licensed by the department specifically to provide these services. As a condition of licensure to provide intercountry adoption services, any private full-service adoption agency and any noncustodial adoption agency shall be accredited by the Council on Accreditation, or supervised by an accredited primary provider, or acting as an exempted provider, in compliance with Subpart F (commencing with Section 96.29) of Part 96 of Title 22 of the Code of Federal Regulations.
(b) A private full-service adoption agency or a noncustodial adoption agency, when acting as the primary provider and using a supervised provider, shall ensure that each supervised provider operates under a written agreement with the primary provider pursuant to subdivision (b) of Section 96.45 of Title 22 of the Code of Federal Regulations.
(c) The primary provider shall provide to the department a copy of the written agreement with each supervised provider containing all provisions required pursuant to subdivision (b) of Section 96.45 of Title 22 of the Code of Federal Regulations.[180]

8900.5. As used in this chapter:
(a) "Accredited agency" means an agency that has been accredited by an accrediting entity, in accordance with the standards in Subpart F (commencing with Section 96.29) of Part 96 of Title 22 of the Code of Federal Regulations, to provide adoption services in the United States in cases subject to the convention. Accredited agency does not include a temporarily accredited agency.
(b) "Adoption service" means any of the following services:
(1) Identifying a child for adoption and arranging an adoption.
(2) Securing the necessary consent to termination of parental rights and to

adoption.

(3) Performing a background study on a child or a home study on any prospective adoptive parent, and reporting on the study.

(4) Making nonjudicial determinations of the best interests of a child and the appropriateness of an adoptive placement for the child.

(5) Monitoring a case after a child has been placed with any prospective adoptive parent until final adoption.

(6) If necessary because of a disruption before final adoption, assuming custody and providing or facilitating child care or any other social service pending an alternative placement.

(c) "Central authority" means the entity designated under paragraph (1) of Article 6 of the convention by a convention country. The United States Department of State is designated as the United States Central Authority pursuant to the federal Intercountry Adoption Act of 2000 (42 U.S.C. Sec. 14911).

(d) "Convention" means the Hague Convention on Protection of Children and Co-operation in Respect of Intercountry Adoption, May 29, 1993.

(e) "Convention adoption" means the adoption of a child resident in a convention country by a United States citizen, or an adoption of a child resident in the United States by an individual or individuals residing in a convention country, if, in connection with the adoption, the child has moved or will move between the United States and the convention country.

(f) "Convention country" means a country that is party to the convention and with which the convention is in force for the United States.

(g) "Exempted provider" means a social work professional or organization that performs a home study on any prospective adoptive parent, or a child background study, or both, in the United States in connection with a convention adoption, and who is not currently providing and has not previously provided any other adoption service in the case.

(h) "Hague adoption certificate" means a certificate issued by the secretary in an outgoing case (where the child is emigrating from the United States to another convention country) certifying that a child has been adopted in the United States in accordance with the convention and, except as provided in subdivision (b) of Section 97.4 of Title 22 of the Code of Federal Regulations, the Intercountry Adoption Act of 2000 (42 U.S.C. Sec. 14901 et seq.; the IAA).

(i) "Hague custody declaration" means a declaration issued by the secretary in an outgoing case (where the child is emigrating from the United States to another convention country) declaring that custody of a child for purposes of adoption has been granted in the United States in accordance with the convention and, except as provided in subdivision (b) of Section 97.4 of Title 22 of the Code of Federal Regulations, the IAA.

(j) "Legal service" means any service, other than those defined in this section as an adoption service, that relates to the provision of legal advice and information or to the drafting of legal instruments. Legal service includes, but is not limited to, any of the following services:

(1) Drafting contracts, powers of attorney, and other legal instruments.

(2) Providing advice and counsel to an adoptive parent on completing forms for the State Department of Health Care Services or the United States Department of State.
(3) Providing advice and counsel to accredited agencies, temporarily accredited agencies, approved persons, or prospective adoptive parents on how to comply with the convention, the IAA, and any regulations implementing the IAA.
(k) "Primary provider" means the accredited agency that is identified pursuant to Section 96.14 of Title 22 of the Code of Federal Regulations as responsible for ensuring that all adoption services are provided and responsible for supervising any supervised providers when used.
(l) "Public domestic authority" means an authority operated by a state, local, or tribal government.
(m) "Secretary" means the United States Secretary of State, and includes any official of the United States Department of State exercising the authority of the Secretary of State under the convention, the IAA, or any regulations implementing the IAA, pursuant to a delegation of authority.
(n) "Supervised provider" means any agency, person, or other nongovernmental entity that is providing any adoption service in a convention adoption under the supervision and responsibility of an accredited agency that is acting as the primary provider in the case.[181]

8901. The department shall adopt regulations to administer the intercountry adoption program.[1]

8902. For intercountry adoptions that will be finalized in this state, the licensed adoption agency shall provide all of the following services:
(a) Assessment of the suitability of the applicant's home.
(b) Placement of the foreign-born child in an approved home.
(c) Postplacement supervision.
(d) Submission to the court of a report on the intercountry adoptive placement with a recommendation regarding the granting of the petition.
(e) Services to applicants seeking to adopt related children living in foreign countries. The Legislature recognizes that these children have an impelling need for adoptive placement with their relatives.[1]

8903. (a) For each intercountry adoption finalized in this state, the licensed adoption agency shall assume all responsibilities for the child including care, custody, and control as if the child had been relinquished for adoption in this state from the time the child left the child's native country.
(b) Notwithstanding subdivision (a), if the child's native country requires and has given full guardianship to the prospective adoptive parents, the prospective adoptive parents shall assume all responsibilities for the child including care, custody, control, and financial support.
(c) If the licensed adoption agency or prospective adoptive parents fail to meet the responsibilities under subdivision (a) or (b) and the child becomes a dependent of the court pursuant to Section 300 of the Welfare and Institutions Code, the state shall assume responsibility for the cost of care for the child. When the child becomes a dependent of the court and if, for any reason, is ineligible for AFDC under Section 14005.1 of the

Welfare and Institutions Code and loses Medi-Cal eligibility, the child shall be deemed eligible for Medi-Cal under Section 14005.4 of the Welfare and Institutions Code and the State Director of Health Services has authority to provide payment for the medical services to the child that are necessary to meet the child's needs.[1]

8904. For an intercountry adoption that will be finalized in a foreign country, the licensed adoption agency shall provide all of the following services:
(a) Assessment of the suitability of the applicant's home.
(b) Certification to the United States Citizenship and Immigration Services that this state's intercountry adoption requirements have been met.
(c) Readoption services as required by the United States Citizenship and Immigration Services.
(d) Postadoption services pursuant to any written agreement between the licensed adoption agency and any other person or entity for which the postadoption services have been paid.

8905. Licensed adoption agencies may work only with domestic and foreign adoption agencies with whom they have written agreements that specify the responsibilities of each. The agreements may not violate any statute or regulation of the United States or of this state.[1]

8906. Nothing in this chapter may be construed to prohibit the licensed adoption agency from entering into an agreement with the prospective adoptive parents to share or transfer financial responsibility for the child.[1]

8907. The costs incurred by a licensed adoption agency pursuant to programs established by this chapter shall be funded by fees charged by the agency for services required by this chapter. The agency's fee schedule is required to be approved by the department initially and whenever it is altered

8908. (a) A licensed adoption agency shall require each person filing an application for adoption to be fingerprinted and shall secure from an appropriate law enforcement agency any criminal record of that person to determine if the person has ever been convicted of a crime other than a minor traffic violation. The licensed adoption agency may also secure the person's full criminal record, if any, with the exception of any convictions for which relief has been granted pursuant to Section 1203.49 of the Penal Code. Any federal-level criminal offender record requests to the Department of Justice shall be submitted with fingerprint images and related information required by the Department of Justice for the purposes of obtaining information as to the existence and content of a record of an out-of-state or federal conviction or arrest of a person or information regarding any out-of-state or federal crimes or arrests for which the Department of Justice establishes that the person is free on bail, or on their own recognizance pending trial or appeal. The Department of Justice shall forward to the Federal Bureau of Investigation any requests for federal summary criminal history information received pursuant to this section. The Department of Justice shall review the information returned from the Federal Bureau of Investigation and shall compile and disseminate a fitness determination to the licensed adoption agency.

(b) Notwithstanding subdivision (c), the criminal record, if any, shall be taken into consideration when evaluating the prospective adoptive parent, and an assessment of the effects of any criminal history on the ability of the prospective adoptive parent to provide adequate and proper care and guidance to the child shall be included in the report to the court.

(c) (1) A licensed adoption agency shall not give final approval for an adoptive placement in any home in which the prospective adoptive parent, or any adult living in the prospective adoptive home, has a felony conviction for either of the following:

(A) A felony conviction for child abuse or neglect, spousal abuse, crimes against a child, including child pornography, or for a crime involving violence, including rape, sexual assault, or homicide, but not including other physical assault and battery. For purposes of this subdivision, crimes involving violence means those violent crimes contained in clause (i) of subparagraph (A), and subparagraph (B), of paragraph (1) of subdivision (g) of Section 1522 of the Health and Safety Code.

(B) A felony conviction that occurred within the last five years for physical assault, battery, or a drug- or alcohol-related offense.

(2) This subdivision shall become operative on October 1, 2008, and shall remain operative only to the extent that compliance with its provisions is required by federal law as a condition of receiving funding under Title IV-E of the federal Social Security Act (42 U.S.C. Sec. 670 et seq.).

(d) Any fee charged by a law enforcement agency for fingerprinting or for checking or obtaining the criminal record of the applicant shall be paid by the applicant. The licensed adoption agency may defer, waive, or reduce the fee if its payment would cause economic hardship to the prospective adoptive parents detrimental to the welfare of the adopted child.

8909. (a) An agency may not place a child for adoption unless a written report on the child's medical background and, if available, the medical background of the child's biological parents so far as ascertainable, has been submitted to the prospective adoptive parents and they have acknowledged in writing the receipt of the report.

(b) The report on the child's background shall contain all known diagnostic information, including current medical reports on the child, psychological evaluations, and scholastic information, as well as all known information regarding the child's developmental history and family life.

(c) (1) The biological parents may provide a blood sample at a clinic or hospital approved by the State Department of Health Services. The biological parents' failure to provide a blood sample shall not affect the adoption of the child.

(2) The blood sample shall be stored at a laboratory under contract with the State Department of Health Services for a period of 30 years following the adoption of the child.

(3) The purpose of the stored sample of blood is to provide a blood sample from which DNA testing can be done at a later date after entry of the order of adoption at the request of the adoptive parents or the adopted child. The cost of drawing and storing the

blood samples shall be paid for by a separate fee in addition to any fee required under Section 8907. The amount of this additional fee shall be based on the cost of drawing and storing the blood samples but at no time shall the additional fee be more than one hundred dollars ($100).

(d) (1) The blood sample shall be stored and released in such a manner as to not identify any party to the adoption.

(2) Any results of the DNA testing shall be stored and released in such a manner as to not identify any party to the adoption.

8910. (a) In no event may a child who has been placed for adoption be removed from the county in which the child was placed, by any person who has not petitioned to adopt the child, without first obtaining the written consent of the licensed adoption agency responsible for the child.

(b) During the pendency of an adoption proceeding:

(1) The child proposed to be adopted shall not be concealed from the agency that is investigating the adoption or from the court with jurisdiction over the adoption proceeding.

(2) The child shall not be removed from the county of the petitioner's residence at the time of placement, unless the petitioners or other interested persons first obtain permission for the removal from the court, after giving advance written notice of intent to obtain the court's permission to the licensed adoption agency responsible for the child. Upon proof of giving notice, permission may be granted by the court if, within a period of 15 days after the date of giving notice, no objections are filed with the court by the licensed adoption agency responsible for the child. If the licensed adoption agency files objections within the 15-day period, upon the request of the petitioners the court shall immediately set the matter for hearing and give to the objector, the petitioners, and the party or parties requesting permission for the removal reasonable notice of the hearing by certified mail, return receipt requested, to the address of each as shown in the records of the adoption proceeding. Upon a finding that the objections are without good cause, the court may grant the requested permission for removal of the child, subject to any limitations that appear to be in the child's best interest.

(c) This section does not apply in any of the following situations:

(1) When the child is absent for a period of not more than 30 days from the county of the petitioner's residence at the time of placement, unless a notice of recommendation of denial of petition has been personally served on the petitioners or the court has issued an order prohibiting the removal of the child from the county of the petitioner's residence at the time of placement, pending consideration of any of the following:

(A) The suitability of the petitioners.

(B) The care provided the child.

(C) The availability of the legally required agency consents to the adoption.

(2) Where the child has been returned to and remains in the custody and control of the child's birth parent or parents.

(3) Where written consent for the removal of the child is obtained from the licensed adoption agency re-

sponsible for the child.
(d) A violation of this section is a violation of Section 280 of the Penal Code.
(e) Neither this section nor Section 280 of the Penal Code may be construed to render lawful any act that is unlawful under any other applicable law.[513]
8911. As a condition of placement, the prospective adoptive parents shall file a petition to adopt the child under Section 8912 within 30 days of placement.[1]

8912. (a) An international adoption or readoption request may be filed by a resident of this state in a county authorized by Section 8609.5. The court clerk shall immediately notify the department at Sacramento in writing of the pendency of the proceeding and of any subsequent action taken.
(b) The caption of the adoption request shall contain the names of the petitioners, but not the child's name. The request shall state the child's sex, date of birth, and the name the child had before adoption.
(c) If the child is the subject of a guardianship petition, the adoption request shall so state and shall include the caption and docket number or have attached a copy of the letters of the guardianship or temporary guardianship. The petitioners shall notify the court of any petition for guardianship or temporary guardianship filed after the adoption petition. The guardianship proceeding shall be consolidated with the adoption proceeding.
(d) The order of adoption shall contain the child's adopted name and the name the child had before adoption.
(e) If the petitioner has entered into a postadoption contact agreement as set forth in Section 8616.5, the petitioner shall file the agreement, signed by the participating parties, with the court before the adoption is finalized.[569]

8913. The prospective adoptive parents and the child proposed to be adopted shall appear before the court pursuant to Sections 8612 and 8613.[1]

8914. If the licensed adoption agency is a party to or joins in the adoption petition, it shall submit a full report of the facts of the case to the court. The department may also submit a report.[1]

8915. When any report or findings are submitted to the court by a licensed adoption agency, a copy of the report or findings, whether favorable or unfavorable, shall be given to the petitioner's attorney in the proceeding, if the petitioner has an attorney of record, or to the petitioner.[1]
8916. (a) If the petitioners move to withdraw the adoption petition or to dismiss the proceeding, the court clerk shall immediately notify the department at Sacramento of the action. The licensed adoption agency shall file a full report with the court recommending a suitable plan for the child in every case where the petitioners desire to withdraw the adoption petition or where the licensed adoption agency recommends that the adoption petition be denied and shall appear before the court for the purpose of representing the child.
(b) Notwithstanding the petitioners' withdrawal or dismissal, the court may retain jurisdiction over the child for the purpose of making any order for the child's custody that the court deems to be in the child's best interest.[1]

8917. (a) If the licensed adoption

agency finds that the home of the petitioners is not suitable for the child or that the required agency consents are not available and the agency recommends that the petition be denied, or if the petitioners desire to withdraw the petition and the agency recommends that the petition be denied, the clerk upon receipt of the report of the licensed adoption agency shall immediately refer it to the court for review.

(b) Upon receipt of the report, the court shall set a date for a hearing of the petition and shall give reasonable notice of the hearing to the licensed adoption agency and the petitioners by certified mail, return receipt requested, to the address of each as shown in the proceeding.

(c) The licensed adoption agency shall appear to represent the child.[1]

8918. At the hearing, if the court sustains the recommendation that the child be removed from the home of the petitioners because the licensed adoption agency has recommended denial or the petitioners desire to withdraw the petition or the court dismisses the petition and does not return the child to the child's parents, the court shall commit the child to the care of the licensed adoption agency for the agency to arrange adoptive placement or to make a suitable plan.[1]

8919. (a) In order to establish a record by which an adoptee can prove the facts of the foreign adoption, a state resident who has finalized an intercountry adoption in a foreign country shall file the petition to readopt within the earlier of 60 days of the adoptee's entry into the United States or the adoptee's 16th birthday. The petition shall include all of the following:

(1) A certified or otherwise official copy of the foreign decree, order, or certification of adoption that reflects finalization of the adoption in the foreign country.

(2) A certified or otherwise official copy of the child's foreign birth certificate.

(3) A certified translation of all documents described in this subdivision that are not written in English. The court shall accept the certified translation, if any, that was completed abroad for purposes of obtaining the child's visa or passport.

(4) Proof that the child was granted lawful entry into the United States as an immediate relative of the adoptive parent or parents.

(5) A report from at least one post-placement home visit by an intercountry adoption agency or a contractor of that agency licensed to provide intercountry adoption services in the State of California.

(6) A copy of the home study report previously completed for the international finalized adoption by an adoption agency authorized to provide intercountry adoption services pursuant to Section 8900.

(b) A readoption order shall not be granted unless the court receives a copy of the reports listed in paragraphs (5) and (6) of subdivision (a). The court shall consider the postplacement visit or visits and the previously completed home study when deciding whether to grant or deny the petition for readoption.

(c) If an adoptive parent who has adopted a child through an intercountry adoption that is finalized in a foreign country fails to file a petition pursuant to this section by the earlier of 60 days of the child's entry into the United States or the child's 16th birthday or fails to provide a copy of the petition to each adoption agency that provided the adoption services to the adoptive parent, then the adoption agency that facilitated the adoption shall file a petition within 90 days of the child's entry into the United States, and shall provide a file-marked copy of the petition to the adoptive parent and to any other adoption agency that provided services to the adoptive parent within five business days of filing. An adoptive parent shall be liable to the adoption agency for all costs and fees incurred as a result of good faith actions taken by the adoption agency to fulfill its requirement pursuant to this subdivision. If the adoption agency fails to file a petition as required by this subdivision, the department may take appropriate disciplinary action against the adoption agency if it is licensed in the State of California and the department has actual or constructive knowledge that the petition was not filed.

(d) If the court finds that the child may be the subject of human trafficking or may be a child who is described in Section 300 of the Welfare and Institutions Code, the court shall, in accordance with existing law, notify all appropriate authorities.

(e) Within 10 business days, the clerk of the court shall submit to the State Registrar the order granting the petition to readopt. Upon receipt, the State Registrar shall issue a delayed registration of birth in accordance with Section 102695 of the Health and Safety Code that lists the adoptive parent or parents as the child's legal parent or parents.

(f) A state resident who has adopted a child through an intercountry adoption that is finalized in a foreign country may obtain a birth certificate for that child pursuant to Section 102635 or 103450 of the Health and Safety Code.

8919.5. (a) An intercountry adoption agency shall report the arrival of an adoptee whose adoption was finalized in a foreign country to the department within 14 calendar days of the adoptee's arrival in California.

(b) If the adoption agency fails to report to the department pursuant to subdivision (a), the department may take appropriate disciplinary action against the adoption agency if it is licensed in the State of California.

8920. (a) A child who was adopted as part of a sibling group and who has been separated from the child's sibling or siblings through readoption by a resident of this state may petition the court to enforce any agreement for visitation to which the separate adoptive families of the siblings subscribed prior to the child's readoption or to order visitation if such agreement does not exist. The court may order that the agreement be enforced or grant visitation rights upon a finding that visitation is in the best interest of the child.

(b) In making a finding that enforcement of an existing agreement or the granting of visitation rights is in the best interest of the child under subdivision (a), the court shall take into consideration the nature and extent of the child's sibling relationship, including, but not limited to, whether the child was raised with a sibling in the same home, whether the child shares significant common experiences or has close and strong bonds with a sibling, and whether ongoing contact with a sibling is in the child's best interest, including the child's long-term interest.

(c) As used in this section, "sibling" means full-siblings or half-siblings.

(d) As used in this section, "readoption" means the process by which a child who belongs to a foreign-born sibling group that was adopted together through an intercountry adoption is subsequently adopted by a different set of adoptive parents who are residents of the state.

8923. (a) A complaint against an accredited agency or approved person in connection with a convention adoption shall be filed according to the procedures set forth in Subpart J (commencing with Section 96.68) of Part 96 of Title 22 of the Code of Federal Regulations.

(b) Each private full-service adoption agency and noncustodial adoption agency licensed by the department under this chapter shall notify the department of any complaint filed against it pursuant to Subpart J (commencing with Section 96.68) of Part 96 of Title 22 of the Code of Federal Regulations.

(c) The department may revoke the license of any agency that fails to comply with the provisions of this chapter and Part 96 of Title 22 of the Code of Federal Regulations.[182]

8924. (a) For cases in which a child is emigrating from California to a convention country, an accredited agency or approved person providing any adoption service described in this chapter, shall perform all of the following:

(1) A background study on the child prepared in accordance with all requirements set forth in subdivisions (a) and (b) of Section 96.53 of Title 22 of the Code of Federal Regulations, Section 8706, and applicable state law.

(2) Consents are obtained in accordance with subdivision (c) of Section 96.53 of Title 22 of the Code of Federal Regulations and applicable state law.

(3) If the child is 12 years of age or older, the agency or person has given due consideration to the child's wishes or opinions before determining that an intercountry adoption is in the child's best interests and in accordance with applicable state law.

(4) Transmission to the United States Department of State or other competent authority, or accredited bodies of the convention country, of the child background study, proof that the necessary consents have been obtained, and the reasons for the determination that the placement is in the child's best interests.

(b) The accredited agency shall comply with all placement standards set forth in Section 96.54 of Title 22 of the Code of Federal Regulations for children emigrating from California to a convention country.

(c) The accredited agency shall keep the central authority of the convention country and the Secretary informed as necessary about the adoption process and the measures taken to complete it for children emigrating from California to a convention country, in accordance with all communication and coordination functions set forth in Section

96.55 of Title 22 of the Code of Federal Regulations.

(d) For all convention and nonconvention adoption cases involving children emigrating from California to a convention country, the agency, person, or public domestic authority providing adoption services shall report information to the Secretary in accordance with Part 99 of Title 22 of the Code of Federal Regulations.

8925. A Hague adoption certificate or, in outgoing cases, a Hague custody declaration, obtained pursuant to Part 97 of Title 22 of the Code of Federal Regulations shall be recognized as a final valid adoption for purposes of all state and local laws.

Chapter 5: Stepparent Adoptions

9000. (a) A stepparent desiring to adopt a child of the stepparent's spouse may for that purpose file a petition in any county authorized by Section 8609.5.

(b) A domestic partner, as defined in Section 297, desiring to adopt a child of the other domestic partner may, for that purpose, file a petition in any county authorized pursuant to Section 8609.5.

(c) The caption of the adoption petition shall contain the names of the petitioners, but not the child's name. The petition shall state the child's sex and date of birth and the name the child had before adoption.

(d) If the child is the subject of a guardianship petition, the adoption petition shall so state and shall include the caption and docket number or have attached a copy of the letters of the guardianship or temporary guardianship. The petitioners shall notify the court of any petition for guardianship or temporary guardianship filed after the adoption petition. The guardianship proceeding shall be consolidated with the adoption proceeding.

(e) The order of adoption shall contain the child's adopted name and the name the child had before adoption.

(f) If the petitioner has entered into a postadoption contact agreement pursuant to Section 8616.5, the petitioner shall file the agreement, signed by the participating parties, with the court before the adoption is finalized.

(g) For the purposes of this chapter, stepparent adoption includes adoption by a domestic partner, as defined in Section 297.[570]

9000.5. (a) The procedures provided in this section apply to a stepparent adoption where the child was born during the marriage or domestic partnership, including a registered domestic partnership or civil union from another jurisdiction, and either of the following circumstances applies:

(1) One of the spouses or partners gave birth to the child.

(2) The child was born through a gestational surrogacy process brought about by one or both of the spouses or partners, and the parentage of only one spouse or partner was established pursuant to the Uniform Parentage Act (Part 3 (commencing with Section 7600) of Division 12) or another parentage proceeding related to the surrogacy.

(b) (1) The following are not required in stepparent adoptions under this section unless otherwise ordered by the court for good cause:

(A) A home investigation pursuant to

Section 9001 or a home study.

(B) Costs incurred pursuant to Section 9002.

(C) A hearing pursuant to Section 9007.

(2) In stepparent adoptions under this section, the parties shall not be required to have been married or in a domestic partnership, including a registered domestic partnership or civil union from another jurisdiction, for a minimum period of time prior to the adoption being granted or to provide verification of their income or education.

(c) For stepparent adoptions filed under this section, the following shall be filed with the petition for adoption:

(1) A copy of the parties' marriage certificate, registered domestic partner certificate, or civil union from another jurisdiction.

(2) A copy of the child's birth certificate.

(3) Declarations by the parent who gave birth, or who caused the birth through gestational surrogacy, and the spouse or partner who is adopting explaining the circumstances of the child's conception in detail sufficient to identify whether there may be other persons with a claim to parentage of the child who are required to be provided notice of, or who must consent to, the adoption.

(d) The court may order a hearing to ascertain whether there are additional persons who must be provided notice of, or who must consent to, the adoption if it appears from the face of the pleadings and the evidence that proper notice or consent have not been provided.

(e) The court shall grant the stepparent adoption under this section upon finding both of the following:

(1) That the parent who gave birth, or who caused the birth through gestational surrogacy, and the spouse or partner who is adopting were married or in a domestic partnership, including a registered domestic partnership or civil union from another jurisdiction, at the time of the child's birth.

(2) Any other person with a claim to parentage of the child who is required to be provided notice of, or who must consent to, the adoption has been noticed or provided consent to the adoption.[492]

9001. (a) Except as provided in Section 9000.5, before granting or denying a stepparent adoption request, the court shall review and consider a written investigative report. The report in a stepparent adoption case shall not require a home study unless so ordered by the court upon request of an investigator or interested person, or on the court's own motion. "Home study" as used in this section means a physical investigation of the premises where the child is residing.

(b) At the time of filing the adoption request, the petitioner shall inform the court in writing if the petitioner is electing to have the investigation and written report completed by a licensed clinical social worker, a licensed marriage and family therapist, a licensed professional clinical counselor, or a private licensed adoption agency, in which cases the petitioner shall not be required to pay an investigation fee pursuant to Section 9002 at the time of filing, but shall pay these fees directly to the investigator. Absent that notification, the court may, at the time of filing, collect an investigation fee pursuant to Section 9002, and may assign

one of the following to complete the investigation: a probation officer, a qualified court investigator, or the county welfare department, if so authorized by the board of supervisors of the county where the action is pending.
(c) If a private licensed adoption agency conducts the investigation, it shall assign the investigation to a licensed clinical social worker, licensed professional clinical counselor, or licensed marriage and family therapist associated with the agency. A grievance regarding the investigation shall be directed to the licensing authority of the clinical social worker, licensed professional clinical counselor, or marriage and family therapist, as applicable.
(d) This section does not require the State Department of Social Services to issue regulations for stepparent adoptions.[375]

9002. Except as provided in Section 9000.5, in a stepparent adoption, the prospective adoptive parent is liable for all reasonable costs incurred in connection with the stepparent adoption, including, but not limited to, costs incurred for the investigation required by Section 9001, up to a maximum of seven hundred dollars ($700). The court, probation officer, qualified court investigator, or county welfare department may defer, waive, or reduce the fee if its payment would cause economic hardship to the prospective adoptive parent detrimental to the welfare of the adopted child.[313]

9003. (a) In a stepparent adoption, the consent of either or both birth parents shall be signed in the presence of a notary public, court clerk, probation officer, qualified court investigator, authorized representative of a licensed adoption agency, or county welfare department staff member of any county of this state. The petitioner, petitioner's counsel, or person before whom the consent is signed shall immediately file the consent with the clerk of the court where the adoption request is filed. If the request has not been filed at the time the consent has been signed, the consent shall be filed simultaneously with the adoption request. Upon filing of the adoption request, the clerk shall immediately notify the probation officer or, at the option of the board of supervisors, the county welfare department of that county.
(b) If the birth parent of a child to be adopted is outside this state at the time of signing the consent, the consent may be signed before an authorized representative of an adoption agency licensed in the state or country where the consent is being signed, a notary, or other person authorized to perform notarial acts.
(c) The consent, when reciting that the person giving it is entitled to sole custody of the child and when acknowledged before any authorized witness specified in subdivision (a), is prima facie evidence of the right of the person signing the consent to the sole custody of the child and that person's sole right to consent.
(d) A birth parent who is a minor has the right to sign a consent for the adoption of the birth parent's child and the consent is not subject to revocation by reason of the minority.

9004. In a stepparent adoption, the form prescribed by the department for the consent of the birth parent shall contain substantially the following notice:

"Notice to the parent who gives the child for adoption: If you and your child lived together at any time as parent and child, the adoption of your child through a stepparent adoption does not affect the child's right to inherit your property or the property of other blood relatives."

9005. (a) Consent of the birth parent to the adoption of the child through a stepparent adoption may not be withdrawn except with court approval. Request for that approval may be made by motion, or a birth parent seeking to withdraw consent may file with the clerk of the court where the adoption petition is pending, a petition for approval of withdrawal of consent, without the necessity of paying a fee for filing the petition. The petition or motion shall be in writing, and shall set forth the reasons for withdrawal of consent, but otherwise may be in any form.

(b) The court clerk shall set the matter for hearing and shall give notice thereof to the probation officer, qualified court investigator, or county welfare department, to the prospective adoptive parent, and to the birth parent or parents by certified mail, return receipt requested, to the address of each as shown in the proceeding, at least 10 days before the time set for hearing.

(c) The probation officer, qualified court investigator, or county welfare department shall, before the hearing of the motion or petition for withdrawal, file a full report with the court and shall appear at the hearing to represent the interests of the child.

(d) At the hearing, the parties may appear in person or with counsel. The hearing shall be held in chambers, but the court reporter shall report the proceedings and, on court order, the fee therefor shall be paid from the county treasury. If the court finds that withdrawal of the consent to adoption is reasonable in view of all the circumstances and that withdrawal of the consent is in the child's best interest, the court shall approve the withdrawal of the consent. Otherwise, the court shall withhold its approval. Consideration of the child's best interest shall include, but is not limited to, an assessment of the child's age, the extent of bonding with the prospective adoptive parent, the extent of bonding or the potential to bond with the birth parent, and the ability of the birth parent to provide adequate and proper care and guidance to the child. If the court approves the withdrawal of consent, the adoption proceeding shall be dismissed.

(e) A court order granting or withholding approval of a withdrawal of consent to an adoption may be appealed in the same manner as an order of the juvenile court declaring a person to be a ward of the juvenile court.

9006. (a) If the petitioner moves to withdraw the adoption petition or to dismiss the proceeding, the court clerk shall immediately notify the probation officer, qualified court investigator, or county welfare department of the action, unless a home investigation was not required pursuant to Section 9000.5.

(b) If a birth parent has refused to give the required consent, the adoption petition shall be dismissed.[314]

9007. Except as provided in Section 9000.5, the prospective adoptive parent and the child proposed to be adopted shall appear before the court pursuant to Sections 8612, 8613, and 8613.5.[315]

Chapter 6: Vacation of Adoption

9100. (a) If a child adopted pursuant to the law of this state shows evidence of a developmental disability or mental illness as a result of conditions existing before the adoption to an extent that the child cannot be relinquished to an adoption agency on the grounds that a plan of adoption is not currently suitable, and of which conditions the adoptive parents or parent had no knowledge or notice before the entry of the order of adoption, a petition setting forth those facts may be filed by the adoptive parents or parent with the court that granted the adoption petition. If these facts are proved to the satisfaction of the court, it may make an order setting aside the order of adoption.
(b) The petition shall be filed within five years after the entry of the order of adoption.
(c) (1) The court clerk shall immediately notify the department at Sacramento of the petition. Within 60 days after the notice, the department shall file a full report with the court and shall appear before the court for the purpose of representing the adopted child.
(2) Notwithstanding any other law, an adoption case file, including a juvenile case file, as defined in subdivision (e) of Section 827 of the Welfare and Institutions Code, may be inspected and copied by the department for the purpose of completing the duties pursuant to this subdivision.[529]

9101. (a) If an order of adoption is set aside as provided in Section 9100, the court making the order shall direct the district attorney, the county counsel, or the county welfare department to take appropriate action under the Welfare and Institutions Code. The court may also make any order relative to the care, custody, or confinement of the child pending the proceeding the court sees fit.
(b) The county in which the proceeding for adoption was had is liable for the child's support until the child is able to be self-supporting.

9102. (a) Except as provided in Section 9100, an action or proceeding of any kind to vacate, set aside, or otherwise nullify an order of adoption on any ground, except fraud, shall be commenced within one year after entry of the order.
(b) Except as provided in Section 9100, an action or proceeding of any kind to vacate, set aside, or nullify an order of adoption, based on fraud, shall be commenced within three years after entry of the order, or within 90 days of discovery of the fraud, whichever is earlier.
(c) In any action to set aside an order of adoption pursuant to this section or Section 9100, the court shall first determine whether the facts presented are legally sufficient to set aside the order of adoption. If the facts are not legally sufficient, the petition shall be denied. If the facts are legally sufficient, the court's final ruling on the matter shall take into consideration the best interests of the child, in conjunction with all other factors required by law.

(d) The department shall not be required under any circumstances to investigate a petition filed pursuant to this section or to represent a child who is the subject of a proceeding under this section.[223]

Chapter 7: Disclosure of Information

9200. (a) The petition, relinquishment or consent, agreement, order, report to the court from any investigating agency, and any power of attorney and deposition filed in the office of the clerk of the court pursuant to this part is not open to inspection by any person other than the parties to the proceeding and their attorneys and the department, except upon the written authority of the judge of the superior court. A judge of the superior court may not authorize anyone to inspect the petition, relinquishment or consent, agreement, order, report to the court from any investigating agency, or power of attorney or deposition or any portion of any of these documents, except in exceptional circumstances and for good cause approaching the necessitous. The petitioner may be required to pay the expenses for preparing the copies of the documents to be inspected.

(b) Upon written request of any party to the proceeding and upon the order of any judge of the superior court, the clerk of the court shall not provide any documents referred to in this section for inspection or copying to any other person, unless the name of the child's birth parents or any information tending to identify the child's birth parents is deleted from the documents or copies thereof.

(c) Upon the request of the adoptive parents or the child, a clerk of the court may issue a certificate of adoption that states the date and place of adoption, the child's birth date, the names of the adoptive parents, and the name the child has taken. Unless the child has been adopted by a stepparent, the certificate shall not state the name of the child's birth parents.[90]

9201. (a) Except as otherwise permitted or required by statute, neither the department nor a licensed adoption agency shall release information that would identify persons who receive, or have received, adoption services.

(b) Employees of the department and licensed adoption agencies shall release to the department at Sacramento any requested information, including identifying information, for the purposes of recordkeeping and monitoring, evaluation, and regulation of the provision of adoption services.

(c) Prior to the placement of a child for adoption, the department or licensed adoption agency may, upon the written request of both a birth and a prospective adoptive parent, arrange for contact between these birth and prospective adoptive parents that may include the sharing of identifying information regarding these parents.

(d) The department and any licensed adoption agency may, upon written authorization for the release of specified information by the subject of that information, share information regarding a prospective adoptive parent or birth parent with other social service agencies, including the department, other licensed adoption agencies, counties or licensed foster family agencies for purposes of approving a resource family pursuant to subparagraph (A) of paragraph (4) of subdivision (p) of Section 16519.5 of the Welfare and Institutions Code, or providers of health care as defined in Section 56.05 of the Civil Code.

(e) Notwithstanding any other law, the department and any licensed adoption agency may furnish information relating to an adoption petition or to a child in the custody of the department or any licensed adoption agency to the juvenile court, county welfare department, public welfare agency, private welfare agency licensed by the department, provider of foster care services, potential adoptive parent, or provider of health care as defined in Section 56.05 of the Civil Code, if it is believed the child's welfare will be promoted thereby.

(f) The department and any licensed adoption agency may make adoption case records, including identifying information, available for research purposes, provided that the research will not result in the disclosure of the identity of the child or the parties to the adoption to anyone other than the entity conducting the research.[363]

9202. (a) Notwithstanding any other law, the department or licensed adoption agency that made a medical report required by Section 8706, 8817, or 8909 shall provide a copy of the medical report, in the manner the department prescribes by regulation, to any of the following persons upon the person's request:

(1) A person who has been adopted pursuant to this part and who has attained the age of 18 years or who presents a certified copy of the person's marriage certificate.

(2) The adoptive parent of a person under the age of 18 years who has been adopted pursuant to this part.

(b) A person who is denied access to a medical report pursuant to regulations adopted pursuant to this section may petition the court for review of the reasonableness of the department's or licensed adoption agency's decision.

(c) The names and addresses of any persons contained in the report shall be removed unless the person requesting the report has previously received the information.

9202.5. (a) Notwithstanding any other law, the laboratory that is storing a blood sample pursuant to Section 8706, 8817, or 8909 shall provide access to the blood sample to only the following persons upon the person's request:

(1) A person who has been adopted pursuant to this part.

(2) The adoptive parent of a person under the age of 18 years who has been adopted pursuant to this part. The adoptive parent may receive access to the blood sample only after entry of the order of adoption.

(b) The birth parent or parents shall be given access to any DNA test results related to the blood sample on request.

(c) Except as provided in subdivision (b), no person other than the adoptive parent and the adopted child shall have access to the blood sample or any DNA test results related to the blood sample, unless the adoptive parent or the child authorizes another person or entity to have that access.

9203. (a) The department or a licensed adoption agency shall do the following:

(1) Upon the request of a person who has been adopted pursuant to this part and who has attained 21 years of age, disclose the identity of the

person's birth parent or parents and their most current address shown in the records of the department or licensed adoption agency, if the birth parent or parents have indicated consent to the disclosure in writing.

(2) Upon the request of the birth parent of a person who has been adopted pursuant to this part and who has attained 21 years of age, disclose the adopted name of the adoptee and the adoptee's most current address shown in the records of the department or licensed adoption agency, if the adult adoptee has indicated in writing, pursuant to the registration program developed by the department, that the adult adoptee wishes the adult adoptee's name and address to be disclosed.

(3) Upon the request of the adoptive parent of a person under 21 years of age who has been adopted pursuant to this part, disclose the identity of a birth parent and the birth parent's most current address shown in the records of the department or licensed adoption agency if the department or licensed adoption agency finds that a medical necessity or other extraordinary circumstances justify the disclosure.

(b) The department shall prescribe the form of the request required by this section. The form shall provide for an affidavit to be executed by the requester that to the best of the requester's knowledge the requester is an adoptee, the adoptee's birth parent, or the adoptee's adoptive parent. The department may adopt regulations requiring any additional means of identification from a requester that it deems necessary. The request shall advise an adoptee that if the adoptee consents, the adoptee's adoptive parents will be notified of the filing of the request before the release of the name and address of the adoptee's birth parent.

(c) Subdivision (a) is not applicable if a birth parent or an adoptee has indicated a desire that the name or address of the birth parent or adoptee not be disclosed.

(d) Within 20 working days of receipt of a request for information pursuant to this section, the department shall either respond to the request or forward the request to a licensed adoption agency that was a party to the adoption.

(e) Notwithstanding any other law, the department shall announce the availability of the present method of arranging contact among an adult adoptee, the adult adoptee's birth parents, and adoptive parents authorized by Section 9204 utilizing a means of communication appropriate to inform the public effectively.

(f) The department or licensed adoption agency may charge a reasonable fee in an amount the department establishes by regulation to cover the costs of processing requests for information made pursuant to subdivision (a). The department or licensed adoption agency shall waive fees authorized by this section for a person who is receiving public assistance pursuant to Part 3 (commencing with Section 11000) of Division 9 of the Welfare and Institutions Code. The revenue resulting from the fees so charged shall be utilized by the department or licensed adoption agency to increase existing staff as needed to process these requests. Fees received by the department shall be deposited in the Adoption Information Fund. This revenue shall be in addition to any other funds appropriated in support of the state adoption program.

(g) This section applies only to adoptions in which the relinquishment for or consent to adoption was signed or the birth parent's rights were involuntarily terminated by court action on or after January 1, 1984.

9203.1. (a) The department or a licensed adoption agency shall, upon the request of a prospective adoptive parent, disclose an adoption homestudy and any updates to an adoption homestudy to a county or licensed foster family agency for the purpose of approving the prospective adoptive parent as a resource family pursuant to subparagraph (A) of paragraph (4) of subdivision (p) of Section 16519.5 of the Welfare and Institutions Code.

(b) The department shall prescribe the form of the request described in subdivision (a).

(c) The department or a licensed adoption agency shall respond to a request made pursuant to subdivision (a) within 20 working days of receiving it.

(d) The department or a licensed adoption agency may charge a fee to cover the reasonable costs of processing requests made pursuant to subdivision (a). The department or a licensed adoption agency shall waive fees authorized by this subdivision for any person who is receiving public assistance pursuant to Part 3 (commencing with Section 11000) of Division 9 of the Welfare and Institutions Code.[364]

9204. (a) Notwithstanding any other law, if an adult adoptee and the adult adoptee's birth parents have each filed a written consent with the department or licensed adoption agency, the department or licensed adoption agency may arrange for contact between those persons. Neither the department nor a licensed adoption agency may solicit, directly or indirectly, the execution of a written consent.

(b) The written consent authorized by this section shall be in a form prescribed by the department.[1]

9205. (a) Notwithstanding any other law, the department, county adoption agency, or licensed adoption agency that joined in the adoption petition shall release the names and addresses of siblings to one another if both of the siblings have attained 18 years of age and have filed the following with the department or agency:

(1) A current address.

(2) A written request for contact with any sibling whose existence is known to the person making the request.

(3) A written waiver of the person's rights with respect to the disclosure of the person's name and address to the sibling, if the person is an adoptee.

(b) Upon inquiry and proof that a person is the sibling of an adoptee who has filed a waiver pursuant to this section, the department, county adoption agency, or licensed adoption agency may advise the sibling that a waiver has been filed by the adoptee. The department, county adoption agency, or licensed adoption agency may charge a reasonable fee, not to exceed fifty dollars ($50), for providing the service required by this section.

(c) An adoptee may revoke a waiver filed pursuant to this section by giving written notice of revocation to the department or agency.

(d) The department shall adopt a form for the request authorized by this section. The form shall provide for an affidavit to be executed by a person seeking to employ the procedure provided by this section that, to the best of the person's knowledge, the person is an adoptee or sibling of an adoptee. The form also shall contain a notice of an adoptee's rights pursuant to subdivision (c) and a statement that information will be disclosed only if there is a currently valid waiver on file with the department or agency. The department may adopt regulations requiring any additional means of identification from a person making a request pursuant to this section as it deems necessary.

(e) The department, county adoption agency, or licensed adoption agency may not solicit the execution of a waiver authorized by this section. However, the department shall announce the availability of the procedure authorized by this section, utilizing a means of communication appropriate to inform the public effectively.

(f) Notwithstanding the age requirement described in subdivision (a), an adoptee or sibling who is under 18 years of age may file a written waiver of confidentiality for the release of the person's name, address, and telephone number pursuant to this section provided that, if an adoptee, the adoptive parent consents, and, if a sibling, the sibling's legal parent or guardian consents. If the sibling is under the jurisdiction of the dependency court and has no legal parent or guardian able or available to provide consent, the dependency court may provide that consent.

(g) Notwithstanding subdivisions (a) and (e), an adoptee or sibling who seeks contact with the other for whom no waiver is on file may petition the court to appoint a confidential intermediary. If the sibling being sought is the adoptee, the intermediary shall be the department, county adoption agency, or licensed adoption agency that provided adoption services as described in Section 8521 or 8533. If the sibling being sought was formerly under the jurisdiction of the juvenile court, but is not an adoptee, the intermediary shall be the department, the county child welfare agency that provided services to the dependent child, or the licensed adoption agency that provided adoption services to the sibling seeking contact, as appropriate. If the court finds that the agency that conducted the adoptee's adoption is unable, due to economic hardship, to serve as the intermediary, then the agency shall provide all records related to the adoptee or the sibling to the court and the court shall appoint an alternate confidential intermediary. The court shall grant the petition unless it finds that it would be detrimental to the adoptee or sibling with whom contact is sought. The intermediary shall have access to all records of the adoptee or the sibling and shall make all reasonable efforts to locate and attempt to obtain the consent of the adoptee, sibling, or adoptive or birth parent, as required to make the disclosure authorized by this section. The confidential intermediary shall notify any located adoptee, sibling, or adoptive or birth parent that consent is optional, not required by law, and does not affect the status of the adoption. If that individual denies the request for consent, the confidential intermediary shall not make any further attempts to obtain consent. The confidential intermediary shall use information found in the records of the adoptee or the sibling for authorized purposes only, and may not disclose that information without authorization. If contact is sought with an adoptee or sibling who is under 18 years of age, the confidential intermediary shall contact and obtain the consent of that child's legal parent before contacting the child. If the sibling is under 18 years of age, under the jurisdiction of the dependency court, and has no legal parent or guardian able or available to provide consent, the intermediary shall obtain that consent from the dependency court. If the adoptee is seeking information regarding a sibling who is known to be a dependent child of the juvenile court, the procedures set forth in subdivision (b) of Section 388 of the Welfare and Institutions Code shall be utilized. If the adoptee is foreign born and was the subject of an intercountry adoption as defined in Section 8527, the adoption agency may fulfill the reasonable efforts requirement by utilizing all information in the agency's case file, and any information received upon request from the foreign adoption agency that conducted the adoption, if any, to locate and attempt to obtain the consent of the adoptee, sibling, or adoptive or birth parent. If that information is neither in the agency's case file, nor received from the foreign adoption agency, or if the attempts to locate are unsuccessful, then the agency shall be relieved of any further obligation to search for the adoptee or the sibling.

(h) For purposes of this section, "sibling" means a biological sibling, half-sibling, or step-sibling of the adoptee.

(i) It is the intent of the Legislature that implementation of some or all of the changes made to this section by Chapter 386 of the Statutes of 2006 shall continue, to the extent possible.

(j) Beginning in the 2011–12 fiscal year, and each fiscal year thereafter, funding and expenditures for programs and activities under this section shall be in accordance with the requirements provided in Sections 30025 and 30026.5 of the Government Code.

9206. (a) Notwithstanding any other law, the department or licensed adoption agency shall release any letters, photographs, or other items of personal property in its possession to an adoptee, birth parent, or adoptive parent, upon written request. The material may be requested by any of the following persons:

(1) The adoptee, if the adoptee has attained the age of 18 years.

(2) The adoptive parent or parents, on behalf of an adoptee under the age of 18 years, as long as instructions to the contrary have not been made by the depositor.

(3) The birth parent or parents.

(b) Notwithstanding any other law, all identifying names and addresses shall be deleted from the letters, photographs, or items of personal property before delivery to the requester.

(c) Letters, photographs, and other items of personal property deposited on or after January 1, 1985, shall be accompanied by a release form or similar document signed by the person depositing the material, specifying to whom the material may be released. At its discretion, the department or licensed adoption agency may refuse for deposit items of personal property that, because of value or bulk, would pose storage problems.

(d) Notwithstanding subdivisions (a) and (b), only the following photographs deposited before January 1, 1985, shall be released:

(1) Photographs of the adoptee that have been requested by the adoptee.

(2) Photographs that have been deposited by the adoptee, the adoptive parent or parents, or the birth parent or parents, and for which there is a letter or other document on file indicating that person's consent to the release of the photographs.

(e) The department and licensed adoption agencies may charge a fee to cover the actual costs of any services required by this section in excess of normal postadoptive services provided by the department or agency. The department shall develop a fee schedule that shall be implemented by the department and licensed adoption agencies in assessing charges to the person who deposits the material or the person to whom the material is released. The fee may be waived by the department or licensed adoption agencies in cases in which it is established that a financial hardship exists.

(f) "Photograph" as used in this section means a photograph of the person depositing the photograph or the person making the request for the release.[1]

9208. (a) The clerk of the superior court entering a final order of adoption concerning an Indian child shall provide the United States Secretary of the Interior or a designee with a copy of the order within 30 days of the date of the order, together with any information necessary to show the following:

(1) The name and tribal affiliation of the child.

(2) The names and addresses of the biological parents.

(3) The names and addresses of the adoptive parents.

(4) The identity of any agency having files or information relating to that adoptive placement.

(b) If the court records contain an affidavit of the biological parent or parents that their identity remain confidential, the court shall include that affidavit with the other information.

9209. (a) Upon application by an Indian individual who has reached the age of 18 years and who was the subject of an adoptive placement, the court which entered the final decree of adoption shall inform that individual of the tribal affiliation, if any, of the individual's biological parents and provide any other information as may be necessary to protect any rights flowing from the individual's tribal relationship, including, but not limited to, tribal membership rights or eligibility for federal or tribal programs or services available to Indians.

(b) If the court records contain an affidavit of the biological parent or parents that their identity remain confidential, the court shall inform the individual that the Secretary of the Interior may, upon request, certify to the individual's tribe that the individual's parentage and other circumstances of birth entitle the individual to membership under the criteria established by the tribe.[147]

Chapter 8: Adoption Proceedings: Conflict of Laws

9210. (a) Except as otherwise provided in subdivisions (b) and (c), a court of this state has jurisdiction over a proceeding for the adoption of a minor commenced under this part if any of the following applies:

(1) Immediately before commencement of the proceeding, the minor lived in this state with a parent, a guardian, a prospective adoptive parent, or another person acting as parent, for at least six consecutive months, excluding periods of temporary absence, or, in the case of a minor under six months of age, lived in this state with any of those individuals from soon after birth and there is available in this state substantial evidence concerning the minor's present or future care.

(2) Immediately before commencement of the proceeding, the prospective adoptive parent lived in this state for at least six consecutive months, excluding periods of temporary absence, and there is available in this state substantial evidence concerning the minor's present or future care.

(3) The agency that placed the minor for adoption is located in this state and both of the following apply:

(A) The minor and the minor's parents, or the minor and the prospective adoptive parent, have a significant connection with this state.

(B) There is available in this state substantial evidence concerning the minor's present or future care.

(4) The minor and the prospective adoptive parent are physically present in this state and the minor has been abandoned or it is necessary in an emergency to protect the minor because the minor has been subjected to or threatened with mistreatment or abuse or is otherwise neglected.

(5) The minor was born in this state and either of the following apply:

(A) A proceeding to free the minor from the custody and control of one or both parents is not required to make the minor available for adoption.

(B) The proceeding to free the minor from the custody and control of one or both parents to make the minor available for adoption is being brought in this state.

(6) It appears that no other state would have jurisdiction under requirements substantially in accordance with paragraphs (1) to (5), inclusive, or another state has declined to exercise jurisdiction on the ground that this state is the more appropriate forum to hear a petition for adoption of the minor, and there is available in this state substantial evidence concerning the minor's present or future care.

(b) A court of this state may not exercise jurisdiction over a proceeding for adoption of a minor if at the time the petition for adoption is filed a proceeding concerning the custody or adoption of the minor is pending in a court of another state exercising jurisdiction substantially in conformity with this part, unless the proceeding is stayed by the court of the other state because this state is a more appropriate forum or for another reason.

(c) If a court of another state has issued a decree or order concerning the custody of a minor who may be the subject of a proceeding for adoption in this state, a court of this state may not exercise jurisdiction over a proceeding for adoption of the minor, unless both of the following apply:

(1) The requirements for modifying an order of a court of another state under this part are met, the court of

another state does not have jurisdiction over a proceeding for adoption substantially in conformity with paragraphs (1) to (5), inclusive, of subdivision (a), or the court of another state has declined to assume jurisdiction over a proceeding for adoption.
(2) The court of this state has jurisdiction under this section over the proceeding for adoption.
(d) For purposes of subdivisions (b) and (c), "a court of another state" includes, in the case of an Indian child, a tribal court having and exercising jurisdiction over a custody proceeding involving the Indian child.
(e) Nothing in this section shall limit jurisdiction that is otherwise permitted under Part 5 (commencing with Section 7900) of Division 12.[148]

9212. (a) Sections 9210 and 9211 apply to interstate adoptions if the prospective adoptive parents reside outside of the state.
(b) This section shall become operative only if Assembly Bill 746 of the 2001–02 Regular Session is enacted. If Assembly Bill 746 is not enacted, the application of Sections 9210 and 9211 is not intended to expand jurisdiction to apply to interstate adoptions if the prospective adoptive parents reside outside of the state.[96]

PART 3: ADOPTION OF ADULTS AND MARRIED MINORS

enacted by Stats. 1992, Ch. 162, Sec. 10

Chapter 1: General Provisions

9300. (a) An adult may be adopted by another adult, including a stepparent, as provided in this part.
(b) A married minor may be adopted in the same manner as an adult under this part.

9301. A married person who is not lawfully separated from the person's spouse may not adopt an adult without the consent of the spouse, provided that the spouse is capable of giving that consent.[1]

9302. (a) A married person who is not lawfully separated from the person's spouse may not be adopted without the consent of the spouse, provided that the spouse is capable of giving that consent.
(b) The consent of the parents of the proposed adoptee, of the department, or of any other person is not required.[1]

9303. (a) Except as permitted by the court, upon a finding of good cause, a person shall not adopt more than one unrelated adult pursuant to this part within one year of the person's adoption of an unrelated adult unless the proposed adoptee is the biological sibling of a person previously adopted pursuant to this part or unless the proposed adoptee is disabled or physically handicapped. An order finding good cause shall be in writing or stated on the record.
(b) Except as permitted by the court, upon a finding of good cause, a person shall not adopt an unrelated adult pursuant to this part within one year of an adoption of another person pursuant to this part by the prospective adoptive parent's spouse unless the proposed adoptee is a biological sibling of a person previously adopted pursuant to this part. An order finding good cause shall be in writing or stated on the record.[563]

9304. A person adopted pursuant to this part may take the family name of the adoptive parent.[1]

9305. After adoption, the adoptee and the adoptive parent or parents shall sustain towards each other the legal relationship of parent and child and have all the rights and are subject to all the duties of that relationship.[1]

9306. (a) Except as provided in subdivisions (b) and (c), the birth parents of a person adopted pursuant to this part are, from the time of the adoption, relieved of all parental duties towards, and all responsibility for, the adopted person, and have no right over the adopted person.
(b) If an adult is adopted by the spouse of a birth parent, the parental rights and responsibilities of that birth parent are not affected by the adoption.
(c) An adult being adopted pursuant to this part may waive the termination of the parental duties and responsibilities of an existing parent or parents under subdivision (a) by signing a waiver at any time prior to the finalization of the adoption. The waiver may be included in the adoption agreement or in a separate writing filed with the court.

9307. A hearing with regard to adoption under Chapter 2 (commencing with Section 9320) or termination of a parent and child relationship under Chapter 3 (commencing with Section 9340) may, in the discretion of the court, be open and public.[1]

Chapter 2: Procedure for Adult Adoption

9320. (a) An adult may adopt another adult who is younger, except the spouse of the prospective adoptive parent, by an adoption agreement approved by the court, as provided in this chapter.
(b) The adoption agreement shall be in writing, executed by the prospective adoptive parent and the proposed adoptee, and shall state that the parties agree to assume toward each other the legal relationship of parent and child and to have all of the rights and be subject to all of the duties and responsibilities of that relationship.[1]

9321. (a) The prospective adoptive parent and the proposed adoptee may file in the county in which either person resides a petition for approval of the adoption agreement.
(b) The petition for approval of the adoption agreement shall state all of the following:
(1) The length and nature of the relationship between the prospective adoptive parent and the proposed adoptee.
(2) The degree of kinship, if any.
(3) The reason the adoption is sought.
(4) A statement as to why the adoption would be in the best interest of the prospective adoptive parent, the proposed adoptee, and the public.
(5) The names and addresses of any living birth parents or adult children of the proposed adoptee.
(6) Whether the prospective adoptive parent or the prospective adoptive parent's spouse has previously adopted any other adult and, if so, the name of the adult, together with the date and place of the adoption.[1]

9321.5. (a) Notwithstanding Section 9321, a person who is a resident of this state may file a petition for adult adoption with the court in any of the following:

(1) The county in which the prospective adoptive parent resides.
(2) The county in which the proposed adoptee was born or resides at the time the petition was filed.
(3) The county in which an office of the public or private agency that placed the proposed adoptee for foster care or adoption as a minor or dependent child is located.
(b) A petitioner who is not a resident of this state may file a petition for adult adoption with the court in a county specified in paragraph (3) of subdivision (a).[253]

9322. When the petition for approval of the adoption agreement is filed, the court clerk shall set the matter for hearing.[1]

9323. The court may require notice of the time and place of the hearing to be served on any other interested person and any interested person may appear and object to the proposed adoption.[1]

9324. Both the prospective adoptive parent and the proposed adoptee shall appear at the hearing in person, unless the court allows otherwise pursuant to Section 8613.5.[514]

9325. No investigation or report to the court by any public officer or agency is required, but the court may require the county probation officer or the department to investigate the circumstances of the proposed adoption and report thereon, with recommendations, to the court before the hearing.[1]

9326. The prospective adoptive parent shall mail or personally serve notice of the hearing and a copy of the petition to the director of the regional center for the developmentally disabled, established pursuant to Chapter 5 (commencing with Section 4620) of Division 4.5 of the Welfare and Institutions Code, and to any living birth parents or adult children of the proposed adoptee, at least 30 days before the day of the hearing on an adoption petition in any case in which both of the following conditions exist:
(a) The proposed adoptee is an adult with developmental disabilities.
(b) The prospective adoptive parent is a provider of board and care, treatment, habilitation, or other services to persons with developmental disabilities or is a spouse or employee of a provider.[1]

9327. If the prospective adoptive parent is a provider of board and care, treatment, habilitation, or other services to persons with developmental disabilities, or is a spouse or employee of a provider, and seeks to adopt an unrelated adult with developmental disabilities, the regional center for the developmentally disabled notified pursuant to Section 9326 shall file a written report with the court regarding the suitability of the proposed adoption in meeting the needs of the proposed adoptee and regarding any known previous adoption by the prospective adoptive parent.[1]

9328. (a) At the hearing the court shall examine the parties, or the counsel of any party not present in person.
(b) If the court is satisfied that the adoption will be in the best interests of the persons seeking the adoption and in the public interest and that there is no reason why the petition should not be granted, the court shall approve the adoption agreement and make an order of adoption declaring that the

person adopted is the child of the adoptive parent. Otherwise, the court shall withhold approval of the agreement and deny the petition.
(c) In determining whether or not the adoption of any person pursuant to this part is in the best interests of the persons seeking the adoption or the public interest, the court may consider evidence, oral or written, whether or not it is in conformity with the Evidence Code.[1]

Chapter 3: Procedure for Terminating Adult Adoption

9340. (a) Any person who has been adopted under this part may, upon written notice to the adoptive parent, file a petition to terminate the relationship of parent and child. The petition shall state the name and address of the petitioner, the name and address of the adoptive parent, the date and place of the adoption, and the circumstances upon which the petition is based.
(b) If the adoptive parent consents in writing to the termination, an order terminating the relationship of parent and child may be issued by the court without further notice.
(c) If the adoptive parent does not consent in writing to the termination, a written response shall be filed within 30 days of the date of mailing of the notice, and the matter shall be set for hearing. The court may require an investigation by the county probation officer or the department.[1]

DIVISION 14: FAMILY LAW FACILITATOR ACT

ADDED BY STATS. 1996, CH. 957, SEC. 9.
SECTION 10000-10015

10000. This division shall be known and may be cited as the Family Law Facilitator Act.[64]

10001. (a) The Legislature finds and declares the following:

(1) Child and spousal support are serious legal obligations. The entry of a child support order is frequently delayed while parents engage in protracted litigation concerning custody and visitation. The current system for obtaining child and spousal support orders is suffering because the family courts are unduly burdened with heavy caseloads and do not have sufficient personnel to meet increased demands on the courts.

(2) Reports to the Legislature regarding the family law pilot projects in the Superior Courts of the Counties of Santa Clara and San Mateo indicate that the pilot projects have provided a cost-effective and efficient method for the courts to process family law cases that involve unrepresented litigants with issues concerning child support, spousal support, and health insurance.

(3) The reports to the Legislature further indicate that the pilot projects in both counties have been successful in making the process of obtaining court orders concerning child support, spousal support, and health insurance more accessible to unrepresented parties. Surveys conducted by both counties indicate a high degree of satisfaction with the services provided by the pilot projects.

(4) There is a compelling state interest in having a speedy, conflict-reducing system for resolving issues of child support, spousal support, and health insurance that is cost-effective and accessible to families that cannot afford legal representation.

(b) Therefore, it is the intent of the Legislature to make the services provided in the family law pilot projects in the Counties of Santa Clara and San Mateo available to unrepresented parties in the superior courts of all California counties.[64]

10002. Each superior court shall maintain an office of the family law facilitator. The office of the family law facilitator shall be staffed by an attorney licensed to practice law in this state who has mediation or litigation experience, or both, in the field of family law. The family law facilitator shall be appointed by the superior court.[64]

10003. This division shall apply to all actions or proceedings for temporary or permanent child support, spousal support, health insurance, child custody, or visitation in a proceeding for dissolution of marriage, nullity of marriage, legal separation, or exclusive child custody, or pursuant to the Uniform Parentage Act (Part 3 (commencing with Section 7600) of Division 12) or the Domestic Violence Prevention Act (Division 10 (commencing with Section 6200)).[75]

10004. Services provided by the family law facilitator shall include, but are not limited to, the following: providing educational materials to parents concerning the process of establishing parentage and establishing, modifying, and enforcing child support and spousal support in the courts; distributing necessary court forms and voluntary declarations of paternity; providing assistance in completing forms; preparing support schedules based upon statutory guidelines; and providing referrals to the local child support agency, family court services, and other community agencies and resources that provide services for parents and children. In counties where a family law information center exists, the family law facilitator shall provide assistance on child support issues.[75]

10005. (a) By local rule, the superior court may designate additional duties of the family law facilitator, which may include, but are not limited to, the following:

(1) Meeting with litigants to mediate issues of child support, spousal support, and maintenance of health insurance, subject to Section 10012. Actions in which one or both of the parties are unrepresented by counsel shall have priority.

(2) Drafting stipulations to include all issues agreed to by the parties, which may include issues other than those specified in Section 10003.

(3) If the parties are unable to resolve issues with the assistance of the family law facilitator, prior to or at the hearing, and at the request of the court, the family law facilitator shall review the paperwork, examine documents, prepare support schedules, and advise the judge whether or not the matter is ready to proceed.

(4) Assisting the clerk in maintaining records.

(5) Preparing formal orders consistent with the court's announced order in cases where both parties are unrepresented.

(6) Serving as a special master in proceedings and making findings to the court unless the family law facilitator has served as a mediator in that case.

(7) Providing the services specified in Section 10004 concerning the issues of child custody and visitation as they relate to calculating child support, if funding is provided for that purpose.

(b) If staff and other resources are available and the duties listed in subdivision (a) have been accomplished, the duties of the family law facilitator may also include the following:

(1) Assisting the court with research and any other responsibilities that will enable the court to be responsive to the litigants' needs.

(2) Developing programs for bar and community outreach through day and evening programs, video recordings, and other innovative means that will assist unrepresented and financially disadvantaged litigants in gaining meaningful access to family court. These programs shall specifically include information concerning underutilized legislation, such as expedited child support orders (Chapter 5 (commencing with Section 3620) of Part 1 of Division 9), and preexisting, court-sponsored programs, such as supervised visitation and appointment of attorneys for children.

10006. The court shall adopt a protocol wherein all litigants, both unrepresented by counsel and represented by counsel, have ultimate access to a hearing before the court.[64]

10007. The court shall provide the family law facilitator at no cost to the parties.[64]

10008. (a) Except as provided in subdivision (b), nothing in this chapter shall be construed to apply to a child for whom services are provided or required to be provided by a local child support agency pursuant to Section 17400.
(b) In cases in which the services of the local child support agency are provided pursuant to Section 17400, either parent may utilize the services of the family law facilitator that are specified in Section 10004. In order for a custodial parent who is receiving the services of the local child support agency pursuant to Section 17400 to utilize the services specified in Section 10005 relating to support, the custodial parent must obtain written authorization from the local child support agency. It is not the intent of the Legislature in enacting this section to limit the duties of local child support agencies with respect to seeking child support payments or to in any way limit or supersede other provisions of this code respecting temporary child support.

10010. The Judicial Council shall adopt minimum standards for the office of the family law facilitator and any forms or rules of court that are necessary to implement this division.[64]

10011. The Director of the State Department of Social Services shall seek approval from the United States Department of Health and Human Services, Office of Child Support Enforcement, to utilize funding under Title IV-D of the Social Security Act for the services provided pursuant to this division.[64]

10012. (a) In a proceeding in which mediation is required pursuant to paragraph (1) of subdivision (a) of Section 10005, where there has been a history of domestic violence between the parties or where a protective order as defined in Section 6218 is in effect, at the request of the party alleging domestic violence in a written declaration under penalty of perjury or protected by the order, the family law facilitator shall meet with the parties separately and at separate times.
(b) Any intake form that the office of the family law facilitator requires the parties to complete before the commencement of mediation shall state that, if a party alleging domestic violence in a written declaration under penalty of perjury or a party protected by a protective order so requests, the mediator will meet with the parties separately and at separate times.[64]

10013. The family law facilitator shall not represent any party. No attorney-client relationship is created between a party and the family law facilitator as a result of any information or services provided to the party by the family law facilitator. The family law facilitator shall give conspicuous notice that no attorney-client relationship exists between the facilitator, its staff, and the family law litigant. The notice shall include the advice that the absence of an attorney-client relationship means that communications between the party and the family law facilitator are not privileged and that the family law facilitator may provide services to the other party.[75]

10014. A person employed by, or directly supervised by, the family law facilitator shall not make any public comment about a pending or impending proceeding in the court as provided by paragraph (9) of subdivision (B) of Canon 3 of the Code of Judicial Ethics. All persons employed by or directly supervised by the family law facilitator shall be provided a copy of paragraph (9) of subdivision (B) of Canon 3 of the Code of Judicial Ethics, and shall be required to sign an acknowledgment that the person is aware of its provisions.

10015. The Judicial Council shall create any necessary forms to advise the parties of the types of services provided, that there is no attorney-client relationship, that the family law facilitator is not responsible for the outcome of any case, that the family law facilitator does not represent any party and will not appear in court on the party's behalf, and that the other party may also be receiving information and services from the family law facilitator.[75]

DIVISION 17: SUPPORT SERVICES

ADDED BY STATS. 1999, CH. 478, SEC. 1.
SECTION 17000-17804

Chapter 1: Department of Child Support Services

Article 1: General

17000. The definitions contained in this section, and definitions applicable to Division 9 (commencing with Section 3500), shall govern the construction of this division, unless the context requires otherwise.

(a) "Child support debt" means the amount of money owed as child support pursuant to a court order.

(b) "Child support order" means a court order for the payment of a set or determinable amount of support by a parent or a court order requiring a parent to provide for health insurance coverage. "Child support order" includes any court order for spousal support or for medical support to the extent these obligations are to be enforced by a single state agency for child support under Title IV-D.

(c) "Court" means any superior court of this state and any court or tribunal of another state that has jurisdiction to determine the liability of persons for the support of another person.

(d) "Court order" means a judgment, decree, or order of any court of this state that orders the payment of a set or determinable amount of support by a parent. It does not include any order or decree of any proceeding in which a court did not order support.

(e) "Department" means the Department of Child Support Services.

(f) "Dependent child" means any of the following:

(1) Any person under 18 years of age who is not emancipated, self-supporting, married, or a member of the Armed Forces of the United States.

(2) Any unmarried person who is at least 18 years of age but who has not reached 19 years of age, is not emancipated, and is a student regularly attending high school or a program of vocational or technical training designed to train that person for gainful employment.

(g) "Director" means the Director of Child Support Services or an authorized representative.

(h) "Local child support agency" means the county department of child support services created pursuant to this chapter and with which the department has entered into a cooperative agreement, to secure child and spousal support, medical support, and determine paternity. Local child support agency includes county programs in multiple counties that have been consolidated into a single agency pursuant to subdivision (a) of Section 17304.

(i) "Parent" means the natural or adoptive father or mother of a dependent child, and includes any person who has an enforceable obligation to support a dependent child.

(j) "Public assistance" means any amount paid under the California Work Opportunity and Responsibility to Kids Act (Chapter 2 (commencing with Section 11200) of Part 3 of Division 9 of the Welfare and Institutions Code), or any Medi-Cal benefit, for the benefit of any dependent child or the caretaker of a child.

(k) "Public assistance debt" means any amount paid under the California Work Opportunity and Responsibility to Kids Act, contained in Chapter 2 (commencing with Section 11200) of Part 3 of Division 9 of the Welfare and Institutions Code, for the benefit of a dependent child or the caretaker of a child for whom the department is authorized to seek recoupment under this division, subject to applicable federal law.

(l) "Title IV-D" or "IV-D" means Part D of Title IV of the federal Social Security Act (42 U.S.C. Sec. 651 et seq.).

Article 2: Organization

17200. The Department of Child Support Services is hereby created within the California Health and Human Services Agency. The department shall administer all services and perform all functions necessary to establish, collect, and distribute child support.

17202. (a) The department is hereby designated the single organizational unit whose duty it shall be to administer the Title IV-D state plan for securing child and spousal support, medical support, and determining paternity. State plan functions shall be performed by other agencies as required by law, by delegation of the department, or by cooperative agreements.

(b) The department shall appoint the local child support agency, as defined in Section 17304, or any other entity receiving federal tax information in performance of its child support duties as its designee for purposes of paragraph (26) of subdivision (b) of Section 11105 of the Penal Code.

(c) For purposes of this section, "federal tax information" is as defined in Section 1044 of the Government Code.[365]

17204. The department consists of the director and such division or other administrative units as the director may find necessary.

17206. The department shall ensure that there is an adequate organizational structure and sufficient staff to perform functions delegated to any governmental unit relating to Part D (commencing with Section 651) of Subchapter 4 of Chapter 7 of Title 42 of the United States Code, including a sufficient number of attorneys to ensure that all requirements of due process are satisfied in the establishment and enforcement of child support orders.

17208. (a) The department shall reduce the cost of, and increase the speed and efficiency of, child support enforcement operations. It is the intent of the Legislature to operate the child support enforcement program through local child support agencies without a net increase in state General Fund or county general fund costs, considering all increases to the General Fund as a result of increased collections and welfare recoupment.

(b) The department shall maximize the use of federal funds available for the costs of administering a child support services department, and to the maximum extent feasible, obtain funds from federal financial incentives for the efficient collection of child support, to defray the remaining costs of administration of the department consistent with effective and efficient support enforcement.

(c) Effective October 1, 2019, the Department of Child Support Services shall impose an administrative service fee in the amount of thirty-five dollars ($35) on a never-assisted custodial party receiving services from the California child support program for order establishment, enforcement, and collection services provided. The annual amount of child support payments collected on behalf of the custodial party must be five hundred fifty dollars ($550) or more before an administrative service fee is imposed pursuant to this subdivision. The fee shall be deducted from the custodial party's collection payment at the time the collection payments for that year have reached levels specified by the department.[409]

17210. The department shall ensure that the local child support agency offices and services are reasonably accessible throughout the counties, and shall establish systems for informing the public, including custodial and noncustodial parents of dependent children, of its services and operations.

17211. The department shall administer the Child Support Assurance Demonstration Project established by Article 5 (commencing with Section 18241) of Chapter 3.3 of Part 6 of the Welfare and Institutions Code, and the county demonstration projects to provide employment and training services to nonsupporting noncustodial parents authorized by Section 18205.5 of the Welfare and Institutions Code. However, the department may contract with the State Department of Social Services to continue development and implementation of these demonstration projects until they have been fully implemented. After the demonstration projects have been fully implemented, the department shall consult with the State Department of Social Services on the administration of the projects. The contracts for evaluation of the demonstration projects shall continue to be maintained by the State Department of Social Services. The department shall be responsible for the final evaluation of the projects.

17212. (a) It is the intent of the Legislature to protect individual rights of privacy, and to facilitate and enhance the effectiveness of the child and spousal support enforcement program, by ensuring the confidentiality of support enforcement and child abduction records, and to thereby encourage the full and frank disclosure of information relevant to all of the following:

(1) The establishment or maintenance of parent and child relationships and support obligations.

(2) The enforcement of the child support liability of absent parents.

(3) The enforcement of spousal support liability of the spouse or former spouse to the extent required by the state plan under Section 17604 and Part 6 (commencing with Section 5700.101) of Division 9.

(4) The location of absent parents.

(5) The location of parents and children abducted, concealed, or detained by them.

(b) (1) (A) Except as provided in subdivision (c), all files, applications, papers, documents, and records established or maintained by a public entity pursuant to the administration and implementation of the child and spousal support enforcement program established pursuant to Part D (commencing with Section 651) of Subchapter IV of Chapter 7 of Title 42 of the United States Code and this division, shall be confidential, and shall not be open to examination or released for disclosure for any purpose not directly connected with the administration of the child and spousal support enforcement program. A public entity shall not disclose any file, application, paper, document, or record, or the information contained therein, except as expressly authorized by this section.

(B) For purposes of this section, "public entity" does not include the court. This subparagraph is declaratory of existing law.

(2) Information shall not be released or the whereabouts of one party or the child disclosed to another party, or to the attorney of any other party, if a protective order has been issued by a court or administrative agency with respect to the party, a good cause claim under Section 11477.04 of the Welfare and Institutions Code has been approved or is pending, or the public agency responsible for establishing paternity or enforcing support has reason to believe that the release of the information may result in physical or emotional harm to the party or the child. When a local child support agency is prohibited from releasing information pursuant to this subdivision, the information shall be omitted from any pleading or document to be submitted to the court and this subdivision shall be cited in the pleading or other document as the authority for the omission. The information shall be released only upon an order of the court pursuant to paragraph (6) of subdivision (c).

(3) Notwithstanding any other law, a proof of service filed by the local child support agency shall not disclose the address where service of process was accomplished. Instead, the local child support agency shall keep the address in its own records. The proof of service shall specify that the address is on record at the local child support agency and that the address may be released only upon an order from the court pursuant to paragraph (6) of subdivision (c). The local child support agency shall, upon request by a party served, release to that person the address where service was effected.

(c) Disclosure of the information described in subdivision (b) is authorized as follows:

(1) All files, applications, papers, documents, and records as described in subdivision (b) shall be available and may be used by a public entity for all administrative, civil, or criminal investigations, actions, proceedings, or prosecutions conducted in connection with the administration of the child and spousal support enforcement program approved under Part D (commencing with Section 651) of Subchapter IV of Chapter 7 of Title 42 of the United States Code and to the county welfare department responsible for administering a program operated under a state plan pursuant to Part A, Subpart 1 or 2 of Part B, or Part E of Subchapter IV of

Chapter 7 of Title 42 of the United States Code.

(2) A document requested by a person who wrote, prepared, or furnished the document may be examined by or disclosed to that person or a designee.

(3) The payment history of an obligor pursuant to a support order may be examined by or released to the court, the obligor, or the person on whose behalf enforcement actions are being taken or that person's designee.

(4) An income and expense declaration of either parent may be released to the other parent for the purpose of establishing or modifying a support order.

(5) Public records subject to disclosure under the California Public Records Act (Division 10 (commencing with Section 7920.000) of Title 1 of the Government Code) may be released.

(6) After a noticed motion and a finding by the court, in a case in which establishment or enforcement actions are being taken, that release or disclosure to the obligor or obligee is required by due process of law, the court may order a public entity that possesses an application, paper, document, or record as described in subdivision (b) to make that item available to the obligor or obligee for examination or copying, or to disclose to the obligor or obligee the contents of that item. Article 9 (commencing with Section 1040) of Chapter 4 of Division 8 of the Evidence Code shall not be applicable to proceedings under this part. At any hearing of a motion filed pursuant to this section, the court shall inquire of the local child support agency and the parties appearing at the hearing if there is reason to believe that release of the requested information may result in physical or emotional harm to a party. If the court determines that harm may occur, the court shall issue any protective orders or injunctive orders restricting the use and disclosure of the information as are necessary to protect the individuals.

(7) To the extent not prohibited by federal law or regulation, information indicating the existence or imminent threat of a crime against a child, or location of a concealed, detained, or abducted child, or the location of the concealing, detaining, or abducting person, may be disclosed to a district attorney, an appropriate law enforcement agency, or to a state or county child protective agency, or may be used in any judicial proceedings to prosecute that crime or to protect the child.

(8) The social security number, most recent address, and the place of employment of the absent parent may be released to an authorized person as defined in Section 653(c) of Title 42 of the United States Code, only if the authorized person has filed a request for the information, and only if the information has been provided to the California Parent Locator Service by the federal Parent Locator Service pursuant to Section 653 of Title 42 of the United States Code.

(9) A parent's or relative's name, social security number, most recent address, telephone number, place of employment, or other contact information may be released to a county child welfare agency or county proba-

tion department pursuant to subdivision (c) of Section 17506.

(d) (1) "Administration and implementation of the child and spousal support enforcement program," as used in this division, means the carrying out of the state and local plans for establishing, modifying, and enforcing child support obligations, enforcing spousal support orders, and determining paternity pursuant to Part D (commencing with Section 651) of Subchapter IV of Chapter 7 of Title 42 of the United States Code and this article.

(2) For purposes of this division, "obligor" means a person owing a duty of support.

(3) As used in this division, "putative parent" shall refer to any person reasonably believed to be the parent of a child for whom the local child support agency is attempting to establish paternity or establish, modify, or enforce support pursuant to Section 17400.

(e) A person who willfully, knowingly, and intentionally violates this section is guilty of a misdemeanor.

(f) This section does not compel the disclosure of information relating to a deserting parent who is a recipient of aid under a public assistance program for which federal aid is paid to this state, if that information is required to be kept confidential by the federal law or regulations relating to the program.[509]

Article 3: Director of Child Support Services

17300. (a) With the consent of the Senate, the Governor shall appoint, to serve at the Governor's pleasure, an executive officer who shall be director of the department. In making the appointment the Governor shall consider training, demonstrated ability, experience, and leadership in organized child support enforcement administration. The director shall receive the salary provided for by Chapter 6 (commencing with Section 11550) of Part 1 of Division 3 of Title 2 of the Government Code.

(b) The Governor also may appoint, to serve at the Governor's pleasure, not to exceed two chief deputy directors of the department, and one deputy director of the department. The salaries of the chief deputy directors and the deputy director shall be fixed in accordance with law.

17302. The director shall do all of the following:

(a) Be responsible for the management of the department.

(b) Administer all federal and state laws and regulations pertaining to the administration of child support enforcement obligations.

(c) Perform all duties as may be prescribed by law, and any other administrative and executive duties imposed by law.

(d) Observe, and report to the Governor, the Legislature, and the public on, the conditions of child support enforcement activities throughout the state pursuant to subdivision (e) of Section 17602.

17303. The Legislature finds and declares all of the following:

(a) Title IV-D of the federal Social Security Act, contained in Part D (commencing with Section 651) of Subchapter 4 of Chapter 7 of Title 42 of the United States Code, requires that there be a single state agency for child support enforcement. California's child support enforcement system is extremely complex, involving numerous state and local agencies. The state's system was divided between the State Department of Social Services, the Attorney General's office, the Franchise Tax Board, the Employment Development Department, the Department of Motor Vehicles, and the 58 county district attorneys' offices.

(b) The lack of coordination and integration between state and local child support agencies has been a major impediment to getting support to the children of this state. An effective child support enforcement program must have strong leadership and effective state oversight and management to best serve the needs of the children of the state.

(c) The state would benefit by centralizing its obligation to hold counties responsible for collecting support. Oversight would be best accomplished by direct management by the state.

(d) A single state agency for child support enforcement with strong leadership and direct accountability for local child support agencies will benefit the taxpayers of the state by reducing the inefficiencies introduced by involving multiple layers of government in child support enforcement operations.

17304. To address the concerns stated by the Legislature in Section 17303, each county shall establish a new county department of child support services. Each department is also referred to in this division as the local child support agency. The local child support agency shall be separate and independent from any other county department and shall be responsible for promptly and effectively establishing, modifying, and enforcing child support obligations, including medical support, enforcing spousal support orders established by a court of competent jurisdiction, and determining paternity in the case of a child born out of wedlock. The local child support agency shall refer all cases requiring criminal enforcement services to the district attorney and the district attorney shall prosecute those cases, as appropriate. If a district attorney fails to comply with this section, the director shall notify the Attorney General and the Attorney General shall take appropriate action to secure compliance. The director shall be responsible for implementing and administering all aspects of the state plan that direct the functions to be performed by the local child support agencies relating to their Title IV-D operations. In developing the new system, all of the following shall apply:

(a) The director shall negotiate and enter into cooperative agreements with county and state agencies to carry out the requirements of the state plan and provide services relating to the establishment of paternity or the establishment, modification, or enforcement of child support obligations as required pursuant to Section 654 of Title 42 of the United States Code. The cooperative agreements shall require that the local child support agencies are reasonably accessible to the citizens of each county and are visible and accountable to the public for their activities. The director, in consultation with the impacted counties, may consolidate the local child support agencies, or any function of the agencies, in more than one county into a single local child support agency, if the director determines that the consolidation will increase the efficiency of the state Title IV-D program and each county has at least one local child support office accessible to the public.

(b) The director shall have direct oversight and supervision of the Title IV-D operations of the local child support agency, and no other local or state agency shall have any authority over the local child support agency as to any function relating to its Title IV-D operations. The local child support agency shall be responsible for the performance of child support enforcement activities required by law and regulation in a manner prescribed by the department. The administrator of the local child support agency shall be responsible for reporting to and responding to the director on all aspects of the child support program.

(c) Nothing in this section prohibits the local child support agency, with the prior approval of the director, from entering into cooperative arrangements with other county departments, as necessary to carry out the responsibilities imposed by this section pursuant to plans of cooperation submitted to the department and approved by the director. The local child support agency may not enter into a cooperative agreement or contract with any county department or independently elected official, including the office of the district attorney, to run, supervise, manage, or oversee the Title IV-D functions of the local child support agency. Until September 1, 2004, the local child support agency may enter into a cooperative agreement or contract of restricted scope and duration with a district attorney to utilize individual attorneys as necessary to carry out limited attorney services. Any cooperative agreement or contract for the attorney services shall be subject to approval by the department and contingent upon a written finding by the department that either the relatively small size of the local child support agency program, or other serious programmatic needs, arising as a result of the transition make it most efficient and cost-effective to contract for limited attorney services. The department shall ensure that any cooperative agreement or contract for attorney services provides that all attorneys be supervised by, and report directly to, the local child support agency, and comply with all state and federal child support laws and regulations. The office of the Legislative Analyst shall review and assess the efficiency and effectiveness of that cooperative agreement or contract, and shall report its findings to the Legislature by January 1, 2004. Within 60 days of receipt of a plan of cooperation or contract from the local child support agency, the department shall either approve the plan of cooperation or contract or notify the agency that the plan is denied. If an agency is notified that the plan is denied, the agency shall have the opportunity to resubmit a revised plan of cooperation or contract. If the director fails to respond in writing within 60 days of receipt, the plan shall otherwise be deemed approved. Nothing in this section shall be deemed an approval of program costs relative to the cooperative arrangements entered into by the counties with other county departments.

(d) In order to minimize the disruption of services provided and to capitalize on the expertise of employees, the director shall create a program that builds on existing staff and facilities to the fullest extent possible. All assets of the family support division in the district attorney's office shall become assets of the local child support agency.

(e) (1) (A) Except as provided in subparagraph (B), all employees and other personnel who serve the office of the district attorney and perform child support collection and enforcement activities shall become the employees and other personnel of the county child support agency at their existing or equivalent classifications, and at their existing salaries and benefits that include, but are not limited to, accrued and unused vacation, sick leave, personal leave, and health and pension plans.

(B) The Title IV-D director is entitled to become an employee of the local child support agency or may be selected as the administrator pursuant to the provisions of subdivision (f).

(2) Permanent employees of the office of the district attorney on the effective date of this chapter shall be deemed qualified, and no other qualifications shall be required for employment or retention in the county child support agency. Probationary employees on the effective date of this chapter shall retain their probationary status and rights, and shall not be deemed to have transferred, so as to require serving a new probationary period.

(3) Employment seniority of an employee of the office of the district attorney on the effective date of this chapter shall be counted toward seniority in the county child support agency and all time spent in the same, equivalent, or higher classification shall be counted toward classification seniority.

(4) An employee organization that has been recognized as the representative or exclusive representative of an established appropriate bargaining unit of employees who perform child support collection and enforcement activities shall continue to be recognized as the representative or exclusive representative of the same employees of the county.

(5) An existing memorandum of understanding or agreement between the county or the office of the district attorney and the employee organization shall remain in effect and be fully binding on the parties involved for the term of the agreement.

(6) Nothing in this section shall be construed to limit the rights of employees or employee organizations to bargain in good faith on matters of wages, hours, or other terms and conditions of employment, including the negotiation of workplace standards within the scope of bargaining as authorized by state and federal law.

(7) (A) Except as provided in subparagraph (B), a public agency shall, in implementing programs affected by the act of addition or amendment of this chapter to this code, perform program functions exclusively through the use of merit civil service employees of the public agency.

(B) Prior to transition from the district attorney to the local child support agency under Section 17305, the district attorney may continue existing contracts and their renewals, as appropriate. After the transition under Section 17305, any contracting out of program functions shall be approved by the director consistent with Section 31000 and following of the Government Code, except as otherwise provided in subdivision (c) with regard to attorney services. The director shall approve or disapprove a proposal to contract out within 60 days. Failure of the director to respond to a request to contract out within 60 days after receipt of the request shall be deemed approval, unless the director submits an extension to respond, which in no event shall be longer than 30 days.

(f) The administrator of the local child support agency shall be an employee of the county selected by the board of supervisors, or in the case of a city and county, selected by the mayor, pursuant to the qualifications established by the department. The administrator may hire staff, including attorneys, to fulfill the functions required by the agency and in conformity with any staffing requirements adopted by the department, including all those set forth in Section 17306. All staff shall be employees of the county and shall comply with all local, state, and federal child support laws, regulations, and directives.

17305. (a) In order to achieve an orderly and timely transition to the new system with minimal disruption of services, the director shall begin the transition from the office of the district attorney to the local child support agencies pursuant to Section 17304, commencing January 1, 2001. The director shall transfer the appropriate number of counties, equaling at least 50 percent of the statewide caseload into the new system by January 1, 2002. The transition shall be completed by January 1, 2003. A county that has appointed an administrator for the local child support agency and has complied with the requirements of subdivision (b) may transition prior to January 1, 2001, subject to the approval of the director. In determining the order in which counties will be transferred from the office of the district attorney to the local child support agencies, the director shall do all of the following:

(1) Consider the performance of the counties in establishing and collecting child support.

(2) Minimize the disruption of the services provided by the counties.

(3) Optimize the chances of a successful transition.

(b) In order to achieve an orderly transition with minimal disruption of services, a county shall submit a plan of transition which shall be approved by the department prior to transition.

(c) The director shall consult with the district attorney to achieve an orderly transition and to minimize the disruption of services. Each district attorney shall cooperate in the transition as requested by the director.

(d) To minimize any disruption of services provided under the child support enforcement program during the transition, each district attorney shall:

(1) Continue to be designated the single organizational unit whose duty it shall be to administer the Title IV-D state plan for securing child and spousal support, medical support, and determining paternity for that county until such time as the county

is notified by the director that the county has been transferred pursuant to subdivision (a) or sooner under Section 17602.

(2) At a minimum, maintain all levels of funding, staffing, and services as of January 1, 1999, to administer the Title IV-D state plan for securing child and spousal support, medical support, and determining paternity. If the director determines that a district attorney has lowered the funding, staffing, or services of the child support enforcement program, the director may withhold part or all state and federal funds, including incentive funds, from the district attorney. Before the director withholds part of or all state and federal funds, including incentive funds, the district attorney shall have the opportunity to demonstrate good cause for any reductions in funding, staffing, or services. Good cause exceptions for reductions shall include, but not be limited to, natural staff attrition and caseload changes.

17306. (a) The Department of Child Support Services shall develop uniform forms, policies, and procedures to be employed statewide by all local child support agencies. Pursuant to this subdivision, the department shall:

(1) Adopt uniform procedures and forms.

(2) Establish standard caseload-to-staffing ratios, adjusted as appropriate to meet the varying needs of local programs.

(3) Institute a consistent statewide policy on the appropriateness of closing cases to ensure that, without relying solely on federal minimum requirements, all cases are fully and pragmatically pursued for collections prior to closing.

(4) Evaluate the best practices for the establishment, enforcement, and collection of child support, for the purpose of determining which practices should be implemented statewide in an effort to improve performance by local child support agencies. In evaluating the best practices, the director shall review existing practices in better performing counties within California, as well as practices implemented by other state Title IV-D programs nationwide.

(5) Evaluate the best practices for the management of effective child support enforcement operations for the purpose of determining what management structure should be implemented statewide in an effort to improve the establishment, enforcement, and collection of child support by local child support agencies, including an examination of the need for attorneys in management level positions. In evaluating the best practices, the director shall review existing practices in better performing counties within California, as well as practices implemented by other state Title IV-D programs nationwide.

(6) Set priorities for the use of specific enforcement mechanisms for use by local child support agencies. As part of establishing these priorities, the director shall set forth caseload processing priorities to target enforcement efforts and services in a way that will maximize collections.

(7) Develop uniform training protocols, require periodic training of all child support staff, and conduct training sessions as appropriate.

(8) Review and approve annual budgets submitted by the local child support agencies to ensure each local child support agency operates an effective and efficient program that complies with all federal and state laws, regulations, and directives, including the directive to hire sufficient staff.

(b) The director shall submit any forms intended for use in court proceedings to the Judicial Council for approval at least six months prior to the implementation of the use of the forms.

(c) In adopting the forms, policies, and procedures, the director shall consult with appropriate organizations representing stakeholders in California, such as the California State Association of Counties, the Child Support Directors Association of California, labor organizations, parent advocates, child support commissioners, family law facilitators, and the appropriate committees of the Legislature.[410]

17306.1. (a) Commencing with the 2019–20 fiscal year, the department shall implement a revised local child support agency funding methodology that was developed in consultation with the California Child Support Directors Association. The methodology shall consist of both of the following components in the 2019–20 fiscal year:

(1) Casework operations, which consists of a statewide standard case-to-staff ratio, the respective labor costs for each local child support agency, and an operating expense and equipment complement based on a percentage of staffing costs. The department shall propose a specific ratio informed by the working sessions described in subdivision (c) and as part of the required update to the Legislature required by subdivision (d).

(2) Call center operations, which consists of a standard statewide ratio of calls to call center agents, the respective labor costs for each local child support agency, and an operating expense and equipment complement based on a percentage of staffing costs.

(b) Any increased state costs that result, either directly or indirectly, from implementation of the funding methodology described in subdivision (a) shall be implemented to the extent of an appropriation of funds in the annual Budget Act.

(c) (1) The Department of Child Support Services shall convene a series of stakeholder working sessions to develop the ongoing methodology, which shall take effect in the 2020–21 fiscal year. There shall be at least three working sessions during the summer and fall of 2019, beginning as early as possible after July 1, 2019.

(2) The working sessions shall include, but not be limited to, representatives from the Child Support Directors Association, the Legislative Analyst's Office, the Department of Finance, consultants from the Assembly and Senate Health and Human Services budget subcommittees, any other interested Legislative consultants, antipoverty advocates, advocacy organizations representing custodial and noncustodial parents, including fathers' rights advocates, impacted families, and any other interested advocates or stakeholders for the child support program.

(3) The working sessions shall do all

of the following:

(A) Further refine or change the local child support agency funding methodology defined in subdivision (a), including accounting for performance incentives to be provided in future years.

(B) Discuss additional strategies that might improve the customer service, pragmatic collectability, and cost efficiency of the child support program and assess fiscal impact to operations and collections.

(C) Consider any policy changes that may affect the workload and associated funding needs of the local child support agencies and assess fiscal impact to operations and collections.

(D) Consider the ways that child support collection improves outcomes for children, impacts the well-being of children in relationship to their parents who are ordered to pay support, particularly their fathers, and impacts the racial wealth gap and further analyze the impact that child support has on parents ordered to pay support who do not have the capacity to pay.

(d) The department shall provide a written update describing recommended changes to the funding methodology described in subdivision (a) to the relevant policy committees and budget subcommittee of the Legislature on February 1, 2020. The written update shall include, but not be limited to, a description of the programmatic and policy changes discussed in the working sessions, the feasibility of implementing the discussed programmatic and policy changes, the impact that the discussed programmatic and policy changes would have on operations, collections, and families served, and additional required statutory changes.[479]

17307. (a) The Legislature hereby finds and declares that the Department of Child Support Services has the authority and discretion to prevent, correct, or remedy the effects of changes in the timing of the receipt of child support payments resulting solely from the initial implementation of the federally required State Disbursement Unit. This authority shall not be construed to supplant existing statutory appropriation and technology project approval processes, limits, and requirements.

(b) The Legislature hereby finds and declares that this section is declaratory of existing law.[126]

17308. The director shall assume responsibility for implementing and managing all aspects of a single statewide automated child support system that will comply with state and federal requirements. The director may delegate responsibility to, or enter into an agreement with, any agency or entity that it deems necessary to satisfy this requirement.

17309. Effective October 1, 1998, the state shall operate a State Disbursement Unit as required by federal law (42 U.S.C. Secs. 654 (27), 654a(g), and 654b).

17309.5. (a) An employer who is required to withhold and, by electronic fund transfer, pay tax pursuant to Section 19011 of the Revenue and Taxation Code or Section 13021 of the Unemployment Insurance Code, shall make child support payments to the

State Disbursement Unit by electronic fund transfer. All child support payments required to be made to the State Disbursement Unit shall be remitted to the State Disbursement Unit by electronic fund transfer pursuant to Division 11 (commencing with Section 11101) of the Commercial Code.

(b) An employer not required to make payment to the State Disbursement Unit pursuant to paragraph (a), may elect to make payment by electronic fund transfer under the following conditions:

(1) The election shall be made in a form, and shall contain information, as prescribed by the Director of the Department of Child Support Services, and shall be subject to approval of the department.

(2) The election may be terminated upon written request to the Department of Child Support Services.

(c) For the purposes of this section:

(1) "Electronic fund transfer" means any transfer of funds, other than a transaction originated by check, draft, or similar paper instrument, that is initiated through an electronic terminal, telephonic instrument, or computer or magnetic tape, so as to order, instruct, or authorize a financial institution to debit or credit an account. Electronic fund transfers shall be accomplished by an automated clearinghouse debit, an automated clearinghouse credit, or by Federal Reserve Wire Transfer (Fedwire).

(2) "Automated clearinghouse" means any federal reserve bank, or an organization established in agreement with the National Automated Clearinghouse Association, that operates as a clearinghouse for transmitting or receiving entries between banks or bank accounts and that authorizes an electronic transfer of funds between these banks or bank accounts.

(3) "Automated clearinghouse debit" means a transaction in which the state, through its designated depository bank, originates an automated clearinghouse transaction debiting the person's bank account and crediting the state's bank account for the amount of tax. Banking costs incurred for the automated clearinghouse debit transaction shall be paid by the state.

(4) "Automated clearinghouse credit" means an automated clearinghouse transaction in which the person, through their own bank, originates an entry crediting the state's bank account and debiting the person's own bank account. Banking costs incurred for the automated clearinghouse credit transaction charged to the state shall be paid by the person originating the credit.

(5) "Fedwire transfer" means a transaction originated by a person and utilizing the national electronic payment system to transfer funds through the federal reserve banks, when that person debits their own bank account and credits the state's bank account. Electronic fund transfers pursuant to this section may be made by Fedwire only if payment cannot, for good cause, be made according to subdivision (a), and the use of Fedwire is preapproved by the department. Banking costs incurred for the Fedwire transaction charged to the person and to the state shall be paid by the person originating the transaction.

17310. (a) The director shall formulate, adopt, amend, or repeal regulations and general policies affecting the purposes, responsibilities, and jurisdiction of the department that are consistent with law and necessary for the administration of the state plan for securing child support and enforcing spousal support orders and determining paternity.

(b) Notwithstanding any other provision of law, all regulations, including, but not limited to, regulations of the State Department of Social Services and the State Department of Health Services, relating to child support enforcement shall remain in effect and shall be fully enforceable by the department. The department may readopt, amend, or repeal the regulations in accordance with Section 17312 as necessary and appropriate.

17311. (a) The Child Support Payment Trust Fund is hereby created in the State Treasury. The department shall administer the fund.

(b) (1) The state may deposit child support payments received by the State Disbursement Unit, including those amounts that result in overpayment of child support, into the Child Support Payment Trust Fund, for the purpose of processing and providing child support payments. Notwithstanding Section 13340 of the Government Code, the fund is continuously appropriated for the purposes of disbursing child support payments from the State Disbursement Unit.

(2) The state share of the interest and other earnings that accrue on the fund shall be available to the department and used to offset the following General Fund costs in this order:

(A) Any transfers made to the Child Support Payment Trust Fund from the General Fund.

(B) The cost of administering the State Disbursement Unit, subject to appropriation by the Legislature.

(C) Other child support program activities, subject to appropriation by the Legislature.

(c) The department may establish and administer a revolving account in the Child Support Payment Trust Fund in an amount not to exceed six hundred million dollars ($600,000,000) to ensure the timely disbursement of child support. This amount may be adjusted by the Director of Finance upon notification of the Legislature as required, to meet payment timeframes required under federal law.

(d) It is the intent of the Legislature to provide transfers from the General Fund to provide startup funds for the Child Support Payment Trust Fund so that, together with the balances transferred pursuant to Section 17311.7, the Child Support Payment Trust Fund will have sufficient cash on hand to make all child support payments within the required timeframes.

(e) Notwithstanding any other law, an ongoing loan shall be made available from the General Fund, from funds not otherwise appropriated, to the Child Support Payment Trust Fund, not to exceed one hundred fifty million dollars ($150,000,000) to ensure the timely disbursement of child support payments when funds have not been recorded to the Child Support Payment Trust Fund or due to other fund liabilities, including, but not limited to, Internal Revenue Service negative adjustments to tax intercept payments. Whenever an adjustment of this amount is required to meet payment timeframes under federal law,

the amount shall be adjusted after approval of the Director of Finance. In conjunction with the Department of Finance and the Controller's office, the department shall establish repayment procedures to ensure the outstanding loan balance does not exceed the average daily cash needs. The ongoing evaluation of the fund as detailed in these procedures shall occur no less frequently than monthly.
(f) Notwithstanding any other law, the Controller may use the moneys in the Child Support Payment Trust Fund for loans to the General Fund as provided in Sections 16310 and 16381 of the Government Code. However, interest shall be paid on all moneys loaned to the General Fund from the Child Support Payment Trust Fund. Interest payable shall be computed at a rate determined by the Pooled Money Investment Board to be the current earning rate of the fund from which loaned. This subdivision does not authorize any transfer that will interfere with the carrying out of the object for which the Child Support Payment Trust Fund was created.[190]

17311.5. (a) The department may enter into a trust agreement with a trustee or fiscal intermediary to receive or disburse child support collections. The trust agreement may contain provisions the department deems reasonable and proper for the security of the child support payments. Any trust accounts created by the trust agreements may be held outside the State Treasury.
(b) For the 2012–13 fiscal year only, trust account moneys may be invested in any of the types of securities listed in Section 16430 of the Government Code or alternatives offering comparable security, including, but not limited to, mutual funds and money market funds. This subdivision does not authorize investments or transfers that would interfere with carrying out the objective for which the Child Support Payment Trust Fund was created.[249]

17311.7. (a) Any payment required to be made to a family through the State Disbursement Unit shall be made directly to the obligee parent in the child support order requiring the payment, the conservator or guardian of the obligee parent, a special needs trust for the benefit of the obligee parent, the guardian of the person and the estate of the child subject to the order, any caregiver relative having custody or responsibility for the child, pursuant to a written record, or an alternate caregiver to whom the obligee under the child support order directs, in a written record, that payments be made.
(b) For purposes of this section, "alternate caregiver" means a nonrelative caregiver who is designated in writing by the obligee parent to take care of the child for a limited time.[379]

17312. (a) The department shall adopt regulations, orders, or standards of general application to implement, interpret, or make specific the law enforced by the department. Regulations, orders, and standards shall be adopted, amended, or repealed by the director only in accordance with Chapter 3.5 (commencing with Section 11340) of Part 1 of Division 3 of Title 2 of the Government Code.
(b) In adopting regulations, the department shall strive for clarity of language that may be readily understood

by those administering public social services or subject to those regulations.

(c) The rules of the department need not specify or include the detail of forms, reports, or records, but shall include the essential authority by which any person, agency, organization, association, or institution subject to the supervision or investigation of the department is required to use, submit, or maintain the forms, reports, or records.

(d) The department's regulations and other materials shall be made available pursuant to the California Code of Regulations and in the same manner as are materials of the State Department of Social Services under the provisions of Section 205.70 of Title 45 of the Code of Federal Regulations.

17314. (a) Subject to the State Civil Service Act (Part 2 (commencing with Section 18500) of Division 5 of Title 2 of the Government Code), the director shall appoint any assistants and other employees that are necessary for the administration of the affairs of the department and shall prescribe their duties and, subject to the approval of the Department of Finance, fix their salaries.

(b) As the director adopts a plan for a local child support agency to assume responsibility for child support enforcement activities in any county served by a district attorney pursuant to Section 17304, the director shall hire a sufficient number of regional state administrators to oversee the local child support agencies to ensure compliance with all state and federal laws and regulations. The regions shall be divided based on the total caseload of each local child support agency. The responsibilities of the regional state administrators shall include all of the following:

(1) Conducting regular and comprehensive site visits to the local child support agencies assigned to their region and preparing quarterly reports to be submitted to the department. The local child support agencies shall fully cooperate with all reasonable requests made by the regional state administrators, including providing all requested data on the local child support agency's program.

(2) Notifying a local child support agency of any potential or actual noncompliance with any state or federal law or regulation by the agency and working with the local child support agency to develop an immediate plan to ensure compliance.

(3) Participating in program monitoring teams as set forth in subdivision (c) of Section 17602.

(4) Participating in meetings with all regional state administrators and the director on at least a monthly basis to promote statewide uniformity as to the functions and structure of the local child support agencies. The regional state administrators may recommend proposals for approval and adoption by the director to achieve this goal.

(5) Responding to requests for management or technical assistance regarding program operations by local child support agencies.

17316. No person, while holding the office of director, shall be a trustee, manager, director, or other officer or employee of any agency performing any function supervised by the department or any institution that is subject to examination, inspection, or supervision by the department.

17318. Except as otherwise expressly provided, Part 1 (commencing with Section 11000) of Division 3 of Title 2 of the Government Code, as it may be added to or amended from time to time, shall apply to the conduct of the department.

17320. The department shall coordinate with the State Department of Social Services to avoid the imposition of any federal penalties that cause a reduction in the state's Temporary Assistance to Needy Families grant, payable pursuant to Section 603(a)(1) of Title 42 of the United States Code.

17325. (a) (1) Notwithstanding any other law, if child support payments are directly deposited to an account of the recipient's choice, as authorized under the federal Electronic Fund Transfer Act (EFTA) (15 U.S.C. Sec. 1693 et seq.), the payments may only be deposited to an account that meets the requirements of a qualifying account, as defined in paragraph (2), for deposit of child support payments.

(2) For purposes of this section, a "qualifying account" is one of the following:

(A) A demand deposit or savings account at an insured depository financial institution that is offered directly by the insured depository financial institution on its internet website or through its branches and that is in the name of the person entitled to the receipt of child support payments.

(B) A prepaid account, or a demand deposit or savings account offered by, or through, an entity other than an insured depository financial institution, that meets all of the following:

(i) The account is held at an insured depository financial institution.

(ii) The account is set up to meet the requirements for direct or passthrough deposit or share insurance payable to the person entitled to the receipt of child support payments by the Federal Deposit Insurance Corporation in accordance with Part 330 of Title 12 of the Code of Federal Regulations, or the National Credit Union Share Insurance Fund in accordance with Part 745 of Title 12 of the Code of Federal Regulations.

(iii) The account is not attached to a credit or overdraft feature that is automatically repaid from the account unless the credit or overdraft feature has no fee, charge, or cost, whether direct, required, voluntary, or involuntary, or the credit or overdraft feature complies with the requirements for credit offered in connection with a prepaid account under the federal Truth in Lending Act (15 U.S.C. Sec. 1601 et seq.) and its implementing regulations.

(iv) The account complies with all of the requirements, and provides the holder of the account with all of the consumer protections, that apply to an account under the rules implementing the EFTA.

(3) A person or entity that is not an insured depository financial institution that offers, maintains, or manages an account that does not comply with paragraph (2) shall not solicit, accept, or facilitate the direct deposit of child support payments to the account.

(b) For purposes of this section, the department shall not be held liable for authorizing a direct deposit of child support payments into an account designated by the recipient that does not comply with paragraph (2) of subdivision (a). The department has no obligation to determine whether an account at the insured depository financial institution of the recipient's choice is a qualifying account as described in subdivision (a).

(c) For the purposes of this section, the following definitions shall apply:

(1) "Insured depository financial institution" means a state or national bank, a state or federal savings and loan association, a mutual savings bank, or a state or federal credit union that holds deposits insured by the Federal Deposit Insurance Corporation or the National Credit Union Administration.

(2) "Prepaid account" has the same meaning as that term is defined in regulations under the EFTA.[496]

Article 4: Statewide Registry for Child Support

17390. (a) The Legislature finds and declares that there is no single statewide database containing statistical data regarding child support orders.

(b) The California Child Support Enforcement System or its replacement may be utilized to provide a single statewide registry of all child support orders in California, including orders for cases under Title IV-D of the Social Security Act and all cases with child support orders.[357]

17391. (a) The department shall develop an implementation plan for the Statewide Child Support Registry. The Statewide Child Support Registry shall be operated by the agency responsible for operation of the California Child Support Enforcement System or its replacement. The Statewide Child Support Registry shall include storage and data retrieval of the data elements specified in Section 17392 for all California child support orders. The Statewide Child Support Registry will operate to ensure that all data in the Statewide Child Support Registry can be accessed and integrated for statistical analysis and reporting purposes with all child support order data contained in the California Child Support Enforcement System.

(b) Each clerk of the court shall provide the information specified in Section 17392 within 20 days to the department or the Statewide Child Support Registry from each new or modified child support order, including child support arrearage orders.

(c) The department shall maintain a system for compiling the child support data received from the clerks of the court, ensure that all child support data received from the clerks of the court are entered into the Statewide Child Support Registry within five business days of receipt in the Statewide Child Support Registry, and ensure that the Statewide Child Support Registry is fully implemented statewide.

(d) The department shall provide aggregate data on a periodic basis on the data maintained by the Statewide Child Support Registry to the Judicial Council, the appropriate agencies of the executive branch, and the Legislature for statistical analysis and review. The data shall not include individual identifying information for specific cases.

(e) Any information maintained by the Statewide Child Support Registry received from clerks of the court shall be provided to local child support agencies, the courts, and others as provided by law.[357]

17392. (a) The Judicial Council shall develop any forms that may be necessary to implement the Statewide Child Support Registry. The forms may be in electronic form or in hardcopy, as appropriate. The forms shall be developed so as not to delay implementation, and shall be available no later than 30 days prior to the implementation, of the Statewide Child Support Registry.
(b) The information transmitted from the clerks of the court to the Statewide Child Support Registry shall include all of the following:
(1) Any information required under federal law.
(2) Any other information the department and the Judicial Council find appropriate.[357]

17393. The Judicial Council shall develop the forms necessary to implement this article.[357]

Chapter 2: Child Support Enforcement

Article 1: Support Obligations

17400. (a) (1) Each county shall maintain a local child support agency, as specified in Section 17304, that shall have the responsibility for promptly and effectively establishing, modifying, and enforcing child support obligations, including medical support, enforcing spousal support orders established by a court of competent jurisdiction, and determining paternity in the case of a child born out of wedlock. The local child support agency shall take appropriate action, including criminal action in cooperation with the district attorneys, to establish, modify, and enforce child support and, if appropriate, enforce spousal support orders if the child is receiving public assistance, including Medi-Cal, and, if requested, shall take the same actions on behalf of a child who is not receiving public assistance, including Medi-Cal.
(2) (A) Provided that no reduction in aid or payment to a custodial parent would result, the local child support agency shall cease enforcement of child support arrearages assigned to the state and other fees and costs owed to the state that the department or the local child support agency has determined to be uncollectible. If enforcement is ceased pursuant to this paragraph, cases shall be closed to the maximum extent permitted under Section 303.11 of Title 45 of the Code of Federal Regulations, as adopted under Section 118203 of Title 22 of the California Code of Regulations.
(B) In determining the meaning of uncollectible for purposes of arrearages assigned to the state and other fees and costs owed to the state, the department and the local child support agency shall consider, but not be limited to, the following factors:
(i) Income and assets available to pay the arrearage or other fees and costs.
(ii) Source of income.
(iii) Age of the arrearage or other fees and costs.
(iv) The number of support orders.

(v) Employment history.

(vi) Payment history.

(vii) Incarceration history.

(viii) Whether the order was based on imputed income.

(ix) Other readily ascertainable debts.

(C) Notwithstanding subparagraph (B), the department and a local child support agency shall deem an arrearage assigned to the state or fees and costs owed to the state as uncollectible if the noncustodial parent's sole income is from any of the following:

(i) Supplemental Security Income/State Supplementary Program for the Aged, Blind, and Disabled (SSI/SSP) benefits.

(ii) A combination of SSI/SSP benefits and Social Security Disability Insurance (SSDI) benefits.

(iii) Cash Assistance Program for Aged, Blind, and Disabled Legal Immigrants (CAPI) benefits.

(iv) Veterans Administration Disability Compensation Benefits in an amount equal to or less than the amount the noncustodial arent would receive in SSI/SSP benefits.

(D) Notwithstanding the Administrative Procedure Act (Chapter 3.5 (commencing with Section 11340) of Part 1 of Division 3 of Title 2 of the Government Code), the department may implement and administer this subdivision through a child support services letter or similar instruction until regulations are adopted. Thereafter, the department shall adopt regulations to implement this subdivision by July 1, 2024.

(b) (1) Notwithstanding Sections 25203 and 26529 of the Government Code, attorneys employed within the local child support agency may direct, control, and prosecute civil actions and proceedings in the name of the county in support of child support activities of the Department of Child Support Services and the local child support agency.

(2) Notwithstanding any other law, and except for pleadings or documents required to be signed under penalty of perjury, a local child support agency may substitute original signatures of the agent of the local child support agency with any form of electronic signatures, including, but not limited to, typed, digital, or facsimile images of signatures, digital signatures, or other computer-generated signatures, on pleadings filed for the purpose of establishing, modifying, or enforcing paternity, child support, or medical support. A substituted signature used by a local child support agency shall have the same effect as an original signature, including, but not limited to, the requirements of Section 128.7 of the Code of Civil Procedure.

(3) Notwithstanding any other law, effective July 1, 2016, a local child support agency may electronically file pleadings signed by an agent of the local child support agency under penalty of perjury. An original signed pleading shall be executed prior to, or on the same day as, the day of electronic filing. Original signed pleadings shall be maintained by the local child support agency for the period of time prescribed by subdivision (a) of Section 68152 of the Government Code. A local child support agency may maintain the original signed pleading by way of an electronic copy in the Statewide Automated Child

Support System. The Judicial Council, by July 1, 2016, shall develop rules to implement this subdivision.

(4) (A) Notwithstanding any other law, a local child support agency may substitute any original signatures, including, but not limited to, signatures of agents of the local child support agencies, support obligors, support obligees, other parents, witnesses, and the attorneys for the parties to the action, with a printed copy or electronic image of an electronic signature obtained in compliance with the rules of court adopted pursuant to paragraph (2) of subdivision (e) of Section 1010.6 of the Code of Civil Procedure, on pleadings or documents filed for the purpose of establishing, modifying, or enforcing paternity, child support, or medical support. If the pleading or document is signed under the penalty of perjury or the signature does not belong to an agent of the local child support agency, the local child support agency represents, by the act of filing, that the declarant electronically signed the pleading or document before, or on the same day as, the date of filing.

(B) The local child support agency shall maintain the electronic form of the pleading or document bearing the original electronic signature for the period of time prescribed by subdivision (a) of Section 68152 of the Government Code, and shall make it available for review upon the request of the court or any party to the action or proceeding in which it is filed. Printed copies or electronic images of electronic signatures used by a local child support agency in this manner shall have the same effect as an original signature, including, but not limited to, the requirements of Section 128.7 of the Code of Civil Procedure.

(c) Actions brought by the local child support agency to establish paternity or child support or to enforce child support obligations shall be completed within the time limits set forth by federal law. The local child support agency's responsibility applies to spousal support only if the spousal support obligation has been reduced to an order of a court of competent jurisdiction. In any action brought for modification or revocation of an order that is being enforced under Title IV-D of the Social Security Act (42 U.S.C. Sec. 651 et seq.), the effective date of the modification or revocation shall be as prescribed by federal law (42 U.S.C. Sec. 666(a)(9)), or any subsequent date.

(d) (1) The Judicial Council, in consultation with the department, the Senate Committee on Judiciary, the Assembly Committee on Judiciary, and a legal services organization providing representation on child support matters, shall develop simplified summons, complaint, and answer forms for any action for support brought pursuant to this section or Section 17404. The Judicial Council may combine the summons and complaint in a single form.

(2) The simplified complaint form shall provide notice of the amount of child support that is sought pursuant to the guidelines set forth in Article 2 (commencing with Section 4050) of Chapter 2 of Part 2 of Division 9 based upon the income or income history of the support obligor as known to the local child support

agency. If the support obligor's income or income history is unknown to the local child support agency, the complaint shall inform the support obligor that income shall be presumed to be the amount of the minimum wage, at 40 hours per week, established by the Industrial Welfare Commission pursuant to Section 1182.11 of the Labor Code unless information concerning the support obligor's income is provided to the court. The complaint form shall be accompanied by a proposed judgment. The complaint form shall include a notice to the support obligor that the proposed judgment will become effective if the obligor fails to file an answer with the court within 30 days of service. Except as provided in paragraph (2) of subdivision (a) of Section 17402, if the proposed judgment is entered by the court, the support order in the proposed judgment shall be effective as of the first day of the month following the filing of the complaint.

(3) (A) The simplified answer form shall be written in simple English and shall permit a defendant to answer and raise defenses by checking applicable boxes. The answer form shall include instructions for completion of the form and instructions for proper filing of the answer.

(B) The answer form shall be accompanied by a blank income and expense declaration or simplified financial statement and instructions on how to complete the financial forms. The answer form shall direct the defendant to file the completed income and expense declaration or simplified financial statement with the answer, but shall state that the answer will be accepted by a court without the income and expense declaration or simplified financial statement.

(C) The clerk of the court shall accept and file answers, income and expense declarations, and simplified financial statements that are completed by hand provided they are legible.

(4) (A) The simplified complaint form prepared pursuant to this subdivision shall be used by the local child support agency or the Attorney General in all cases brought under this section or Section 17404.

(B) The simplified answer form prepared pursuant to this subdivision shall be served on all defendants with the simplified complaint. Failure to serve the simplified answer form on all defendants shall not invalidate any judgment obtained. However, failure to serve the answer form may be used as evidence in any proceeding under Section 17432 of this code or Section 473 of the Code of Civil Procedure.

(C) The Judicial Council shall add language to the governmental summons, for use by the local child support agency with the governmental complaint to establish parental relationship and child support, informing defendants that a blank answer form should have been received with the summons and additional copies may be obtained from either the local child support agency or the superior court clerk.

(e) In any action brought or enforcement proceedings instituted by the local child support agency pursuant to this section for payment of child or spousal support, an action to recover an arrearage in support payments may be maintained by the local child support agency at any time within the period otherwise specified for the enforcement of a support judgment, notwithstanding the fact that the child has attained the age of majority.

(f) The county shall undertake an outreach program to inform the public that the services described in subdivisions (a) to (c), inclusive, are available to persons not receiving public assistance. There shall be prominently displayed in every public area of every office of the agencies established by this section a notice, in clear and simple language prescribed by the Director of Child Support Services, that the services provided in subdivisions (a) to (c), inclusive, are provided to all individuals, whether or not they are recipients of public assistance.

(g) (1) In any action to establish a child support order brought by the local child support agency in the performance of duties under this section, the local child support agency may make a motion for an order effective during the pendency of that action, for the support, maintenance, and education of the child or children that are the subject of the action. This order shall be referred to as an order for temporary support. This order has the same force and effect as a like or similar order under this code.

(2) The local child support agency shall file a motion for an order for temporary support within the following time limits:

(A) If the defendant is the mother, a presumed father under Section 7611, or any father if the child is at least six months old when the defendant files the answer, the time limit is 90 days after the defendant files an answer.

(B) In any other case in which the defendant has filed an answer prior to the birth of the child or not more than six months after the birth of the child, then the time limit is nine months after the birth of the child.

(3) If more than one child is the subject of the action, the limitation on reimbursement shall apply only as to those children whose parental relationship and age would bar recovery were a separate action brought for support of that child or those children.

(4) If the local child support agency fails to file a motion for an order for temporary support within the time limits specified in this section, the local child support agency shall be barred from obtaining a judgment of reimbursement for any support provided for that child during the period between the date the time limit expired and the date the motion was filed, or, if no motion is filed, when a final judgment is entered.

(5) Except as provided in Section 17304, this section does not prohibit the local child support agency from entering into cooperative arrangements with other county departments as necessary to carry out the responsibilities imposed by this section pursuant to plans of cooperation with the departments approved by the Department of Child Support Services.

(6) This section does not otherwise limit the ability of the local child support agency from securing and enforcing orders for support of a spouse or former spouse as authorized under any other law.

(h) As used in this article, "enforcing

obligations" includes, but is not limited to, all of the following:

(1) The use of all interception and notification systems operated by the department for the purpose of aiding in the enforcement of support obligations.

(2) The obtaining by the local child support agency of an initial order for child support that may include medical support or that is for medical support only, by civil or criminal process.

(3) The initiation of a motion or order to show cause to increase an existing child support order, and the response to a motion or order to show cause brought by an obligor parent to decrease an existing child support order, or the initiation of a motion or order to show cause to obtain an order for medical support, and the response to a motion or order to show cause brought by an obligor parent to decrease or terminate an existing medical support order, without regard to whether the child is receiving public assistance.

(4) The response to a notice of motion or order to show cause brought by an obligor parent to decrease an existing spousal support order if the child or children are residing with the obligee parent and the local child support agency is also enforcing a related child support obligation owed to the obligee parent by the same obligor.

(5) The referral of child support delinquencies to the department under subdivision (c) of Section 17500 in support of the local child support agency.

(i) As used in this section, "out of wedlock" means that the biological parents of the child were not married to each other at the time of the child's conception.

(j) (1) The local child support agency is the public agency responsible for administering wage withholding for current support for the purposes of Title IV-D of the Social Security Act (42 U.S.C. Sec. 651 et seq.).

(2) This section does not limit the authority of the local child support agency granted by other sections of this code or otherwise granted by law.

(k) In the exercise of the authority granted under this article, the local child support agency may intervene, pursuant to subdivision (b) of Section 387 of the Code of Civil Procedure, by ex parte application, in any action under this code, or other proceeding in which child support is an issue or a reduction in spousal support is sought. By notice of motion, order to show cause, or responsive pleading served upon all parties to the action, the local child support agency may request any relief that is appropriate that the local child support agency is authorized to seek.

(l) The local child support agency shall comply with all regulations and directives established by the department that set time standards for responding to requests for assistance in locating noncustodial parents, establishing paternity, establishing child support awards, and collecting child support payments.

(m) As used in this article, medical support activities that the local child support agency is authorized to perform are limited to the following:

(1) The obtaining and enforcing of court orders for health insurance coverage.

(2) Any other medical support activity mandated by federal law or regulation.

(n) (1) Notwithstanding any other law, except when a court of competent jurisdiction under Section 4251 hearing the action or proceeding under this division transfers the action or proceeding pursuant to Section 397.5 of the Code of Civil Procedure pursuant to a directly filed motion, a redirected motion, or on the court's own motion under Section 397.5 of the Code of Civil Procedure, venue for an action or proceeding under this division shall be determined as follows:

(A) Venue shall be in the superior court in the county that is currently expending public assistance.

(B) If public assistance is not currently being expended, venue shall be in the superior court in the county where the child who is entitled to current support resides or is domiciled.

(C) If current support is no longer payable through, or enforceable by, the local child support agency, venue shall be in the superior court in the county that last provided public assistance for actions to enforce arrearages assigned pursuant to Section 11477 of the Welfare and Institutions Code.

(D) If subparagraphs (A), (B), and (C) do not apply, venue shall be in the superior court in the county of residence of the support obligee.

(E) If the support obligee does not reside in California, and subparagraphs (A), (B), (C), and (D) do not apply, venue shall be in the superior court of the county of residence of the obligor.

(2) Notwithstanding paragraph (1), if the child becomes a resident of another county after an action under this part has been filed, venue may remain in the county where the action was filed until the action is completed. Nothing in this paragraph shall be construed to limit the court hearing the action or proceeding under this division from exercising its discretion under Section 397.5 of the Code of Civil Procedure.

(o) The local child support agency of one county may appear on behalf of the local child support agency of any other county in an action or proceeding under this part.

(p) This section shall become inoperative on January 1, 2026, and, as of January 1, 2027, is repealed.[601]

17400. (a) (1) Each county shall maintain a local child support agency, as specified in Section 17304, that shall have the responsibility for promptly and effectively establishing, modifying, and enforcing child support obligations, including medical support, enforcing spousal support orders established by a court of competent jurisdiction, and determining paternity in the case of a child born out of wedlock. The local child support agency shall take appropriate action, including criminal action in cooperation with the district attorneys, to establish, modify, and enforce child support and, if appropriate, enforce spousal support orders if the child is receiving public assistance, including Medi-Cal, and, if requested, shall take the same actions on behalf of a child who is not receiving public assistance, including Medi-Cal.

(2) (A) Provided that no reduction in aid or payment to a custodial parent would result, the local child support

agency shall cease enforcement of child support arrearages assigned to the state and other fees and costs owed to the state that the department or the local child support agency has determined to be uncollectible. If enforcement is ceased pursuant to this paragraph, cases shall be closed to the maximum extent permitted under Section 303.11 of Title 45 of the Code of Federal Regulations, as adopted under Section 118203 of Title 22 of the California Code of Regulations.

(B) In determining the meaning of uncollectible for purposes of arrearages assigned to the state and other fees and costs owed to the state, the department and the local child support agency shall consider, but not be limited to, the following factors:

(i) Income and assets available to pay the arrearage or other fees and costs.

(ii) Source of income.

(iii) Age of the arrearage or other fees and costs.

(iv) The number of support orders.

(v) Employment history.

(vi) Payment history.

(vii) Incarceration history.

(viii) Whether the order was based on imputed income.

(ix) Other readily ascertainable debts.

(C) Notwithstanding subparagraph (B), the department and a local child support agency shall deem an arrearage assigned to the state or fees and costs owed to the state as uncollectible if the noncustodial parent's sole income is from any of the following:

(i) Supplemental Security Income/State Supplementary Program for the Aged, Blind, and Disabled (SSI/SSP) benefits.

(ii) A combination of SSI/SSP benefits and Social Security Disability Insurance (SSDI) benefits.

(iii) Cash Assistance Program for Aged, Blind, and Disabled Legal Immigrants (CAPI) benefits.

(iv) Veterans Administration Disability Compensation Benefits in an amount equal to or less than the amount the noncustodial parent would receive in SSI/SSP benefits.

(D) Notwithstanding the Administrative Procedure Act (Chapter 3.5 (commencing with Section 11340) of Part 1 of Division 3 of Title 2 of the Government Code), the department may implement and administer this subdivision through a child support services letter or similar instruction until regulations are adopted. Thereafter, the department shall adopt regulations to implement this subdivision by July 1, 2024.

(b) (1) Notwithstanding Sections 25203 and 26529 of the Government Code, attorneys employed within the local child support agency may direct, control, and prosecute civil actions and proceedings in the name of the county in support of child support activities of the Department of Child Support Services and the local child support agency.

(2) Notwithstanding any other law, and except for pleadings or documents required to be signed under penalty of perjury, a local child support agency may substitute original signatures of the agent of the local child support agency with any form of electronic signatures, including, but

not limited to, typed, digital, or facsimile images of signatures, digital signatures, or other computer-generated signatures, on pleadings filed for the purpose of establishing, modifying, or enforcing paternity, child support, or medical support. A substituted signature used by a local child support agency shall have the same effect as an original signature, including, but not limited to, the requirements of Section 128.7 of the Code of Civil Procedure.

(3) Notwithstanding any other law, a local child support agency may electronically file pleadings signed by an agent of the local child support agency under penalty of perjury. An original signed pleading shall be executed prior to, or on the same day as, the day of electronic filing. Original signed pleadings shall be maintained by the local child support agency for the period of time prescribed by subdivision (a) of Section 68152 of the Government Code. A local child support agency may maintain the original signed pleading by way of an electronic copy in the Statewide Automated Child Support System. The Judicial Council shall develop rules to implement this subdivision.

(4) (A) Notwithstanding any other law, a local child support agency may substitute any original signatures, including, but not limited to, signatures of agents of the local child support agencies, support obligors, support obligees, other parents, witnesses, and the attorneys for the parties to the action, with a printed copy or electronic image of an electronic signature obtained in compliance with the rules of court adopted pursuant to paragraph (2) of subdivision (e) of Section 1010.6 of the Code of Civil Procedure, on pleadings or documents filed for the purpose of establishing, modifying, or enforcing paternity, child support, or medical support. If the pleading or document is signed under the penalty of perjury or the signature does not belong to an agent of the local child support agency, the local child support agency represents, by the act of filing, that the declarant electronically signed the pleading or document before, or on the same day as, the date of filing.

(B) The local child support agency shall maintain the electronic form of the pleading or document bearing the original electronic signature for the period of time prescribed by subdivision (a) of Section 68152 of the Government Code, and shall make it available for review upon the request of the court or any party to the action or proceeding in which it is filed. Printed copies or electronic images of electronic signatures used by a local child support agency in this manner shall have the same effect as an original signature, including, but not limited to, the requirements of Section 128.7 of the Code of Civil Procedure.

(c) Actions brought by the local child support agency to establish paternity or child support or to enforce child support obligations shall be completed within the time limits set forth by federal law. The local child support agency's responsibility applies to spousal support only if the spousal support obligation has been reduced to an order of a court of competent jurisdiction. In any action brought for modification or revocation of an order that is being enforced under Title IV-

D of the Social Security Act (42 U.S.C. Sec. 651 et seq.), the effective date of the modification or revocation shall be as prescribed by federal law (42 U.S.C. Sec. 666(a)(9)), or any subsequent date.

(d) (1) The Judicial Council, in consultation with the department, the Senate Committee on Judiciary, the Assembly Committee on Judiciary, and a legal services organization providing representation on child support matters, shall develop simplified summons, complaint, and answer forms for any action for support brought pursuant to this section or Section 17404. The Judicial Council may combine the summons and complaint in a single form.

(2) (A) The simplified complaint form shall provide notice of the amount of child support that is sought pursuant to the guidelines set forth in Article 2 (commencing with Section 4050) of Chapter 2 of Part 2 of Division 9 based upon one of the following methods used to determine income:

(i) If sufficient information is available to determine actual income, pursuant to subdivision (a) of Section 4058 and Section 4060, the local child support agency shall use actual income as the basis of the proposed support obligation, unless the local child support agency has sufficient information to proceed under clause (ii).

(ii) If the local child support agency has sufficient information that the earning capacity is greater than the actual income, and sufficient evidence is available to establish earning capacity pursuant to subdivision (b) of Section 4058, the local child support agency may use earning capacity as the basis of the proposed support obligation.

(iii) If the actual income of the support obligor is unknown to the local child support agency, and sufficient evidence is available to establish earning capacity pursuant to subdivision (b) of Section 4058, the local child support agency shall use earning capacity as the basis of the proposed support obligation. A complaint seeking child support under this clause shall set forth the steps first taken by the local child support agency to establish the support obligor's actual income prior to considering earning capacity, which must include, but are not limited to:

(I) Attempting to contact the support obligor through telephonic, electronic, and postal means, to the extent contact information is known or can be discovered through reasonably available means. At least three attempts to contact the support obligor shall be made.

(II) Seeking information about the support obligor's expenses and work history from the party seeking support.

(III) Searching in available databases for information relating to the support obligor's employment, income, or both.

(B) The complaint shall inform the support obligor of the basis for the proposed support amount. If the basis of the proposed support amount is the support obligor's earning capacity rather than actual income, the complaint shall inform the obligor of the factors considered by the local child support agency and used to determine the obligor's earning capacity.

(C) The complaint form shall be accompanied by a proposed judgment. The complaint form shall include a notice to the support obligor that the proposed judgment may become effective if the obligor fails to file an answer with the court within 30 days of the service. If the proposed judgment is entered by the court, the support order in the proposed judgment shall be effective as of the first day of the month following the filing of the complaint.

(D) If the proposed judgment is based on the support obligor's earning capacity pursuant to clause (ii) or (iii) of subparagraph (A), the local child support agency shall file a motion for judgment, as provided in subdivision (b) of Section 17404. The motion for judgment filed pursuant to this subparagraph shall be served on the defendant in compliance with Section 1013 of the Code of Civil Procedure or otherwise as provided by law. If the hearing on the motion for judgment under this subdivision is continued, the court may make a temporary order as authorized by Section 17404.

(E) Notwithstanding the Administrative Procedure Act (Chapter 3.5 (commencing with Section 11340) of Part 1 of Division 3 of Title 2 of the Government Code), the department may implement and administer this subdivision through a child support services letter or similar instruction until permanent regulations are adopted. The department shall adopt regulations to implement this subdivision by January 1, 2028.

(3) (A) The simplified answer form shall be written in simple English and shall permit a defendant to answer and raise defenses by checking applicable boxes. The answer form shall include instructions for completion of the form and instructions for proper filing of the answer.

(B) The answer form shall be accompanied by a blank income and expense declaration or simplified financial statement and instructions on how to complete the financial forms. The answer form shall direct the defendant to file the completed income and expense declaration or simplified financial statement with the answer, but shall state that the answer will be accepted by a court without the income and expense declaration or simplified financial statement.

(C) The clerk of the court shall accept and file answers, income and expense declarations, and simplified financial statements that are completed by hand provided they are legible.

(4) (A) The simplified complaint form prepared pursuant to this subdivision shall be used by the local child support agency or the Attorney General in all cases brought under this section or Section 17404.

(B) The simplified answer form prepared pursuant to this subdivision shall be served on all defendants with the simplified complaint. Failure to serve the simplified answer form on all defendants shall not invalidate any judgment obtained. However, failure to serve the answer form may be used as evidence in any proceeding under Section 17432 of this code or Section 473 of the Code of Civil Procedure.

(C) The Judicial Council shall add language to the governmental summons, for use by the local child support agency with the governmental complaint to establish parental relationship and child support, informing defendants that a blank answer form should have been received with the summons and additional copies may be obtained from either the local child support agency or the superior court clerk.

(e) In any action brought or enforcement proceedings instituted by the local child support agency pursuant to this section for payment of child or spousal support, an action to recover an arrearage in support payments may be maintained by the local child support agency at any time within the period otherwise specified for the enforcement of a support judgment, notwithstanding the fact that the child has attained the age of majority.

(f) The county shall undertake an outreach program to inform the public that the services described in subdivisions (a) to (c), inclusive, are available to persons not receiving public assistance. There shall be prominently displayed in every public area of every office of the agencies established by this section a notice, in clear and simple language prescribed by the Director of Child Support Services, that the services provided in subdivisions (a) to (c), inclusive, are provided to all individuals, whether or not they are recipients of public assistance.

(g) (1) In any action to establish a child support order brought by the local child support agency in the performance of duties under this section, the local child support agency may make a motion for an order effective during the pendency of that action, for the support, maintenance, and education of the child or children that are the subject of the action. This order shall be referred to as an order for temporary support. This order has the same force and effect as a like or similar order under this code.

(2) The local child support agency shall file a motion for an order for temporary support within the following time limits:

(A) If the defendant is the mother, a presumed father under Section 7611, or any father if the child is at least six months old when the defendant files the answer, the time limit is 90 days after the defendant files an answer.

(B) In any other case in which the defendant has filed an answer prior to the birth of the child or not more than six months after the birth of the child, then the time limit is nine months after the birth of the child.

(3) If more than one child is the subject of the action, the limitation on reimbursement shall apply only as to those children whose parental relationship and age would bar recovery were a separate action brought for support of that child or those children.

(4) If the local child support agency fails to file a motion for an order for temporary support within the time limits specified in this section, the local child support agency shall be barred from obtaining a judgment of reimbursement for any support provided for that child during the period between the date the time limit expired and the date the motion was filed, or, if no motion is filed, when a final judgment is entered.

(5) Except as provided in Section

17304, this section does not prohibit the local child support agency from entering into cooperative arrangements with other county departments as necessary to carry out the responsibilities imposed by this section pursuant to plans of cooperation with the departments approved by the Department of Child Support Services.

(6) This section does not otherwise limit the ability of the local child support agency from securing and enforcing orders for support of a spouse or former spouse as authorized under any other law.

(h) As used in this article, "enforcing obligations" includes, but is not limited to, all of the following:

(1) The use of all interception and notification systems operated by the department for the purpose of aiding in the enforcement of support obligations.

(2) The obtaining by the local child support agency of an initial order for child support that may include medical support or that is for medical support only, by civil or criminal process.

(3) The initiation of a motion or order to show cause to increase an existing child support order, and the response to a motion or order to show cause brought by an obligor parent to decrease an existing child support order, or the initiation of a motion or order to show cause to obtain an order for medical support, and the response to a motion or order to show cause brought by an obligor parent to decrease or terminate an existing medical support order, without regard to whether the child is receiving public assistance.

(4) The response to a notice of motion or order to show cause brought by an obligor parent to decrease an existing spousal support order if the child or children are residing with the obligee parent and the local child support agency is also enforcing a related child support obligation owed to the obligee parent by the same obligor.

(5) The referral of child support delinquencies to the department under subdivision (c) of Section 17500 in support of the local child support agency.

(i) As used in this section, "out of wedlock" means that the biological parents of the child were not married to each other at the time of the child's conception.

(j) (1) The local child support agency is the public agency responsible for administering wage withholding for current support for the purposes of Title IV-D of the Social Security Act (42 U.S.C. Sec. 651 et seq.).

(2) This section does not limit the authority of the local child support agency granted by other sections of this code or otherwise granted by law.

(k) In the exercise of the authority granted under this article, the local child support agency may intervene, pursuant to subdivision (b) of Section 387 of the Code of Civil Procedure, by ex parte application, in any action under this code, or other proceeding in which child support is an issue or a reduction in spousal support is sought. By notice of motion, order to show cause, or responsive pleading served upon all parties to the action, the local child support agency may request any relief that is appropriate that the local child support agency is authorized to seek.

(l) The local child support agency shall comply with all regulations and directives established by the department that set time standards for responding to requests for assistance in locating noncustodial parents, establishing paternity, establishing child support awards, and collecting child support payments.

(m) As used in this article, medical support activities that the local child support agency is authorized to perform are limited to the following:

(1) The obtaining and enforcing of court orders for health insurance coverage.

(2) Any other medical support activity mandated by federal law or regulation.

(n) (1) Notwithstanding any other law, except when a court of competent jurisdiction under Section 4251 hearing the action or proceeding under this division transfers the action or proceeding pursuant to Section 397.5 of the Code of Civil Procedure pursuant to a directly filed motion, a redirected motion, or on the court's own motion under Section 397.5 of the Code of Civil Procedure, venue for an action or proceeding under this division shall be determined as follows:

(A) Venue shall be in the superior court in the county that is currently expending public assistance.

(B) If public assistance is not currently being expended, venue shall be in the superior court in the county where the child who is entitled to current support resides or is domiciled.

(C) If current support is no longer payable through, or enforceable by, the local child support agency, venue shall be in the superior court in the county that last provided public assistance for actions to enforce arrearages assigned pursuant to Section 11477 of the Welfare and Institutions Code.

(D) If subparagraphs (A), (B), and (C) do not apply, venue shall be in the superior court in the county of residence of the support obligee.

(E) If the support obligee does not reside in California, and subparagraphs (A), (B), (C), and (D) do not apply, venue shall be in the superior court of the county of residence of the obligor.

(2) Notwithstanding paragraph (1), if the child becomes a resident of another county after an action under this part has been filed, venue may remain in the county where the action was filed until the action is completed. Nothing in this paragraph shall be construed to limit the court hearing the action or proceeding under this division from exercising its discretion under Section 397.5 of the Code of Civil Procedure.

(o) The local child support agency of one county may appear on behalf of the local child support agency of any other county in an action or proceeding under this part.

(p) This section shall become operative January 1, 2026.[602]

17400.5. If an obligor has an ongoing child support order being enforced by a local child support agency pursuant to Title IV-D of the Social Security Act and the obligor is disabled, meets the SSI resource test, and is receiving Supplemental Security Income/State Supplemental Payments (SSI/SSP) or, but for excess income as described in Section 416.1100 et seq. of Part 416 of

Title 20 of the Code of Federal Regulations, would be eligible to receive as SSI/SSP, pursuant to Section 12200 of the Welfare and Institutions Code, and the obligor has supplied the local child support agency with proof of eligibility for, and, if applicable, receipt of, SSI/SSP or Social Security Disability Insurance benefits, then the local child support agency shall prepare and file a motion to modify the support obligation within 30 days of receipt of verification from the noncustodial parent or any other source of the receipt of SSI/SSP or Social Security Disability Insurance benefits. The local child support agency shall serve the motion on both the noncustodial parent and custodial person and any modification of the support order entered pursuant to the motion shall be effective as provided in Section 3653 of the Family Code.

17401. If the parent who is receiving support enforcement services provides to the local child support agency substantial, credible, information regarding the residence or work address of the support obligor, the agency shall initiate an establishment or enforcement action and serve the defendant, if service is required, within 60 days and inform the parent in writing when those actions have been taken. If the address or any other information provided by the support obligee is determined by the local child support agency to be inaccurate and if, after reasonable diligence, the agency is unable to locate and serve the support obligor within that 60-day period, the local child support agency shall inform the support obligee in writing of those facts. The requirements of this section shall be in addition to the time standards established by the Department of Child Support Services pursuant to subdivision (l) of Section 17400.

17401.5. (a) All of the following shall include notice of, and information about, the child support service hearings available pursuant to Section 17801, provided that there is federal financial participation available as set forth in subdivision (j) of Section 17801:

(1) The booklet required by subdivision (a) of Section 17434.

(2) Any notice required by subdivision (c) or (h) of Section 17406.

(b) To the extent not otherwise required by law, the local child support agency shall provide notice of, and information about, the child support services hearings available pursuant to Section 17801 in any regularly issued notices to custodial and noncustodial parents subject to Section 17400, provided that there is federal financial participation available as set forth in subdivision (e) of Section 17801.

Notice of and information about the child support service hearings and the child support complaint resolution process required under Section 17800 shall be easily accessible and shall be provided in a single section of the booklet.

17402. (a) In any case of separation or desertion of a parent or parents from a child or children that results in aid under Chapter 2 (commencing with Section 11200) of Part 3 of Division 9 of the Welfare and Institutions Code being granted to that family, the noncustodial parent or parents shall be obligated to the county for an amount equal to the amount specified in an order for the support and maintenance of the family issued by a court of competent jurisdiction.

(b) The local child support agency shall take appropriate action pursuant to this section as provided in subdivision (l) of Section 17400. The local child support agency may establish liability for child support as provided in subdivision (a) when public assistance was provided by another county or by other counties.

(c) The amount of the obligation established for each parent with a liability under subdivision (a) shall be determined by using the appropriate child support guideline currently in effect and shall be computed as follows:

(1) If one parent remains as a custodial parent, the support shall be computed according to the guideline.

(2) If the parents reside together and neither father nor mother remains as a custodial parent, the guideline support shall be computed by combining the noncustodial parents' incomes. The combined incomes shall be used as the high earner's net monthly disposable income in the guideline formula. Income shall not be attributed to the caretaker or governmental agency. The amount of guideline support resulting shall be proportionately shared between the noncustodial parents based upon their net monthly disposable incomes.

(3) If the parents reside apart and neither father nor mother remains as a custodial parent, the guideline support shall be computed separately for each parent by treating each parent as a noncustodial parent. Income shall not be attributed to the caretaker or government agency.

(d) A parent shall pay the amount of support specified in the support order to the local child support agency.

17402.1. (a) Each local child support agency shall, on a monthly basis, remit to the department both the federal and state public assistance child support payments received pursuant to Section 17402.

(b) The department shall promulgate regulations to implement this section.

17404. (a) Notwithstanding any other statute, in any action brought by the local child support agency for the support of a minor child or children, the action may be prosecuted in the name of the county on behalf of the child, children, or a parent of the child or children. The parent who has requested or is receiving support enforcement services of the local child support agency shall not be a necessary party to the action but may be subpoenaed as a witness. Except as provided in subdivision (e), in an action under this section there shall be no joinder of actions, or coordination of actions, or cross-complaints, and the issues shall be limited strictly to the question of parentage, if applicable, and child support, including an order for medical support. A final determination of parentage may be made in any action under this section as an incident to obtaining an order for support. An action for support or parentage pursuant to this section shall not be delayed or stayed because of the pendency of any other action between the parties.

(b) (1) Judgment in an action brought pursuant to this section, and in an action brought pursuant to Section 17402, if at issue, may be rendered pursuant to a noticed motion, that shall inform the defendant that in order to exercise the right to trial, the defendant shall appear at the hearing on the motion.

(2) If the defendant appears at the hearing on the motion, the court shall inquire of the defendant if the defendant desires to subpoena evidence and witnesses, if parentage is at issue and genetic tests have not already been conducted whether the defendant desires genetic tests, and if the defendant desires a trial. If the defendant's answer is in the affirmative, a continuance shall be granted to allow the defendant to exercise those rights. A continuance shall not postpone the hearing to more than 90 days from the date of service of the motion. If a continuance is granted, the court may make an order for temporary support without prejudice to the right of the court to make an order for temporary support as otherwise allowed by law.

(c) In any action to enforce a spousal support order the action may be pled in the name of the county in the same manner as an action to establish a child support obligation. The same restrictions on joinder of actions, coordination of actions, cross-complaints, and delay because of the pendency of any other action as relates to actions to establish a child support obligation shall also apply to actions to enforce a spousal support order.

(d) This section does not prevent the parties from bringing an independent action under other provisions of this code and litigating the issues of support, custody, visitation, or protective orders. In that event, any support, custody, visitation, or protective order issued by the court in an action pursuant to this section shall be filed in the action commenced under the other provisions of this code and shall continue in effect until modified by a subsequent order of the court. To the extent that the orders conflict, the court order last issued shall supersede all other orders and be binding upon all parties in that action.

(e) (1) After a support order, including a temporary support order and an order for medical support only, has been entered in an action brought pursuant to this section, the parent who has requested or is receiving support enforcement services of the local child support agency shall become a party to the action brought pursuant to this section, only in the manner and to the extent provided by this section, and only for the purposes allowed by this section.

(2) Notice of the parent's status as a party shall be given to the parent by the local child support agency in conjunction with the notice required by subdivision (e) of Section 17406. The complaint shall contain this notice. Service of the complaint on the parent in compliance with Section 1013 of the Code of Civil Procedure, or as otherwise provided by law, shall constitute compliance with this section. In all actions commenced under the procedures and forms in effect on or before December 31, 1996, the parent who has requested or is receiving support enforcement services of the local child support agency shall not become a party to the action until joined as a party pursuant to an ex parte application or

noticed motion for joinder filed by the local child support agency or a noticed motion filed by either parent. The local child support agency shall serve a copy of any order for joinder of a parent obtained by the local child support agency's application on both parents in compliance with Section 1013 of the Code of Civil Procedure.

(3) Once both parents are parties to an action brought pursuant to this section in cases where Title IV-D services are currently being provided, the local child support agency shall be required, within five days of receipt, to mail the nonmoving party in the action all pleadings relating solely to the support issue in the action that have been served on the local child support agency by the moving party in the action, as provided in subdivision (f) of Section 17406. There shall be a rebuttable presumption that service on the local child support agency consistent with the provisions of this paragraph constitutes valid service on the nonmoving party. Where this procedure is used to effectuate service on the nonmoving party, the pleadings shall be served on the local child support agency not less than 30 days prior to the hearing.

(4) The parent who has requested or is receiving support enforcement services of the local child support agency is a party to an action brought under this section for issues relating to the support, custody, and visitation of a child, and for restraining orders, and for no other purpose. The local child support agency shall not be required to serve or receive service of papers, pleadings, or documents, or participate in, or attend any hearing or proceeding relating to issues of custody or visitation, except as otherwise required by law. Orders concerning custody and visitation may be made in an action pursuant to this subdivision only if orders concerning custody and visitation have not been previously made by a court of competent jurisdiction in this state or another state and the court has jurisdiction and is the proper venue for custody and visitation determinations. All issues regarding custody and visitation shall be heard and resolved in the manner provided by this code. Except as otherwise provided by law, the local child support agency shall control support and parentage litigation brought pursuant to this section, and the manner, method, and procedures used in establishing parentage and in establishing and enforcing support obligations unless and until the parent who requested or is receiving support enforcement services has requested in writing that the local child support agency close the case and the case has been closed in accordance with state and federal regulation or policy.

(f) (1) A parent who has requested or is receiving support enforcement services of the local child support agency may take independent action to modify a support order made pursuant to this section while support enforcement services are being provided by the local child support agency. The parent shall serve the local child support agency with notice of any action filed to modify the support order and provide the local child support agency with a copy of the modified order within 15 calendar days after the date the order is issued.

(2) A parent who has requested or is

receiving support enforcement services of the local child support agency may take independent action to enforce a support order made pursuant to this section while support enforcement services are being provided by the local child support agency with the written consent of the local child support agency. At least 30 days prior to filing an independent enforcement action, the parent shall provide the local child support agency with written notice of the parent's intent to file an enforcement action that includes a description of the type of enforcement action the parent intends to file. Within 30 days of receiving the notice, the local child support agency shall either provide written consent for the parent to proceed with the independent enforcement action or notify the parent that the local child support agency objects to the parent filing the proposed independent enforcement action. The local child support agency may object only if the local child support agency is currently using an administrative or judicial method to enforce the support obligation or if the proposed independent enforcement action would interfere with an investigation being conducted by the local child support agency. If the local child support agency does not respond to the parent's written notice within 30 days, the local child support agency shall be deemed to have given consent.

(3) The court shall order that all payments of support shall be made to the local child support agency in any action filed under this section by the parent who has requested, or is receiving, support enforcement services of the local child support agency unless support enforcement services have been terminated by the local child support agency by case closure as provided by state and federal law. Any order obtained by a parent prior to support enforcement services being terminated in which the local child support agency did not receive proper notice pursuant to this section shall be voidable upon the motion of the local child support agency.

(g) Any notice from the local child support agency requesting a meeting with the support obligor for any purpose authorized under this section shall contain a statement advising the support obligor of the right to have an attorney present at the meeting.

(h) For the purpose of this section, "a parent who is receiving support enforcement services" includes a parent who has assigned their rights to support pursuant to Section 11477 of the Welfare and Institutions Code.

(i) The Judicial Council shall develop forms to implement this section.

17404.1. (a) Upon receipt of a petition or comparable pleading pursuant to Part 6 (commencing with Section 5700.101) of Division 9, the local child support agency or petitioner may either (1) request the issuance of a summons or (2) request the court to issue an order requiring the respondent to appear personally at a specified time and place to show cause why an order should not be issued as prayed in the petition or comparable pleading on file.

(b) The respondent may also be served with a proposed judgment consistent with the relief sought in the petition or other comparable pleading. If the respondent's income or income history is unknown to the local child support agency, the local child support agency may serve a form of proposed judgment with the petition and other documents on the respondent that shall inform the respondent that income shall be presumed to be the amount of the state minimum wage, at 40 hours per week, unless information concerning the respondent's income is provided to the court. The respondent shall also receive notice that the proposed judgment will become effective if the respondent fails to file a response with the court within 30 days after service.

(c) If a summons is issued for a petition or comparable pleading pursuant to Part 6 (commencing with Section 5700.101) of Division 9, the local child support agency or petitioner shall cause a copy of the summons, petition, and other documents to be served upon the respondent according to law.

(d) If an order to show cause is issued on a petition or comparable pleading pursuant to Part 6 (commencing with Section 5700.101) of Division 9 requiring the respondent to appear at a specified time and place to respond to the petition, a copy of the order to show cause, the petition, and other documents shall be served upon the respondent at least 15 days prior to the hearing.

(e) A petition or comparable pleading served upon a respondent in accordance with this section shall be accompanied by a blank responsive form that shall permit the respondent to answer the petition and raise any defenses by checking applicable boxes and by a blank income and expense declaration or simplified financial statement together with instructions for completion of the forms.

(f) In any action pursuant to Part 6 (commencing with Section 5700.101) of Division 9 in which the judgment was obtained pursuant to presumed income, as set forth in this section, the court may set aside that part of the judgment or order concerning the amount of child support to be paid on the grounds specified and in the manner set forth in Section 17432.

(g) This section shall become inoperative on January 1, 2026, and, as of January 1, 2027, is repealed.

17404.1. (a) Upon receipt of a petition or comparable pleading pursuant to Part 6 (commencing with Section 5700.101) of Division 9, the local child support agency or petitioner may either (1) request the issuance of a summons or (2) request the court to issue an order requiring the respondent to appear personally at a specified time and place to show cause why an order should not be issued as prayed in the petition or comparable pleading on file.

(b) The respondent may also be served with a proposed judgment consistent with the relief sought in the petition or other comparable pleading. The petition or other comparable pleading shall provide notice to the obligor of the amount of child support that is being sought pursuant to the guidelines set forth in Article 2 (commencing with Section 4050) of Chapter 2 of Part 2 of Division 9 based upon the methodology for determining the obligor's income for purposes of a simplified complaint as required by subparagraph (A) of paragraph (2) of subdivision (d) of Section 17400.

(c) If the proposed judgment is based

on the support obligor's earning capacity pursuant to clause (ii) or (iii) of subparagraph (A) of paragraph (2) of subdivision (d) of Section 17400, the local child support agency shall file a motion for judgment, as provided in subdivision (b) of Section 17404.

(d) If a summons is issued for a petition or comparable pleading pursuant to Part 6 (commencing with Section 5700.101) of Division 9, the local child support agency or petitioner shall cause a copy of the summons, petition, and other documents to be served upon the respondent according to law.

(e) If an order to show cause is issued on a petition or comparable pleading pursuant to Part 6 (commencing with Section 5700.101) of Division 9 requiring the respondent to appear at a specified time and place to respond to the petition, a copy of the order to show cause, the petition, and other documents shall be served upon the respondent at least 15 days prior to the hearing.

(f) A petition or comparable pleading served upon a respondent in accordance with this section shall be accompanied by a blank responsive form that shall permit the respondent to answer the petition and raise any defenses by checking applicable boxes and by a blank income and expense declaration or simplified financial statement together with instructions for completion of the forms.

(g) This section shall become operative January 1, 2026.[555]

17404.2. (a) If, prior to filing, a petition or comparable pleading pursuant to Part 6 (commencing with Section 5700.101) of Division 9 is received by the local child support agency or the superior court and the county in which the pleadings are received is not the appropriate jurisdiction for trial of the action, the court or the local child support agency shall forward the pleadings and any accompanying documents to the appropriate court of this state or to the jurisdiction of another state without filing the pleadings or order of the court, and shall notify the petitioner, the California Central Registry, and the local child support agency of the receiving county where and when the pleading was sent.

(b) If, after a petition or comparable pleading has been filed with the superior court of a county pursuant to Part 6 (commencing with Section 5700.101) of Division 9, it appears that the respondent is not or is no longer a resident of the county in which the action has been filed, upon ex parte application by the local child support agency or petitioner, the court shall transfer the action to the appropriate court of this state or to the appropriate jurisdiction of another state and shall notify the petitioner, the respondent, the California Central Registry, and the local child support agency of the receiving county where and when the pleading was sent.

(c) If, after entry of an order by a court of this state or an order of another state registered in a court of this state for enforcement or modification pursuant to Part 6 (commencing with Section 5700.101) of Division 9, it appears that the respondent is not or is no longer a resident of the county in which the foreign order has been registered, upon ex parte application by the local child support agency of the transferring or receiving county or the

petitioner, the court shall transfer the registered order and all documents subsequently filed in that action to the appropriate court of this state and shall notify the petitioner, the respondent, the California Central Registry, and the local child support agency of the transferring and receiving county where and when the registered order and all other appropriate documents were sent. Transfer of certified copies of documents shall meet the requirements of this section.
(d) If, in an action initiated in a court of this state pursuant to Part 6 (commencing with Section 5700.101) of Division 9 or a predecessor law for interstate enforcement of support, the petitioner is no longer a resident of the county in which the action has been filed, upon ex parte application by the petitioner or the local child support agency, the court shall transfer the action to the appropriate court of this state and shall notify the responding jurisdiction where and when the action was transferred.
(e) Notwithstanding subdivisions (b) and (c), if the respondent becomes a resident of another county or jurisdiction after an action or registered order has been filed pursuant to Part 6 (commencing with Section 5700.101) of Division 9, the action may remain in the county where the action was filed until the action is completed.[340]

17404.3. Hearings by telephone, audiovisual means, or other electronic means shall be permitted in child support cases in which the local child support agency is providing child support services. The Judicial Council shall adopt court rules implementing this provision and subdivision (f) of Section 5700.316 on or before July 1, 2016.[341]

17404.4. In exercising the jurisdiction under Section 5700.319, either the department or the local child support agency shall issue a notice to change payee on a support order issued in this state, upon request from the support enforcement agency of another state where a custodial party has either assigned the right to receive support or has requested support enforcement services. Notice of the administrative change of payee shall be filed with the court in which the order was issued or last registered.

17405. In carrying out duties under this article, the local child support agency shall interview the custodial parent within 10 business days of opening a child support case. This interview shall solicit financial and all other information about the noncustodial parent. This information shall be acted upon immediately. The local child support agency shall reinterview the custodial parent as needed.[75]

17406. (a) In all actions involving paternity or support, including, but not limited to, other proceedings under this code, and under Division 9 (commencing with Section 10000) of the Welfare and Institutions Code, the local child support agency and the Attorney General represent the public interest in establishing, modifying, and enforcing support obligations. No attorney-client relationship shall be deemed to have been created between the local child support agency or Attorney General and any person by virtue of the action of the local child support agency or the Attorney General in carrying out these statutory duties.

(b) Subdivision (a) is declaratory of existing law.

(c) In all requests for services of the local child support agency or Attorney General pursuant to Section 17400 relating to actions involving paternity or support, not later than the same day an individual makes a request for these services in person, and not later than five working days after either (1) a case is referred for services from the county welfare department, (2) receipt of a request by mail for an application for services, or (3) an individual makes a request for services by telephone, the local child support agency or Attorney General shall give notice to the individual requesting services or on whose behalf services have been requested that the local child support agency or Attorney General does not represent the individual or the children who are the subject of the case, that no attorney-client relationship exists between the local child support agency or Attorney General and those persons, and that no such representation or relationship shall arise if the local child support agency or Attorney General provides the services requested. Notice shall be in bold print and in plain English and shall be translated into the language understandable by the recipient when reasonable. The notice shall include the advice that the absence of an attorney-client relationship means that communications from the recipient are not privileged and that the local child support agency or Attorney General may provide support enforcement services to the other parent in the future.

(d) The local child support agency or Attorney General shall give the notice required pursuant to subdivision (c) to all recipients of services under Section 17400 who have not otherwise been provided that notice, not later than the date of the next annual notice required under Section 11476.2 of the Welfare and Institutions Code. This notice shall include notification to the recipient of services under Section 17400 that the recipient may inspect the clerk's file at the office of the clerk of the court, and that, upon request, the local child support agency, or, if appropriate, the Attorney General, will furnish a copy of the most recent order entered in the case.

(e) The local child support agency or, if appropriate, the Attorney General shall serve a copy of the complaint for paternity or support, or both, on recipients of support services under Section 17400, as specified in paragraph (2) of subdivision (e) of Section 17404. A notice shall accompany the complaint that informs the recipient that the local child support agency or Attorney General may enter into a stipulated order resolving the complaint, and that the recipient shall assist the prosecuting attorney, by sending all information on the noncustodial parent's earnings and assets to the prosecuting attorney.

(f) (1) (A) The local child support agency or Attorney General shall provide written notice to recipients of services under Section 17400 of the initial date and time, and purpose of every hearing in a civil action for paternity or support.

(B) Once the parent who has requested or is receiving support enforcement services becomes a party to the action pursuant to subdivision (e) of Section 17404, in lieu of the above, the local child support agency or Attorney General shall serve on a parent all pleadings relating to paternity or support that have been served on the local child support agency by the other parent. The pleading shall be accompanied by a notice.

(C) The notice provided subject to subparagraphs (A) and (B) shall include the following language:

IMPORTANT NOTICE

It may be important that you attend the hearing. The local child support agency does not represent you or your children. You may have information about the other parent, such as information about that parent's income or assets that will not be presented to the court unless you attend the hearing. You have the right to attend the hearing and to be heard in court and tell the court what you think the court should do with the child support order. This hearing could change your rights or your children's rights to support.

(2) The notice shall state the purpose of the hearing or be attached to the motion or other pleading which caused the hearing to be scheduled.

(3) The notice shall be provided separate from all other material and shall be in at least 14-point type. The failure of the local child support agency or Attorney General to provide the notice required pursuant to subparagraph (A) of paragraph (1) does not affect the validity of any order.

(4) (A) The notice required pursuant to subparagraph (A) of paragraph (1) shall be provided not later than seven calendar days prior to the hearing, or, if the local child support agency or Attorney General receives notice of the hearing less than seven days prior to the hearing, within two days of the receipt by the local child support agency or Attorney General of the notice of the hearing.

(B) Service of the notice and the pleadings required pursuant to subparagraph (B) of paragraph (1) shall be completed not later than five days after receipt of the pleadings served on the local child support agency by the parent.

(5) The local child support agency or Attorney General shall, in order to implement this subdivision, make reasonable efforts to ensure that the local child support agency or Attorney General has current addresses for all parties to the child support action.

(g) The local child support agency or Attorney General shall give notice to recipients of services under Section 17400 of every order obtained by the local child support agency or Attorney General that establishes or modifies the support obligation for the recipient or the children who are the subject of the order, by sending a copy of the order to the recipient. The notice shall be made within the time specified by federal law after the order has been filed. The local child support agency or Attorney General shall also give notice to these recipients of every order obtained in any other jurisdiction that establishes or modifies the support obligation for the recipient or the children who are the subject of the order, and which is received by the local child support agency or Attorney General, by sending a copy of the order to the recipient within the timeframe specified by federal law after the local child support agency or Attorney General has received a copy of the order. In any action enforced under Part 6 (commencing with Section 5700.101) of Division 9, the notice shall be made in compliance with the requirements of that chapter. The failure of the local child support agency or Attorney General to comply with this subdivision does not affect the validity of any order.

(h) The local child support agency or Attorney General shall give notice to the noncustodial parent against whom a civil action is filed that the local child support agency or Attorney General is not the attorney representing any individual, including, but not limited to, the custodial parent, the child, or the noncustodial parent.

(i) This section does not preclude a person who is receiving services under Section 17400 from filing and prosecuting an independent action to establish, modify, and enforce an order for current support on behalf of that person or a child if that person is not receiving public assistance.

(j) A person who is receiving services under Section 17400 but who is not currently receiving public assistance on their own behalf or on behalf of a child shall be asked to execute, or consent to, any stipulation establishing or modifying a support order in any action in which that person is named as a party, before the stipulation is filed. The local child support agency or Attorney General may not submit to the court for approval a stipulation to establish or modify a support order in the action without first obtaining the signatures of all parties to the action, their attorneys of record, or persons authorized to act on their behalf. Any stipulation approved by the court in violation of this subdivision shall be void.

(k) The local child support agency or Attorney General may not enter into a stipulation that reduces the amount of past due support, including interest and penalties accrued pursuant to an order of current support, on behalf of a person who is receiving support enforcement services under Section 17400 and who is owed support arrearages that exceed unreimbursed public assistance paid to the recipient of the support enforcement services, without first obtaining the consent of the person who is receiving services under Section 17400 on their own behalf or on behalf of the child.

(l) The notices required in this section shall be provided in the following manner:

(1) In all cases in which the person receiving services under Section 17400 resides in California, notice shall be provided by mailing the item by first-class mail to the last known address of, or personally delivering the item to, that person.

(2) In all actions enforced under Part 6 (commencing with Section 5700.101) of Division 9, unless otherwise specified, notice shall be provided by mailing the item by first-class mail to the initiating court.

(m) Notwithstanding any other provision of this section, the notices provided for pursuant to subdivisions (c) to (g), inclusive, are not required in foster care cases.

17407. (a) If the Attorney General is of the opinion that a support order or support-related order is erroneous and presents a question of law warranting an appeal, or that an order is sound and should be defended on appeal, in the public interest the Attorney General may:

(1) Perfect or oppose an appeal to the proper appellate court if the order was issued by a court of this state.
(2) If the order was issued in another state, cause an appeal to be taken or opposed in the other state.
(b) In either case, expenses of the appeal may be paid on order of the Attorney General from funds appropriated for the Office of the Attorney General.[75]

17407.5. A declaration of state reciprocity issued by the Attorney General on or before December 31, 2015, and a declaration issued pursuant to subdivision (b) of Section 5700.308, shall remain in full force and effect unless one of the following occurs:
(a) The declaration is revoked or declared invalid by the Attorney General, in consultation with the department, or by the other party to the reciprocity agreement.
(b) The declaration is superseded by a subsequent federal bilateral agreement with the other party.
(c) The declaration is superseded by the other party's ratification of or accession to the Hague Convention on the International Recovery of Child Support and Other Forms of Family Maintenance.[342]

17408. (a) Notwithstanding Section 17404, upon noticed motion of the local child support agency, the superior court may consolidate or combine support or reimbursement arrearages owed by one obligor to one obligee in two or more court files into a single court file, or combine or consolidate two or more orders for current child support into a single court file. A motion to consolidate may be made by a local child support agency only if it is seeking to enforce the orders being consolidated. The motion shall be filed only in the court file the local child support agency is seeking to have designated as the primary file.
(b) Orders may be consolidated regardless of the nature of the underlying action, whether initiated under the Welfare and Institutions Code, this code, or another law. Orders for support shall not be consolidated unless the children involved have the same mother and father and venue is proper pursuant to Section 17400.
(c) Upon consolidation of orders, the court shall designate which court file the support orders are being consolidated into the primary file, and which court files are subordinate. Upon consolidation, the court shall order the local child support agency to file a notice in the subordinate court actions indicating the support orders in those actions were consolidated into the primary file. The notice shall state the date of the consolidation, the name of the court, and the primary file number.
(d) Upon consolidation of orders, the superior court shall not issue further orders pertaining to support in a subordinate court file; and all enforcement and modification of support orders shall occur in the primary court action.
(e) After consolidation of court orders, a single wage assignment for current support and arrearages may be issued when possible.

17410. In any action filed by the local child support agency pursuant to Section 17402 or 17404, the local child support agency shall provide the mother and the alleged father the opportunity to voluntarily acknowledge paternity by signing a paternity declaration as described in Section 7574 prior to a hearing or trial where the paternity of a minor child is at issue. The opportunity to voluntarily acknowledge paternity may be provided either before or after an action pursuant to Section 17402 or 17404 is filed and served upon the alleged father. For the purpose of meeting the requirements of this section, the local child support agency may afford the defendant an opportunity to enter into a stipulation for judgment of paternity after an action for paternity has been filed in lieu of the voluntary declaration of paternity.

17412. (a) Notwithstanding any other law, an action for child support may be brought by the local child support agency on behalf of a minor child or caretaker parent based upon a voluntary declaration of parentage as provided in Chapter 3 (commencing with Section 7570) of Part 2 of Division 12.
(b) Except as provided in Sections 7580 and 7581, the voluntary declaration of parentage shall be given the same force and effect as a judgment for parentage entered by a court of competent jurisdiction. The court shall make appropriate orders for support of the minor child based upon the voluntary declaration of parentage unless evidence is presented that the voluntary declaration of parentage has been rescinded by the parties or set aside by a court as provided in Section 7575, 7576, or 7577.
(c) The Judicial Council shall develop the forms and procedures necessary to implement this section.
(d) This section shall become operative on January 1, 2020.

17414. In any action or proceeding brought by the local child support agency to establish parentage pursuant to Section 17400, the court shall enter a judgment establishing parentage upon the filing of a written stipulation between the parties provided that the stipulation is accompanied by a written advisement and waiver of rights which is signed by the defendant. The written advisement and waiver of rights shall be developed by the Judicial Council.

17415. (a) It shall be the duty of the county welfare department to refer all cases in which a parent is absent from the home, or in which the parents are unmarried and parentage has not been established by the completion and filing of a voluntary declaration of paternity pursuant to Section 7573 or a court of competent jurisdiction, to the local child support agency immediately at the time the application for public assistance, including Medi-Cal benefits, or certificate of eligibility, is signed by the applicant or recipient, except as provided in Section 17552 and Sections 11477 and 11477.04 of the Welfare and Institutions Code. If an applicant is found to be ineligible, the applicant shall be notified in writing that the referral of the case to the local child support agency may be terminated at the applicant's request. The county welfare department shall cooperate with the local child support agency and shall make available all pertinent information pursuant to Section 17505.
(b) Upon referral from the county

welfare department, the local child support agency shall investigate the question of nonsupport or paternity and shall take all steps necessary to obtain child support for the needy child, enforce spousal support as part of the state plan under Section 17604, and determine paternity in the case of a child born out of wedlock. Upon the advice of the county welfare department that a child is being considered for adoption, the local child support agency shall delay the investigation and other actions with respect to the case until advised that the adoption is no longer under consideration. The granting of public assistance or Medi-Cal benefits to an applicant shall not be delayed or contingent upon investigation by the local child support agency.

(c) In cases where Medi-Cal benefits are the only assistance provided, the local child support agency shall provide child and spousal support services unless the recipient of the services notifies the local child support agency that only services related to securing health insurance benefits are requested.

(d) Whenever a court order has been obtained, any contractual agreement for support between the local child support agency or the county welfare department and the noncustodial parent shall be deemed null and void to the extent that it is not consistent with the court order.

(e) Whenever a family that has been receiving public assistance, including Medi-Cal, ceases to receive assistance, including Medi-Cal, the local child support agency shall, to the extent required by federal regulations, continue to enforce support payments from the noncustodial parent until the individual on whose behalf the enforcement efforts are made sends written notice to the local child support agency requesting that enforcement services be discontinued.

(f) The local child support agency shall, when appropriate, utilize reciprocal arrangements adopted with other states in securing support from an absent parent. In individual cases where utilization of reciprocal arrangements has proven ineffective, the local child support agency may forward to the Attorney General a request to utilize federal courts in order to obtain or enforce orders for child or spousal support. If reasonable efforts to collect amounts assigned pursuant to Section 11477 of the Welfare and Institutions Code have failed, the local child support agency may request that the case be forwarded to the United States Treasury Department for collection in accordance with federal regulations. The Attorney General, when appropriate, shall forward these requests to the Secretary of Health and Human Services, or a designated representative.[280]

17416. (a) When the local child support agency has undertaken enforcement of support, the local child support agency may enter into an agreement with the noncustodial parent, on behalf of a minor child or children, a spouse, or former spouse for the entry of a judgment without action determining paternity, if applicable, and for periodic child and spousal support payments based on the noncustodial parent's reasonable ability to pay or, if for spousal support, an amount previously ordered by a court of competent jurisdiction. An agreement for entry of a judgment under this section may be executed prior to the birth of the child and may include a provision that the judgment is not to be entered until after the birth of the child.

(b) A judgment based on the agreement shall be entered only if one of the following requirements is satisfied:

(1) The noncustodial parent is represented by legal counsel and the attorney signs a certificate stating: "I have examined the proposed judgment and have advised my client concerning their rights in connection with this matter and the consequences of signing or not signing the agreement for the entry of the judgment and my client, after being so advised, has agreed to the entry of the judgment."

(2) A judge of the court in which the judgment is to be entered, after advising the noncustodial parent concerning their rights in connection with the matter and the consequences of agreeing or not agreeing to the entry of the judgment, makes a finding that the noncustodial parent has appeared before the judge and the judge has determined that under the circumstances of the particular case the noncustodial parent has willingly, knowingly, and intelligently waived due process rights in agreeing to the entry of the judgment.

(c) The clerk shall file the agreement, together with any certificate of the attorney or finding of the court, without the payment of any fees or charges. If the requirements of this section are satisfied, the court shall enter judgment thereon without action. The provisions of Article 4 (commencing with Section 4200) of Chapter 2 of Part 2 of Division 9 or Chapter 4 (commencing with Section 4350) of Part 3 of Division 9 shall apply to the judgment. A judgment for support so entered may be enforced by any means by which any other judgment for support may be enforced.

(d) Upon request of the local child support agency in any case under this section, the clerk shall set the matter for hearing by the court. The hearing shall be held within 10 days after the clerk receives the request. The local child support agency may require the person who signed the agreement for the entry of judgment to attend the hearing by process of subpoena in the same manner as the attendance of a witness in a civil action may be required. The presence of the person who signed the agreement for entry of judgment at the hearing shall constitute the presence of the person in court at the time the order is pronounced for the purposes of Section 1209.5 of the Code of Civil Procedure if the court makes the findings required by paragraph (2) of subdivision (b).

(e) The local child support agency shall cause the following to be served, in the manner specified in Section 415.10, 415.20, 415.30, or 415.40 of the Code of Civil Procedure, upon the person who signed the agreement for entry of the judgment and shall file proof of service thereof with the court:

(1) A copy of the judgment as entered.

(2) If the judgment includes an order for child or spousal support payments, a notice stating the substance of the following: "The court has continuing authority to make an order increasing or decreasing the amount of the child or

spousal support payments. You have the right to request that the court order the child and spousal support payments be decreased or eliminated entirely."

(f) An order for child and spousal support included in a judgment entered under this section may be modified or revoked as provided in Article 1 (commencing with Section 3650) of Chapter 6 of Part 1 of Division 9 and in (1) Article 1 (commencing with Section 4000) of Chapter 2 of Part 2 of Division 9 or (2) Chapter 2 (commencing with Section 4320) and Chapter 3 (commencing with Section 4330) of Part 3 of Division 9. The court may modify the order to make the support payments payable to a different person.

(g) For the purposes of this section, in making a determination of the noncustodial parent's reasonable ability to pay, any relevant circumstances set out in Section 4005 shall be considered.

(h) After arrest and before plea or trial, or after conviction or plea of guilty, under Section 270 of the Penal Code, if the defendant appears before the court in which the criminal action is pending and the requirements of paragraph (1) or (2) of subdivision (b) have been satisfied, the court may suspend proceedings or sentence in the criminal action, but this does not limit the later institution of a civil or criminal action or limit the use of any other procedures available to enforce the judgment entered pursuant to this section.

(i) Nothing in this section applies to a case where a civil action has been commenced.

17418. In enforcing the provisions of this division, the local child support agency shall inquire of both the custodial and noncustodial parent as to the number of minor children each is legally obligated to support. The local child support agency shall consider the needs of all of these children in computing the level of support requested to be ordered by the court.

17420. After judgment in any court action brought to enforce the support obligation of a noncustodial parent pursuant to the provisions of this division, the court shall issue an earnings assignment order for support pursuant to Chapter 8 (commencing with Section 5200) of Part 5 of Division 9.

17422. (a) The state medical insurance form required in Article 1 (commencing with Section 3750) of Chapter 7 of Part 1 of Division 9 shall include, but shall not be limited to, all of the following:

(1) The parent or parents' names, addresses, and social security numbers.

(2) The name and address of each parent's place of employment.

(3) The name or names, addresses, policy number or numbers, and coverage type of the medical insurance policy or policies of the parents, if any.

(4) The name, CalWORKs case number, social security number, and Title IV-E foster care case number or Medi-Cal case numbers of the parents and children covered by the medical insurance policy or policies.

(b) (1) In an action brought or enforcement proceeding instituted by the local child support agency under this division for payment of child or spousal support, a completed state medical insurance form shall be obtained and sent by the local child support agency to the State Department of Health Care Services in the manner prescribed by the State Department of Health Care Services.

(2) Where it has been determined under Section 3751 that health insurance coverage is not available at no or reasonable cost, the local child support agency shall seek a provision in the support order that provides for health insurance coverage should it become available at no or reasonable cost.

(3) Health insurance coverage shall be considered reasonable in cost if the cost to the responsible parent providing medical support does not exceed 5 percent of the parent's gross income. In applying the 5 percent for the cost of health insurance, the cost is the difference between self-only and family coverage. If the obligor is entitled to a low-income adjustment as provided in paragraph (7) of subdivision (b) of Section 4055, health insurance shall not be enforced, unless the court determines that not requiring medical support would be unjust and inappropriate in the particular case. As used in this section, "health insurance coverage" also includes providing for the delivery of health care services by a fee for service, health maintenance organization, preferred provider organization, or any other type of health care delivery system under which medical services could be provided to the dependent child or children of an absent parent.

(c) (1) The local child support agency shall request employers and other groups offering health insurance coverage that is being enforced under this division to notify the local child support agency if there has been a lapse in insurance coverage. The local child support agency shall be responsible for forwarding information pertaining to the health insurance policy secured for the dependent children for whom the local child support agency is enforcing the court-ordered medical support to the custodial parent.

(2) The local child support agency shall periodically communicate with the State Department of Health Care Services to determine if there have been lapses in health insurance coverage for public assistance applicants and recipients. The State Department of Health Care Services shall notify the local child support agency when there has been a lapse in court-ordered insurance coverage.

(3) The local child support agency shall take appropriate action, civil or criminal, to enforce the obligation to obtain health insurance when there has been a lapse in insurance coverage or failure by the responsible parent to obtain insurance as ordered by the court.

(4) The local child support agency shall inform all individuals upon their application for child support enforcement services that medical support enforcement services are available.

17424. (a) A parent who has been served with a medical insurance form shall complete and return the form to the local child support agency's office within 20 calendar days of the date the form was served.

(b) The local child support agency

shall send the completed medical insurance form to the department in the manner prescribed by the department.

17428. In any action or judgment brought or obtained pursuant to Section 17400, 17402, 17404, or 17416, a supplemental complaint may be filed, pursuant to Section 464 of the Code of Civil Procedure and Section 2330.1, either before or after a final judgment, seeking a judgment or order of paternity or support for a child of the mother and father of the child whose paternity and support are already in issue before the court. A supplemental judgment entered in the proceedings shall include, when appropriate and requested in the supplemental complaint, an order establishing or modifying support for all children named in the original or supplemental actions in conformity with the statewide uniform guideline for child support. A supplemental complaint for paternity or support of children may be filed without leave of court either before or after final judgment in the underlying action. Service of the supplemental summons and complaint shall be made in the manner provided for the initial service of a summons by the Code of Civil Procedure.

17430. (a) Notwithstanding any other law, in an action filed by the local child support agency pursuant to Section 17400, 17402, or 17404, a judgment shall be entered without hearing, without the presentation of any other evidence or further notice to the defendant, upon the filing of proof of service by the local child support agency evidencing that more than 30 days have passed since the simplified summons and complaint, proposed judgment, blank answer, blank income and expense declaration, and all notices required by this division were served on the defendant.

(b) If the defendant fails to file an answer with the court within 30 days of having been served as specified in subdivision (d) of Section 17400, or at any time before the default judgment is entered, the proposed judgment filed with the original summons and complaint shall be conformed by the court as the final judgment and a copy provided to the local child support agency, unless the local child support agency has filed a declaration and amended proposed judgment pursuant to subdivision (c).

(c) If the local child support agency receives additional financial information within 30 days of service of the complaint and proposed judgment on the defendant and the additional information would result in a support order that is different from the amount in the proposed judgment, the local child support agency shall file a declaration setting forth the additional information and an amended proposed judgment. The declaration and amended proposed judgment shall be served on the defendant in compliance with Section 1013 of the Code of Civil Procedure or otherwise as provided by law. The defendant's time to answer or otherwise appear shall be extended to 30 days from the date of service of the declaration and amended proposed judgment.

(d) Upon entry of the judgment, the clerk of the court shall provide a conformed copy of the judgment to the local child support agency. The local child support agency shall mail by first-class mail, postage prepaid, a notice of entry of judgment by default and a copy of the judgment to the defendant to the address where the summons and complaint were served and last known address if different from that address.

(e) This section shall become inoperative on January 1, 2026, and, as of January 1, 2027, is repealed.[553]

17430. (a) (1) Notwithstanding any other law, in an action filed by the local child support agency pursuant to Section 17400, 17402, 17404, or 17404.1, in which the proposed child support amount is based on actual income, a judgment shall be entered without hearing, without the presentation of any other evidence or further notice to the defendant, upon the filing of proof of service by the local child support agency evidencing that more than 30 days have passed since the simplified summons and complaint, proposed judgment, blank answer, blank income and expense declaration, and all notices required by this division were served on the defendant.

(2) If the defendant fails to file an answer with the court within 30 days of having been served as specified in subdivision (d) of Section 17400 in an action in which the proposed child support amount is based on actual income, or at any time before the default judgment is entered, the proposed judgment filed with the original summons and complaint shall be conformed by the court as the final judgment and a copy provided to the local child support agency, unless the local child support agency has filed a declaration and amended proposed judgment pursuant to subdivision (c).

(b) (1) If the proposed judgment is based on the support obligor's earning capacity pursuant to clause (ii) or (iii) of subparagraph (A) of paragraph (2) of subdivision (d) of Section 17400, the local child support agency shall file a motion for judgment, as provided in subdivision (b) of Section 17404. The motion for judgment filed pursuant to this paragraph shall be served on the defendant in compliance with Section 1013 of the Code of Civil Procedure or otherwise as provided by law.

(2) At the motion for judgment hearing, the court shall permit the appearance and participation of the defendant and the other parent in the hearing, including, but not limited to, sworn testimony and the introduction of evidence, regardless of whether the defendant has filed an answer to the complaint.

(3) If the defendant fails to file an answer with the court and does not appear at the motion for judgment hearing, the judgment shall be entered by way of default after the court considers the factors set forth in subdivision (b) of Section 4058 and states its findings on the record. When considering those factors or any other relevant matter, the court may inquire of the local child support agency regarding the factors set forth in subdivision (b) of Section 4058 or any other relevant matter. If after consideration of the factors set forth in subdivision (b) of Section 4058 and the evidence presented by the local child support agency or the other parent the court determines that child support pursuant to the guidelines set forth in Article 2 (commencing with Section 4050) of Chapter 2 of Part 2 of Divi-

sion 9 would be lower than the proposed support obligation listed in the proposed judgment, the court shall enter an order for guideline child support. This paragraph does not limit the court's discretion to order an amount higher than, lower than, or equal to the proposed support obligation listed in the proposed judgment based on the evidence presented if the defendant files an answer or appears at the motion for judgment hearing.

(c) If the local child support agency receives additional information before the answer is filed and the additional information would result in a support order that is different from the amount in the proposed judgment, the local child support agency shall file a declaration setting forth the additional information and an amended proposed judgment. The local child support agency shall be permitted to file the amended proposed judgment at any time after the filing of the initial summons and complaint and before the answer is filed. The declaration and amended proposed judgment shall be served on the defendant in compliance with Section 1013 of the Code of Civil Procedure or otherwise as provided by law. The defendant's time to answer or otherwise appear shall be extended to 30 days from the date of service of the declaration and amended proposed judgment.

(d) Upon entry of the judgment, the clerk of the court shall provide a conformed copy of the judgment to the local child support agency. The local child support agency shall mail by first-class mail, postage prepaid, a notice of entry of judgment by default and a copy of the judgment to the defendant to the address where the summons and complaint were served and last known address if different from that address.

(e) (1) (A) Notwithstanding any other law, if the judgment is entered by way of default from a proposed support order that is based on earning capacity pursuant to clause (iii) of subparagraph (A) of paragraph (2) of subdivision (d) of Section 17400, within one year after entry of judgment and then annually thereafter, until a modified order is entered, the local child support agency shall conduct a review of the case to determine if there is sufficient additional evidence of income or earning capacity as described by Section 4058 available to establish actual income of the defendant or a different earning capacity, as described by subdivision (b) of Section 4058, from that which was the basis of the initial support order.

(B) If after any review pursuant to subparagraph (A), the local child support agency determines sufficient additional evidence exists, the local child support agency shall file a motion to modify the support order prospectively with the court within 60 days of its determination, and additional evidence shall constitute a change in circumstances to obtain a modification of the support order. This subdivision does not prohibit the local child support agency from filing the motion to modify pursuant to this subdivision prior to the expiration of any annual review period if additional evidence is discovered sooner.

(2) (A) Notwithstanding any other law, if the judgment is entered by way of default from a proposed support

order that is based on earning capacity pursuant to clause (iii) of subparagraph (A) of paragraph (2) of subdivision (d) of Section 17400, the defendant or the other parent may file a motion to modify the initial support order prospectively if sufficient additional evidence becomes available to establish actual income of the defendant or a different earning capacity.

(B) Additional evidence available pursuant to subparagraph (A) shall constitute a change in circumstances to obtain a modification of the initial support order.

(f) This section shall become operative January 1, 2026.[556]

17432. (a) In any action filed by the local child support agency pursuant to Section 17400, 17402, or 17404, the court may, on any terms that may be just, set aside that part of the judgment or order concerning the amount of child support to be paid. This relief may be granted after the six-month time limit of Section 473 of the Code of Civil Procedure has elapsed, based on the grounds, and within the time limits, specified in this section.

(b) This section shall apply only to judgments or orders for support that were based upon presumed income as specified in subdivision (d) of Section 17400 and that were entered after the entry of the default of the defendant under Section 17430. This section shall apply only to the amount of support ordered and not that portion of the judgment or order concerning the determination of parentage.

(c) The court may set aside the child support order contained in a judgment described in subdivision (b) if the defendant's income was substantially different for the period of time during which judgment was effective compared with the income the defendant was presumed to have. A "substantial difference" means that amount of income that would result in an order for support that deviates from the order entered by default by 10 percent or more.

(d) Application for relief under this section shall be filed together with an income and expense declaration or simplified financial statement or other information concerning income for any relevant years. The Judicial Council may combine the application for relief under this section and the proposed answer into a single form.

(e) The burden of proving that the actual income of the defendant deviated substantially from the presumed income shall be on the party seeking to set aside the order.

(f) A motion for relief under this section shall be filed within one year of the first collection of money by the local child support agency or the obligee. The one-year time period shall run from the date that the local child support agency receives the first collection.

(g) Within three months from the date the local child support agency receives the first collection for any order established using presumed income, the local child support agency shall check all appropriate sources for income information, and if income information exists, the local child support agency shall make a determination whether the order qualifies for set aside under this section. If the order qualifies for set aside, the local child support agency shall bring a motion for relief under this section.

(h) In all proceedings under this

section, before granting relief, the court shall consider the amount of time that has passed since the entry of the order, the circumstances surrounding the defendant's default, the relative hardship on the child or children to whom the duty of support is owed, the caretaker parent, and the defendant, and other equitable factors that the court deems appropriate.

(i) If the court grants the relief requested, the court shall issue a new child support order using the appropriate child support guidelines currently in effect. The new order shall have the same commencement date as the order set aside.

(j) The Judicial Council shall review and modify any relevant forms for purposes of this section. Any modifications to the forms shall be effective July 1, 2005. Prior to the implementation of any modified Judicial Council forms, the local child support agency or custodial parent may file any request to set aside a default judgment under this section using Judicial Council Form FL-680 entitled "Notice of Motion (Governmental)" and Form FL-684 entitled "Request for Order and Supporting Declaration (Governmental)."

(k) This section shall become inoperative on January 1, 2026, and, as of January 1, 2027, is repealed.[554]

17432. (a) In any action filed by the local child support agency pursuant to Section 17400, 17402, 17404, or 17404.1, the court may, on any terms that may be just, set aside that part of the judgment or order concerning the amount of child support to be paid. This relief may be granted after the six-month time limit of Section 473 of the Code of Civil Procedure has elapsed, based on the grounds, and within the time limits, specified in this section.

(b) This section shall apply only to judgments or orders for support that were based upon presumed income or earning capacity and that were entered after the entry of the default of the support obligor as specified in Sections 17400, 17404.1, and 17430 or any predecessors of those sections in the Family Code or the Welfare and Institutions Code. This section shall apply only to the amount of support ordered and not that portion of the judgment or order concerning the determination of parentage or the obligation of medical support or health insurance.

(c) (1) The court may set aside the child support order contained in a judgment described in subdivision (b) if the support obligor's income or earning capacity was substantially different for the period of time during which judgment was effective compared with the income or earning capacity the support obligor was presumed to have.

(2) For purposes of this section, "substantially different" means that amount of income that would result in an order for support that deviates from the order entered by default by 10 percent or more.

(d) The court, in its discretion, may set aside and reinstate child support for all or partial relevant periods of time depending on the income or earning capacity information available at the time the motion is filed. Relief setting aside the child support order for less than the full period of time that the judgment was effective shall not preclude a subsequent review within the timeframe provided pursuant to subdivision (g).

(e) Application for relief under this section shall be filed together with an income and expense declaration or simplified financial statement or other information concerning income or earning capacity for any relevant years. The Judicial Council may combine the application for relief under this section and the proposed answer into a single form.

(f) The party seeking to set aside the order has the burden of proving that the actual income or earning capacity of the support obligor was substantially different from the presumed income or earning capacity.

(g) (1) A party to the action described in subdivision (a), including the local child support agency, may file a motion for relief pursuant to this section within two years of the local child support agency's first collection of money through an earnings assignment order or an order or notice to withhold income for child support. The two-year time period shall run from the date that the local child support agency receives the first collection of money from one of the sources listed in this subdivision. Immediately upon receipt of the first collection of money from an earnings assignment order or order or notice to withhold income for child support, the local child support agency shall notify the support obligor and the support obligee in writing of the first collection, including the source of the collection, and the commencement of the two-year time period to file a motion for relief under this section.

(2) This subdivision does not prohibit any party to the action, including the local child support agency, from filing a motion for relief under this section prior to the commencement of the two-year time period.

(h) Within three months from the date the local child support agency receives the first collection for an order established using presumed income or earning capacity when the order was entered by default, the local child support agency shall check all appropriate sources for income information, and, if income information exists, the local child support agency shall determine whether the order qualifies for set aside under this section. If the order qualifies for set aside, the local child support agency shall bring a motion for relief under this section. When a party to the action, including the local child support agency, has taken subsequent legal action to modify the support prospectively, but did not address a possible set aside under this section, the subsequent modification shall not preclude the filing of a potential set aside at a later date.

(i) In all proceedings under this section, before granting relief, the court shall consider the amount of time that has passed since the entry of the order, the circumstances surrounding the support obligor's default, the relative hardship on the child or children to whom the duty of support is owed, the caretaker parent, and the support obligor, and other equitable factors that the court deems appropriate.

(j) If the court grants the relief requested, the court shall issue a new child support order using the appropriate child support guidelines currently in effect. The new order shall have the same commencement date as the order set aside.

(k) This section shall become operative on January 1, 2026.[557]

17432.5. No later than September 1, 2024, the Judicial Council shall adopt and approve any forms necessary to implement Sections 17400, 17404.1, 17430, and 17432 as added by the act that added this section. Forms adopted pursuant to this section shall have an effective date of January 1, 2026.[558]

17433. In an action in which a judgment or order for support was entered after the entry of the default of the defendant under Section 17430, the court shall relieve the defendant from that judgment or order if the defendant establishes that the defendant was mistakenly identified in the order or in any subsequent documents or proceedings as the person having an obligation to provide support. The defendant shall also be entitled to the remedies specified in subdivisions (d) and (e) of Section 17530 with respect to any actions taken to enforce that judgment or order. This section is only intended to apply where an order has been entered against a person who is not the support obligor named in the judgment or order.

17433.5. In any action enforced pursuant to this article, no interest shall accrue on an obligation for current child, spousal, family, or medical support due in a given month until the first day of the following month.[127]

17434. (a) The department shall publish a booklet describing the proper procedures and processes for the collection and payment of child and spousal support. The booklet shall be written in language understandable to the lay person and shall direct the reader to obtain the assistance of the local child support agency, the family law facilitator, or legal counsel where appropriate. The department may contract on a competitive basis with an organization or individual to write the booklet.

(b) The department shall have primary responsibility for the design and development of the contents of the booklet. The department shall solicit comment regarding the content of the booklet from the Director of the Administrative Office of the Courts. The department shall verify the appropriateness and accuracy of the contents of the booklet with at least one representative of each of the following organizations:

(1) A local child support agency.

(2) The State Attorney General's office.

(3) A community organization that advocates for the rights of custodial parents.

(4) A community organization that advocates for the rights of supporting parents.

(c) Upon receipt of booklets on support collection, each county welfare department shall provide a copy to each head of household whose application for public assistance under Division 9 (commencing with Section 10000) of the Welfare and Institutions Code has been approved and for whom support rights have been assigned pursuant to Section 11477 of the Welfare and Institutions Code. The department shall provide copies of the booklet to local child support agencies for distribution, and to any person upon request. The department shall also distribute the booklets to all superior courts. Upon receipt of those booklets, each clerk of the court shall provide two copies of the booklet to the petitioner or plaintiff in any action involving the support of a minor child. The moving party shall serve a copy of the booklet on the responding party.

(d) The department shall expand the information provided under its toll-free information hotline in response to inquiries regarding the process and procedures for collection and payment of child and spousal support. This toll-free number shall be advertised as providing information on child and spousal support. The hotline personnel shall not provide legal consultation or advice, but shall provide only referral services.

(e) The department shall maintain a file of referral sources to provide callers to the telephone hotline with the following information specific to the county in which the caller resides:

(1) The location and telephone number of the local child support agency, the county welfare office, the family law facilitator, and any other government agency that handles child and spousal support matters.

(2) The telephone number of the local bar association for referral to attorneys in family law practice.

(3) The name and telephone number of at least one organization that advocates the payment of child and spousal support or the name and telephone number of at least one organization that advocates the rights of supporting parents, if these organizations exist in the county.[358]

17440. (a) The Department of Child Support Services shall work with all branches of the United States military and the National Guard to ensure that information is made available regarding the rights and abilities of activated service members to have their support orders modified based on a change in income resulting from their activation, or other change of circumstance affecting the child support calculation, or to have a portion of their child support arrearages compromised pursuant to Section 17560.

(b) No later than 90 days after the effective date of this section, the department shall develop a form for completion by the service member that will allow the local child support agency to proceed with a motion for modification without the service member being required to appear. The form shall contain only the information necessary for the local child support agency to proceed with the motion.

(c) Within five business days of receipt of a properly completed form, the local child support agency shall bring a motion to modify the support order. The local child support agency shall bring the motion if the change in circumstances would result in any change in the dollar amount of the support order.

(d) The department shall work with the United States military to have this form and the form developed pursuant to Section 3651 distributed at all mobilization stations or other appropriate locations to ensure timely notification to all activated personnel of their rights and responsibilities.

Article 1.5: Delinquent Child Support Obligations and Financial Institution Data Match

17450. (a) For purposes of this article:

(1) "Child support delinquency" means a delinquency defined in subdivision (c) of Section 17500.

(2) "Earnings" shall include the items described in Section 5206.

(b) (1) When a delinquency is submitted to the department pursuant to subdivision (c) of Section 17500, the amount of the child support delinquency shall be collected by the department in any manner authorized under state or federal law.

(2) Any compensation, fee, commission, expense, or other fee for service incurred by the department in the collection of a child support delinquency authorized under this article shall not be an obligation of, or collected from, the obligated parent.

(c) (1) The department may return or allow a local child support agency to retain a child support delinquency for a specified purpose for collection where the department determines that the return or retention of the delinquency for the purpose so specified will enhance the collectibility of the delinquency. The department shall establish a process whereby a local child support agency may request and shall be allowed to withdraw, rescind, or otherwise recall the submittal of an account that has been submitted.

(2) If an obligor is disabled, meets the federal Supplemental Security Income resource test, and is receiving Supplemental Security Income/State Supplementary Payments (SSI/SSP), or, but for excess income as described in Section 416.1100 and following of Part 416 of Title 20 of the Code of Federal Regulations, would be eligible to receive as SSI/SSP, pursuant to Section 12200 of the Welfare and Institutions Code, and the obligor has supplied the local child support agency with proof of eligibility for, and, if applicable, receipt of, SSI/SSP or Social Security Disability Insurance benefits, then the child support delinquency shall not be referred to the department for collection, and, if referred, shall be withdrawn, rescinded, or otherwise recalled from the department by the local child support agency. The department shall not take any collection action, or if the local child support agency has already taken collection action, shall cease collection actions in the case of a disabled obligor when the delinquency is withdrawn, rescinded, or otherwise recalled by the local child support agency in accordance with the process established as described in paragraph (1).

(d) It is the intent of the Legislature that when the California Child Support Enforcement System (CSE) is fully operational, any statutes that should be modified based upon the status of the system shall be revised. During the development and implementation of CSE, the department, as the Title IV-D agency, may, through appropriate interagency agreement, delegate any and all of the functions or procedures specified in this article to the Franchise Tax Board. The Franchise Tax Board shall perform those functions or procedures as specified in Sections 19271 to 19275, inclusive, of the Revenue and Taxation Code until the director, by letter to the executive officer of the Franchise Tax Board, revokes the delegation of Title IV-D functions. Sections 19271 to 19275, inclusive, of the Revenue and Taxation Code shall be effective for these purposes until the revocation of delegation to the Franchise Tax Board.

(e) Consistent with the development and implementation of the California Child Support Enforcement System, the Franchise Tax Board and the department shall enter into a letter of agreement and an interagency agreement whereby the department shall assume responsibility for collection of child support delinquencies and the Financial Institution Data Match System as set forth in this article. The letter of agreement and interagency agreement shall, at a minimum, set forth all of the following:

(1) Contingent upon the enactment of the Budget Act, and staffing authorization from the Department of Finance and the Department of Human Resources, the department shall assume responsibility for leadership and staffing of the collection of child support delinquencies and the Financial Institution Data Match System.

(2) All employees and other personnel who staff or provide support for the collection of child support delinquencies and the Financial Institution Data Match System at the Franchise Tax Board shall become the employees of the department at their existing or equivalent classification, salaries, and benefits.

(3) Any other provisions necessary to ensure continuity of function and meet or exceed existing levels of service, including, but not limited to, agreements for continued use of automated systems used by the Franchise Tax Board to locate child support obligors and their assets.

17452. (a) Subject to state and federal privacy and information security laws, the Franchise Tax Board shall make tax return information available to the department, upon request, for the purpose of collecting child support delinquencies referred to the department.

(b) For purposes of this article, the Franchise Tax Board shall incur no obligation or liability to any person arising from any of the following:

(1) Furnishing information to the department as required by this section.

(2) Failing to disclose to a taxpayer or accountholder that the name, address, social security number, or other taxpayer identification number or other identifying information of that person was included in the data exchange with the department required by this section.

(3) Any other action taken in good faith to comply with the requirements of this section.

(c) It is the intent of the Legislature that any provision of income tax return information by the Franchise Tax Board to the department pursuant to this article shall be done in accordance with the privacy and confidential information laws of this state and of the United States, and to the satisfaction of the Franchise Tax Board.

17453. (a) The department, in coordination with financial institutions doing business in this state, shall operate a Financial Institution Data Match System utilizing automated data exchanges to the maximum extent feasible. The Financial Institution Data Match System shall be implemented and maintained pursuant to guidelines prescribed by the department. These guidelines shall include a structure by which financial institutions, or their designated data-processing agents, shall receive from the department the file or files of past-due support obligors compiled in accordance with subdivision (c), so that the institution shall match with its own list of accountholders to identify past-due support obligor accountholders at the institution. To the extent allowed by the federal Personal Responsibility and Work Opportunity Reconciliation Act of 1996 (P.L. 104-193), the guidelines shall include an option by which financial institutions without the technical ability to process the data exchange, or without the ability to employ a third-party data processor to process the data exchange, may forward to the department a list of all accountholders and their social security numbers, so that the department shall match that list with the file or files of past-due support obligors compiled in accordance with subdivision (c).

(b) The Financial Institution Data Match System shall not be subject to any limitation set forth in Chapter 20 (commencing with Section 7460) of Division 7 of Title 1 of the Government Code. However, any use of the information provided pursuant to this section for any purpose other than the enforcement and collection of a child support delinquency, as set forth in Section 17450, shall be a violation of Section 17212.

(c) (1) Until implementation of the California Child Support Automation System, each county shall compile a file of support obligors with judgments and orders that are being enforced by local child support agencies pursuant to Section 17400, and who are past due in the payment of their support obligations. The file shall be compiled, updated, and forwarded to the department, in accordance with the guidelines prescribed by the department.

(2) The department shall compile a file of obligors with support arrearages from requests made by other states for administrative enforcement in interstate cases, in accordance with federal requirements pursuant to paragraph 14 of subsection (a) of Section 666 of Title 42 of the United States Code. The file shall include, to the extent possible, the obligor's address.

(d) To effectuate the Financial Institution Data Match System, financial institutions subject to this section shall do all of the following:

(1) Provide to the department on a quarterly basis, the name, record address and other addresses, social security number or other taxpayer identification number, and other identifying information for each noncustodial parent who maintains an account at the institution and who owes past-due support, as identified by the department by name and social security number or other taxpayer identification number.

(2) Except as provided in subdivision (j), in response to a notice or order to withhold issued by the department, withhold from any accounts of the obligor the amount of any past-due support stated on the notice or order and transmit the amount to the

department in accordance with Section 17454.

(e) Unless otherwise required by applicable law, a financial institution furnishing a report or providing information to the department pursuant to this section shall not disclose to a depositor, accountholder, codepositor, or coaccountholder, that the name, address, social security number, or other taxpayer identification number or other identifying information of that person has been received from, or furnished to, the department.

(f) A financial institution shall incur no obligation or liability to any person arising from any of the following:

(1) Furnishing information to the department as required by this section.

(2) Failing to disclose to a depositor, accountholder, codepositor, or coaccountholder, that the name, address, social security number, or other taxpayer identification number or other identifying information of that person was included in the data exchange with the department required by this section.

(3) Withholding or transmitting any assets in response to a notice or order to withhold issued by the department as a result of the data exchange. This paragraph shall not preclude any liability that may result if the financial institution does not comply with subdivision (b) of Section 17456.

(4) Any other action taken in good faith to comply with the requirements of this section.

(g) (1) With respect to files compiled under paragraph (1) of subdivision (c), the department shall forward to the counties, in accordance with guidelines prescribed by the department, information obtained from the financial institutions pursuant to this section. No county shall use this information for directly levying on any account. Each county shall keep the information confidential as provided by Section 17212.

(2) With respect to files compiled under paragraph (2) of subdivision (c), the amount collected by the department shall be deposited and distributed to the referring state in accordance with Section 17458.

(h) For those noncustodial parents owing past-due support for which there is a match under paragraph (1) of subdivision (d), the amount past due as indicated on the file or files compiled pursuant to subdivision (c) at the time of the match shall be a delinquency under this article for the purposes of the department taking any collection action pursuant to Section 17454.

(i) A child support delinquency need not be referred to the department for collection if a jurisdiction outside this state is enforcing the support order.

(j) (1) Each county shall notify the department upon the occurrence of the circumstances described in the following subparagraphs with respect to an obligor of past-due support:

(A) A court has ordered an obligor to make scheduled payments on a child support arrearages obligation and the obligor is in compliance with that order.

(B) An earnings assignment order or an order/notice to withhold income that includes an amount for past-due support has been served on the obligated parent's employer and earnings are being withheld pursuant to the earnings assignment order or an order/notice to withhold income.

(C) At least 50 percent of the obligated parent's earnings are being withheld for support.

(2) Notwithstanding Section 704.070 of the Code of Civil Procedure, if any of the conditions set forth in paragraph (1) exist, the assets of an obligor held by a financial institution are subject to levy as provided by paragraph (2) of subdivision (d). However, the first three thousand five hundred dollars ($3,500) of an obligor's assets are exempt from collection under this subdivision without the obligor having to file a claim of exemption.

(3) If any of the conditions set forth in paragraph (1) exist, an obligor may apply for a claim of exemption pursuant to Article 2 (commencing with Section 703.510) of Chapter 4 of Division 2 of Title 9 of Part 2 of the Code of Civil Procedure for an amount that is less than or equal to the total amount levied. The sole basis for a claim of exemption under this subdivision shall be the financial hardship for the obligor and the obligor's dependents.

(4) For the purposes of a claim of exemption made pursuant to paragraph (3), Section 688.030 of the Code of Civil Procedure shall not apply.

(5) For claims of exemption made pursuant to paragraph (3), the local child support agency responsible for enforcement of the obligor's child support order shall be the levying officer for the purpose of compliance with the provisions set forth in Article 2 (commencing with Section 703.510) of Chapter 4 of Division 2 of Title 9 of Part 2 of the Code of Civil Procedure except for the release of property required by subdivision (e) of Section 703.580 of the Code of Civil Procedure.

(6) The local child support agency shall notify the department within two business days of the receipt of a claim of exemption from an obligor. The department shall direct the financial institution subject to the order to withhold to hold any funds subject to the order pending notification by the department to remit or release the amounts held.

(7) The superior court in the county in which the local child support agency enforcing the support obligation is located shall have jurisdiction to determine the amount of exemption to be allowed. The court shall consider the needs of the obligor, the obligee, and all persons the obligor is required to support, and all other relevant circumstances in determining whether to allow any exemption pursuant to this subdivision. The court shall give effect to its determination by an order specifying the extent to which the amount levied is exempt.

(8) Within two business days of receipt of an endorsed copy of a court order issued pursuant to subdivision (e) of Section 703.580 of the Code of Civil Procedure, the local child support agency shall provide the department with a copy of the order. The department shall instruct the financial institution to remit or release the obligor's funds in accordance with the court's order.

(k) Out of any money received from the federal government for the purpose of reimbursing financial institutions for their actual and reasonable costs incurred in complying with this section, the state shall reimburse those institutions. To the extent that money is not provided by the federal government for that purpose, the state shall not reimburse financial institutions for their costs in complying with this section.

(l) For purposes of this section:

(1) "Account" means any demand deposit account, share or share draft account, checking or negotiable withdrawal order account, savings account, time deposit account, or a money market mutual fund account, whether or not the account bears interest.

(2) "Financial institution" has the same meaning as defined in paragraph (1) of subsection (d) of Section 669A of Title 42 of the United States Code.

17454. (a) At least 45 days before sending a notice to withhold, the department shall request that a depository institution provide the department with a designated address for receiving notices to withhold.

(b) Once the depository institution has specified a designated address pursuant to subdivision (a), the department shall send all notices to that address unless the depository institution provides notification of another address. The department shall send all notices to withhold to a new designated address 30 days after notification.

(c) If a notice to withhold is mailed to the branch where the account is located or principal banking office, the depository institution shall be liable for a failure to withhold only to the extent that the accounts can be identified in information normally maintained at that location in the ordinary course of business.

(d) The department may by notice, served by magnetic media, electronic transmission, or other electronic technology, require any depository institution, as defined in the Federal Reserve Act (12 U.S.C.A. Sec. 461 (b)(1)(A)), that the department, in its sole discretion, has reason to believe may have in its possession, or under its control, any credits or other personal property or other things of value, belonging to a child support obligor, to withhold, from the credits or other personal property or other things of value, the amount of any child support delinquency, and interest, due from an obligor and transmit that amount withheld to the department at the times that it may designate, but not less than 10 business days from receipt of the notice. The notice shall state the amount due from the obligor and shall be delivered or transmitted to the branch or office reported pursuant to subdivision (a), or other address designated by that depository institution for purposes of the department serving notice by magnetic media, electronic transmission, or other electronic technology.

(e) For purposes of this section, the term "address" shall include telephone or modem number, facsimile number, or any other number designated by the depository institution to receive data by electronic means.

17456. (a) Any person required to withhold and transmit any amount pursuant to this article shall comply with the requirement without resort to any legal or equitable action in a court of law or equity. Any person paying to the department any amount required by it to be withheld is not liable therefore to the person from whom withheld unless the amount withheld is refunded to the withholding agent. However, if a depository institution, as defined in the Federal Reserve Act (12 U.S.C.A. Sec. 461(b)(1)(A)) withholds and pays to the department pursuant to this article any moneys held in a deposit account in which the delinquent obligor and another person or persons have an interest, or in an account held in the name of a third party or parties in which the delinquent obligor is ultimately determined to have no interest, the depository institution paying those moneys to the department is not liable therefore to any of the persons who have an interest in the account, unless the amount withheld is refunded to the withholding agent.

(b) In the case of a deposit account or accounts for which this notice to withhold applies, the depository institution shall send a notice by first-class mail to each person named on the account or accounts included in the notice from the department, provided that a current address for each person is available to the institution. This notice shall inform each person as to the reason for the hold placed on the account or accounts, the amount subject to being withheld, and the date by which this amount is to be remitted to the department. An institution may assess the account or accounts of each person receiving this notice a reasonable service charge not to exceed three dollars ($3).

17460. (a) As necessary, the department shall seek reciprocal agreements with other states to improve its ability to collect child support payments from out-of-state obligated parents on behalf of custodial parents residing in California. The department may pursue agreements with the Internal Revenue Service, as permitted by federal law, to improve collections of child support delinquencies from out-of-state obligated parents through cooperative agreements with the service.

(b) The California Child Support Enforcement System shall, for purposes of this article, include the capacity to interface and exchange information, if feasible, with the Internal Revenue Service, to enable the immediate reporting and tracking of obligated parent information.

(c) The department shall enter into any interagency agreements that are necessary for the implementation of this article. State departments and boards shall cooperate with the department to the extent necessary for the implementation of this article. Out of any money received from the federal government for the purpose of reimbursing state departments and boards for their actual and reasonable costs incurred in complying with this section, the department shall reimburse those departments and boards. To the extent that money is not provided by the federal government for that purpose, and subject to the annual Budget Act, the state shall fund departments and boards for their costs in complying with this section.

Article 2: Collections and Enforcement

17500. (a) In carrying out its obligations under Title IV-D of the Social Security Act (42 U.S.C. Sec. 651 et seq.), the department and the local child support agency shall have the responsibility for promptly and effectively collecting and enforcing child support obligations.

(b) The department and the local child support agency are the public agencies responsible for administering wage withholding for the purposes of Title IV-D of the Social Security Act (42 U.S.C. Sec. 651 et seq.).

(c) Except as provided in Section 17450, the local child support agency shall submit child support delinquencies to the department for purposes of supplementing the collection efforts of the local child support agencies. Submissions shall be in the form and manner and at the time prescribed by the department. Collection shall be made by the department in accordance with Section 17450. For purposes of this subdivision, "child support delinquency" means an arrearage or otherwise past due amount that accrues when an obligor fails to make any court-ordered support payment when due, which is more than 60 days past due, and the aggregate amount of which exceeds one hundred dollars ($100).

(d) If a child support delinquency exists at the time a case is opened by the local child support agency, the responsibility for the collection of the child support delinquency shall be submitted to the department no later than 30 days after receipt of the case by the local child support agency.

17502. A local child support agency that is collecting child support payments on behalf of a child and who is unable to deliver the payments to the obligee because the local child support agency is unable to locate the obligee shall make all reasonable efforts to locate the obligee for a period of six months. If the local child support agency is unable to locate the obligee within the six-month period, it shall return the undeliverable payments to the obligor, with written notice advising the obligor that (a) the return of the funds does not relieve the obligor of the support order, and (b) the obligor should consider placing the funds aside for purposes of child support in case the obligee appears and seeks collection of the undistributed amounts. No interest shall accrue on any past-due child support amount for which the obligor made payment to the local child support agency for six consecutive months, or on any amounts due thereafter until the obligee is located, provided that the local child support agency returned the funds to the obligor because the local child support agency was unable to locate the obligee and, when the obligee was located, the obligor made full payment for all past-due child support amounts.

17504. (a) The first fifty dollars ($50) of any amount of child support collected in a month in payment of the required support obligation for that month shall be paid to a recipient of aid under Article 2 (commencing with Section 11250) of Chapter 2 of Part 3 of Division 9 of the Welfare and Institutions Code, except recipients of foster care payments under Article 5 (commencing with Section 11400) of Chapter 2 of Part 3 of Division 9 of the Welfare and Institutions Code shall not be considered income or resources of the recipient family, and shall not be deducted from the amount of aid to which the family would otherwise be eligible. The local child support agency in each county shall ensure that payments are made to recipients as required by this section.

(b) This section shall become inoperative on January 1, 2022, or when the State Department of Social Services and the Department of Child Support Services notify the Legislature that the Statewide Automated Welfare System and the Child Support Enforcement System can perform the necessary automation to implement this section, as amended by the act that added this subdivision, whichever date is later, and as of that date, or, if this section becomes inoperative on a date other than January 1, 2022, on January 1 of the following year, is repealed.

(c) The State Department of Social Services shall issue an all-county letter or similar instruction no later than September 1, 2020, to facilitate automation changes necessary to implement this section and Section 17504, as added by Section 2 of the act that added this subdivision.[486]

17504. (a) The first one hundred dollars ($100) of any amount of child support collected in a month for a family with one child, or the first two hundred dollars ($200) for a family with two or more children, in payment of the required support obligation for that month shall be paid to a recipient of aid under Article 2 (commencing with Section 11250) of Chapter 2 of Part 3 of Division 9 of the Welfare and Institutions Code, except recipients of foster care payments under Article 5 (commencing with Section 11400) of Chapter 2 of Part 3 of Division 9 of the Welfare and Institutions Code, and shall not be considered income or resources of the recipient family, and shall not be deducted from the amount of aid to which the family would otherwise be eligible. The local child support agency in each county shall ensure that payments are made to recipients as required by this section.

(b) Notwithstanding the rulemaking provisions of the Administrative Procedure Act (Chapter 3.5 (commencing with Section 11340) of Part 1 of Division 3 of Title 2 of the Government Code), the State Department of Social Services and the Department of Child Support Services may implement, interpret, or make specific this section by means of all-county letters or similar instructions from the department until regulations are adopted. These all-county letters or similar written instructions shall have the same force and effect as regulations until the adoption of regulations.

(c) This section shall become operative on January 1, 2022, or when the State Department of Social Services and the Department of Child Support Services notify the Legislature that the Statewide Automated Welfare System and Child Support Enforcement System can perform the necessary automation to implement this section, whichever date is later.

17504.2. (a) (1) Any amount of support collected in a month in payment of an assigned support obligation shall be passed through to a former recipient of aid under Article 2 (commencing with Section 11250) of Chapter 2 of Part 3 of Division 9 of the Welfare and Institutions Code, except recipients of foster care payments under Article 5 (commencing with Section 11400) of Chapter 2 of Part 3 of Division 9 of the Welfare and Institutions Code.

(2) The local child support agency in each county shall ensure that payments are made to former recipients of aid when required by this section.

(3) The Department of Child Support Services and the local child support agencies shall provide written or electronic informational materials, which shall be developed by the Department of Child Support Services in collaboration with the Department of Social Services, to child support case participants, who are former recipients of aid, to notify them of the potential impacts of passthrough collections pursuant to this section on eligibility for public benefit programs.

(b) Notwithstanding Section 17502 of the Family Code, any passthrough payments under this section that cannot be delivered to a former recipient of aid pursuant to paragraph (2) of subdivision (a) for a period of six months shall not be returned to the obligor and shall be sent to recoup aid paid on behalf of the recipient pursuant to Section 11477 of the Welfare and Institutions Code. If the former recipient of aid makes a claim for the passthrough payment within 12 months of the payment being sent to recoupment, the payment shall be removed from recoupment and sent to the former recipient of aid. The Department of Child Support Services shall monitor the number of claims made after payments are sent for recoupment. The department shall provide that information to the Legislature no later than April 1, 2025, or two years and three months after the operative date of this section as established by subdivision (e), whichever date is later.

(c) Nothing in this section shall be construed to discontinue assignments under Section 11477 of the Welfare and Institutions Code.

(d) Notwithstanding the rulemaking provisions of the Administrative Procedure Act (Chapter 3.5 (commencing with Section 11340) of Part 1 of Division 3 of Title 2 of the Government Code), the State Department of Social Services and the Department of Child Support Services may implement, interpret, or make specific this section by means of all-county letters or similar instructions from the department until regulations are adopted. These all-county letters or similar written instructions shall have the same force and effect as regulations until the adoption of regulations.

(e) This section shall become operative on July 1, 2023, or on the date the department notifies the Legislature that the Child Support Enforcement System can perform the necessary automation to implement this section, and the Department of Child Support Services has developed and provided the written materials pursuant to subdivision (a), whichever date is later.[522]

17504.4. On a monthly basis, the local child support agency shall provide to any CalWORKs recipient or former recipient for whom an assignment pursuant to subdivision (a) of Section 11477 of the Welfare and Institutions Code is currently effective, a notice of the amount of assigned support payments made on behalf of the recipient or former recipient or any other family member for whom public assistance is received.

17505. (a) All state, county, and local agencies shall cooperate with the local child support agency (1) in the enforcement of any child support obligation or to the extent required under the state plan under Part 6 (commencing with Section 5700.101) of Division 9, Section 270 of the Penal Code, and Section 17604, and (2) the enforcement of spousal support orders and in the location of parents or putative parents. The local child support agency may enter into an agreement with and shall secure from a municipal, county, or state law enforcement agency, pursuant to that agreement, state summary criminal record information through the California Law Enforcement Telecommunications System. This subdivision applies irrespective of whether the children are or are not receiving aid to families with dependent children. All state, county, and local agencies shall cooperate with the district attorney in implementing Chapter 8 (commencing with Section 3130) of Part 2 of Division 8 concerning the location, seizure, and recovery of abducted, concealed, or detained minor children.

(b) On request, all state, county, and local agencies shall supply the local child support agency of any county in this state or the California Parent Locator Service with all information on hand relative to the location, income, or property of any parents, putative parents, spouses, or former spouses, notwithstanding any other provision of law making the information confidential, and with all information on hand relative to the location and prosecution of any person who has, by means of false statement or representation or by impersonation or other fraudulent device, obtained aid for a child under this chapter.

(c) The California Child Support Automation System, or its replacement, shall be entitled to the same cooperation and information provided to the California Parent Locator Service, to the extent allowed by law. The California Child Support Automation System, or its replacement, shall be allowed access to criminal offender record information only to the extent that access is allowed by law.

(d) Information exchanged between the California Parent Locator Service or the California Child Support Automation System, or its replacement, and state, county, or local agencies as specified in Sections 653(c)(4) and 666(c)(1)(D) of Title 42 of the United State Code shall be through automated processes to the maximum extent feasible.[343]

17506. (a) There is in the department a California Parent Locator Service and Central Registry that shall collect and disseminate all of the following, with respect to any parent, putative parent, spouse, or former spouse:

(1) The full and true name of the parent together with any known aliases.

(2) Date and place of birth.

(3) Physical description.

(4) Social security number, individual taxpayer identification number, or other uniform identification number.

(5) Employment history and earnings.

(6) Military status and Veterans Administration or military service serial number.

(7) Last known address, telephone number, and date thereof.

(8) Driver's license number or identification card number issued by the Department of Motor Vehicles, driving record, and vehicle registration information.

(9) Criminal, licensing, and applicant records and information.

(10) (A) Any additional location, asset, and income information, including income tax return information obtained pursuant to Section 19548 of the Revenue and Taxation Code, and to the extent permitted by federal law, the address, telephone number, and social security number obtained from a public utility, cable television corporation, a provider of electronic digital pager communication, or a provider of mobile telephony services that may be of assistance in locating the parent, putative parent, abducting, concealing, or detaining parent, spouse, or former spouse, in establishing a parent and child relationship, in enforcing the child support liability of the absent parent, or enforcing the spousal support liability of the spouse or former spouse to the extent required by the state plan pursuant to Section 17604.

(B) For purposes of this subdivision, "income tax return information" means all of the following regarding the taxpayer:

(i) Assets.

(ii) Credits.

(iii) Deductions.

(iv) Exemptions.

(v) Identity.

(vi) Liabilities.

(vii) Nature, source, and amount of income.

(viii) Net worth.

(ix) Payments.

(x) Receipts.

(xi) Address.

(xii) Social security number, individual taxpayer identification number, or other uniform identification number.

(b) Pursuant to a letter of agreement entered into between the Department of Child Support Services and the Department of Justice, the Department of Child Support Services shall assume responsibility for the California Parent Locator Service and Central Registry. The letter of agreement shall, at a minimum, set forth all of the following:

(1) Contingent upon funding in the Budget Act, the Department of Child Support Services shall assume responsibility for leadership and staff of the California Parent Locator Service and Central Registry commencing July 1, 2003.

(2) All employees and other personnel who staff or provide support for the California Parent Locator Service and Central Registry shall, at the time of the transition, at their option, become the employees of the Department of Child Support Services at their existing or equivalent classification, salaries, and benefits.

(3) Until the department's automation system for the California Parent Locator Service and Central Registry functions is fully operational, the department shall use the automation system operated by the Department of Justice.

(4) Any other provisions necessary to ensure continuity of function and meet or exceed existing levels of service.

(c) To effectuate the purposes of this section, the California Child Support Enforcement System and the California Parent Locator Service and Central Registry shall utilize the federal Parent Locator Service to the extent necessary, and may request and shall receive from all departments, boards, bureaus, or other agencies of the state, or any of its political subdivisions, and those entities shall provide, that assistance and data that will enable the Department of Child Support Services and other public agencies to carry out their powers and duties to locate parents, spouses, and former spouses, and to identify their assets, to establish parent-child relationships, and to enforce liability for child or spousal support, and for any other obligations incurred on behalf of children, and shall also provide that information to any local child support agency in fulfilling the duties prescribed in Section 270 of the Penal Code, and in Chapter 8 (commencing with Section 3130) of Part 2 of Division 8 of this code, relating to abducted, concealed, or detained children and to any county child welfare agency or county probation department in fulfilling the duties prescribed in Article 5.5 (commencing with Section 290.1) of Chapter 2 of Part 1 of Division 2 of the Welfare and Institutions Code, and prescribed in Article 6 (commencing with Section 300) of Chapter 2 of Part 1 of Division 2 of the Welfare and Institutions Code to identify, locate, and notify parents or relatives of children who are the subject of juvenile court proceedings, to establish parent and child relationships pursuant to Section 316.2 of the Welfare and Institutions Code, and to assess the appropriateness of placement of a child with a noncustodial parent pursuant to Section 361.2 of the Welfare and Institutions Code. Consistent with paragraph (1) of subdivision (e) of Section 309 of, and paragraph (2) of subdivision (d) of Section 628 of, the Welfare and Institutions Code, in order for county child welfare and probation departments to carry out their duties to identify and locate all grandparents, adult siblings, and other adult relatives of the child as defined in paragraph (2) of subdivision (f) of Section 319 of the Welfare and Institutions Code, including any other adult relatives suggested by the parents, county personnel are permitted to request and receive information from the California Parent Locator Service and Federal Parent Locator Service. County child welfare agencies and probation departments shall be entitled to the information described in this subdivision regardless of whether an all-county letter or similar instruction is issued pursuant to subparagraph (C) of paragraph (8) of subdivision (c) of Section 11478.1 of the Welfare and Institutions Code. The California Child Support Enforcement System shall be entitled to the same cooperation and information as the California Parent Locator Service and Central Registry to the extent allowed by law. The California Child Support Enforcement System shall be allowed access to criminal record information only to the extent that access is allowed by state and federal law.

(d) (1) To effectuate the purposes of this section, and notwithstanding any other law, regulation, or tariff, and to the extent permitted by federal law, the California Parent Locator Service and Central Registry and the California Child Support Enforcement System may request and shall receive from public utilities, as defined in Section 216 of the Public Utilities Code, customer service information, including the full name, address, telephone number, date of birth, employer name and address, and social security number of customers of the public utility, to the extent that this information is stored within the computer database of the public utility.

(2) To effectuate the purposes of this section, and notwithstanding any other law, regulation, or tariff, and to the extent permitted by federal law, the California Parent Locator Service and Central Registry and the California Child Support Enforcement System may request and shall receive from cable television corporations, as defined in Section 216.4 of the Public Utilities Code, the providers of electronic digital pager communication, as defined in Section 629.51 of the Penal Code, and the providers of mobile telephony services, as defined in Section 224.4 of the Public Utilities Code, customer service information, including the full name, address, telephone number, date of birth, employer name and address, and social security number of customers of the cable television corporation, customers of the providers of electronic digital pager communication, and customers of the providers of mobile telephony services.

(3) In order to protect the privacy of utility, cable television, electronic digital pager communication, and mobile telephony service customers, a request to a public utility, cable television corporation, provider of electronic digital pager communication, or provider of mobile telephony services for customer service information pursuant to this section shall meet the following requirements:

(A) Be submitted to the public utility, cable television corporation, provider of electronic digital pager communication, or provider of mobile telephony services in writing, on a transmittal document prepared by the California Parent Locator Service and Central Registry or the California Child Support Enforcement System and approved by all of the public utilities, cable television corporations, providers of electronic digital pager communication, and providers of mobile telephony services. The transmittal shall be deemed to be an administrative subpoena for customer service information.

(B) Have the signature of a representative authorized by the California Parent Locator Service and Central Registry or the California Child Support Enforcement System.

(C) Contain at least three of the following data elements regarding the person sought:

(i) First and last name, and middle initial, if known.

(ii) Social security number.

(iii) Driver's license number or identification card number issued by the Department of Motor Vehicles.

(iv) Birth date.

(v) Last known address.

(vi) Spouse's name.

(D) The California Parent Locator Service and Central Registry and the California Child Support Enforcement System shall ensure that each public utility, cable television corporation, provider of electronic digital pager communication services, and provider of mobile telephony services has at all times a current list of the names of persons authorized to request customer service information.

(E) The California Child Support

Enforcement System and the California Parent Locator Service and Central Registry shall ensure that customer service information supplied by a public utility, cable television corporation, provider of electronic digital pager communication, or provider of mobile telephony services is applicable to the person who is being sought before releasing the information pursuant to subdivision (d).

(4) During the development of the California Child Support Enforcement System, the department shall determine the necessity of additional locate sources, including those specified in this section, based upon the cost-effectiveness of those sources.

(5) The public utility, cable television corporation, electronic digital pager communication provider, or mobile telephony service provider may charge a fee to the California Parent Locator Service and Central Registry or the California Child Support Enforcement System for each search performed pursuant to this subdivision to cover the actual costs to the public utility, cable television corporation, electronic digital pager communication provider, or mobile telephony service provider for providing this information.

(6) No public utility, cable television corporation, electronic digital pager communication provider, or mobile telephony service provider or official or employee thereof, shall be subject to criminal or civil liability for the release of customer service information as authorized by this subdivision.

(e) Notwithstanding Section 14203 of the Penal Code, any records established pursuant to this section shall be disseminated only to the Department of Child Support Services, the California Child Support Enforcement System, the California Parent Locator Service and Central Registry, the parent locator services and central registries of other states as defined by federal statutes and regulations, a local child support agency of any county in this state, and the federal Parent Locator Service. The California Child Support Enforcement System shall be allowed access to criminal offender record information only to the extent that access is allowed by law.

(f) (1) At no time shall any information received by the California Parent Locator Service and Central Registry or by the California Child Support Enforcement System be disclosed to any person, agency, or other entity, other than those persons, agencies, and entities specified pursuant to Section 17505, this section, or any other provision.

(2) This subdivision shall not otherwise affect discovery between parties in any action to establish, modify, or enforce child, family, or spousal support, that relates to custody or visitation.

(g) (1) The Department of Justice, in consultation with the Department of Child Support Services, shall promulgate rules and regulations to facilitate maximum and efficient use of the California Parent Locator Service and Central Registry. Upon implementation of the California Child Support Enforcement System, the Department of Child Support Services shall assume all responsibility for promulgating rules and regulations for use of the California Parent Locator Service and Central Registry.

(2) The Department of Child Support Services, the Public Utilities Commission, the cable television corporations, providers of electronic digital pager communication, and the providers of mobile telephony services shall develop procedures for obtaining the information described in subdivision (c) from public utilities, cable television corporations, providers of electronic digital pager communication, and providers of mobile telephony services and for compensating the public utilities, cable television corporations, providers of electronic digital pager communication, and providers of mobile telephony services for providing that information.

(h) The California Parent Locator Service and Central Registry may charge a fee not to exceed eighteen dollars ($18) for any service it provides pursuant to this section that is not performed or funded pursuant to Section 651 and following of Title 42 of the United States Code.

(i) This section shall be construed in a manner consistent with the other provisions of this article.[387]

17508. (a) The Employment Development Department shall, when requested by the Department of Child Support Services local child support agency, the federal Parent Locator Service, or the California Parent Locator Service, provide access to information collected pursuant to Division 1 (commencing with Section 100) of the Unemployment Insurance Code to the requesting department or agency for purposes of administering the child support enforcement program, and for purposes of verifying employment of applicants and recipients of aid under this chapter or CalFresh under Chapter 10 (commencing with Section 18900) of Part 6 of Division 9 of the Welfare and Institutions Code.

(b) (1) To the extent possible, the Employment Development Department shall share information collected under Sections 1088.5 and 1088.8 of the Unemployment Insurance Code immediately upon receipt. This sharing of information may include electronic means.

(2) This subdivision shall not authorize the Employment Development Department to share confidential information with any individuals not otherwise permitted by law to receive the information or preclude batch runs or comparisons of data.[359]

17509. Once the statewide automated system is fully implemented, the Department of Child Support Services shall periodically compare Employment Development Department information collected under Division 1 (commencing with Section 100) of the Unemployment Insurance Code to child support obligor records and identify cases where the obligor is employed but there is no earning withholding order in effect. The department shall immediately notify local child support agencies in those cases.[75]

17510. To assist local agencies in child support enforcement activities, the department shall operate a workers' compensation notification project based on information received pursuant to Section 138.5 of the Labor Code or any other source of information.

17512. (a) Upon receipt of a written

request from a local child support agency enforcing the obligation of parents to support their children pursuant to Section 17400, or from an agency of another state enforcing support obligations pursuant to Section 654 of Title 42 of the United States Code, every employer, as specified in Section 5210, and every labor organization shall cooperate with and provide relevant employment and income information that they have in their possession to the local child support agency or other requesting agency for the purpose of establishing, modifying, or enforcing the support obligation. No employer or labor organization shall incur any liability for providing this information to the local child support agency or other requesting agency.

(b) Relevant employment and income information shall include, but not be limited to, all of the following:

(1) Whether a named person has or has not been employed by an employer or whether a named person has or has not been employed to the knowledge of the labor organization.

(2) The full name of the employee or member or the first and middle initial and last name of the employee or member.

(3) The employee's or member's last known residence address.

(4) The employee's or member's date of birth.

(5) The employee's or member's social security number.

(6) The dates of employment.

(7) All earnings paid to the employee or member and reported as W-2 compensation in the prior tax year and the employee's or member's current basic rate of pay.

(8) Other earnings, as specified in Section 5206, paid to the employee or member.

(9) Whether dependent health insurance coverage is available to the employee through employment or membership in the labor organization.

(c) The local child support agency or other agency shall notify the employer and labor organization of the local child support agency case file number in making a request pursuant to this section. The written request shall include at least three of the following elements regarding the person who is the subject of the inquiry: (A) first and last name and middle initial, if known; (B) social security number; (C) driver's license number; (D) birth date; (E) last known address; or (F) spouse's name.

(d) The local child support agency or other requesting agency shall send a notice that a request for this information has been made to the last known address of the person who is the subject of the inquiry.

(e) An employer or labor organization that fails to provide relevant employment information to the local child support agency or other requesting agency within 30 days of receiving a request pursuant to subdivision (a) may be assessed a civil penalty of a maximum of one thousand dollars ($1,000), plus attorneys' fees and costs. Proceedings to impose the civil penalty shall be commenced by the filing and service of an order to show cause.

(f) "Labor organization," for the purposes of this section means a labor organization as defined in Section 1117 of the Labor Code or any related benefit trust fund covered under the federal Employee Retirement Income Security Act of 1974 (Chapter 18 (commencing with Section 1001) of Title 29 of the United States Code).

(g) Any reference to the local child support agency in this section shall apply only when the local child support agency is otherwise ordered or required to act pursuant to existing law. Nothing in this section shall be deemed to mandate additional enforcement or collection duties upon the local child support agency beyond those imposed under existing law on the effective date of this section.

17514. (a) It is the intent of the Legislature to protect individual rights of privacy, and to facilitate and enhance the effectiveness of the child abduction and recovery programs, by ensuring the confidentiality of child abduction records, and to thereby encourage the full and frank disclosure of information relevant to all of the following:

(1) The establishment or maintenance of parent and child relationships and support obligations.

(2) The enforcement of the child support liability of absent parents.

(3) The enforcement of spousal support liability of the spouse or former spouse to the extent required by the state plan under Section 17400, and Chapter 6 (commencing with Section 4800) of Part 5 of Division 9.

(4) The location of absent parents.

(5) The location of parents and children abducted, concealed, or detained by them.

(b) (1) Except as provided in this subdivision, all files, applications, papers, documents, and records, established or maintained by a public entity for the purpose of locating an abducted child, locating a person who has abducted a child, or prosecution of a person who has abducted a child shall be confidential, and shall not be open to examination or released for disclosure for any purpose not directly connected with locating or recovering the abducted child or abducting person or prosecution of the abducting person.

(2) Except as provided in subdivision (c), a public entity shall not disclose any file, application, paper, document, or record described in this section, or the information contained therein.

(c) (1) All files, applications, papers, documents, and records as described in subdivision (b) shall be available and may be used by a public entity for all administrative, civil, or criminal investigations, actions, proceedings, or prosecution conducted in connection with the child abduction or prosecution of the abducting person.

(2) A document requested by a person who wrote, prepared, or furnished the document may be examined by or disclosed to that person or a designee.

(3) Public records subject to disclosure under Division 10 (commencing with Section 7920.000) of Title 1 of the Government Code may be released.

(4) After a noticed motion and a finding by the court, in a case in which child recovery or abduction prosecution actions are being taken, that release or disclosure is required by due process of law, the court may order a public entity that possesses an application, paper, document, or record described in this subdivision to make that item available to the defendant or

other party for examination or copying, or to disclose to an appropriate person the contents of that item. Article 9 (commencing with Section 1040) of Chapter 4 of Division 8 of the Evidence Code shall not be applicable to proceedings under this part.

(5) To the extent not prohibited by federal law or regulation, information indicating the existence or imminent threat of a crime against a minor child, or location of a concealed or abducted child, or the location of the concealing or abducting person, may be disclosed to any appropriate law enforcement agency, or to any state or county child protective agency, or may be used in any judicial proceedings to prosecute that crime or to protect the child.

(6) Information may be released to any state or local agency for the purposes connected with establishing, modifying, and enforcing child support obligations, enforcing spousal support orders, and determining paternity as required by Part D (commencing with Section 651) of Subchapter IV of Chapter 7 of Title 42 of the United States Code and this article.

17516. In no event shall public social service benefits, as defined in Section 10051 of the Welfare and Institutions Code, or benefits paid pursuant to Title XVI of the Social Security Act be employed to satisfy a support obligation.

17518. (a) As authorized by subdivision (d) of Section 704.120 of the Code of Civil Procedure, the following actions shall be taken in order to enforce support obligations that are not being met. Whenever a support judgment or order has been rendered by a court of this state against an individual who is entitled to unemployment compensation benefits or unemployment compensation disability benefits, the local child support agency may file a certification of support judgment or support order with the Department of Child Support Services, verifying under penalty of perjury that there is or has been a judgment or an order for support with sums overdue thereunder. The department shall periodically present and keep current, by deletions and additions, a list of the certified support judgments and orders and shall periodically notify the Employment Development Department of individuals certified as owing support obligations.

(b) If the Employment Development Department determines that an individual who owes support may have a claim for unemployment compensation disability insurance benefits under a voluntary plan approved by the Employment Development Department in accordance with Chapter 6 (commencing with Section 3251) of Part 2 of Division 1 of the Unemployment Insurance Code, the Employment Development Department shall immediately notify the voluntary plan payer. When the department notifies the Employment Development Department of changes in an individual's support obligations, the Employment Development Department shall promptly notify the voluntary plan payer of these changes. The Employment Development Department shall maintain and keep current a record of individuals who owe support obligations who may have claims for unemployment compensation or unemployment compensation disability benefits.

(c) Notwithstanding any other law, the Employment Development Department shall withhold the amounts specified below from the unemployment compensation benefits or unemployment compensation disability benefits of individuals with unmet support obligations. The Employment Development Department shall forward the amounts to the Department of Child Support Services for distribution to the appropriate certifying county.

(d) Notwithstanding any other law, during the payment of unemployment compensation disability benefits to an individual, with respect to whom the Employment Development Department has notified a voluntary plan payer that the individual has a support obligation, the voluntary plan payer shall withhold the amounts specified below from the individual's unemployment compensation disability benefits and shall forward the amounts to the appropriate certifying county.

(e) The amounts withheld in subdivisions (c) and (d) shall be equal to 25 percent of each weekly unemployment compensation benefit payment or periodic unemployment compensation disability benefit payment, rounded down to the nearest whole dollar, which is due the individual identified on the certified list. However, the amount withheld may be reduced to a lower whole dollar amount through a written agreement between the individual and the local child support agency or through an order of the court.

(f) The department shall ensure that the appropriate certifying county shall resolve any claims for refunds in the amounts overwithheld by the Employment Development Department or voluntary plan payer.

(g) No later than the time of the first withholding, the individuals who are subject to the withholding shall be notified by the payer of benefits of all of the following:

(1) That the individual's unemployment compensation benefits or unemployment compensation disability benefits have been reduced by a court-ordered support judgment or order pursuant to this section.

(2) The address and telephone number of the local child support agency that submitted the certificate of support judgment or order.

(3) That the support order remains in effect even though the individual is unemployed or disabled unless it is modified by court order, and that if the amount withheld is less than the monthly support obligation, an arrearage will accrue.

(h) The individual may ask the appropriate court for an equitable division of the individual's unemployment compensation or unemployment compensation disability amounts withheld to take into account the needs of all the persons the individual is required to support.

(i) The Department of Child Support Services and the Employment Development Department shall enter into any agreements necessary to carry out this section.

(j) For purposes of this section, "support obligations" means the child and related spousal support obligations that are being enforced pursuant to a plan described in Section 454 of the

Social Security Act and as that section may hereafter be amended. However, to the extent "related spousal support obligation" may not be collected from unemployment compensation under federal law, those obligations shall not be included in the definition of support obligations under this section.

17520. (a) As used in this section:
(1) "Applicant" means a person applying for issuance or renewal of a license.
(2) "Board" means an entity specified in Section 101 of the Business and Professions Code, the entities referred to in Sections 1000 and 3600 of the Business and Professions Code, the State Bar of California, the Department of Real Estate, the Department of Motor Vehicles, the Secretary of State, the Department of Fish and Wildlife, and any other state commission, department, committee, examiner, or agency that issues a license, certificate, credential, permit, registration, or any other authorization to engage in a business, occupation, or profession, or to the extent required by federal law or regulations, for recreational purposes. This term includes all boards, commissions, departments, committees, examiners, entities, and agencies that issue a license, certificate, credential, permit, registration, or any other authorization to engage in a business, occupation, or profession. The failure to specifically name a particular board, commission, department, committee, examiner, entity, or agency that issues a license, certificate, credential, permit, registration, or any other authorization to engage in a business, occupation, or profession does not exclude that board, commission, department, committee, examiner, entity, or agency from this term.
(3) "Certified list" means a list provided by the local child support agency to the Department of Child Support Services in which the local child support agency verifies, under penalty of perjury, that the names contained therein are support obligors found to be out of compliance with a judgment or order for support in a case being enforced under Title IV-D of the federal Social Security Act.
(4) "Compliance with a judgment or order for support" means that, as set forth in a judgment or order for child or family support, the obligor is no more than 30 calendar days in arrears in making payments in full for current support, in making periodic payments in full, whether court ordered or by agreement with the local child support agency, on a support arrearage, or in making periodic payments in full, whether court ordered or by agreement with the local child support agency, on a judgment for reimbursement for public assistance, or has obtained a judicial finding that equitable estoppel as provided in statute or case law precludes enforcement of the order. The local child support agency is authorized to use this section to enforce orders for spousal support only when the local child support agency is also enforcing a related child support obligation owed to the obligee parent by the same obligor, pursuant to Sections 17400 and 17604.
(5) "License" includes membership in the State Bar of California, and a cer-

tificate, credential, permit, registration, or any other authorization issued by a board that allows a person to engage in a business, occupation, or profession, or to operate a commercial motor vehicle, including appointment and commission by the Secretary of State as a notary public. "License" also includes any driver's license issued by the Department of Motor Vehicles, any commercial fishing license issued by the Department of Fish and Wildlife, and to the extent required by federal law or regulations, any license used for recreational purposes. This term includes all licenses, certificates, credentials, permits, registrations, or any other authorization issued by a board that allows a person to engage in a business, occupation, or profession. The failure to specifically name a particular type of license, certificate, credential, permit, registration, or other authorization issued by a board that allows a person to engage in a business, occupation, or profession, does not exclude that license, certificate, credential, permit, registration, or other authorization from this term.

(6) "Licensee" means a person holding a license, certificate, credential, permit, registration, or other authorization issued by a board, to engage in a business, occupation, or profession, or a commercial driver's license as defined in Section 15210 of the Vehicle Code, including an appointment and commission by the Secretary of State as a notary public. "Licensee" also means a person holding a driver's license issued by the Department of Motor Vehicles, a person holding a commercial fishing license issued by the Department of Fish and Wildlife, and to the extent required by federal law or regulations, a person holding a license used for recreational purposes. This term includes all persons holding a license, certificate, credential, permit, registration, or any other authorization to engage in a business, occupation, or profession, and the failure to specifically name a particular type of license, certificate, credential, permit, registration, or other authorization issued by a board does not exclude that person from this term. For licenses issued to an entity that is not an individual person, "licensee" includes an individual who is either listed on the license or who qualifies for the license.

(b) The local child support agency shall maintain a list of those persons included in a case being enforced under Title IV-D of the federal Social Security Act against whom a support order or judgment has been rendered by, or registered in, a court of this state, and who are not in compliance with that order or judgment. The local child support agency shall submit a certified list with the names, social security numbers, individual taxpayer identification numbers, or other uniform identification numbers, and last known addresses of these persons and the name, address, and telephone number of the local child support agency who certified the list to the department. The local child support agency shall verify, under penalty of perjury, that the persons listed are subject to an order or judgment for the payment of support and that these persons are not in compliance with the order or judgment. The local child support agency shall submit to the department an updated certified list on a monthly basis.

(c) The department shall consolidate the certified lists received from the local child support agencies and, within 30 calendar days of receipt, shall provide a copy of the consolidated list to each board that is responsible for the regulation of licenses, as specified in this section.

(d) On or before November 1, 1992, or as soon thereafter as economically feasible, as determined by the department, all boards subject to this section shall implement procedures to accept and process the list provided by the department, in accordance with this section. Notwithstanding any other law, all boards shall collect social security numbers or individual taxpayer identification numbers from all applicants for the purposes of matching the names of the certified list provided by the department to applicants and licensees and of responding to requests for this information made by child support agencies.

(e) (1) Promptly after receiving the certified consolidated list from the department, and prior to the issuance or renewal of a license, each board shall determine whether the applicant is on the most recent certified consolidated list provided by the department. The board shall have the authority to withhold issuance or renewal of the license of an applicant on the list.

(2) If an applicant is on the list, the board shall immediately serve notice as specified in subdivision (f) on the applicant of the board's intent to withhold issuance or renewal of the license. The notice shall be made personally or by mail to the applicant's last known mailing address on file with the board. Service by mail shall be complete in accordance with Section 1013 of the Code of Civil Procedure.

(A) The board shall issue a temporary license valid for a period of 150 days to any applicant whose name is on the certified list if the applicant is otherwise eligible for a license.

(B) Except as provided in subparagraph (D), the 150-day time period for a temporary license shall not be extended. Except as provided in subparagraph (D), only one temporary license shall be issued during a regular license term and it shall coincide with the first 150 days of that license term. As this paragraph applies to commercial driver's licenses, "license term" shall be deemed to be 12 months from the date the application fee is received by the Department of Motor Vehicles. A license for the full or remainder of the license term shall be issued or renewed only upon compliance with this section.

(C) In the event that a license or application for a license or the renewal of a license is denied pursuant to this section, any funds paid by the applicant or licensee shall not be refunded by the board.

(D) This paragraph shall apply only in the case of a driver's license, other than a commercial driver's license. Upon the request of the local child support agency or by order of the court upon a showing of good cause, the board shall extend a 150-day temporary license for a period not to exceed 150 extra days.

(3) (A) The department may, when it is economically feasible for the

department and the boards to do so as determined by the department, in cases where the department is aware that certain child support obligors listed on the certified lists have been out of compliance with a judgment or order for support for more than four months, provide a supplemental list of these obligors to each board with which the department has an interagency agreement to implement this paragraph. Upon request by the department, the licenses of these obligors shall be subject to suspension, provided that the licenses would not otherwise be eligible for renewal within six months from the date of the request by the department. The board shall have the authority to suspend the license of any licensee on this supplemental list.

(B) If a licensee is on a supplemental list, the board shall immediately serve notice as specified in subdivision (f) on the licensee that the license will be automatically suspended 150 days after notice is served, unless compliance with this section is achieved. The notice shall be made personally or by mail to the licensee's last known mailing address on file with the board. Service by mail shall be complete in accordance with Section 1013 of the Code of Civil Procedure.

(C) The 150-day notice period shall not be extended.

(D) In the event that any license is suspended pursuant to this section, any funds paid by the licensee shall not be refunded by the board.

(E) This paragraph shall not apply to licenses subject to annual renewal or annual fee.

(f) Notices shall be developed by each board in accordance with guidelines provided by the department and subject to approval by the department. The notice shall include the address and telephone number of the local child support agency that submitted the name on the certified list, and shall emphasize the necessity of obtaining a release from that local child support agency as a condition for the issuance, renewal, or continued valid status of a license or licenses.

(1) In the case of applicants not subject to paragraph (3) of subdivision (e), the notice shall inform the applicant that the board shall issue a temporary license, as provided in subparagraph (A) of paragraph (2) of subdivision (e), for 150 calendar days if the applicant is otherwise eligible and that upon expiration of that time period the license will be denied unless the board has received a release from the local child support agency that submitted the name on the certified list.

(2) In the case of licensees named on a supplemental list, the notice shall inform the licensee that the license will continue in its existing status for no more than 150 calendar days from the date of mailing or service of the notice and thereafter will be suspended indefinitely unless, during the 150-day notice period, the board has received a release from the local child support agency that submitted the name on the certified list. Additionally, the notice shall inform the licensee that any license suspended under this section will remain so until the expiration of the remaining license term, unless the board receives a release along with applications and fees, if applicable, to reinstate the license

during the license term.

(3) The notice shall also inform the applicant or licensee that if an application is denied or a license is suspended pursuant to this section, any funds paid by the applicant or licensee shall not be refunded by the board. The Department of Child Support Services shall also develop a form that the applicant shall use to request a review by the local child support agency. A copy of this form shall be included with every notice sent pursuant to this subdivision.

(g) (1) Each local child support agency shall maintain review procedures consistent with this section to allow an applicant to have the underlying arrearage and any relevant defenses investigated, to provide an applicant information on the process of obtaining a modification of a support order, or to provide an applicant assistance in the establishment of a payment schedule on arrearages if the circumstances so warrant.

(2) It is the intent of the Legislature that a court or local child support agency, when determining an appropriate payment schedule for arrearages, base its decision on the facts of the particular case and the priority of payment of child support over other debts. The payment schedule shall also recognize that certain expenses may be essential to enable an obligor to be employed. Therefore, in reaching its decision, the court or the local child support agency shall consider both of these goals in setting a payment schedule for arrearages.

(h) If the applicant wishes to challenge the submission of their name on the certified list, the applicant shall make a timely written request for review to the local child support agency who certified the applicant's name. A request for review pursuant to this section shall be resolved in the same manner and timeframe provided for resolution of a complaint pursuant to Section 17800. The local child support agency shall immediately send a release to the appropriate board and the applicant, if any of the following conditions are met:

(1) The applicant is found to be in compliance or negotiates an agreement with the local child support agency for a payment schedule on arrearages or reimbursement.

(2) The applicant has submitted a request for review, but the local child support agency will be unable to complete the review and send notice of its findings to the applicant within the time specified in Section 17800.

(3) The applicant has filed and served a request for judicial review pursuant to this section, but a resolution of that review will not be made within 150 days of the date of service of notice pursuant to subdivision (f). This paragraph applies only if the delay in completing the judicial review process is not the result of the applicant's failure to act in a reasonable, timely, and diligent manner upon receiving the local child support agency's notice of findings.

(4) The applicant has obtained a judicial finding of compliance as defined in this section.

(i) An applicant is required to act with diligence in responding to notices from the board and the local child support agency with the recognition that the temporary license will lapse or the license suspension will go into effect after 150 days and that the local child support agency and, where appropriate, the court must have time to act within that period. An applicant's delay in acting, without good cause, which directly results in the inability of the local child support agency to complete a review of the applicant's request or the court to hear the request for judicial review within the 150-day period shall not constitute the diligence required under this section which would justify the issuance of a release.

(j) Except as otherwise provided in this section, the local child support agency shall not issue a release if the applicant is not in compliance with the judgment or order for support. The local child support agency shall notify the applicant, in writing, that the applicant may, by filing an order to show cause or notice of motion, request any or all of the following:

(1) Judicial review of the local child support agency's decision not to issue a release.

(2) A judicial determination of compliance.

(3) A modification of the support judgment or order.

The notice shall also contain the name and address of the court in which the applicant shall file the order to show cause or notice of motion and inform the applicant that their name shall remain on the certified list if the applicant does not timely request judicial review. The applicant shall comply with all statutes and rules of court regarding orders to show cause and notices of motion.

This section does not limit an applicant from filing an order to show cause or notice of motion to modify a support judgment or order or to fix a payment schedule on arrearages accruing under a support judgment or order or to obtain a court finding of compliance with a judgment or order for support.

(k) The request for judicial review of the local child support agency's decision shall state the grounds for which review is requested and judicial review shall be limited to those stated grounds. The court shall hold an evidentiary hearing within 20 calendar days of the filing of the request for review. Judicial review of the local child support agency's decision shall be limited to a determination of each of the following issues:

(1) Whether there is a support judgment, order, or payment schedule on arrearages or reimbursement.

(2) Whether the petitioner is the obligor covered by the support judgment or order.

(3) Whether the support obligor is or is not in compliance with the judgment or order of support.

(4) (A) The extent to which the needs of the obligor, taking into account the obligor's payment history and the current circumstances of both the obligor and the obligee, warrant a conditional release as described in this subdivision.

(B) The request for judicial review shall be served by the applicant upon the local child support agency that submitted the applicant's name on the certified list within seven calendar days of the filing of the petition. The court has the authority to uphold the action, unconditionally release the license, or conditionally release the license.

(C) If the judicial review results in a finding by the court that the obligor is in compliance with the judgment or order for support, the local child support agency shall immediately send a release in accordance with subdivision (l) to the appropriate board and the applicant. If the judicial review results in a finding by the court that the needs of the obligor warrant a conditional release, the court shall make findings of fact stating the basis for the release and the payment necessary to satisfy the unrestricted issuance or renewal of the license without prejudice to a later judicial determination of the amount of support arrearages, including interest, and shall specify payment terms, compliance with which are necessary to allow the release to remain in effect.

(l) (1) The department shall prescribe release forms for use by local child support agencies. When the obligor is in compliance, the local child support agency shall mail to the applicant and the appropriate board a release stating that the applicant is in compliance. The receipt of a release shall serve to notify the applicant and the board that, for the purposes of this section, the applicant is in compliance with the judgment or order for support. A board that has received a release from the local child support agency pursuant to this subdivision shall process the release within five business days of its receipt.

(2) When the local child support agency determines, subsequent to the issuance of a release, that the applicant is once again not in compliance with a judgment or order for support, or with the terms of repayment as described in this subdivision, the local child support agency may notify the board, the obligor, and the department in a format prescribed by the department that the obligor is not in compliance.

(3) The department may, when it is economically feasible for the department and the boards to develop an automated process for complying with this subdivision, notify the boards in a manner prescribed by the department, that the obligor is once again not in compliance. Upon receipt of this notice, the board shall immediately notify the obligor on a form prescribed by the department that the obligor's license will be suspended on a specific date, and this date shall be no longer than 30 days from the date the form is mailed. The obligor shall be further notified that the license will remain suspended until a new release is issued in accordance with subdivision (h). This section does not limit the obligor from seeking judicial review of suspension pursuant to the procedures described in subdivision (k).

(m) The department may enter into interagency agreements with the state agencies that have responsibility for the administration of boards necessary to implement this section, to the extent that it is cost effective to implement this section. These agreements shall provide for the receipt by the other state agencies and boards of federal funds to cover that portion of costs allowable in federal law and regulation and incurred by the state agencies and boards in implementing this section. Notwithstanding any other law, revenue generated by a board or state agency shall be used to fund the nonfederal share of costs incurred pursuant to this section. These agreements shall provide that boards shall reimburse the department for the nonfederal share of costs incurred by the department in implementing this section. The boards shall reimburse the department for the nonfederal share of costs incurred pursuant to this section from moneys collected from applicants and licensees.

(n) Notwithstanding any other law, in order for the boards subject to this section to be reimbursed for the costs incurred in administering its provisions, the boards may, with the approval of the appropriate department director, levy on all licensees and applicants a surcharge on any fee or fees collected pursuant to law, or, alternatively, with the approval of the appropriate department director, levy on the applicants or licensees named on a certified list or supplemental list, a special fee.

(o) The process described in subdivision (h) shall constitute the sole administrative remedy for contesting the issuance of a temporary license or the denial or suspension of a license under this section. The procedures specified in the administrative adjudication provisions of the Administrative Procedure Act (Chapter 4.5 (commencing with Section 11400) and Chapter 5 (commencing with Section 11500) of Part 1 of Division 3 of Title 2 of the Government Code) shall not apply to the denial, suspension, or failure to issue or renew a license or the issuance of a temporary license pursuant to this section.

(p) In furtherance of the public policy of increasing child support enforcement and collections, on or before November 1, 1995, the State Department of Social Services shall make a report to the Legislature and the Governor based on data collected by the boards and the district attorneys in a format prescribed by the State Department of Social Services. The report shall contain all of the following:

(1) The number of delinquent obligors certified by district attorneys under this section.

(2) The number of support obligors who also were applicants or licensees subject to this section.

(3) The number of new licenses and renewals that were delayed, temporary licenses issued, and licenses suspended subject to this section and the number of new licenses and renewals granted and licenses reinstated following board receipt of releases as provided by subdivision (h) by May 1, 1995.

(4) The costs incurred in the implementation and enforcement of this section.

(q) A board receiving an inquiry as to the licensed status of an applicant or licensee who has had a license denied or suspended under this section or has been granted a temporary license under this section shall respond only that the license was denied or suspended or the temporary license was issued pursuant to this section. Information collected pursuant to this section by a state agency, board, or department shall be subject to the Information Practices Act of 1977 (Chapter 1 (commencing with Section 1798) of Title 1.8 of Part 4 of Division 3 of the Civil Code).

(r) Any rules and regulations issued pursuant to this section by a state agency, board, or department may be adopted as emergency regulations in accordance with the rulemaking provisions of the Administrative Procedure Act (Chapter 3.5 (commencing with Section 11340) of Part 1 of Division 3 of Title 2 of the Government Code). The adoption of these regulations shall be deemed an emergency and necessary for the immediate preservation of the public peace, health, and safety, or general welfare. The regulations shall become effective immediately upon filing with the Secretary of State.

(s) The department and boards, as appropriate, shall adopt regulations necessary to implement this section.

(t) The Judicial Council shall develop the forms necessary to implement this section, except as provided in subdivisions (f) and (l).

(u) The release or other use of information received by a board pursuant to this section, except as authorized by this section, is punishable as a misdemeanor.

(v) The State Board of Equalization shall enter into interagency agreements with the department and the Franchise Tax Board that will require the department and the Franchise Tax Board to maximize the use of information collected by the State Board of Equalization, for child support enforcement purposes, to the extent it is cost effective and permitted by the Revenue and Taxation Code.

(w) (1) The suspension or revocation of a driver's license, including a commercial driver's license, under this section shall not subject the licensee to vehicle impoundment pursuant to Section 14602.6 of the Vehicle Code.

(2) Notwithstanding any other law, the suspension or revocation of a driver's license, including a commercial driver's license, under this section shall not subject the licensee to increased costs for vehicle liability insurance.

(x) If any provision of this section or the application thereof to any person or circumstance is held invalid, that invalidity shall not affect other provisions or applications of this section which can be given effect without the invalid provision or application, and to this end the provisions of this section are severable.

(y) All rights to administrative and judicial review afforded by this section to an applicant shall also be afforded to a licensee.

17520.5. (a) (1) Notwithstanding any other law, the department shall not include in the list sent to the Department of Motor Vehicles pursuant to Section 17520, for the purpose of denying, withholding, or suspending a driver's license, the information of a support obligor found to be out of compliance with a judgment or order for support in a case being enforced under Title IV-D of the federal Social Security Act, if the annual household income of the support obligor is at or below 70 percent of the median income for the county in which the department or the local child support agency believes the support obligor resides, based on the most recent available data published by the Department of Housing and Community Development pursuant to Section 6932 of Title 25 of the California Code of Regulations or successor regulation thereto.

(2) Commencing January 1, 2027, this subdivision shall apply only with respect to noncommercial driver's

licenses.

(b) This section shall be implemented to the extent allowed under federal law.

(c) This section shall become operative on January 1, 2025.[606]

17521. The order to show cause or notice of motion described in subdivision (j) of Section 17520 shall be filed and heard in the superior court.[91]

17522. (a) Notwithstanding any other law, if a support obligor is delinquent in the payment of support for at least 30 days and the local child support agency is enforcing the support obligation pursuant to Section 17400, the local child support agency may collect the delinquency or enforce a lien by levy served on all persons having in their possession, or who will have in their possession or under their control, credits or personal property belonging to the delinquent support obligor, or who owe any debt to the obligor at the time they receive the notice of levy.

(b) A levy may be issued by a local child support agency for a support obligation that accrued under a court order or judgment if the obligor had notice of the accrued support arrearage as provided in this section, and did not make a timely request for review.

(c) The notice requirement shall be satisfied by the local child support agency sending a statement of support arrearages to the obligor at the obligor's last known address by first-class mail, postage prepaid. The notice shall advise the obligor of the amount of the support arrearage. The notice shall advise the obligor that the obligor may have the arrearage determination reviewed by administrative procedures and state how the review may be obtained. The local child support agency shall conduct the review pursuant to this section in the same manner and timeframe provided for resolution of a complaint pursuant to Section 17800. The notice shall also advise the obligor of the right to seek a judicial determination of arrearages pursuant to Section 17526 and shall include a form to be filed with the court to request a judicial determination of arrearages. If the obligor requests an administrative review of the arrearage determination within 20 days from the date the notice was mailed to the obligor, the local child support agency may not issue the levy for a disputed amount of support until the administrative review procedure is completed.

(d) If the obligor requests a judicial determination of the arrearages within 20 days from the date the notice was mailed to the obligor, the local child support agency shall not issue the levy for a disputed amount of support until the judicial determination is complete.

(e) A person upon whom a levy has been served who possesses or controls any credits or personal property belonging to the delinquent support obligor or owing any debts to the delinquent support obligor at the time of receipt of the levy or coming into the person's possession or control within one year of receipt of the notice of levy, shall surrender the credits or personal property to the local child support agency or pay to the local child support agency the amount of any debt owing the delinquent support obligor within 10 days of service of the levy, and shall surrender the credits or personal property, or the amount of any debt owing to the delinquent support obligor coming into the person's possession or control within one year of receipt of the notice of levy, within 10 days of the date of coming into possession or control of the credits or personal property or the amount of any debt owing to the delinquent support obligor.

(f) A person who surrenders any credits or personal property or pays the debts owing the delinquent support obligor to the local child support agency pursuant to this section shall be discharged from any obligation or liability to the delinquent support obligor to the extent of the amount paid to the local child support agency as a result of the levy.

(g) When the levy is made on a deposit or credits or personal property in the possession or under the control of a bank, savings and loan association, or other financial institution as defined by Section 669A(d)(1) of Title 42 of the United States Code, the notice of levy may be delivered or mailed to a centralized location designated by the bank, savings and loan association, or other financial institution pursuant to Section 689.040 of the Code of Civil Procedure.

(h) A person who is served with a levy pursuant to this section and who fails or refuses to surrender any credits or other personal property or pay any debts owing to the delinquent support obligor shall be liable in their own person or estate to the local child support agency in an amount equal to the value of the credits or other personal property or in the amount of the levy, up to the amount specified in the levy.

(i) If an amount required to be paid pursuant to a levy under this section is not paid when due, the local child support agency may issue a warrant for enforcement of a lien and for the collection of any amount required to be paid to the local child support agency under this section. The warrant shall be directed to any sheriff, marshal, or the Department of the California Highway Patrol and shall have the same force and effect as a writ of execution. The warrant shall be levied and sale made pursuant to it in the manner and with the same force and effect as a levy and sale pursuant to a writ of execution. The local child support agency may pay or advance to the levying officer the same fees, commissions, and expenses for services under this section as are provided by law for similar services pursuant to a writ of execution, except for those fees and expenses for which a district attorney is exempt by law from paying. The local child support agency, and not the court, shall approve the fees for publication in a newspaper.

(j) The fees, commissions, expenses, and the reasonable costs associated with the sale of property levied upon by warrant or levy pursuant to this section, including, but not limited to, appraisers' fees, auctioneers' fees, and advertising fees are an obligation of the support obligor and may be collected from the obligor by virtue of the warrant or levy or in any other manner as though these items were support payments delinquent for at least 30 days.[466]

17522.5. (a) Notwithstanding Section 8112 of the Commercial Code and Section 700.130 of the Code of Civil Procedure, when a local child support agency pursuant to Section 17522, or the department pursuant to Section 17454 or 17500, issues a levy upon, or requires by notice any employer, person, political officer or entity, or depository institution to withhold the amount of, as applicable, a financial asset for the purpose of collecting a delinquent child support obligation, the person, financial institution, or securities intermediary (as defined in Section 8102 of the Commercial Code) in possession or control of the financial asset shall liquidate the financial asset in a commercially reasonable manner within 20 days of the issuance of the levy or the notice to withhold. Within five days of liquidation, the person, financial institution, or securities intermediary shall transfer to the State Disbursement Unit, established under Section 17309, the proceeds of the liquidation, less any reasonable commissions or fees, or both, which are charged in the normal course of business.

(b) If the value of the financial assets exceed the total amount of support due, the obligor may, within 10 days after the service of the levy or notice to withhold upon the person, financial institution, or securities intermediary, instruct the person, financial institution, or securities intermediary who possesses or controls the financial assets as to which financial assets are to be sold to satisfy the obligation for delinquent support. If the obligor does not provide instructions for liquidation, the person, financial institution, or securities intermediary who possesses or controls the financial assets shall liquidate the financial assets in a commercially reasonable manner and in an amount sufficient to cover the obligation for delinquent child support, and any reasonable commissions or fees, or both, which are charged in the normal course of business, beginning with the financial assets purchased most recently.

(c) For the purposes of this section, a financial asset shall include, but not be limited to, an uncertificated security, certificated security, or security entitlement (as defined in Section 8102 of the Commercial Code), security (as defined in Section 8103 of the Commercial Code), or a securities account (as defined in Section 8501 of the Commercial Code).[360]

17523. (a) Notwithstanding any other provision of law, if a support obligor is delinquent in the payment of support and the local child support agency is enforcing the support obligation pursuant to Section 17400 or 17402, a lien for child support shall arise against the personal property of the support obligor in either of the following circumstances:

(1) By operation of law for all amounts of overdue support, regardless of whether the amounts have been adjudicated or otherwise determined.

(2) When either a court having continuing jurisdiction or the local child support agency determines a specific amount of arrearages is owed by the support obligor.

(b) The lien for child support shall be perfected by filing a notice of child support lien with the Secretary of State pursuant to Section 697.510 of the Code of Civil Procedure. Once filed, the child support lien shall have the same priority, force, and effect as a judgment lien on personal property pursuant to Article 3 (commencing with Section 697.510) of Chapter 2 of Division 2 of Article 9 of the Code of Civil Procedure.

(c) For purposes of this section, the following definitions shall apply:

(1) "Notice of child support lien" means a document filed with the Secretary of State that substantially complies with the requirements of Section 697.530 of the Code of Civil Procedure.

(2) "Support obligor is delinquent in payment of support" means that the support obligor has failed to make payment equal to one month's support obligation.

(3) "Personal property" means that property that is subject to attachment by a judgment lien pursuant to Section 697.530 of the Code of Civil Procedure.

(d) Nothing in this section shall affect the priority of any of the following interests:

(1) State tax liens as set forth in Article 2 (commencing with Section 7170) of Division 7 of Title 1 of the Government Code.

(2) Liens or security interests as set forth in Article 3 (commencing with Section 697.510) of Chapter 2 of Division 2 of Article 9 of the Code of Civil Procedure.

(e) As between competing child support liens and state tax liens, a child support lien arising under this section shall have priority over a state tax lien if (1) the child support lien is filed with the Secretary of State, (2) the notice of child support lien is filed in an action or proceeding in which the obligor may become entitled to property or money judgment, or (3) the levy for child support on personal property is made, before a notice of state tax lien is filed with the Secretary of State pursuant to Section 7171 of the Government Code or filed in an action or proceeding in accordance with Section 7173 of the Government Code.

(f) A personal property lien for child support arising in another state may be enforced in the same manner and to the same extent as a personal property lien arising in this state.

17523.5. (a) (1) Notwithstanding any other law, in connection with the duty of the department and the local child support agency to promptly and effectively collect and enforce child support obligations under Title IV-D, the transmission, filing, and recording of a lien record by departmental and local child support agency staff that arises pursuant to subdivision (a) of Section 4506 of this code or Section 697.320 of the Code of Civil Procedure against the real property of a support obligor in the form of a digital or a digitized electronic record shall be permitted and governed only by this section.

(2) A facsimile signature that complies with the requirements of paragraph (2) of subdivision (b) of Section 27201 of the Government Code shall be accepted on any document relating to a lien that is filed or recorded pursuant to this section.

(3) The department and the local child support agency may use the California Child Support Enforcement System to transmit, file, and record a lien record under this section.

(b) Nothing in this section shall be construed to require a county recorder to establish an electronic recording delivery system or to enter into a contract with an entity to implement this section.

(c) For purposes of this section, the following terms have the following meanings:

(1) "Digital electronic record" means a record containing information that is created, generated, sent, communicated, received, or stored by electronic means, but not created in original paper form.

(2) "Digitized electronic record" means a scanned image of the original paper document.[361]

17524. (a) Upon making application to the local child support agency for child support enforcement services pursuant to Section 17400, every applicant shall be requested to give the local child support agency a statement of arrearages stating whether any support arrearages are owed. If the applicant alleges arrearages are owed, the statement shall be signed under penalty of perjury.

(b) For all cases opened by the district attorney or local child support agency after December 31, 1995, the local child support agency shall enforce only arrearages declared under penalty of perjury pursuant to subdivision (a), arrearages accrued after the case was opened, or arrearages determined by the court in the child support action. Arrearages may be determined by judgment, noticed motion, renewal of judgment, or registration of the support order.

(c) For all cases opened by the district attorney on or before December 31, 1995, the local child support agency shall enforce only arrearages that have been based upon a statement of arrearages signed under penalty of perjury or where the local child support agency has some other reasonable basis for believing the amount of claimed arrearages to be correct.

17525. (a) Whenever a state or local governmental agency issues a notice of support delinquency, the notice shall state the date upon which the amount of the delinquency was calculated, and shall notify the obligor that the amount calculated may, or may not, include accrued interest. This requirement shall not be imposed until the local child support agency has instituted the California Child Support Enforcement System implemented and maintained by the Department of Child Support Services pursuant to Section 17308. The notice shall further notify the obligor of the right to an administrative determination of arrears by requesting that the local child support agency review the arrears, but that payments on arrears continue to be due and payable unless and until the local child support agency notifies the obligor otherwise. A state agency shall not be required to suspend enforcement of any arrearages as a result of the obligor's request for an administrative determination of arrears, unless the agency receives notification of a suspension pursuant to subdivision (b) of Section 17526.

(b) For purposes of this section, "notice of support delinquency" means a notice issued to a support obligor that includes a specific statement of the amount of delinquent support due and payable.

(c) This section does not require a state or local entity to calculate the amount of a support delinquency, except as otherwise required by law.[466]

17526. (a) Upon request of an obligor

or obligee, the local child support agency shall review the amount of arrearages alleged in a statement of arrearages that may be submitted to the local child support agency by an applicant for child support enforcement services. The local child support agency shall complete the review in the same manner and pursuant to the same timeframes as a complaint submitted pursuant to Section 17800. In the review, the local child support agency shall consider all evidence and defenses submitted by either parent on the issues of the amount of support paid or owed.
(b) The local child support agency may, in its discretion, suspend enforcement or distribution of arrearages if it believes there is a substantial probability that the result of the administrative review will result in a finding that there are no arrearages.
(c) Any party to an action involving child support enforcement services of the local child support agency may request a judicial determination of arrearages. The party may request an administrative review of the alleged arrearages prior to requesting a judicial determination of arrearages. The local child support agency shall complete the review in the same manner and pursuant to the same timeframes specified in subdivision (a). Any motion to determine arrearages filed with the court shall include a monthly breakdown showing amounts ordered and amounts paid, in addition to any other relevant information.
(d) A county that submits a claim for reimbursement as a state-mandated local program of costs incurred with respect to the administrative review of alleged child support arrearages under this section shall be ineligible for state subventions or, to the extent permitted by federal law, state-administered federal subventions, for child support in the amount of any local costs under this section.[93]

17528. (a) As authorized by subdivision (c) of Section 704.110 of the Code of Civil Procedure, the following actions shall be taken in order to enforce support obligations that are not being met:
(1) Within 18 months of implementation of the California Child Support Enforcement System (CSE), or its replacement as prescribed by former Section 10815 of the Welfare and Institutions Code, and certification of CSE or its replacement by the United States Department of Health and Human Services, the department shall compile a file of all support judgments and orders that are being enforced by local child support agencies pursuant to Section 17400 that have sums overdue by at least 60 days or by an amount equal to 60 days of support.
(2) The file shall contain the name and social security number of the person who owes overdue support, the amount of overdue support as of the date the file is created, the name of the county in which the support obligation is being enforced by the local child support agency, and any other information that is deemed necessary by the department and the Public Employees' Retirement System.
(3) The department shall provide the certified file to the Public Employees' Retirement System for the purpose of matching the names in the file with members and beneficiaries of the

Public Employees' Retirement System that are entitled to receive Public Employees' Retirement System benefits. The department and the Public Employees' Retirement System shall work cooperatively to develop an interface in order to match the names in their respective electronic data processing systems. The interface required to intercept benefits that are payable periodically shall be done as soon as it is technically feasible.

(4) The department shall update the certified file no less than on a monthly basis to add new cases within the local child support agencies or existing cases that become delinquent and to delete persons who are no longer delinquent. The department shall provide the updated file no less than on a monthly basis to the Public Employees' Retirement System.

(5) Information contained in the certified file provided to the Public Employees' Retirement System by the department and the local child support agencies and information provided by the Public Employees' Retirement System to the department shall be used exclusively for child support enforcement purposes and may not be used for any other purpose.

(b) Notwithstanding any other law, the Public Employees' Retirement System shall withhold the amount certified from the benefits and refunds to be distributed to members with overdue support obligations or from benefits to be distributed to beneficiaries with overdue support obligations. If the benefits are payable periodically, the amount withheld pursuant to this section shall not exceed the amount permitted to be withheld for an earnings withholding order for support under Section 706.052 of the Code of Civil Procedure.

(c) The Public Employees' Retirement System shall forward the amounts withheld pursuant to subdivision (b) within 10 days of withholding to the department for distribution to the appropriate county.

(d) On an annual basis, the department shall notify individuals with overdue support obligations that PERS benefits or PERS contribution refunds may be intercepted for the purpose of enforcing family support obligations.

(e) No later than the time of the first withholding, the Public Employees' Retirement System shall send those persons subject to withholding the following:

(1) Notice that the person's benefits or retirement contribution refund have been reduced by payment on a support judgment pursuant to this section.

(2) A form developed by the department that the applicant shall use to request either a review by the local child support agency or a court hearing, as appropriate.

(f) The notice shall include the address and telephone number of the local child support agency that is enforcing the support obligation pursuant to Section 17400, and shall specify that the form requesting either a review by the local child support agency or a court hearing must be received by the local child support agency within 20 days of the date of the notice.

(g) The form shall include instructions that are designed to enable the member or beneficiary to obtain a review or a court hearing as appropriate on their own behalf. The form shall specify that if the member or beneficiary disputes the amount of support arrearages certified by the local child support agency pursuant to this section, the member or beneficiary may request a review by the local child support agency.

(h) The department shall develop procedures that are consistent with this section to be used by each local child support agency in conducting the requested review. The local child support agency shall complete the review in accordance with the procedures developed by the department and shall notify the member or beneficiary of the result of the review within 20 days of receiving the request for review. The notification of review results shall include a request for hearing form and shall inform the member or beneficiary that if the member or beneficiary returns the completed request for hearing form within 20 days of the date of the notice of review results, the local child support agency shall calendar the matter for court review. If the local child support agency cannot complete the review within 20 days, the local child support agency shall calendar the matter for hearing as specified in subdivision (k).

(i) The form specified in subdivision (g) shall also notify the member or beneficiary that the member or beneficiary may request a court hearing to claim an exemption of any benefit not payable periodically by returning the completed form to the local child support agency within 20 days. If the local child support agency receives a timely request for a hearing for a claim of exemption, the local child support agency shall calendar a court hearing. The amount of the exemption, if any, shall be determined by the court in accordance with the procedures set forth in Section 703.070 of the Code of Civil Procedure.

(j) If the local child support agency receives the form requesting either a review by the local child support agency or a court hearing within the 20 days specified in subdivision (f), the local child support agency shall not distribute the amount intercepted until the review by the local child support agency or the court hearing is completed. If the local child support agency determines that all or a portion of the member's or beneficiary's benefits were intercepted in error, or if the court determines that any amount of the benefits are exempt, the local child support agency shall refund any amount determined to be exempt or intercepted in excess of the correct amount to the member or beneficiary within 10 days of determination that a refund is due.

(k) A hearing properly requested pursuant to this section shall be calendared by the local child support agency. The hearing shall be held within 20 days from the date that the local child support agency receives the request for hearing. The local child support agency shall provide notice of the time and place for hearing by first-class mail no later than five days prior to the hearing.

(l) This section does not limit any existing rights of the member or beneficiary, including, but not limited to, the right to seek a determination of arrearages or other appropriate relief directly from the court. However, if the procedures of this section are not utilized by the member or beneficiary, the court may not require the local child support agency to refund any money that was distributed to the child support obligee prior to the local child support agency receiving notice of a court determination that a refund is due to the member or beneficiary.

(m) The Department of Child Support Services and the Public Employees' Retirement System shall enter into any agreement necessary to implement this section, which shall include provisions for the department to provide funding to the Public Employees' Retirement System to develop, implement, and maintain the intercept process described in this section.

(n) The Public Employees' Retirement System shall not assess service charges on members or beneficiaries in order to recover any administrative costs resulting from complying with this section.[33]

17530. (a) Notwithstanding any other law, this section applies to any actions taken to enforce a judgment or order for support entered as a result of action filed by the local child support agency pursuant to Section 17400, 17402, or 17404, where it is alleged that the enforcement actions have been taken in error against a person who is not the support obligor named in the judgment or order.

(b) A person claiming that a support enforcement action has been taken against that person, or the person's wages or assets, in error, shall file a claim of mistaken identity with the local child support agency. The claim shall include verifiable information or documentation to establish that the person against whom the enforcement actions have been taken is not the person named in the support order or judgment. The local child support agency shall resolve a claim of mistaken identity submitted pursuant to this section in the same manner and timeframes provided for resolution of a complaint pursuant to Section 17800.

(c) If the local child support agency determines that a claim filed pursuant to this section is meritorious, or if the court enters an order pursuant to Section 17433, the agency shall immediately take the steps necessary to terminate all enforcement activities with respect to the claimant, to return to the claimant any assets seized, to terminate any levying activities or attachment or assignment orders, to release any license renewal or application being withheld pursuant to Section 17520, to return any sums paid by the claimant pursuant to the judgment or order, including sums paid to any federal, state, or local government, but excluding sums paid directly to the support obligee, and to ensure that all other enforcement agencies and entities cease further actions against the claimant. With respect to a claim filed under this section, the local child support agency shall also provide the claimant with a statement certifying that the claimant is not the support obligor named in the support order or judgment, which statement shall be prima facie evidence of the claimant's identity in any subsequent enforcement proceedings or actions with respect to that support order or judgment.

(d) If the local child support agency rejects a claim pursuant to this section, or if the agency, after finding a claim to be meritorious, fails to take any of the remedial steps provided in subdivision (c), the claimant may file an action with the superior court to establish the mistaken identity or to obtain the remedies described in subdivision (c), or both.

(e) Filing a false claim pursuant to this section shall be a misdemeanor.[34]

17531. When a local child support agency closes a child support case containing summary criminal history information, the local child support agency shall delete or purge from the file and destroy any documents or information concerning or arising from offenses for or of which the parent has been arrested, charged, or convicted, other than offenses related to the parent's having failed to provide support for minor children, no later than four years and four months, or any other timeframe that is consistent with federal regulations controlling child support records retention, after the date the local child support agency closes the case.

17540. (a) (1) Commencing July 1, 2000, the department shall pay only those county claims for federal or state reimbursement under this division which are filed with the department within nine months of the end of the calendar quarter in which the costs are paid. A claim filed after that time may only be paid if the claim falls within the exceptions set forth in federal law.

(2) The department may change the nine-month limitation specified in paragraph (1), as deemed necessary by the department to comply with federal changes which affect time limits for filing a claim.

(b) (1) The department may waive the time limit imposed by subdivision (a) if the department determines there was good cause for a county's failure to file a claim or claims within the time limit.

(2) (A) For purposes of this subdivision, "good cause" means circumstances which are beyond the county's control, including acts of God and documented action or inaction by the state or federal government.

(B) "Circumstances beyond the county's control" do not include neglect or failure on the part of the county or any of its offices, officers, or employees.

(C) A county shall request a waiver of the time limit imposed by this section for good cause in accordance with regulations adopted and promulgated by the department.

(3) The department's authority to waive the time limit under this subdivision shall be subject to the availability of funds and shall not apply to claims submitted more than 18 months after the end of the calendar quarter in which costs were paid.

17550. (a) The Department of Child Support Services, in consultation with the State Department of Social Services, shall establish regulations by which the local child support agency, in any case of separation or desertion of a parent from a child that results in aid under Chapter 2 (commencing with Section 11200) of Part 3 of Division 9 of the Welfare and Institutions Code being granted to the child, may compromise the obligor parent or parents' liability for public assistance debt, including interest thereon, owed to the state where the child for whom public assistance was paid is residing with the obligor parent, and all of the following conditions are met:

(1) The obligor parent establishes one of the following:

(A) The child has been adjudged a dependent of the court under Section 300 of the Welfare and Institutions Code and the child has been reunified with the obligor parent pursuant to a court order.

(B) The child received public assistance while living with a guardian or relative caregiver and the child has been returned to the custody of the obligor parent, provided that the obligor parent for whom the debt compromise is being considered was the parent with whom the child resided prior to the child's placement with the guardian or relative caregiver.

(2) The obligor parent, for whom the debt compromise is being considered, has an income less than 250 percent of the current federal poverty level.

(3) The local child support agency, pursuant to regulations set forth by the department, has determined that the compromise is necessary for the child's support.

(b) Prior to compromising an obligor parent's liability for debt incurred for either AFDC-FC payments provided to a child pursuant to Section 11400 of the Welfare and Institutions Code, or incurred for CalWORKs payments provided on behalf of a child, the local child support agency shall consult with the county child welfare department.

(c) This section does not relieve an obligor, who has not been reunified with their child, of any liability for public assistance debt.

(d) For the purposes of this section, the following definitions apply:

(1) "Guardian" means the legal guardian of the child, who assumed care and control of the child while the child was in the guardian's control, and who is not a biological or adoptive parent.

(2) "Relative caregiver" means a relative as defined in subdivision (c) of Section 11362 of the Welfare and Institutions Code, who assumed primary responsibility for the child while the child was in the relative's care and control, and who is not a biological or adoptive parent.

(e) The department shall promulgate all necessary regulations pursuant to this section on or before October 1, 2002, including regulations that set forth guidelines to be used by the local child support agency when compromising public assistance debt.[35]

17552. (a) (1) The State Department of Social Services, in consultation with the Department of Child Support Services, shall promulgate regulations by which the county child welfare department, in any case of separation or desertion of a parent or parents from a child that results in foster care assistance payments under Section 11400 of, or a voluntary placement under Section 11401.1 of, or the payments for a minor child placed in the same home as a minor or nonminor dependent parent under Section 11401.4 of, the Welfare and Institutions Code, or CalWORKs payments to a caretaker relative of a child who comes within the jurisdiction of the juvenile court under Section 300, 601, or 602 of the Welfare and Institutions Code, who has been removed from the parental home and placed with the caretaker relative by court order, and who is under the supervision of the county child welfare agency or probation department under Section 11250 of, or Kin-GAP payments under Article 4.5 (commencing with Section 11360) or Article 4.7 (commencing with Section 11385) of, or aid under subdivision (b) of Section 10101 of, the Welfare and Institutions Code, shall determine whether it is in the best interests of the child or nonminor to have the case referred to the local child support agency for child support services. If reunification services are not offered or are terminated, the case may be referred to the local child support agency, unless the child's permanent plan is legal guardianship with a relative who is receiving Kin-GAP and the payment of support by the parent may compromise the stability of the current placement with the related guardian, or the permanent plan is transitional foster care for the nonminor under Section 11403 of the Welfare and Institutions Code. In making the determination, the department regulations shall provide the factors the county child welfare department shall consider, including:

(A) Whether the payment of support by the parent will pose a barrier to the proposed reunification, in that the payment of support will compromise the parent's ability to meet the requirements of the parent's reunification plan.

(B) Whether the payment of support by the parent will pose a barrier to the proposed reunification in that the payment of support will compromise the parent's current or future ability to meet the financial needs of the child.

(2) The department's regulations shall require the county welfare department, in making the determination pursuant to paragraph (1), to presume that the payment of support by the parent is likely to pose a barrier to the proposed reunification.

(b) The department regulations shall provide that, when the county child welfare department determines that it is not in the best interest of the child to seek a support order against the parent, the county child welfare department shall refrain from referring the case to the local child support agency. The regulations shall define those circumstances in which it is not in the best interest of the child to refer the case to the local child support agency. The regulations shall include the presumption described in paragraph (2) of subdivision (a) that the payment of support by the parent is likely to pose a barrier to the proposed reunification.

(c) The department regulations shall provide, when the county child welfare department determines that it is not in the child's best interest to have the case referred to the local child support agency, the county child welfare department shall review that determination periodically to coincide with the redetermination of AFDC-FC eligibility under Section 11401.5 of, or the CalWORKs eligibility under Section 11265 of, or Kin-GAP eligibility under Article 4.5 (commencing with Section 11360) or Article 4.7 (commencing with Section 11385) of Chapter 2 of Part 3 of Division 9 of, the Welfare and Institutions Code, and shall refer the child's case to the local child support agency upon a determination that, due to a change in the child's circumstances, it is no longer contrary to the child's best interest to have the case referred to the local child support agency.

(d) Notwithstanding any other law, a nonminor dependent, as described in subdivision (v) of Section 11400 of the Welfare and Institutions Code, who is over 19 years of age, is not a child for purposes of referral to the local child support agency for collection or enforcement of child support.

(e) Notwithstanding any other law, a minor or a nonminor dependent, as defined in subdivision (v) of Section 11400 of the Welfare and Institutions Code, who has a minor child placed in the same licensed or approved facility pursuant to Section 11401.4 of the Welfare and Institutions Code is not a parent for purposes of referral to the local child support agency for collection or enforcement of child support.

(f) The State Department of Social Services shall revise its regulations to implement the changes made by the act that added this subdivision on or before October 1, 2023.[544]

17555. (a) Any appropriation made available in the annual Budget Act for the purposes of augmenting funding for local child support agencies in the furtherance of their revenue collection responsibilities shall be subject to all of the following requirements:

(1) Each local child support agency shall submit to the department an early intervention plan with all components to take effect upon receipt of their additional allocation as a result of this proposal.

(2) Funds shall be distributed to counties based on their performance on the following two federal performance measures:

(A) Measure 3: Collections on Current Support.

(B) Measure 4: Cases with Collections on Arrears.

(3) A local child support agency shall be required to use and ensure that 100 percent of the new funds allocated are dedicated to maintaining caseworker staffing levels in order to stabilize child support collections.

(4) At the end of each fiscal year that this augmentation is in effect, the department shall provide a report on the cost-effectiveness of this augmentation, including an assessment of caseload changes over time.

(b) It is the intent of the Legislature to review the results of this augmentation and the level of related appropriation during the legislative budget review process.[265]

17556. On or before March 1, 2019, and annually thereafter, the department shall submit a report to the Legislature providing information on the status of all of the following:

(a) Case-to-staff ratios for each local child support agency.

(b) Collections to families and recoupment collections to county, state, and federal governmental agencies.

(c) Cost avoidance benefits.

(d) The number of families served by the child support program.[369]

17560. (a) The department shall establish and operate a statewide compromise of arrears program pursuant to which the department may accept offers in compromise of child support arrears and interest accrued thereon owed to the state for reimbursement of aid paid pursuant to Chapter 2 (commencing with Section 11200) of Part 3 of Division 9 of the Welfare and Institutions Code. The program shall operate uniformly across California and shall take into consideration the needs of the children subject to the child support order and the obligor's ability to pay.

(b) If the obligor owes current child support, the offer in compromise shall require the obligor to be in compliance with the current support order for a set period of time before any arrears and interest accrued thereon may be compromised.

(c) Absent a finding of good cause, or a determination by the director that it is in the best interest of the state to do otherwise, any offer in compromise entered into pursuant to this section shall be rescinded, all compromised liabilities shall be reestablished notwithstanding any statute of limitations that otherwise may be applicable, and no portion of the amount offered in compromise may be refunded, if either of the following occurs:

(1) The department or local child support agency determines that the obligor did any of the following acts regarding the offer in compromise:

(A) Concealed from the department or local child support agency any income, assets, or other property belonging to the obligor or any reasonably anticipated receipt of income, assets, or other property.

(B) Intentionally received, withheld, destroyed, mutilated, or falsified any information, document, or record, or intentionally made any false statement, relating to the financial conditions of the obligor.

(2) The obligor fails to comply with any of the terms and conditions of the offer in compromise.

(d) Pursuant to subdivision (k) of Section 17406, in no event may the administrator, director, or director's designee within the department, accept an offer in compromise of any child support arrears owed directly to the custodial party unless that party consents to the offer in compromise in writing and participates in the agreement. Prior to giving consent, the custodial party shall be provided with a clear written explanation of the rights with respect to child support arrears owed to the custodial party and the compromise thereof.

(e) Subject to the requirements of this section, the director shall delegate to the administrator of a local child support agency the authority to compromise an amount of child support arrears up to five thousand dollars ($5,000), and may delegate additional authority to compromise up to an amount determined by the director to support the effective administration of the offers in compromise program.

(f) For an amount to be compromised under this section, the following conditions shall exist:

(1) (A) The administrator, director or director's designee within the department determines that acceptance of an offer in compromise is in the best interest of the state and that the compromise amount equals or exceeds what the state can expect to collect for reimbursement of aid paid pursuant to Chapter 2 (commencing with Section 11200) of Part 3 of Division 9 of the Welfare and Institutions

Code in the absence of the compromise, based on the obligor's ability to pay.

(B) Acceptance of an offer in compromise shall be deemed to be in the best interest of the state, absent a finding of good cause to the contrary, with regard to arrears that accrued as a result of a decrease in income when an obligor was a reservist or member of the National Guard, was activated to United States military service, and failed to modify the support order to reflect the reduction in income. Good cause to find that the compromise is not in the best interest of the state shall include circumstances in which the service member's failure to seek, or delay in seeking, the modification were not reasonable under the circumstances faced by the service member. The director, no later than 90 days after the effective date of the act adding this subparagraph, shall establish rules that compromise, at a minimum, the amount of support that would not have accrued had the order been modified to reflect the reduced income earned during the period of active military service.

(2) Any other terms and conditions that the director establishes that may include, but may not be limited to, paying current support in a timely manner, making lump-sum payments, and paying arrears in exchange for compromise of interest owed.

(3) The obligor shall provide evidence of income and assets, including, but not limited to, wage stubs, tax returns, and bank statements as necessary to establish all of the following:

(A) That the amount set forth in the offer in compromise of arrears owed is the most that can be expected to be paid or collected from the obligor's present assets or income.

(B) That the obligor does not have reasonable prospects of acquiring increased income or assets that would enable the obligor to satisfy a greater amount of the child support arrears than the amount offered, within a reasonable period of time.

(C) That the obligor has not withheld payment of child support in anticipation of the offers in compromise program.

(g) A determination by the administrator, director or the director's designee within the department that it would not be in the best interest of the state to accept or rescind an offer in compromise in satisfaction of child support arrears shall be final and not subject to the provisions of Chapter 5 (commencing with Section 17800) of Division 17, or subject to judicial review.

(h) Any offer in compromise entered into pursuant to this section shall be filed with the appropriate court. The local child support agency shall notify the court if the compromise is rescinded pursuant to subdivision (c).

(i) Any compromise of child support arrears pursuant to this section shall maximize to the greatest extent possible the state's share of the federal performance incentives paid pursuant to the Child Support Performance and Incentive Act of 1998 and shall comply with federal law.

(j) The department shall ensure uniform application of this section across the state.

Article 3: Program Compliance

17600. (a) The Legislature finds and

declares all of the following:

(1) The Legislative Analyst has found that county child support enforcement programs provide a net increase in revenues to the state.

(2) The state has a fiscal interest in ensuring that county child support enforcement programs perform efficiently.

(3) The state does not provide information to counties on child support enforcement programs, based on common denominators that would facilitate comparison of program performance.

(4) Providing this information would allow county officials to monitor program performance and to make appropriate modifications to improve program efficiency.

(5) This information is required for effective management of the child support program.

(b) Except as provided in this subdivision commencing with the 1998–99 fiscal year, and for each fiscal year thereafter, each county that is participating in the state incentive program described in Section 17704 shall provide to the department, and the department shall compile from this county child support information, monthly and annually, all of the following performance-based data, as established by the federal incentive funding system, provided that the department may revise the data required by this paragraph in order to conform to the final federal incentive system data definitions:

(1) One of the following data relating to paternity establishment, as required by the department, provided that the department shall require all counties to report on the same measurement:

(A) The total number of children in the caseload governed by Part D (commencing with Section 451) of Title IV of the federal Social Security Act (42 U.S.C. Sec. 651 et seq.), as of the end of the federal fiscal year, who were born to unmarried parents for whom paternity was established or acknowledged, and the total number of children in that caseload, as of the end of the preceding federal fiscal year, who were born to unmarried parents.

(B) The total number of minor children who were born in the state to unmarried parents for whom paternity was established or acknowledged during a federal fiscal year, and the total number of children in the state born to unmarried parents during the preceding calendar year.

(2) The number of cases governed by Part D (commencing with Section 451) of Title IV of the federal Social Security Act (42 U.S.C. Sec. 651 et seq.) during the federal fiscal year and the total number of those cases with support orders.

(3) The total dollars collected during the federal fiscal year for current support in cases governed by Part D (commencing with Section 451) of Title IV of the federal Social Security Act (42 U.S.C. Sec. 651 et seq.) and the total number of dollars owing for current support during that federal fiscal year in cases governed by those provisions.

(4) The total number of cases for the federal fiscal year governed by Part D (commencing with Section 451) of Title IV of the federal Social Security Act (42 U.S.C. Sec. 651 et seq.) in

which payment was being made toward child support arrearages and the total number of cases for that fiscal year governed by these federal provisions that had child support arrearages.

(5) The total number of dollars collected and expended during a federal fiscal year in cases governed by Part D (commencing with Section 451) of Title IV of the federal Social Security Act (42 U.S.C. Sec. 651 et seq.).

(6) The total amount of child support dollars collected during a federal fiscal year, and, if and when required by federal law, the amount of these collections broken down by collections distributed on behalf of current recipients of federal Temporary Assistance for Needy Families block grant funds or federal foster care funds, on behalf of former recipients of federal Temporary Assistance for Needy Families block grant funds or federal foster care funds, or on behalf of persons who have never been recipients of these federal funds.

(c) In addition to the information required by subdivision (b), the department shall collect, on a monthly basis, from each county that is participating in the state incentive program described in Section 17704, information on the local child support agency for each federal fiscal year, and shall report semiannually on all of the following performance measurements:

(1) The percentage of cases with collections of current support. This percentage shall be calculated by dividing the number of cases with an order for current support by the number of those cases with collections of current support. The number of cases with support collected shall include only the number of cases actually receiving a collection, not the number of payments received. Cases with a medical support order that do not have an order for current support may not be counted.

(2) The average amount collected per case for all cases with collections.

(3) The percentage of cases that had a support order established during the period. A support order shall be counted as established only when the appropriate court has issued an order for child support, including an order for temporary child support, or an order for medical support.

(4) The total cost of administering the local child support agency, including the federal, state, and county share of the costs, and the federal and state incentives received by each county. The total cost of administering the program shall be broken down by the following:

(A) The direct costs of the program, broken down further by total employee salaries and benefits, a list of the number of employees broken down into at least the following categories: attorneys, administrators, caseworkers, investigators, and clerical support; contractor costs; space charges; and payments to other county agencies. Employee salaries and numbers need only be reported in the annual report.

(B) The indirect costs, showing all overhead charges.

(5) In addition, the local child support agency shall report monthly on measurements developed by the department that provide data on the following:

(A) Locating obligors.

(B) Obtaining and enforcing medical

support.

(C) Providing customer service.

(D) Any other measurements that the director determines to be an appropriate determination of a local child support agency's performance.

(6) A county may apply for an exemption from any or all of the reporting requirements of this subdivision for a fiscal year by submitting an application for the exemption to the department at least three months prior to the commencement of the fiscal year or quarter for which the exemption is sought. A county shall provide a separate justification for each data element under this subdivision for which the county is seeking an exemption and the cost to the county of providing the data. The department may not grant an exemption for more than one year. The department may grant a single exemption only if both of the following conditions are met:

(A) The county cannot compile the data being sought through its existing automated system or systems.

(B) The county cannot compile the data being sought through manual means or through an enhanced automated system or systems without significantly harming the child support collection efforts of the county.

(d) After implementation of the statewide automated system, in addition to the information required by subdivision (b), the Department of Child Support Services shall collect, on a monthly basis, from each county that is participating in the state incentive program described in Section 17704, information on the county child support enforcement program beginning with the 1998–99 fiscal year or a later fiscal year, as appropriate, and for each subsequent fiscal year, and shall report semiannually on all of the following measurements:

(1) For each of the following support collection categories, the number of cases with support collected shall include only the number of cases actually receiving a collection, not the number of payments received.

(A) (i) The number of cases with collections for current support.

(ii) The number of cases with arrears collections only.

(iii) The number of cases with both current support and arrears collections.

(B) For cases with current support only due:

(i) The number of cases in which the full amount of current support owed was collected.

(ii) The number of cases in which some amount of current support, but less than the full amount of support owed, was collected.

(iii) The number of cases in which no amount of support owed was collected.

(C) For cases in which arrears only were owed:

(i) The number of cases in which all arrears owed were collected.

(ii) The number of cases in which some amount of arrears, but less than the full amount of arrears owed, was collected.

(iii) The number of cases in which no amount of arrears owed was collected.

(D) For cases in which both current support and arrears are owed:

(i) The number of cases in which the full amount of current support and arrears owed was collected.

(ii) The number of cases in which

some amount of current support and arrears, but less than the full amount of support owed, was collected.

(iii) The number of cases in which no amount of support owed was collected.

(E) The total number of cases in which an amount was due for current support only.

(F) The total number of cases in which an amount was due for both current support and arrears.

(G) The total number of cases in which an amount was due for arrears only.

(H) For cases with current support due, the number of cases without orders for medical support and the number of cases with an order for medical support.

(2) The number of alleged fathers or obligors who were served with a summons and complaint to establish paternity or a support order, and the number of alleged fathers or obligors for whom it is required that paternity or a support order be established. In order to be counted under this paragraph, the alleged father or obligor shall be successfully served with process. An alleged father shall be counted under this paragraph only once if served with process simultaneously for both a paternity and a support order proceeding for the same child or children. For purposes of this paragraph, a support order shall include a medical support order.

(3) The number of new asset seizures or successful initial collections on a wage assignment for purposes of child support collection. For purposes of this paragraph, a collection made on a wage assignment shall be counted only once for each wage assignment issued.

(4) The number of children requiring paternity establishment and the number of children for whom paternity has been established during the period. Paternity may only be established once for each child. A child for whom paternity is not at issue shall not be counted in the number of children for whom paternity has been established. For this purpose, paternity is not at issue if the parents were married and neither parent challenges paternity or a voluntary paternity declaration has been executed by the parents prior to the local child support agency obtaining the case and neither parent challenges paternity.

(5) The number of cases requiring that a support order be established and the number of cases that had a support order established during the period. A support order shall be counted as established only when the appropriate court has issued an order for child support, including an order for temporary child support, or an order for medical support.

(6) The total cost of administering the local child support agency, including the federal, state, and county share of the costs and the federal and state incentives received by each county. The total cost of administering the program shall be broken down by the following:

(A) The direct costs of the program, broken down further by total employee salaries and benefits, a list of the number of employees broken down into at least the following categories: attorneys, administrators, caseworkers, investigators, and clerical support; contractor costs; space charges; and payments to other county agencies. Employee salaries and numbers need only be reported in the annual report.

(B) The indirect costs, showing all overhead charges.

(7) The total child support collections due, broken down by current support, interest on arrears, and principal, and the total child support collections that have been collected, broken down by current support, interest on arrears, and principal.

(8) The actual case status for all cases in the county child support enforcement program. Each case shall be reported in one case status only. If a case falls within more than one status category, it shall be counted in the first status category of the list set forth below in which it qualifies. The following shall be the case status choices:

(A) No support order, location of obligor parent required.

(B) No support order, alleged obligor parent located and paternity required.

(C) No support order, location and paternity not at issue but support order must be established.

(D) Support order established with current support obligation and obligor is in compliance with support obligation.

(E) Support order established with current support obligation, obligor is in arrears, and location of obligor is necessary.

(F) Support order established with current support obligation, obligor is in arrears, and location of obligor's assets is necessary.

(G) Support order established with current support obligation, obligor is in arrears, and no location of obligor or obligor's assets is necessary.

(H) Support order established with current support obligation, obligor is in arrears, the obligor is located, but the local child support agency has established satisfactorily that the obligor has no income or assets and no ability to earn.

(I) Support order established with current support obligation and arrears, obligor is paying the current support and is paying some or all of the interest on the arrears, but is paying no principal.

(J) Support order established for arrears only and obligor is current in repayment obligation.

(K) Support order established for arrears only, obligor is not current in arrears repayment schedule, and location of obligor is required.

(L) Support order established for arrears only, obligor is not current in arrears repayment schedule, and location of obligor's assets is required.

(M) Support order established for arrears only, obligor is not current in arrears repayment schedule, and no location of obligor or obligor's assets is required.

(N) Support order established for arrears only, obligor is not current in arrears repayment, and the obligor is located, but the local child support agency has established satisfactorily that the obligor has no income or assets and no ability to earn.

(O) Support order established for arrears only and obligor is repaying some or all of the interest, but no principal.

(P) Other, if necessary, to be defined in the regulations promulgated under subdivision (e).

(e) Upon implementation of the statewide automated system, or at the time that the department determines that compliance with this subdivision is possible, whichever is earlier, each county that is participating in the state incentive program described in Section 17704 shall collect and report, and the department shall compile for each participating county, information on the county child support program in each fiscal year, all of the following data, in a manner that facilitates comparison of counties and the entire state, except that the department may eliminate or modify the requirement to report any data mandated to be reported pursuant to this subdivision if the department determines that the local child support agencies are unable to accurately collect and report the information or that collecting and reporting of the data by the local child support agencies will be onerous:

(1) The number of alleged obligors or fathers who receive CalWORKs benefits, CalFresh benefits, and Medi-Cal benefits.

(2) The number of obligors or alleged fathers who are in state prison or county jail.

(3) The number of obligors or alleged fathers who do not have a social security number.

(4) The number of obligors or alleged fathers whose address is unknown.

(5) The number of obligors or alleged fathers whose complete name, consisting of at least a first and last name, is not known by the local child support agency.

(6) The number of obligors or alleged fathers who filed a tax return with the Franchise Tax Board in the last year for which a data match is available.

(7) The number of obligors or alleged fathers who have no income reported to the Employment Development Department during the third quarter of the fiscal year.

(8) The number of obligors or alleged fathers who have income between one dollar ($1) and five hundred dollars ($500) reported to the Employment Development Department during the third quarter of the fiscal year.

(9) The number of obligors or alleged fathers who have income between five hundred one dollars ($501) and one thousand five hundred dollars ($1,500) reported to the Employment Development Department during the third quarter of the fiscal year.

(10) The number of obligors or alleged fathers who have income between one thousand five hundred one dollars ($1,501) and two thousand five hundred dollars ($2,500) reported to the Employment Development Department during the third quarter of the fiscal year.

(11) The number of obligors or alleged fathers who have income between two thousand five hundred one dollars ($2,501) and three thousand five hundred dollars ($3,500) reported to the Employment Development Department during the third quarter of the fiscal year.

(12) The number of obligors or alleged fathers who have income between three thousand five hundred one dollars ($3,501) and four thousand five hundred dollars ($4,500) reported to the Employment Development Department during the third quarter of the fiscal year.

(13) The number of obligors or al-

leged fathers who have income between four thousand five hundred one dollars ($4,501) and five thousand five hundred dollars ($5,500) reported to the Employment Development Department during the third quarter of the fiscal year.

(14) The number of obligors or alleged fathers who have income between five thousand five hundred one dollars ($5,501) and six thousand five hundred dollars ($6,500) reported to the Employment Development Department during the third quarter of the fiscal year.

(15) The number of obligors or alleged fathers who have income between six thousand five hundred one dollars ($6,501) and seven thousand five hundred dollars ($7,500) reported to the Employment Development Department during the third quarter of the fiscal year.

(16) The number of obligors or alleged fathers who have income between seven thousand five hundred one dollars ($7,501) and nine thousand dollars ($9,000) reported to the Employment Development Department during the third quarter of the fiscal year.

(17) The number of obligors or alleged fathers who have income exceeding nine thousand dollars ($9,000) reported to the Employment Development Department during the third quarter of the fiscal year.

(18) The number of obligors or alleged fathers who have two or more employers reporting earned income to the Employment Development Department during the third quarter of the fiscal year.

(19) The number of obligors or alleged fathers who receive unemployment benefits during the third quarter of the fiscal year.

(20) The number of obligors or alleged fathers who receive state disability benefits during the third quarter of the fiscal year.

(21) The number of obligors or alleged fathers who receive workers' compensation benefits during the third quarter of the fiscal year.

(22) The number of obligors or alleged fathers who receive Social Security Disability Insurance benefits during the third quarter of the fiscal year.

(23) The number of obligors or alleged fathers who receive Supplemental Security Income/State Supplementary Program for the Aged, Blind and Disabled benefits during the third quarter of the fiscal year.

(f) The department, in consultation with the Legislative Analyst's Office, the Judicial Council, the California Family Support Council, and child support advocates, shall develop regulations to ensure that all local child support agencies report the data required by this section uniformly and consistently throughout California.

(g) For each federal fiscal year, the department shall provide the information for all participating counties to each member of a county board of supervisors, county executive officer, local child support agency, and the appropriate policy committees and fiscal committees of the Legislature on or before June 30, of each fiscal year. The department shall provide data semiannually, based on the federal fiscal year, on or before December 31, of each year. The department shall present the information in a manner that facilitates comparison of county performance.

(h) For purposes of this section, "case" means a noncustodial parent, whether mother, father, or putative father, who is, or eventually may be, obligated under law for support of a child or children. For purposes of this definition, a noncustodial parent shall be counted once for each family that has a dependent child they may be obligated to support.

(i) This section shall be operative only for as long as Section 17704 requires participating counties to report data to the department.

17601. The department shall provide to the Legislature actual performance data on child support collections within 60 days of the end of each quarter. This data shall include all comparative data for managing program performance currently provided to local child support agencies, including national, state, and local performance data, as available. The department shall prominently post the data on its Web site, and shall require all local child support agency Web sites to prominently post a link to the state Web site. The department shall update the Legislature during the annual budget subcommittee hearing process, commencing in 2008, on the state and local progress on child support federal performance measures and collections.[133]

17602. (a) The department shall adopt the federal minimum standards as the baseline standard of performance for the local child support agencies and work in consultation with the local child support agencies to develop program performance targets on an annual federal fiscal year basis. The performance measures shall include, at a minimum, the federal performance measures and the state performance measures, as described in subdivision (c) of Section 17600. The program performance targets shall represent ongoing improvement in the performance measures for each local child support agency, as well as the department's statewide performance level.

(b) In determining the performance measures in subdivision (a), the department shall consider the total amount of uncollected child support arrearages that are realistically collectible. The director shall analyze, in consultation with local child support agencies and child support advocates, the current amount of uncollected child support arrearages statewide and in each county to determine the amount of child support that may realistically be collected. The director shall consider, in conducting the analysis, factors that may influence collections, including demographic factors such as welfare caseload, levels of poverty and unemployment, rates of incarceration of obligors, and age of delinquencies. The director shall use this analysis to establish program priorities as provided in paragraph (7) of subdivision (b) of Section 17306.

(c) The department shall use the performance-based data, and the criteria for that data, as set forth in Section 17600 to determine a local child support agency's performance measure for the quarter.

(d) The director shall adopt a three-phase process to be used statewide when a local child support agency is out of compliance with the performance standards adopted pursuant to subdivision (a), or the director determines that the local child support agency is failing in a substantial manner to comply with any provision of the state plan, the provisions of this code, the requirements of federal law, the regulations of the department, or the cooperative agreement. The director shall adopt policies as to the implementation of each phase, including requirements for measurement of progress and improvement, which shall be met as part of the performance improvement plan specified in paragraphs (1) and (2), in order to avoid implementation of the next phase of compliance. The director shall not implement any of these phases until July 1, 2001, or until six months after a local child support agency has completed its transition from the office of the district attorney to the new county department of child support services, whichever is later. The phases shall include the following:

(1) Phase I: Development of a performance improvement plan that is prepared jointly by the local child support agency and the department, subject to the department's final approval. The plan shall provide performance expectations and goals for achieving compliance with the state plan and other state and federal laws and regulations that must be reviewed and assessed within specific timeframes in order to avoid execution of Phase II.

(2) Phase II: Onsite investigation, evaluation, and oversight of the local child support agency by the department. The director shall appoint program monitoring teams to make site visits, conduct educational and training sessions, and help the local child support agency identify and attack problem areas. The program monitoring teams shall evaluate all aspects of the functions and performance of the local child support agency, including compliance with state and federal laws and regulations. Based on these investigations and evaluations, the program monitoring team shall develop a final performance improvement plan and shall oversee implementation of all recommendations made in the plan. The local child support agency shall adhere to all recommendations made by the program monitoring team. The plan shall provide performance expectations and compliance goals that must be reviewed and assessed within specific timeframes in order to avoid execution of Phase III.

(3) Phase III: The director shall assume, either directly or through agreement with another entity, responsibility for the management of the child and spousal support enforcement program in the county until the local child support agency provides reasonable assurances to the director of its intention and ability to comply. During the period of state management responsibility, the director or an authorized representative shall have all of the powers and responsibilities of the local child support agency concerning the administration of the program. The local child support agency shall be responsible for providing any funds necessary for the continued operation of the program. If the local child support agency fails or refuses to provide these funds, including a sufficient

amount to reimburse any and all costs incurred by the department in managing the program, the Controller may deduct an amount certified by the director as necessary for the continued operation of the program by the department from any state or federal funds payable to the county for any purpose.

(e) The director shall report in writing to the Legislature semiannually, beginning July 1, 2001, on the status of the state child support enforcement program. The director shall submit data semiannually to the Legislature, the Governor, and the public, on the progress of all local child support agencies in each performance measure, including identification of the local child support agencies that are out of compliance, the performance measures that they have failed to satisfy, and the performance improvement plan that is being taken for each.

17604. (a) (1) If at any time the director considers any public agency, that is required by law, by delegation of the department, or by cooperative agreement to perform functions relating to the state plan for securing child and spousal support and determining paternity, to be failing in a substantial manner to comply with any provision of the state plan, the director shall put that agency on written notice to that effect.

(2) The state plan concerning spousal support shall apply only to spousal support included in a child support order.

(3) In this chapter the term spousal support shall include support for a former spouse.

(b) After receiving notice, the public agency shall have 45 days to make a showing to the director of full compliance or set forth a compliance plan that the director finds to be satisfactory.

(c) If the director determines that there is a failure on the part of that public agency to comply with the provisions of the state plan, or to set forth a compliance plan that the director finds to be satisfactory, or if the state certifies to the director that the public agency is not in conformity with applicable merit system standards under Part 2.5 (commencing with Section 19800) of Division 5 of Title 2 of the Government Code, and that sanctions are necessary to secure compliance, the director shall withhold part or all of state and federal funds, including incentive funds, from that public agency until the public agency shall make a showing to the director of full compliance.

(d) After sanctions have been invoked pursuant to subdivision (c), if the director determines that there remains a failure on the part of the public agency to comply with the provisions of the state plan, the director may remove that public agency from performing any part or all of the functions relating to the state plan.

(e) In the event of any other audit or review that results in the reduction or modification of federal funding for the program under Part D (commencing with Section 652) of Subchapter IV of Title 42 of the United States Code, the sanction shall be assessed against those counties specifically cited in the federal findings in the amount cited in those findings.

(f) The department shall establish a process whereby any county assessed a portion of any sanction may appeal the department's decision.

(g) Nothing in this section shall be construed as relieving the board of supervisors of the responsibility to provide funds necessary for the continued operation of the state plan as required by law.[270]

Article 4: Program Costs

17701. (a) There is established within California's child support program a quality assurance and performance improvement program, pursuant to which local child support agencies, in partnership with the Department of Child Support Services, shall monitor and measure program performance and compliance, and ensure the implementation of actions necessary to meet state and federal requirements and to continuously improve the quality of child support program services.

(b) Under the direction and oversight of the department, each local child support agency shall implement a quality assurance and performance improvement program that shall include, at a minimum, all of the following:

(1) An annual planning process that incorporates statewide standards and requirements, and establishes local performance goals that the department and local agency agree are appropriate.

(2) The inclusion of local performance goals and other performance-related measures in the local child support agency's Plan of Cooperation agreement with the department.

(3) Implementation of actions necessary to promote the delivery of enhanced program services and improved performance.

(4) An ongoing self-assessment process that evaluates progress in achieving performance improvement and compliance with program requirements.

(5) Regular and ongoing oversight by the department, including onsite reviews and the provision of technical assistance.

(c) The department shall promulgate regulations to implement this section.[100]

17702. (a) The department shall assess, at least once every three years, each county's compliance with federal and state child support laws and regulations in effect for the time period being reviewed, using a statistically valid sample of cases. Counties found to be out of compliance shall be assessed annually, until they are found to be in compliance. The information for the assessment shall be based on reviews conducted and reports produced by either state or county staff, as determined by the department.

In addition, in order to meet federal self-assessment requirements, the department shall conduct an annual assessment of the state's compliance, using a statistically valid statewide sample of cases.

(b) A county shall be eligible for the state incentives under Section 17704 only if the department determines that the county is in compliance with all federal and state laws and regulations or if the county has a corrective action plan in place that has been certified by the department pursuant to this subdivision. If a county is determined not to be in compliance the county shall develop and submit a corrective action plan to the department. The department shall certify a corrective action plan if the department determines that the plan will put the county into compliance with federal and state laws and regulations. A county shall be eligible for state incentives under Section 17704 only for any quarter the county remains in compliance with a corrective action plan that has been certified by the department.

(c) Counties under a corrective action plan shall be assessed on a quarterly basis until the department determines that they are in compliance with federal and state child support program requirements.[101]

17702.5. (a) The Child Support Collections Recovery Fund is hereby created in the State Treasury, and shall be administered by the department for the purposes specified in subdivision (c).

(b) Except as otherwise provided in this section, the fund shall consist of both of the following:

(1) All public moneys transferred by public agencies to the department for deposit into the fund, as permitted under Section 304.30 of Title 45 of the Code of Federal Regulations or any other applicable federal statutes.

(2) Any interest that accrues on amounts in the fund.

(c) Upon appropriation by the Legislature, all moneys in the fund shall be used to make payments or advances to local child support agencies of the federal share of administrative payments for costs incurred pursuant to this article.

(d) Upon repeal of this section, the Legislature intends that any moneys remaining in the fund shall be returned to the federal agency that provides federal financial participation to the department.

17703. (a) A revolving fund in the State Treasury is hereby created to be known as the Child Support Services Advance Fund. All moneys deposited into the fund are for the purpose of making a consolidated payment or advance to counties, state agencies, or other governmental entities, comprised of the state and federal share of costs associated with the programs administered by the Department of Child Support Services, inclusive of the payment of refunds. In addition, the fund may be used for the purpose of making a consolidated payment to a payee, comprised of the state and federal shares of local assistance costs associated with the programs administered by the Department of Child Support Services.

(b) Payments or advances of funds to counties, state agencies, or other governmental agencies and other payees doing business with the state that are properly chargeable to appropriations or other funds in the State Treasury, may be made by a Controller's warrant drawn against the Child Support Services Advance Fund. For every warrant so issued, a remittance advice shall be issued by the Department of Child Support Services to identify the purposes and amounts for which it was drawn.

(c) The amounts to be transferred to the Child Support Services Advance Fund at any time shall be determined by the department, and, upon order of the Controller, shall be transferred from the funds and appropriations otherwise properly chargeable.

(d) Refunds of amounts disbursed from the Child Support Services Advance Fund shall, on order of the

Controller, be deposited in the Child Support Services Advance Fund, and, on order of the Controller, shall be transferred therefrom to the funds and appropriations from which those amounts were originally derived. Claims for amounts erroneously deposited into the Child Support Services Advance Fund shall be submitted by the department to the Controller who, if the claims are approved, shall draw a warrant in payment thereof against the Child Support Services Advance Fund.

(e) All amounts increasing the cash balance in the Child Support Services Advance Fund, that were derived from the cancellation of warrants issued therefrom, shall, on order of the Controller, be transferred to the appropriations from which the amounts were originally derived.

17704. (a) For the 1998–99 fiscal year the department shall pay to each county a child support incentive payment. Every county shall receive the federal child support incentive. A county shall receive the state child support incentive if it elects to do both of the following:

(1) Comply with the reporting requirements of Section 17600 while federal financial participation is available for collecting and reporting data.

(2) Comply with federal and state child support laws and regulations, or has a corrective action plan certified by the department pursuant to Section 17702. The combined federal and state incentive payment shall be 13.6 percent of distributed collections. If the amount appropriated by the Legislature for the state incentives is less than the amount necessary to satisfy each county's actual incentives pursuant to this section, each county shall receive its proportional share of incentives.

(b) (1) Beginning July 1, 1999, the department shall pay to each county a child support incentive for child support collections. Every county shall receive the federal child support incentive. The combined federal and state incentive payments shall be 13.6 percent of distributed collections. In addition to the federal child support incentive, each county may also receive a state child support incentive. A county shall receive the state child support incentive if it elects to do both of the following:

(A) Comply with the reporting requirements of Section 17600 while federal financial participation is available for collecting and reporting data.

(B) Be in compliance with federal and state child support laws and regulations, or have a performance improvement plan certified by the department pursuant to Section 17702.

(2) (A) For purposes of paragraph (1), the federal incentive component shall be each county's share of the child support incentive payments that the state receives from the federal government, based on the county's collections.

(B) (i) Effective July 1, 1999, and annually thereafter, state funds appropriated for child support incentives shall first be used to fund the administrative costs incurred by local child support agencies in administering the child support program, excluding automation costs as set forth in

Section 10085 of the Welfare and Institutions Code, after subtracting all federal financial participation for administrative costs and all federal child support incentives received by the state and passed on to the local child support agencies. The department shall allocate sufficient resources to each local child support agency to fully fund the remaining administrative costs of its budget as approved by the director pursuant to paragraph (9) of subdivision (b) of Section 17306, subject to the appropriation of funding in the annual Budget Act. No later than January 1, 2000, the department shall identify allowable administrative costs that may be claimed for reimbursement from the state, which shall be limited to reasonable amounts in relation to the scope of services and the total funds available. If the total amount of administrative costs claimed in any year exceeds the amount appropriated in the Budget Act, the amount provided to local child support agencies shall be reduced by the percentage necessary to ensure that projected General Fund expenditures do not exceed the amount authorized in the Budget Act.

(ii) Effective July 1, 2001, and annually thereafter, after allowable administrative costs are funded under clause (i), the department shall use any remaining unallocated incentive funds appropriated from the prior fiscal year which are hereby reappropriated to implement an incentive program that rewards up to 10 local child support agencies in each year, based on their performance or increase in performance on one or more of the federal performance standards set forth in Section 458 of the federal Social Security Act (42 U.S.C. Sec. 658), or state performance standards set forth in subdivision (a) of Section 17602, as determined by the department. The department shall determine the number of local agencies that receive state incentive funds under this program, subject to a maximum of 10 agencies and shall determine the amount received by each local agency based on the availability of funds and each local child support agency's proportional share based on the performance standard or standards used.

(iii) Any funds received pursuant to this subdivision shall be used only for child support enforcement activities.

(c) Each county shall continue to receive its federal child support incentive funding whether or not it elects to participate in the state child support incentive funding program.

(d) The department shall provide incentive funds pursuant to this section only during any fiscal year in which funding is provided for that purpose in the Budget Act.

17708. (a) This section shall apply to any county that elects to participate in the state incentive program described in Section 17704.

(b) Each participating county child support enforcement program shall provide the data required by Section 17600 to the department on a quarterly basis. The data shall be provided no later than 15 days after the end of each quarter.

(c) On and after July 1, 1998, a county shall be required to comply with the provisions of this section only during fiscal years in which funding is provided for that purpose in the Budget Act.

17710. (a) Each county shall be responsible for any administrative expenditures for administering the child support program not covered by federal and state funds.
(b) Notwithstanding subdivision (a), effective July 1, 1991, to June 30, 1992, inclusive, counties shall pay the nonfederal share of the administrative costs of conducting the reviews required under former Section 15200.8 of the Welfare and Institutions Code from the savings counties will obtain as a result of the reduction in the maximum aid payments specified in Section 11450. Effective July 1, 1992, to June 30, 1993, inclusive, the state shall pay the nonfederal share of administrative costs of conducting the reviews required under former Section 15200.8 of the Welfare and Institutions Code. Funding for county costs after June 30, 1993, shall be subject to the availability of funds in the annual Budget Act.[362]

17712. Notwithstanding subdivision (a) of Section 17708, and to the extent funds are appropriated by the annual Budget Act, funds shall be provided to the Judicial Council for the nonfederal share of costs for the costs of child support commissioners pursuant to Section 4251 and family law facilitators pursuant to Division 14 (commencing with Section 10000). The Judicial Council shall distribute the funds to the counties for the purpose of matching federal funds for the costs of child support commissioners and family law facilitators and related costs. Funds distributed pursuant to this section may also be used to offset the nonfederal share of costs incurred by the Judicial Council for performing the duties specified in Sections 4252 and 10010.

17714. (a) (1) Any funds paid to a county pursuant to this chapter prior to June 30, 1999, which exceed the county's cost of administering the child support program of the local child support agency pursuant to Section 17400 to that date, hereafter referred to as "excess funds," shall be expended by the county only upon that program. All these excess funds shall be deposited by the county into a special fund established by the county for this purpose.
(2) Performance incentive funds shall include, but not be limited to, incentive funds paid pursuant to Section 17704, and performance incentive funds paid pursuant to Section 14124.93 of the Welfare and Institutions Code and all interest earned on deposits in the special fund. Performance incentive funds shall not include funds paid pursuant to Section 17706. Performance incentive funds shall be expended by the county only upon that program. All performance incentive funds shall be deposited by the county into a special fund established by the county for this purpose.
(b) All excess funds and performance incentive funds shall be expended by the county on the support enforcement program of the local child support agency within two fiscal years following the fiscal year of receipt of the funds by the county. Except as provided in subdivision (c), any excess funds or performance incentive funds

paid pursuant to this chapter since July 1, 1992, that the department determines have not been spent within the required two-year period shall revert to the state General Fund, and shall be distributed by the department only to counties that have complied with this section. The formula for distribution shall be based on the number of CalWORKs cases within each county.

(c) A county that submits to the department a written plan approved by that county's local child support agency for the expenditure of excess funds or performance incentive funds shall be exempted from the requirements of subdivision (b), if the department determines that the expenditure will be cost-effective, will maximize federal funds, and the expenditure plan will require more than the time provided for in subdivision (b) to expend the funds. Once the department approves a plan pursuant to this subdivision, funds received by a county and designated for an expenditure in the plan shall not be expended by the county for any other purpose.

(d) Nothing in this section shall be construed to nullify the recovery and reversion to the General Fund of unspent incentive funds as provided in Section 6 of Chapter 479 of the Statutes of 1999.

Chapter 5: Complaint Resolution

17800. Each local child support agency shall maintain a complaint resolution process. The department shall specify by regulation, no later than July 1, 2001, uniform forms and procedures that each local child support agency shall use in resolving all complaints received from custodial and noncustodial parents. A complaint shall be made within 90 days after the custodial or noncustodial parent affected knew or should have known of the child support action complained of. The local child support agency shall provide a written resolution of the complaint within 30 days of the receipt of the complaint. The director of the local child support agency may extend the period for resolution of the complaint an additional 30 days in accordance with the regulations adopted pursuant to Section 17804.

17801. (a) A custodial or noncustodial parent who is dissatisfied with the local child support agency's resolution of a complaint shall be accorded an opportunity for a state hearing when one or more of the following actions or failures to take action by the department or the local child support agency is claimed by the parent:

(1) An application for child support services has been denied or has not been acted upon within the required timeframe.

(2) The child support services case has been acted upon in violation of state or federal law or regulation or department letter ruling, or has not yet been acted upon within the required timeframe, including services for the establishment, modification, and enforcement of child support orders and child support accountings.

(3) Child support collections have not been distributed or have been distributed or disbursed incorrectly, or the amount of child support arrears, as calculated by the department or the local child support agency is inaccurate. The amount of the court order

for support, including current support and arrears, is not subject to a state hearing under this section.

(4) The child support agency's decision to close a child support case.

(b) Prior to requesting a hearing pursuant to subdivision (a), the custodial or noncustodial parent shall exhaust the complaint resolution process required in Section 17800, unless the local child support agency has not, within the 30-day period required by that section, submitted a written resolution of the complaint. If the custodial or noncustodial parent does not receive that timely written resolution, the custodial parent may request a hearing pursuant to subdivision (a).

(c) A hearing shall be provided under subdivision (a) when the request for a hearing is made within 90 days after receiving the written notice of resolution required in Section 17800 or, if no written notice of resolution is provided within 30 days from the date the complaint was made, within 90 days after making the complaint.

(d) (1) A hearing under subdivision (a) shall be set to commence within 45 days after the request is received by the state hearing office, and at least 10 days prior to the hearing, all parties shall be given written notice of the time and place of the hearing. Unless the time period is waived by the complainant, the proposed hearing decision shall be rendered by the state hearing office within 75 days after the request for a state hearing is received by the state hearing office. The department shall have 15 days from the date the proposed decision is rendered to act upon the decision. When a hearing is postponed, continued, or reopened with the consent of the complainant, the time for issuance of the decision, and action on the decision by the department, shall be extended for a period of time consistent with the postponement, continuance, or reopening.

(2) For purposes of this subdivision, the "state hearing office" refers to the division of the office or agency designated by the department to carry out state hearings, that conducts those state hearings.

(e) To the extent not inconsistent with this section, hearings under subdivision (a) shall be provided in the same manner in which hearings are provided in Sections 10950 to 10967 of the Welfare and Institutions Code and the State Department of Social Services' regulations implementing and interpreting those sections.

(f) Pendency of a state hearing shall not affect the obligation to comply with an existing child support order.

(g) A child support determination that is subject to the jurisdiction of the superior court and that is required by law to be addressed by motion, order to show cause, or appeal under this code shall not be subject to a state hearing under this section. The director shall, by regulation, specify and exclude from the subject matter jurisdiction of state hearings provided under subdivision (a), grievances arising from a child support case in the superior court that must, by law, be addressed by motion, order to show cause, or appeal under this code.

(h) The local child support agency shall comply with, and execute, every decision of the director rendered pursuant to this section.

(i) The director shall contract with the State Department of Social Services or the Office of Administrative Hearings for the provision of state hearings in accordance with this section.

(j) This section shall be implemented only to the extent that there is federal financial participation available at the child support funding rate set forth in Section 655(a)(2) of Title 42 of the United States Code.

17803. The custodial or noncustodial parent, within one year after receiving notice of the director's final decision, may file a petition with the superior court, under Section 1094.5 of the Code of Civil Procedure, praying for a review of the entire proceedings in the matter, upon questions of law involved in the case. The review, if granted, shall be the exclusive remedy available to the custodial or noncustodial parent for review of the director's decision. The director shall be the sole respondent in the proceedings. A filing fee shall not be required for the filing of a petition pursuant to this section. Any such petition to the superior court shall be entitled to a preference in setting a date for hearing on the petition. A bond shall not be required in the case of any petition for review, nor in any appeal therefrom. The custodial or noncustodial parent shall be entitled to reasonable attorney's fees and costs, if the parent obtains a decision in their favor.

17804. Each local child support agency shall establish the complaint resolution process specified in Section 17800. The department shall implement the state hearing requirements specified in Section 17801 no later than July 1, 2001.

DIVISION 20: PILOT PROJECTS

ENACTED BY STATS. 1992, CH. 162, SEC. 10.
SECTION 20000-20043

PART 1: FAMILY LAW PILOT PROJECTS

enacted by Stats. 1992, Ch. 162, Sec. 10.

Chapter 1: General Provisions

20000. (a) The Legislature finds and declares the following:

(1) Child and spousal support are serious legal obligations. In addition, children are frequently left in limbo while their parents engage in protracted litigation concerning custody and visitation. The current system for obtaining child and spousal support orders is suffering because the family courts are unduly burdened with heavy case-loads and personnel insufficient to meet the needs of increased demands on the courts.

(2) There is a compelling state interest in the development of a child and spousal support system that is cost-effective and accessible to families with middle or low incomes.

(3) There is a compelling state interest in first implementing such a system on a small scale.

(4) There is a compelling state interest in the development of a speedy, conflict-reducing method of resolving custody and visitation disputes.

(b) Therefore, it is the intent of the Legislature in enacting this part to provide a means for experimenting with and evaluating procedural innovations with significant potential to improve the California child and spousal support systems, and the system for mediation, evaluation, and litigation of custody and visitation disputes.

20001. The Superior Courts of the Counties of Santa Clara and San Mateo may conduct pilot projects pursuant to this part. Chapter 2 (commencing with Section 20010) shall govern the San Mateo County Pilot Project, and Chapter 3 (commencing with Section 20030) shall govern the Santa Clara County Pilot Project.

20002. The duration of the pilot projects shall be two years.

Chapter 2: San Mateo County Pilot Project

20010. The San Mateo County Pilot Project shall apply to hearings on motions for temporary child support, temporary spousal support, and temporary health insurance issuable in proceedings under this code, where at least one party is unrepresented by counsel.

20011. Motions for temporary orders under this chapter shall be heard as soon as practicable, consistent with the rules governing other civil actions.

20012. The court shall appoint a Family Law Evaluator, who shall be available to assist parties. By local rule the superior court may designate the duties of the Family Law Evaluator, which may include, but are not limited to, the following:

(a) Requiring litigants in actions which involve temporary child support, temporary spousal support, and temporary maintenance of health insurance in which at least one litigant is unrepresented, to meet with the Family Law Evaluator prior to the support hearing.

(b) Preparing support schedules based on standardized formulae accessed through existing up-to-date computer technology.

(c) Drafting stipulations to include all issues agreed to by the parties.

(d) Prior to, or at, any hearing pursuant to this chapter, reviewing the paperwork by the court, advising the judge whether or not the matter is ready to proceed, and making a recommendation to the court regarding child support, spousal support, and health insurance.

(e) Assisting the clerk in maintaining records.

(f) Preparing a formal order consistent with the court's announced oral order, unless one of the parties is represented by an attorney.

(g) Assisting the court with research and any other responsibilities which will enable the court to be responsive to the litigants' needs.

20013. The court shall provide the Family Law Evaluator at no cost to the parties.

20014. The clerk shall stamp all moving papers in which a party is not represented by counsel with a notice of a requirement to see the Family Law Evaluator. The unrepresented party shall serve the stamped pleadings on the other party.

20015. The court shall adopt a protocol wherein all litigants, both unrepresented by counsel and represented by counsel, have ultimate access to a hearing before the court.

20016. The court may elect to publish a low-cost booklet describing this program.

20017. The Family Law Evaluator shall be an attorney, licensed to practice in this state.

20018. Orders for temporary support issued pursuant to this chapter shall comply with the statewide uniform guideline set forth in Article 2 (commencing with Section 4050) of Chapter 2 of Part 2 of Division 9 and shall be based on the economic evidence supplied by the parties or otherwise available to the court.

20019. Where it appears from a party's application for an order under this chapter or otherwise in the proceedings that the custody of, or visitation with, a minor child is contested, the court shall set those issues for mediation pursuant to Section 3170. The pendency of the mediation proceedings shall not delay a hearing on any other matter for which a temporary order is required, including child support, and a separate hearing, if required, shall be scheduled respecting the custody and visitation issues following mediation in accordance with Section 3170. However, the court may grant a continuance for good cause shown.

20020. In a contested proceeding for temporary child or spousal support under this chapter, both the moving party and the responding party shall provide all of the following documents

to the Family Law Evaluator, and to the court at the time of the hearing:
(a) Copies of the last two federal and state income tax returns filed.
(b) Paycheck stubs for all paychecks received in the four months immediately prior to the hearing.
(Added by Stats. 1993, Ch. 219, Sec. 210. Effective January 1, 1994.)

20021. A party who fails to submit documents to the court as required by Section 20020 may, in the court's discretion, not be granted the relief requested, or the court may impose evidentiary sanctions.

20022. The tax return submitted pursuant to Section 20020 may be reviewed by the other party. A party may be examined by the other party as to the contents of the tax return.

20023. (a) Except as provided in subdivision (c):
(1) Nothing in this chapter shall be construed to apply to a child for whom services are provided or required to be provided by a district attorney pursuant to Section 11475.5 of the Welfare and Institutions Code.
(2) The court shall not hear or enter any order under this chapter in a matter involving such a child.
(b) Any order entered contrary to the provisions of subdivision (a) is void and without legal effect.
(c) For purposes of enabling a custodial parent receiving assistance under Chapter 2 (commencing with Section 11200) of Part 3 of Division 9 of the Welfare and Institutions Code to participate in a pilot project authorized by this chapter, the district attorney, upon the request of the custodial parent, may execute a limited waiver of the obligation or representation under Section 11475.1 of the Welfare and Institutions Code. These limited waivers shall be signed by both the district attorney and custodial parent and shall only permit the custodial parent to participate in the proceedings under this chapter. It is not the intent of the Legislature in enacting this section to limit the duties of district attorneys with respect to seeking child support payments or to in any way limit or supersede other provisions of this code respecting temporary child support.

20026. (a) It is estimated that under the pilot project authorized by this chapter, approximately 2,200 litigants will be served annually and that the following savings will occur:
(1) The program would save 520 hours, or 65 days, of court time per year.
(2) There would be a concomitant saving of time by litigants due to the expedited proceedings and, in addition, there would be a saving to litigants of wages that would otherwise be lost due to time off from work.
(b) The estimated costs of the pilot project are as follows:
(1) The salaries of the Family Law Evaluator and any staff necessary for the evaluator to carry out the evaluator's functions.
(2) The cost of a booklet, if any, describing the program.
(c) There would be no cost for the following:
(1) Computers, printers, or other equipment. This equipment is already available in the family law department.
(2) Training for the Family Law Evaluator or the evaluator's staff. They will be trained by already

existing judicial personnel.

Chapter 3: Santa Clara County Pilot Project

20030. The Superior Court of the County of Santa Clara may conduct a pilot project pursuant to this chapter.

20031. The pilot project applies to all hearings, for temporary or permanent child or spousal support, modifications thereof, health insurance, custody, or visitation in a proceeding for dissolution of marriage, nullity of marriage, legal separation of the parties, exclusive custody, or pursuant to the Uniform Parentage Act (Part 3 (commencing with Section 7600) of Division 12).

20032. (a) Each and every hearing in a proceeding described in Section 20031 in which child or spousal support is at issue, including related contempt matters, shall be set by the clerk of the court for hearing within 30 days of filing.
(b) At any hearing in which child or spousal support is at issue, each party, both moving and responding, shall bring to the hearing, copies of the last two federal and state income tax returns filed by the party and pay stubs from the last four full months immediately preceding the hearing received by the party, and shall serve those documents on the opposing party at least five days in advance of the hearing date. Willful failure to comply with these requirements or any of the requirements of this pilot project may result in a citation for contempt under Title 5 (commencing with Section 1209) of Part 3 of the Code of Civil Procedure, or in the court's discretion, the court may refuse to grant relief requested or may impose evidentiary sanctions on a party who fails to submit these documents. The clerk shall cause to be placed on the face sheet of any moving papers for child or spousal support at the time of filing, a notice informing the parties of the requirements of this section. The notice shall also inform the parties that prior to the hearing, they must meet with the Attorney-Mediator pursuant to Section 20034. That meeting may occur in advance of the hearing dates by agreement of the parties, or on the day of the hearing.
(c) No continuance of any hearing involving child or spousal support shall be granted by a court without an order setting an interim support level unless the parties stipulate otherwise or the court finds good cause therefor.

20033. The court may pass a local rule that suspends the use of the Income and Expense Declaration mandated by California Rule of Court 1285.50 in some or all proceedings during the pendency of the pilot project, provided that substitute forms are developed and adopted to solicit substantially the same information in a simplified format. The court may, notwithstanding the adoption of a local form, require the use of the Income and Expense Declaration mandated by California Rule of Court 1285.50 in appropriate cases on the motion of either party or on the court's own motion.

20034. (a) An attorney, known as an Attorney-Mediator, shall be hired to assist the court in resolving child and spousal support disputes, to develop community outreach programs, and to undertake other duties as assigned by the court.

(b) The Attorney-Mediator shall be an attorney, licensed to practice in this state, with mediation or litigation experience, or both, in the field of family law.

(c) By local rule, the superior court may designate the duties of the Attorney-Mediator, which may include, but are not limited to, the following:

(1) Meeting with litigants to mediate issues of child support, spousal support, and maintenance of health insurance. Actions in which one or both of the parties are unrepresented by counsel shall have priority.

(2) Preparing support schedules based on statutory guidelines accessed through existing up-to-date computer technology.

(3) Drafting stipulations to include all issues agreed to by the parties, which may include issues other than those specified in Section 20031.

(4) If the parties are unable to resolve issues with the assistance of the Attorney-Mediator, prior to or at the hearing, and at the request of the court, the Attorney-Mediator shall review the paperwork, examine documents, prepare support schedules, and advise the judge whether or not the matter is ready to proceed.

(5) Assisting the clerk in maintaining records.

(6) Preparing formal orders consistent with the court's announced order in cases where both parties are unrepresented.

(7) Serving as a special master to hearing proceedings and making findings to the court unless the individual has served as a mediator in that case.

(8) Assisting the court with research and any other responsibilities that will enable the court to be responsive to the litigants' needs.

(9) Developing programs for bar and community outreach through day and evening programs, video recordings, and other innovative means that will assist unrepresented and financially disadvantaged litigants in gaining meaningful access to family court. These programs shall specifically include information concerning underutilized legislation, such as expedited temporary support orders (Chapter 5 (commencing with Section 3620) of Part 1 of Division 9), modification of support orders (Article 3 (commencing with Section 3680) of Chapter 6 of Part 1 of Division 9), and preexisting, court-sponsored programs, such as supervised visitation and appointment of attorneys for children.

(d) The court shall develop a protocol wherein all litigants, both unrepresented by counsel and represented by counsel, have ultimate access to a hearing before the court.

20035. Orders for temporary support issued pursuant to this chapter shall comply with the statewide uniform guideline set forth in Article 2 (commencing with Section 4050) of Chapter 2 of Part 2 of Division 9 and shall be based on the economic evidence supplied by the parties or otherwise available to the court.

20036. Upon motion by either party or on the court's own motion, any proceeding that would otherwise fall within this pilot project may by judicial order be exempted from its requirements.

20037. (a) Except as provided in subdivision (c):

(1) Nothing in this chapter shall be construed to apply to a child for whom services are provided or required to be provided by a district attorney pursuant to Section 11475.1 of the Welfare and Institutions Code.

(2) The court shall not hear or enter any order` under this chapter in a matter involving such a child.

(b) Any order entered contrary to subdivision (a) is void and without legal effect.

(c) For purposes of enabling a custodial parent receiving assistance under Chapter 2 (commencing with Section 11200) of Part 3 of Division 9 of the Welfare and Institutions Code to participate in a pilot project authorized by this chapter, the district attorney, upon the request of the custodial parent, may execute a limited waiver of the obligation of representation under Section 11475.1 of the Welfare and Institutions Code. These limited waivers shall be signed by both the district attorney and custodial parent and shall only permit the custodial parent to participate in the proceedings under this chapter. It is not the intent of the Legislature in enacting this section to limit the duties of district attorneys with respect to seeking child support payments or to in any way limit or supersede other provisions of this code respecting temporary child support.

20038. (a) In any case where either party has filed a motion regarding a custody or visitation dispute and has not yet scheduled an appointment for the mediation orientation class by the time of the hearing on the order to show cause, the court shall order all parties to go to Family Court Services that day to schedule an appointment. The mediation orientation shall be scheduled within 14 days. Mediation orientation shall be conducted by Family Court Services and shall include general information on the effect of separation and dissolution on children and parents, the developmental and emotional needs of children in those circumstances, time-sharing considerations and various options concerning legal and physical custody of children, the effect of exposure to domestic violence and extreme conflict on children and parents, the nature of the mediation process and other Family Court Services procedures, and related community resources.

(b) After the mediation orientation, the parties may elect to utilize private mental health professionals, in which case the parties or the court may modify the fast-track time guidelines provided for in this section.

(c) If, after orientation, either party requests mediation, and both parties complete Family Court Services mediation petitions, an appointment shall be scheduled within four weeks after both petitions are submitted and both parties shall attend the mediation as scheduled.

(d) At the mediation, if the parties agree to all of the issues regarding custody or visitation, the mediator shall memorialize the agreement in writing, and shall mail copies of the document to the attorneys and parents. Unless written objections to the agreement are sent to Family Court Services within 20 days of mailing the agreement, it will be submitted to the court and become a court order. A copy of the order shall be sent with proof of service to the parties and attorneys by the Family Court.

(e) If mediation is completed and there are remaining disputes, the mediator shall write a memorandum of any partial agreement and shall outline the remaining disputes which shall be sent to the attorneys and parties acting in propria persona. The mediator shall refer the parties to the Early Resolution Project. The parties shall meet and confer within 14 days of the referral to determine if a solution can be formulated. If there are remaining issues to be settled after the meeting, an early resolution judicial conference shall be scheduled within 30 days of the request of either party.

(f) At the early resolution conference, the judge may take stipulations resolving the issues of custody or visitation. The judge may also request the staff of Family Court Services to provide assessments and expedited evaluations to be held on the same day as the conference, in which case the judge, upon stipulation of the parties, may also order a hearing as soon as the same day on the issues. The judge may also order counseling, a mental health special master, psychological testing, or an extended evaluation by Family Court Services or a private evaluator on some or all issues.

(g) When the court at the early resolution judicial conference orders an extended evaluation, the parties shall complete all paperwork, submit deposits to Family Court Services, or both, within five days of the early resolution judicial conference. An evaluator shall be assigned to the case within 10 days thereafter.

(h) Evaluation shall be completed within 60 days of assignment to the evaluator, and the evaluator shall submit a report and recommendations which include a proposed order resolving all disputed issues. This report shall be served by certified mail on the attorneys of record, or on the parties if they are appearing in propria persona. If there are objections to the proposed order, the parties shall file written objections, meet with the evaluator within 30 days of service of the report, and serve a copy of the order on Family Court Services within the 30-day period. If a stipulation is reached, it shall be filed with the court. If a dispute remains, a judicial settlement conference shall be scheduled within 14 days of the meeting with the evaluator. Parties, counsel, and the evaluator shall be present at this judicial settlement conference. If there is no resolution at this settlement conference, a trial shall be set within 30 days from the settlement conference by the settlement conference judge. If no objections are filed, Family Court Services shall file the proposed order with the court, and it shall become the court's order.

(i) For good cause shown, all deadlines in this section may be altered by the court.

20040. The court may elect to publish a low-cost booklet describing the program.

20041. The court shall centralize, augment, `and coordinate all presently existing programs under the court's supervision that relate to children, including, but not limited to, mental health special masters, appointment of attorneys for children, supervised visitation, and other supporting personnel.

20043. (a) It is estimated for Santa Clara County's participation in the pilot project authorized by this chapter, that 4,000 litigants will be served annually, and that the following savings will occur:

(1) With an estimated 20 percent reduction in the use of court time over the current system, the county would save approximately 178 hours per year of court time, or approximately 22 workdays per year.

(2) With an estimated cost savings in incomes of judges, court reporters, clerks, bailiffs, and sheriffs, the project is expected to save approximately twenty thousand dollars ($20,000) per year. Cases involving child support obligations which the district attorney's office was required to handle in one participating county, for the 1989–90 fiscal year, number 2,461. The average time spent on a typical child support order is approximately five hours. There is a potential of 12,500 man-hours per year that could be saved, resulting in a savings of three hundred sixty-seven thousand eight hundred seventy-five dollars ($367,875) per year in attorney salaries alone. This does not take into consideration costs for documents, filing, and other district attorney personnel.

(3) The average savings personally to litigants who otherwise would require private representation would be from fifty dollars ($50) to two hundred fifty dollars ($250) per hour of court time and other preparation work.

(b) The satisfaction of participating parties will be determined by requiring the litigants using the pilot project to fill out a simple exit poll. The response of at least 70 percent of those questionnaires will be analyzed to decide whether the program has been deemed satisfactory by the participants.

(c) The estimated cost of the program is as follows:

(1) The estimated salary for an Attorney-Mediator is sixty thousand dollars ($60,000) to sixty-five thousand dollars ($65,000) per year, plus an additional 25 percent of salary to cover the costs of benefits for that position. In addition, there may be other costs connected with this position for support staff at the court.

(2) The costs of exit polling and any informational materials to be handed out to the public by the Attorney-Mediator is undetermined and cannot be estimated.

(d) The estimated income to cover the costs of this program will be as follows:

(1) There are approximately 10,000 dissolution of marriage petitions filed in Santa Clara County each year. Of those cases, approximately one-third of them have responses filed. At the present time, it costs one hundred sixty-five dollars ($165) to have a petition for dissolution of marriage filed and one hundred twenty-seven dollars ($127) to have a response filed, for a cost differential of thirty-eight dollars ($38). By equalizing the response fee with the petition fee, income generated would be approximately one hundred twenty-five thousand four hundred dollars ($125,400) per year. This does not include the cost of fourteen dollars ($14) for each responsive declaration filed to a motion or order to show cause, the annual number of which is significantly greater than 3,300. It is estimated that

an additional fifty thousand dollars ($50,000) per year could be generated by equalizing the responsive fees to a motion or order to show cause with the filing of those motions. These fees generated would more than offset the costs of the program.

(2) It is also anticipated that the Attorney-Mediator will develop public information and outreach programs which will be paid for by any excess revenue generated from the pilot project and ultimately will result in savings to the public and the court. The public will save by not having to pay attorneys for certain information regarding child support matters, and the court will save by not having to educate the public from the bench, thus expediting the handling of support and custody cases.

(e) The cost of computers, printers, and other equipment will be defrayed by contributions.

ENDNOTES

1 Enacted by Stats. 1992, Ch. 162, Sec. 10. Operative January 1, 1994.

2 Added by Stats. 1993, Ch. 1101, Sec. 11. Effective October 11, 1993; operative January 1, 1994.

3 Added by Stats. 1993, Ch. 1101, Sec. 13. Effective October 11, 1993; operative January 1, 1994.

4 Added by Stats. 1993, Ch. 1101, Sec. 14. Effective October 11, 1993; operative January 1, 1994.

5 Added by Stats. 1993, Ch. 219, Sec. 79. Effective January 1, 1994.

6 Added by Stats. 1993, Ch. 219, Sec. 79.3. Effective January 1, 1994.

7 Added by Stats. 1993, Ch. 219, Sec. 81. Effective January 1, 1994.

8 Repealed and added by Stats. 1993, Ch. 219, Sec. 87. Effective January 1, 1994.

9 Added by Stats. 1993, Ch. 219, Sec. 99.5. Effective January 1, 1994.

10 Added by Stats. 1993, Ch. 219, Sec. 106.7. Effective January 1, 1994.

11 Added by Stats. 1993, Ch. 219, Sec. 107. Effective January 1, 1994.

12 Added by Stats. 1993, Ch. 219, Sec. 108. Effective January 1, 1994.

13 Added by Stats. 1993, Ch. 219, Sec. 108.5. Effective January 1, 1994.

14 Amended by Stats. 1993, Ch. 219, Sec. 110. Effective January 1, 1994.

15 Amended by Stats. 1993, Ch. 219, Sec. 111. Effective January 1, 1994.

16 Repealed and added by Stats. 1993, Ch. 219, Sec. 115.5. Effective January 1, 1994.

17 Added by renumbering Section 3021 by Stats. 1993, Ch. 219, Sec. 116.12. Effective January 1, 1994.

18 Amended by Stats. 1993, Ch. 219, Sec. 116.14. Effective January 1, 1994.

19 Amended by Stats. 1993, Ch. 219, Sec. 116.16. Effective January 1, 1994.

20 Added by Stats. 1993, Ch. 219, Sec. 116.18. Effective January 1, 1994.

21 Added by Stats. 1993, Ch. 219, Sec. 116.19. Effective January 1, 1994.

22 Repealed and added by Stats. 1993, Ch. 219, Sec. 116.50. Effective January 1, 1994.

23 Added by Stats. 1993, Ch. 219, Sec. 116.61. Effective January 1, 1994.

24 Amended by Stats. 1993, Ch. 219, Sec. 116.70. Effective January 1, 1994.

25 Amended by Stats. 1993, Ch. 219, Sec. 116.71. Effective January 1, 1994.

26 Amended by Stats. 1993, Ch. 219, Sec. 116.72. Effective January 1, 1994.

27 Amended by Stats. 1993, Ch. 219, Sec. 116.73. Effective January 1, 1994

28 Repealed and added by Stats. 1993, Ch. 219, Sec. 116.76. Effective January 1, 1994.

29 Repealed and added by Stats. 1993, Ch. 219, Sec. 116.81. Effective January 1, 1994.

30 Repealed and added by Stats. 1993, Ch. 219, Sec. 116.87. Effective January 1, 1994.

31 Amended by Stats. 1993, Ch. 219, Sec. 121. Effective January 1, 1994

32 Amended by Stats. 1993, Ch. 219, Sec. 158. Effective January 1, 1994

33 Added by Stats. 1993, Ch. 219, Sec. 159. Effective January 1, 1994.

34 Added by Stats. 1993, Ch. 219, Sec. 160. Effective January 1, 1994.

35 Added by Stats. 1993, Ch. 219, Sec. 161. Effective January 1, 1994.
36 Added by Stats. 1993, Ch. 219, Sec. 165. Effective January 1, 1994.
37 Added by Stats. 1993, Ch. 219, Sec. 166. Effective January 1, 1994.
38 Added by Stats. 1993, Ch. 219, Sec. 167. Effective January 1, 1994.
39 Added by Stats. 1993, Ch. 219, Sec. 168. Effective January 1, 1994.
40 Added by Stats. 1993, Ch. 219, Sec. 169. Effective January 1, 1994.
41 Added by Stats. 1993, Ch. 219, Sec. 170. Effective January 1, 1994.
42 Added by Stats. 1993, Ch. 219, Sec. 177. Effective January 1, 1994.
43 Amended by Stats. 1994, Ch. 1269, Sec. 9. Effective January 1, 1995.
44 Amended by Stats. 1994, Ch. 1269, Sec. 10. Effective January 1, 1995.
45 Amended by Stats. 1994, Ch. 1269, Sec. 12. Effective January 1, 1995.
46 Amended by Stats. 1994, Ch. 1269, Sec. 15. Effective January 1, 1995.
47 Amended by Stats. 1994, Ch. 1269, Sec. 16. Effective January 1, 1995.
48 Amended by Stats. 1994, Ch. 1269, Sec. 17. Effective January 1, 1995.
49 Amended by Stats. 1994, Ch. 1269, Sec. 18. Effective January 1, 1995.
50 Amended by Stats. 1994, Ch. 1269, Sec. 19. Effective January 1, 1995.
51 Amended by Stats. 1994, Ch. 1269, Sec. 20. Effective January 1, 1995.
52 Amended by Stats. 1994, Ch. 1269, Sec. 21. Effective January 1, 1995.
53 Amended by Stats. 1994, Ch. 1269, Sec. 22. Effective January 1, 1995.
54 Amended by Stats. 1994, Ch. 1269, Sec. 23. Effective January 1, 1995.
55 Added by Stats. 1994, Ch. 1286, Sec. 1. Effective January 1, 1995.
56 Amended by Stats. 1995, Ch. 246, Sec. 1. Effective January 1, 1996.
57 Amended by Stats. 1995, Ch. 506, Sec. 3. Effective January 1, 1996.
58 Added by Stats. 1995, Ch. 884, Sec. 9. Effective January 1, 1996.
59 Added by Stats. 1995, Ch. 904, Sec. 2. Effective January 1, 1996.
60 Added by Stats. 1996, Ch. 490, Sec. 1. Effective January 1, 1997.
61 Added by Stats. 1996, Ch. 761, Sec. 3. Effective January 1, 1997.
62 Added by Stats. 1996, Ch. 761, Sec. 4. Effective January 1, 1997.
63 Added by Stats. 1996, Ch. 957, Sec. 5. Effective January 1, 1997.
64 Added by Stats. 1996, Ch. 957, Sec. 9. Effective January 1, 1997.
65 Amended by Stats. 1997, Ch. 849, Sec. 5. Effective January 1, 1998.
66 Amended by Stats. 1997, Ch. 849, Sec. 6. Effective January 1, 1998.
67 Added by Stats. 1998, Ch. 225, Sec. 1. Effective January 1, 1999.
68 Amended by Stats. 1998, Ch. 229, Sec. 1. Effective January 1, 1999.
69 Amended by Stats. 1998, Ch. 511, Sec. 1. Effective January 1, 1999.
70 Amended by Stats. 1998, Ch. 581, Sec. 4. Effective January 1, 1999.
71 Amended by Stats. 1998, Ch. 581, Sec. 5. Effective January 1, 1999.
72 Amended by Stats. 1998, Ch. 581, Sec. 12. Effective January 1, 1999.
73 Amended by Stats. 1998, Ch. 581, Sec. 13. Effective January 1, 1999.
74 Added by Stats. 1998, Ch. 981, Sec. 2. Effective January 1, 1999.
75 Added by Stats. 1999, Ch. 652. Effective January 1, 2000.
76 Repealed and added by Stats. 1999, Ch. 867, Sec. 3. Effective January 1, 2000.
77 Added by Stats. 1999, Ch. 1004, Sec. 4. Effective January 1, 2000.
78 Added by Stats. 2000, Ch. 808, Sec. 21. Effective September 28, 2000.
79 Amended by Stats. 2001, Ch. 703,

Sec. 2. Effective January 1, 2002.

80 Amended by Stats. 2001, Ch. 703, Sec. 4. Effective January 1, 2002.

81 Amended by Stats. 2001, Ch. 703, Sec. 7. Effective January 1, 2002.

82 Added by Stats. 2002, Ch. 192, Sec. 1. Effective January 1, 2003.

83 Added by Stats. 2002, Ch. 260, Sec. 7. Effective January 1, 2003.

84 Added by Stats. 2002, Ch. 374. Effective January 1, 2003.

85 Amended by Stats. 2002, Ch. 784, Sec. 105. Effective January 1, 2003.

86 Amended by Stats. 2002, Ch. 784, Sec. 107. Effective January 1, 2003.

87 Amended by Stats. 2002, Ch. 784, Sec. 108. Effective January 1, 2003.

88 Amended by Stats. 2002, Ch. 784, Sec. 109. Effective January 1, 2003

89 Amended by Stats. 2002, Ch. 784, Sec. 113. Effective January 1, 2003.

90 Amended by Stats. 2002, Ch. 784, Sec. 114. Effective January 1, 2003.

91 Amended by Stats. 2002, Ch. 784, Sec. 115. Effective January 1, 2003.

92 Amended by Stats. 2002, Ch. 927, Sec. 2. Effective January 1, 2003.

93 Amended by Stats. 2002, Ch. 927, Sec. 6.5. Effective January 1, 2003.

94 Amended by Stats. 2002, Ch. 1077, Sec. 3. Effective January 1, 2003.

95 Added by Stats. 2002, Ch. 1118. Effective January 1, 2003.

96 Amended by Stats. 2003, Ch. 62, Sec. 90. Effective January 1, 2004.

97 Amended by Stats. 2003, Ch. 134, Sec. 1. Effective January 1, 2004.

98 Amended by Stats. 2003, Ch. 134, Sec. 2. Effective January 1, 2004.

99 Amended by Stats. 2003, Ch. 251, Sec. 5. Effective January 1, 2004.

100 Added by Stats. 2003, Ch. 308, Sec. 6. Effective January 1, 2004.

101 Amended by Stats. 2003, Ch. 308, Sec. 7. Effective January 1, 2004.

102 Amended by Stats. 2003, Ch. 365. Effective January 1, 2004.

103 Amended by Stats. 2003, Ch. 387, Sec. 3. Effective January 1, 2004.

104 Amended by Stats. 2003, Ch. 387, Sec. 8. Effective January 1, 2004.

105 Amended by Stats. 2003, Ch. 387, Sec. 9. Effective January 1, 2004.

106 Amended by Stats. 2003, Ch. 387, Sec. 10. Effective January 1, 2004.

107 Amended by Stats. 2003, Ch. 468, Sec. 3. Effective January 1, 2004.

108 Amended by Stats. 2003, Ch. 667, Sec. 3. Effective January 1, 2004.

109 Added by Stats. 2003, Ch. 674. Effective January 1, 2004.

110 Repealed and added by Stats. 2004, Ch. 45, Sec. 2. Effective June 7, 2004.

111 Amended by Stats. 2004, Ch. 476, Sec. 1. Effective September 10, 2004.

112 Amended by Stats. 2004, Ch. 299. Effective January 1, 2005.

113 Amended by Stats. 2004, Ch. 305, Sec. 3. Effective January 1, 2005.

114 Amended by Stats. 2004, Ch. 305, Sec. 4. Effective January 1, 2005.

115 Amended by Stats. 2004, Ch. 339, Sec. 3. Effective January 1, 2005.

116 Amended by Stats. 2004, Ch. 472, Sec. 2. Effective January 1, 2005.

117 Amended by Stats. 2004, Ch. 182, Sec. 34. Effective January 1, 2005. Operative July 1, 2005, by Sec. 64 of Ch. 182.

118 Amended by Stats. 2005, Ch. 154, Sec. 3. Effective August 30, 2005.

119 Amended by Stats. 2005, Ch. 22, Sec. 61. Effective January 1, 2006.

120 Amended by Stats. 2005, Ch. 22, Sec. 63. Effective January 1, 2006.

121 mended by Stats. 2005, Ch. 75, Sec. 45. Effective July 19, 2005. Operative January 1, 2006, by Sec.

156 of Ch. 75.

122 Amended by Stats. 2005, Ch. 125, Sec. 2. Effective January 1, 2006.

123 Added by Stats. 2005, Ch. 483, Sec. 3. Effective January 1, 2006.

124 Added by Stats. 2005, Ch. 472, Sec. 2. Effective January 1, 2006.

125 Amended by Stats. 2005, Ch. 489, Sec. 2. Effective January 1, 2006.

126 Added by Stats. 2006, Ch. 75, Sec. 6. Effective July 12, 2006.

127 Added by Stats. 2006, Ch. 75, Sec. 7. Effective July 12, 2006.

128 Added by Stats. 2006, Ch. 60, Sec. 1. Effective January 1, 2007.

129 Added by Stats. 2006, Ch. 82, Sec. 1. Effective January 1, 2007.

130 Added by Stats. 2006, Ch. 86. Effective January 1, 2007.

131 Repealed and added by Stats. 2006, Ch. 86, Sec. 6. Effective January 1, 2007.

132 Amended by Stats. 2006, Ch. 130, Sec. 1. Effective January 1, 2007.

133 Added by Stats. 2007, Ch. 177, Sec. 1. Effective August 24, 2007.

134 Amended by Stats. 2006, Ch. 207, Sec. 1. Effective January 1, 2007.

135 Added by Stats. 2006, Ch. 496, Sec. 2. Effective January 1, 2007.

136 Added by Stats. 2006, Ch. 496, Sec. 3. Effective January 1, 2007.

137 Amended by Stats. 2006, Ch. 538, Sec. 156. Effective January 1, 2007

138 Amended by Stats. 2006, Ch. 538, Sec. 157. Effective January 1, 2007

139 Added by Stats. 2006, Ch. 797, Sec. 1. Effective January 1, 2007.

140 Amended by Stats. 2006, Ch. 802, Sec. 2. Effective January 1, 2007.

141 Added by Stats. 2006, Ch. 806, Sec. 1. Effective January 1, 2007.

142 Amended by Stats. 2006, Ch. 806, Sec. 4. Effective January 1, 2007.

143 Added by Stats. 2006, Ch. 838, Sec. 1. Effective January 1, 2007.

144 Amended by Stats. 2006, Ch. 838, Sec. 4. Effective January 1, 2007.

145 Added by Stats. 2006, Ch. 838, Sec. 6. Effective January 1, 2007.

146 Added by Stats. 2006, Ch. 838, Sec. 7. Effective January 1, 2007.

147 Added by Stats. 2006, Ch. 838, Sec. 14. Effective January 1, 2007.

148 Amended by Stats. 2025, Ch. 757, Sec. 3. (SB 450) Effective January 1, 2026.

149 Amended by Stats. 2006, Ch. 816, Sec. 4. Effective January 1, 2007. Operative January 1, 2008, by Sec. 56 of Ch. 816.

150 Amended by Stats. 2006, Ch. 816, Sec. 6. Effective January 1, 2007. Operative January 1, 2008, by Sec. 56 of Ch. 816.

151 Amended by Stats. 2006, Ch. 816, Sec. 8. Effective January 1, 2007. Operative January 1, 2008, by Sec. 56 of Ch. 816.

152 Added by Stats. 2006, Ch. 816, Sec. 8.5. Effective January 1, 2007. Operative January 1, 2008, by Sec. 56 of Ch. 816.

153 Amended by Stats. 2006, Ch. 816, Sec. 12. Effective January 1, 2007. Operative January 1, 2008, by Sec. 56 of Ch. 816.

154 Amended by Stats. 2006, Ch. 816, Sec. 20. Effective January 1, 2007. Operative January 1, 2008, by Sec. 56 of Ch. 816.

155 Added by Stats. 2006, Ch. 816, Sec. 21. Effective January 1, 2007. Operative January 1, 2008, by Sec. 56 of Ch. 816.

156 Added by Stats. 2006, Ch. 816, Sec. 22. Effective January 1, 2007. Operative January 1, 2008, by Sec. 56 of Ch. 816.

157 Amended by Stats. 2006, Ch. 816,

Sec. 24. Effective January 1, 2007. Operative January 1, 2008, by Sec. 56 of Ch. 816.

158 Amended by Stats. 2006, Ch. 816, Sec. 25. Effective January 1, 2007. Operative January 1, 2008, by Sec. 56 of Ch. 816.

159 Amended by Stats. 2006, Ch. 816, Sec. 26. Effective January 1, 2007. Operative January 1, 2008, by Sec. 56 of Ch. 816.

160 Amended by Stats. 2006, Ch. 816, Sec. 27. Effective January 1, 2007. Operative January 1, 2008, by Sec. 56 of Ch. 816.

161 Amended by Stats. 2006, Ch. 816, Sec. 28. Effective January 1, 2007. Operative January 1, 2008, by Sec. 56 of Ch. 816.

162 Amended by Stats. 2006, Ch. 816, Sec. 31. Effective January 1, 2007. Operative January 1, 2008, by Sec. 56 of Ch. 816.

163 Amended by Stats. 2006, Ch. 816, Sec. 32. Effective January 1, 2007. Operative January 1, 2008, by Sec. 56 of Ch. 816.

164 Amended by Stats. 2006, Ch. 816, Sec. 33. Effective January 1, 2007. Operative January 1, 2008, by Sec. 56 of Ch. 816.

165 Amended by Stats. 2006, Ch. 816, Sec. 34. Effective January 1, 2007. Operative January 1, 2008, by Sec. 56 of Ch. 816.

166 Amended by Stats. 2006, Ch. 816, Sec. 35. Effective January 1, 2007. Operative January 1, 2008, by Sec. 56 of Ch. 816.

167 Amended by Stats. 2006, Ch. 816, Sec. 36. Effective January 1, 2007. Operative January 1, 2008, by Sec. 56 of Ch. 816.

168 Amended by Stats. 2006, Ch. 816, Sec. 37. Effective January 1, 2007. Operative January 1, 2008, by Sec. 56 of Ch. 816.

169 Amended by Stats. 2006, Ch. 816, Sec. 38. Effective January 1, 2007. Operative January 1, 2008, by Sec. 56 of Ch. 816.

170 Amended by Stats. 2007, Ch. 47, Sec. 3. Effective January 1, 2008.

171 Amended by Stats. 2007, Ch. 130, Sec. 85. Effective January 1, 2008.

172 Amended by Stats. 2007, Ch. 130, Sec. 87. Effective January 1, 2008.

173 Amended by Stats. 2007, Ch. 441, Sec. 1. Effective January 1, 2008.

174 Amended (as amended by Stats. 2006, Ch. 816) by Stats. 2007, Ch. 483, Sec. 9. Effective January 1, 2008.

175 Amended by Stats. 2007, Ch. 488, Sec. 1. Effective January 1, 2008.

176 Amended (as amended by Stats. 2006, Ch. 816) by Stats. 2007, Ch. 567, Sec. 8. Effective January 1, 2008. Operative January 1, 2009, by Sec. 13 of Ch. 567.

177 Amended by Stats. 2007, Ch. 567, Sec. 9. Effective January 1, 2008.

178 Added by Stats. 2007, Ch. 583, Sec. 1. Effective January 1, 2008.

179 Added by Stats. 2007, Ch. 583, Sec. 2. Effective January 1, 2008.

180 Amended by Stats. 2007, Ch. 583, Sec. 5. Effective January 1, 2008.

181 Added by Stats. 2007, Ch. 583, Sec. 6. Effective January 1, 2008.

182 Added by Stats. 2007, Ch. 583, Sec. 8. Effective January 1, 2008.

183 Amended by Stats. 2007, Ch. 617, Sec. 2. Effective January 1, 2008.

184 Amended by Stats. 2007, Ch. 738, Sec. 13. Effective January 1, 2008.

185 Repealed (in Sec. 13) and added by Stats. 2008, Ch. 759, Sec. 14. Effective September 30, 2008. Section operative October 1, 2008,

by its own provisions.

186 Amended by Stats. 2008, Ch. 534, Sec. 4. Effective January 1, 2009.

187 Amended by Stats. 2008, Ch. 534, Sec. 9. Effective January 1, 2009.

188 Amended by Stats. 2008, Ch. 699, Sec. 2. Effective January 1, 2009.

189 Amended by Stats. 2008, Ch. 699, Sec. 3. Effective January 1, 2009.

190 Amended by Stats. 2009, 3rd Ex. Sess., Ch. 9, Sec. 4. Effective February 20, 2009.

191 Amended by Stats. 2009, Ch. 412, Sec. 2. (AB 130) Effective January 1, 2010.

192 Amended by Stats. 2009, Ch. 492, Sec. 2. (AB 941) Effective January 1, 2010.

193 Amended by Stats. 2009, Ch. 552, Sec. 3. (SB 40) Effective January 1, 2010.

194 Repealed (in Sec. 1) and added by Stats. 2007, Ch. 249, Sec. 2. Effective January 1, 2008. Section operative January 1, 2011, by its own provisions.

195 Amended by Stats. 2010, Ch. 65, Sec. 1. (AB 2674) Effective January 1, 2011.

196 Amended by Stats. 2010, Ch. 65, Sec. 2. (AB 2674) Effective January 1, 2011.

197 Added by Stats. 2010, Ch. 179, Sec. 1. (SB 1188) Effective January 1, 2011.

198 Added by Stats. 2010, Ch. 352, Sec. 3. (AB 939) Effective January 1, 2011.

199 Amended by Stats. 2010, Ch. 352, Sec. 4. (AB 939) Effective January 1, 2011.

200 Amended by Stats. 2010, Ch. 352, Sec. 7. (AB 939) Effective January 1, 2011.

201 Amended by Stats. 2010, Ch. 352, Sec. 9. (AB 939) Effective January 1, 2011.

202 Amended by Stats. 2010, Ch. 352, Sec. 10. (AB 939) Effective January 1, 2011.

203 Amended by Stats. 2010, Ch. 352, Sec. 12. (AB 939) Effective January 1, 2011.

204 Amended by Stats. 2010, Ch. 352, Sec. 13. (AB 939) Effective January 1, 2011.

205 Amended by Stats. 2010, Ch. 352, Sec. 14. (AB 939) Effective January 1, 2011.

206 Amended by Stats. 2010, Ch. 352, Sec. 15. (AB 939) Effective January 1, 2011.

207 Amended by Stats. 2010, Ch. 352, Sec. 16. (AB 939) Effective January 1, 2011.

208 Amended by Stats. 2010, Ch. 352, Sec. 17. (AB 939) Effective January 1, 2011.

209 Amended by Stats. 2010, Ch. 397, Sec. 1. (AB 2700) Effective January 1, 2011.

210 Amended by Stats. 2010, Ch. 397, Sec. 2. (AB 2700) Effective January 1, 2011.

211 Amended by Stats. 2010, Ch. 178, Sec. 25. (SB 1115) Effective January 1, 2011. Operative January 1, 2012, by Sec. 107 of Ch. 178.

212 Amended by Stats. 2010, Ch. 352, Sec. 11. (AB 939) Effective January 1, 2011. Amended version operative January 1, 2012, pursuant to earlier operation of new subdivision (d).

213 Amended by Stats. 2010, Ch. 572, Sec. 6. (AB 1596) Effective January 1, 2011. Operative January 1, 2012, by Sec. 28 of Ch. 572.

214 Amended by Stats. 2010, Ch. 572, Sec. 9. (AB 1596) Effective January

1, 2011. Operative January 1, 2012, by Sec. 28 of Ch. 572.

215 Amended by Stats. 2010, Ch. 572, Sec. 11. (AB 1596) Effective January 1, 2011. Operative January 1, 2012, by Sec. 28 of Ch. 572.

216 Added by Stats. 2010, Ch. 572, Sec. 12. (AB 1596) Effective January 1, 2011. Operative January 1, 2012, by Sec. 28 of Ch. 572.

217 Amended by Stats. 2010, Ch. 572, Sec. 18. (AB 1596) Effective January 1, 2011. Operative January 1, 2012, by Sec. 28 of Ch. 572.

218 Amended by Stats. 2010, Ch. 572, Sec. 21. (AB 1596) Effective January 1, 2011. Operative January 1, 2012, by Sec. 28 of Ch. 572.

219 Amended by Stats. 2010, Ch. 572, Sec. 22. (AB 1596) Effective January 1, 2011. Operative January 1, 2012, by Sec. 28 of Ch. 572.

220 Amended by Stats. 2011, Ch. 296, Sec. 92. (AB 1023) Effective January 1, 2012.

221 Added by Stats. 2011, Ch. 462, Sec. 5. (AB 687) Effective January 1, 2012.

222 Added by Stats. 2011, Ch. 462, Sec. 6. (AB 687) Effective January 1, 2012.

223 Amended by Stats. 2011, Ch. 462, Sec. 9. (AB 687) Effective January 1, 2012.

224 Amended by Stats. 2011, Ch. 652, Sec. 1. (AB 499) Effective January 1, 2012.

225 Amended by Stats. 2011, Ch. 721, Sec. 4. (SB 651) Effective January 1, 2012.

226 Amended by Stats. 2012, Ch. 35, Sec. 2. (SB 1013) Effective June 27, 2012.

227 Amended by Stats. 2012, Ch. 35, Sec. 3. (SB 1013) Effective June 27, 2012.

228 Amended by Stats. 2012, Ch. 35, Sec. 4. (SB 1013) Effective June 27, 2012.

229 Amended by Stats. 2012, Ch. 35, Sec. 5. (SB 1013) Effective June 27, 2012.

230 Amended by Stats. 2012, Ch. 35, Sec. 7. (SB 1013) Effective June 27, 2012.

231 Amended by Stats. 2012, Ch. 35, Sec. 9. (SB 1013) Effective June 27, 2012.

232 Amended by Stats. 2012, Ch. 35, Sec. 10. (SB 1013) Effective June 27, 2012.

233 Amended by Stats. 2012, Ch. 35, Sec. 11. (SB 1013) Effective June 27, 2012.

234 Amended by Stats. 2012, Ch. 35, Sec. 15. (SB 1013) Effective June 27, 2012.

235 Amended by Stats. 2012, Ch. 35, Sec. 16. (SB 1013) Effective June 27, 2012.

236 Amended by Stats. 2012, Ch. 35, Sec. 17. (SB 1013) Effective June 27, 2012.

237 Amended by Stats. 2012, Ch. 35, Sec. 18. (SB 1013) Effective June 27, 2012.

238 Amended by Stats. 2012, Ch. 35, Sec. 19. (SB 1013) Effective June 27, 2012.

239 Amended by Stats. 2012, Ch. 35, Sec. 20. (SB 1013) Effective June 27, 2012.

240 Amended by Stats. 2012, Ch. 35, Sec. 22. (SB 1013) Effective June 27, 2012.

241 Amended by Stats. 2012, Ch. 35, Sec. 23. (SB 1013) Effective June 27, 2012.

242 Amended by Stats. 2012, Ch. 35, Sec. 24. (SB 1013) Effective June

27, 2012.

243 Amended by Stats. 2012, Ch. 35, Sec. 25. (SB 1013) Effective June 27, 2012.

244 Amended by Stats. 2012, Ch. 35, Sec. 29. (SB 1013) Effective June 27, 2012.

245 Amended by Stats. 2012, Ch. 35, Sec. 30. (SB 1013) Effective June 27, 2012.

246 Amended by Stats. 2012, Ch. 35, Sec. 31. (SB 1013) Effective June 27, 2012.

247 Amended by Stats. 2012, Ch. 35, Sec. 34. (SB 1013) Effective June 27, 2012.

248 Amended by Stats. 2012, Ch. 35, Sec. 35. (SB 1013) Effective June 27, 2012.

249 Amended by Stats. 2012, Ch. 47, Sec. 1. (SB 1041) Effective June 27, 2012.

250 Amended by Stats. 2012, Ch. 440, Sec. 6. (AB 1488) Effective September 22, 2012.

251 Amended by Stats. 2012, Ch. 77, Sec. 1. (AB 1727) Effective January 1, 2013.

252 Amended by Stats. 2012, Ch. 107, Sec. 3. (AB 1406) Effective January 1, 2013

253 Added by renumbering Section 9213 by Stats. 2012, Ch. 162, Sec. 48. (SB 1171) Effective January 1, 2013.

254 Amended by Stats. 2012, Ch. 258, Sec. 2. (AB 2365) Effective January 1, 2013.

255 Amended by Stats. 2012, Ch. 276, Sec. 3. (SB 1206) Effective January 1, 2013.

256 Amended by Stats. 2012, Ch. 470, Sec. 12. (AB 1529) Effective January 1, 2013.

257 Amended by Stats. 2012, Ch. 470, Sec. 13. (AB 1529) Effective January 1, 2013.

258 Amended by Stats. 2012, Ch. 470, Sec. 14. (AB 1529) Effective January 1, 2013.

259 Amended by Stats. 2012, Ch. 470, Sec. 15. (AB 1529) Effective January 1, 2013.

260 Amended by Stats. 2012, Ch. 470, Sec. 16. (AB 1529) Effective January 1, 2013 .

261 Amended by Stats. 2012, Ch. 470, Sec. 20. (AB 1529) Effective January 1, 2013. Section operative as provided in subd. (b).).

262 Amended by Stats. 2012, Ch. 470, Sec. 22. (AB 1529) Effective January 1, 2013.

263 Amended by Stats. 2012, Ch. 638, Sec. 4. (AB 1757) Effective January 1, 2013.

264 Amended by Stats. 2012, Ch. 638, Sec. 5. (AB 1757) Effective January 1, 2013.

265 Amended by Stats. 2012, Ch. 728, Sec. 38. (SB 71) Effective January 1, 2013.

266 Amended by Stats. 2013, Ch. 61, Sec. 1. (SB 826) Effective January 1, 2014.

267 Amended by Stats. 2013, Ch. 145, Sec. 1. (AB 238) Effective January 1, 2014.

268 Added by Stats. 2013, Ch. 261, Sec. 1. (AB 161) Effective January 1, 2014. Section operative July 1, 2014, by its own provisions.

269 Amended by Stats. 2013, Ch. 263, Sec. 3. (AB 176) Effective January 1, 2014. Operative July 1, 2014, by Sec. 5 of Ch. 263.

270 Amended by Stats. 2013, Ch. 427, Sec. 1. (AB 1062) Effective January 1, 2014.

271 Amended by Stats. 2013, Ch. 510,

Sec. 2. (AB 1403) Effective January 1, 2014.

272 Amended by Stats. 2013, Ch. 510, Sec. 6. (AB 1403) Effective January 1, 2014.

273 Amended by Stats. 2013, Ch. 510, Sec. 9. (AB 1403) Effective January 1, 2014.

274 Amended by Stats. 2013, Ch. 510, Sec. 11. (AB 1403) Effective January 1, 2014.

275 Amended by Stats. 2013, Ch. 510, Sec. 12. (AB 1403) Effective January 1, 2014.

276 Amended by Stats. 2013, Ch. 510, Sec. 14. (AB 1403) Effective January 1, 2014.

277 Amended by Stats. 2013, Ch. 510, Sec. 20. (AB 1403) Effective January 1, 2014.

278 Amended by Stats. 2013, Ch. 510, Sec. 23. (AB 1403) Effective January 1, 2014.

279 Amended by Stats. 2013, Ch. 564, Sec. 5.5. (SB 274) Effective January 1, 2014

280 Amended by Stats. 2014, Ch. 29, Sec. 1. (SB 855) Effective June 20, 2014.

281 Added by Stats. 2014, Ch. 202, Sec. 1. (AB 414) Effective August 15, 2014.

282 Amended by Stats. 2014, Ch. 82, Sec. 2. (SB 1306) Effective January 1, 2015.

283 Amended by Stats. 2014, Ch. 82, Sec. 3. (SB 1306) Effective January 1, 2015.

284 Amended by Stats. 2014, Ch. 82, Sec. 11. (SB 1306) Effective January 1, 2015.

285 Amended by Stats. 2014, Ch. 82, Sec. 13. (SB 1306) Effective January 1, 2015.

286 Amended by Stats. 2014, Ch. 82, Sec. 14. (SB 1306) Effective January 1, 2015.

287 Amended by Stats. 2014, Ch. 82, Sec. 15. (SB 1306) Effective January 1, 2015.

288 Amended by Stats. 2014, Ch. 82, Sec. 16. (SB 1306) Effective January 1, 2015.

289 Amended by Stats. 2014, Ch. 82, Sec. 17. (SB 1306) Effective January 1, 2015.

290 Amended by Stats. 2014, Ch. 82, Sec. 19. (SB 1306) Effective January 1, 2015..

291 Amended by Stats. 2014, Ch. 82, Sec. 21. (SB 1306) Effective January 1, 2015.

292 Amended by Stats. 2014, Ch. 82, Sec. 22. (SB 1306) Effective January 1, 2015.

293 Amended by Stats. 2014, Ch. 82, Sec. 23. (SB 1306) Effective January 1, 2015.

294 Amended by Stats. 2014, Ch. 82, Sec. 24. (SB 1306) Effective January 1, 2015.

295 Amended by Stats. 2025, Ch. 633, Sec. 1. (AB 1134) Effective January 1, 2026. Repealed as of January 1, 2027, by its own provisions. See later operative version added by Sec. 2 of Stats. 2025, Ch. 633.

296 Amended by Stats. 2014, Ch. 82, Sec. 27. (SB 1306) Effective January 1, 2015.

297 Amended by Stats. 2014, Ch. 82, Sec. 28. (SB 1306) Effective January 1, 2015.

298 Amended by Stats. 2014, Ch. 82, Sec. 30. (SB 1306) Effective January 1, 2015.

299 Amended by Stats. 2014, Ch. 82, Sec. 31. (SB 1306) Effective January 1, 2015.

300 Amended by Stats. 2014, Ch. 82,

Sec. 32. (SB 1306) Effective January 1, 2015.

301 Amended by Stats. 2014, Ch. 82, Sec. 33. (SB 1306) Effective January 1, 2015.

302 Amended by Stats. 2014, Ch. 82, Sec. 34. (SB 1306) Effective January 1, 2015.

303 Amended by Stats. 2014, Ch. 82, Sec. 35. (SB 1306) Effective January 1, 2015.

304 Amended by Stats. 2014, Ch. 82, Sec. 36. (SB 1306) Effective January 1, 2015.

305 Amended by Stats. 2014, Ch. 144, Sec. 9. (AB 1847) Effective January 1, 2015.

306 Amended by Stats. 2014, Ch. 144, Sec. 10. (AB 1847) Effective January 1, 2015.

307 Amended by Stats. 2014, Ch. 144, Sec. 11. (AB 1847) Effective January 1, 2015.

308 Amended by Stats. 2014, Ch. 144, Sec. 12. (AB 1847) Effective January 1, 2015.

309 Added by Stats. 2014, Ch. 169, Sec. 1. (AB 2586) Effective January 1, 2015.

310 Amended by Stats. 2014, Ch. 311, Sec. 1. (AB 2745) Effective January 1, 2015.

311 Amended by Stats. 2014, Ch. 328, Sec. 1. (AB 1628) Effective January 1, 2015.

312 Amended by Stats. 2014, Ch. 635, Sec. 3. (AB 2089) Effective January 1, 2015.

313 Amended by Stats. 2014, Ch. 636, Sec. 5. (AB 2344) Effective January 1, 2015.

314 Amended by Stats. 2014, Ch. 636, Sec. 6. (AB 2344) Effective January 1, 2015.

315 Amended by Stats. 2014, Ch. 636, Sec. 7. (AB 2344) Effective January 1, 2015.

316 Added by Stats. 2014, Ch. 763, Sec. 4. (AB 1701) Effective January 1, 2015.

317 Amended by Stats. 2014, Ch. 763, Sec. 5. (AB 1701) Effective January 1, 2015.

318 Amended by Stats. 2014, Ch. 763, Sec. 6. (AB 1701) Effective January 1, 2015.

319 Amended by Stats. 2014, Ch. 763, Sec. 9. (AB 1701) Effective January 1, 2015.

320 Amended by Stats. 2014, Ch. 763, Sec. 11. (AB 1701) Effective January 1, 2015.

321 Amended by Stats. 2025, Ch. 757, Sec. 2. (SB 450) Effective January 1, 2026.

322 Amended by Stats. 2014, Ch. 763, Sec. 13. (AB 1701) Effective January 1, 2015.

323 Amended by Stats. 2014, Ch. 763, Sec. 15. (AB 1701) Effective January 1, 2015.

324 Added by Stats. 2014, Ch. 772, Sec. 1. (SB 1460) Effective January 1, 2015.

325 Amended by Stats. 2014, Ch. 913, Sec. 16. (AB 2747) Effective January 1, 2015.

326 Amended by Stats. 2015, Ch. 46, Sec. 3. (SB 340) Effective January 1, 2016.

327 Amended by Stats. 2015, Ch. 46, Sec. 4. (SB 340) Effective January 1, 2016.

328 Amended by Stats. 2015, Ch. 73, Sec. 1. (AB 536) Effective January 1, 2016.

329 Amended by Stats. 2015, Ch. 91, Sec. 4. (AB 1049) Effective January 1, 2016.

330 Amended by Stats. 2015, Ch. 196,

Sec. 1. (AB 380) Effective January 1, 2016.

331 Amended by Stats. 2015, Ch. 293, Sec. 1. (AB 139) Effective January 1, 2016.

332 Added by renumbering Section 3201 (as added by Stats. 1999, Ch. 1004, Sec. 2) by Stats. 2015, Ch. 303, Sec. 145. (AB 731) Effective January 1, 2016.

333 Amended by Stats. 2015, Ch. 303, Sec. 149. (AB 731) Effective January 1, 2016.

334 Amended by Stats. 2015, Ch. 411, Sec. 4. (AB 1081) Effective January 1, 2016.

335 Amended by Stats. 2015, Ch. 411, Sec. 5. (AB 1081) Effective January 1, 2016.

336 Amended by Stats. 2015, Ch. 411, Sec. 6. (AB 1081) Effective January 1, 2016..

337 Added by Stats. 2015, Ch. 415, Sec. 2. (AB 1407) Effective January 1, 2016.

338 Amended by Stats. 2015, Ch. 493, Sec. 3. (SB 646) Effective January 1, 2016.

339 Added by Stats. 2015, Ch. 493, Sec. 5. (SB 646) Effective January 1, 2016.

340 Added by Stats. 2015, Ch. 493, Sec. 9. (SB 646) Effective January 1, 2016.

341 Added by Stats. 2015, Ch. 493, Sec. 10. (SB 646) Effective January 1, 2016.

342 Added by Stats. 2015, Ch. 493, Sec. 13. (SB 646) Effective January 1, 2016.

343 Added by Stats. 2015, Ch. 493, Sec. 14. (SB 646) Effective January 1, 2016.

344 Added by Stats. 2016, Ch. 50, Sec. 35. (SB 1005) Effective January 1, 2017.

345 Amended by Stats. 2016, Ch. 67, Sec. 1. (AB 1735) Effective January 1, 2017.

346 Amended by Stats. 2016, Ch. 114, Sec. 2. (SB 1255) Effective January 1, 2017.

347 Amended by Stats. 2016, Ch. 114, Sec. 3. (SB 1255) Effective January 1, 2017.

348 Amended by Stats. 2016, Ch. 114, Sec. 4. (SB 1255) Effective January 1, 2017.

349 Amended by Stats. 2016, Ch. 114, Sec. 5. (SB 1255) Effective January 1, 2017.

350 Amended by Stats. 2016, Ch. 130, Sec. 1. (AB 2128) Effective January 1, 2017.

351 Amended by Stats. 2016, Ch. 385, Sec. 3. (AB 2349) Effective January 1, 2017.

352 Amended by Stats. 2016, Ch. 474, Sec. 4. (AB 2882) Effective January 1, 2017.

353 Amended by Stats. 2016, Ch. 474, Sec. 5. (AB 2882) Effective January 1, 2017.

354 Amended by Stats. 2016, Ch. 474, Sec. 6. (AB 2882) Effective January 1, 2017.

355 Amended by Stats. 2016, Ch. 474, Sec. 7. (AB 2882) Effective January 1, 2017.

356 Amended by Stats. 2016, Ch. 474, Sec. 9. (AB 2882) Effective January 1, 2017.

357 Added by Stats. 2016, Ch. 474, Sec. 13. (AB 2882) Effective January 1, 2017.

358 Amended by Stats. 2016, Ch. 474, Sec. 15. (AB 2882) Effective January 1, 2017.

359 Amended by Stats. 2016, Ch. 474, Sec. 21. (AB 2882) Effective

January 1, 2017.

[360] Amended by Stats. 2016, Ch. 474, Sec. 22. (AB 2882) Effective January 1, 2017.

[361] Amended by Stats. 2016, Ch. 474, Sec. 23. (AB 2882) Effective January 1, 2017.

[362] Amended by Stats. 2016, Ch. 474, Sec. 26. (AB 2882) Effective January 1, 2017.

[363] Amended by Stats. 2016, Ch. 612, Sec. 11. (AB 1997) Effective January 1, 2017.

[364] Added by Stats. 2016, Ch. 612, Sec. 12. (AB 1997) Effective January 1, 2017.

[365] Amended by Stats. 2017, Ch. 19, Sec. 7. (AB 111) Effective June 27, 2017.

[366] Added by Stats. 2017, Ch. 98, Sec. 1. (SB 204) Effective January 1, 2018.

[367] Amended by Stats. 2017, Ch. 732, Sec. 2. (AB 404) Effective January 1, 2018.

[368] Amended by Stats. 2017, Ch. 732, Sec. 3. (AB 404) Effective January 1, 2018

[369] Added by Stats. 2018, Ch. 35, Sec. 2. (AB 1811) Effective June 27, 2018.

[370] Amended by Stats. 2018, Ch. 83, Sec. 1. (AB 2792) Effective January 1, 2019.

[371] Amended by Stats. 2018, Ch. 219, Sec. 2. (AB 2694) Effective January 1, 2019.

[372] Amended by Stats. 2018, Ch. 219, Sec. 3. (AB 2694) Effective January 1, 2019.

[373] Amended by Stats. 2018, Ch. 389, Sec. 13. (AB 2296) Effective January 1, 2019.

[374] Amended by Stats. 2018, Ch. 389, Sec. 14. (AB 2296) Effective January 1, 2019.

[375] Amended by Stats. 2018, Ch. 389, Sec. 17. (AB 2296) Effective January 1, 2019.

[376] Amended by Stats. 2018, Ch. 423, Sec. 25. (SB 1494) Effective January 1, 2019.

[377] Amended by Stats. 2018, Ch. 504, Sec. 2. (AB 3248) Effective January 1, 2019.

[378] Amended by Stats. 2018, Ch. 504, Sec. 3. (AB 3248) Effective January 1, 2019.

[379] Repealed and added by Stats. 2018, Ch. 504, Sec. 6. (AB 3248) Effective January 1, 2019

[380] Added by Stats. 2018, Ch. 660, Sec. 2. (SB 273) Effective January 1, 2019.

[381] Amended by Stats. 2018, Ch. 660, Sec. 3. (SB 273) Effective January 1, 2019.

[382] Amended by Stats. 2018, Ch. 660, Sec. 4. (SB 273) Effective January 1, 2019.

[383] Amended by Stats. 2018, Ch. 660, Sec. 6. (SB 273) Effective January 1, 2019.

[384] Amended by Stats. 2018, Ch. 660, Sec. 7. (SB 273) Effective January 1, 2019.

[385] Amended by Stats. 2018, Ch. 660, Sec. 9. (SB 273) Effective January 1, 2019.

[386] Added by Stats. 2018, Ch. 820, Sec. 1. (AB 2274) Effective January 1, 2019.

[387] Amended by Stats. 2018, Ch. 838, Sec. 6. (SB 695) Effective January 1, 2019.

[388] Amended by Stats. 2018, Ch. 850, Sec. 1. (SB 1129) Effective January 1, 2019.

[389] Repealed and added by Stats. 2018, Ch. 876, Sec. 5. (AB 2684)

Effective January 1, 2019.

390 Repealed and added by Stats. 2018, Ch. 876, Sec. 9. (AB 2684) Effective January 1, 2019

391 Added by Stats. 2018, Ch. 876, Sec. 10. (AB 2684) Effective January 1, 2019.

392 Repealed and added by Stats. 2018, Ch. 876, Sec. 14. (AB 2684) Effective January 1, 2019.

393 Amended by Stats. 2018, Ch. 876, Sec. 15. (AB 2684) Effective January 1, 2019.

394 Repealed and added by Stats. 2018, Ch. 876, Sec. 19. (AB 2684) Effective January 1, 2019.

395 Amended by Stats. 2018, Ch. 876, Sec. 20. (AB 2684) Effective January 1, 2019.

396 Amended by Stats. 2018, Ch. 876, Sec. 21. (AB 2684) Effective January 1, 2019.

397 Added by Stats. 2018, Ch. 876, Sec. 22. (AB 2684) Effective January 1, 2019.

398 Added by Stats. 2018, Ch. 876, Sec. 23. (AB 2684) Effective January 1, 2019.

399 Added by Stats. 2018, Ch. 876, Sec. 24. (AB 2684) Effective January 1, 2019.

400 Amended by Stats. 2018, Ch. 876, Sec. 46. (AB 2684) Effective January 1, 2019.

401 Amended by Stats. 2018, Ch. 876, Sec. 52. (AB 2684) Effective January 1, 2019.

402 Amended by Stats. 2018, Ch. 876, Sec. 53. (AB 2684) Effective January 1, 2019.

403 Amended by Stats. 2018, Ch. 876, Sec. 57. (AB 2684) Effective January 1, 2019.

404 Amended by Stats. 2018, Ch. 876, Sec. 59. (AB 2684) Effective January 1, 2019.

405 Amended by Stats. 2018, Ch. 876, Sec. 60. (AB 2684) Effective January 1, 2019.

406 Amended by Stats. 2018, Ch. 876, Sec. 62. (AB 2684) Effective January 1, 2019.

407 Amended by Stats. 2018, Ch. 876, Sec. 63. (AB 2684) Effective January 1, 2019.

408 Amended by Stats. 2018, Ch. 938, Sec. 1. (AB 929) Effective January 1, 2019.

409 Amended by Stats. 2019, Ch. 27, Sec. 4. (SB 80) Effective June 27, 2019.

410 Amended by Stats. 2019, Ch. 27, Sec. 5. (SB 80) Effective June 27, 2019.

411 Repealed (in Sec. 1) and added by Stats. 2017, Ch. 330, Sec. 2. (AB 1692) Effective January 1, 2018. Section operative January 1, 2020, by its own provisions.

412 Amended by Stats. 2019, Ch. 43, Sec. 1. (AB 327) Effective January 1, 2020.

413 Amended by Stats. 2019, Ch. 115, Sec. 1. (AB 1817) Effective January 1, 2020.

414 Amended by Stats. 2019, Ch. 115, Sec. 2. (AB 1817) Effective January 1, 2020.

415 Amended by Stats. 2019, Ch. 115, Sec. 6. (AB 1817) Effective January 1, 2020.

416 Amended by Stats. 2019, Ch. 115, Sec. 7. (AB 1817) Effective January 1, 2020.

417 Amended by Stats. 2019, Ch. 115, Sec. 8. (AB 1817) Effective January 1, 2020.

418 Amended by Stats. 2019, Ch. 115, Sec. 9. (AB 1817) Effective January 1, 2020.

419 Amended by Stats. 2019, Ch. 115, Sec. 10. (AB 1817) Effective January 1, 2020.

420 Amended by Stats. 2019, Ch. 115, Sec. 11. (AB 1817) Effective January 1, 2020.

421 Amended by Stats. 2019, Ch. 115, Sec. 14. (AB 1817) Effective January 1, 2020.

422 Amended by Stats. 2019, Ch. 115, Sec. 15. (AB 1817) Effective January 1, 2020.

423 Amended by Stats. 2019, Ch. 115, Sec. 16. (AB 1817) Effective January 1, 2020.

424 Amended by Stats. 2025, Ch. 48, Sec. 1. (AB 1297) Effective January 1, 2026. Repealed as of January 1, 2027, by its own provisions. See later operative version added by Sec. 2 of Stats. 2025, Ch. 48.

425 Amended by Stats. 2019, Ch. 115, Sec. 18. (AB 1817) Effective January 1, 2020.

426 Amended by Stats. 2019, Ch. 115, Sec. 19. (AB 1817) Effective January 1, 2020.

427 Amended by Stats. 2019, Ch. 115, Sec. 20. (AB 1817) Effective January 1, 2020.

428 Amended by Stats. 2019, Ch. 115, Sec. 21. (AB 1817) Effective January 1, 2020.

429 Amended by Stats. 2019, Ch. 115, Sec. 22. (AB 1817) Effective January 1, 2020.

430 Amended by Stats. 2019, Ch. 115, Sec. 24. (AB 1817) Effective January 1, 2020.

431 Amended by Stats. 2019, Ch. 115, Sec. 25. (AB 1817) Effective January 1, 2020.

432 Amended by Stats. 2019, Ch. 115, Sec. 26. (AB 1817) Effective January 1, 2020.

433 Amended by Stats. 2019, Ch. 115, Sec. 27. (AB 1817) Effective January 1, 2020.

434 Amended by Stats. 2019, Ch. 115, Sec. 30. (AB 1817) Effective January 1, 2020.

435 Amended by Stats. 2019, Ch. 115, Sec. 31. (AB 1817) Effective January 1, 2020.

436 Amended by Stats. 2019, Ch. 115, Sec. 32. (AB 1817) Effective January 1, 2020.

437 Amended by Stats. 2019, Ch. 115, Sec. 34. (AB 1817) Effective January 1, 2020.

438 Amended by Stats. 2019, Ch. 115, Sec. 35. (AB 1817) Effective January 1, 2020.

439 Amended by Stats. 2019, Ch. 115, Sec. 37. (AB 1817) Effective January 1, 2020.

440 Amended by Stats. 2019, Ch. 115, Sec. 38. (AB 1817) Effective January 1, 2020.

441 Amended by Stats. 2019, Ch. 115, Sec. 39. (AB 1817) Effective January 1, 2020.

442 Amended by Stats. 2019, Ch. 115, Sec. 40 (AB 1817) Effective January 1, 2020.

443 Amended by Stats. 2019, Ch. 115, Sec. 41 (AB 1817) Effective January 1, 2020.

444 Amended by Stats. 2019, Ch. 115, Sec. 42 (AB 1817) Effective January 1, 2020.

445 Amended by Stats. 2019, Ch. 115, Sec. 43 (AB 1817) Effective January 1, 2020.

446 Amended by Stats. 2019, Ch. 115, Sec. 44 (AB 1817) Effective January 1, 2020.

447 Amended by Stats. 2019, Ch. 115, Sec. 45 (AB 1817) Effective January 1, 2020.

[448] Amended by Stats. 2019, Ch. 115, Sec. 47 (AB 1817) Effective January 1, 2020.

[449] Amended by Stats. 2019, Ch. 115, Sec. 48 (AB 1817) Effective January 1, 2020.

[450] Amended by Stats. 2019, Ch. 115, Sec. 49 (AB 1817) Effective January 1, 2020.

[451] Amended by Stats. 2019, Ch. 115, Sec. 50 (AB 1817) Effective January 1, 2020.

[452] Amended by Stats. 2019, Ch. 115, Sec. 51 (AB 1817) Effective January 1, 2020.

[453] Amended by Stats. 2019, Ch. 115, Sec. 52 (AB 1817) Effective January 1, 2020.

[454] Amended by Stats. 2019, Ch. 115, Sec. 53 (AB 1817) Effective January 1, 2020.

[455] Amended by Stats. 2019, Ch. 115, Sec. 54 (AB 1817) Effective January 1, 2020.

[456] Amended by Stats. 2019, Ch. 115, Sec. 55 (AB 1817) Effective January 1, 2020.

[457] Amended by Stats. 2019, Ch. 115, Sec. 56 (AB 1817) Effective January 1, 2020.

[458] Amended by Stats. 2019, Ch. 115, Sec. 57 (AB 1817) Effective January 1, 2020.

[459] Amended by Stats. 2019, Ch. 115, Sec. 58 (AB 1817) Effective January 1, 2020.

[460] Amended by Stats. 2019, Ch. 115, Sec. 60 (AB 1817) Effective January 1, 2020.

[461] Amended by Stats. 2019, Ch. 115, Sec. 61. (AB 1817) Effective January 1, 2020.

[462] Amended by Stats. 2019, Ch. 115, Sec. 62. (AB 1817) Effective January 1, 2020.

[463] Amended by Stats. 2019, Ch. 115, Sec. 64. (AB 1817) Effective January 1, 2020

[464] Amended by Stats. 2019, Ch. 115, Sec. 66. (AB 1817) Effective January 1, 2020.

[465] Amended by Stats. 2019, Ch. 115, Sec. 69. (AB 1817) Effective January 1, 2020.

[466] Amended by Stats. 2019, Ch. 115, Sec. 157. (AB 1817) Effective January 1, 2020.

[467] Amended by Stats. 2019, Ch. 135, Sec. 1. (SB 30) Effective January 1, 2020.

[468] Amended by Stats. 2019, Ch. 135, Sec. 2. (SB 30) Effective January 1, 2020.

[469] Amended by Stats. 2019, Ch. 135, Sec. 3. (SB 30) Effective January 1, 2020.

[470] Amended by Stats. 2019, Ch. 135, Sec. 4. (SB 30) Effective January 1, 2020.

[471] Amended by Stats. 2019, Ch. 135, Sec. 5. (SB 30) Effective January 1, 2020.

[472] Amended by Stats. 2019, Ch. 135, Sec. 6. (SB 30) Effective January 1, 2020.

[473] Amended by Stats. 2019, Ch. 135, Sec. 7. (SB 30) Effective January 1, 2020.

[474] Amended by Stats. 2019, Ch. 193, Sec. 1. (AB 1380) Effective January 1, 2020.

[475] Amended by Stats. 2019, Ch. 497, Sec. 110. (AB 991) Effective January 1, 2020.

[476] Amended by Stats. 2019, Ch. 551, Sec. 2. (SB 495) Effective January 1, 2020.

[477] Amended by Stats. 2019, Ch. 823, Sec. 1. (AB 1165) Effective January 1, 2020.

478 Amended by Stats. 2020, Ch. 36, Sec. 27. (AB 3364) Effective January 1, 2021.

479 Amended by Stats. 2020, Ch. 370, Sec. 116. (SB 1371) Effective January 1, 2021.

480 Amended by Stats. 2021, Ch. 86, Sec. 3. (AB 153) Effective July 16, 2021.

481 Amended by Stats. 2021, Ch. 86, Sec. 4. (AB 153) Effective July 16, 2021.

482 (Repealed and added by Stats. 2021, Ch. 86, Sec. 6. (AB 153) Effective July 16, 2021.

483 Repealed and added by Stats. 2021, Ch. 86, Sec. 8. (AB 153) Effective July 16, 2021.

484 Amended by Stats. 2021, Ch. 86, Sec. 9. (AB 153) Effective July 16, 2021.

485 Added by Stats. 2021, Ch. 620, Sec. 5. (AB 583) Effective October 7, 2021.

486 Amended by Stats. 2020, Ch. 11, Sec. 1. (AB 79) Effective June 29, 2020. Inoperative on or after January 1, 2022, as prescribed by its own provisions. Repealed as of January 1, 2022, or a later January 1, pursuant to its own provisions. See later operative version added by Sec. 2 of Stats. 2020, Ch. 11.

487 Added by Stats. 2020, Ch. 245, Sec. 1. (AB 2517) Effective January 1, 2021. Operative January 1, 2022, by its own provisions.

488 Added by Stats. 2021, Ch. 58, Sec. 7. (AB 627) Effective January 1, 2022.

489 Amended by Stats. 2021, Ch. 124, Sec. 27. (AB 938) Effective January 1, 2022.

490 Amended by Stats. 2021, Ch. 124, Sec. 28. (AB 938) Effective January 1, 2022.

491 Amended by Stats. 2025, Ch. 676, Sec. 3. (SB 50) Effective January 1, 2026.

492 Amended by Stats. 2021, Ch. 199, Sec. 1. (AB 746) Effective January 1, 2022.

493 Amended by Stats. 2021, Ch. 213, Sec. 2. (AB 1579) Effective January 1, 2022.

494 Amended by Stats. 2021, Ch. 440, Sec. 6. (AB 462) Effective January 1, 2022.

495 Added by Stats. 2021, Ch. 457, Sec. 1. (AB 277) Effective January 1, 2022.

496 Amended by Stats. 2021, Ch. 546, Sec. 1. (SB 497) Effective January 1, 2022.

497 Amended by Stats. 2021, Ch. 626, Sec. 11. (AB 1171) Effective January 1, 2022.

498 Added by Stats. 2021, Ch. 681, Sec. 1. (AB 887) Effective January 1, 2022.

499 Added by Stats. 2021, Ch. 681, Sec. 2. (AB 887) Effective January 1, 2022.

500 Amended by Stats. 2021, Ch. 685, Sec. 3. (SB 320) Effective January 1, 2022.

501 Added by Stats. 2021, Ch. 685, Sec. 5. (SB 320) Effective January 1, 2022.

502 Amended by Stats. 2021, Ch. 685, Sec. 6. (SB 320) Effective January 1, 2022.

503 Amended by Stats. 2021, Ch. 686, Sec. 1. (SB 538) Effective January 1, 2022.

504 Amended by Stats. 2021, Ch. 768, Sec. 2. (SB 654) Effective January 1, 2022.

505 Amended by Stats. 2022, Ch. 76, Sec. 2. (AB 1621) Effective June 30,

2022.

506 Amended by Stats. 2022, Ch. 573, Sec. 3. (AB 207) Effective September 27, 2022.

507 Added by Stats. 2022, Ch. 573, Sec. 5. (AB 207) Effective September 27, 2022.

508 Added by renumbering Section 17504.1 by Stats. 2022, Ch. 573, Sec. 6. (AB 207) Effective September 27, 2022.

509 Amended by Stats. 2021, Ch. 615, Sec. 106. (AB 474) Effective January 1, 2022. Operative January 1, 2023, pursuant to Sec. 463 of Stats. 2021, Ch. 615.

510 Amended by Stats. 2022, Ch. 159, Sec. 2. (AB 2495) Effective January 1, 2023.

511 Amended by Stats. 2022, Ch. 159, Sec. 3. (AB 2495) Effective January 1, 2023.

512 Amended by Stats. 2022, Ch. 159, Sec. 6. (AB 2495) Effective January 1, 2023.

513 Amended by Stats. 2022, Ch. 159, Sec. 7. (AB 2495) Effective January 1, 2023.

514 Amended by Stats. 2022, Ch. 159, Sec. 10. (AB 2495) Effective January 1, 2023.

515 Added by Stats. 2022, Ch. 385, Sec. 2. (SB 1182) Effective January 1, 2023.

516 Amended by Stats. 2022, Ch. 385, Sec. 3. (SB 1182) Effective January 1, 2023.

517 Amended by Stats. 2022, Ch. 420, Sec. 15. (AB 2960) Effective January 1, 2023.

518 Amended by Stats. 2025, Ch. 267, Sec. 2. (AB 561) Effective January 1, 2026.

519 Amended by Stats. 2025, Ch. 267, Sec. 3. (AB 561) Effective January 1, 2026.

520 Amended by Stats. 2022, Ch. 420, Sec. 19. (AB 2960) Effective January 1, 2023.

521 Amended by Stats. 2022, Ch. 420, Sec. 20. (AB 2960) Effective January 1, 2023.

522 Added by Stats. 2022, Ch. 573, Sec. 7. (AB 207) Effective September 27, 2022. Conditionally operative on or after July 1, 2023, as prescribed by its own provisions.

523 Repealed and added by Stats. 2022, Ch. 591, Sec. 2. (AB 2369) Effective January 1, 2023

524 Amended by Stats. 2022, Ch. 810, Sec. 4. (SB 107) Effective January 1, 2023.

525 Amended by Stats. 2022, Ch. 810, Sec. 5. (SB 107) Effective January 1, 2023.

526 Amended by Stats. 2022, Ch. 810, Sec. 6. (SB 107) Effective January 1, 2023.

527 Amended by Stats. 2022, Ch. 810, Sec. 7. (SB 107) Effective January 1, 2023.

528 Amended by Stats. 2022, Ch. 810, Sec. 8. (SB 107) Effective January 1, 2023.

529 Amended by Stats. 2022, Ch. 870, Sec. 1. (AB 2711) Effective January 1, 2023.

530 Amended by Stats. 2023, Ch. 43, Sec. 2. (AB 120) Effective July 10, 2023.

531 Amended by Stats. 2023, Ch. 43, Sec. 3. (AB 120) Effective July 10, 2023.

532 Amended by Stats. 2023, Ch. 43, Sec. 4. (AB 120) Effective July 10, 2023.

533 Amended by Stats. 2023, Ch. 43, Sec. 7. (AB 120) Effective July 10, 2023.

534 Repealed and added by Stats. 2023, Ch. 43, Sec. 10. (AB 120) Effective July 10, 2023.

535 Repealed and added by Stats. 2023, Ch. 43, Sec. 11. (AB 120) Effective July 10, 2023.

536 Repealed and added by Stats. 2023, Ch. 43, Sec. 9. (AB 120) Effective July 10, 2023.

537 Amended by Stats. 2023, Ch. 192, Sec. 1. (SB 138) Effective September 13, 2023.

538 Amended by Stats. 2023, Ch. 192, Sec. 2. (SB 138) Effective September 13, 2023.

539 Repealed (in Sec. 1) and added by Stats. 2021, Ch. 620, Sec. 2. (AB 583) Effective October 7, 2021. Operative January 1, 2024, by its own provisions.

540 Repealed (in Sec. 3) and added by Stats. 2021, Ch. 620, Sec. 4. (AB 583) Effective October 7, 2021. Operative January 1, 2024, by its own provisions.

541 Amended by Stats. 2023, Ch. 67, Sec. 1. (AB 1179) Effective January 1, 2024.

542 Amended by Stats. 2023, Ch. 131, Sec. 59. (AB 1754) Effective January 1, 2024.

543 Amended by Stats. 2023, Ch. 131, Sec. 60. (AB 1754) Effective January 1, 2024.

544 Amended by Stats. 2023, Ch. 131, Sec. 61. (AB 1754) Effective January 1, 2024.

545 Added by Stats. 2023, Ch. 152, Sec. 1. (SB 457) Effective January 1, 2024.

546 Amended by Stats. 2023, Ch. 152, Sec. 2. (SB 457) Effective January 1, 2024.

547 Repealed (in Sec. 2) and added by Stats. 2023, Ch. 213, Sec. 3. (SB 343) Effective January 1, 2024. Operative September 1, 2024, by its own provisions.

548 Repealed (in Sec. 4) and added by Stats. 2023, Ch. 213, Sec. 3. (SB 343) Effective January 1, 2024. Operative September 1, 2024, by its own provisions.

549 Repealed (in Sec. 6) and added by Stats. 2023, Ch. 213, Sec. 3. (SB 343) Effective January 1, 2024. Operative September 1, 2024, by its own provisions.

550 Repealed (in Sec. 8) and added by Stats. 2023, Ch. 213, Sec. 3. (SB 343) Effective January 1, 2024. Operative September 1, 2024, by its own provisions.

551 Repealed (in Sec. 10) and added by Stats. 2023, Ch. 213, Sec. 3. (SB 343) Effective January 1, 2024. Operative September 1, 2024, by its own provisions.

552 Repealed (in Sec. 12) and added by Stats. 2023, Ch. 213, Sec. 3. (SB 343) Effective January 1, 2024. Operative September 1, 2024, by its own provisions.

553 Amended by Stats. 2023, Ch. 213, Sec. 18. (SB 343) Effective January 1, 2024. Inoperative January 1, 2026, by its own provisions. Repealed as of January 1, 2027, by its own provisions. See later operative version added by Sec. 19 of Stats. 2023, Ch. 21.

554 Amended by Stats. 2023, Ch. 213, Sec. 20. (SB 343) Effective January 1, 2024. Inoperative January 1, 2026, by its own provisions. Repealed as of January 1, 2027, by its own provisions. See later operative version added by Sec. 21 of Stats. 2023, Ch. 213.

555 Repealed (in Sec. 16) and added by

Stats. 2023, Ch. 213, Sec. 21. (SB 343) Effective January 1, 2024. Operative January 1, 2026, by its own provisions.

556 Repealed (in Sec. 18) and added by Stats. 2023, Ch. 213, Sec. 21. (SB 343) Effective January 1, 2024. Operative January 1, 2026, by its own provisions.

557 Repealed (in Sec. 20) and added by Stats. 2023, Ch. 213, Sec. 21. (SB 343) Effective January 1, 2024. Operative January 1, 2026, by its own provisions.

558 Added by Stats. 2023, Ch. 213, Sec. 22. (SB 343) Effective January 1, 2024.

559 Amended by Stats. 2023, Ch. 242, Sec. 1. (AB 818) Effective January 1, 2024.

560 Repealed (in Sec. 2) and added by Stats. 2023, Ch. 338, Sec. 3. (AB 665) Effective January 1, 2024. Operative July 1, 2024, by its own provisions.

561 Amended by Stats. 2023, Ch. 456, Sec. 1. (AB 816) Effective January 1, 2024.

562 Added by Stats. 2023, Ch. 456, Sec. 2. (AB 816) Effective January 1, 2024.

563 Amended by Stats. 2023, Ch. 478, Sec. 22. (AB 1756) Effective January 1, 2024.

564 Amended by Stats. 2023, Ch. 851, Sec. 3. (AB 1650) Effective January 1, 2024.

565 Amended by Stats. 2023, Ch. 851, Sec. 4. (AB 1650) Effective January 1, 2024.

566 Amended by Stats. 2023, Ch. 851, Sec. 5. (AB 1650) Effective January 1, 2024.

567 Amended by Stats. 2023, Ch. 851, Sec. 7. (AB 1650) Effective January 1, 2024.

568 Amended by Stats. 2023, Ch. 851, Sec. 8. (AB 1650) Effective January 1, 2024.

569 Amended by Stats. 2023, Ch. 851, Sec. 9. (AB 1650) Effective January 1, 2024.

570 Amended by Stats. 2023, Ch. 851, Sec. 10. (AB 1650) Effective January 1, 2024.

571 Amended by Stats. 2023, Ch. 493, Sec. 2. (SB 599) Effective January 1, 2024.

572 Amended by Stats. 2023, Ch. 493, Sec. 4. (SB 599) Effective January 1, 2024.

573 Added by Stats. 2023, Ch. 503, Sec. 1. (SB 741) Effective January 1, 2024.

574 Amended by Stats. 2023, Ch. 565, Sec. 1. (AB 1148) Effective January 1, 2024.

575 Amended by Stats. 2023, Ch. 874, Sec. 2. (SB 459) Effective January 1, 2024.

576 Amended by Stats. 2024, Ch. 80, Sec. 43. (SB 1525) Effective January 1, 2025.

577 Amended by Stats. 2024, Ch. 169, Sec. 1. (AB 3209) Effective January 1, 2025.

578 Amended by Stats. 2024, Ch. 190, Sec. 1. (SB 1427) Effective January 1, 2025.

579 Amended by Stats. 2024, Ch. 190, Sec. 2. (SB 1427) Effective January 1, 2025.

580 Amended by Stats. 2024, Ch. 190, Sec. 3. (SB 1427) Effective January 1, 2025.

581 Added by Stats. 2024, Ch. 190, Sec. 4. (SB 1427) Effective January 1, 2025. Operative January 1, 2026, by its own provisions.

582 Added by Stats. 2024, Ch. 190, Sec.

5. (SB 1427) Effective January 1, 2025.

583 Amended by Stats. 2024, Ch. 190, Sec. 6. (SB 1427) Effective January 1, 2025.

584 Amended by Stats. 2024, Ch. 190, Sec. 7. (SB 1427) Effective January 1, 2025.

585 Amended by Stats. 2024, Ch. 303, Sec. 1. (AB 1974) Effective January 1, 2025.

586 Amended by Stats. 2024, Ch. 317, Sec. 1. (AB 3072) Effective January 1, 2025.

587 Amended by Stats. 2024, Ch. 317, Sec. 2. (AB 3072) Effective January 1, 2025.

588 Amended by Stats. 2024, Ch. 495, Sec. 1. (SB 1518) Effective January 1, 2025.

589 Amended by Stats. 2024, Ch. 541, Sec. 2. (AB 3083) Effective January 1, 2025.

590 (Repealed in 2026 Edition)

591 Repealed (in Sec. 6) and added by Stats. 2024, Ch. 544, Sec. 7. (SB 899) Effective January 1, 2025. Operative January 1, 2026, by its own provisions.

592 Amended (as added by Stats. 2024, Ch. 544, Sec. 9.5) by Stats. 2025, Ch. 241, Sec. 6. (SB 857) Effective January 1, 2026.

593 Amended by Stats. 2024, Ch. 610, Sec. 1. (AB 1880) Effective January 1, 2025.

594 Added by Stats. 2024, Ch. 611, Sec. 1. (SB 764) Effective January 1, 2025.

595 Amended by Stats. 2024, Ch. 648, Sec. 1. (AB 2024) Effective January 1, 2025.

596 Amended by Stats. 2024, Ch. 652, Sec. 2. (SB 554) Effective January 1, 2025.

597 Amended by Stats. 2024, Ch. 780, Sec. 2. (SB 1150) Effective January 1, 2025.

598 Amended by Stats. 2024, Ch. 780, Sec. 3. (SB 1150) Effective January 1, 2025.

599 Amended by Stats. 2024, Ch. 780, Sec. 4. (SB 1150) Effective January 1, 2025.

600 Amended by Stats. 2024, Ch. 845, Sec. 1. (AB 2929) Effective January 1, 2025.

601 Amended (as amended by Stats. 2023, Ch. 213, Sec. 14) by Stats. 2024, Ch. 853, Sec. 21. (AB 3281) Effective January 1, 2025. Inoperative January 1, 2026, by its own provisions. Repealed as of January 1, 2027, by its own provisions. See later operative version added by Sec. 15 of Stats. 2023, Ch. 213.

602 Amended (as added by Stats. 2023, Ch. 213, Sec. 21) by Stats. 2024, Ch. 853, Sec. 22. (AB 3281) Effective January 1, 2025.

603 Amended by Stats. 2025, Ch. 136, Sec. 12. (AB 260) Effective September 26, 2025.

604 Amended by Stats. 2025, Ch. 664, Sec. 4. (AB 495) Effective January 1, 2026.

605 Amended by Stats. 2025, Ch. 664, Sec. 5. (AB 495) Effective January 1, 2026.

606 Added by Stats. 2022, Ch. 830, Sec. 1. (SB 1055) Effective January 1, 2023. Operative January 1, 2025, by its own provisions.

607 Amended by Stats. 2024, Ch. 25, Sec. 1. (AB 2397) Effective January 1, 2025.

608 Added by Stats. 2025, Ch. 757, Sec. 1. (SB 450) Effective January 1, 2026.

609 Repealed (in Sec. 1) and added by Stats. 2025, Ch. 48, Sec. 2. (AB 1297) Effective January 1, 2026. Operative January 1, 2027, by its own provisions.

610 Repealed (in Sec. 1) and added by Stats. 2025, Ch. 633, Sec. 2. (AB 1134) Effective January 1, 2026. Operative January 1, 2027, by its own provisions.

611 Added by Stats. 2025, Ch. 452, Sec. 1. (AB 1375) Effective January 1, 2026.

612 Added by Stats. 2025, Ch. 574, Sec. 2. (AB 1363) Effective January 1, 2026.

APPENDIX 1:
STATUTORY DEADLINES AND TIME BARS

(Reference Only)

Scope and Use

This appendix summarizes statutory deadlines, time limits, and absolute bars contained in the California Family Code as in effect on January 1, 2026. It is intended as a quick confirmation reference only.

Risk Classification

Jurisdictional: Court lacks authority if deadline is missed
Reversible: Order vulnerable on appeal if misapplied
Procedural: Deadline may be extended, waived, or cured by statute or order

Relief After Deadline indicates whether the court retains statutory authority to grant any form of relief after the specified deadline has passed. It does not imply tolling, exception, or equitable discretion.

Editorial Statement

This appendix is intended to identify statutory deadlines and absolute time bars that affect court authority or appellate vulnerability. It does not include case law, commentary, or practice guidance.

Sections include:

Section 1.1: Responsive Pleadings and Initial Procedural Deadlines
Section 1.2: Mandatory Financial Disclosure Deadlines
Section 1.3: Motions to Set Aside Judgment
Section 1.4: Absolute Statutory Bars
Section 1.5: Statements of Decision
Section 1.6: Support Modification Effective Dates and Retroactivity
Section 1.7: Applicability and Finality

SECTION 1.1: RESPONSIVE PLEADINGS AND INITIAL PROCEDURAL DEADLINES

Issue	Trigger	Deadline / Limit	Authority	Risk Class	Relief After Deadline
Response to Petition	Service of petition and summons	30 days	FC §2020	Procedural	Yes
Joinder of Interested Party	Court determination	As ordered	FC §2021	Procedural	Yes

SECTION 1.2: MANDATORY FINANCIAL DISCLOSURE DEADLINES

Issue	Trigger	Deadline / Limit	Authority	Risk Class	Relief After Deadline
Preliminary Declaration of Disclosure (Petitioner)	Filing of petition	Concurrent with petition	FC §2104	Procedural	Yes
Preliminary Declaration of Disclosure (Respondent)	Filing of response	Concurrent or within 60 days	FC §2104	Procedural	Yes
Extension of Preliminary Disclosure	Agreement or court order	As ordered	FC §2104	Procedural	Yes
Final Declaration of Disclosure	Agreement or trial setting	Before agreement or ≥45 days before first assigned trial date	FC §2105(a)	Reversible	Yes
Waiver of Final Disclosure	After preliminary disclosures completed	Mutual waiver only	FC §2105(d)	Reversible	Yes

SECTION 1.3: MOTIONS TO SET ASIDE JUDGMENT

Ground	Trigger	Deadline	Authority	Risk Class	Relief After Deadline
Actual Fraud	Discovery or constructive discovery	1 year	FC §2122(a)	Jurisdictional	No
Perjury	Discovery or constructive discovery	1 year	FC §2122(b)	Jurisdictional	No
Duress	Entry of judgment	2 years	FC §2122(c)	Jurisdictional	No
Mental Incapacity	Entry of judgment	2 years	FC §2122(d)	Jurisdictional	No
Mistake (stipulated or uncontested judgment)	Entry of judgment	1 year	FC §2122(e)	Jurisdictional	No
Failure to Comply with Disclosure Requirements	Discovery or constructive discovery	1 year	FC §2122(f)	Jurisdictional	No

SECTION 1.4: ABSOLUTE STATUTORY BARS

(No Timing Cure)

Issue	Limitation	Authority	Risk Class
Inequity Alone	Judgment may not be set aside solely because it was inequitable when made	FC §2123	Jurisdictional
Attorney Negligence	Not imputed absent client knowledge and failure to self-protect	FC §2124	Jurisdictional
Scope of Set-Aside Relief	Relief limited to provisions materially affected, unless equity requires otherwise	FC §2125	Reversible

SECTION 1.5: STATEMENTS OF DECISION

Issue	Trigger	Rule	Authority	Risk Class
Statement of Decision	Timely request after trial	Court shall issue where controverted factual issues resolved	FC §2127	Reversible

SECTION 1.6: SUPPORT MODIFICATION EFFECTIVE DATES AND RETROACTIVITY

Issue	Trigger	Limitation	Authority	Risk Class	Relief After Deadline
Child Support Modification	Filing of motion or order to show cause	Retroactive only to filing date unless statute permits otherwise	FC §3653(a)	Reversible	Yes (prospective)
Temporary Support Orders	Request for pendente lite relief	Subject to court discretion within statutory limits	FC §3600	Procedural	Yes
Permanent Support Orders	Entry of judgment or subsequent request	Governed by modification statutes	FC §§3651–3653	Reversible	Yes (prospective)

SECTION 1.7: APPLICABILITY AND FINALITY

Issue	Rule	Authority	Risk Class
Relief From Judgment Chapter	Applies to judgments entered on or after January 1, 1993	FC §2129	Jurisdictional

APPENDIX 2: MANDATORY AND DISCRETIONARY AUTHORITY

(Reference Only)

Scope and Use

This appendix classifies selected provisions of the California Family Code as Mandatory, Discretionary, or Prohibited, based solely on statutory language as in effect on January 1, 2026. This appendix does not address how discretion should be exercised and does not limit the court's authority beyond express statutory language.

Classification Key

Mandatory (Consideration Required) – Court shall consider/shall make findings
Mandatory (Order Required) – Court shall issue/shall enter/shall divide
Discretionary – Court may
Prohibited (No Authority) – Court may not/shall not

Editorial Statement

Classifications above are based on express statutory verbs (shall, may, may not, shall not) and conditional clauses within the cited provisions. No case law, commentary, or practice guidance is included.

Sections include:

Section 2.1: Child Support Guideline and Deviation
Section 2.2: Support Modification and Retroactivity (Child And Spousal)
Section 2.3: Spousal Support Factors
Section 2.4: Division of Property
Section 2.5: Relief from Judgment (Selected)
Section 2.6: Attorney's Fees and Sanctions

SECTION 2.1: CHILD SUPPORT GUIDELINE AND DEVIATION

Issue	Authority Classification	Statutory Verb	Condition or Trigger	Statutory Basis
Adherence to statewide uniform guideline	Mandatory (Order Required)	shall	Guideline applies; departures limited to circumstances set forth in article	FC §4052
Guideline amount presumed correct	Mandatory (Consideration Required)	presumed	Presumption applies to formula amount	FC §4057(a)
Rebuttal of guideline presumption	Discretionary	may	Only if admissible evidence shows guideline unjust/inappropriate and factor(s) found applicable	FC §4057(b)
Required information when ordering amount different from guideline	Mandatory (Order Required)	shall	Only when support ordered differs from guideline formula amount	FC §4056(a)
Information used to determine guideline amount (upon request)	Mandatory (Order Required)	shall	Only at request of any party	FC §4056(b)

SECTION 2.2: SUPPORT MODIFICATION AND RETROACTIVITY (CHILD AND SPOUSAL)

Issue	Authority Classification	Statutory Verb	Condition or Trigger	Statutory Basis
Modification or termination of support order	Discretionary	may	Subject to listed statutory limits and exceptions	FC §3651(a)
Past-due amounts before filing	Prohibited (No Authority)	may not	Accrued amounts before filing of notice of motion / RFO / OSC (subject to stated exceptions)	FC §3651(c)(1)
Retroactivity window (general rule)	Discretionary	may	Retroactive to filing date, or later, subject to subdivisions and federal law	FC §3653(a)
Retroactivity when unemployment basis	Mandatory (Order Required)	shall	If modification entered due to unemployment, retroactive to later of service date or unemployment date unless good cause stated	FC §3653(b)
Nonmodifiable spousal support by agreement	Prohibited (No Authority)	may not	To extent an agreement specifically provides spousal support is not modifiable/terminable	FC §3651(d)

SECTION 2.3: SPOUSAL SUPPORT FACTORS

Issue	Authority Classification	Statutory Verb	Condition or Trigger	Statutory Basis
Consideration of spousal support factors	Mandatory (Consideration Required)	shall consider	When ordering spousal support under Part 3	FC §4320

SECTION 2.4: DIVISION OF PROPERTY

Issue	Authority Classification	Statutory Verb	Condition or Trigger	Statutory Basis
Equal division of community estate	Mandatory (Order Required)	shall	In dissolution or legal separation, absent qualifying agreement/stipulation or other statutory provision	FC §2550
Valuation timing (default rule)	Mandatory (Order Required)	shall	Value as near as practicable to time of trial (except as provided)	FC §2552(a)
Alternate valuation date	Discretionary	may	Upon 30 days' notice and good cause shown, value after separation and before trial	FC §2552(b)

SECTION 2.5:
RELIEF FROM JUDGMENT (SELECTED)

Issue	Authority Classification	Statutory Verb	Condition or Trigger	Statutory Basis
Set-aside based solely on inequity	Prohibited (No Authority)	may not	Inequitable when made or later inequitable circumstances alone	FC §2123
Scope of relief (materially affected provisions)	Mandatory (Order Required)	shall	When granting relief under Chapter 10	FC §2125 (first sentence)
Set aside entire judgment	Discretionary	has discretion	Only if necessary for equitable considerations	FC §2125 (second sentence)
Statement of decision	Mandatory (Order Required)	shall	If timely request made and controverted factual evidence resolved	FC §2127

SECTION 2.6: ATTORNEY'S FEES AND SANCTIONS

A. Need-based fees (access to representation)

Issue	Authority Classification	Statutory Verb	Condition or Trigger	Statutory Basis
Ensure access to legal representation	Mandatory (Order Required)	shall ensure	In dissolution and related postjudgment proceedings	FC §2030(a)(1)
Required findings when fees requested	Mandatory (Consideration Required)	shall make findings	When request for fees and costs is made	FC §2030(a)(2)
Fee award when findings show disparity and ability to pay	Mandatory (Order Required)	shall make an order	Only if findings demonstrate disparity in access and ability to pay	FC §2030(a)(2)

B. Sanctions for litigation conduct (Fam Code §271)

Issue	Authority Classification	Statutory Verb	Condition or Trigger	Statutory Basis
Award fees and costs as a sanction	Discretionary	may	Based on extent conduct furthers or frustrates settlement policy and cooperation	FC §271(a)
Consideration of financial evidence	Mandatory (Consideration Required)	shall take into consideration	When making an award under §271	FC §271(a)
Unreasonable financial burden limit	Prohibited (No Authority)	shall not	Court shall not impose sanction that imposes unreasonable financial burden	FC §271(a)
Notice and opportunity to be heard	Mandatory (Order Required)	shall be imposed only after	Before imposing §271 sanction	FC §271(b)

www.ingramcontent.com/pod-product-compliance
Lightning Source LLC
LaVergne TN
LVHW021001300926
849160LV00007B/215
9798901130537